To

My family and friends

*Special thanks to Sunil and Shaurya
who have been my greatest strength*

VINNIE JAUHARI

To

*The two pillars of guidance and support
who gave meaning to my existence—
my parents—Mrs and Mr K.K.M. Mehta
and
The one who guides and motivates me
through the ebb and flow of life—
my husband—Anil
and my two angels—Yoshita and Ridhima*

KIRTI DUTTA

SERVICES
Marketing, Operations, and Management

VINNIE JAUHARI

Director
Institute of International Management and Technology (IIMT)
Gurgaon

KIRTI DUTTA

Assistant Professor
Bharatiya Vidya Bhavan's
Usha and Lakshmi Mittal Institute of Management
New Delhi

OXFORD
UNIVERSITY PRESS

OXFORD

UNIVERSITY PRESS

Oxford University Press is a department of the University of Oxford.
It furthers the University's objective of excellence in research, scholarship,
and education by publishing worldwide. Oxford is a registered trademark of
Oxford University Press in the UK and in certain other countries.

Published in India by
Oxford University Press
YMCA Library Building, 1, Jai Singh Road, New Delhi 110001, India

First Edition published in 2009
Fourth impression 2011

ISBN-13: 978-0-19-568908-2
ISBN-10: 0-19-568908-9

Typeset In Baskerville
by Le Studio Graphique, Gurgaon 122001
Printed in India by Adage Printers (P) Ltd, Noida 201301 U.P.

Preface

The contribution of the services sector in the growth of the global economy is significant. Business operations are getting more complex on account of liberalization of economies and rapid changes in technology. In light of the changing market structures, aspirations of the consumers, and internationalization of firms, it is important to understand the changing business dynamics in India and other emerging economies. India is one of the faster growing economies in the world. The estimates of the Organisation for Economic Co-operation and Development (OECD) indicate that India would emerge to be the third largest economy by 2026. The service industry in India contributes to more than 53 per cent of the GDP (World Development Indicators 2007). This book is an attempt to understand the dynamics of the services industry, especially in the Indian and South Asian context.

About the Book

Services: Marketing, Operations, and Management is targeted to meet the requirements of management students, faculty, and practitioners by presenting a comprehensive overview of services management. To understand services management, it is important to have an understanding of the specific characteristics of the services industry. There is a need to understand the broad economic environment as well as elements of the service mix, such as the service product, price, place, promotion, people, physical evidence, and process. A business manager should also have an understanding of consumer behaviour, segmentation, targeting, positioning, perceptions, and customer expectations to deliver a commercially viable service product. The understanding of services management also requires an insight into technological issues, ethical issues, and future options available for growth of the business. There is a need to appreciate alternatives to implement excellence in service businesses, as short-term approach may not be conducive for long-term survival.

Pedagogical Features

The book explores the emerging issues in the services sector from an Indian perspective. It touches upon various key concepts by bringing in examples from the business world. The practices at Indian and global companies, such as HDFC, Hewlett–Packard, ITC, HUL, KFC, and McDonald's, have been discussed.

Every chapter begins with outlining the scope of the chapter. The key definitions and summary at the end of each chapter help the reader in better assimilation of the content.

The text in each chapter is interspersed with the suitable corporate examples in the form of boxed exhibits to facilitate the understanding of various concepts relating to services.

The book captures the changing business dynamics of the services sector. It discusses emerging issues in the services sector, which business managers would need to address—excellence, innovation, technology, and strategy. The Internet-based exercises will provide the reader with a wider exposure to the key areas in services management.

The following are the key highlights of the book:

- Integrates theory with corporate examples
- Provides rich insights into the dynamics of the service sector
- Includes aspects such as technology management, ethics, strategies for growth, business excellence, and balanced scorecard approach
- Gives a perspective on emerging service sectors such as software and ITES, healthcare, banking, and retailing
- Discusses the practices of Indian and global companies such as HDFC, Hewlett–Packard, LIC, Ferns 'n' Petals, KFC, and McDonald's
- Contains exhibits which give insights into the Indian service industry
- Explains concepts through examples, exhibits, tables, caselets, and case studies
- Includes Internet-based exercises which will help the students to apply the theory to business situations

Coverage and Structure

The book is divided into 19 chapters. It discusses various aspects of the services industry. The chapters have a case study in the end, which is an application of the concepts discussed in the chapters. The case studies are contemporary and will develop the analytical skills of the students. The book has critical review questions, caselets, and Internet-based exercises, which help the students to apply the theory to real-life situations.

Chapter 1, *Introduction to Service Industry*, gives an introduction to the services sector in the global and Indian context. The chapter delineates the characteristics of services and compares it with the characteristics of the products. It also brings out the importance of services in case of manufactured products. The challenges for the service industry have been discussed and the critical success factors have also been elaborated on. The chapter also covers international trade regulations and their impact on the services sector. The services marketing environment has been elaborated on and the service mix elements—product, price, place, promotion, people, physical evidence, and process—have been explained.

Chapter 2, *Service Product*, gives an understanding of the product in the context of services. It discusses the levels of service offering and the steps involved in new product development. The concept of the product life cycle as well as the strategies involved in managing the product during the different stages of the life cycle have also been discussed. The relevance of branding a services product has been elaborated on.

Chapter 3, *Marketing Research in Service Industry*, emphasizes the importance of market research in understanding and delivering services to markets. The chapter gives an overview of the marketing research process. The methodology for conducting research and the tools and techniques of research have been elaborated on. The chapter also gives an insight into the marketing research strategies followed by firms in the Indian market. It also gives insights into the challenges faced by the marketing research firms.

Chapter 4, *Understanding Consumer Behaviour*, gives insights on understanding consumer behaviour before, during, and after consuming the service. It analyses the values and perceptions of customers and their disposition towards the purchase process. The chapter discusses the dynamics of Indian consumers and examines the factors leading to increased consumption of new services. The chapter gives an overview of factors influencing consumer behaviour. It also discusses the concepts of relationship marketing, consumer loyalty, customer delight, and consumerism in the context of the services sector.

Chapter 5, *Segmentation, Targeting, and Positioning*, gives an overview of the strategies involved in helping the service marketer to arrive at the basis of segmentation in the market place. The chapter delineates the criteria that help service organizations to choose the segment in which they are going to focus on for marketing the service product. Keeping the target segment in mind, the chapter highlights the different strategies for positioning the service in the mind of the consumers.

Chapter 6, *Consumer Perception*, highlights the service quality dimensions affecting the customers' perception of services. It further discusses the gaps in service delivery and their effect on consumer perceptions. It also delineates the concept of service encounter and touches upon service Gap model. It discusses the concept of service quality and the SERVQUAL model as well.

Chapter 7, *Consumer Expectations*, examines customers' anticipation about a service based on their perceptions. The chapter also gives a perspective on managing customer expectations, thus leading to customer satisfaction and even 'delight' with the services provided.

Chapter 8, *Physical Evidence*, delineates the different factors, which have a bearing on the customer's perception about the service provider. It further elaborates on the management of different dimensions of physical evidence to create a perception, which is in line with the services being provided.

Chapter 9, *Understanding Service Operations and Processes*, analyses the management of service processes by service firms. The chapter establishes the relationship between profitability and service process. It details the blueprinting process which maps all the activities right from the time that the customer begins the contact with the marketer to the time that the customer departs from the service provider's premises. The chapter also gives insight into managing the demand and supply dynamics. Demand management is an important aspect of services as it greatly impacts the profitability of the firm and has a strong bearing on the customer satisfaction level. The waiting-time strategies have also been discussed in the chapter. It goes on to discuss the role played by customers in the delivery process. The service delivery process should ensure homogeneity of customers in order to ensure that the customer experience is unaffected. The chapter also discusses issues related with service guarantees and explains the service process matrix. It addresses how the decisions related with customization and mass service are taken by service providers.

Chapter 10, *Customer Feedback and Service Recovery*, examines the issues that need to be managed when the service delivered falls short of customer expectations. It discusses strategies to retain customers after a service delivery failure. Customer feedback is an extremely important way to improvise the service processes. The recovery mechanism enables a firm to reduce the attrition level and could have an immense bearing on consumer loyalty. It discusses various ways of managing the service recovery and also examines the issue of service warranties.

Chapter 11, *Distribution Channels*, discusses the distribution channels available for the services sector. It discusses the management of these channels so that there is optimization of service availability for the customer. It also studies the impact of the Internet on distribution.

Chapter 12, *Managing People*, provides an understanding of the importance of managing people in the process of service delivery. Individuals employed in the services industry have to be involved and highly motivated as well as committed to the job to deliver to the best of their abilities. This has numerous implications for the service managers to manage their teams well. The kind of people recruited by the service organization depends on the availability of people in the labour market in a country or region. The demand and supply dynamics in labour markets also influences the availability of skills and competencies for a particular industry. The chapter also gives an understanding of the role of culture, which influences individuals' behaviour in the organizational setting. The chapter discusses service culture and the aspects that influence it. The issues of recruitment, retention, teamwork, training and development, rewards, and job security have been explained.

Chapter 13, *Pricing Strategies*, explains the various pricing strategies which could be adopted by service firms. These could be cost-based or market-based strategies. There are a range of options that service firms could initiate in each category. The chapter helps to bring in a perspective on implications of pricing strategies for the service provider. It gives insights into the pricing strategies adopted by the current service providers in India.

Chapter 14, *Promotion Mix*, discusses the management of the marketing communications for a service organization. It covers advertising, sales promotion, personal selling, direct marketing and public relations and focuses on the management of these different channels of marketing communications to position the product in the minds of the customers and creating realistic expectations. It also explains the concept of e-marketing.

Chapter 15, *Impact of Technology*, gives an overview of the technology issues that are faced by the service firms. Technology influences the strategies adopted by the service firms. They impact the way the service is provided. The chapter delineates the impact of technology on different aspects of the business such as productivity, new services, control mechanisms, distribution networks, new relationships, and customer relationships. The chapter also traces the impact of online technologies on services businesses. It also discusses the concepts of service innovation and key influencers in the same. The concepts of data mining and data warehousing have also been discussed.

Chapter 16, *Managing Quality and Excellence*, gives a perspective on the management of services in totality. It discusses different service excellence models such as the Malcolm Baldrige Quality Award, ISO, European Quality Award, and CII awards in India. It develops a critique on these models and discusses a blueprint for service excellence in the form of the Balanced Scorecard model.

Chapter 17, *Ethics in Services Businesses*, introduces the concepts of ethics and values. The global businesses will have to imbibe models of sustainable development in order to perform well. The chapter argues the need for pursuing ethical business practices.

Chapter 18, *Strategies for Business Growth*, gives insight into the strategies adopted by service firms for growth. The chapter discusses the various options such as green-field ventures, joint ventures, mergers and acquisitions, strategic alliances, franchising, and management contracts. The advantages and disadvantages of the same have also been elaborated on.

Chapter 19, *Emerging Service Sectors in India*, discusses four emerging sectors in India—biotechnology, healthcare, banking, and retailing. Each sector is discussed in detail, along with the industry structure, critical success factors, and major challenges faced by it.

Acknowledgements

We would like to express our heartfelt gratitude to a number of institutions, publications, and individuals without whose support and encouragement we would have not been able to complete this work.

First of all, we would like to thank our host institutions which have been supportive of our efforts. The leadership at IIMT, Dr R. Kapur, Mr K.B. Kachru, and the entire team, including Dr Kamlesh Misra, Dr Umashankar Venkatesh, and Kamal Manaktola, have all been wonderful colleagues and have always stood by us. Ashok Sahu has always been a source of great strength and his contribution is beyond description. Amit Sexena and Manjit have always worked very hard in our endeavours and have rendered outstanding support.

The team at Hewlett–Packard, especially Michel Benard and Rob Bouzon, have been a source of inspiration.

A very warm word of thanks to dear Shivangi Gupta and Himani Kaul whose support has been immeasurable during very tough periods. They played a very important role in evolving the final draft version of this book. We would remember their contribution forever.

We would like to express deep thanks to the following publications and institutions, which have been very supportive of sharing the resources for publication:

Emerald group of journals, *The Business Standard, Hindustan Times, The Times of India, Business World, Journal of Services Research, International Journal of Contemporary Hospitality Management, Indian Management, Economic Times*, World Bank, and Institute for International Management and Technology (IIMT), and Institute of Chartered Financial Analysts of India (ICFAI).

The role of Prof. Chihiro Watanabe for all his motivation and support is gratefully acknowledged. His constant encouragement has had a big influence on the book. The presence of friends, such as Amee Yajnik, Charla-Griffy Brown, Meenakshi, Jagdeep, Ajay Jugran, Vinayshil Gautam, Vipin Gogia, Pankaj, and Kirti Madan, is also appreciated.

We would like to express our heartfelt thanks to our families. Our respective spouses Sunil and Anil as well as children Shaurya and Yoshita, and Ridhima, brothers Shallen and Yash, sister Jaya, parents, and in-laws, who have always been on our side to help us progress in our professional careers. Without them it would never have been possible to accomplish all this.

We would like to thank the entire team of Oxford University Press for the standards laid by them and in motivating us to improve our earlier drafts. The painstaking efforts of the team are indeed commendable.

VINNIE JAUHARI

KIRTI DUTTA

Contents

1 Introduction to Service Industry

OBJECTIVES

After reading this chapter you will be able to understand the:

- essentials of a service economy
- concept of a service and its characteristics
- difference between a service and a product
- classification of services, and the importance of classification
- difference between goods and services
- factors responsible for the growth of service sector and the challenges thereof
- critical factors for success of the services sector
- dimensions of international trade regulations for the service sector
- concepts of service management
- ingredients of the traditional marketing mix

INTRODUCTION

As the economy grows, the demand for services increases. The services sector, which has registered a nine per cent annual growth since the mid 1990s, accounts for 54 per cent of India's GDP and is currently the fastest growing sector of the economy (Planning Commission, 2006). The services sector, which witnessed a double-digit annual growth, includes transportation (air, rail, or road), telecom, healthcare, financial services such as banking and insurance, business services such as advertising, legal services, etc. The growth of the service industry has been uniform, with sectors such as accountancy, facility management, hospitality, entertainment, and personal services also showing impressive growth. Among the services, 'transport and communications' has been the fastest growing sector with growth averaging 15.3 per cent per annum during the Tenth Five Year Plan period followed by construction. The growth of financial services comprising banking, insurance, and business services in the year 2006–07 was 13.9 per cent (*India Economic Survey 2007–08*). In line with the boom in the global services economy, India's export of services worth $76.2 billion grew by 32.1 per cent in 2006–2007. (*India Economic Survey 2007–08*). Software services, business services, financial services and communication services, were the main drivers of growth. Table 1.1

Table 1.1 The growth of commercial services exports by category and region for 1990–2006 (Annual percentage change)

		World	North America	South and Central America	Europe	CIS	Africa	Middle East	Asia
Commercial services									
	1990–96	9	8	9	–	–	7	...	...
	1995–2000	5	7	6	...	...	4	...	4
	2000–06	11	6	8	12	19	13	12	12
	2004	20	13	15	20	28	21	16	27
	2005	11	10	18	9	20	12	14	15
	2006	12	9	13	11	23	11	14	17
Transportation services									
	1990–95	6	4	7	–	–	5	...	11
	1995–2000	3	3	2	3	...	0	...	3
	2000–06	10	6	10	11	16	12	13	13
	2004	25	19	21	25	21	21	17	28
	2005	13	13	21	12	16	17	17	13
	2006	10	11	8	7	18	12	11	23
Travel									
	1990–95	9	7	10	–	–	9	...	...
	1995–2000	3	6	7	2	...	6	...	2
	2000–06	8	2	7	9	18	14	8	10
	2004	18	14	14	15	39	22	8	32
	2005	8	8	13	6	10	15	13	9
	2006	9	5	11	8	22	12	7	14
Other commercial services									
	1990–95	10	12	10	–	–	5	...	16
	1995–2000	7	11	9	...	...	6	...	6
	2000–06	13	8	10	14	27	10	14	14
	2004	19	11	13	20	30	19	22	12
	2005	12	11	24	10	35	3	13	19
	2006	15	11	20	13	30	9	21	21

Source: Adapted from The WTO data on 'Trade in Commercial Services by Category 2008'.

depicts the growth of commercial services exports by category and region between 1990–2006.

The distinction between goods and services is slowly getting blurred. Given the demands of global competition, and thanks to the increasingly sophisticated production, it makes more economic sense for companies to combine services with the product they offer. Manufacturers are now moving downstream (towards the customer) as they are appreciating the fact that, it is in services that the profit lies (Wise and Baumgartner

Table 1.2   Services: The new profit imperative in manufacturing

Category	Total expenditure
Personal computers	5 times the product cost
Locomotives	21 times the product cost
Automobiles	5 times the product cost

Source: Adapted from Howells (2004).

1999). They now understand that the sale of product forms just a small portion of the overall revenue and it is services, which generate the big money. It is the experience dimension of the product consumption which is becoming important. Table 1.2 shows the product cost in terms of total expenditure for a manufacturer. As manufacturers have an intimate knowledge of their products and the market, they are in a better position to provide the service activities related to their products. Today, they consider product sales as an entry point for foraying into services.

For instance, Ford had long been engaged in finance (Ford Credit), and in maintenance and car components (Visteon). Eventually, the company moved into car insurance and general after-sales care and web retailing (fordjourney.com). To add to its list of customer services, it formed a joint venture, Wingcast, with Qualcomm, a wireless electronics company, and Cartell, a telematics equipment supplier, to provide 'in-vehicle' navigational assistance, and Internet and entertainment services. Similarly, Fiat took over full control of Toro Assicurazioni some years ago to provide insurance and other financial services to its customers. Primarily, all these activities are closely associated with selling the manufactured product, the car. IBM and Siemens derive more than half of their turnover from services activities (Howells 2004).

This trend is also evident in the aerospace industry wherein aircraft builders are offering finance and leasing options along with providing repair and overhaul facilities. For example, GE has a major finance and leasing company (GE Capital Services), and also provides a range of purchasing, leasing and rental options. Thus, engines can be rented from GE Engine Services (GEES) for a period ranging from 24 hours to more than a year. It also offers 'GE On Wing Support', which provides wide ranging maintenance service package including engine inventory, long-term preservation, and facilities support. Similarly, Rolls Royce has acquired aero-engine repair and maintenance companies worldwide. This aspect of marketing or 'servicization' phenomenon is termed as 'service encapsulation' of goods and materials. Table 1.3 highlights the service encapsulation phenomenon, wherein goods are not offered to the consumers in their own right, but in terms of their wider service attributes.

More and more countries are finding that the majority of their gross national product (GNP) is being generated by the services sector. An examination of the World Bank development indicators for 2007–08 indicates that the services sector is the major source of economic activity across the world (Table 1.4).

South Asia, which includes India, shows a 54 per cent contribution to GDP from the services sector. Although the export figures for the region are low as compared to Europe

Table 1.3   Service dimensions through life cycle of a product

Pre-purchase activities	During purchase activities	Post-purchase activities
□ Seeking advice □ Consultation services □ Purchase facilitation	□ Financing □ Leasing □ Information sharing	□ Disposal □ Recycling □ Repair and maintenance □ Delivery

Source: Adapted from Howells (2004).

and the Americas, the average growth figure for per capita GDP is 7 per cent. The overall trend in the world's economic activities shows that barring the services sector, all other major activities such as agriculture and industry have showed a downward curve. An insight into the kind of profits generated by the services industry can be seen in Table 1.5. According to a sector-wise analysis of India by CapitalinePlus, some 5,344 services listed in the country, netted a profit of Rs 100,959.86 crore during the financial year 2007–08 compared to the manufacturing sector that earned a profit of Rs 119,587.23 crore from 7,053 listed companies. The total number of service firms in the country might be larger, but they do not feature here as many of them are unlisted firms.

India's hospitality industry is another service segment that is poised for growth and has very bright prospects in terms of generating revenue as well as jobs. Increasing business activity, flourishing leisure travel, and a booming middle class are encouraging global brands to line up for a slice of the Indian hospitality pie (Exhibit 1.1).

Table 1.4   World Bank Development Indicators 2008

	GNI Atlas method[b] $ billions 2006	GNI per capita Atlas[b] $ 2006	 PPP[c] $ 2006	GDP per capita Average annual real growth % 2005–06	Services % of GDP 2006	Gross capital formation % of GDP 2006	Exports of goods and services $ billions 2006	Total debt service to exports % 2006
East Asia and Pacific	3,525	1,860	4,360	8.6	41	39	1,632	1,316
Europe and Central Asia	2,217	4,810	9,790	6.7	60	23	1,014	583
Latin America and Caribbean	2,661	4,790	8,680	4.2	62	21	761	313
Middle East and North Africa	779	2,510	6,710	3.3	48	26	...	256
South Asia	1,151	770	2,290	7.0	54	32	244	220
Sub-Saharan Africa	648	830	1,680	3.0	55	21	230	118

Source: Adapted from Facts and Figures: The World Bank Development Indicators (2008).

Table 1.5 Sector-wise comparison statistics from India

Name	Number of companies	Year 2007–08	
		Sales Rs (crore)	Net profit Rs (crore)
All companies	15370	3,132,136.80	262,657.13
Commodities	833	194,150.71	32,552.97
Diversified	32	30,798.18	3,019.93
Manufacturing	7053	1,859,228.56	119,587.23
Miscellaneous	1335	49,912.04	4,984.38
Services	5344	822,233.98	100,959.86
Trading	747	165,631.79	1,069.67

Source: Adapted from CapitalinePlus (2006).

SERVICES: CONCEPT AND CHARACTERISTICS

What exactly are services? There are several definitions of services in services marketing literature. Grönroos (1990) defines services as 'An activity or series of activities of more or less intangible nature that normally, but not necessarily, take place in interactions between the customer and service employees and/or physical resources or goods and/or systems of the service provider, which are provided as a solutions to customer problems.' Kotler (1991) defines services as 'Any act or performance that one party can

Exhibit 1.1 Growth of the Indian hospitality industry

The Indian hospitality sector is poised for a huge inflow of world's leading hotel brands. With ever increasing business activity, flourishing leisure travel, booming middle class, and of course, the Commonwealth Games in 2010 in Delhi, the prospects for growth are only too bright.

At an estimated 426,668 job requirement, this sector is expected to generate the maximum number of employment in 2008. Industry experts expect that nearly $11.41 billion would be pumped into the sector over the next two years and India is likely to have around 40 international hotel brands by 2011. India could be the third largest market in hospitality and tourism by 2015.

The boom in tourism industry evidently has had a cascading effect on the hospitality sector, which has seen an increase in the occupancy ratios and average room rates. With the demand continuing to surge, many a global hospitality major has shown a keen interest in the Indian hospitality sector. For example, US-based brand Starwood is all set to enter India with its tie-up with ITC group. Unitech has joined hands with Marriott to operate three new hotels in Kolkata, Gurgaon, and Noida. DLF has already developed plans to set up over 100 business and 4-star hotels in 50 cities over the next 10 years.

Indian hotels are expected to flourish as there is a severe shortage of quality rooms. With prospects being so bright, Indians can look forward to exciting management career opportunities in the field of international hospitality. Due to the severe shortage of skilled workforce in this industry, well-educated hospitality managers with an international perspective and professional experience will be in high demand.

Source: Adapted from The Economic Times (2008, 2006).

Table 1.6 Tangibility element in various service sectors

Higher intangible content	Higher tangible content
◻ Teaching	◻ Cosmetics
◻ Consulting	◻ Detergents
◻ Financial investment	◻ Furniture
◻ Hospitality	◻ IT equipment
	◻ Sugar

Source: Adapted from Shostack (1977).

offer to another that is essentially intangible and does not result in the ownership of anything. Its production may not be tied to a physical product.'

Valarie et al. (2006) have reflected upon services as, 'An act or performance offered by one party to other. Although the process may be tied to a physical product, the performance is transitory, often intangible in nature and does not normally result in ownership of any of the factors of production.' Kasper et al. (1999) define services as, 'Services are originally intangible and relatively quickly perishable activities whose buying takes place in an interaction process aimed at creating customer satisfaction but during this interactive consumption this does not always lead to material possession.' The various definitions of services include several features such as element of tangibility, which could vary on a spectrum of being very high to low. This would mean that services such as consultancy could be highly intangible while certain others, such as education may be more tangible. Thus we can define services as 'A set of activities or benefits which produce a product, which is normally intangible in nature, perishable, involving temporary transfer of ownership or as long as the service is being used and which gratify the customers needs or problems. Services can also be provided in connection with sale of tangible goods for creating value perceptions among customers.' Table 1.6 highlights the element of tangibility in various services areas.

Characteristics of Services

A review on the subject by Lovelock and Gummesson (2004) and Parker (1960), identified intangibility and perishability as the two most important characteristics of services. Regan (1963) identified intangibility, inseparability, perishability, and ubiquity as the four characteristic features of a service. However, he neither defined nor explained them. Rathmell (1966) identified as many as thirteen characteristic differences between goods and services. The first authors, according to the review, to cite all four characteristics were Sasser et al. (1978), who presented them in a pioneering services operations textbook. However, they used the term 'simultaneity' instead of 'inseparability'. Zeithaml et al. (1985) identified four characteristics of services that all service marketers must bear in mind—intangibility, inseparability, variability, and perishability.

Intangibility

Services are 'experiences' created for customers. They comprise actions rather than objects. Bateson (1977) first described services as intangibles because 'Services are performances rather than objects, they cannot be seen, felt, tasted or touched in same manner in which goods can be touched.' He identified intangibility as the critical difference between goods and services from which all the other differences emerge. Bateson further categorized intangibility into *physical intangibility*, which is 'not palpable or cannot be touched' and *mental intangibility*, which is difficult for the consumer to grasp or measure even mentally. For example, it is not easy to judge how thoroughly a car has been serviced immediately after the service. He thus concluded that services are doubly intangible.

The intangibility of services results in the following implications for marketers*:

- Services cannot be stored.
- Services cannot be patented legally, hence they can be easily copied by competitors.
- Services cannot be readily displayed or easily communicated leading to difficulty in assessing its quality.
- Decisions regarding advertising and promotions are difficult.
- Pricing services is difficult as it is hard to determine the actual cost of a 'unit of service' and price/quality relationship is complex.
- It is less efficient than goods production.
- Design of total service package is not possible.

Some of the possible solutions for service marketers to overcome intangibility issues can be:

- use tangible cues
- stimulate, manage, and promote word-of-mouth communication
- use personal sources of information more than non-personal sources
- use post-purchase communication
- strengthen internal and external marketing
- use relationship marketing
- create strong organizational image
- use cost accounting to help set prices.

Inseparability

This stands for inseparability of production and consumption. Services are created (by the provider) and consumed (by the client/user) simultaneously and cannot be stored like goods. Hence a mobile phone (product), which is manufactured in Korea and shipped to Sweden, is sold four months later, and is used for years. On the other hand, the transportation services of an airplane are first sold, and then produced and experienced or consumed simultaneously (Zeithaml et al. 1985). This also implies that the customers have to be present during service production. Consumers frequently interact with each

---

Source: * Adapted from Zeithaml et al. 1985; Rampal and Gupta 2002; Rao 2005; Hoffman and Bateson 2002.

other and may influence each other's experience. Thus a service must be provided at the right time, in the right place, and in the right way. Service producers themselves play an important role as part of the product itself, as well as an essential ingredient in the service experience for consumers.

We can thus summarize that 'Inseparability involves the presence of the customer, customer's role as co-producer, customer to employee and customer to customer interaction' (Lovelock and Gummesson 2004). A case in point has been the emergence of healthcare tourism in India. Efficient and skilled healthcare at affordable costs has made India a favourite global health destination. As services are 'inseparable' and aimed at giving the customer an 'experience of a lifetime', several leading medical care chains are tying up with hospitality chains to provide a unique combination of health and tourism. Exhibit 1.2 highlights this facet of the service sector.

The inseparability of services results in the following challenges for those marketing services:

- Centralized mass production becomes difficult if not impossible.
- Customer experience depends upon the action of employees and interaction between employees (service providers) and customers.
- Operations need to be decentralized so that the service can be delivered directly to consumers at convenient locations.
- Due to simultaneous production and consumption, the customer involvement is high and this influences the outcome of the service transaction.

Exhibit 1.2 Booming healthcare tourism in India

The Indian healthcare sector is emerging as the preferred choice for 'medical' tourists from Britain, US, and Canada. The year 2007 was not only a record year for India's inbound tourism, but it was the fifth consecutive year showing a double-digit increase in foreign tourist arrivals. The growth of tourist inflow into India was well above the world average, leading to a rise of the country's share in global arrivals from 0.37 per cent in 2001 to 0.53 per cent in 2006.

Tourism is an important industry in India, contributing around 6.8 per cent to the national GDP, and providing employment to over 41 million people. Medical tourism is playing a significant role in this upsurge. This is mainly due to the fact that private hospitals in India are world class and have the latest medical technologies in place. The doctors and nurses in the country have a very high degree of proficiency and have the capability to outshine any hospital in the West. India's knowledge of Ayurveda, Unani, Reiki and other alternate forms of medicine is also highly valued across the world.

According to a Planning Commission report, India is a cheaper option for healthcare as compared to countries such as Thailand, UK, or US. A cosmetic surgery would cost $3500 in Thailand, $20,000 in US, and about $10,000 in UK. The same in India would cost just about $2000!

Besides being home to some of the best privately-owned hospitals, tourists from the West face relatively lesser communication problems as English is a widely spoken language here. Moreover, the waiting list for these foreign patients is low. All these advantages point towards one main point—medical tourism is riding a growth curve and is all set to drive India's economy in the years to come.

Source: Adapted from *The Times of India* (2008) and http://www.ibef.org (2008).

- Involvement of other customers in the production process becomes an imperative.

Some of the probable solutions to overcome inseparability problems of services can be:

- having strong selection and training programmes for personnel who would be dealing with public/clients
- announcing strong incentives and motivations to attract and satisfy the customer
- marketing at multi-site locations
- innovating techniques of indirect interaction
- achieving standardization to the maximum extent possible
- resorting to consumer management
- focusing on personal attention
- developing a distribution network with quality control mechanism.

Variability

Services face the difficulty of achieving uniform output, especially labour-intensive services. Olsen and Wyckoff (1978) described the challenge of setting up standards when the behaviour and performance vary not only among service workers, but even between the same employee's dealings with different customers, and on different days. Variability or heterogeneity also results because no two customers are alike in their demands.

Thus, quality and essence of service vary from producer to producer, customer to customer, and from day to day (Zeithaml et al. 1985), and is largely the result of human interaction and all the vagaries that accompany it. The implications for marketing due to variability in services are:

- difficulty in achieving standardization
- difficulty in setting quality controls
- determination of quality possible only after performance of service
- difficulty in communicating to the clients what exactly they would get.

The strategies that can help in overcoming this aspect of services are:

- stress upon standardization and performance
- focus on employee training programme, performance evaluation, and internal marketing.
- consider licensing and other forms of credential requirements
- position variation as a strength of innovation
- promote research and innovation
- industrialize service: Levitt (1972) suggested 'Specific techniques to substitute organized pre-planned systems for individual service operations (for example, travel agents could offer pre-packaged vacation tours to obviate the need for the selling, tailoring, and haggling involved in customization). This strategy is the opposite of customization.'
- customize services.

Perishability

This implies that 'services cannot be saved' (Zeithaml et al. 1985). Goods once produced can be stored and then sold at a later date but services peter out. They cannot be stored. An unutilized service capacity cannot be utilized further. For example, an unoccupied hotel room, airline seats, etc. cannot be saved, stored for reuse later, resold, or even returned if the customer is unhappy (Lovelock and Gummesson 2004). The marketing implications as a result of perishability of services are:

- short-lived value of services
- services cannot be inventoried
- there is a lot of time pressure in sales
- capacity of services is finite.

Marketing strategies that can be adopted to overcome the marketing implications are:

- demand forecasting and creative planning for capacity utilization to close gaps between demand and supply
- formulate strategies to cope with fluctuating demand
- devise strong recovery strategies when things go wrong
- focus on competence and expertise
- continuous study of demand patterns and competitive parameters
- develop creative pricing options such as early bird or frequent flier specials.

Lovelock and Gummesson (2004) have applied the four characteristics of services to categorize services into four types based on whether the service offering is physical or non-physical in nature and whether people themselves, owned objects, or information, represent the central element that is processed to create the service. These four categories are—(1) physical actions to the person of the customer (people processing); (2) physical actions to an object belonging to the customer (possession processing); (3) non-physical actions directed at the customer's mind (mental stimulus processing); and (4) non-physical actions directed at data or intangible assets (information processing). Representative examples of services in each category are highlighted in the Table 1.7.

Table 1.7 Applicability of unique characteristics of services to different types of services

Physical action to a person	Physical action to the object of a customer	Non-physical action at the mind	Non-physical action directed at data
□ Hair cut	□ Repair and maintenance of equipment	□ Advertising	□ Information processing
□ Beauty treatment		□ Theatre	
□ Medical surgeries	□ Interior designing	□ Lectures/talks	□ Consulting
□ Restaurant food service	□ Transportation of goods		

Source: Adapted from Lovelock and Gummesson (2004).

CLASSIFICATION OF SERVICES

Services can be classified in several ways. Various authors have tried to classify services on the basis of different features/aspects such as the market segment, tangibility factor, skill type, etc. Figure 1.1 shows the numerous factors along which services can be classified. They are enlisted as follows:

- tangibility component
- skill-type involved
- goals of the business
- regulatory dimension
- intensity of labour used
- consumer contact
- place and timing
- customization
- relationship with customers
- demand and supply.

Categorizing Service Processes

Various authors have classified services on the basis of the processes, which in turn are differentiated on numerous factors. The various service classifications are discussed in detail in this section.

Market segment Services can be classified on the basis of market segment they are catering to. Thus we can have services catering to end-consumers, such as the hair salon and beauty services, coaching classes, and car wash services or services catering to organizational consumers such as management consulting, repair and maintenance services for machines, and legal services (Lovelock 1983, and Rampal and Gupta 2002).

Degree of tangibility According to Lovelock and Wright (1999) services can be classified into tangible offerings, such as food services or dry cleaning, and intangible services, such as teaching and medical services. Judd (1964) classified services as rental goods services, such as hotel and lodging services, and car rental; owned-goods services such as laundry, cleaning, repair of gadgets, etc. which involves repair or improvement of goods owned by the customer; and non-goods services that cover personal experiences such as legal services, educational services, and social services (family and counselling services, job training, etc.).

Skills of the service provider Services can be provided by highly skilled labour or unskilled labour (Rampal and Gupta 2002). Thus services can be classified as professional, such as health/medical services, engineering, accounting, research, management, etc., and non-professional services such as shoe shining, laundry, cleaning services, etc.

Goals of the service provider At times, services are differentiated on the basis of the goals they pursue—whether they are profit making or non-profit making. For

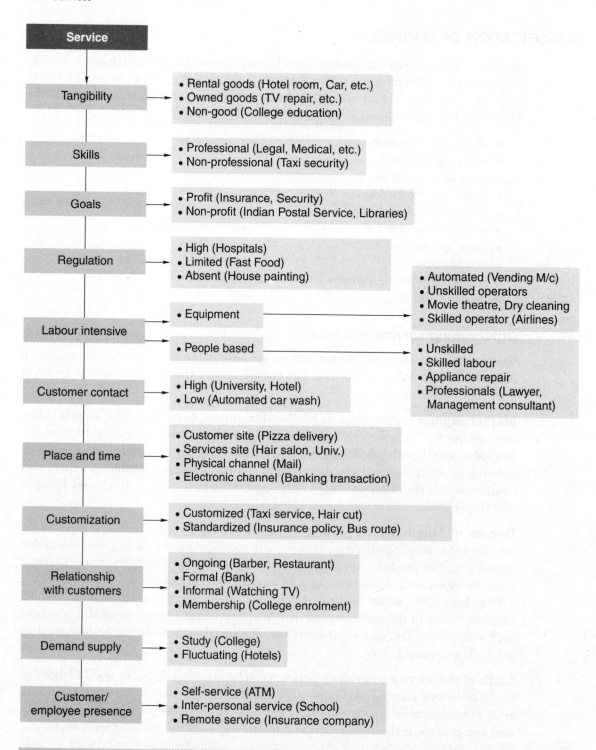

Fig. 1.1 Classification of service

example, an organization can be a profit-oriented entity, such as airlines, hotels, or restaurants. Non-profit organizations or services include state-owned post and telegraph services, public libraries, etc. (Kotler 1980).

Degree of regulation   Services are also classified according to the extent of government regulation on them (Rathmell 1974). Services, such as mass transportation systems, which include airlines, railways, and roadways are highly-regulated, while some face limited regulations. The hospitality sector faces limited government regulation. There are some services that are not regulated at all; for example, barber and beauty services, domestic help services, etc.

Degree of labour intensiveness   Service employees play a vital role in the delivery of services and sometimes are also a part of the service delivery (Varoglu and Eser 2006). However, services may vary according to the extent of the labour involved. Thus, there can be equipment-based services on the one hand and people-based services on the other (Thomas 1978). Equipment-based services, as the name suggests, could include completed automated services such as ATMs and vending machines, or an offering through a machine with little or unskilled human intervention, as in movie theaters, dry cleaners, etc. They also include services that are operated by skilled professionals, such as airlines, BPOs, etc. People-based services can again be classified into unskilled (guards and cleaning services); skilled (appliance repair, printing, catering, etc.); and professionals like engineering, management consulting, data processing, medical services, etc.

Degree of customer contact   Chase (1978) classified organizations on the basis of the contact time between the customers and the service staff. Thus organizations could be high-contact or low-contact ones depending upon the time a customer spent with the service provider. High contact services are those, where the customer spends hours, days or weeks in the service system, like in education and hospitality industry; while low contact service is one in which the contact with service system ranges from a few minutes to some hours. For example, appliance repair services, postal services, etc.

Place and time   According to Lovelock (1983), services can be classified on the basis of the place and time of service delivery (Table 1.8). Thus, there can be service-site, customer-site, and service-delivery services. In case of a service-site service, the customer needs to visit the service location to avail the service; for example, watching a movie in a theatre. In customer-site service, the service is delivered to the customer, like home delivery of food items. Service delivery involves the interaction between the customer and the service provider through a physical channel such as e-mail, as in case of online reservations of airline, railway tickets, etc.

Customization   According to Silvestro et al. (1992), 'a high degree of customization is when the service process can be adapted to suit the needs of individual customers'. Lovelock (1983) has also classified services as customized and standardized. A standardized service is where the service to be provided is predetermined and pre-designed. A customer may be offered several options, all of which are predetermined and the customer can make a choice. Table 1.9 provides an insight on customization of services.

Table 1.8 Methods of service delivery

Nature of interaction between customer and service organization	Availability of service outlets	
	Single	Multiple site
Customer goes to service organization	Salon	Train transport
Service organization comes to customer	□ Home delivery for various services □ Repair and maintenance	□ Courier services □ Movers and packers services
Customer and service organization transact at arms length (mail or electronic communication)	Online buying websites such as eBay, Amazon, etc.	Online banking

Source: Adapted from Lovelock (1983). Reprinted with the permission of the American Marketing Association.

Relationship with customers Lovelock (1983) classified services according to the nature of relationship with customers. According to him, the relationship can be formal, informal, ongoing, or a membership-based one. A formal relationship is exemplified in banks, where each transaction is noted; while an informal relationship is one in which customers are anonymous and the transactions are short-lived, as in case of watching television. An ongoing relationship is epitomized by services of a barber or in a restaurant, where proactive measures need to be taken to enjoy continued patronage of clients. A membership relationship is one in which patrons (clients) must apply to become members and their performance is reviewed over time. Sometimes service providers create special memberships or frequent user programmes to reward loyal users. For example, airline companies offer frequent flyer programmes for regular customers. Table 1.10 highlights differentiation of services based on customer relationship.

Table 1.9 Customization and judgment in service delivery

Extent to which customer contact personnel exercise judgment in meeting individual customer needs	Extent to which service characteristics are customized	
	High	Low
High	□ Legal services □ Healthcare/surgery □ Architectural design	□ Education (large classes) □ Preventive health programmes
Low	□ Internet broadband services □ Hotel services □ Loans	□ Public transportation □ Fast-food restaurant □ Movie theatre

Source: Adapted from Lovelock (1983).

Table 1.10   Relationships with customers

Nature of service delivery	Type of relationship between the service organization and its customers	
	Membership relationship	No formal relationship
Continuous delivery of service	❑ Insurance ❑ Telephone subscription ❑ Newspaper/magazine subscription	Police protection National highway
Discrete transactions	Long-distance phone calls	Postal service

Source: Adapted from Lovelock (1983).

Demand and supply   Some service organizations can be classified according to the demand for the service and the ability of the service organizations to match the demand (Lovelock 1983). Thus the grouping can be categorized as steady, like colleges where there is a 'steady' demand for the services; or 'fluctuating' as in the hospitality industry where the demand is not constant over a period of time (Table 1.11).

Facilities, equipment, and people   Equipment, facilities, and people form the tangible elements of service delivery. It is important because customers use tangible clues to assess the quality of a service provided. The more intangible a service is, the greater is the need to make it tangible (Rafiq and Pervaiz 1995). For example, in a college the classrooms, tables and chairs, the overhead projector, and the faculty form a part of the tangible elements (Lovelock and Wright 1999).

Degree of discretion   Silvestro et al. (1992) classified services according to the degree of discretion. A high degree of discretion is exercised when front office personnel can use judgment in altering the service package or process without referring to superiors, as in case of management consultancy. A low degree of discretion is where changes to service provision can be made only with authorization from superiors, like in services by news agents and confectioners.

Table 1.11   Nature of demand for service with respect to supply

Extent to which supply is constrained	Extent of demand fluctuations over time	
	Wide	Narrow
Peak demand can usually be met without a major delay	❑ Electricity ❑ Natural gas	❑ Insurance ❑ Legal service
Peak demand regularly exceeds capacity	❑ Accounting and tax preparation ❑ Passenger transportation	❑ Services similar to those above but that have insufficient capacity for their base level of business

Source: Adapted from Lovelock (1983).

Value addition Silvestro et al. (1992) grouped services on the basis of value addition done by the front-office or the back-office staff. According to this parameter, services can be classified into back-office and front-office services. 'A back-office-oriented service is (one) where proportion of front-office (customer contact) staff to total staff is small, and a front-office-oriented service is (one) where proportion of front-office staff to total staff is large.' For example, in management consultancy and in hospitality sector the focus is on front-office orientation, whereas in transport service back-office orientation is predominant.

Product and process Silvestro et al. (1992) also classified services as product-oriented, where emphasis is on what the customer buys, and process-oriented, where the focus is on how the service is delivered to the customer. Thus, restaurants and transport services are product-focused, whereas hotels are process focused.

Utility creation perspective Hsieh and Chu (1992) classified the services business from the utility creation perspective. According to them, the value of a service business depends on its ability to create a utility. They identified time utility and space utility as dimensions of the service product, and people or things as the service recipients. For example, they classified hair styling and beauty salon as time utilities where recipients could obtain better appearance in a short while. Similarly, a space utility for people is created by a hotel to widen the area of lodgers' activities.

Service as a Process

A process involves the conversion of an input into an output. In services, two broad categories—people and objects—are processed. The nature of service act can be tangible or intangible. From an operational perspective, Lovelock and Wright (1999) categorized service process into four broad groups—people processing, possession processing, mental stimulus processing, and information processing (Table 1.12). All categories have different forms of process with vital implications for marketing, operations, and human resource managers.

Table 1.12   Understanding the nature of the service

What is the nature of the service action?	Who or what is the direct recipient of the service?	
	People	**Things**
Tangible actions	Services directed at people, on their person: (people processing)	Services directed at goods and other physical possessions: (possession processing)
Intangible actions	Services directed at people's minds: (mental stimulus processing)	Services directed at intangible assets: (information processing)

Source: Adapted from Lovelock (1983).

People processing This involves noteworthy actions directed towards people, in particular, the bodies of persons, such as haircut, surgery, etc. Here customers must enter the service factory/location where service providers (people/machines or both) deliver the service benefits to them. Sometimes service providers, come to the customers along with their tools to provide the desired benefits at locations of customers' choice.

Management implications If managers think about the process and output in terms of people/or objects being processed, it helps them to identify the benefits being created and the non-financial costs—time, fear, pain, and mental and physical effort—that customers incur.

Possession processing This includes concrete actions to physical goods belonging to customers. In this case, customers need not be present, but objects requiring processing must be present. For example, lawn mowing, warehousing, laundry, etc. Many such activities are quasi-manufacturing operations, and do not always involve simultaneous production and consumption.

Management implications The managers should note that the output in each instance should be a satisfactory solution to the customer's problem/need or there must be some tangible enhancement/improvement of the item in question.

The nature of services needs to be understood. Depending on the target segment, the offering needs to be packaged appropriately. Table 1.12 provides an insight on the segment at which the services are targeted.

For examples of the service actions illustrated in Table 1.12, please refer to Table 1.7.

Mental stimulus processing This kind of service focuses on intangible actions directed at the minds of people. It includes education, news, entertainment, sport, theatre, etc. In such instances customers must be present mentally, but could be physically located either in specific service facility, or in a remote place connected by broadcast signals or telecommunication linkages. This is in sharp contrast to people processing where people must be present physically, e.g. hair cut, or air travel. As these kind of services, i.e. advertising, consulting, etc. pertain to people's minds and have the power to influence attitudes, there is lot of scope for manipulation; hence, strong moral standards and cautious oversight is required on the part of the service providers.

Management implication As core content of all services in this category is information-based, which can easily be recorded and transformed to manufactured product, this service can thus be 'inventoried'.

Information processing This describes indistinguishable actions directed at the customer's belongings or assets. In service sectors such as insurance and banking, little direct contact is needed with the customer, once the request for service has been set in motion. The extent of customer involvement is determined more by convention, and a personal desire to meet the supplier face to face than by operational need.

Management implication   Information is the most intangible form of service output but can be transformed into more enduring tangible forms such as reports, books, tapes, diskettes, etc. Although professionals and clients prefer one-to-one meetings to know more about each other's needs and disposition, management should try to build successful personal relationships based on trust. This relationship can also be created and maintained through telephone or e-mail, thus saving the firm from all the complexities of managing people-processing service.

Importance of Classification System

The purpose of the development of classification system for services can be multi-dimensional. Hafer (1987) compiled the following reasons to classify products/services and the advantages thereof:

- Classification helps to understand the needs of consumers and their motivation for making purchases. This helps a marketer to stay abreast of changes in the needs of the consumers.
- It helps a marketer to understand pre-purchase and post-purchase the buyer behaviour. This provides insights into the consumers approach at evaluating services, their sources of information, and judgment of a product's absolute and relative performance.
- Classification can help service providers formulate strategies for groups of products/services. Such strategies save time and effort and can become the foundation for the marketing mix of the firm.
- Classification helps to identify whether products/services have complements in other industries or businesses and identify strategies for possible adoption. It is a benchmark to list the service types or organizations, which are felt to fit into the groupings.
- Classifying services acts as a checklist of service dimensions possessed by service providers and helps to determine their strategic positioning. This further helps to determine the strengths and weaknesses of a particular service, i.e., determine areas of excellence as well as areas that need to be worked upon, abolished, or reduced.
- It also helps to determine the competitor set. This also leads to the determination of the competitor's strengths and weaknesses, which could enable a marketer to identify strategic gaps that represent growth potential or high risk.

DIFFERENTIATION BETWEEN GOODS AND SERVICES

A product is the core output of a firm. It can either be a service or a manufactured good produced by the firm. Goods are described as physical objects or devices that provide benefits to the customer through ownership or use. In contrast, services are actions, deeds, or performances. The basic differences between goods and services are:

Ownership   On purchasing goods customers obtain tangible ownership of a product. But while purchasing services, customers do not obtain permanent ownership of tangible elements. They can only derive values or some mental satisfaction either by renting, or hiring or availing the benefits of using certain products. Here they purchase the experience of using the service product, instead of the service itself.

Performance The performance of goods is tangible, and the products can be used to perform their functions time and again. Services on the other hand are intangibility predominant performances. The benefits of owning and using manufactured products emanate from their physical characteristics whereas in services benefits arise from the nature of performance.

Another interesting way to distinguish between goods and services is to place them on a scale from tangible dominant to intangible dominant. This section describes some of the parameters of this scale.

Customer involvement Performance of a service involves the participation of the customer, either actively (e.g. ATM) or by their cooperation with service personnel (e.g. hotels, schools, etc.), in the production process. In contrast during the production of goods, customers do not have to play an active role—they just purchase the standard finished goods.

People as part of the product In high-contact services, such as the hospitality sector, customers not only come in contact with service personnel but with other customers as well. Thus the distinction between service businesses often lies in the quality of employees who are serving the customers and type of customers patronizing the service business. People constitute an important part of the product in many services. It is the task of the management (service providers) to manage the service encounters in such a manner as to create favourable experiences for the customers in order to generate customer loyalty.

Variability Products can be standardized but there is a great degree of variability in services. Since service personnel, influenced by other customers in the system, perform operational inputs and outputs, this makes it difficult to standardize and control variability in services. However, service providers are trying hard to customize services to the maximum extent possible.

Evaluation Since goods are made up of tangible attributes, it is easier to search for a product suiting the customer's requirements. In services, on the other hand, the entire emphasis is on experience attributes, which makes it harder for even customers to evaluate it after consumption. For example, the service aspects related to a surgery are difficult to evaluate.

Inventory Goods can be inventoried till they are sold or consumed. In contrast, services are perishable and cannot be stored.

Distribution channel Goods are distributed through proper distribution channels which are industry specific. Services, however, either use electronic channels or combine the service factory, retail outlet, and point of consumption at a single location. Also, service firms have to manage the behaviour of their personnel as well as customers to ensure smooth running of operations.

FACTORS RESPONSIBLE FOR GROWTH OF SERVICES SECTOR

There are both global factors as well country-specific factors, which have led to the growth of services sector across the world over the last two decades. This section discusses the factors that led to the growth of the services sector in India.

Liberalization of service sector Certain service sectors in India have been liberalized and thrown open to private sector. This has led to enhanced competition leading to higher degree of entrepreneurship in these areas. In India, for example the insurance and banking sectors have been opened to foreign direct investment (FDI). Similarly, the software and telecommunication sectors have been liberalized. Figure 1.2 indicates that the more liberalized sectors, such as information technology (IT) and telecommunications, have attracted significant FDI, created more employment opportunities, and galvanized other sectors of the economy as well. According to a Planning Commission report (2006), 'Liberalization of trade and investment in high technology goods and the development of efficient basic telecommunication have brought India to the forefront of developing nations supplying IT-enabled and knowledge-related services.' However, sectors such as, retail and other professional services, that have not been exposed to

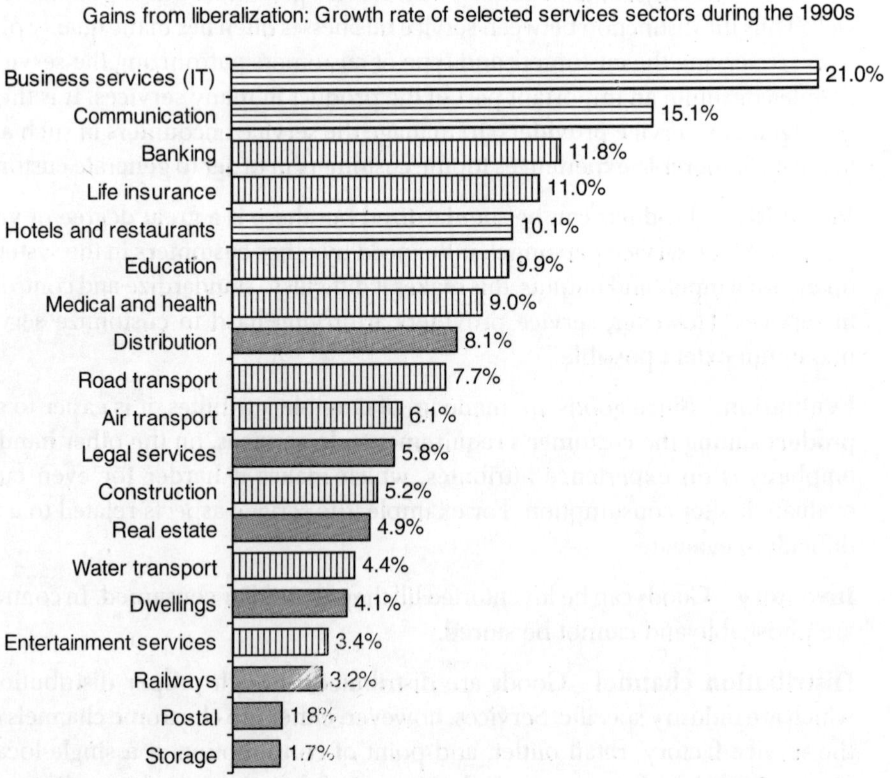

Gains from liberalization: Growth rate of selected services sectors during the 1990s

Sector	Growth rate
Business services (IT)	21.0%
Communication	15.1%
Banking	11.8%
Life insurance	11.0%
Hotels and restaurants	10.1%
Education	9.9%
Medical and health	9.0%
Distribution	8.1%
Road transport	7.7%
Air transport	6.1%
Legal services	5.8%
Construction	5.2%
Real estate	4.9%
Water transport	4.4%
Dwellings	4.1%
Entertainment services	3.4%
Railways	3.2%
Postal	1.8%
Storage	1.7%

Source: The World Bank (2008).

Fig. 1.2   Growth of liberalized sectors

sufficient domestic and foreign competition, and where the regulatory framework is weak, have failed to create income or employment opportunities for the economy.

Foreign direct investment Liberalization has led to increased foreign direct investment (FDI) in the services sector. This has led to increased investment by multinationals in India and hence stiffer competition. Domestic firms have also tried to meet the growing customer aspirations resulting in commitment to offering superior services. The flow of FDI in India in 2005–06 amounted to $6 billion and is expected to increase significantly in the years to come, according to the Planning Commission, 2006 report. Figure 1.3 highlights the positive co-relation between FDI and growth in various service sectors.

Higher flows of FDI have also been associated with more exports in the services sector. Among the individual segments of the services sector, there appears to be a strong association between FDI growth and exports. The IT sector is a case in point. Figure 1.4 illustrates the relationship between FDI and IT exports in select states in India.

Better living standards The standards of living are getting better thanks to increased employment opportunities for people. This has been led by high disposable income, double household income, and convenience factors.

High disposable incomes The incomes of consumers have increased manifold in the years of liberalization. People now have bigger amounts of money to spend. With more disposable incomes consumers tend to spend on services that make their life convenient. A case in point is the proliferation of mobile phone services in the country. The percolation of the mobile phones to literally every segment of the society has made life convenient and improved lifestyles as also the way of doing business. Thus, several

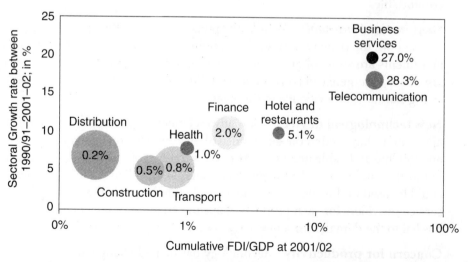

Source: The World Bank.

Fig. 1.3 Positive association between FDI and growth

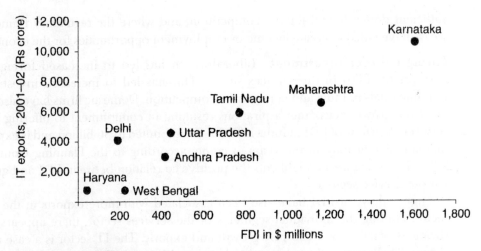

Source: NASSCOM (2008).

Fig. 1.4   FDI and IT exports in some Indian states

cellular phone service providers keep devising new attractive schemes for consumers to make it easier for them to acquire mobile phones as well as services.

Convenience factors   As incomes of people rise, there is a proclivity towards convenience-related services. For example, laundry services, house-keeping, and repairing are some of the services which are increasingly being outsourced. There is also a rush for baby-sitting services, home delivery grocery outlets, and transport providers. The idea is to utilize money in improving one's lifestyle and making it comfortable.

Dual income households   With both spouses working, the spending power increases and so does the paucity of time. Thus, home-care services, salon services, and service apartments are some of areas that have seen a lot of growth in recent years. This has also led to emergence of convenience retailing formats. The success of superstores such as Big Bazaar is an evidence of this change.

New technological devices   New advancements in technology and their commercial applications have led to the emergence of new services such as gaming, entertainment, and satellite and cable networks. Also, convergence of technological applications have led to the emergence of new products, such as the iPod, mobile phones, etc. which could be used to download text, video, and audio signals. This creates a new room for service providers for such products. Thus the creation of new platforms of technology has led to the demand for a new stream of content developers for the new services.

Concern for productivity   Technology has helped change the dynamics of business transactions. For instance, banking has become so convenient with new standards being set in customer delivery. The options of ATMs, online banking, payments through the

Internet, and credit cards have all contributed to convenience, and at the same time resulted in more business and cost savings by the provider. Many product and service firms have set up call centres that take care of customer queries and after-sales servicing. These factors have contributed to higher revenues and business growth in the services segment.

CHALLENGES CONFRONTED BY THE SERVICE SECTOR

The services sector faces a lot of challenges. If we take into account the various stakeholders into account, then there are numerous challenges that need to be addressed. These stakeholders are the government, consumers, society, financial investors, suppliers, and the firms or service providers themselves.

Infrastructure

The growth of any segment depends upon the presence of adequate and good infrastructure. Despite India's average performance in the manufacturing segment as compared to China, it fares better in terms of service industry, especially the software industry. The support by the government in terms of providing and developing software technology parks has been largely instrumental in the emergence of world-class Indian software firms such as Infosys and Tata Consultancy Services. Technology facilitates a lot of value drivers in the service industry. For instance, call centres help in putting together a customer response system. But these can function well and are meaningful only if the roads are proper, the transport sector is well developed, and the power, water and bandwidth availability is adequate. Thus, the biggest challenge in India is creation of world-class infrastructure to match the demands of the growing economy. The airports and local transport system needs to be revamped, and investments in civic amenities need to be hiked.

Technology

Technology has dramatically changed the nature of business. E-commerce, for instance, has opened up an additional channel for sales for many organizations. This has implications on nature of transactions, procurement, and delivery processes for firms that have integrated IT in their business. Distribution channels stand greatly enhanced due to instance availability of e-tickets for airline and train travel, direct room reservations, etc. Also, shopping on the Internet opens up new options for consumers. While IT enables convenient purchase for consumers, it throws up several issues of secure transactions and security of consumer databases for the service firms. Also, firms will have to look for larger volumes of business to make their online businesses commercially viable. Technology sophistication and availability also implies that the same service can be copied as anyone can buy the technology off the shelf. It is a challenge to remain competitive in the long run. It implies that firms need to invest in enduring relationships with consumers to survive.

Employees

It is a big challenge to find the right kind of people who can create a distinct experience for consumers. Sectors such as retail and IT enabled services (ITES) operating in India face the challenge of high attrition. This implies that new people have to be hired continuously and trained. In fact, many BPOs frequently place large recruitment ads for walk-in interviews. There are also high attrition rates in the Indian hospitality sector, and firms face a big challenge in retaining talented workers. The employee attitude is a key factor that influences the service experience of a customer. It is, therefore, important that an employee has the right attitude, and is well trained so that services could be standardized, and deviations on account of human errors be avoided. Service firms will have the following challenges relating to the workforce:

- How to recruit the right talent and nurture it as well?
- How to retain the people?
- How to imbibe the right competencies in the manpower?
- What interventions are required at the education level to have both the right output for the industry, and the right trainers?
- How could best practices be instituted and benchmarked?

Consumers

Consumers are becoming more and more literate as most economies are investing increased amounts on education. This results in higher levels of consumer awareness. Higher incomes have also resulted in higher expectations on delivery. With competition having increased, consumers are willing to experiment to get maximum value for their money. Thus, for a service firm sustaining growth is a big challenge. Today, the consumers benchmark internationally and their expectations are also higher, thanks to the Internet and global satellite channels. Also, the level of domestic and international travel has gone up dramatically, which has contributed to higher aspirations and expectations. Many desperate service firms, in the name of relationship marketing, make innumerable unsolicited calls for selling credit cards or offering loans in order to achieve higher sales. These are not viable solutions for the businesses. Better ways of engaging customers would have to be thought of rather than hitting the same database with the same enquiries about potential association. The consumer courts have also become stronger in India. They provide relief to hassled consumers, thus making the business of providing services more challenging than before.

Competition

Competition also becomes an important challenge for service firms. With similar technologies available, the search for different value drivers becomes difficult. The firms face a tough time constantly striving to achieve a higher market share. The long-term solution should be not to compete against each other, but go in for cooperative arrangements to prevent wastage of resources. For example, global majors in the business of sustainable energy sources have fostered alliances for commercializing alternate fuel technologies. Similarly, in the field of information technology (IT), Intel, Hewlett-Packard (HP), and Princeton University have fostered an alliance, 'Planetlab' which works on Linux technologies on Itanium platform.

Suppliers

Suppliers are becoming more and more dynamic, and this has given rise to new kind of industry relationships in the services sector. In certain high-technology industries these relationships have a profound impact on the business and the shape of the industry itself. For instance, the relationship of Intel with various personal computer (PC) manufacturers has set new technology standards. Similarly, the alliance of Microsoft with various PC vendors has led to several tie ups for the operating systems. These alliances have long-term impacts on the nature of industry relationships. In the travel industry, the global reservation systems, which most firms adopt, have become the default standards, and, hence have a unique place for suppliers of such software. In the years to come, service providers will have to ponder over the following questions:

- How will the supplier impact my future growth?
- Should I go with a few exclusive suppliers, or should I deal with multiple vendors?
- How would future change in technology influence the relationship with current vendors?

Service firms will have to assess the above-mentioned challenges and devise a strategy to cope with them.

CRITICAL FACTORS FOR SUCCESS

Every service segment has some distinct aspects that contribute towards its success. However, there are some generic aspects which can be addressed keeping in mind the general characteristics of the service industry.

Focus on Customers

It is always important for a service firm to remember that the consumer is the most important entity and all its processes and activities need to be aligned to ensure a better service delivery. Many a time, in the process of adopting a particular technology system or quality initiatives, firms alter the processes of service delivery, which may or may not be convenient for the customer. For example, the automatic response system set up by many service providers, such as banks or airlines, sometimes takes a lot of time for resolving a query. The technology, people, systems, and policies are all facilitators, and are not an end by themselves. So a service firm always needs to address issues such as:

- Who are my customers?
- What do they want?
- How much are they willing to pay?
- What could be the quickest way of delivery without compromising quality?

Caring for Employees

People management is one of the most critical factors in services management. Employee satisfaction leads to better performance at work resulting in customer satisfaction and hence increased market share. This has been discussed extensively in Chapter 17. It is, therefore, important for companies to care of their employees. Satisfied and loyal employees could facilitate a happy experience for customers, which is translated into increased business. Thus, managing attrition, training people, and helping chart a bright career path for them, are key challenges in managing human resources.

Identification of Value Drivers

Every business has its own value chain as has been pointed out by Porter (1985) in his theory of value chain analysis. In some businesses, it is the experience such as multiples as in adventure; tourism or in some service sectors it may be technological superiority, which are the essential or key value drivers that can be identified and worked upon. A firm, if it does not have a unique or a distinct advantage, will not last long in business. Hence, identification of unique elements, which would extend longevity is one of the critical challenges for these companies.

Deploying Technology to a Firm's Advantage

Technology opens new vistas of business for a service firm. It is, therefore, important to identify the technology which could add value to the service being provided and the firm. The Internet offers an immense challenge. The dynamics of online purchase are also very different as compared to traditional channels of marketing. Also, it offers new ways of reaching out to consumers through various portals. One critical success factor is to evolve the right communication strategy to drive the business.

Demand Management

Since services cannot be stored, it is a big challenge to manage the demand. The pricing strategy has to be such that it generates volumes to keep the business going. Necessity-based entrepreneurship always leads to lot of challenges for service firms. In India, the small-scale sector faces a huge challenge of demand management. A survey conducted by the Department of Small Scale Industries in 2005, showed that lack of demand was one of the key contributors to sickness in Indian small scale industries (SSI). Technology can be utilized to leap frog to higher growth, provided customer focus is in place.

Adequate Systems

It is essential to invest in adequate systems and procedures. Lack of proper service delivery systems can ruin the brand. Work flow systems have to be in place with clear reporting relationships. The implementation of services need to be closely monitored.

INTERNATIONAL TRADE REGULATIONS FOR SERVICE SECTOR

The General Agreement on Trade in Services (GATS) is a treaty of the World Trade Organization (WTO) and the first multilateral trade agreement to cover trade in services at the global level. This intergovernmental agreement, which entered into force from 1 January 1995, is regarded as a major achievement of the Uruguay Round of trade negotiations from 1986 to 1993. It provides for the extension of the multilateral trading system to the services sector. However, GATS is considered to be more complex than the General Agreement on Trade and Tariffs (GATT) in global merchandise trade. This because the global service sector is highly differentiated as it covers both retail consumers, and industrial and institutional customers (Hibbert 2003). Little wonder, it was almost half a century after GATT was enforced in 1947 that GATS became a reality. All members of WTO are signatories to GATS. The basic WTO principle of 'most favoured nation' applies to GATS as well. The first round of service negotiations among WTO members started in January 2000.

Perspective

The need for an international regulation in global services trade has long been questioned. This because certain services, such as the hospitality sector and personal services, were generally considered as domestic activities, while sectors like rail transport and telecommunications were viewed as domains of the government. It was also widely considered that social sectors, such as health, education, and insurance, should be regulated by governments. However, finance and marine transport have largely remained open for centuries due to international trade. The advancements in communication technology, the IT revolution, as well as the development of the Internet has changed the ways of conducting global trade. Hibbert (2003) identified the following global trends resulting in increased business opportunities in services trade internationally:

- Information technology coupled with telecommunications has made virtually all services tradable via one mode of supply or the other.
- Information technology has helped in unbundling the production and consumption.
- Both goods and services organizations are outsourcing their non-core products to increase their competitiveness and creating more opportunities.

Services have, in recent times, become the most effervescent segment of international trade. Since 1980, world services trade has grown from 20 per cent to 24 per cent on balance of payment (BoP) basis. Given the continued impetus of global services trade, the need for internationally recognized rules became increasingly imperative.

Basic Purpose of GATS

According to the WTO, 'GATS is intended to contribute to trade expansion under conditions of transparency and progressive liberalization and as a means of promoting the economic growth of all trading partners and the development of developing countries.'

Thus we can conclude that the contribution of GATS to world services trade rests on two main pillars:

- ensuring increased transparency and predictability of relevant rules and regulations
- promoting progressive liberalization through successive rounds of negotiations.

Scope and Application

'A service is traded when the supplier and customer are from different countries, regardless of the location of the transaction' (Hibbert 2003). GATS allows members to take any measure affecting trade in specific services sectors. The measure can be taken at the federal, regional, or local government level, or by non-governmental bodies exercising delegated powers. The relevant definition covers any measure, 'whether in the form of a law, regulation, rule, procedure, decision, administrative action, or any other form, ... in respect of the:

- purchase, payment or use of a service
- access to and use of, in connection with the supply of a service, services which are required by members to be offered to the public generally
- presence, including commercial presence, of persons of a member for the supply of a service in the territory of another member.'

For purposes of structuring their commitments, WTO members have generally used a classification system comprising 12 core service sectors (WTO 2006).

1. Business services (including professional services and computer services)
2. Communication services
3. Construction and related engineering services
4. Distribution services
5. Educational services
6. Environmental services
7. Financial services (including insurance and banking)
8. Health-related and social services
9. Tourism and travel-related services
10. Recreational, cultural, and sporting services
11. Transport services
12. Other services not included elsewhere

Basic principles   The following are the basic principles of GATS:

- All services are covered by GATS.
- Most-favoured-nation treatment applies to all services, except the one-off temporary exemptions.
- National treatment applies in the areas where commitments are made.
- Transparency in regulations, inquiry points.
- Regulations have to be objective and reasonable.
- International payments: normally unrestricted.
- Individual countries' commitments: negotiated and bound.
- Progressive liberalization: through further negotiations.

Please refer to Exhibit 1.3 for an insight on the Doha Development Agenda.

Thus we can conclude that overall the business community stands to gain due to the increased predictability or legal certainty within the services trading environment. Commitments have been made to ensure that there are no arbitrary regulatory interventions by governments. GATS is still at a nascent stage, and limitations and restrictions are bound to exist. But at least they have been identified and can be anticipated (Hibbert 2003). Also, once members have made commitments they cannot renege on those commitments without compensating other members.

SERVICE MANAGEMENT

This section discusses the traditional marketing mix, the expanded marketing mix, and the variables and elements of the marketing mix.

Traditional Marketing Mix

Culiton (1948) developed the idea of a marketing mix from the notion of a marketer as a 'mixer of ingredients' where a marketer plans various means of competition and blends them together so that a profit function is optimized. The term and concept of 'marketing mix' was introduced by Neil Borden in the 1950s. According to Baron et al. (1991), the marketing mix is defined as 'those activities that show similarities to the overall process of marketing, requiring the combination of individual elements'. After the Second World War, Cullotin coined the 'P' philosophy of marketing, proposing a long list of Ps which typified profit, planning, production etc. and represented the key activities of running a business. According to Czinkota, one could differentiate between a 'sales orientated' and a 'manufacture oriented' company by examining the amount of emphasis given to the various 'Ps'. Thus, the idea, and eventually, the practice of a marketing-orientated company emerged. MaCarthy (1960) further developed this idea and refined the principle to what is today generally known as the four 'Ps'—product, place (distribution), promotion, and price.

Product

The definition of the first 'P', that is, product, according to Kotler et al. (2006) is, 'anything that can be offered to a market for attention, acquisition, use or consumption; it includes physical objects, services, personalities, places, organization services and ideas'.

The service industry has to develop the right service package. A service package includes the service delivery process also, because, in services, the delivery process is part of the product. Since the product is the main offering which the clients covet, any failure in it will ring a death knell for the service.

Place

'Place' in marketing stands for distribution of services. A client can engage a service if he/she has possession of it, at the right time and location convenient to him/her. Thus place is concerned with the 'possession of service that is accessible to the client at the right place and at the right time'. It includes distribution channels, levels of distribution, logistics, etc. However, for service industries, strategic location is of prime importance, and by occupying strategic locations the advantages and resources can be optimized (Low and Tan 1995).

Promotion

Once the organization has decided to market their services they need to inform the customers or the public in general about their existence, what services they can provide, and how they are different from the other providers of the same service so that they can influence the purchasing decisions of the customers. Promotion, or the third 'P' in marketing, is all about this. In order to effectively strengthen the customer's view of the organization, the promotion mix must be integrated with the marketing mix to deliver a consistent message and strategically position the company and the product. The four main promotion tools are advertising, sales promotion, public relations, and personal selling.

Price

This is the only marketing mix element which generates revenue and is set in relation to the other three 'Ps' as all the others represent cost. According to Kotler et al. (2006), 'Price is the amount of money charged for a good or service'. It is 'The sum of the values consumers exchange for the benefits of having or using the product or service'. Pricing is a difficult area of marketing due to the number of variables such as capacity, efficiency of the firm, competitors' prices, relationships with suppliers, economic conditions, and company's policy on the mark-up.

Expanded Marketing Mix for Services

Services are produced and consumed simultaneously (Bitner 1990). Thus the customers are present 'in the firm's factory' and 'interact directly with the firm's personnel'. The contact employees are then playing a dual role—that of marketing and operations.

According to Shostack (1977), customers are frequently searching for 'surrogates' or 'cues' to help determine a firm's capabilities to overcome 'intangibility'. And often the only cues available are the physical facility and the employees. On the basis of this reasoning Booms and Bitner (1981) broadened the traditional four 'Ps' into seven 'Ps' of services by adding 'physical evidence (the physical surroundings and all tangible cues), participants (all human actors in the service encounter including firm personnel and other customers) and process (procedures, mechanisms and flow of activities)' thus including all elements, which an organization can control in order to satisfy its target market. Although these new elements could be covered within the traditional mix, separating them draws attention to the factors that are significant to service firm managers.

People

Booms and Bitner (1981) included all the 'human actors in the service encounter including firm's personnel and other customers' in the *people* concept. Organizational personnel are very important in a services firm as they are the only component that can deliver the services. In many services customers influence the service delivery and thus affect the service quality not only of their own services but of services of other customers as well. Bitner (1992) identified three types of service organizations based on who performs actions within the 'servicescape' (i.e. physical facility where the service is offered). These are as follows:

Self-service   Organizations in which few employees are present, and level of customer activity is high. For example, ATMs, vending machines, etc.

Inter-personal service   These are organizations where both employees and customers are present, and perform actions within the servicescape. For example, restaurants and hospitals.

Remote service   This is the other extreme of the spectrum. Organizations of such kind have little or no customer involvement, and sometimes even little employee involvement in the servicescape. For example, voice messaging services.

Physical Evidence

According to Zeithaml and Bitner (2003), physical evidence is 'The environment in which the service is delivered and where the firm and customer interact and any tangible components that facilitate performance or communication of the service'. It is important because customers use tangible clues to assess the quality of service provided. Hence if a service is highly intangible, the marketing need is to make it more tangible so that customers can evaluate it easily. The physical evidence thus includes all the tangible representations of the service such as layout/decor, ambience, cleanliness, equipment, employee dress, quantity, guarantees, etc. Bitner (1992) emphasized the importance of managing the physical aspects of the servicescape as a:

- sensory package designed to elicit emotional responses
- facilitator to shape customer behaviour and enable efficient flow of activities
- differentiator to distinguish a service provider from its competitors.

These signal the intended market segments at which the service is targeted, and differentiate higher priced offerings from the less expensive ones. Customers may be specifically attracted to an expensive service by the availability of superior tangible elements, such as a more elegant and better equipped hotel room.

According to Bitner (1992) the servicescape can be of any of the following kinds:

Lean These environments are very simple with few elements, few spaces, and few forms. For example, Federal Express drops off kiosks where the service is provided from one simple structure. For lean servicescapes, design decisions are relatively straightforward, especially in self-service or remote service situations in which there are no interactions between customers and employees.

Elaborate Servicescapes which are very complicated with many elements and many forms are termed elaborate environments. For example, a hospital with many floors, rooms, sophisticated equipment, and complex variability in functions performed within the physical facility. Firms positioned in the elaborate interpersonal service cell face the most complex servicescape decisions.

Process

Process is the actual manner in which the services are delivered. Since the customers are present at the time of service delivery the service process is a prime consideration in customer satisfaction. Services, by concentrating on this aspect, can turn customer satisfaction into customer delight and thus gain a customer for a lifetime.

The importance of physical setting depends on the nature of the job and the nature of the consumption experience.

In Exhibit 1.4 the 7Ps have been applied to the McDonald's fast food chain to give a fair understanding of the marketing mix elements and variables.

Expanded Mix for Services

Within the marketing mix elements we can have a number of variables. Variables can be defined as 'A set of controllable factors that a firm can use to influence the buyer's response' (Vignali and Davies 1994). The variables and elements of the extended marketing mix are illustrated in Table 1.13.

An Integrated Approach

From the earlier discussion it is clear that an intelligent marketer should balance all parts of the marketing mix to convey a harmonious message.

SERVICES MARKETING ENVIRONMENT

A company's marketing mix must be designed after considering the business environment it operates in. This environment is made up of political, economic, demographic, socio-cultural, and technological factors, and the company's competitors (Fig. 1.5). In the

Exhibit 1.4 McDonald's marketing mix elements and variables

The concept of marketing mix can be further illustrated by examining the practices followed by McDonald's, the world's largest fast food chain. It has 25,000 restaurants in over 100 countries and continues to expand its presence globally.

Product

Although McDonald's aims to create standardized items, adaptation to local cultures, tastes, laws, and customs has become a key feature of its marketing strategy. While India was the first outlet where the beef burger was not sold, in Malaysia and Singapore, the chain underwent rigorous inspections to ensure the absence of pork products. Quality assurance remains its main focus and is the global practice that distinguishes the chain from others in the market.

McDonald's is a very good example of prudent and strategic expansion. About 4403 restaurants in 1825 days were added during 1999–2004, i.e., more than 2 restaurants each day for 5 years. This reflects globalization with a glocal focus.

Price

Even the pricing strategy of McDonald's is one of localization than globalization. In order to select the right price for the right market, a price objective is selected, demand is determined, cost is estimated, competitor's cost is analysed, a pricing method is selected, and a final price is determined.

Promotion

Although the company's overall objective is to promote a global image, the entire marketing communications strategy is localized to adapt to the cultural differences that are faced in each country. Footballers Alan Shearer and Fabien Barthez advertise for the company in UK and France respectively. In India, McDonald's is promoted as a family restaurant. The company sponsors a vast array of sports and seeks to enhance a brand name during the Olympic Games and the World Cup. It paid an estimated 20 million pounds for the right to use its logo in an international football event.

McDonald's concentrates on helping children and families facing problems. The company is strongly committed to staffing locally and promoting from within its ranks. Its policy of satisfying all its customers all the time is one of the main reasons for its sustained success.

Process

Stringent criteria are followed for each food item and these procedures are identical globally.

Physical Evidence

'To focus on consistent delivery of quality, service and cleanliness through excellence in our restaurants.' This message is visible in every McDonald's franchise around the world. Thus all around the world, every McDonald's restaurant offers a family environment to its customers.

Source: Adapted from Vignali (2001).

figure, apart from the seven Ps, there are two more Ps—political power and personal relations. These were introduced by Kotler (1984) for firms venturing overseas into new markets. In the new market they have to satisfy not only target clients but other parties, such as government, trade unions, and other interest groups, who act as gatekeepers in their markets (Low and Tan 1995). Kotler coined the term 'megamarketing' to include political power and public relations as part of the marketing tool.

Competitors

Competitors are an important aspect of a company's macro-environment. A successful company has to satisfy the needs and wants of the customers better than its competitors. According to Kotler et al. (2006) a company has to face four levels of competition (Fig. 1.6).

Table 1.13   The extended marketing mix—variables and elements for services

Elements	Product	Place	Promotion	Price

Variables	▫ Brand
	▫ Features
	▫ Quality
	▫ Quantity
	▫ Style
	▫ Accessories
	▫ Packaging
	▫ Warranties
	▫ Product lines
		▫ Outlet type
		▫ Outlet nos
		▫ Accessibility
		▫ Location
		▫ Stocks
		▫ Intermediaries
		▫ Transportation
		▫ Managing channels
			▫ Personal selling
			  – Selection
			  – Training
			  – Incentives
			▫ Advertising
			  – Targets
			  – Media types
			▫ Sales promotion
			▫ Public relations
				▫ Price level
				▫ Strategy
				▫ Determinants
				▫ Discount
				▫ Trade-ins
				▫ Credit
				▫ Terms

Elements	**People**	**Physical evidence**	**Process**	
Variables	▫ Customers ▫ Age ▫ Social group ▫ Employees ▫ Quantity ▫ Quality ▫ Training ▫ Motivation ▫ Promotion ▫ Rewards ▫ Teamwork	▫ Layout/Decor ▫ Ambience ▫ Cleanliness ▫ Equipment ▫ Employee dress ▫ Quantity ▫ Guarantees	▫ Blueprinting ▫ Automation ▫ Control procedures	

Source: Adapted from Zeithaml and Bitner (2003), Vignali and Davies (1994), and Vignali (2001).

Product form competition   This includes all competitors who offer similar products and services to the same segment of customers at a similar price. To illustrate, for a south Indian restaurant all other restaurants offering south Indian dishes are competitors. Coke and Thums Up are product form competitors of Pepsi (Fig. 1.6).

Product category competition   This includes all the companies making the same class of products. Thus Mirinda, 7UP, Sprite, and Limca are product category competitors of Pepsi.

General competition   This includes all companies providing the same service. Hence, different forms of fruit juices (packaged and fresh), flavoured drinks such as Frooti, Rooh Afza, Haldiram's Rose, etc., and home-made drinks, such as fresh lime and lassi (a drink made from curd), provide a general competition to Pepsi.

Budget competition   This broadly includes all companies who compete for the same consumer rupees. Thus restaurants, movie theatres, and snacks provide a budget competition to Pepsi.

A competitor analysis is important for a company as it is essential to identify rivals, ascertain the market share of the different players in the market, comprehend their marketing strategies, and emulate their best practices.

Source: Adapted from Low and Tan (1995) and Kotler (2006).

Fig. 1.5 An overview of the marketing environment

Political Environment

According to Kotler et al. (2006) the 'political environment is made up of laws, government agencies and pressure groups that influence and limit the activities of various organizations and individuals in society' and its basic purpose is to protect:

- companies from unfair competition
- consumers from unfair practices
- the society from unimpeded business behaviour.

In India a number of laws have been constituted to protect the rights of the stakeholders of a business. For instance, laws relating to working hours, conditions of services and employment, employment and training, labour laws, wage laws, etc. protect the rights of employees. Apart from this there are over around 30,000 non-governmental organizations (NGO) working in the area of social welfare. An NGO is a non-profit group or association that acts outside the political structure and pursues matters of interest to its members by lobbying, persuasion, or direct action. The political environment of a country is important for a company's business in view of various legal parameters. Also, all the mandatory requirements should be adhered to and a continuous monitoring of the environment is required so that any future laws or rules, which can affect the functioning of an organization, can be incorporated into marketing strategies without delay.

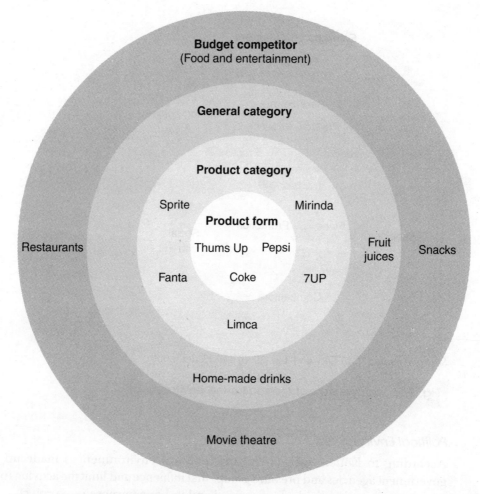

Source: Adapted from Kotler et al. (2006).

Fig. 1.6   Levels of competition

Economic Environment

This consists of factors that affect consumer purchasing power and spending patterns. Marketers should pay attention to both income distribution and average income. Rising income levels have a bearing on the spending power of customers. The importance of income in marketing of services has been discussed in detail in Chapter 5. Consumer spending slows down during times of economic slowdown. Companies should undertake innovative steps to tide over the economic slumps. The global economy is also important for the hospitality industry with the increase in international tourism. According to India Brand Equity Foundation (IBEF), the growth of tourist inflow into India was well above the world average, leading to a rise of India's share in world arrivals from 0.37 per cent in 2001 to 0.53 per cent in 2006.

Demographic Environment

According to Kotler et al. (2006) 'Demography is the study of human population in terms of size, density, location, age, gender, race, occupation and other statistics'. The demographics of a country is of major interest to marketers because it represents the target customers for products and services. Market segmentation on the basis of demographics is practised by most marketers. This concept has been elaborated in detail in Chapter 5.

Socio-cultural Environment

The society plays a major role in shaping the basic beliefs and values of its members. A society's cultural environment includes institutions and other forces that affect the basic values, perceptions, preferences, and behaviours of its members. Indian culture is diverse and varies like its vast geography. People speak in different languages, dress differently, follow different religions, eat different food but are of the same temperament. A festival or a celebration is never confined to a family or a home. The whole community or neighbourhood is involved in bringing liveliness to an occasion. Companies announce special packages along with different programmes to attract customers during the festive season. An occasion such as Holi or New Year results in increased revenues for the hospitality sector. For example, Hotel Umaid Palace in Jodhpur targets its prospective clients during the Holi festival. The hotel offers special activities at premium prices during the peak season. According to Mr Mandeep Lamba, President, Fortune Park Hotels Ltd, the trend of people visiting their relatives' homes is now being replaced by the inclination for taking vacations at hotels and resorts. India's domestic tourism has grown by 40 per cent in the last four years. Keeping in line with this social trend, Fortune Park plans to build 52 hotels by 2010 and the number of rooms is expected to go up to 4200 from the current 1600 rooms.

Technological Environment

The most remarkable force that is shaping our destiny today is technology. We are still at the threshold of Internet technology, which has given us countless opportunities at a negligible cost.

It is very important for organizations to be aware of the changes taking place in the macroenvironment. This helps them at the strategic planning level to formulate effective strategies. The scanning of the environment for future predictions should be a continuous process for organizations keeping in line with the adage 'forewarned is forearmed'. An organization can convert a threat into an opportunity by preparing itself with strategies. On the other hand, lack of focus at the strategic planning level can result in the company losing its market share to rivals. Exhibit 1.5 illustrates the use of technology in the hospitality sector.

Exhibit 1.5 Use of technology in the hospitality sector

Technology in India has come a long way. The hotel industry is adapting the latest technologies, thanks to increasing competition. It has been closely observed that technology acts as a key differentiator to retain international clientele. Research indicates that hotels and resorts with websites without a real-time reservation facility lose 30% of their potential customers. Online hotel bookings across the industry have witnessed an upward trend keeping in view the large number of computer users in the country.

As the hospitality industry started looking for ways to improve efficiencies, efforts and investments in the field of information technology intensified. Highly sophisticated accounting systems are in place and are constantly fine tuned to suit the customer. For instance, The Taj Group of Hotels has implemented a WAN named TajNet that connects the group's 55 properties in India, Nepal, and Sri Lanka. Such a centralized system has tremendous benefits, such as greater economies of scale, when the group wants to announce a special scheme for all its member hotels. In addition, the group can monitor the performance of each member hotel and summarize the sales performance of the whole group.

Customer relationship management (CRM) is also being implemented in all major hotels as it helps them to store complete profiles of their customers, which in turn helps to build one-to-one customized service experience.

Wireless Internet access has become commonplace in hotels. To ensure complete satisfaction, some hotels have even deployed wireless equipped handheld phones with the purpose of tracking the person anywhere in the hotel premises. This service is really useful for mobile staff, who are able to attend to a complaint immediately.

A growing trend has been observed as far as online reservations are concerned. There has been a shift towards 'direct-to-customer' sales strategy. This increasing demand for direct access using the online hotel reservation system is greatly reducing the hotel's need to rely on travel agents and tour operators for their business. Online hotel reservation software helps by saving operating costs substantially and minimizing the cost of acquiring and retaining a customer. This facility ensures that bookings can be made 24/7. It also displays the availability of rooms. All major hotel groups, such as The Taj, Le Meridien, and Maurya Sheraton, have online reservation systems, which are safe and convenient. Utilizing the strength of the Internet, more and more of such hotels are ensuring 24/7 room reservations. This not only reaches out to a greater number of people but also enables greater visibility of services.

Source: Adapted from ExpressComputerOnline (2008).

SUMMARY

Services constitute a major portion of the world trade and are growing at an increasing rate. However, they are different from the traditional product marketing in a number of ways. These differences make the marketing of services challenging for the management. This chapter highlights some of the strategies the marketers can adopt to overcome these concerns. The chapter also gives an understanding of the factors responsible for the growth of the service sector and the critical factors for its success. This is important to understand the service sector and form a background for a detailed study in services management. Infrastructure, technology, employees, etc. are some of the issues discussed in the section on the challenges faced by the service sector. International trade regulations concerning services have been discussed under GATS. This section highlights the initiatives taken to promote trade in the services sector. The next section discusses the various aspects of marketing mix applicable to services. A rationale has been developed for the extended marketing mix and an integrated approach to

Contd

Summary Contd

services management is discussed. The last section deals with the services environment as well as the internal and external environment affecting the delivery. All these sections help to develop a basic understanding of the service sector before going into the finer nuances of management of the same.

KEY TERMS

Foreign investment   Investment in the domestic economy by foreign individuals or companies. Foreign investment takes the form of either direct investment in productive enterprises or investment in financial instruments, such as a portfolio of shares.

Liberalization   To remove or loosen restrictions on an economic or political system.

Marketing mix   The factors controlled by a company that can influence consumers' buying of its products. Product, pricing, promotion, and place are the four components of a marketing mix. The potential profitability of a particular marketing mix and its acceptability to its market are assessed by marketing research.

Product   Anything that can be offered to a market for attention, acquisition, use, or consumption that might satisfy a need. It includes physical objects and services.

Pricing   The setting of selling prices for the products and services supplied by an organization. Prices can be based either on market prices or costs.

Promotion   An activity designed to boost the sales of a product or service. It may include an advertising campaign, increased PR activity, a free-sample campaign, offering free gifts or trading stamps, arranging demonstrations or exhibitions, setting up competitions with attractive prizes, temporary price reductions, door-to-door selling, telemarketing, mailers, etc.

Place   Activities such as sales and distribution of the product, transportation services, and desirable stock levels.

Service   Any activity or benefit that one party can offer to another that is intangible and does not result in the transfer of ownership of any physical object.

Service economy   With the decline of heavy engineering and rise of the knowledge-based economy, the service industry constitutes an ever-increasing proportion of the national income in nearly all the developed countries.

CONCEPT REVIEW QUESTIONS

1. Critically discuss the importance of services in the economic growth of a developing country.

2. Which extended elements of the marketing mix are absent in the marketing of traditional products. Critically discuss their importance in the marketing of services.

3. What are the different ways by which services can be classified? Discuss any two.

4. Should services be classified? Discuss.

5. What are the different challenges being confronted by the services industry. Which according to you is most important and why?

6. What is the marketing environment? Discuss any two factors of marketing environment, which affect the services sector the most.

CRITICAL THINKING QUESTIONS

1. Discuss how services are increasingly forming an important component in the marketing of traditional products.

2. Identify any three services you are using the most in your daily life. Discuss the levels of their intangibility.

3. Visit any pure services outlet, such as a hotel or a bank, and examine the marketing strategies employed to overcome the different characteristics of services.

INTERNET EXERCISES

1. Visit the government website of any developing Asian country and try to identify the importance of the service sector in the development of their economy. (*Hint*: you can consider services as a percentage of GDP, employment generated, exports and imports of services, etc.)

2. Visit the website of the WTO and find out the latest developments pertaining to the GATS.

3. Identify two organizations whose services are possible only because of the Internet.

CASE STUDY

The Housing Finance Sector in India: A Focus on HDFC

The mortgage financing industry, which is primarily known as the housing finance industry in India, has grown by leaps and bounds in the past few years. The sector has emerged as one of the outstanding successes over the last decade, second, perhaps, only to the country's software industry. Total home loan disbursements by banks and housing finance companies (HFCs) increased from Rs 19,723 crore in 1999–2000 to Rs 53,679 crore in 2003–04. However, the mortgage to GDP ratio (ratio of outstanding home loans to GDP), which is used to determine the extent of penetration of housing finance in the country, is one of the lowest for India as compared to developed countries where it ranges from 25 per cent to 60 per cent. The mortgage to GDP ratio stood at an abysmal 2 per cent in India when compared to 20 per cent in Southeast Asia, 57 per cent in UK, 54 per cent in USA, 40 per cent in the EU, 7 per cent in China and 14 per cent in Thailand. Hence, there is a great deal of promise for this industry in India, as the penetration of housing is very low and there are immense growth

opportunities in the long-run. (CapitalinePlus, 2006). The housing finance industry has grown at an estimated compounded annual growth rate (CAGR) of 28 to 30 per cent during this period.

Factors Driving the Mortgage Market

According to the National Housing Board the age-old concept of a house as a 'shelter' has transformed with time to mean a popular 'investment' for a significant segment of the population who consider this as a good source of return on capital. This has further been facilitated by low and stable interest rates. Some of the main fiscal, social, and regulatory drivers that have fuelled the growth are:

1. Changes in demographic profile, including increase in the rate of household formation, due to a structural shift from joint family system to nuclear family.

2. Ever increasing middle class, migration of population, and increasing urbanization resulting in acute shortage of housing units.

3. Increase in disposable income levels due to decrease in marginal tax rates and increase in total income levels.

4. Tax benefits and other fiscal incentives announced in the Union budget.

5. Increasing affordability of housing property purchase due to declining interest rates and stable property prices.

6. Increased demand from software and other services sectors.

7. Decline in the average house cost to annual income ratio to around 4–5 from 11–14 during the last decade, resulting in an affordable equated monthly instalments (EMI) as a percentage of monthly income.

Apart from this, India, with vast untapped opportunities, is already on its way to becoming the desired location for real estate investors.

o The Indian real estate market is growing at an annual rate of 30 per cent with steady growth in residential properties, shopping malls, multiplexes, food outlets, office spaces, and convention and business centres across India.

o 80 per cent of the demand for commercial space is being fuelled by the IT and ITES sector with the emergence of India as the knowledge capital of the world.

Foreign developers, architects, and planners are playing a crucial role in the development of integrated/luxury townships.

Structure of Housing Finance System in India

The housing finance industry can be broadly classified into the formal and informal sector. In the formal sector there are housing finance companies, HUDCO, commercial banks, etc., accounting for around 30 per cent of the total housing finance needs. The remaining 70 per cent is met by the informal sector sources such as household savings, disposal of existing property, borrowings from friends, relatives, and local moneylenders, etc.

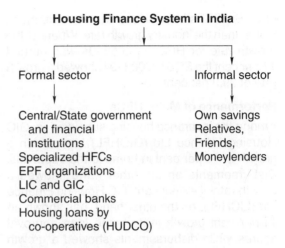

Housing Finance System in India

Formal sector

Central/State government and financial institutions
Specialized HFCs
EPF organizations
LIC and GIC
Commercial banks
Housing loans by co-operatives (HUDCO)

Informal sector

Own savings
Relatives,
Friends,
Moneylenders

Increasing Share of Banks

The Housing Development Finance Corporation Limited (HDFC) pioneered individual lending based on market principles for homeownership in India. The success of HDFC over the years indicates that financing houses can be a profitable business. This has motivated many new housing finance companies to venture into the housing finance business. An important event of the 1980s was the formation of the National Housing Bank (NHB) in 1987. The objective of NHB is to channel formal sector resources to housing finance (urban and rural) through the promotion of a sound, healthy, and cost-effective housing finance system.

Despite being a late entrant, banks have overtaken the HFCs in the home loan market. The share of banks in total home loan disbursements has risen from 50 per cent in the year 1999–2000 to 61 per cent in 2003–04. Banks have increased their focus on the retail finance market, particularly in housing finance due to lower non-performing assets (NPA) levels.

During 1999–2000 the share of home loan (HL) disbursements among HFCs and scheduled commercial banks (SCB), (which include public sector banks, private sector banks, and foreign banks in India) stood equal. However, with gradual progress, SCBs have outpaced its counterpart and in 2003–04 the ratio stood at 39:61 in favour of SCBs. SCBs have also grown at a rate much higher than the industry growth rate. Whereas the growth rate for HFCs in 2003–04 was around 17 per cent the SCB in 2003–04 showed a growth rate of 39.3 per cent.

Performance of Major HFCs

Among the insurance housing subsidiaries, GIC Housing Finance Ltd (GICHFL) has shown a growth of 46 per cent in home loans approvals. Disbursements on the other hand showed a growth rate of 47 per cent. LIC Housing Finance Ltd (LICHFL), on the other hand, has shown an 11 per cent growth in its home loan approval figures, while disbursements showed a growth rate of 13 per cent.

Among the private players, HDFC has shown a 30 per cent growth in its home loan approval figures. Disbursements have shown a growth rate of 28 per cent. DHFL, on the other hand, has shown a 41 per cent growth in its home loan approval figures while disbursements have had a growth rate of 35 per cent.

HDFC, the market leader with over 50 per cent market share in housing loans, has consistently clocked a 40–50 per cent growth rate during the last six years as against the industry growth rate of 33 per cent (*Business India* 2002). In 2004–05 HDFC performed well with the highest profit after tax of Rs 1036.58 crore and a growth rate of 21.7 per cent. Amongst other HFCs, GICHFL shows the maximum growth during 2004–05, at 59.9 per cent.

Among SCBs, ICICI Bank is the leader in the retail finance arena with a market share of 30 per cent. Its retail assets showed a growth of 68 per cent in 2004. In the public sector bank (PSB) segment, State Bank of India (SBI) has significant presence in the retail segment. Retail loans constitute 24 per cent of the bank's total loan book of which 53.8 per cent is housing loans. SBI's home loans segment grew by 46 per cent (Rs 7,906 crore). The total housing loan book for SBI stands at Rs 24,988 crore as on March 2005.

HDFC Bank

HDFC was amongst the first to receive an 'in principle' approval from the Reserve Bank of India (RBI) to set up a bank in the private sector, as part of the RBI's liberalization of the Indian banking industry in 1994. The bank was incorporated in August 1994 in the name of 'HDFC Bank Limited', with its registered office in Mumbai, India. HDFC Bank commenced operations as a scheduled commercial bank in January 1995.

HDFC is India's premier housing finance company and enjoys an impeccable track record in India as well as in international markets. Since its inception in 1977, the company has maintained a consistent and healthy growth in its operations to remain the market leader in mortgages. Its outstanding loan portfolio covers well over a million dwelling units. HDFC has developed significant expertise in retail mortgage loans to different market segments and also has a large corporate client base for its housing-related credit facilities.

Business Focus

HDFC Bank's mission is to be a world-class Indian bank. The objective is to build sound customer franchises across distinct businesses so as to be the preferred provider of banking services for target retail and wholesale customer segments, and to achieve healthy growth in profitability, consistent with the bank's risk appetite. The bank is committed to maintain the highest level of ethical standards, professional integrity, corporate governance, and regulatory compliance. HDFC Bank's business philosophy is based on four core values—operational excellence, customer focus, product leadership, and people. In a study conducted by Apnaloan.com to discover how the different institutions score, HDFC has emerged as the top scorer in two categories and one of the top scorers in two other categories, and clearly leads the other institutions.

Distribution Network

HDFC Bank is headquartered in Mumbai. The bank, at present has an enviable network of over 531 branches spread over 228 cities across India. All branches are linked on an online real-time basis. Customers in over 120 locations are also serviced through telephone banking. The bank's expansion plans take into account the need to have a presence in all major industrial and commercial centres where its corporate customers are located as well as the need to build a strong retail customer base for both deposits and loan products. Being a clearing/settlement bank to various leading stock exchanges, the bank has branches in the centres where the NSE/BSE have a strong and active member base. The bank also has a network of about over 1054 networked ATMs across these cities. Moreover, all domestic and international Visa/MasterCard, Visa Electron/Maestro, Plus/Cirrus and American Express credit cardholders can access HDFC Bank's ATM network.

In a milestone transaction in the Indian banking industry, Times Bank Limited (another new private sector bank promoted by Bennett, Coleman & Co/Times Group) was merged with HDFC Bank Ltd, effective 26 February 2000. The acquisition added significant value to HDFC Bank in terms of increased branch network, expanded geographic reach, enhanced customer base, skilled manpower, and the opportunity to cross-sell and leverage alternative delivery channels.

Apart from giving housing loans HDFC also provides services such as HDFC realty in which they provide assistance required at various stages of property dealings for financial, legal, taxation and valuation, and for sale, purchase, and lease of commercial and residential property. As a good-will gesture, HDFC has come up with a grievance cell where, if you are at your wits end regarding a newly purchased property, all you have to do is provide details like name and address of your building, name of the developer, date of purchase, etc., mention your problem as briefly as possible, and HDFC takes it up with the developers.

Outlook for the Housing Finance Industry

The Indian housing finance industry is on solid ground and has interesting prospects ahead. Given the size of the market, and the huge shortage of housing and low penetration levels, housing loans will continue to grow rapidly and show strong growth for the next few years. Realistic property prices, low interest rates, tax incentives, and innovative products offered by housing finance companies augurs very well for the growth of the housing sector. Further, the Indian housing finance industry mainly caters to the organized or the employed sector, and is traditionally confined to metros and other big cities. The housing finance industry has to go a long way to cover the vast populace of semi-urban and rural towns that live outside the formal sector. However, the HFCs will face stiff challenges from banks, which will definitely put pressure on their margins. Hence, profitability growth will come mainly from loan growth. The Q1FY06 profits for the six leading HFCs grew by 21.8 per cent to Rs 318.07 crore in comparison to Rs 261.12 crore reported in Q1FY05. The second quarter results are expected to be in line or better than the first quarter results for most HFCs.

Questions

1. What are the different factors driving the growth of the home loan industry in India. Can you draw similes with the growth of the service sector in India?

2. Critically evaluate the growth of the home loan sector vis-à-vis the different institutions providing the loans.

3. Evaluate HDFC's strategy to capture the home loan market. What critical factors is it focusing on for its success?

4. Comment on the distribution of services employed by HDFC.

SELECT REFERENCES

Bitner, M.J. (1990), 'Evaluating the service encounters: The effects of physical surroundings and employee responses', *Journal of Marketing*, April, vol. 54, no. 2, pp. 69–82.

Bitner, M.J. (1992), 'Servicescapes: The impact of physical surroundings on customers and employees', *Journal of Marketing*, vol. 56, no. 2, pp. 57–71.

CapitalinePlus (2006), 'Services: Banks and housing finance', *Capitaline Plus*, Mumbai.

Freeman, N.L. (2005), 'Extended marketing mix drives service delivery', *Opthalmology Times*, vol. 30, no. 20, p. 106.

Grönroos, C. (1994), 'From marketing mix to relationship marketing: Towards a paradigm shift in marketing', *Management Decision*, vol. 32, no. 2, pp. 4–22.

Hafer, J.C. (1987), 'Developing and operationalizing a product/service classification system for health care providers', *Journal of Health Care Marketing*, vol. 7, no. 3, pp. 25–36.

Hibbert, E. (2003), 'The new framework for global trade in services–All about GATS', *The Service Industries Journal*, vol. 23, no. 2, pp. 67–78.

Hoffman, K.D. and J.E.G. Bateson (2002), *Essentials of Services Marketing: Concepts, Strategies and Cases*, 2nd edn, Orlando, Harcourt College.

Howells J. (2004), 'Innovation, consumption and services: Encapsulation and the combinatorial role of services', *The Services Industries Journal,* vol. 24, no. 1, pp. 19–36.

'ITC upgrades hotel brand', *Business Standard*, 7 August 2006, http://www.itcportal.com/newsroom/press_dec16_04.htm

Hsieh, Charng-Horng and Tzong-Yau Chu (1992), 'Classification of service businesses from a utility creation rerspective', *The Service Industries Journal*, vol. 12, no. 4, pp. 545–557.

Kasper, H., P.V. Helsdingen, and Wouter de Vries Jr (1999), *Services Marketing Management: An International Perspective*, John Wiley and Sons, New York.

Kotler, P., J.T. Bowen, and J.C. Makens (2006), *Marketing for Hospitality and Tourism*, Pearson Education Inc., New Jersey.

Lovelock, C. (1983), 'Classifying services to gain strategic marketing insights', *Journal of Marketing*, vol. 47, pp. 9–20.

Lovelock, C. and E. Gummesson (2004), 'Whither services marketing? In search of a new paradigm and fresh rerspectives', *Journal of Services Research*, vol. 7, no. 1, pp. 20–41.

Lovelock, C. and J. Wirtz (2006), *Services Marketing*, 5th edn, Pearson Education, New Delhi.

Lovelock, C. and L. Wright (1999), *Principles of Services Marketing and Management*, Prentice Hall, New Jersey, p. 14.

Low, Sui Pheng and C.S. Martin Tan (1995), 'A convergence of western marketing mix concepts and oriental strategic thinking', *Marketing Intelligence and Planning*, vol. 13, no. 2, pp. 36–46.

National Housing Board (2004), *Report on trend and progress of housing in India*, June.

Porter, M. (1985), *The Competitive Advantage*, Free Press, New York.

Rafiq, Mohammed and Pervaiz K. Ahmed (1995), 'Using the 7Ps as a generic marketing mix: An exploratory survey of UK and European marketing academics', *Marketing Intelligence and Planning*, vol. 13, no. 9, pp. 4–16.

Rampal, M.K. and S.L. Gupta (2002), *Service Marketing: Concepts, Applications and Cases*, Galgotia Publishing Company, New Delhi.

Rao, R.M. (2005), *Services Marketing*, Pearson Education, New Delhi.

Shostack, G. Lynn (1977), 'Breaking free from product marketing', *Journal of Marketing*, vol. 41, no. 2, pp. 73–80.

Silvestro, R., L. Fitzgerald, and R. Johnston (1992), 'Towards a classification of service processes', *International Journal of Service Industry Management*, vol. 3, no. 3, pp. 62–75.

Sinha, Kounteya (2008), 'Medical tourism booming in India', *The Times of India*, 4 April, p. 19.

'The art of leveraged living' (2002), *Business India,* April 15–28, pp. 47–53.

Unnikrishnan, Rajesh and Prince Matthew Thomas (2006), 'Global brands line up for a slice of the Indian hospitality pie', *The Economic Times*, 24 July.

Vargo, S.L. and R.F. Lusch (2004), 'The four service marketing myths: Remnants of a goods-based manufacturing model', *Journal of Service Research*, vol. 6, no. 4, pp. 324–335.

Varoglu, D. and Z. Eser (2006), 'How service employees can be treated as internal customers in hospitality industry', *The Business Review,* Cambridge, vol. 5, no. 2, pp. 30–36.

Vignali, C. (2001), 'McDonald's: Think global, act local–the marketing mix', *British Food Journal*, vol. 103, no. 2, pp. 97–108.

Vignali, C. and B.J. Davies (1994), 'The marketing mix redefined and mapped: Introducing the MIX', *Management Decision*, vol. 32, no. 8, London, pp. 6, 11.

Wise, R. and P. Baumgartner (1999), 'Go downstream the new profit imperative in manufacturing', *Harvard Business Review*, Sep–Oct 1999.

World Trade Organization (2001), *Trading into the Future: WTO*, The World Trade Organization, 2nd edn.

Zeithaml, V.A., A. Parasuraman, and L.L. Berry (1985), 'Problems and strategies in services marketing', *Journal of Marketing*, vol. 49, no. 2, pp. 33–46.

Zeithaml, V.A. and M.J. Bitner (2003), *Services Marketing*, Tata McGraw-Hill Publishing Company Limited, New Delhi.

http://economictimes.indiatimes.com/News/News_By_Industry/Jobs/One_million_new_jobs_in_India_in_2008/rssarticleshow/2851629.cms, accessed on 23 April 2008.

http://planningcommission.nic.in, accessed on 23 April 2008.

http://siteresources.worldbank.org/INTRANETTRADE/Resources/Topics/Services/IndiaSerRep-Chapt2.pdf, accessed on 25 April 2008.

http://siteresources.worldbank.org/INTRANETTRADE/Resources/Topics/Services/IndiaSerRep-Chapt2.pdf, accessed on 25 April 2008.

http://stats.unctad.org/Handbook/TableViewer/chartView.aspx, accessed on 23 April 2008.

http://www.capitaline.com, accessed on 23 April 2008.

http://www.expresscomputeronline.com/20021209/indtrend1.shtml, accessed on 22 April 2008.

http://www.hdfcrealty.com/general/realtyguide, accessed on 5 September 2006.

http://www.hdfc.com, accessed on 5 September 2006.

http://www.ibef.org/industry/tourismhospitality.aspx, accessed on 24 April 2008.

http://www.indianngos.com/listing.htm, accessed on 24 April 2008.

http://www.india.gov.in/business/laws.php, accessed on 24 April 2008.

http://www.india.gov.in/knowindia/lifestyle.php, accessed on 24 April 2008.

http://www.unctad.org/en/docs/tdstat31ch8_enfr.pdf, accessed on 24 April 2008. http://www.unctad.org/Templates/Page.asp?intItemID=1890&lang=1, accessed on 23 April 2008.

http://www.wto.org/english/tratop_e/serv_e/gsintr_e.doc, accessed on 24 April 2008.

www.ehotelier.com, accessed on 22 April 2008.

www.encyclopedia.com, accessed on 24 April 2008.

www.fhrai.com, accessed on 24 April 2008.

www.wikipedia.com, accessed on 24 April 2008.

2 The Service Product

OBJECTIVES

After reading this chapter you will be able to understand the:
- features of a services product
- process of new product development
- concept of product life cycle and the strategies adopted for the different stages of a service product
- relevance of branding in services

INTRODUCTION

A product/service forms the core focus around which the firm's activities revolve. All the grand plans of marketing activities can fail if the product/service is flawed or does not meet the customer expectations. The marketing environment is dynamic and to be successful, the product/service offering should be reconsidered from time to time so that it can cater to the changing demands. Competitive pressures compel an organization to reconsider its service offering.

In traditional product marketing, a product is a physical commodity, which is an outcome of a production process. The marketing activities revolve around this pre-produced product. However, services are different as there is no readymade, pre-produced article of marketing and utilization. They is only a process; some part of which may be prepared before the customer enters, but the crucial part of the service cannot start until the consumer or user enters the process and interacts with the service providers. The service is ultimately performed and delivered in the presence of the customer. Thus, Grönroos (1998) came up with the idea of the 'missing product' and stated that, 'Services are processes, and hence service firms do not offer products that are comparable to pre-produced bundles of physical resources and features that are provided by manufacturing companies. Instead the outcome of the process is an integral part of the service process, which is consumed by customers as a solution to perceived problems. Thus the use of a service can be characterized as process consumption as opposed to outcome consumption, where only the outcome of a process is consumed or used'. Thus in services marketing a product can be a vacation package, a meal at a restaurant, a financial service, a health service, educational service, etc.

THE SERVICE PRODUCT

There are numerous perspectives on a service product. Kotler et al. (2006) defines a product as, 'Anything that can be offered to a market for attention, acquisition, use, or consumption that might satisfy a need or want. It includes physical objects, services, place, organizations, and ideas'. This definition includes both tangible and intangible offerings. It also places emphasis on meeting the customer expectations.

The American Marketing Association defines a product as, 'Anything that can be offered to a market for attention, acquisition or consumption including physical objects, services, personalities, organizations and desires'. In this definition the focus has been on the offering to the consumer. The emphasis is not on satisfaction.

Adcock and Halborg (2001) define services as 'Everything that the customer receives that is of value in terms of perceived want, need or problem'. This definition attaches importance to the value that is offered to the consumer.

Thus it can be seen that a product can be a tangible object, or an intangible service or idea, which a marketer has to offer to satisfy the needs and wants of the customers. A service is an offering, including both tangible and intangible offerings, which satisfies customer needs through an integrated approach and at the same time contributes to the societal welfare.

Nature of a Service Offering

Customers adopt a product based on the perception that the benefits derived are worth more than the cost of the product. Thus, service organizations must develop and offer a service product that meets or exceeds customer expectation (Gordon et al. 1993). According to Gibney and Luscombe (2000), 'When industries are competing at equal price and functionality, design is the only differential that matters'. When designing the service product marketers need to strategize, keeping in mind the customers wants and expectations regarding the service product. The element of experience in the service product is of prime importance. The design of the service product must thus address three key components (Lovelock and Wirtz 2006):

- core product
- augmented service offering
- delivery process.

Core Product

According to Lovelock and Wirtz (2006), the core product is a vital constituent of the services offering and basically addresses two questions:

- What do the buyers get when they purchase the product?
- What business are we in?

It is the bare minimum of a particular service without any frills or specific features and is the heart of the service. Thus, schools solve the need to provide basic education to children, airlines solve the need to move a person from one location to another, and a hotel provides a clean room for the night.

Augmented Product

According to Lovelock and Wirtz (2006), the core product and the supplementary services together constitute the augmented product. However, according to Kotler et al. (2006), the accessibility, atmosphere, customer interaction with service organization, customer participation and customers' interaction with each other along with the core and supporting products create the augmented product. In 1977, Lynn Shostack gave the molecular model for the augmented product. For example, Shostack's molecular model for airline services explains how vehicles, and food and drinks form the tangible elements of the airlines while the service frequency, transport, in-flight service and pre- and post-flight services form the intangible elements of the airlines product. For instance, in an economy hotel, supplementary services consist of check-in and check-out whereas in a first class corporate hotel it consists of check-in, check-out, telephones, restaurant, valet service, etc. Thus, by adding more of supplementary services the service provider can charge a higher price for the product. For example, the spa industry creates packages around an occasion and markets it as a product. So, there are different offerings in the spa category (Exhibit 2.1).

Delivery Process

This component consists of the manner in which the core and supplementary product is delivered to the final customer. Since the delivery of services involves constant interaction between the service provider and the customer, the delivery process must be planned in detail—the prescribed procedures for delivery of various services, and how and where customers fit in.

Exhibit 2.1 Spa time

The spa industry is going the greeting cards companies' way. In a bid to attract people, spas are creating packages around an occasion and marketing it as a product. So there are spa cuisines, spas with couple suites and four-hand experience (two masseurs working on an individual), and even Raksha Bandhan packages that can be gifted to one's sister on this special occasion. To make spa treatment a holistic experience, various spas have introduced meditation sessions, yoga sessions, and spa cuisine. While the spa at the Leela Kovalam Beach Resort, Kerala, offers its guests refreshing coconut water after a massage, the one at Trident Hilton hotel, Gurgaon, offers herbal tea. Tejas Spa located in the Taj Mansingh hotel, Delhi, offers four-hand massage for Rs 4,200. One can experience the romance of a spa at the Kama Suite of Ananda in Uttaranchal, India's only destination spa. The romantic package costs Rs 9,200 and includes a massage for two, foot-bath rituals, a body scrub, and Jacuzzi bath. At Kairali Day Spa in Delhi one can avail a relaxation package—ten massages in six months for Rs 6,500. Also popular among travellers is the Panchkarma therapy package at Kairali Ayurvedic Health Resort, Kerala.

Hotels, which cater to business travellers, also see a big opportunity in spas with a margin as high as 95 per cent. Though ayurvedic products rule the market, Thai and French products are also used by various spas. To create a niche in the market, spas are launching their own product lines. Jiva Spa will launch 37 Indian beauty products labelled as 'Jiva'. Kairali too has a range of ayurvedic shampoos and oils. The spa industry is still at its nascent stage and highly unorganized, but worldwide the spa business is a $5 billion industry and is expected to become a $20 billion industry by 2010.

Source: Adapted from Talreja (2006).

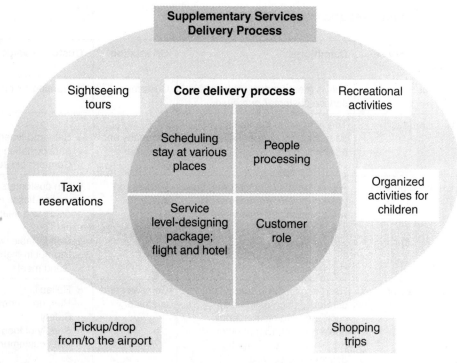

Source: Adapted from Lovelock and Wirtz (2006).

Fig. 2.1 Service offering for a packaged trip

The integration of these three activities is incorporated in Fig. 2.1, which illustrates the service offering for a packaged trip. Thus, for a packaged tour operator the core delivery process consists of designing the package, flight and hotel reservation, scheduling stay at various places along with the people processing and customer role. The supplementary services include sightseeing tours, taxi reservations, recreational activities during the scheduled stay, organized activities for children, etc. These services and the manner in which all this is handled forms the delivery process.

Various Levels of Service Product

According to Kotler (2002) there are five levels of service product the marketer needs to think about. They are:

- Core or generic product/service: This is the most fundamental product/service that customers purchase. For example, customers purchase transportation when buying airline tickets.
- Basic product/service: This is how the marketer translates the core benefit into a service product.
- Expected product/service: This includes the attributes, such design, quality, packaging, etc., which customers expect when purchasing a service product.

Table 2.1   Product level and customer value in services

Level	Product/service level	Definitions	Orientation	Customer value
1.	Core or generic	This is most fundamental product/ service customer purchase.	Customer	▫ Transportation
2.	Basic product	This is how the marketer translates the core benefit into a service product.	Company and customer	▫ Safe and timely transportation ▫ Comfortable seat
3.	Expected product	A set of attributes along with basic product buyers normally expect while purchasing a service.	Market and customer	When customers buy an airline ticket, in addition to a seat they expect: ▫ Comfortable waiting area ▫ Prompt in-flight service ▫ Good meals
4.	Augmented product	Basic product and something different, which delights the customer and differentiates one's product from another, e.g., incentives, warranty, delivery and service.	Company and customer	▫ Reliability ▫ Responsiveness ▫ Safety ▫ Supply of food that suits customer's health
5.	Potential product	New ways of attracting and satisfying the customer, which have not been offered yet.	Company and customer	▫ Offering gifts, which 'wows' the customer and wins loyalty

Source: Adapted from Kotler (2002), Rampal and Gupta (2002), and Rao (2005).

- Augmented product/service: This includes the supplementary services the marketer offers to differentiate their product offering from other players in the same market segment.
- Potential product/service: This consists of new ways of attracting and satisfying the customers.

These five levels of the product constitute the customer value hierarchy (CVH). Taking air transportation by a customer as the backdrop for customer value, a brief explanation of the various levels is provided in Table 2.1.

Classifying Supplementary Services

If we study a variety of services we observe that though the core product may differ widely as there are common supplementary elements such as billing, order-taking, problem-solving, etc. Lovelock classifies them as facilitating or enhancing services. He personifies the services as a flower and maintains that if a service is poorly or badly executed it is like an unattractive flower with missing, wilted, or discoloured petals (Lovelock and Wirtz 2006). Depending upon the nature of the product we can have different supplementary services along with the core product. Generally, people processing services and high-contact services have comparatively more supplementary services. For example, let us take the case of a budget hotel in India. A clean room with bath facilities, telephone, and television is a basic core offering. Any services such as transport, business centre, safekeeping, or travel desk are referred to as facilitating or enhancing services.

NEW PRODUCT DEVELOPMENT

In this section 'product' is being used as a reference to the service product. Every service product has a life cycle. It passes through different stages such as introduction, growth, maturity, and decline. The challenge for companies is to prolong the age of the service product. The task of the company is to keep introducing new products before the decline in sale of the old product in order to stay profitable. Today, the marketing environment is characterized by intense global competition and a fast pace of technological development and this in turn pressurizes firms to develop new products to maintain profitability and market position (Ali 2000). Companies that have a new product strategy in place are more successful than those that do not. New product development, in a conventional buying environment, is largely driven by the need to innovate. More profitable and faster growing firms are found to engage in sustained innovative activities (Vermeulen et al. 2005). Thus, product development is 'An essential process for competitive success, survival and renewal of organizations' (Brown and Eisenhardt 1995). Also, the company must understand how the old product ages and then change the 'Marketing strategies as it passes through the life cycle stages' (Kotler et al. 2006).

Kotler et al. (2006) state that a company can obtain new products either by acquisition of existing companies or by setting up a research and development department for new product development. New product refers to:

- original products
- product improvements
- product modifications
- new brands that firms develop.

Failure is an intrinsic part of innovation (Davis 1997). Firms introduce many new products but 50 per cent of the products disappear within four years (Asplund and Sandin 1999). This occurs because sometimes the cost of developing a new product is higher or the competitors fight back more than expected. 'Successful new services result from an appropriately designed structure and a carefully orchestrated process and are rarely mere happenstance' (Scheuing and Johnson 1989).

Stages in New Product Development

New product development involves the conversion of novel ideas into viable and marketable products. It is a complex process, which involves a complex range of activities. Exhibit 2.2 provides an insight on music downloads as a service offering. Product development is illustrated in Fig. 2.2. The main stages are as listed and are

Exhibit 2.2   Download music while listening to digital radio

Now downloading music from digital radio is becoming a reality, at least for the people in Britain. Players such as London-based UBC Media have announced a download service which plans to roll out the digital music download (DMD) service to generate 95 million pounds (about 173 million dollars) of turnover by 2012, with a profit of nearly 10 million. Even mobile phones will be equipped with such a service and as per the forecast, 25 per cent of all mobile phones will be equipped with this latest technology in the next 6 years and 10 per cent of people who own them will buy downloads.

UBC media plans to work with other players, such as BT group and Carphone Warehouse, to come up with plans in which consumers will pre-pay for the songs using a credit plan. Analysts say that it is not destined to turn into 'Mobile iTunes', as its dominance on the PC is far greater. The mobile technology has so many dynamics in the strategy chain that no dominant model can exist. Upgrades in technology like these are sure to develop the digital media market like never before.

Source: Adapted from Reuters (2006).

subsequently explained.

- Objectives and strategy
- New service idea
  - Idea generation
  - Idea screening
- Concept development and testing
- Budget analysis
  - Budget development
  - Market assessment
- Service process
  - Design
  - Development
  - Testing
- Strategy formulation
  - Marketing
  - HR
- Commercialization
- Review and control

New Service Objective and Strategy

This is important for a well-conceived and carefully implemented new service development process. Lack of formulation of objective is like lifting anchor without determining the desired destination. The company's objective can be high cash flow or it could focus on a particular market share. The environmental analysis and the corporate objectives, and the mission of the business influence these objectives and strategy. These in turn 'drive and direct the entire service innovation effort and instil it with effectiveness and efficiency'. For example, AT&T has redefined itself as being in the information

Source: Adapted from Scheuing and Johnson (1989).

Fig. 2.2   New service development model

management and movement business instead of telecommunications equipment and services. Thus, it now concentrates on all aspects of information management and movement (Scheuing and Johnson 1989).

New Service Idea

The new service idea consists of new idea generation as well as screening of these ideas to come up with the most feasible option.

Idea generation   This is the systematic search for new ideas by an organization. Sometimes a number of ideas have to be generated to find a few excellent ones, which are compatible with the business. Now, there is a paradigm shift as to how companies generate new ideas for product innovation. In the old model of 'closed innovation' companies believed 'successful innovation requires control'. As one cannot be sure of the quality, availability, and capability of others' ideas the innovative ideas must come from within the organization and they should develop, manufacture, market, and distribute the product/service themselves. Increasingly this approach to innovation is no longer sustainable and 'open innovation' is emerging in its place. Using open innovation, an organization can and should use the external and internal ideas and paths to market for new product development. Adding external sources of technology also increases the possible number of sources for innovation (Chesbrough 2004). New product development ideas can come from any of the following sources.

Internal sources   According to a study more than 55 per cent of all new ideas come from within a company (Kotler et al. 2006). Internal search, consultation, and brainstorming can be some ways to generate ideas internally. Also, employees in direct contact with the customers, be it the marketing staff or the service personnel, can be excellent sources for new ideas. Companies are increasingly motivating their staff to be unconventional and encourage out-of-the-box thinking to generate innovation across products and services. This helps them to tap the collective innovation talent inside the company rather than isolating it to a particular department such as R&D.

Customers   Companies are increasingly focusing on customer involvement in new product development to reduce uncertainty and achieve a more favourable cost/time product development curve. They feel that customers are 'Sources of information and knowledge and their involvement can enhance product concept effectiveness' (Lundkvist and Yakhlef 2004). Bonner (1999) stated that, the higher the customer involvement in the new product development, the greater is the likelihood of product success.

Competitors   Many companies get new product ideas from their competitors or other players in the market in the same product category, in the same market, or other markets. Keeping an eye on competitors' activities is one way in which companies can adopt their strategies as well as be at par with the services being offered in the market segment.

Distributors and suppliers   Distributors are in constant contact with the customers. They are a valuable source of information for problems faced by consumers and the new features, facilities, and services the consumer is looking for. Studies suggest that supplier involvement in new product development can 'Help reduce cost, reduce concept-to-customer development time, improve quality, and provide innovative technologies that can help capture market share' (Handfield et al. 1999). It is generally seen that during the process of new product development many problems emerge, such as cost, performance, timing, quality, etc., which results in tradeoffs and design changes. However, if the suppliers are involved in the product development right from the idea generation stage then potential technologies can be assessed and breakthrough ideas can be achieved. The suppliers can also be used to gather information about the new products being developed by rival companies.

Other sources   Companies can get ideas through 'other sources like trade magazines, shows, seminars, government agencies, new product consultants, market research firms, university, and inventors' (Kotler et al. 2006).

Idea screening   Once a number of ideas are generated the next step is to screen the ideas to 'separate the chaff from the grain' i.e., to select more meritorious ideas from the less promising ones (Scheuing and Johnson 1989). A good idea could be too expensive for the company to produce. Therefore, it looks for new ideas that the existing workforce can produce in the existing assembly line, which are profitable for the organization to produce, and fit in with the objective and strategy of the organization. Kotler et al. (2006) identified the following issues the new product should:

- fulfil the company's mission
- meet corporate objectives
- protect and promote the core business
- protect and please key customers
- result in better utilization of existing resources
- support and enhance existing product lines.

Concept Development and Testing

The product ideas selected after screening all the new product ideas are then to be developed into a product concept. A product idea is a possible product that the company may launch in the market. A product concept on the other hand, is a detailed version of the product idea stated in meaningful consumer terms. It is a description of the potential new service. According to Scheuing and Johnson (1989), a typical concept statement includes:

- a description of a problem a prospect might experience
- the reasons why the new service is to be offered
- an outline of the features and benefits of the new service
- rationale for the purchase of the new service offering.

A successful services firm cannot market an untested product. It has to first test the service offering in a limited market to see the market response.

Once the product concept is developed it is tested on the target customers to examine the buyers' response to the service concept. This can be done in the form of simple attitude surveys or by other statistical techniques. A concept test is a technique used in marketing research to assess the reactions of consumers to a new product or a proposed change to an existing product (*Oxford Dictionary of Business and Management* 2006). It evaluates whether a prospective user understands the idea of the proposed service offering, reacts favourably to it, and feels it offers benefits that answer unmet needs (Scheuing and Johnson 1989).

Smaller organizations, however, move over directly from product idea to full implementation without going into concept testing. Ultimately, if the financial implication of the new service developed is enormous, it is always better to test the feasibility of the new service offering rather than regret a disastrous mistake later.

Business Analysis

This represents an exhaustive analysis of the business implications, such as sales, costs, and profit projections, of the new product concept. It involves both market assessment and drafting of the budget for the development and launch of the new service. The purpose of business analysis is to develop recommendations for the top management as to how to implement the new service offering.

Service Design and Development

Till now the new product exists only as a concept. It must now be developed into a physical concept, an operational entity, which customers can perceive as an imperative service and which can be produced within the estimated budgeted cost. The core product for the market offering is developed when the service is designed. This is different from concept development as it involves the help of prospective users and customer contact personnel, who tell the company what customers desire in a new service. The service design and development on the other hand, is done with the help of the users and the operational staff who will deliver the service. While designing the service we also have to design the delivery process and system. This should be instated, refined, and restructured in order to ensure smooth delivery upon introduction.

Test marketing   Once the product has been designed, marketing strategy worked out, and the personnel trained to handle queries for and delivery of the new service, the next step is to launch the product in the market. Test marketing field-tests the service product within a limited sample of customers. This allows the marketer to gain experience of marketing the product and in the process, to find potential problem areas, and determine how the service product can be refined and made 'irresistible' to the target market.

Strategy Formulation

This stage involves the development of marketing strategy and training of employees.

Marketing strategy   Once the service has been developed, that is, the product of the marketing mix has been decided, the next step is to develop the marketing strategy for the introduction of the product into the market. According to Kotler et al. (2006) the marketing strategy includes:

- the price, distribution, and marketing budget for the first year
- target market, product positioning and sales, market share, and profit goals for the first few years
- the planned long-run sales, profit goals, and marketing mix strategy.

Personnel training   To complete the design part of the new product development the employees have to be familiarized with the elucidation and operational details of the new service. Personnel training is critical to the success of new product development as services have often failed due to lack of proper training of the personnel who sell and deliver the service (Scheuing and Johnson 1989).

Commercialization

Once test marketing has been carried out and the product has been fine-tuned to the market, the next step is to launch the new service in the entire market area. According to Kotler et al. (2006) the following four considerations have to be made while launching the new service.

1. When: The first decision is, when is the right time to introduce the new service?
2. Where: The company must decide whether to launch the service in a single/multiple region or national/international markets. Since a lot of investment is required to launch the product nationally, organizations generally opt for a planned market rollout.
3. To whom: Once the service has been launched in the market, the management has to determine the profiles of prime prospects, i.e., it has to look for early adopters, heavy users, and opinion leaders.
4. How: The company must develop the action plan and spend the marketing budget appropriately on the marketing mix.

Post-launch Review

Even after carefully testing the new product idea before commercialization of the service, market conditions may require further modifications. For example, after introduction in the market, Courier Pak, the document delivery service of Federal Express, realized that the key purchase decision-makers for the new service were executives and secretaries rather than traffic managers and shipping clerks. Consequently, they had to develop a separate advertising and sales approach. Also, the pickup and delivery locations were different and required additional ground operations. After making these changes Courier Pak became a successful new service venture (Scheuing and Johnson 1989).

PRODUCT LIFE CYCLE STRATEGIES

This section provides a detailed explanation of the various stages of the product life cycle, the marketing strategies adopted during each stage, and finally, the limitations of the theory.

Product Life Cycle Stages

Each product passes through a distinct stage. These stages constitute the life cycle of the product. There are four such stages (Kotler et al. 2006) in the life cycle of a product (Fig. 2.3). These are as follows:

Introductory stage   This is the stage immediately after the launch of a new product in the market. This period is characterized by slow sales growth and negligible profit as heavy expenditure is incurred for introduction of the product. If the product introduced is really innovative it is at an advantage as the competition is then minimized. Examples of services in the introductory stage are broadband, Internet banking, direct-to-home (DTH) services, etc.

Growth stage   The growth stage follows the introductory stage. This stage is characterized by high sales growth rate and increasing profits. Due to the heavy marketing expenditure in the introductory, stage people increasingly accept the product and hence the high

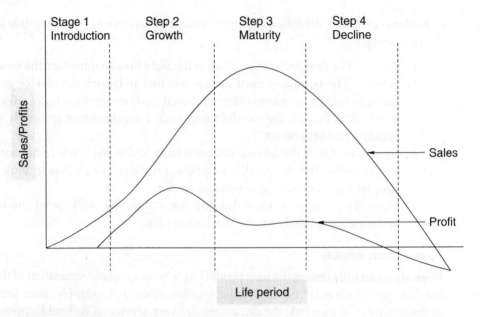

Source: Oxford Dictionary of Business and Management (2006).

Fig. 2.3 Product life cycle

sales growth rate. Since increasing profits marks this stage it is the task of the marketing department to protract this period. For example, cable services in India are in their growth stage.

Maturity stage   This stage arises when all the potential buyers have accepted the product and consequently the sales of the product have now reached a plateau. The waning of profits marks this stage, as expenses have to be incurred again in marketing the product. For example, cinema halls have reached their maturity stage.

Decline stage   This is the stage characterized by a fall in sales and hence profits of the product and soon the firm incurs a loss. Services in the decline stage are post office services, rail transport, manual banking, etc.

This is the life cycle that most products follow. The understanding of this concept is essential as it guides the strategies to be made by an organization at various intervals of time. From this we can summarize that:

1. Products have a life and they pass through different stages, as in a life cycle.
2. Sales of the product pass through distinct phases and each phase is characterized by unique challenges, opportunities, and problems.
3. Profits vary with the stage of the life cycle.
4. Different strategies are required during the different life cycle stages for the products to stay profitable for a longer duration.

It has been observed that three other types of patterns of the product life cycle are possible. They are as follows.

1. Growth–slump–maturity pattern: This pattern is characteristic of services, which pass through the introductory sales and maturity cycle and then instead of the decline there is a constant demand for the service; for example, life insurance products in India.

2. Cycle–recycle pattern: This pattern is characteristic of the hospitality industry where initially when a new property comes up, there is a demand represented by the initial cycle. However, later as the sales decline, efforts are made to push the sales with increased marketing strategies and this results in the second cycle, which is lower in magnitude and duration than the first.

3. Scalloped product life cycle: Here the product passes through the succession of life cycles based on discovery of new service features/characteristics, uses, or users. For example, the insurance sector in India received a boost due to the different features it introduced from time to time. Schemes, such as the money-back policy, tax-saving schemes, child welfare, girl child policies, etc. resulted in the Life Insurance Corporation (LIC) becoming the number one service brand in India (*Brand Equity* 2006).

Marketing Strategies

We have seen that a product passes through different phases in its lifetime. Each stage has unique characteristics and needs to be handled differently so that:

- the product can develop a competitive advantage
- it can stay profitable
- resources can be allocated properly.

The detailed strategies for a product as it passes through its different stages are elaborated in this section.

Introduction Stage

The introduction phase is very important for services marketing because it is during this period that customers or consumers, on the basis of initial experimentation with the service, form their opinions about the service. If the introduction phase is not appropriately handled it the service introduced may be 'nipped in the bud', as it will lead to negative word-of-mouth publicity. Since in this phase the service is launched for the first time, logistics or other difficulties may emerge. This is a learning phase where staff skills have to be developed and systems have to be redesigned on the basis of experience (Lazer and Layton 1999). Thus, this stage is marked by frequent service modifications. Hence the more carefully thought out the new service is in the planning stage, the less difficulty it will encounter in the introductory stage leading to the successful launch of the service. According to Michael (1971), quality has the largest impact on sales in this stage followed by advertising and price. Advertising is done mainly to create awareness among customers and can be accompanied by sampling and couponing.

Growth Stage

If the introduction of the service is successful, i.e., customers accept the offer and have a favourable experience, it will result in positive word-of-mouth followed by hectic sales activities. Service firms can review their strategies at this stage and can:

- get customer feedback as to how to further improve the service offered
- develop customer loyalty
- re-price the product to achieve market penetration
- strengthen distributor network
- shift from product awareness to product preference advertising.

This stage is marked by an expanded number of services and frequent modifications in the services. Advertising is done primarily to build awareness and interest in the mass market. However, the sales promotion followed in the introductory stage is reduced to take advantage of the heavy demand. The Indian insurance sector is likely to register unprecedented growth of 200 per cent and attain a size of Rs 200 lakh crore by 2009–10. Within this, the private sector insurance business will achieve a growth rate of 140 per cent as a result of the aggressive marketing technique being adopted by them, as against 35–40 per cent growth rate of the state-owned insurance companies (The Associated Chambers of Commerce and Industry of India 2008). The insurance sector in India, which ranked twentieth in 2000, is seventeenth (in 2006) in the global life insurance business and has a share of 1.02 per cent of the world market. The sector has been growing exceptionally since liberalization with the introduction of new investment type unit-linked insurance plans. The total premium underwritten by the life insurance industry has grown from Rs 34,898 crore in 2000–01 to Rs 1,56,041 crore in 2006–07. The industry has reported a growth of 1.41 per cent in new business premium underwritten during the period April–November 2007 (Economic Survey-Insurance and Pension Funds 2008).

Maturity Stage

This stage is marked by slow sales. In this stage most of the consumers have tried the services, competitors have come up with similar services, and profits are constricted. The sales slowdown leads to overcapacity in the market, which further intensifies the competition. If the service providers have managed their growth period sales well and have been able to deliver 'customer delight' they will be in a better position to sustain sales in the maturity period. Most of the price-insensitive buyers have already tried the product; so this stage is marked by frequent markdowns, increased advertising, and sales promotion budget (to encourage brand switching), and aggressive selling so that the weaker competition withdraws and the dominant firms take over.

Decline Stage

The final stage in the product life cycle is that of decline. This stage is marked by plummeting sales. At this stage again it is the quality of service that is important and price cuts have virtually no impact (Michael 1971). However a decline in sales does not necessarily mean that the service has left the maturity stage. Vyas (1993) has

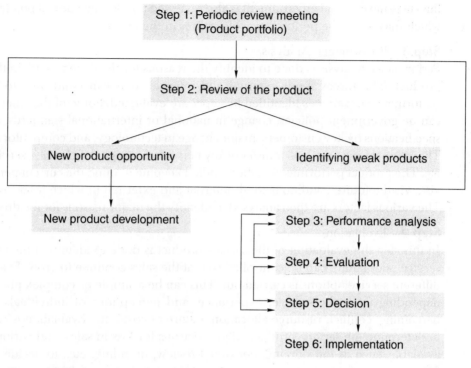

Source: Adapted from Vyas (1993).

Fig. 2.4   Process for product replacement/elimination

recommended a strategy whereby the product sales can be enhanced by replacing the service with the enhanced version of the same service or by eliminating the service (Fig. 2.4).

Step 1   Periodic Review Meeting (Product Portfolio)
During the scheduled meetings (can be monthly or bi-monthly depending upon the policies adopted by different organizations) product improvement opportunities, availability of new technologies, competitors' activities, and feedback from customers and channel partners is reviewed. New ideas for enhancement of service are identified. The product portfolio is reviewed in totality and with relation to its market segment.

Step 2   Product Review
When the product portfolio is reviewed in totality it leads to detection of new product ideas or opportunities and weak performing products are differentiated from performing products. The improved service ideas are detected; feasibility plans are prepared, which include development cost, sales/profit estimates, ROI analysis, etc. The new product is then developed as per the stages of new product development discussed earlier. Along with the identification of new product opportunities, the existing products are also reviewed to identify the products that are not performing as per expectations. During

this stage the external environment is also reviewed for identification of potential forces, which may affect the performance of services in the future.

Step 3 Performance Analysis

Performance analysis is done to identify the reasons for the drop in sales in the service product. The forces (both external and internal) that can contribute to the weak performance of services identified in step 2 are evaluated. Some of the external forces can be government policies, change in national or international standards, change in specifications by key customers, major change in technology, and competitor strategies. The internal forces are loss/transfer of key personnel, design deficiencies, service delays, etc. The product performance is then studied keeping in mind the current performance vis-à-vis the future conditions (both internal and external) in which it has to perform. The various factors are then analysed to identify the major reasons for the drop in sales.

Step 4 Evaluation

In this step the evaluation of the service product is done to identify if the reasons for service sales failure can be controlled so that the sales continue to grow. Evaluation of different service options is carried out. This can be a simple or complex phenomenon depending upon the service, experience, and perceptions of individuals involved, bargaining, conflict, resource allocation, nature of costs, etc. Evaluation is carried out to determine the service product failure, reasons for loss in sales, and various options available, such as outsourcing, personnel review, branding, etc., to decide about the future course of action for the service product.

Step 5 Decision

Product elimination suggestions are scrutinized thoroughly. If there is no market demand for the service and hence no substitute product is required, the product is eliminated. However, a number of factors have to be considered before this decision can be finalized, such as whether the generic sales for the service category exists, the industry growth rate, customer feedback, channel partners feedback, sales and marketing personnel feedback, impact on organizations image, effect on product mix, etc. (discussed in steps 2, 3, and 4). On the basis of the analysis of these factors organizations can go in for a service replacement decision instead of a service elimination decision. Thus, this step is the most difficult and several iterations may occur among steps 3, 4, and 5 before the final decision can be made.

Step 6 Implementation

This is the final implementation of the decision taken in step 5. The decision taken is relevant if it is completed within a specific timeframe.

It is clear from this discussion that the marketing environment keeps on changing and companies have to review their strategies at regular intervals to match their competitive positions (Lazer and Layton 1999). Table 2.2 illustrates how organizations can match their characteristics, objectives, and strategies with the product life cycle to gain a competitive edge by effective resource allocation. In order to survive in the long run, organizations should introduce a new service before the complete decline in sales of the previous service so that the overall growth curve remains constant. According to

Table 2.2 Summary of product life cycle characteristics, objectives, and strategies

	Introduction	Growth	Maturity	Decline
Characteristics				
Sales	Low sales	Rapidly rising sales	Peak sales	Declining sales
Costs	High cost per customer	Average cost per customer	Low cost per customer	Low cost per customer
Profits	Negative	Rising profits	High profits	Declining profits
Customers	Innovators	Early adopters	Middle majority	Laggards
Competitors	Few	Growing number	Stable number beginning to decline	Declining number
Marketing objective	Create product awareness and trial	Maximize market share	Maximize profit while defending market share	Reduce expenditure and milk the brand
Cash flow	Negative	Moderate	High	Moderate
Focus	Non-users	New segments	Defend share	Cut costs
Differential advantage	Service quality	Brand image	Price and service	Service quality and price
Strategies				
Product	Offer a basic product/service	Offer service extensions, service, and warranty	Diversify brands and services	Phase out the weak
Price	Charge cost-plus	Price to penetrate market	Price to match or best competitors	Cut price
Distribution	Build selective distribution	Build intensive distribution	Build more intensive distribution	Go selective: phase out unprofitable outlets
Advertising	Build product awareness among early adopters and dealers	Build awareness and interest in the mass market	Stress brand differences and benefits	Reduce to level needed to retain hard core loyals
Sales promotion	Use heavy sales promotion to entice trial	Reduce to take advantage of heavy customer demand	Increase to encourage brand switching	Reduce to minimal level
Organization				
Structure	Team	Market focus	Functional	Lean
Focus	Innovation	Marketing	Efficiency	Cost reduction
Culture	Freewheeling	Marketing led	Professional	Pressured

Sources: Adapted from Wasson (1978), Weber (1976), Doyle (1976), and Doyle (2002).

Modis (1994), the thumb rule is that 'When 90 per cent saturation level of the old process is reached the new wave should be at 1 per cent of the way into its own growth process'. This denotes that for a particular service industry the initial introduction phase is composed of services with shorter life cycles (in accordance with the low growth phase the service is in), the growth phase has services with relatively longer life cycles (in accordance with the high growth period) and again at maturity the services life cycles are short showing a decline in the marketability of the service organization. If in the same service level, all organizations have a short life cycle it might reflect a changing social pattern. If we consider the life cycles of a number of unrelated services and products and observe a general shorter life cycle for all, it may reflect a global economic recession.

Weaknesses of Product Life Cycle Concept

Even though the product life cycle concept is very important in the marketing of services, Doyle (2002) has listed the following weaknesses in the product life cycle concept.

Product/service oriented   The marketing concept focuses on the customers, their needs and wants, and how best to satisfy them. However, the focus of the life cycle concept is the product/service. If managers focus on the product, they lose their customer orientation, which might be the other reason for the product to inevitably fall in the product life cycle stages of maturity and decline.

Undefined concept   As there are different driving forces for demands, technologies, product categories, etc., there is no agreement as to the level of aggregation the concept refers to.

No common shape   As is evident from the discussion, there are different shapes for the life cycles of different types of products/services, so there is no standardization as to the common shape for the services.

Unpredictability   How long a particular product or service is going to stay in a particular phase of the product life cycle cannot be predicted. Some services might stay in a particular stage for a few months while others can be there for generations.

Unclear implication   Even where a life cycle pattern can be identified, the implications are not clear. For example, a service shows a decline in sales and is put in the mature phase of the product life cycle whereas this decline in sales can be associated with some production problem at the service providers end or may be due to lack of effective service providing personnel.

Internal   Product life cycle is often a result of management actions and their implications rather than outside market forces. When sales become flat there can be a number of internal problems relating to distribution, production, product, etc. Thus, it is the task of the management to identify the source of low turnover and take remedial actions instead of passing it off as the life cycle stage. Exhibit 2.3 illustrates the concept further.

Exhibit 2.3 Party time: Star hotels reap benefits of room shortage

The booming hospitality sector in India has also led to a lot of other transformations. The average room rates (ARR) of hotels in India have kept pace with those in the West. The ARR is increasing at the rate of over 20 per cent, almost equal to those in Europe or US. There is also significant variation in the trends within India. For example, the ARR increase in Bangalore and Gurgaon is as high as 50 per cent. The high demand and shortage of five-star accommodation is the main reason for the spiralling ARR rates. The tourism sector is booming and the rooms in India meet high standards, hence high occupancy rates have led to shortage of rooms. Business travellers, who do not book rooms in advance, end up opting for a higher category room that costs about 40 dollars more. With most of the hotels witnessing a room occupancy rate of more than 80 per cent, the trend will just be moving upward. Most of the hotels are planning to add more rooms in the coming years and tie-ups are in force with foreign brands ready to enter India.

Source: Adapted from Talreja (2006).

BRANDING THE SERVICE PRODUCT

The biggest challenge for marketing professionals is their ability to create, maintain, and enhance brands. Branding is a major issue to be tackled in product strategy, as successful branding is one of the most potent tools for businesses to create and preserve value (Singhal 2004; Rio et al. 2001). Branding is an immensely challenging process, which requires intensive investment, building an element of trust with consumers, and delivering promises made to the consumer. It takes many years of efforts and investments to create global brands. The American Marketing Association defines a brand as, 'A name, term, sign, symbol, or design, or a combination of them, intended to identify the goods or services of one seller or group of sellers and to differentiate them from competitors' (Kotler 2002). Some of the notable brands names are Coca-Cola, Colgate, Disney, Goodyear, Heinz, Kellogg's, and Kodak. According to Ries and Ries (1999), 'marketing is branding' or branding is the glue that holds the marketing functions together. The concept of 'selling' is being replaced by 'purchasing' due to the rise of brands and so branding is important as it 'pre-sells' the product or service to the customer. Thus, branding is the most important activity for companies to become more profitable and more powerful. Branding helps marketers to be competitive in a fluctuating environment. Market conditions force marketers to adopt innovative branding strategies. Brand orientation is seen as a powerful tool for creating shareholder and long-term value (Simoes and Dibb 2001). A brand can convey up to six levels of meaning (Kotler 2002).

Attributes   There may be features/attributes associated with the brand. For example, a bank may list the services offered in its portfolio such as loans, savings accounts, demat account, online transactions, etc.

Benefits   A brand represents functional and/or emotional benefits. For example, a bank may offer a 24/7 service or ease of transactions, or an unforgettable experience as mentioned by some airlines.

Values These relate to the product/service values. For example, 'Made in Switzerland' for watches or 'Made in Japan' for electronics products evoke feelings of trust. For example, the 'Incredible India' campaign promotes unique Indian cultural aspects as a pull factor for foreign tourists.

Culture A brand represents a culture. For example, Sony and Toyota represent Japanese precision and quality.

Personality A brand may project a personality of the consumer. For example, a Diner's Card is evidence of a customer's long association with the bank.

User A brand points out the categories of users. For example, tour operators specifically target age groups of customers when they advertise travel packages such as family destinations, honeymoon couples, girls-only groups, etc.

Levine (2003) remarks that branding is a complex process, but its goal is simple. It is the creation and development of a specific identity for a company, product, commodity, group, or person. According to him, branding is the process by which a brand comes to be. The role of public relations in creation of a brand has been overlooked in conventional literature. Advertising has been used to create mass awareness about the products or services.

Uses of Branding

A brand connotes a certain service offering and the choice of a branded service assumes a certain level of service. Consumers feel that service providers would like to uphold the brand and will honour their commitment. This reduces risk because a brand inspires confidence in the mind of the consumer. For example, when one chooses Marriott as a brand, a certain service assurance comes with it. It also reduces search cost as a customer is assured of specific standards. To sum up, a consumer associates a brand with the following aspects (Keller 2003):

- identification of source of product
- assignment of responsibility to product maker
- reduction of risk
- reduction of search costs
- promise, bond, or pact with maker of product
- symbolic device
- signal of quality.

The brand helps manufacturers or service providers by helping them to create a unique positioning for themselves, legally protecting the features, associating a distinct quality expectation, source of competitive advantage, and distinct returns.

Branding Challenges

Kotler (2003) has enumerated various branding challenges faced by a marketer.

To brand or not to brand   There are instances in service segments such as home loans and credit collection agencies, which work for leading banking brands, such as ICICI and HDFC. On their own, they would find it difficult to sustain their operations.

Brand sponsor decisions   These decisions are about whether the brand would be a manufacturer's brand, distributor's brand, or licensed brand. Firms such as Wills Lifestyle have opened their own stores for retailing its brand of clothes. Superstores, such as Marks and Spencers, retail products using their own brand names. Certain firms, such as Disney Stores, sell their products under license.

Brand name decisions   These decisions are related to whether individual names, blanket family names, separate family names, or company trade names should be combined with an individual product name.

Brand strategy decisions   These are related to brand positioning decisions.

The challenge for the service provider is how to place the brand in the mind of the consumer. These questions have been addressed in detail in Chapter 5. Four strategic questions need to be addressed:

1. Who am I? (corporate identity, endorsement)
2. What am I? (category-related, benefit-related, usage and time)
3. For whom am I? (segmentation)
4. Why me? (unique attribute, competitor)

Brands are important because they act as the communication tool between increasingly physically separated businesses and consumers. According to Ellwood (2002), a brand is the area that surrounds a product or service that communicates its benefits and differentiates it from the competition for the consumer. The seven Ps of marketing must be integrated well to give the right perception of the brand product, price, place, promotion, place, people, process, and physical evidence. Ellwood (2002) has discussed the 'brand DNA' model. He relates DNA with brand proposition, brand personality, emotional benefits, and rational benefits. This has an impact on business culture, consumer culture, social image, and self-image.

Singh (1997) has discussed about the brand's competence and its relationship with the external world. It is the relationship which dictates competitive advantage. The consumer choices of a brand are governed by numerous factors. These could be the attributes, emotions, and price factors, among others. Brands help consumers to arrive at decisions as they simplify the decision-making process. Choosing a commodity is far more complex than choosing a brand. This is because in case of selecting a commodity, the decision is based on logical deductions and evaluation of rational attributes and parameters, necessitating volumes of data collection, assimilation, and comparison. Brands come with certain attributes and expectations that are clearly mapped. Brands allow consumers the luxury of engaging in emotional experiences. Singh (1997) postulates that brands have barely exposed the tip of a customer's emotional iceberg, using primarily three key emotions—warmth, humour, and fear.

Most marketers adopt the logical route to branding and benefit communication. The brand is positioned in the left brain offering a rational explanation of its key attributes, how they work, and the results they produce. As a result, the consumers respond to these with greater rational reasoning, which results in their minds ruling their hearts. If the marketer influences a consumer's right side of the brain, as frequently done in the fashion and fragrance industries, the brand is able to emotionally connect with the consumer. Once the consumer is bonded to the brand, faith in functional superiority follows, because emotionally the consumer is convinced of its benefits and quality. It is possible to impact the consumers' decision-making process through the route chosen to enter their mind space. How can the brand enter the consumer's right brain first? This can be done either by enhancing the intrinsic worth, that is, helping them to feel better about their own selves or through enhancement of their extrinsic worth (by helping them look better to the world around them). When a brand employs its core capability to enhance the consumer's intrinsic or extrinsic worth, it accomplishes a successful right brain entry.

Singh (1997) quotes the Plutchik's emotion solid scale where there is a range of emotions, such as adoration, ecstasy, terror, amazement, grief, rage, vigilance, loathing, disgust, sadness, fear, anger, surprise, apprehension, distraction, pensiveness, boredom, or annoyance, could be targeted. It is essential that some of the following factors be considered for successful brand building in the service industry. Each of these is explained in detail in this section.

Evoke feeling of trust   Service industry is primarily a people-oriented industry. The challenge for the service firms is to ensure uniformity of experience event after event. In order to ensure this, it is essential that adequate investments be made in training of employees and experience as per the expectations that are built in the consumers.

Unlike products, wherein there are quality certifications, a consumer perceives a higher level of risk especially in high-involvement and high-priced service categories such as buying time-share options, travelling to a particular country, or making financial investments. The consumer needs to be assured of a pleasant experience and endorsements by other consumers could evoke feelings of trust. Exhibit 2.4 illustrates the concept further.

Trained manpower   Employees of the firm are the face of the company as they communicate a lot about the service culture of the firm. Well-dressed employees with polite behaviour as well as product knowledge go a long way in developing relationships with the consumers. Taj Hotels connotes a luxury brand in India. Premium pricing strategy and attention to details, such as the ambience of the rooms, further reinforce the image of luxury.

Service blueprint   The service processes should be mapped and the flow of activities from one stage to another should be well thought of. In a service operation critical time for each activity needs to be assessed and respected. The details are discussed in Chapter 9.

Exhibit 2.4 Life Insurance Corporation of India

A case of an Indian brand, which evokes an element of trust in consumers, is Life Insurance Corporation of India (LIC). It is a public sector organization that has received numerous awards:

□ Loyalty Awards 2008 (Insurance category)

□ Reader's Digest 'Most Trusted Brand' Award 2007

□ Web 18 Genius of the Web Awards 2007

□ Outlook Money NDTV Profit Awards 2007

□ NDTV Profit Business Leadership Award 2007

□ CNBC Awaaz Consumer Awards 2007

□ Golden Peacock Award for Excellence in Corporate Governance

□ Webby's People's Voice Award (Insurance category)

□ NDTV Profit Business Leadership Awards

In 2005 the company's profit was Rs 5,800 crore. The business has been operating for the last 50 years. Life insurance in its modern form came to India from England in the year 1818. Oriental Life Insurance started by the Europeans in Calcutta was the first life insurance company on Indian soil. All the insurance companies established during that period were brought up with the purpose of looking after the needs of the European community. The Parliament of India passed the Life Insurance Corporation Act on 19 June 1956 and LIC was created on 1 September 1956 with the objective of spreading life insurance particularly in rural areas. Despite so many multinationals operating this domain, LIC still has a leading market share in the life insurance segment. At present, LIC has 7 zonal offices, 100 divisional offices, 2,048 branch offices and close to 1,002,149 insurance agents called 'producers'.

Source: Adapted from Life Insurance Corporation of India (2008).

Physical evidence Tangible cues help to create a high degree of confidence in consumers. Well-groomed employees, well-maintained building and ambience, visual imagery created at contact points, usage of state-of-the-art equipment, all contribute to creating a pleasant experience for the consumer (Exhibit 2.5). Great promises and advertisements devoid of tangible evidence do not influence customers for too long.

Exhibit 2.5 Tanishq—India's largest jewellery brand

Tanishq is India's largest, most desirable, and fastest growing jewellery brand. The brand is the jewellery business group of Titan Industries Ltd and is promoted by the TATA Group. Tanishq had retail sales worth Rs 1,200 crore in 2007 and is expected to hit Rs 2,000 crore in 2008. Continuing to expand, at present there are 91 Tanishq showrooms in 64 cities across India.

Tanishq is prominent in the form of standalone boutiques. Each outlet has a distinct ambience with chic lighting and green plants. The sales staff wears uniforms and as soon as consumers enter an outlet, they are escorted by staff members and directed to a counter depending on their requirements. Beverages are offered to consumers and there is an air of professionalism. Tanishq promises pure gold jewellery and certifies the quality of the precious/semi-precious stones in writing. It offers the most modern, scientific, and non-destructive process to measure the exact purity of the gold jewellery using a karat meter. The entire process and experience that a consumer goes through right from entering to leaving the boutique signifies trust.

Source: Adapted from Tanishq (2008).

Mechanisms for consumers to reach the service provider A service firm needs to redress consumer grievances. More importantly, it should be able to anticipate consumer requirements and deliver services, which exceed consumer expectations. Obstacles, which inhibit consumer access to the service firm, need to be removed. The feedback and research process initiation should not be undertaken because it is politically correct to do so but because they help consumers to voice their concerns and suggestions. This in turn helps the firm to continuously improve itself.

Connecting to consumers Marketers deploy various strategies to reach out to consumers. Advertising, sales promotion, personal selling, and public relations (PR) are some of these ways. However, PR could be deployed very meaningfully and be used as a tool to create a bonding with the consumer. For example, ITC initiated a unique intervention in rural India by studying the lives of the farmers very closely. In doing so, it identified the use of information technology (IT) to help farmers sell their soya crop at the market rate. This led to higher returns to farmers for their produce. On the other hand, ITC saved a lot of money on procurement of the soya crop. Therefore, it was a win-win strategy for both the company and the farmers. Similarly, The Body Shop, a retail firm based in UK, associated itself with social and environmentally active groups and initiated a campaign for banning testing of cosmetics on animals. This led to an instant bond with over six million European consumers who participated in a signature campaign. When firms stand up for a right cause, a lot more is achieved than by simple advertising initiatives.

SUMMARY

This chapter discussed in detail the concept of the product in services management. Along with the definition and nature of services it discussed the different levels of the service product, which is crucial as before discussing the different management techniques for services we need to be clear about the product and its various levels. The chapter also discussed the different levels involved in the development of a new product. The various strategies used in different product life cycle stages were discussed along with the limitations of the same. The last section dealt with branding strategies for the service product. This section is crucial as it discussed the strategic importance of branding. It delineates the different branding strategies the organization can opt for in the process of differentiating its services in the market place. This gives a comprehensive understanding of the service product and forms a basis for discussion of strategies for the management of the same.

KEY TERMS

Augmented product Additional consumer services and benefits sold with a core product. The augmented product can be a critical factor in the success of the core product.

Commercialization The stage in the development of a new product during which a decision is made to embark on its full-scale production and distribution.

Concept test A technique used in marketing research to assess the reactions of consumers to a new product or a proposed change to an existing product.

Core product The problem-solving service or core benefit that a consumer is really buying when purchasing a product.

Idea generation The systematic search for new product ideas.

Idea screening Screening new product ideas in order to identify and develop good ideas and drop poor ones as soon as possible.

Marketing strategy A plan identifying what marketing goals and objectives will be pursued to sell a particular product line and how these objectives will be achieved in the time available.

New product development A marketing procedure in which new ideas are developed into viable new products or extensions to existing products or product ranges.

Product life cycle The course of a product's sales and profitability over its lifetime. The model describes stages, each of which represents a different opportunity for the marketer. The duration of each stage is unique to each product. The concept of product life cycle underpins the strategic management concept of product portfolios. The various stages of a product's life cycle are—introduction, growth, maturity, and decline.

Service product An offering that includes both tangible and intangible offerings, which satisfies customer needs through an integrated approach and at the same time contributes to societal welfare.

Test marketing A procedure for launching a new product in a restricted geographical area to test consumers' reactions. If the product is unsuccessful, the company will have to minimize its costs and make the necessary changes before a wider launch. Test marketing has the disadvantage that competitors learn about the new product before its full launch.

CONCEPT REVIEW QUESTIONS

1. Discuss what a service product is and how is it different from the traditional product.

2. Enumerate the different components of service offering with the help of examples.

3. What is new product development? How would you develop a new product for the tourism industry in India?

4. Critically discuss the product life cycle. Discuss with the help of examples from the Indian hospitality sector.

5. Evaluate the different strategies in the growth phase of the product life cycle.

6. What is the cascading life cycle? Critically discuss with the help of examples from any service sector.

7. What are the prerequisites for the success of a services brand?

8. Evaluate the decisions that need to be taken when branding services.

CRITICAL THINKING QUESTIONS

1. You have to introduce a new Italian dish in the Indian market. What steps are you going to take and why?

2. Discuss the different components of a product for the education sector.

3. You have to introduce a new airline in the Indian market. What strategies are you going to adopt initially, after a year, and after five years to market your airline?

PROJECT ASSIGNMENTS

1. Identify any two new firms in a similar service industry. What are the similarities and differences in the product offering?

2. Visit the site for a service firm and try to identify which product life cycle stage it is in.

3. Identify a service firm, which has been launched within the past two years in India. Identify a similar one in China. Critically evaluate their strategies for the marketing of their service product. Can any similarities be drawn?

CASE STUDY

Growth of Insurance Sector in India: The 'Insurance Product' of LIC

Brief History of Insurance

The story of insurance is probably as old as the story of mankind. The same instinct that prompts modern businesspeople today to secure themselves against loss and disaster existed in primitive humans also. They too sought to avert the evil consequences of fire and flood, and loss of life, and were willing to make some sort of sacrifice in order to achieve security. Although the concept of insurance is largely a development of the recent past, particularly after the industrial era, its beginnings date back almost 6,000 years.

Life insurance in its modern form came to India from England in the year 1818. Oriental Life Insurance Company started by Europeans in Calcutta was the first life insurance company on Indian soil. All the insurance companies established during that period were started with the purpose of looking after the needs of the European community. These companies did not insure the Indian natives. However, later with the efforts of eminent people, such as Babu Muttylal Seal, foreign life insurance companies started insuring Indian lives. However, Indians lives were treated as sub-standard and heavy premiums were charged on them. Bombay Mutual Life Assurance Society heralded the birth of the first Indian life insurance company, in the year 1870, and covered Indian lives at normal rates. Starting as Indian enterprises with highly patriotic motives, insurance companies came into existence to carry the message of insurance and social security to various sectors of society. Bharat Insurance Company (1896) was one such company that was inspired by nationalism. The Swadeshi movement of 1905–07 gave rise to more insurance companies. The United India in Madras, National Indian and National Insurance in Calcutta, and the Co-operative Assurance in Lahore, were established in 1906. In 1907, Hindustan Co-operative Insurance Company took birth in one of the rooms of Jorasanko, the house of the great poet Rabindranath Tagore, in Kolkata. Indian Mercantile, General Assurance, and Swadeshi Life (later Bombay Life) were some of the companies established during the same period.

Prior to 1912, India had no legislation to regulate the insurance business. In the year 1912, the Life Insurance Companies Act and the Provident Fund Act were passed. The Life Insurance Companies Act, 1912 made it mandatory for the premium rate tables and periodical valuations of companies to be certified by an actuary. However, the Act discriminated between foreign and Indian companies on many accounts, putting the Indian companies at a disadvantage.

The first two decades of the twentieth century saw substantial growth in the insurance business. From 44 companies with total business-in-force at Rs 22.44 crore, it rose to 176 companies with total business-in-force at Rs 298 crore in 1938. During the mushrooming of insurance business many companies, which were financially unsound, failed miserably.

The Insurance Act, 1938 was the first legislation governing not only life insurance, but also non-life insurance to provide strict state control over insurance business. The demand for nationalization of the life insurance industry was made repeatedly in the past but it gathered momentum in 1944 when a bill to amend the Life Insurance Act, 1938 was introduced in the legislative assembly. However, it was much later, on 19 January 1956 that life insurance in India was nationalized. About 154 Indian insurance companies and 16 non-Indian companies, were operating in India at the time of nationalization. Nationalization was accomplished in two stages; initially the management of the companies was taken over by means of an ordinance, and later, the ownership too by means of a comprehensive bill.

Life Insurance

Life insurance in India made its debut well over 100 years ago. In our country, which is one of the most populated in the world, the prominence of insurance is not as widely understood as it ought to be. What follows is an attempt to acquaint readers with some of the concepts of life insurance, with special reference to LIC. Life insurance is a contract that pledges payment of an amount to the person assured (or his/her nominee) on the happening of the event insured against. The contract is valid for payment of the insured amount during:

o the date of maturity, or
o specified dates at periodic intervals, or
o unfortunate death, if it occurs earlier.

Among other things, the contract also provides for the payment of premium periodically to the corporation by the policyholder. Life insurance is universally acknowledged to be an institution, which eliminates 'risk', substituting certainty for uncertainty, and comes to the timely aid of the family in the unfortunate event of death of the breadwinner. By and large, life insurance is civilization's partial solution to the problems caused by death. Life insurance, in short, is concerned with two hazards that stand across the life-path of every person:

o that of dying prematurely leaving a dependent family to fend for itself, or

o that of living till old age without visible means of support.

Life Insurance in India: Milestones

1818: Oriental Life Insurance Company, the first life insurance company on Indian soil started its operations.

1870: Bombay Mutual Life Assurance Society, the first Indian life insurance company started its business.

1912: The Indian Life Assurance Companies Act enacted as the first statute to regulate the life insurance business.

1928: The Indian Insurance Companies Act enacted to enable the government to collect statistical information about both life and non-life insurance businesses.

1938: Earlier legislation consolidated and amended by the Insurance Act with the objective of protecting the interests of the insuring public.

1956: 245 Indian and foreign insurers and provident societies are taken over by the central government and nationalized. LIC formed by an Act of Parliament, namely, LIC Act, 1956, with a capital contribution of Rs 5 crore from the Government of India.

The general insurance business in India, on the other hand, can trace its roots to the Triton Insurance Company Ltd, the first general insurance company established in the year 1850 in Calcutta by the British.

Some of the important milestones in the general insurance business in India are:

1907: The Indian Mercantile Insurance Ltd set up as the first company to transact all classes of general insurance business.

1957: General Insurance Council, a wing of the Insurance Association of India, frames a code of conduct for ensuring fair conduct and sound business practices.

1968: The Insurance Act amended to regulate investments and set minimum solvency margins, and the Tariff Advisory Committee set up.

1972: The General Insurance Business (Nationalization) Act, 1972 nationalized the general insurance business in India with effect from 1 January 1973.

One hundred and seven insurers amalgamated and grouped into four companies, namely, the National Insurance Company Ltd, the New India Assurance Company Ltd, the Oriental Insurance Company Ltd, and the United India Insurance Company Ltd.

The 'Life Insurance Product'

Contract of insurance   A contract of insurance is a contract of utmost good faith technically known as 'uberrima fides'. The doctrine of disclosing all material facts is embodied in this important principle, which applies to all forms of insurance.

At the time of taking a policy, the policyholder should ensure that all questions in the proposal form are correctly answered. Any misrepresentation, non-disclosure, or fraud in any document leading to the acceptance of the risk renders the insurance contract null and void.

Protection   Savings through life insurance guarantees full protection against risk of death of the saver. Also, in case of demise, life insurance assures payment of the entire amount assured (with bonuses wherever applicable), whereas in other savings schemes only the amount saved (with interest) is payable.

Aid to thrift   Life insurance encourages 'thrift'. It allows long-term savings since payments can be made effortlessly because of the 'easy instalment' facility built into the scheme. Premium payment for insurance is monthly, quarterly, half-yearly, or yearly. For example, the salary saving scheme, popularly known as SSS, provides a convenient method of paying premium each month by deduction from one's salary. In this case, the employer directly pays the deducted premium to the insurance company. The SSS is ideal for any institution or establishment subject to specified terms and conditions.

Liquidity   In case of insurance, it is easy to acquire loans on the sole security of any policy that has acquired loan value. Besides, a life insurance policy is also generally accepted as security, even for a commercial loan.

Tax relief   Life insurance is the best way to enjoy tax deductions on income tax and wealth tax. This is available for amounts paid by way of premium for life insurance subject to income tax rates in force. Assessees can also avail of provisions in the law for tax relief. In such cases, the assured in effect pays a lower premium for insurance than otherwise.

Monetary needs   A policy that has a suitable insurance plan or a combination of different plans can be effectively used to meet certain monetary needs that may arise from time-to-time. Children's education, start-in-life, marriage provision, or even periodical needs for cash over a stretch of time can be less stressful with the help of these policies. Alternatively, policy money can be made available at the time of one's retirement from service and used for any specific purpose, such as purchase of a house or for other investments. Also, loans are granted to policyholders for house-building or for purchase of flats (subject to certain conditions).

Insurance for women   Prior to nationalization (1956) of life insurance, many private insurance companies would offer insurance to women with some extra premium or on restrictive conditions. However, after nationalization, the terms under which life insurance is granted to female lives have been reviewed from time-to-time. At present, women who work and earn an income are treated at par with men. In other cases, a restrictive clause is imposed only if the age of the female is up to 30 years and if she does not have an income attracting income tax.

Medical and non-medical schemes   Life insurance is normally offered after a medical examination of the person to be assured. However, to facilitate greater spread of insurance and also to avoid inconvenience, insurance companies, such as LIC, have been extending insurance cover without any medical examination, subject to certain conditions.

With profit and without profit plans An insurance policy can be 'with' or 'without' profit. In the former, bonuses disclosed, if any, after periodical valuations are allotted to the policy and are payable along with the contracted amount. In 'without' profit plan the contracted amount is paid without any addition. The premium rate charged for a 'with' profit policy is, therefore, higher than for a 'without' profit policy.

Key man insurance Key man insurance is taken by a business firm on the life of key employee(s) to protect the firm against financial losses, which may occur due to the premature demise of the person.

The Life Insurance Corporation of India

The Parliament of India passed the Life Insurance Corporation Act on 19 June 1956, and the Life Insurance Corporation (LIC) of India was created on 1 September 1956, with the objective of spreading life insurance much more widely and in particular to the rural areas, with a view to reach all insurable persons in the country, providing them adequate financial cover at a reasonable cost.

LIC had 5 zonal offices, 33 divisional offices, and 212 branch offices, apart from its corporate office, in the year 1956. Since life insurance contracts are long-term agreements and during the currency of the policy a variety of services are required, it later needed to expand the operations and place a branch office at each district headquarter. LIC was re-organized and a large numbers of new branch offices were opened. As a result, servicing functions were transferred to the branches and branches were made accounting units. It worked wonders with the performance of the corporation. It may be seen that from about Rs 200 crore of new business in 1957 the corporation crossed Rs 1,000 crore in the year 1969–70, and it took another ten years for LIC to cross the Rs 2,000 crore mark. However, with re-organization in the early eighties, by 1985–86 LIC had already crossed Rs 7,000 crore sum assured on new policies.

Today, LIC functions with 2,048 fully computerized branch offices, 100 divisional offices, 7 zonal offices, and the corporate office. LIC's wide area network covers 100 divisional offices and connects all the branches through a metro area network. LIC has tied up with some banks and service providers to offer online premium collection facility in selected cities. The company's ECS and ATM premium payment facility is an additional customer convenience. Apart from online kiosks and IVRS, info centres have been commissioned at Mumbai, Ahmedabad, Bangalore, Chennai, Hyderabad, Kolkata, New Delhi, Pune, and many other cities. With a vision of providing easy access to its policyholders, LIC has launched its Satellite Sampark offices. The satellite offices are smaller, leaner, and closer to the customer. The digitalized records of the satellite offices will facilitate 'anywhere' servicing and many other conveniences in the future.

LIC continues to be the dominant life insurer even in the liberalized scenario of Indian insurance and is moving fast on a new growth trajectory surpassing its own past records. LIC has issued over one crore policies during the current year. It had crossed the milestone of issuing 10,132,955 new policies by 15 October 2005, posting a healthy growth rate of 16.67 per cent over the corresponding period of the previous year.

From then to now, LIC has crossed many milestones and has set unprecedented performance records in various aspects of the life insurance business. The same motives which inspired our forefathers to bring insurance into existence in this country inspire LIC to take this message of protection, to light the lamps of security in as many homes as possible, and help people to provide security to their families.

Mission and Vision of LIC

The mission of LIC is to 'Explore and enhance the quality of life of people through financial security by providing products and services of aspired attributes with competitive returns, and by rendering resources for economic development'. The company's vision is to be 'A transnationally competitive financial conglomerate of significance to societies and pride of India'.

LIC and IT

LIC has been one of the pioneering organizations in India that introduced the leverage of information technology in servicing, and in their business. Data pertaining to almost ten crore policies is being stored on computers in LIC. Over the years it has adopted relevant and appropriate technology. 1964 saw the introduction of computers in LIC. Unit record machines introduced in the late 1950s were phased out in the 1980s and replaced by microprocessor-based computers in branch and divisional offices for back office computerization. Standardization of hardware and software commenced in 1990s. Standard computer packages were developed and implemented for ordinary and SSS policies.

Front-end operations   In July 1995, LIC started a drive of online service to policyholders and agents through computers, with a view to enhancing customer responsiveness and services. This online service enabled policyholders to receive immediate policy status reports, prompt acceptance of their premium, and get revival quotations and loan quotation on demand. Incorporating change of address can be done online. Quicker completion of proposals and dispatch of policy documents have become a reality. All the 2,048 branches across the country have been covered under front-end operations. Thus, all the 100 divisional offices have achieved the distinction of 100 per cent branch computerization. New payment-related modules pertaining to both ordinary and SSS policies have been added to the front-end package catering to loan, claims, and development officers' appraisal. All these modules help to reduce time lag and ensure accuracy.

Metropolitan area network   A metropolitan area network, connecting 74 branches in Mumbai was commissioned in November 1997, enabling policyholders in Mumbai to pay their premium or get their status report, surrender value quotation, loan quotation, etc., from any branch in the city. The system has been working successfully. More than 10,000 transactions are carried out over this network on any given working day. Such networks have been implemented in other cities also.

Wide area network   All seven zonal offices and all the MAN centres are connected through a wide area network (WAN). This will enable a customer to view his policy data and pay premium from any branch of any MAN city. As at November 2005, there were 91 centres in India with more than 2,035 branches networked under WAN.

Interactive voice response systems (IVRS) IVRS has already been made functional in 59 centres all over the country. This enables customers to call LIC and receive information (e.g., next premium due, status, loan amount, maturity payment due, accumulated bonus, etc.) about their policies on the telephone. This information can also be faxed to the customer on demand.

LIC on the Internet   The LIC website is an information bank. Information is displayed about LIC and its offices. Efforts have been made to make the web site dynamic and interactive. The addresses/e-mail ids of the zonal offices, zonal training centres, management development centre, overseas branches, divisional offices, and also all branch offices, with a view to speed up the communication process.

Payment of premium and policy status on Internet   LIC has given its policyholders a unique facility to pay premiums through the Internet absolutely free and also view their policy details on Internet premium payments. There are 11 service providers with whom LIC has signed the agreement to provide this service. Customers have to register themselves to avail of these services.

Information kiosks   LIC has set up 150 interactive touch-screen based multimedia kiosks in prime locations in metros and some major cities for disseminating information to the general public on products and services. These kiosks can provide policy details and accept premium payments.

Info centres   LIC has also set up eight call centres manned by skilled employees to provide customers with information about the company's products, policy services, branch addresses, and other organizational information (LIC 2006).

Products offered by LIC

LIC offers a number of products, which have been divided into the following categories:

1. Insurance plans
2. Pension plans
3. Unit plans
4. Special plans
5. Group schemes

Insurance plans   Keeping in mind the different requirements of different individuals LIC offers a number of insurance plans with unique options that can fit into different requirements.

The company has a number of options under children's plans, plan for handicapped dependents, endowment assurance plan, plan for high worth individuals, money-back plans, special money-back plans for women, etc.

Pension plans   These plans provide customers with financial stability in old age. The different pension plans offered are Jeevan Nidhi, Future Plus, Jeevan Akshay IV, New Jeevan Dhara I, and New Jeevan Suraksha I. They thus provide annuity for life with the return of purchase price on the death of the annuitant.

Unit plans   These are investment plans that help to realize the worth of hard-earned money. These plans yield rich benefits and also help to save tax even if a person does not have a consistent income. Thus, they provide the twin benefits of investment and insurance cover.

Special plans   LIC's special plans are not plans but opportunities that the company offers at a point in time. These plans are a blend of insurance and investment. Currently, LIC offers the Golden Jubilee Plan under Bima Gold and New Bima Gold; Special Plan with Bima Nivesh, 2005; and Jeevan Saral.

Group schemes   These are life insurance schemes for groups of people and are ideal for employers, associations, societies, etc. They allow individuals to enjoy group benefits at really low costs. One can choose from a number of group schemes and social security schemes (LIC 2006).

LIC as a Brand

In *Brand Equity's* 'Most Trusted Brands Survey' (2005), LIC showed a phenomenal rise to secure the sixth position and was the only service brand among the top 50 brands for the last three years. The company's ratings shot up at a time when several parts of the country were wrecked by natural disasters, most notable being the tsunami. In fact, LIC's handling of the situation earned it recognition in the Manila-based Asia Insurance Review. LIC visited the tsunami-affected areas with a list of policyholders, set up camps, and settled the claims immediately. According to Mr A.K. Shukla, Chairman, LIC, 'We are in the business of trust and once these things happen, one should tell people that we live up to our promises'. LIC is focusing on quick claim settlement— 90 per cent of policyholders receive post-dated cheques before the date of maturity. In case of death claims, the time lag has been brought down from 90 days six years ago to 60 days, and the target is 45 days in the near future.

LIC has targeted both the urban and rural market. For the urban market it has increased emphasis on value-added services through its online portal and allowed for premium collection through ATM machines and ECS. The other strategies being followed in the urban areas are given in detail in the section on LIC and IT.

With 50 per cent of the agents based in rural areas, LIC concentrates on personal selling in these regions. LIC has covered one crore below poverty line or marginally above the poverty line families with the help of its social security fund. Nabankur Gupta, marketing consultant and founder, Nobby, attributes LIC's success to a much better brand experience, 'the package they offer is pretty good and refunds are dead on time. It marks a complete revival of the brand growth rate on the policies are on a 15-year high at 23 per cent' (*Brand Equity* 2006).

Questions

1. Comment on the different services being offered by LIC.

2. Which stage of the product life cycle is LIC in? Why?

3. Discuss the branding strategies followed by the company.

SELECT REFERENCES

Adcock, R. and Halborg (2001), *Marketing Principles and Practices*, 4th edn, Prentice Hall, Harlow.

Ali, A. (2000), 'The impact of innovativeness and development time on new product performance for small firms', *Marketing Letters*, vol. 11, no. 2, pp. 151–163.

Asplund, M. and R. Sandin (1999), 'The survival of new products', *Review of Industrial Organization*, vol. 15, no. 3, pp. 219–223.

'Back in the High Life' (2006), Brand Equity, *The Economic Times*, 15 February.

Bonner, J.M. (1999), 'Customer involvement in new product development: Customer interaction intensity and customer network issues', PhD thesis, Graduate School of the University of Minnesota.

Brown, S.L. and K. Eisenhardt (1995), 'Product development: Past research, present findings and future directions', *Academy of Management Review*, vol. 20, no. 2, pp. 343–378.

Chesbrough, H. (2004), 'Managing open innovation', *Research Technology Management*, vol. 47, no. 1, pp. 23–26.

Davis, S.M. (1997), 'Bringing innovation to life', *The Journal of Consumer Marketing*, vol. 14, no. 5, pp. 339–353.

Doyle, P. (1976), 'The realities of the product life cycle', *Quarterly Review of Marketing*, vol. 16, Summer, pp. 1–6.

Doyle, P. (2002), *Marketing Management and Strategy*, 3rd edn, Pearson Education, Essex, Chapter 5.

Ellwood, I. (2002), *The Essential Brand Book*, Kogan Page, London.

Gordon, G.L., R.J. Calantone, and C.A. Benedetto (1993), 'Business to business service marketing—How does it differ from business to business product marketing', *The Journal of Business and Industrial Marketing*, vol. 8, no. 1, pp. 45–57.

Grönroos, C. (1998), 'Marketing services: The case of the missing product', *The Journal of Business and Industrial Marketing*, vol. 13, no. 4/5, pp. 322–336.

Handfield, R.B., G.L. Ragatz, K.J. Petersen, and R.M. Monczka (1999), 'Involving suppliers in new product development', *California Management Review*, vol. 42, no. 1, pp. 59–82.

Keller, K.L. (2003), *Strategic Brand Management*, Pearson, Delhi.

Kotler, P. (2002), *Marketing Management*, Prentice Hall, New Delhi.

Kotler, P. (2003), *Marketing Management*, Prentice Hall, London.

Kotler, P., J.T. Bowens, and J.C. Makens (2006), *Marketing for Hospitality and Tourism*, 4th edn, Pearson Education Inc., New Jersey, Chapter 9.

Lazer, W. and R.A. Layton (1999), *Contemporary Hospitality Marketing—A Service Management Approach*, Education Institute of American Hotel and Motel Association, Michigan, Chapter 10.

Levine, M. (2003), *A Branded World*, John Wiley, New Jersey.

Lovelock, C. and J. Wirtz (2006), *Services Marketing*, 5th edn, Pearson Education, New Delhi, Chapter 4.

Lundkvist, A. and A. Yakhlef (2004), 'Customer involvement in new service development: A conversational approach', *Managing Service Quality*, vol. 14, no. 2/3, pp. 249–257.

Michael, G.C. (1971), 'Product petrification: A new stage in the life cycle theory', *California Management Review*, vol. 14, no. 1, pp. 88–91.

Modis, T. (1994), 'Life cycles: Forecasting the rise and fall of almost anything', *The Futurist*, vol. 28, no. 5, pp. 20–25.

Nicholls, A. (2004), 'Fair trade new product development', *The Service Industries Journal*, vol. 24, no. 2, pp. 102–117.

Oxford Dictionary of Business and Management (2006), 4th edn, Oxford University Press, New Delhi.

Rampal, M.K. and S.L. Gupta (2002), *Service Marketing: Concepts, Applications and Cases*, Galgotia Publishing Company, New Delhi, Chapter 14.

Rao, R.M. (2005), *Services Marketing*, Pearson Education, Delhi, Chapters 1 and 7.

Reuters (2006), 'Download music while listening to digital radio', *The Economic Times*, New Delhi, 21 June.

Ries, A. and L. Ries (1999), 'World-class brands', *Executive Excellence*, vol. 16, no. 3, p. 11.

Rio, A.B., R. Vazquez, and V. Iglesias (2001), 'The role of the brand name in obtaining differential advantages', *Journal of Product and Brand Management*, vol. 10, no. 7, pp. 452–465.

Scheuing, E. and E.M. Johnson (1989), 'A proposed model for new service development', *The Journal of Services Marketing*, vol. 3, no. 2, pp. 25–34.

Shetty, M. (2006), 'India moves to no.17 in global life insurance biz', *The Economic Times*, New Delhi, 20 July.

Shostack, G.L. (1977) 'Breaking free from product marketing', *Journal of Marketing*, vol. 41, no. 2, pp. 73–80.

Simoes, C. and S. Dibb (2001), 'Rethinking the brand concept: New brand orientation', *Corporate Communications: An International Journal*, vol. 6, no. 4, pp. 217–224.

Singh, S. (1997), *Right Brain Positioning in Strategic Marketing*, Indian Institute of Management, Calcutta.

Singhal, A. (2004), 'Creating and preserving brand', *Strategic Brand Management*, vol. 3, no. 5, pp. 18–21.

Talreja, V. (2006), 'Budget hotels catch brands' imagination', *The Economic Times*, New Delhi, 3 November, p. 4.

Talreja, V. (2006), 'Party time: Star hotels reap benefits of room shortage', *The Economic Times*, New Delhi, 26 July.

Talreja, V. (2006), 'Spa time: A massage for every occasion', *The Economic Times*, New Delhi, 7 August.

Verma, R., G.M. Thompson, W.L. Moore, and J.J. Louviere (2001), 'Effective design of products/services: An approach based on integration of marketing and operations management decisions', *Decision Science*, vol. 32, no. 1, pp. 165–193.

Vermeulen, P.A.M., J.P.J.D. Jong, and K.C. O'Shaughnessy (2005), 'Identifying key determinants for new product introductions and firm performance in small service firms', *The Service Industries Journal*, vol. 25, no. 5, pp. 625–640.

Vyas, N.M. (1993), 'Industrial product elimination decisions: Some complex issues', *European Journal of Marketing*, vol. 27, no. 4, pp. 58–76.

Wasson, C.R. (1968), 'How predictable are fashion and other product life cycles', *Journal of Marketing*, vol. 32, no. 3, pp. 36–43.

Wasson, C.R. (1978), *Dynamic Competitive Strategy and Product Life Cycles*, Austin Press, Austin.

Weber, J.A., (1976), 'Planning corporate growth with inverted product life cycles', *Long Range Planning*, vol. 9, no. 5, October.

Economic Survey 2007–08, 'Insurance and pension funds', http://indiabudget.nic.in/es2007–08/chapt 2008/chap56.pdf>, accessed on 29 April 2008.

http://www.licindia.com/history.htm, accessed on 2 April 2008.

http://www.tanishq.co.in/tanishq_aboutus.html, accessed on 28 April 2008.

3

Marketing Research in Service Industry

OBJECTIVES

After reading this chapter you will be able to understand the:

- concept of marketing research
- importance of marketing research for management
- influence of the Internet on marketing research
- developments in the Indian and global marketing research industry
- problems in marketing research
- upcoming trends in marketing research over the next decades
- process of marketing research

INTRODUCTION

The discipline of marketing begins and centres on customer needs. The domain of marketing extends to numerous areas such as researching for development of new ideas for product development; various elements of marketing mix such as product, price, place, promotion, after-sales services, and channels related to setting up customer relationship processes. Marketing research covers all such areas of research related to the domain of marketing. As issues of return for investment become increasingly important, firms compete fiercely for a space in the customer's choice criterion. As the competition becomes intense, they compete with each other to discover the parameters that can keep them ahead of others. Marketing research provides insights into customer and market dynamics.

Marketing research is evolving as a discipline. The most profound effect on marketing research has been the advent of the Internet, globalization (Struce 1999–2000), newer forms of data collection, and developments in data analysis and predictive tools.

This chapter presents an overview of marketing research and leads to an understanding of why marketing research is important for service providers. It gives an insight into emerging dynamics of marketing research as an industry in India and explains the process of marketing research.

The American Marketing Association defines marketing research as follows:

'Marketing research is a function that links the consumer, customer, and public to the marketer through information—information used to identify and define marketing opportunities and problems; generate, refine, and evaluate marketing actions; monitor marketing performance; and improve understanding of marketing as a process. Marketing research specifies the information required to address these issues, designs the method of collecting information, manages and implements the data collection process, and analyses and communicates the findings and their implications.'

As Aaker et al. (1998) have elaborated, this definition highlights the role of marketing research as an aid to decision-making. Too often, marketing research is considered narrowly as the gathering and analysis of data for someone else to use. Firms can achieve and sustain competitive advantage through the creative use of market information. Hence, marketing research is defined as an information input to decisions, and not simply the evaluation of decisions that have been made. Market research alone does not guarantee success; the intelligent use of marketing research is the key to business achievement. A competitive edge is more the result of how information is used than of who does or does not have the information (Boughton 1992).

As the name suggests, marketing research signifies research in the area of marketing. Research per se signifies the scientific technique of data collection, analysis, and presentation of information. When a research technique is applied to the area of marketing it signifies research pertaining to the following—identification of consumer needs, development of product as well as decisions related to the product, namely, packaging, branding, positioning, pricing strategies, distribution aspects, promotion potential estimation, demand forecasting, customer analysis, monitoring performance, competition analysis, and after-sales feedback. The scope of marketing is the scope for marketing research.

Parasuraman et al. (1985) defines marketing research as a set of techniques and principles for systematically collecting, recording, analysing, and interpreting data that can aid decision makers involved in marketing goods, services, or ideas. This definition stresses on both the techniques and principles of marketing research. It also emphasizes the importance of data collection and analysis. It suggests that marketing research is an aid to decision makers.

MARKETING RESEARCH AND MANAGEMENT

Marketing research can be viewed as playing three functional roles—descriptive, diagnostic, and predictive (McDaniel and Gates 1999). The *descriptive role* is about gathering facts and figures, such as, what are the sales for various product categories? What do people buy? How much investment is made on education in urban and rural areas? The second role of research is the *diagnostic function* wherein the data or actions are explained. What happened when pricing was changed? What was the effect of change of the size or shape of the product? What was the impact on demand when the new promotions were launched? The third role is the *predictive function* of research. This helps policy makers to make decisions about the products or service offerings based on data collected and analysis of the same.

Marketing research is an expensive exercise and requires commitment of funds on the part of the marketer. New product development especially is a long drawn process and the success rate is very small. The challenge for service providers is, therefore, to decide the attributes or operations related aspects that should be included in the services, which could lead to higher acceptance by the consumers.

Marketing research could help service providers understand the customers' perception of quality. 'Return on quality' is important for service providers. It is the management objective based on the twin principles—(1) that the quality being delivered is the quality the target market desires; and (2) that quality must have a positive impact on the profitability. The key to making return on quality work is marketing research. It is the mechanism that enables organizations to determine what types and forms of quality are important to the target market. Marketing research can sometimes force marketers to abandon their cherished beliefs.

In a research quoted by McDaniel and Gates (1999), 'United Parcel Service had always assumed that on-time delivery was the paramount concern of its customers; everything else came second. Before long UPS's definition of quality centred almost exclusively on the results of time and motion studies. Everything else came second. Knowing the average time it took elevator doors to open on a city block and figuring how long it took people to answer their doorbells were critical parts of the quality equation. So was pushing drivers to meet exacting schedules. The problem was UPS's marketing research was asking the wrong questions. Its survey asked customers if they were pleased with delivery time and whether they thought delivery could be faster.

On further probing, it was discovered that the clients were not as obsessed with on-time delivery as it was thought. On the other hand, the customers wanted more interaction with the drivers—the only face-to-face contact any of them had with the company. If drivers were less hurried and more willing to chat, customers would get some practical advice on shipping.' According to Honomichl (1996), the factors that influence a manager's decision to use research information are:

- research quality
- conformity with prior expectations
- clarity of presentation
- political acceptability within the firm, and
- challenge to the status quo.

Benefits of Marketing Research

Marketing research enables an organization to get insights into the dynamics of the markets, measure the impact of business environment changes, get perspectives on the service elements mix, and enable service providers to evaluate their strategies, monitor sales patterns, customer behaviour, and future ideas for new service offerings (Exhibit 3.1). The findings of the research may help organizations to take decisions about further investments in products and markets. It may give clues on initiating new interventions for managing their customers better. Market research provides answers to numerous questions such as:

- What will be the demand for my product or service?
- What should the product features be?

Exhibit 3.1 The scope of marketing research

The scope of marketing research extends across the following domains:

Sales Analysis

- Measurement of market potential
- Determination of market characteristics
- Market share estimation
- Emerging buying trends
- Geographical analysis of sales

Sales Methods and Policies

- Evaluating alternate ways of reaching the consumer
- Effectiveness of direct selling
- Effectiveness of e-selling

Service Product Management

- Are the current service options are enough?
- What are the consumer preferences?

Processes Measurement

- Do the delivery processes need to be altered?
- What would make the delivery schedules faster and more effective?
- What should be the delivery time for each critical activity in the entire service delivery process?

Pricing-related Research

- What should be the prices of various services?
- Can price bundling be initiated?
- What would be the impact of changing the prices on the mind of the consumer?

People Management

- How do consumers perceive the service level of the employees?
- How do consumers perceive the service delivery?
- How has the people factor been a criterion in the choice of their decision?

Place-related issues

- What should be the mix of real-time service delivery options and the online delivery options?
- Are consumers happy with the use of technology in service delivery?
- What new interventions could be initiated to make the service more user-friendly?
- How many new outlets should be opened?
- Which new areas should be targeted for expansion?

Promotion

- Which combination of promotion techniques should be used?
- Which one is more effective?
- What is the potential of sales through online channels?
- How effective is the promotional strategy? What kind of images are created in the mind of the consumer?

Physical Evidence

- To explore moments of truth for the consumer.
- What were the positive aspects about the point of consumer contact?
- Which areas of service delivery location need to improve?

- What kind of packaging should be used?
- What price will be able to generate higher sales?
- What should be the target market?
- What are the geographical areas which my firm should target?
- What should be my distribution strategy?
- What media should I use for promoting my products?
- How satisfied are the customers with our services?
- How many customers stop using our services every month?

- How many new customers are added?
- What impact will the new technology have on the usage pattern of our services?

The above indicated areas are very valued by the customer and hence it is important that firms make investments in marketing research. All large international firms have sound investments in marketing research practices. For instance, when Japanese automobile manufacturers entered the American markets, they conducted research in the US to study the consumer behaviour patterns regarding space, preferred colour, taste in music, etc. These features were taken into account to conceptualize the service level.

Marketers also need to study the cultural dimensions of their service delivery. For instance, McDonald's studied the religious and cultural practices in India and initiated the 'Navratra week' wherein no non-vegetarian meals are served in any of their outlets. Radisson Hotels, a Carlson brand, started a new fine-dining restaurant in India named, 'The Great Kebab Factory'. This concept became an instant success and thereby franchising operations started for this chain both as a standalone restaurant in India, as well as the Middle East. The idea, based on research conducted in various culinary traditions across various states in India, was to serve kebabs either as a non-vegetarian or vegetarian option and continuously service numerous helpings.

Let us look at Exhibit 3.2 to understand the current trends in marketing research.

WHEN SHOULD A SERVICE FIRM NOT CONDUCT MARKET RESEARCH?

There are situations when market research should not be carried out. These could be related to the following situations:

1. The decision related to the service/product has already been taken and research is being done in order to be politically correct. This is merely a waste of resources.
2. There is ambiguity about the objectives of conducting research.
3. The data collected is not put to much use. Data collection is an ardous exercise and if this is not used then resources should not be wasted on data collection efforts.
4. In case the sample does not represent the desired population aimed to be covered by the study, it will result in erroneous outcomes.

Mistakes made by the Marketer

Some of the following are the mistakes made by marketers.

1. Jumping to conclusions: The biggest sin marketers commit is jumping to a conclusion first and then commissioning research to back up the idea. This attitude can lead to inherent bias and the research questions may be geared to give marketers precisely the answers they want to hear. The very purpose of research is thus negated.
2. Lack of clear cut objectives for conducting research: There may be a situation wherein the objectives are not very well defined. In this context, the scope of research will not clearly map out the domain of the areas which need to be

Exhibit 3.2   What's your competitor doing?

Market research now has a new dimension. It is competitive intelligence (CI), i.e. knowing what your competitors are doing about their business and customers, as well as yours. It is a fact that the competition is always looking to get your customers, while you want to retain yours and get theirs. It's the need of the hour for market agencies to provide hard 'intelligent' facts to their companies. Strategic intelligence is about knowing 'why' and 'how' the market affects you. Facts state that market data and information are available to most companies but 80 per cent of it is unstructured. Thus, this data may not be relevant and remain unprocessed. What is important now is to convert this data into intelligence, analyse it, and arrive at an actionable strategy.

It is extremely crucial for companies nowadays to pick up relevant information regarding their customers, market movements, changes in technology and trends, competitors, their strategy, their customer feedback, and so on. This process is ongoing and needs to be updated time and again. This will, in turn, help a company to become proactive and not reactive to market changes. Indian firms are considered short-sighted and seem more interested in working towards immediate goals. They currently do not feel the need for CI because there is room for everyone. However, in about 8–10 years, market penetration is going to be deep, leading to 90 per cent saturation.

It is time for companies to realize the need for CI-based marketing and strategy as these are going to be the key to survival of companies across industry sectors. Following are examples of two companies, one that survived with CI and the other, which failed to realize its importance.

Shell: The company analysed and had foreseen a situation where the Middle East would cut/reduce crude supply. It had anticipated this and it happened. While Shell had a strategy and was ready with a plan, other companies were caught unawares and suffered huge losses. This gave Shell an edge over the others.

Motorola: This company was the global leader in mobile technology before it fell to the fourth position to Nokia. Nokia is the current global leader and has a dedicated team working on competitive intelligence. Motorola failed to see the change from analog to digital, and also did not realize that mobile phones are no longer a mere means of communication, but so much more.

Source: Adapted from Uchil (2008).

covered and hence there may be lot of ambiguity in conducting the research. In the end, when action needs to be taken on the research conducted, then information on some aspects may be missing.

3. Misconception: Research findings are entirely different from what the marketer wants to believe. For example, in India, the misconception was that the beauty products market was essentially targeted at the female segment, whereas the male segment has emerged as a key user in this market.

4. Identification of wrong market: Many marketers falter by ignoring category research before specific research. It makes sense to understand the dimensions of a category research clearly.

5. Single research exercise: The other common hurdle in the way of effective research is trying to cover too much area in a single research exercise.

6. Instrument: The instrument selected may be flawed and may have numerous errors. The sequence may not be correct or it may have double-barrelled questions, which use words such as 'and' or 'or', that may yield responses to

number of questions and the conclusions drawn would not be appropriate. For example consider the following question:

Were you happy with the food and the service when you dined at the restaurant?

1. Yes   2. No   3. Neutral

Here there will be an ambiguity in the question as we are asking both for quality of food and service at the same time. If a closed-ended response is required, we would not know whether the person referred to food or service. The person may be happy with the food but not with the service or may be happy with service but not food.

7. Flaws: The sampling method may be flawed and the sample may not represent the true population.
8. Size: The size of the sample also matters. Choosing smaller samples may result in erroneous conclusions.
9. Techniques: The data analysis tools have to be used with care. Using wrong techniques, wherein basic assumptions of testing are not met, may reflect in wrong analysis of the whole situation.
10. Giving a general brief without quantifying the specific areas that need to be checked. The marketer is unable to decide what he/she actually wants to get researched. Thus, the brief tends to point in too many different directions, which may lead to inadequate outcomes.

INFLUENCE OF THE INTERNET ON CONDUCTING MARKETING RESEARCH

The Internet is a major phenomenon in the world. As the use of the Internet spreads, e-commerce will also increase. It is important for firms to understand the nature and characteristics of business conducted through the Internet. The conduct of business using online technologies depends on the infrastructure available in a region or a country, as well as aspects such as, the availability of PCs, bandwidth, and education profile, among other factors. Figure 3.1 provides an indication of the Internet penetration by region across various parts of the world. As it can be observed from the figure, the penetration of Internet is the highest in Europe as compared to other parts of the world.

Figure 3.2 gives an indication of the differences between Internet users in developed and emerging economies. This certainly has an impact on the way business firms conduct their business. For instance, though the population size in emerging economies may be higher than countries in Europe yet the penetration rate of the Internet is higher in Europe. Marketers who want to launch their products online will have to take into account the penetration rate than just absolute population number.

Figure 3.3 also points out the gaps between mobile phone usage between different categories of economies. The level of e-commerce strategies will depend upon the level of percolation and the kind of technologies that have been used by the businesses in a particular country. For example, Japan has already migrated to the third generation

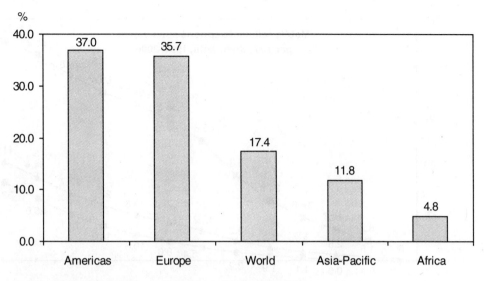

Source: International Telecommunications Union (2008).

Fig. 3.1   Internet penetration by region in 2006

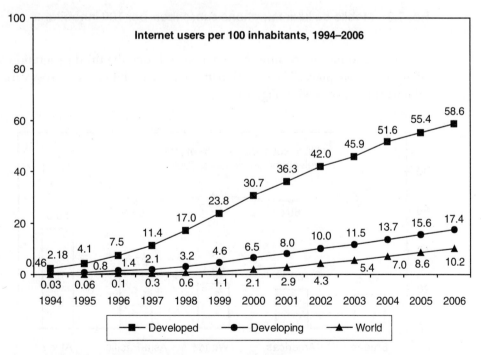

Source: International Telecommunications Union (2008).

Fig. 3.2   Internet users in the world

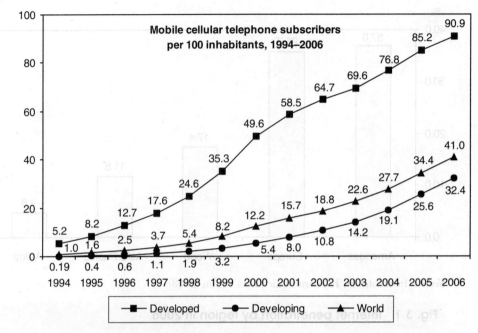

Source: International Telecommunications Union (2008).

Fig. 3.3 Mobile cellular telephone subscribers per 100 inhabitants

technology and mobile commerce, whereas in India, the third generation technology shift needs to take place. The growth pattern in the mobile usage across various regions in the world is indicated in Fig. 3.4.

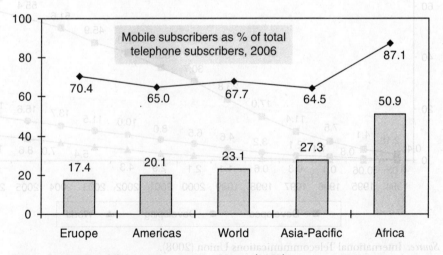

Source: International Telecommunications Union (2008).

Fig. 3.4 Annual average growth rate in mobile subscribers, 2001–06

Table 3.1 Internet subscribers and broadband users in select countries

	Internet				Broadband subscribers	
	Subscribers (000s)	Subscribers per 100 inhab.	Users (000s)	Users per 100 inhab.	Total (000s)	Per 100 inhab.
	2007	2007	2007	2007	2007	2007
China	150,264.0	11.31	210,000.0	15.81	66,464.0	5.00
Hong Kong, China	2,842.0	39.44	3,961.4	54.97	1,879.7	26.09
India	13,490.0	1.15	200,000.0	17.11	3,130.0	0.27
Japan	33,883.9	26.55	94,000.0	73.46	28,300.0	22.12
Macao, China	117.9	24.51	238.0	49.47	110.5	22.97

Source: Adapted from International Telecommunications Union (2008).

The mobile sector has witnessed high growth rate in the past and global mobile penetration rates are expected to reach 50 per cent by 2008 (ITU 2008). India has entered the '100 million club' in 2007, to become the fifth largest mobile nation in the world after China, USA, Japan, and Russia, in terms of total mobile subscribers (CII 2008).

If one looks at the number of main telephone lines per 100 inhabitants, in 2007, USA had 57.15 lines, Japan had 35.80, Germany had 65.07, and China had 27.51, as compared to India which had 3.36 lines (ITU World Telecommunications/ICT Indicators Database 2008). This certainly has implications on the methodologies adopted by the marketing research firms to conduct marketing research. In a country where the reach of telecom and the Internet is still low, the use of such technologies will also be lower. The reliance will be more on more personal surveys. The connectivity in rural areas is still low and to reach nearly 50 per cent of the population will not be possible if the reliance is only on online technologies. Table 3.2 reflects the mobile phone subscription across various countries. Information access on mobile devices is limited by the reach of these devices in a country.

The Internet users per 1000 inhabitants in India in the year 2007 are indicated in Table 3.1. Despite impressive growth in the number of Internet users and the availability of personal computers (PC), India still remains on the wrong side of the divide. The number of Internet users is still a negligible fraction of India's total population. Per capita availability of PCs is also very low.

The typical questions that online marketing research attempts to answer are—What are the purchase patterns for individuals and groups? What factors encourage online purchasing? How can we identify the real buyers from those who are just browsing? How does an individual navigate: do consumers check information first or do they go directly to ordering? What is the optimal web page design? (Turban and King 2003). Online market research methods range from e-mail, moderated focus group discussions, and surveys on the websites, to tracking of customers movement on the web. These days service providers can also look at Internet blogs to get an insight on what consumers

Table 3.2 Mobile phone subscribers in select countries

	Mobile cellular subscribers					As % of total telephone subscribers
	(000s)		CAGR (%)	Per 100 inhabitants	% digital	
	2002	2007	2002–07	2007	2007	2007
China	206,005.0	547,286.0	21.6	41.19	100.0	60.0
India	13,000.0	233,620.0	78.2	19.98	-	85.6
Israel	6,300.0	8,403.8	7.5	122.74	100.0	73.7
Japan	81,118.3	100,525.0	4.4	78.56	100.0	68.7
Macao, China	276.1	794.3	23.5	165.10	100.0	81.7
Asia	443,937.2	1,451,110.8	26.7	36.75	68.2	69.9

Source: Adapted from International Telecommunications Union (2008).

feel about their products and services. Any negative reactions need to be looked into and addressed.

Web surveys: These are becoming popular among companies and researchers. Free software is available to conduct such surveys; for example, zoomrang.com (Turban and King 2003)

Online focus groups: These are conducted using Internet technology. They offer the advantage of reaching to widespread consumers at lower costs.

Tracking consumer movements: These are tracked using cookie files.

Transaction logs: The customers enter their information and knowledge about how they shop and clickstream behaviour can be monitored.

Cookies and web bugs: These can supplement transaction logs. Cookies allow a website to store data on the user's PC which can be used to find what the customer did in the past when they return to the site. Cookies are combined with the web bugs, tiny graphic files embedded on e-mail messages and on websites.

The feasibility of conducting online research offers numerous advantages such as saving time, lower costs, wide coverage, global samples, etc. However, the response rates may be lower than the conventional mail surveys. Also, it is more arduous to fill the forms online in case of lengthy questionnaires. Other issues could be assessing the correctness of the demographic variables and connectivity. Please read Exhibit 3.3 to have a perspective on new types of marketing research.

MARKETING RESEARCH INDUSTRY IN INDIA AND THE WORLD

This section discusses about the issues related to marketing research firms in India and also compares the same with marketing research firms in other countries.

Exhibit 3.3 A marketing research firm with a unique offering

Web portals are gaining popularity in India, and Indians here and all over the world are using this medium to find their soul mates. The organized matrimonial business in India is worth Rs 1,000 crore, with portals such as shaadi.com and bharatmatrimony.com among the leading ones. Years ago, matrimonial services operated as a loose network of friends, astrologers, family priests, and so on. There were also some marriage bureaus, but with the advent of web portals, the industry took off.

Anupam Mittal, Chairman and Managing Director of shaadi.com was sure about the long-term direction the company should take. He wanted to be in the consumer Internet business and develop a few brands in the industry. As he was thinking about the vertical to target, he came across a professional matchmaker in India. 'The business model of the matchmaker intrigued him and he drilled down further to realize that basically this matchmaker went from door-to-door within his community, and to people he knew, and carried 'resumes' with him. Essentially, the choice of a life partner was determined by how far the matchmaker could travel and how much weight he could carry. He wondered what would happen if we took away the spatial and geographical limitations, by putting up profiles on the Internet. The rest, as they say is history. Today, shaadi.com has over 10 million members and 801,764 success stories. A pioneer in the Internet space in India, shaadi.com is today a brand to reckon with' (Merinews 2007).

'Another popular portal, bharatmatrimony.com has successfully developed the concept of matchmaking on the Internet and thus, connected millions of users across the globe. Understanding the customer mindset, it has developed features that transform real life marriages into the virtual world. The special features of the site include horoscope generation, horoscope matching, matrimonial references, and patent pending verification services, among others' (NASSCOM 2007). It is also the only portal in India to provide a voice-based matrimony service, which allows users to record, listen, and reply to any profile, using their mobile phones.

The real advantage for these online portals is that they make available detailed profiles of the members, unlike one-liners in newspapers. Developing the business model further, the brick and mortar model will expand primarily through franchisees sold to the group. The initial investment in the franchisee operation has been pegged at an initial Rs 8–10 lakh and office space requirements to 600–800 sq ft. The franchisee model for both the above brands work on a 50:50 revenue sharing basis. Over 90 per cent of Shaadi Point franchisees are women, while women entrepreneurs run half of bharatmatrimony's 33 franchisee centres. With the aim of finding a suitable match, it helps parents through a wide database. Both claim to have a database of 200,000 profiles each. While Bharatmatrimony focuses on ambience, with tidy spaces and user-friendly infrastructure, which includes contact details and so on, in a bid to make visiting parents feel comfortable, Shaadi Point, has a counsellor to guide them through the entire process of selecting profiles, uploading information, etc.

Other strategies, such as tie-ups with local newspapers to provide editorial content for their matrimonial columns, advertising through fillers, and outdoor hoardings, help these companies to increase their brand visibility and build a strong brand identity.

With 12 million online urban Indians using matrimonial search, making it the thirteenth most popular online activity, it has also been one of the biggest 'gainers' among users, in terms of activities over the last one year.

Source: Adapted from Merinews (2007), NASSCOM (2007), and *Business Standard* (2006).

Marketing Research firms in India

In India, marketing research has grown by 16 per cent last year and crossed the $100 million mark in 2007. Out of the total market of $23 billion worldwide, $100 million worth of business is in India. The significant point worth noting is that India is growing at the rate of 16 per cent, whereas the average worldwide growth is only 5 per cent (*Hindu Business Line* 2007). The amount spent on market research in India in 2007 was about $100 million. The turnover of the industry in the 1970s was Rs 1 crore; it reached Rs 3 crore in 1983, Rs 7 crore in 1987 and Rs 10.06 crore in 1988–9. Clearly, the 1980s saw the mushrooming of many of Indian companies in market research. Growing concern for competitiveness and increased reliance on marketing research ensured that the industry maintained a healthy growth rate of about 25 per cent, and even some of the smaller companies have recorded growth rates as high as 80 per cent. From above Rs 30 crore in the early 1990s, marketing research has blossomed to a Rs 200 crore industry today, employing 3,000 full-time professionals in the late 1990s.

The entire turnover of the industry is very low in comparison to the manufacturing firms. Any single medium-scale manufacturing unit could have that kind of a turnover. ORG-MARG, which merged with ACNielsen, is one of the largest marketing research firms. Industry sources say that most of the marketing research firms in India are growing at more than 80 per cent year-on-year and are expected to grow further in 2008 and 2009 (Rediff Money 2007). Exhibit 3.3 gives a perspective on the growth of marketing research firms in India. Marketing research budgets range typically between 2–10 per cent of the advertising budget. Eighty per cent of the marketing research business is client specific; the marketing research products that different agencies offer account for the rest. The leading clients were HLL (now HUL) and ITC, which retained the marketing research budgets of Rs 10 crore (Annuncio 1998). The marketing research companies invest substantial sums on them, but earn back even up to 100 per cent profit.

The first form of formal research started in 1965 with the Operations Research Group (ORG). In 1971, HTA created IMRB to handle research for clients who were demanding it. Earlier, margins were low and were to the tune of 5–10 per cent.

The share of syndicated research has risen from 15 per cent to 30 per cent. Worldwide syndicated work forms roughly 45 per cent of the total spending on marketing research. Hectic marketing research activity is not limited to FMCG marketers. Today, their share is down to 60 per cent of the total spend. The active areas where a lot of research is being undertaken are:

- pharmaceuticals
- media
- financial services
- automobile industry.

The media fragmentation is quite evident. There are 1,700 TV advertisement spots everyday. The total advertising time beamed out to consumers has moved up from 51 to 214 million seconds over the past five years, in turn, reducing the duration of the commercials (*The Marketing Whitebook* 2007–08). This has added to the high rate of failure and so, marketers now check the films at each stage. One has to ensure that communication is working for the brand and the company image (Annuncio 1998).

There is a great deal of emphasis on the time pressures that really have to be taken into account. The clients insist on weekly reports rather than monthly reports, thereby demanding both quantity and quality at the same time. Exhibit 3.4 reflects the increased number of domestic and outsourcing marketing research firms in India.

Comparison of Marketing Research Industry in India and Other Countries

'The average worldwide per capita spend on market research is about $3.6. Per person spend on market research in the UK is $39, in France it is $36, in North America it is $25, in Europe it is $13, and in APAC it is $0.9. In India, the amount spent on research per person is as low as $0.09. The world average is pulled down because of regions, such as APAC, Central America, West Asia and Africa, which have higher populations, but have low research spends on a per capita basis' (*Hindu Business Line* 2007). The US accounts for only 39 per cent of market research expenditures worldwide. Western Europe accounts for 40 per cent of research expenditure, Japan accounts for nearly 10 per cent, and the rest of the world accounts for the remainder (Aaker et al. 1998).

PROBLEMS IN MARKETING RESEARCH

The industry is beset with a lot of problems. Some of these are as highlighted in this section.

- The population is large and heterogeneous. There is a diversity in languages that are used. This certainly has implications in terms of the level of skills required by the employees. The numbers to be surveyed are large and cultural and linguistic diversity calls for even greater difficulties in adapting research to the local needs.
- There is a whole set of infrastructure problems. There is still a lot of automation that is required. This lack results in lots of delays in the data analysis and compilation.
- There are a whole set of problems with respect to manpower, methodology, and attitude. The industry requires manpower with a good conceptual understanding of the issues, diversified skills relating to understanding of different cultures, analytical skills, and ability to put in a lot of hard work. Currently, there are

individuals working in Indian marketing research firms who are merely graduates, or professionals who have moved into research after working for a few years in the corporate sector. Most of the learning takes place on the job. Common sense is the most sought-after trait. There are no specific institutes that offer specialized training in these particular areas. Marketing research, as a discipline of study in the management institutes, is also not very popular, with very few professionals available who are well-versed in the technique of carrying out research.

- Most Indian organizations do not spend a great deal of the money on market research. Indian organizations are price conscious and it hurts them to pay colossal amounts on research. They still rely more on intuition rather than on the results of formal research.
- There is also a problem of carrying out industry-specific research in certain cases. For instance, there are certain industries that are dominated by two or three large players, as a result of which syndicated research does not make much sense on account of economies of scale. For instance, just two major players dominate the Indian soft drinks industry. There is also a problem of too many players in the field, as a result of which there is a paucity of requisite skilled manpower. Also, research is a process that requires lot of finance. As a result of small size, there is often a problem of handling bigger projects. Again, organizations often subcontract the fieldwork, which results in little control over the research process, resulting in erroneous results.
- There is also a serious problem of data fabrication. Probably, when organizations do take decisions based on these results, they discount this aspect. If an organization subcontracts the jobs, it is important to check the credentials of the research undertaken.
- There is also a lack of professionalism. The delays and lack of sufficient facilities in terms of manpower do contribute to that. In fact, there has been a mushrooming of firms that are characterized by lack of knowledge and experience.
- The turnover rate of employees is also very high. There are too many organizations and a dearth of good people, as a result of which people keep switching jobs for financial gain. Finding an overseas assignment is also seen to be lucrative.
- There are also problems of wrong identification of the problem. The client carries a preconceived notion as a result of which the entire research design is oriented towards a wrong problem. The research briefs given by the client are also sometimes very fuzzy, which further complicate the problem.
- The reports that are generated are often bulky, as a result of which decision-making is not easy. Often, they also lack in adequate recommendations.
- There is also a problem of information databases as a result of which a lot of time is wasted in collecting basic information. Database-building in India is still to develop adequately. There is no detailed information on retail audits and cultural studies, as a result of which there have been many problems of wrong positioning of the products.

TRENDS IN THE COMING DECADES

This section discusses the trends that seem to emerge from the analysis.

- Marketing in India is all about having to deal with tens or hundreds of millions of consumers. For the market researcher, therefore, there is no escape from the tyranny of enormous numbers. When we talk of marketing research, we talk of understanding through marketing research, a population of about 1.5 billion in the year 2020. In the coming decades the consumer in the rural areas will have adopted a far wider range of products and the rural marketing will not be an add-on, but the main event. There will also be shifts in the incomes of the consumers. The number of branded products will increase, but the diversity in the branded consumer base will increase equally. Exhibit 3.5 shows how economic growth in India has led to the shift in advertising spend, and how advertising in India has come of age, and the trends that have been visible over the years.
- There is also going to be a massive market for the rural segments.
- There will also be a shift in the cultural paradigm that has been quite alien to the Indian culture. There will be an increase in hedonism without guilt—a case of, 'I'm doing it because I want to do it'. There will also be a significant increase in consumer spending on products that are low on functionality and high on indulgence.
- There will also be a change in the decision-making systems. There is going to be a shift in the traditional power balance systems. Children will influence many product purchases.
- There is going to be a greater accuracy in data collection and a decline in the traditional door-to-door interviewing methods where findings are totally dependent on the researcher's stimulus and consumer's response. There is going to be a greater amount of data capture through gadgets that will be more objective, and there will be less reliance on human intervention.
- At the level of industry, there is greater likelihood of consolidation. Additional use of sophisticated gadgets will mean capital investment, which means that the industry could end up being dominated by a few, may be only 2–3 large players who have the financial and infrastructural clout.
- The other trend could be a sharper polarization of the market research industry in terms of the services it offers. At one end there will be data suppliers, and on the other hand, there will be professionals whose role could centre round just the delivery of quick, cost-effective data. There will be a breed of value adders cast in the consultancy mode, to make sense of the data.
- Specialization in market research is moving away from the qualitative–quantitative divide, towards industry categories. There is a greater likelihood of having more financial market researchers, pharmaceutical market researchers, and automotive researchers, than focus group or product testing experts.
- Qualitative research budgets are being pumped up. Hindustan Unilever Limited (HUL) now sets aside a third of its budget for qualitative research.

Exhibit 3.5 Advertising in 'New' India

India has changed drastically in the last century and will continue to change in the future as well. The definitive characteristics of the country are changing. *And the change has occurred in less than a time span of a single generation.* It is a fact that a couple of decades ago, there was a man who said that, 'An Indian is one who wishes he wasn't'. But today, an Indian is proud to be one.

Big corporates in India such as Tata, Birla, Wipro, and Infosys are buying companies all around the world. An Indian consumer is aware, and is readily buying foreign brands such as LG, Samsung, L'Oreal, Sony, and Toyota, along with Videocon, Godrej, Lakmé, and Maruti. There is a spur in consumer growth, and growth in advertising follows. Indians have gained economically through the boom in IT, media, telecom, banking, and retail among others. Anand Halve, an IIMA alumnus, says that advertising is the mirror that reflects a society. The following paragraphs reflect some recent developments in advertising in the Indian society.

The most visible aspect of India currently, is that India is being wooed globally. India is catching the world's attention. The importance of Indians is visible from a commercial that teaches the world, how to do 'namaste'. Various universities from all over the world have set up 'educational fairs', and counselling and advisory centres in India. After all, Indians top the list of foreign students in many universities all over the world. While going abroad was a status symbol once, today the same destinations seek the 'Indian flavour'.

The Indian woman too has changed; and this change has not been overnight. It has been a continuous process of significant change. A major change is the fact that she is no longer portrayed as someone who just stays at home, cooks for the family, and looks after her children. The L'Oreal ad shows a woman signing off by saying, 'Because, I am worth it'. The fact is that the Indian woman is well-aware and does not mind spending on herself. The Femina brand has been long associated with belief. Femina encourages women to be self-confident and self-reliant. The new Sunsilk promotion is also based on the same fact. The Scooty ad signs off with the one liner, 'Why should boys have all the fun'. The Asmi brand tag-line is, 'For the woman of spirit'.

As the economy grows, new customers enter new product categories. For example, the introduction of shampoo in sachets got a lot of users who could not afford to buy a shampoo bottle earlier. Mobile phones are a phenomenon, with loads of options available in the lower end segment as well, as shown in an ad that shows parents fearing that their son has turned to bad ways as they see him with an expensive-looking handset. Air Deccan has introduced a no-frill, low-cost service that will bring a common man's dream of flying, to reality.

The Internet is another major phenomenon in the nation. The growth of the Internet seems to reflect a major shift in the power equation between the seller and the buyer. Portals like naukri.com, monster.com, and shaadi.com, have entered the mainstream advertising. Even travel portals like makemytrip.com and yatra.com have become regular advertisers. Though the advertising so far is largely generic, the signs are that online services have certainly established themselves as a part of the larger advertising ecosystem.

The entertainment industry has also come of age and its advertising is not limited to hoardings, on display before a film's release. Movie stars have started to market their movies on their own by associating themselves with a particular brand (which may also feature in the movie) or a reality show on TV. The movie 'Krrish' starring Hrithik Roshan, featured Singapore Tourism Board, Sony, John Players, Bournvita, Tide, and Hero Honda, among others. The recent 'Don' re-make featured, Tag Heuer watches, Motorola phones, while Louis Philippe even came out with the Don range of clothes.

All this points to the fact that Indian advertising is coming of age. All foreign players want to woo India, establish their brands, and want Indian celebrities to endorse their products. This brings the world to India's doorstep and gives the Indian consumer a wide range to choose from. And the fortunate part is that, this is just the beginning.

Source: Adapted from Halve (2007).

- The marketing research agency is seen as a partner in growth and an extension of the marketing arm of the company. Earlier, the marketing research agency was hardly involved in decision-making. Today, because of the width of experience and knowledge base, clients expect the marketing research agencies to attend the strategy meetings.
- At the same time, one must accept that research can at best be a decision support system; there are a whole host of factors that have a bearing on the success or failure of a brand.
- Financial institutions, automobiles, public sector companies, media, and real estate are also taking on intensive studies to examine growth possibilities in the Indian market. Worldwide, government, finance, trade, pharmaceuticals, and media are some of the biggest sources of revenue (Chakraborty 1998).

Though the industry has evolved over a period of time, there is a great deal of potential and changes that are foreseen which have been deliberated upon. There will be a phase of consolidation, sharper polarization in the nature of services that are being offered, and increase in the syndicated research. Marketing research agencies will be seen as partners in the organization's growth and there will be a greater sophistication in the data analysis procedures. Time pressures on the industry are going to be immense; as a result, there will be greater emphasis on the sophisticated techniques of data collection and analysis.

MARKETING RESEARCH PROCESS

The marketing research process consists of the following steps.

1. Identifying the problem
2. Creating the research design
3. Choosing the research methodology
4. Selecting the sampling procedure
5. Collecting the data
6. Analysing the data
7. Preparing and writing the report
8. Follow up

Problem Identification

It is extremely important to have a clear understanding of the problem to be addressed by a marketing research firm. Good problem definition is a prerequisite for a successful marketing research.

Research Design

The research design is a master plan of the research to be undertaken. The function of the research design is to ensure that requisite data in accordance with the problem at hand is collected. It is a blueprint for the research study, which guides the collection and analysis of data (Churchill 1999). As Simon (1969) states, 'There is never a single, standard, correct way of carrying out research. A proper approach is required. There is no single perfect design. A research method for a given problem is not like the solution to a problem in algebra. There are four types of research designs:

1. Exploratory designs
2. Descriptive designs
3. Quasi-experimental designs
4. Experimental designs

Exploratory When not much is known about the problem in hand, exploratory research needs to be initiated. For instance, when mobile phones were launched, there was not much of information on the kind of designs and features consumers would be looking for. So for new products, exploratory studies need to be conducted and these lead to identification of some constructs, which could help in taking decisions. The major emphasis in exploratory research is on the discovery of ideas and insights.

Descriptive Such studies are conducted to answer who, what, when, where, and how questions (McDaniel and Gates 1999).

Here, some basic knowledge is already available with the firm and certain hypothesis could be generated. Based on these, the research design could be formulated, which could further explore relationships between the variables. In comparison to exploratory research, descriptive research is more formal and less flexible. As descriptive design is directed at collecting qualitative and quantitative data, hypothesis testing could be done. Case research designs, longitudinal and cross sectional designs, and focus group studies, are all examples of this category of research design.

Quasi-experimental In this research design, the researcher has control over data collection procedures but lacks control over the scheduling of the treatments and the ability to randomize the test units' exposure to treatments. There are various designs, which fall under this category of research design. Some of these methods are listed here.

1. After–only without control group
2. Before–after without control group
3. The static–group comparison
4. Longitudinal designs
5. Multiple time series design

Experimental Such designs provide a stronger and more reliable basis for the existence of a casual relationship between variables. There could be a control group and there could be another group for which conditions are altered and then measurements are taken. There could be the following possibilities:

1. After–only with one control group
2. Before–after with one control group
3. The Solomon four group design
4. Completely randomized design

5. Randomized block design
6. Latin square design

Data Collection

There are two categories of sources of data—secondary data and primary data.

Secondary data   Secondary data is the data, which could be obtained from published sources. These could be various books, journals, magazines, newspapers, Internet websites, databases, such as Capitaline Plus, Indiastat, Prowess, and Mintel Reports (UK), business insights, annual reports of firms, industry reports, industry association publications, government reports, white papers, etc.

Primary data   This is the data collected by an individual researcher. This involves personal surveys, interviews, telephonic surveys, online surveys, focus group discussions, Delphi studies, observation techniques, mystery shopping techniques, and so on. A firm may use one or a combination of these techniques to collect the data.

Selecting the Sampling Procedure

There are two main methods of sampling—(1) probability sampling methods; and (2) non-probability sampling methods.

Probability sampling   These methods are based on random selection methods. A probability sample is characterized by every element in the population having a non-zero probability of being selected. There are four ways of sampling adopted under the probability sampling method.

Simple random sampling   Each member has known and equal probability of being included in the sample.

It is not widely used in market research because of the following reasons:

- In consumer studies, individuals, households, shops, or areas are selected as sampling units.
- In industry, larger firms are more amenable to such studies.

Systematic sampling   Suppose a population consists of N units. The desired sample size required is k. The sample is chosen in a way that $N/n = k$, where k is the sample interval, and n is the desired sample size.

So if $N = 1000$, $n = 100$, then $k = 10$. So every tenth item would be chosen to be a part of the sample.

Stratified sampling   The entire population is divided into various mutually exclusive categories and collectively exhaustive strata or groups. The criteria for choosing the strata could be:

- income, age, gender, or frequency of purchase
- size of the household
- size of the retail store
- region of the country.

Cluster sampling In this sampling technique all the elements of the population are divided into suitable clusters and a few countries are selected randomly, and all the elements of the selected clusters are used. The collection of data is easier, faster, and more convenient than collecting data over units scattered over a region. The criteria in choosing clusters should be that they are as heterogeneous as possible. The elements between clusters should be homogeneous.

Non-probability sampling It refers to all samples that cannot be considered probability samples. The non-probability sampling methods are convenience sampling, judgment sampling, quota sampling, and snowball sampling.

Convenience sampling The reason for choosing this sample is convenience. There are lower costs and faster results, which could emanate out of the same.

Judgment sampling Samples in which selection criteria are based on personal judgment and the element chosen is a representative of the population under study.

Quota sampling It is selected in such a way that demographic characteristics of interest to the researcher are represented in the sample in the same proportion as they are in the population.

Snowball sampling It involves the selection of additional respondents on the basis of referrals from initial respondents.

Data Collection Techniques

There are number of ways of data collection such as questionnaire surveys, telephonic interviews, face-to-face interviews, focus group discussions, participant observation, etc. The nature of problem, which is being investigated, should determine the combination of methods to be deployed for data collection. The detailed discussion on these methods is out of scope of this book. However, questionnaire-based survey, the most commonly used method for data collection, has been explained in this section. An appropriate questionnaire design is extremely important to get the appropriate data.

Questionnaire A questionnaire is a structured set of questions designed to generate the information required for a specific purpose, especially in marketing research. The questionnaire can make use of multiple-choice questions, with a series of formal questions designed to produce limited responses; alternatively, it can use more open-ended questions, giving respondents an opportunity to air their views. The latter types of questions are often used with small samples to provide the basis of questionnaires for larger samples.

Questionnaire design The questionnaire needs to be designed keeping in mind the objectives of the research and using appropriate scales to facilitate a pragmatic data analysis. A variety of scales are used for this purpose. Some of the scales that are used for questionnaire preparation are nominal scale, ordinal scale, interval scale, semantic differential scale, and ratio scale.

Nominal scale A nominal scale partitions data into mutually exclusive categories. Such data could only be categorized in distinct categories. For instance, the following categories are examples for nominal scale.

Geographic area	Urban	Rural
Gender	Male	Female

Ordinal scale These scales maintain the labelling characteristics along with an ability to order data.

Example:
1. Please rank the following colours in decreasing order of preference with 1 being the most preferred and 5 being the least preferred.
   - Red
   - White
   - Yellow
   - Green
   - Pink

Interval scales These scales contain all the features of the ordinal scales as well as an added dimension that the intervals between the points in scale are equal. Such scales are amenable to statistical techniques such as mean, standard deviation, and correlation, and F tests, t tests, and z tests could be applied on these. Both parametric and non-parametric tests could be applied on these questions.

Example:
1. Mark the following statements:

   I would like to pay extra if the service provider offers a prompt service.

   1. Strongly disagree_____   2. Slightly disagree _____   3. Disagree _____
   4. Neutral _____   5. Agree _____   6. Slightly agree_____
   7. Strongly agree _____

   The different statements are ranked on strongly agree to strongly disagree, on a scale from 1 to 5 or 1 to 7.

Semantic differential scale This is a modified version of the semantic differential test wherein, instead of using strongly disagree to strongly agree statements, pairs of opposite words are used at the end of scale. Examples:

1. The ambience of the restaurant is:

   Very bad ○   Bad ○   Neutral ○   Good ○   Very good ○

2. The colours used in the lobby are:

   Very unpleasant ○   Unpleasant ○   Neutral ○   Pleasant ○   Very pleasant ○

Ratio scales The ratio scales have all the powers of previously discussed scales. This is an agreed absolute zero point which is used in this scale. Physical characteristics of the respondents, such as age, weight, and height, are some examples. Others could be area, distance, money, population counts, elapsed time, and so on.

Design principles The design of the questionnaire needs to be done keeping in mind the survey objectives and constraints.

1. The data collection method needs to be chosen appropriately.
2. The question format needs to be chosen appropriately— should it be a closed format, an open format, or a mixed format.
3. The wordings should be chosen carefully keeping in mind the following.
   - The questions must be clear with no ambiguity.
   - The questions should not use unnecessary jargon.
   - There should not be any double-barrelled questions such as, 'Do you like the service and are you happy with it'?
     The use of words such as *and* or *or* should be avoided.
4. The design should avoid biasing the respondent by using the words such as high class or low quality. This means that you are feeding the biases in the respondent's mind.
5. The ability of the respondent should also be kept in mind while designing the study.
6. The layout of the questionnaire should also be appropriate. The following is the prescribed sequence:
   - Screeners are the first few qualifying questions such as 'Do you use a cell phone?'
   - First few questions such as 'Which brand do you use? How many years have you been using this brand?
   - First third of the questions are transition questions. Questions such as, which features do you like best, should be addressed in this section.
   - Middle half of second third should feature difficult and complicated questions. The questions such as, give a rating to the following questions, should be given here.
   - The last section should cover the demographics.
   - The questionnaire should be pre-tested before implementing to avoid subsequent errors. Sample testing should be done on a small sample and suitable modifications must be made after initial implementation of the questionnaire.

Analysing the Data

There are numerous ways of analysing the data. The quantitative data could be analysed in numerous ways depending upon the scaling techniques used in the questionnaire design. The data analysis could be a combination of techniques involving univariate, bivariate, and multivariate techniques of analysis.

Univariate techniques of data collection involve analysing the single variable by calculating the means, standard deviation, median, mode, etc. *Bivariate* analysis techniques are the analysis of two variables such as correlation analysis, chi square analysis, t test, z test, and F test. *Multivariate* analysis techniques involve testing relationships between more than two variables. Tests such as multiple regression, factor analysis, conjoint analysis, and path analysis MANOVA are used in this case. A discussion on the details of these tests is beyond the scope of this book. For further details please refer to books on statistical techniques and research methodology.

Report Writing

This chapter does not discuss the essentials of report writing. However, the broad guideline is to keep in mind the audience of the report and the specific purpose for which the report is being written. It should be easy to comprehend and should provide necessary details on the different aspects of the research that has been conducted. The report should be prescriptive as well. The limitations of the study need to be indicated.

Follow Up

Whenever consumer surveys or product/service reactions are undertaken, follow-up surveys are important. This is to ascertain whether corrective actions have facilitated a change.

SUMMARY

This chapter delves upon the concept of marketing research. Marketing research is about extending the research to the domains of marketing—need analysis, product, price, place, promotion, process, people and physical evidence, and customer feedback. It is a systematic approach to research. With changing market dynamics and economic environment, market research is considered even more important. As firms expand globally, there are even more challenges in understanding consumers and markets. Marketing research could be used for describing, diagnosing, and predicting various aspects related to consumers and markets. There are numerous advantages for firms to engage in the marketing research, which range from a better understanding of markets and consumers. It helps to channelize investments, and customize and improve upon the service offering. Marketers should be careful to avoid making mistakes related to the research process. A systematic knowledge about the research process is extremely helpful.

The chapter also deals with the influence of the Internet on marketing research. As consumers begin to use Internet extensively marketers will increasingly use this mode. However, the important aspects to be considered are the access to the Internet in an economy, and the kind of product category for which research is being conducted. Online market research methods range from e-mail, moderated focus group discussions, and surveys on the websites, to tracking of customer movements on the web. Online research techniques offer several advantages such as saving time, lower costs, wider coverage, and global samples.

The process of marketing research is also delineated. The important components of marketing research are as follows:

Contd

Summary Contd

Problem identification: This deals with identification of the problem appropriately.

Creating the research design: This deals with identifying the path which will help to achieve the objectives. There are four types of research design—exploratory, descriptive, quasi-experimental, and experimental. Most of the research in the management domain falls in the first two categories. Experimental research in the management area is challenging and resource extensive.

Selecting the sampling technique: This deals with two broad categories of techniques, which are probability and non-probability sampling. There are techniques under both the categories.

Data collection: This includes the mix of a variety of techniques such as, designing the research instrument and using an appropriate way of data collection, such as survey in person or telephoni-cally, and Internet-based data collection. Also, in certain cases interviews may be used for data collection.

Data analysis: There are a range of techniques which can be classified as univariate, bivariate, and multivariate analysis.

Preparing and writing the research report: The report writing must follow a structure for communication and must be clearly written, keeping in mind the objective and audience to which it is directed.

Marketing research should not be carried out as a goal in itself but should have well-defined objectives. A proper research design is important for conducting a proper research. Any biases in design could result in erroneous findings. The findings should also be correlated with the actual phenomenon being observed in the marketplace. Technology tools can be used to enhance the effectiveness of the research.

KEY TERMS

Database An organized collection of information on a computer.

Data analysis The process of systematically applying statistical and logical techniques to describe, summarize, and compare data.

Internet An international network of computers, connected by modems, dedicated lines, telephone cables, and satellite links, with associated software controlling the movement of data. It offers facilities for accessing remote databases, transfer of data between computers, and e-mail.

Marketing research The systematic collection and analysis of data to resolve problems concerning marketing, undertaken to reduce the risk of inappropriate marketing activity. Data is almost always collected from a sample of the target market, by such methods as observation, interviews, and audit of shop sales. Interviews are the most common technique, and can be carried out face-to-face, by telephone, or by post.

Primary data This is first hand data collected by an individual researcher. This involves personal surveys, interviews, telephonic surveys, online surveys, focus group discussions, Delphi studies, observation techniques, mystery shopping techniques, etc. A firm may use one or a combination of these techniques to obtain the data.

Process A specific, structured, and managed set of work activities, with known inputs, designed to produce a specific output.

Research design It is the master plan of the research to be undertaken. The function of the research design is to ensure that the requisite data in accordance with the problem at hand is collected. It is a blueprint for the research study, which guides the collection and analysis of data.

Sampling The process of selecting a group of items or individuals from a population to represent the characteristics of the population as a whole. Samples are often used in market research because it is not feasible to interview every member of a particular market.

Secondary data The data which could be obtained from published sources such as books, journals, magazines, newspaper, Internet websites, databases, annual reports of the firms, industry reports, industry association publications, government reports, white papers, etc.

Questionnaire A structured set of questions designed to generate the information required for a specific purpose, especially in marketing research. The questionnaire can make use of multiple-choice questions, with a series of formal questions designed to produce limited responses; alternatively, it can use more open-ended questions, giving respondents an opportunity to air their views. The latter types of questions are often used with small samples to provide the basis of questionnaires for larger samples.

CONCEPT REVIEW QUESTIONS

1. Evaluate the scope of market research.
2. What are the mistakes made by marketers in conducting market research?
3. Explain the important steps in conducting market research.
4. How has the use of the Internet influenced the use of market research?
5. What are the challenges in conducting market research?
6. What elements should be considered while designing a questionnaire?
7. What are the various sampling techniques deployed in conducting research?
8. What are the challenges faced by small and medium firms in conducting research?

CRITICAL THINKING QUESTIONS

1. In an airline, it was observed on a particular route, that 40 per cent of the passengers did not finish their meals. When the formal feedback was taken it was found that the passengers just rated the meal quality to be average but no further details could be found.

   (i) Please suggest a strategy for research to find the reasons for non-consumption of the meals on the flight.

   (ii) Design a suitable questionnaire to measure consumer preferences for meals in context of the above-described case.

   (iii) Please indicate the data analysis techniques, which you could use with the questionnaire developed in the question above.

2. There is a need for businesses to adopt green practices for conserving the environment. Please suggest the appropriate research design to carry out this study for the hotel industry in India.

3. A bank in India wanted to carry out a customer satisfaction survey and find out whether the customers were happy with the services offered to them. It has 300 branches, with 150 in urban areas and 150 in rural areas. To measure customer satisfaction, it carried out the survey randomly with 100 respondents each in the four metros, namely, Delhi, Mumbai, Chennai, and Kolkata as well as 30 respondents each in Bangalore, Ahmedabad, and Nagpur. Critically evaluate the sampling procedure chosen for the research study.

═══ PROJECT ASSIGNMENTS ═══

1. Make a team of four students and conduct a market assessment of factors influencing the choice of mobile phone in the age group of 18–25 years in India. Identify the objectives, develop an appropriate research design, collect the data, and make an appropriate analysis.

2. Evaluate the Internet usage habits of college students with regard to working on their academic projects.

CASE STUDY

Population Growth and the Urban Poor*

According to the Organisation for Economic Co-operation and Development (OECD) estimates, by the year 2050 India will be the world's third largest economy. The population of India is expected to increase from 1029 million to 1400 million during the period 2001–26, an increase of 36 per cent in 25 years at the rate of 1.2 per cent annually (Census of India). According to the Government of India's projections, urban population in the country, which was 28 per cent in 2001, is expected to increase to 38 per cent by 2026. The urban growth will account for over two-thirds (67 per cent) of total population increase by 2026. Out of the total population increase of 371 million during 2001–26 in the country, the share of increase in urban population is expected to be 249 million. Delhi, for example, will have the highest growth of 102 per cent during 2001–26. States such as Himachal Pradesh, Punjab, West Bengal, Orissa, Andhra Pradesh, and Karnataka will have a projected growth in the range of 20–30 per cent. In states such as Haryana, Rajasthan, Uttar Pradesh, and Madhya Pradesh, the increase is projected to be 40–50 per cent by 2001–26, which is above the national average of 36 per cent. Of the projected increase in population of 371 million in India during 2001–26, 187 million is likely to occur in the seven states of Bihar, Chhattisgarh, Jharkhand, Madhya Pradesh, Rajasthan, Uttar Pradesh, and Uttaranchal. It is interesting to note that nearly 21 per cent of mobile users in India reside in the villages. As on September 2007, out of 209 million mobile users in the country, 43 million were in the rural areas (*The Hindu Business Line* 2008). Table 3.3 shows the rural market share of various mobile operators in India.

Table 3.3   Rural market share of telephone operators in India

New rural ringtone

(in million)

Operator	Total subscribers	Rural subscribers	Rural market share (%)
Bharti	48.88	9.80	22.2
Reliance	36.32	6.11	13.89
Vodafone	35.66	9.73	22.1
BSNL	34.13	10.87	24.7
Tata	19.50	1.04	02.3
Idea Cellular	18.67	3.74	08.5

As on September 2007

Source: The Hindu Business Line (2008).

Rural Marketing in India

The Indian rural market is and will be difficult to ignore. It is true that the heart of India still resides in its villages. It reflects a lot of potential. Table 3.3 indicates that in categories such as mobile phones, rural markets have been gaining on the charts. Today, rural markets are critical for every

* Mirchandani, R., *Rural Marketing in India*, Aries Flash Online, http://business.vsnl.com/ariesagro/rural951.html, accessed on 17 November 2008. Reprinted with the permission of Dr Rahul Mirchandani, Executive Director, Aries Agro Limited, Mumbai, India.

marketer, whether it is branded shampoos, automobiles, soaps, or colour television. The size of the rural market is pegged at more than Rs 700 million in 2006. The time has gone when marketers thought that van campaigns, cinema commercials, and a few wall paintings would be sufficient to entice rural folks to their folds. Thanks to television, today a customer in a rural area is quite aware about myriad products that are on offer in the marketplace.

It is true that all individuals in rural India have the same needs, wants, desires, and aspirations that anyone in urban India has, but the buying behaviour demonstrated by the rural Indian differs tremendously when compared to the typical urban Indian. Further, the same values, aspirations, and needs of the rural people vastly differ from that of the urban population. Basic cultural values still remain the same in rural India, where buying decisions are still made by the eldest male member, whereas even children have started influencing buying decisions in urban areas. Further, buying decisions are highly influenced by social customs, traditions, and beliefs in the rural markets. Many rural purchases require collective social sanction, unheard off in urban areas.

Another contrasting feature is the precision in the assessment of purchasing power of the consumers. In urban markets, income levels are generally used to measure purchasing power and markets are segmented accordingly. However, this measure is not adequate to define the purchasing power in rural areas because of the fact that rural incomes are hugely underestimated. Farmers and rural artisans are paid in cash as well as in kind. However, while reporting their incomes, they report only cash earnings, which in turn, affects the calculation of their purchasing power. This is the main reason why marketers are often surprised to find that their products exist in the households of people who, according to their surveys and estimates, do not have the purchasing power for this. Hence, it is important for every marketing manager to make an attempt to understand the rural consumer better so that the strategies are decided in a manner that they produce the desired results.

Rural marketing mix

The price-sensitivity of a consumer in a village is extremely important to marketers. Rural income levels are largely determined by the vagaries of the monsoon and hence, the demand forecast is not easy. Apart from increasing the geographical width of their product distribution, the focus of corporates should be on the introduction of brands and development of strategies specific to rural consumers. Britannia Industries launched the successful Tiger biscuits especially for the rural market. It clearly paid dividend. Its share of the glucose biscuit market has increased from 7 per cent to 15 per cent. Unfortunately, most marketers of today try to extend marketing plans that they use in urban areas to the rural markets, which is a devastating strategy. They should adopt a strategy that appeals individually to the rural audience, such as price sensitivity and separate annual plans, and sales targets for the rural segment should be formulated. The marketing mix elements such as price, place, product, and promotion, should be customized for the rural market. If corporate marketers start designing goods for the urban markets and subsequently push them in the rural areas, they are bound to face problems.

The unique consumption patterns, tastes, and needs of the rural consumers should be analysed at the product planning stage so that they match the needs of the rural people. Companies such as Hindustan Unilever have successfully used strategies to influence the rural market for its shampoos in sachets. The sachet strategy has proved so successful that, according to an ORG-MARG data, 95 per cent of total shampoo sales in rural India is by sachets. The company had developed a direct access to markets through the wholesale channel and created awareness through media, demonstrations, and on-ground contact. This changed the attitude of the villagers. Today, the young and the educated in the villages are already large in number. And this number is increasing. Already, 40 per cent of all those graduating from colleges are rural youth. They are the decision makers and are not very different in education, exposure, attitudes, and aspirations from their counterparts, at least in smaller cities and towns.

In rural India, annual *melas* organized with a religious or festive significance, are quite popular and provide a very good platform for distribution. Rural markets come alive at *melas*, days with religious significance, and festivals such as Diwali, Holi, Navratras, etc. People visit these fairs to make several purchases. According to the Indian Market Research Bureau, around 8,000 such melas are held in rural India every year. Besides these melas, rural markets have the practice of fixing specific days in a week as market days when exchange of goods and services are carried out. This is another potential low cost distribution channel available to the marketers. Also, one satellite town, where people prefer to go to buy their durable commodities, generally serves every region consisting of several villages. If marketing managers use these towns they will easily be able to cover a large section of the rural population.

While planning promotional strategies in rural markets, marketers must be careful in choosing the right vehicle to be used for communication. It is worth remembering that only 16 per cent of the rural population has access to a vernacular newspaper. Although television is undoubtedly a powerful medium, the audiovisuals must be planned, keeping them in mind, so as to convey a right message to the rural folk. The marketers must try and rely on the rich, traditional media forms such as folk dances, puppet shows, etc. with which the rural consumers are familiar and comfortable, for high impact product campaigns.

Questions

1. Based on the above case on rural markets, what should service providers, such as telecom firms, be doing?

2. Can service providers in India ignore rural markets? Critically analyse this, based on the data provided in the case study.

3. What are the buying preferences for consumers in rural areas in India?

4. As a marketer, if you were to offer healthcare consulting services to rural areas, what aspects would you consider while marketing the same?

SELECT REFERENCES

Aaker, A.D., V. Kumar, and G.S. Day (1998), *Marketing Research*, John Wiley, New York.

Ahluwalia, T. (1995), 'Polarisation in market research', Brand Equity, *The Economic Times*, 4 January.

Annuncio, C. (1998), 'Monitoring the mindset', *Outlook*, New Delhi, 13 July.

Bijapurkar, R. (1996), 'The traps in advertising research', *The Strategist Quarterly*, January–March, vol. 1.

Boughton, Paul (1992), 'Marketing research partnerships: A strategy for the 90s', *Marketing Research: A Magazine of Management and Applications*, 4 December, pp. 8–13.

Chakraborty, A. (1998), 'The new research agenda', *Business India*, 27 July–9 August.

Churchill Jr., Gilbert A. (1999), *Marketing Research*, Dryden Press, New York.

Gaur, A. and S. Nagi (1995), 'Re-engineering marketing', *The Economic Times*, 4 January.

Gupta, I. (1996), 'Mapping your brand', *The Strategist Quarterly*, January–March.

Halve, A. (2007), 'Advertising in changing India', *The Marketing Whitebook 2007–2008*.

Honomichl, J.J. (1996), '1996 Business Report on the marketing research industry', *Marketing News*, 3 June.

Honomichl, J.J. (2005), 'Top 50', *Marketing News*, 15 June.

McDaniel, C. and R. Gates (1999), *Contemporary Marketing Research*, South-Western College Publishing, New York.

Parasuraman, A., V.A. Zeithaml, and L.L. Berry (1985), 'A conceptual model of service quality and its implications for future research', *Journal of Marketing*, vol. 49, no. 4, pp. 41–50.

Rakesh Kumar (2003), 'Analyzing marketing strategy for broadband services of BSNL', Dissertation for Post Graduate Diploma in Business Management, MDI, Gurgaon.

Sharma, S. (1995), 'Push button marketing', *The Economic Times*, 4 January.

Simon, J.L. (1969), *Basic Research Methods in Social Science: The Art of Empirical Investigation*, Random House, New York.

Struce, Doss (1999–2000), 'Marketing research's top 25 influences', *Marketing Research*, Winter/Spring.

Turban, E. and D. King (2003), *Introduction to e-commerce*, Prentice Hall, New Jersey.

Uchil, D. (2008), 'What's your competitor doing?', *The Hindustan Times*, New Delhi, 1 May, p. 30.

Business Standard (2006), http://www.business-standard.com/strategist/storypage.php?tab=r&autono=260362&subLeft=3&.

Confederation of Indian Industry, http://cii.in/menu-contact.php?menu_id=629, accessed on April 2008.

'India to be global hub for market research', http://in.rediff.com/money/2007/may/05india.htm.

International Telecommunication Union, http://www.itu.int.

Merinews (2007), http://www.merinews.com/catFull.jsp?articleID=125367&catID=7&category=Lifestyle&rtFlg=rtFlg.

NASSCOM (2007), http://www.nasscom.in/upload/55199/Bharatmatrimony.pdf.

Rediff (2004), http://www.rediff.com/money/2004/may/18bpo.htm.

The Hindu (2001), 'Rural market—A world of opportunity', http://www.hinduonnet.com/2001/10/11/stories/0611000c.htm.

The Hindu (2008), http://www.hinduonnet.com/2001/10/11/stories/0611000c.htm.

The Hindu Business Line (2006), http://www.thehindubusinessline.com/catalyst/2006/08/17/stories/2006081700250400.htm.

The Hindu Business Line (2007), 'Market research firms must offer insights too', http://www.thehindubusinessline.com/catalyst/2007/02/08/stories/2007020800190200.htm.

The Hindu Business Line (2008), http://www.blonnet.com/2008/01/27/stories/2008012751080100.htm.

The Hindu Business Line (2008), http://www.thehindubusinessline.com/2008/01/27/stories/2008012751080100.htm.

VSNL Business (2006), URL:http://business.vsnl.com/ariesagro/rural951.html.

4 Understanding Consumer Behaviour

OBJECTIVES

After reading this chapter you will be able to understand the:

- basics of consumer behaviour
- process of consumer decision-making
- factors influencing buying behaviour of consumers
- concept of relationship marketing
- meaning of the term customer delight
- concepts relating to customer loyalty
- meaning of consumerism

INTRODUCTION

Consumer behaviour is an inter-disciplinary science that investigates the decision-making activities of individuals in their consumption roles. It describes the reasons for development of consumer behaviour as an academic discipline and an applied science. It is pertinent for marketers to understand the dynamics of consumer buying and consumption patterns to continuously improve their service offering. The service industry is dynamic and hence, it is important to understand the trends and customize the service offering appropriately. Schiffman and Kanuk (1997) define consumer behaviour as the behaviour displayed by consumers in searching for, purchasing, using, evaluating, and disposing of the products, services, and ideas, which are expected to satisfy their needs. It includes understanding questions such as the what, why, where, how, and when of consumer behaviour. Consumer behaviour is an integral factor in the flow of business.

This chapter gives an overview of consumer behaviour in the context of the service industry. It gives an insight into the dynamics of consumer behaviour and the decision-making processes, and delineates the factors affecting consumer behaviour. It also explores the concept of relationship marketing and consumer loyalty and discusses a case study on rural marketing in India. Consumer behaviour helps managers to:

- design the service mix
- segment the marketplace

- position and differentiate the product
- perform environmental analysis
- develop market research studies
- improve the personal ability of an individual to be a more effective consumer
- understand human behaviour and impact the policy decisions in public and organizational domains.

RELEVANCE OF CONSUMER BEHAVIOUR

Consumer behaviour has emerged as a separate area of specialization. Consumer aspirations change with the dynamics of the changing business environment. There is a need to document and understand differences in behaviour, buying, and usage patterns across various countries. There may be a change in the needs, personality, and lifestyle pattern of consumers. The product life cycle is also becoming shorter, and environmental concerns are becoming important. The ethical issues related to service marketing and consumption, and recycling, also need to be understood. Consumer behaviour draws inputs from various disciplines such as psychology, sociology, social psychology, cultural anthropology, economics, and strategic management.

The techniques used to target consumers have changed over the various time cycles. Prior to World War II, companies were production oriented, wherein the focus was on intensive distribution and mass production. The service element was not a consideration. There was then a shift to product orientation, wherein there was greater focus on the product features. For instance, when competition intensified, features such as the best quality, better performance, and maximum number of features, became key selling points. This obsession with product features rather than the assessment of the market need was known as marketing myopia (Levitt 1967). Later there was a shift to sales orientation, wherein the capability to sell predominated the market need. The next focus was on identifying the consumer need and offering a product/service, which satisfied those needs, while at the same time engaging in societal welfare. However, this paradigm shift has been more visibly seen in the case of developed economies. In the services sector, the service offering is decided based on the maturity of the service category and sophistication level of the consumers. Hence, in emerging economies, a sales orientation is still predominant. However, with the opening up of economies, and higher access to media and communication channels, consumers are becoming more discerning. As a result, marketers are making efforts to offer contemporary services in various sectors, such as telecom, ITES, railways, etc. To understand consumer behaviour, one needs to appreciate the following aspects:

1. Consumer behaviour is a process that includes many activities.
2. It is motivated.
3. A consumer may adopt many roles.
4. It is influenced by external factors.
5. It varies for different people.

Consumer Behaviour Process

Consumer behaviour can be understood by understanding the processes at three levels.

1. Stage I: Pre-purchase activities
2. Stage II: Purchasing activities
3. Stage III: Post-purchase activities

The consumption can be analysed during different phases of—acquisition, consumption, and disposition. The acquisition phase analyses the factors influencing the choice exercised by the consumers. The consumption phase analyses the factors affecting their consumption patterns. The disposition phase analyses the consumers' disposition after they have consumed the services. There are three levels of analysis of consumer behaviour—(1) individual level of analysis; (2) micro-environment (interpersonal and situational influences); and (3) macro-environment (culture, sub-culture, social class, and economic conditions).

Decision-making Process

An individual consumer is a complex person who is influenced by numerous factors, which affect his/her decision-making process. One such model, which gives an insight into the customer decision-making process, is explained in this section.

EKB Model

A comprehensive model of consumer decision-making, the Engel, Kollat, and Blackwell (EKB) model maps out a five-step decision process during which a range of internal and external variables continually intervene to influence the final purchase (Fig. 4.1). The model maps out the complex mix of factors that affect the consumer decisions. It identifies five distinct aspects of consumer decision-making—(1) inputs; (2) information processing; (3) decision process; (4) decision process variables; and (5) external influences.

Inputs The consumer experiences numerous stimuli, which are driven by the marketer, such as advertisements, road shows, technical literature, personal selling, or selling, through a network of friends/acquaintances.

Information processing The consumer absorbs the information and tries to collect more information on the various options available. The information processing progresses in stages, such as exposure to information, capture of attention, comprehension of the information, acceptance of the information, and retention of the information by the consumer.

Decision process At any given time, the consumer is exposed to various stimuli through the media and interactions with peer group, family, and friends. These different options vie for the consumer's attention. This information is then comprehended and processed, and the consumer retains the relevant data. The decision process also involves numerous steps. It is a five-step process as outlined below.

- Need/problem recognition: During this stage, the consumer identifies his/her own needs and attempts to look for solutions.

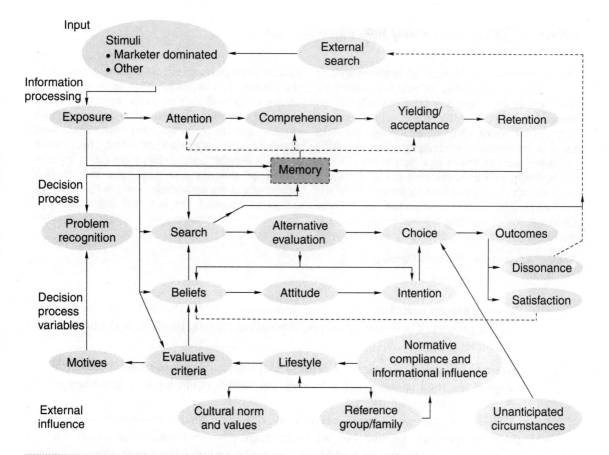

Fig. 4.1 EKB model

- Information search: The consumer searches for information on alternatives available in the marketplace. He/she tries to find more information from various sources on the features of various options. The time spent on information search will depend on the nature of the investment made.
- Alternative evaluation: The consumer evaluates the alternate possibilities and tries to find the option that yields the best outcomes. Alternative evaluation is influenced by the beliefs, attitudes, and intentions of the consumer.
- Choice: The consumer zeroes in on an option, which best meets his/her requirements after having evaluated various options.
- Outcome of the decision: The outcome of the decision results in purchase or consumption.

After the customer has made a choice, he/she may sometimes have a negative evaluation about the purchase. This is known as cognitive dissonance. The attempt of the service provider is to reduce the element of cognitive dissonance.

Exhibit 4.1   M-Commerce may soon mean M-ticketing

The word 'mobile commerce' or 'm-commerce' is being used in a big way in countries, such as Hungary, where elections take place by short messaging service (SMS). In India, however, the scene is completely different; we still use our SMS service for sending messages or for m-voting on shows such as Indian Idol, Star Voice of India, etc. Recently, early adopters, such as PVR Cinemas, have started issuing m-tickets for theatre entry, and the trend is picking up in other sectors too. At Fame Cinemas, the m-ticketing service allows users to utilize the voice-based booking service to choose a movie, make payment via credit card, and confirm the booking. The tickets can then be collected after showing the SMS and the credit card used while making the booking. This can further be used to send regular updates on movies and inform customers about forthcoming movies and offers. The Director of PVR Cinemas, Sanjeev Bijli, says that in the pilot phase the m-ticketing services have seen 20,000 downloads of the application interface (available for select subscribers). The potential of this sector is huge and soon cinema may become an impulse purchase.

Source: Adapted from *Business Standard* (2006).

Decision process variables   There are numerous variables that influence the decision-making process. These are—motives, evaluation criteria, lifestyle, and informational influence.

External influences   It refers to cultural and reference groups. Also included in this category are the unanticipated circumstances, which could have an influence on the decision-making processes.

There are different categories of consumer decisions. There are some decisions where the consumer buys on impulse, while there are others where he/she weighs various alternatives as in the case of healthcare, insurance, or investment in real estate. Exhibit 4.1 illustrates how technology is transforming movie tickets into impulse purchases.

CONSUMER BEHAVIOUR MODELS

There are numerous models for understanding consumer behaviour. A consumer is continuously exposed to market stimuli, which affect his/her decision processes. There

Market stimuli	Other stimuli	Buyers' characteristics	Buyers' decision process	Buyers' decisions
• Product • Price • Place • Promotion • People process • Physical evidence	• Economic • Social • Technological • Political • Cultural	• Cultural • Social • Personal • Psychological	• Problem • Recognition • Information search • Evaluation of alternatives	• Service choice • Brand choice • Dealer choice • Purchase timing • Purchase amount

Fig. 4.2   Understanding consumer behaviour

are numerous factors that influence buyer behaviour. The stimuli along with buyer characteristics and behaviour result in a buyer's decision (Fig. 4.2).

CHANGING DYNAMICS OF INDIAN CONSUMERS

As the Indian economy grows, consumption patterns are witnessing a lot of changes. Some of these changes, such as income growth, increase in disposable income, an ever expanding female workforce, as well as the increased spending on entertainment, education, and healthcare are discussed in this section.

Income growth The income levels of the consumers have been steadily rising. McKinsey Global Institute's analysis shows that if India achieves the current growth path over the next 20 years, the Indian income levels will almost triple (*The Marketing Whitebook* 2007–08).

Increasing disposable income As income grows, expenditure on services and goods, which make life easy, is also increasing. Spending on domestic help and other services such as laundry, eating out, etc. is also increasing. McKinsey Global Institute's study indicates that the average real household disposable income will grow from Rs 113,744 in 2005 to Rs 318,896 by 2025, a compound annual growth rate of 5.3 per cent (*The Marketing Whitebook* 2007–08).

Women participating in workforce As more and more women join the workforce, spendings on healthcare, beauty services, banking, the Internet, and convenience services will increase.

Education and health services People are spending on health insurance and healthcare services are growing. People have started investing in preventive health checkups. The spending on education is increasing as people look for good quality education. So, a lot of international schools and institutions dedicated to higher education are being set up.

Entertainment People are spending larger amounts on entertainment. There is increased spending on restaurants, malls, and movies.

Comfort with technology Online shopping is increasing and consumers are making investments in high-tech products.

Table 4.1 provides an insight into the spending pattern of Indian consumers. The table details the percentage share of total consumption for nine categories.

The KSA Technopak survey on Indian consumers classifies consumers into four segments—(1) technology babies; (2) impatient aspirers; (3) balance seekers; and (4) arrived veterans.

Technology babies This segment in the age group of 8–19 years is estimated to be around 17 million in number. These are the post-liberalization kids with tremendous exposure to satellite and cable network as well as familiarity with gizmos and computers. They are technology savvy and have a high degree of western influence. With 45 per cent of India's population below 20 years, this segment is very attractive to marketers.

Table 4.1 Spending pattern of Indian consumers compared to US and China

Consumption category	US	China	India (2005)	India (2025)
Food, beverages, and tobacco	15%	35%	42%	25%
Apparels	4%	11%	6%	5%
Personal products and services	14%	4%	8%	11%
Housing and utilities	19%	9%	12%	10%
Household products	5%	6%	3%	3%
Education and recreation	12%	15%	5%	9%
Transportation	11%	6%	17%	20%
Communication	1%	7%	2%	6%
Healthcare	19%	7%	7%	13%

Source: Adapted from *The Marketing Whitebook 2008.*

Impatient aspirers   They belong to the age group of 20–25 years and are about 16 million in number. They are young and a wide number of career and education opportunities are available to them. They are more open to experimentation and are able to experiment with unconventional career opportunities. They spend on eating out, books, music, consumer durables, etc.

Balance seekers   At around 41 million, this segment, in the age group of 26–50 years, spends on lifestyle goods due to their rising purchasing power. Looking good is important for this segment. They spend money on vacations and household goods as well. The marketing opportunities exist for entertainment avenues, home decor services, personal grooming chains, and bill payment services.

Arrived veterans   This segment comprises nine million consumers in the age group of 51–60 years. The big spends are on children—their education, settling them, and their marriage. Healthcare is another area of expenditure. This age group spends the maximum money on vacationing.

Exhibit 4.2 illustrates the trend of increased spending by Indian consumers.

FACTORS INFLUENCING BUYING BEHAVIOUR

There are numerous factors, which influence consumers' buying behaviour. These can be classified as cultural, social, personal, and psychological factors.

Cultural Factors

Taylor (1871) defined culture as a complex whole, which includes knowledge, belief, art, morals, customers, and any other capabilities and habits acquired by man as a member of society. Culture can be understood in numerous ways. According to one framework, culture can be analysed by understanding internal and external material culture.

Exhibit 4.2   Insights on Indian consumers

As per an ACNielsen survey, India is supposed to be the most optimistic country in the world. More and more Indians seem to have a positive outlook on job prospects and personal finances. While about 66 per cent Indians are excited to try new products and services, ever-increasing disposable incomes are allowing Indians to invest in the share market (the percentage is as high as 44 per cent). It is a fact that about 87 per cent of Indians think that their personal finances in the future are going to be in good shape.

The optimistic Indian scenario has also led to an increasing number of online shoppers. Although this population is still small when compared globally, it surely offers qualities such as affluence and technology adaptation. As per the report, more than 627 million people have purchased video games and DVDs, and 135 million have made airline reservations. Compared to their global counterparts, Indians have made a high number of online purchases in the most recent months of online purchase. Nearly one-fourth of Indians have purchased items such as electronic equipment (for instance, cameras) and over one-fifth have purchased items such as apparel, music, electronics, and entertainment, among others.

The above data clearly demonstrates that the Indian consumer has come of age and is willing to spend on a wide variety of items.

Source: Adapted from VNU Marketing Information Services (2006).

External material culture   It refers to the external objects, which we experience in our day-to-day living, such as art, music, leisure, sports, buildings, etc. Use of technology has an impact on external material culture. Festivals are an integral part of the Indian culture. Leisure activities in India revolve around shopping, eating out, and watching movies. Bollywood, through its films, reflects the place of music and dance in Indian society. Indians are avid cricket lovers and companies use promotions and advertisements during cricket matches to target consumers. During various festivals, companies come out with special offers, which lead to increased spending by consumers. In India, the festivities begin with the Navratras, wherein the Mother Goddess is worshipped. This is followed by Dusshera, Diwali, and Id, during which gifts are exchanged.

Internal material culture   This refers to the ideas and points of view shared by most members of a society. The most prominent of these include knowledge systems (language, sciences, and objective descriptions of the material culture), belief and value systems (such as religions, political, or social philosophies), and the social normative system. The Indian society is driven by values such as family, respect for elders, and children. Children are the key factor around which families revolve.

However, environmental factors have an impact on the external and internal material culture. These evolve over a period of time. In India, movies reflect Indian values and tradition. The marketing campaigns initiated by various service providers are also a depiction of the mindset of Indian culture.

Sub-culture   Each culture consists of many sub-cultures that help marketers identify consumer consumption trends. India, with its rich cultural diversity, is a melting pot of different sub-cultures. Northern and southern India have some distinctively different consumption patterns. In India, the food habits and consumption patterns differ across various states. North India, for example, is primarily wheat-consuming while south

Exhibit 4.3   Trends in coffee consumption in India

Coffee consumption in India is on a steady rise. From being a traditional beverage consumed mainly in south India, it has a national presence now and is available in various formats. The consumption increased by 6 per cent in 2007 due to better availability and improved market-driven strategies by the Coffee Board of India. Coffee consumption is expected to reach 90,000 tonnes this year from 85,000 tonnes in 2006. As far as facts are concerned, the domestic consumption of coffee is increasing, but out-of-home coffee shows an impressive increase of 12–13 per cent. Specialist coffee centres, such as Barista and Café Coffee Day, have been driving sales of coffee in non-coffee regions such as north India. The northern region of India is traditionally tea consuming, while south India accounts for more than three-fourths of the total annual coffee consumption.

The share of coffee consumption in restaurants and cafes is now 85 per cent of the total out-of-home segment, according to the Coffee Board. However, per capita consumption is still low compared to other developed countries. Per capita consumption in the US is 4.09 kg, in the UK it is 3.03 kg, and in Japan it is 3.41 kg, while in India it is only about 80 grams.

Source: Adapted from Indian Coffee Board (2007).

Indians primarily eat rice. The dress, colours, and fabrics used in south India are very different from those used in north India. For example, in Rajasthan (a state in north-west India), the food habits and colours seen are very different as compared to other parts of India. Exhibit 4.3 illustrates the trends in coffee consumption in India.

The infrastructure availability and the level of development in a country also affect the habits of consumers. People in various states prefer movies in their own regional language. The regional channels also reflect the use of the local language. Cultural factors can also be seen across various services. For instance, the sanitation services and consumer orientation towards them are very different. Exhibit 4.4 illustrates the concept further. The general perceptions on consumers may be different from the reality.

Social Class

According to Kotler (2002), different societies exhibit different social classification. He elaborates, 'Social classes are relatively homogeneous and enduring divisions in a society, which are hierarchically ordered, and whose members share similar values, interests, and behaviour'. Social classes give indications on spending patterns, recreation patterns,

Exhibit 4.4   India is a land of vegetarians—Myth or Fact?

India is a land of vegetarians, right? Wrong, according to a recent study by the National Institute of Nutrition. A majority, 64 per cent, of Indian households are meat eaters. The south, at 92.2 per cent, consumes more meat than the north at 40.4 per cent. Another surprise.

The study on, 'knowledge, attitude, beliefs, practices, and study, on food and drug safety in India' covered over 20,000 households in 82 districts in 28 states.

Source: Adapted from *The Times of India* (2006).

Exhibit 4.5   Lufthansa—How to fly premium passengers?

Lufthansa offers the services of a small private jet, which can fly passengers to over 1,000 airports all over Europe. And, the interesting fact is that, this is not the case with only European passengers; major Indian business houses are used to travelling in company planes in India and expect the same service when in Europe. The Private Jet, in fact, is one instance of how Lufthansa is aiming at the high-end traveller, whether in India or elsewhere. Over the past few years, Lufthansa has been rolling out a lot of initiatives to attract more and more business class passengers by providing them with premium service.

There are some compelling reasons as to why Lufthansa decided to attract the premium segment. This airline, which was once controlled by the German government, was badly hit by low-cost airlines such as Ryan Air and Easy Jet. The unfortunate part for the German airline was that even its loyalists began migrating to these low-cost airlines and it was left with the option of either climbing up the value chain or becoming cost competitive. Since legacy carriers such as Lufthansa can never compete as low-cost, the former was a more suitable option. So,

Lufthansa started to brand itself as a premium airline that offered a quality flying experience. Unable to shield itself from the low-carrier business, Germanwings was set up in 2002 as a separate service, offering low-cost services.

With the new branding, Lufthansa began by improving the quality of food and service, which are two of the most important factors remembered by the customers. A seven-course menu and bone-china service are among the services included. The Private Jet came as a strategy to reduce the connection times at Munich or Frankfurt for the business class passengers. Later, the extremely luxurious First Class Terminal was started, where guests could drive up to the foyer and relax in the luxurious brown toned terminal. Transit passengers can sleep in private rooms, have a bath, and eat a gourmet meal, among other things. They can also be driven directly to the aircraft in a Mercedes S-Class or a Porsche Cayenne. The frequency of flights to India has increased and there are plans to expand it further to East India. This strategy clearly is an example of how analysing consumer behaviour can help a brand to provide the services that suit the consumers.

Source: Adapted from *The Strategist* (2006).

---

values, attitudes, lifestyles, and occupations. For example, in India there are a range of services targeted at the affluent segment of society. With the economy growing every year and with increased job opportunities, the number of rich Indians is also growing every year. Exhibit 4.5 illustrates the strategies used by marketers to target the affluent Indian consumer.

Social Factors

Consumer behaviour is influenced by social factors such as reference groups, family, social roles, and status (Kotler 2002).

Reference Groups

A person's reference group consists of all the groups, which have a direct or indirect impact on the individual. The reference group may be the family, friends, neighbours, and co-workers with whom the person interacts fairly. The family plays an extremely important role. Exhibit 4.6 illustrates the influence of children on the purchase behaviour.

Exhibit 4.7 illustrates how companies are using their understanding of the youth behaviour to improve sales.

Exhibit 4.6   Kids' pester power in India

Children in India constitute 18.7 per cent of the world's kids' population and one-third of India's population is under the age of 15 years. This surely indicates that kids are a huge market and can play a very important role as influencers in brand purchase. An ACNielsen Report (2007) shows that an average child in India watches TV for about three hours on weekdays and 3.7 hours on weekends. Apart from watching programmes, kids also view a lot of advertisements, thus making them better consumers for advertising. A fact that is being considered by most brands is that, since a child's mind is not as cluttered as an adult's mind, they absorb messages faster, and this receptiveness to messages leads to what we know in marketing as a kid's 'pester power'.

An interesting study by Millward Brown and IMRB cited in Live Mint 2008 showed that kids influence decision-making on categories not just meant for kids. It suggests that recognition of corporate logos happens at the age of six months. The brand name requests start at the age of three and differentiating between brand values happens by the age of 10, and brand loyalty starts at 11. Capitalizing on these facts, 'catch them when they are young' is the new mantra. If a teenager gets glued to a brand, she may be a consumer for life.

India's popular airline, Kingfisher, launched its operations in May 2005. Every little girl who flew with them received a Barbie doll dressed up in the trademark 'all red' costume, toting the same luggage as the crew did. This is an example of 'catching them young' and helps build brand recognition with parents and leverages the 'pester power' to the brand's advantage. As per the GM (Marketing) of Kingfisher, children are an important community for the airline, and pester power works well as kids are strategic influencers. Even the popular logistics company DHL hopes to create brand recognition through toys; when a kid sees a yellow delivery truck—synonymous with DHL—on the road, she will definitely make the association. Brands such as Michelin Tyres and Shell, feature regularly in Mattel's creations, and thus ensure an association and quick recall.

In India, the advertising spend per year on products for kids, but purchased by parents, is 12 to 15 per cent of the total Rs 38,000 million; the rate is about 8 per cent for products bought by kids themselves, such as chocolates. Thus, whether it is the Hutch (now Vodafone) ad with a kid or ads for drinks, such as Frooti, or car advertisements for Maruti, and life insurance/mutual fund ads, brands are increasingly using innovative tactics to utilize the pester power of kids.

Source: Adapted from *Live Mint* (2008).

Family

The family plays a very important role in influencing consumer buying behaviour. This may vary across cultures. However, in India, as in other Asian economies, the family influences buying patterns to a great extent. The choice of service providers for telecom, IT, transport, power, travel, resort destinations, etc. are more often family decisions rather than individual decisions. Exhibit 4.8 illustrates this aspect.

Personal Factors

These factors can be understood by evaluating factors such as, age and stage in the life cycle, occupation, economic circumstances, lifestyle, personality, and self-concept. Age and stage in the life cycle are important determinants for purchase decisions. For example, in case of a higher age group, the spending increases on services such as healthcare, and vacation and travelling. Another case in point is Sony's strategy to target PlayStation at an older and more affluent audience (Exhibit 4.9).

Exhibit 4.7 The youth of India

Many big brands in India are developing a set of mixed strategies to attract the youth. Whether it is Pepsi's Youngistaan campaign or MTV's Roadies, leisure, food, and apparel chains are developing youth-centric campaigns to draw teenyboppers and twenty somethings towards their products and services.

The working youth in the age group 22–8, have sufficient disposable incomes to spend on personal accessories and services. There exist some cross-promotional strategies that include youth hangouts such as McDonald's, Nirulas, Café Coffee Day, Barista, etc. Other store-in-store collaborations such as opening up a Barista in a store has enabled youth-centric products to become household names. It is said that pricey gizmos and expensive food do not go down well with the youth in all the cities, as they are usually hard-pressed for cash. Keeping this in mind, Pizza Corner came up with a 'combo meal' at a price of Rs 170. MTNL has started a 'Vidyarthi Plan' to attract youth with its low-priced mobile talk plan. A well-timed promotion, right pricing, and a 'cool' tag line (maybe a desi tag line for the rural youth) can help brands to cash-in on brand-conscious youth.

Also, digital ads and products have the highest penetration among the youth. While 61.2 per cent Indians are below 30 years and 50 per cent are below 25 years, 22 per cent of the advertisements cater to the youth and 59 per cent of the advertisements are youth-oriented. Generation Next is going to drive the future of online marketing in India. The youth of India, who surf the net regularly, flash swanky mobile phones, and are more knowledgeable about the latest products and services in the market, are the ones to watch out for.

Source: Adapted from *The Hindu Business Line* (2006).

Exhibit 4.8 The Indian family today

A study of the Indian consumer is incomplete without considering the Indian family. In India, where family plays a pivotal role, individualist culture did not exist earlier. India had a pre-dominant joint family culture and everyone made a decision with a consensus. Another major reason for this culture was the lack of social security, unlike people in the West. This culture, however, is under pressure, partly because greater access to a range of different foreign media in the form of publications and international channels has made individuals more aware about the wide opportunities that exist in the market.

While earlier, the father was the unquestioned head of the family, today even parents do not have all the answers for the questioning minds of kids, who in turn, prefer to go to their seniors or peers for personal advice. There is a general increase in self-confidence, but the uncertainty has increased as well. While earlier, people would join a company and serve there till retirement, now job-switching for better opportunities is common. There are opportunities everywhere.

The role models who have a high moral grounding are also few; hence, people choose their icons based on their levels of success. Parents are trying to revisit their youth; nowadays they can splurge on things that were not available when they were growing up. The Indian woman is becoming more outgoing, open, and assertive like never before. She is educated and thus seeks a better role in life. The generation gap has widened and parental authority has surely come down on an average in Indian households. Nowadays, children know the tactics to involve parents emotionally and get things done.

This paradigm shift towards the so-called western culture is quite visible, but also true is the fact that Indians feel like Indians as never before. We are proud of our culture and identify with it. As more and more Indians are successful the world over, they have realized that 'Indianness' is nothing to be embarrassed about; in fact, it is something to be proud of.

Source: Adapted from *The Marketing Whitebook 2005.*

Exhibit 4.9 Sony—Shifting focus

The Victoria and Albert Museum in London will display an innovative sculpture soon and this has been designed by 3D, a rapper from Massive Attack and Sony's PlayStation video games business. This move from Sony clearly points to the fact that it is now targeting a different audience as well. The company has created artworks that allow people to interact within the gallery, or through the Internet using PlayStation. There seems to be an expansion—youth-oriented marketing as well as attracting older consumers. The company believes that after evolving the PlayStation brand prominently through close associations with youth-oriented activities, such as music, community football, etc., the brand is big enough to encourage a wider range of people, especially the older consumers. It is time now that the older audience starts recognizing Sony PlayStation as a broad-based entertainment brand willing to engage with culture and not just computer games.

Even other brands, such as Levi's and L'Oreal, which focus on youth-oriented marketing, are now moving towards targeting a wider market. It has been found out that many people start feeling ignored as they get older, though the fact is that it is the older not the younger consumers who are the growth market in both numbers and purchasing power. Even Nintendo, another video game brand, is targeting consumers aged 35 and above to highlight 'brain training' games designed to boost mental agility and memory.

Some brand consultants fear that such a strategy may lead to repulsion from some of the audience, who may not find the brand interesting anymore. To this, PlayStation's Christopher says, 'This strategy definitely does not mean to abandon youth marketing completely; they plan to run it parallel to each other, while constantly introducing new lively products.'

Source: Adapted from Carter (2006).

Roles and Status

A person's position in each group can be defined in terms of role and status. Marketers need to cater to the demands of different categories of consumers. For example, premium consumers expect better quality and wider range of services whereas, low-income group consumers may desire a no-frills, low-priced service. Occupation also determines the choice of service product. For example, the Life Insurance Corporation (LIC) of India has targeted the consumers from the underprivileged segment (Exhibit 4.10).

Consumer Lifestyle

Lindquist and Sirgy (2005) have defined lifestyle as a constellation of individual characteristics that reflect certain behaviours, such as participation in social groups and relationships with significant others, commitment to certain behaviours, and a central life interest. This may vary according to socio-economic characteristics. Psychographics attempt to analyse and measure consumer lifestyle. To obtain a psychographic profile of consumer segments, marketers examine various aspects of personality and behaviour.

1. Personality traits and concept of self
2. Attitude towards brand and product class
3. Activities, interests, and opinions
4. Value systems

The activities, interests, and opinions (AIO) inventory is used to measure lifestyles of consumers (Wells and Tigert 1971).

Exhibit 4.10 LIC ventures into micro finance

Micro finance is the new buzz word at LIC. Although many other insurance companies have been involved in micro finance, it is LIC with more than 70 per cent share in life insurance that will put the nascent micro insurance industry into top gear.

Factors, such as legislation brought about by Insurance Regulatory and Development Authority (IRDA), have created an institutional structure for small ticket policies. Also, the fact that a major portion of the under-privileged segment was not insured also made micro finance a strong viable business option. LIC found that micro finance would be difficult to promote with the normal agent channel, as NGOs work more with this segment. High levels of funding on both equity and debit sides has led to significant skill building within, and ensured that many NGOs and MFIs are LIC's partners.

Some selective policies, such as the 'Auto Cover' facility, have been introduced keeping the target audience in mind. If at least two full years' premium has been paid in respect of any policy, and any subsequent premium not duly paid, full death cover shall continue from the due date of the first unpaid premium (FUP) for a period of two years or till the end of the policy, whichever is earlier.

This is indeed a good step by LIC to address the need of India's millions of poor, who will definitely gain from this small introduction in the financial mainstream.

Source: Adapted from Sarkar (2006).

There is another framework, which is known as the VALS framework. SRI International's Values and Lifestyles is an available psychographic segmentation system, which has gained worldwide acceptance (Kotler 2002). VALS™ is a marketing and consulting tool that helps businesses worldwide to develop and execute more effective strategies. The system identifies current and future opportunities by segmenting the consumer marketplace on the basis of the personality traits that drive consumer behaviour. VALS applies in all phases of the marketing process, from new product development and entry-stage targeting, to communications strategy and advertising. Based on the personality traits of consumers, which can be measured, they are classified into various categories.

VALS framework The SRI International Values and Lifestyles Framework gives a detailed insight into the VALS typology (The VALS™ Segments 2008).

Innovators They are successful, sophisticated, and have high self-esteem. Image is important to them, not as evidence of status or power, but as an expression of their personality.

Thinkers Motivated by ideals, thinkers have moderate respect for the status quo institutions of authority and social decorum, but are open to new ideas.

Achievers They lead a goal-oriented lifestyle, motivated by the desire for achievement. They have many wants and needs and are very active in the consumer marketplace.

Experiencers Self-expression is the prime motivator of experiencers. Young, enthusiastic, and impulsive consumers, they quickly become enthusiastic about new possibilities but are equally quick to cool. These avid consumers are high spenders.

Believers These are conservative and conventional people with concrete beliefs based on tradition. Opting for familiar products and established brands, the believers are predictable consumers.

Strivers Trendy and fun loving, strivers are motivated by achievement. They are also concerned about the opinions and approval of others and like to demonstrate their ability to win over peers.

Makers They are practical people who are motivated by self-expression. Makers have constructive skills and value self-sufficiency. They are suspicious of new ideas and big businesses.

Survivors Leading narrowly-focused lives, survivors are cautious consumers. They represent a very modest market for most products and services.

Psychological Factors

An individual's buying behaviour is influenced by psychological factors such as perception, beliefs and attitudes, learning, and motivation.

Perception

Perception is the process by which an individual selects, organizes, and interprets information inputs to create a meaningful picture of the world. People can perceive the same object on account of perceptual processes—selective, attention, selective distortion, and selective retention. It is important for service providers to create the right perceptions. Consumers' interpretations of perceptions about products can be examined in several areas—consumer categorization, consumer attributions, product/service quality, perceived value, etc.

Beliefs and Attitudes

A belief is a thought that a person holds about something. These may emanate on account of his/her conditioning, culture, religion, etc. An attitude is a person's favourable or unfavourable evaluation, emotional feelings, and action tendencies towards an object or an idea (Krech et al. 1962).

Organizations use a variety of techniques to mould consumer attitudes. For instance, marketers have spent considerable amounts on advertising to create health consciousness among Indian consumers. It has taken many years for firms such as Reebok and Nike, to create a positive disposition towards health. People's perception about the Tata Group is that of reliability. Reliance Industries is associated with big projects.

Learning

Consumer researchers have treated the theme of consumer learning from three perspectives—probability theory, behaviour analysis, and cognitive theory (Lindquist and Sirgy 2003).

Probability theory treats learning as formation of habits. There are numerous models which have been designed to study brand loyalty, brand acceptance, brand switching, and new product forecasting. *Behaviour analysis* focuses on how certain behaviours could be reinforced or modified. *Cognitive theory* is another alternative that emphasizes the thinking, rather than the doing, of learning. It involves a four-stage process (Hach and Deighton 1989):

1. Formulation of hypotheses
2. Exposure
3. Encoding
4. Integration

The consumer develops a hypothesis about the brand and then tests it. If it works, it reinforces his/her belief. Eventually, by seeking more information from diverse sources and experience, the consumer's information horizon widens.

Then his/her experience is encoded in the memory and new information is processed based on prior experience. Established marketers need to reinforce the positive elements of service experience. They could block the strategy and explain why they offer a superior service. For a new service provider, the strategies deployed could be disruption of existing competition and attempting to facilitate a trail by the consumers.

Consumer Motivation

Research indicates that consumers who are motivated to process information are likely to do so at deeper levels of memory. For the service industry, depending upon the impact of the service on the consumer, the motivation to choose a service provider will be different. For instance, in the insurance sector, LIC is the market leader as consumers feel more secure investing with a public sector firm. The underlying motivation is security of the investment. Similarly, for healthcare services, reliability and genuine care are higher degree of concerns for deciding on a hospital or clinic. On the other hand, a choice of a multiplex theatre may be governed more by convenience, and membership of a polo club or a vacation destination may be governed by self-esteem needs. So, there may be diverse motivation factors, which are at play when a consumer makes a buying decision. Human element being an important factor in the services sector, reliability, tangibility, experience, and trust may become important factors rather than the motivation factors listed in Maslow's or Herzberg's framework.

The implication for marketers is to provide information that consumers would retain. The repetition and emotional content of the message makes a difference. The packaging, advertising, and display cues should be such that they assist memory retrieval.

INDIAN SHOPPING HABITS

The retail trade set up in India is changing drastically and it is extremely important for the storeowners to assess their store, and compare the relative development in each country, and usage of private labels. Exhibit 4.11 provides an insight into Indian shopping patterns.

Exhibit 4.11 Shoppers' trends

This exhibit features excerpts taken from a study by ACNielsen. Shopper trends offer an analysis of the changing behavioural patterns of shoppers globally. The study considers when, where, and how often people visit key retailers and provides insights into these changing patterns. It allows the storeowners to assess their stores. Below is an interesting list of key drivers that drive the consumers towards them. Another find is that the number of stores visited has reduced, implying that people are settling down to their own brands and have stopped experimenting, the loyal shoppers have increased, and hence, the average number of stores visited has gone down.

Top choice driver	Rank
Convenient to get to	1
Close to home	2
Attractive and interesting promotions	3
Food and groceries are good value for money	4
Always have what I want in stock	5
Everything I need in one store	6
A place where it is easy to quickly find what I need	7
Low prices for most items	8
Good range of fresh products	9
Better selection of high quality brands and products	10
Staff provide good service	11
Good quality instant cooked food	12

Another advantage of the modern retail format is that the convenience factor is the most important one, followed by good promotions, and value for money items.

The marketing research conducted by ACNielsen has some interesting pointers regarding the trend of online shopping. More than 85 per cent of the world's online population has used the Internet to make a purchase; this is about 40 per cent increase in the past two years. This trend shows that online retail has become an integral part of modern-day life. The following are some findings of the new research on the online market in India.

- About 78 per cent of Indian respondents surfing the Internet have used it to make a purchase.
- About 73 per cent of Indians have purchased online tickets/reservations, highest in the Asia Pacific region. This category is quite suited because of its ability to provide efficient and comprehensive access to a wide range of comparable information.
- Most Indians prefer to make payment via credit card, with 84 per cent opting for this.
- Most Indian online shoppers are loyal to the sites they make purchases from and do not experiment much. About 54 per cent opt for the same site every time.
- As Indians are extremely price sensitive, 48 per cent of the online Indians are influenced by special offers on the sites. This is followed by general surfing (40 per cent), personal recommendation (31 per cent), online advertising (26 per cent), and search engines (22 per cent), which are some of the other factors that influence online shoppers in India.
- Indians love networking with people. While they are one of the heaviest users of mobile phones, being online helps them to keep in touch with family and friends.
- Apart from these online trends, grocery store shopping is also one of the most important activities of the Indian household. With the entry of numerous big players, such as Big Bazaar, Subhiksha, Reliance Fresh, Spencer's Retail, etc., competition has become fierce. Some of the trends observed from the ACNielsen (2007) survey of about 26,486 Internet users in 47 markets from Europe, Asia Pacific, the Americas, and the Middle East were as follows:
- Good value-for-money is the most important criterion for Indian consumers while choosing the grocery shop. Due to this reason, players, such as Big Bazaar, Vishal Mega Mart, and Subhiksha stores, advertise themselves as being the cheapest and the best value-for-money store.
- The second most important factor is better selection of high-quality brands and products (79 per cent), followed by location (54 per cent), and available parking space (54 per cent).
- Price, promotions, and perceptions allow customers to arrive at the perception of value.
- 64 per cent of Indians research and compare prices to decide which store offers good value for money, while 58 per cent decide on the basis of word-of-mouth information.

Source: Adapted from ACNielsen (2008).

Table 4.2 Shifting marketing paradigm

1980s	Current
◻ Mass marketing	◻ Personal
◻ Passive consumer	◻ Participative
◻ One-off, short-term	◻ Lifetime, long-term
◻ Limited use of technology	◻ Widespread use of technology
◻ Serve customers well	◻ Serve customers differently
◻ Success measured by current market share	◻ Success measured by lifetime market share
◻ Success measured by current profits	◻ Success measured by lifetime profits

RELATIONSHIP MARKETING

The market dynamics are changing at an astounding pace. With increasing competition, consumers certainly have a wider choice. In the light of these changes, consumer focus assumes a lot of importance. Marketers are now looking at building long-term relationships with the consumers rather than analysing isolated transactions with them. The whole paradigm of marketing is witnessing a sea change whereby the following shifts are taking place (Table 4.2).

Success, as mentioned earlier, is being measured by lifetime market share and lifetime profits. For instance, a single cigarette could cost just a few rupees, while the lifetime value of one cigarette smoker is Rs 1.10 lakh over a 10-year period, which is roughly 7,000 times the value of a single pack of cigarettes. Another estimate points out that the value of all the consumer products and services, which one could personally use over the next 25 years, would be worth Rs 1.4 crore. The customer becomes important because companies lose roughly 15 per cent of their customers every year, and in three years the company would be left with only half the customers it started with.

Relationship marketing shifts the focus of marketing exchange from transactions to relationships (Foss and Stone 2001). Some organizations have realized the importance of relationship marketing and have tried to cash in on the opportunity. Citibank has launched a product called life-stage marketing wherein it recognizes the needs of the customers, as they grow older. As a student, a customer may need a loan for higher education, a few years into his job he/she will need money to get married, and then, a loan to buy a house.

Apollo Tyres adopted relationship marketing and discovered that there are approximately 1,50,000 truck owners in India and the lifetime value of each was Rs 1.68 crore. Therefore, developing a relationship with all of them made a lot of sense. Apollo Tyres issues privilege cards to its customers. The customers collect points on every purchase. These points could be redeemed for various awards ranging from a music system to a trip to New York. The programme works like an airline's frequent flyer programme. Value Club, the super value programme of Apollo Tyres, already has 42,000 owners collecting miles on their trucks.

Most marketers initiating relationship marketing need to build up a database of their consumers. For instance, General Motors hired McCann to generate a list of 50,000 potential buyers. At the click of a mouse, General Motors can get an idea about how much each of these people earn, the kind of electronic gizmos they possess, how large their families are, what cars they own, and where they holiday. Glaxo has a database of 2,30,000 doctors. It initiated a relationship marketing programme through its Care and Aid programme for medical practitioners and started communicating with each one of them 3–12 times a year.

Appropriate market segmentation is also essential for a right strategy. For that, one needs to answer some of the following questions.

- Do all my customers have the same service needs and expectations?
- If not, can I regroup them into a few manageable clusters?
- Does it leave me with enough communality so that I will have a basic common offer?
- Who belongs to which segment?

Hear Music, a record and CD music chain in California, segments its market. It identified four service segments—passive consumer (interested in only top hits); eclectic (wide tastes, a little bit of jazz and classical); specialist (knows more than the sales people about their selections); and collector (looks for masterpieces). The marketer needs to respond to these segments through appropriate training of service personnel. Relationship marketing entails a lot of effort on the part of the marketer but sustained efforts certainly ensure loyal customers, which is definitely worth all the effort.

CUSTOMER DELIGHT

The new age customer is very different; the expectation has increased, he/she has become more knowledgeable and is aware of multiple options to satisfy his/her needs, and switches over to newer brands for better value for money. There are increasing number of competitors, both domestic and global, offering higher value-added products and processes through innovation. Although achieving customer satisfaction has long been identified as the heart of the entire marketing concept, most companies pay greater attention to their market share than to their customers' satisfaction. This is surely a big mistake as the market share is a backward-looking metric, while customer satisfaction is a forward-looking metric. If customer satisfaction starts slipping, then market share erosion will hit the brand in a big way.

Although meeting customer expectations can satisfy customers, the emotional response, such as an element of surprise, can delight the customers. Even satisfied customers can indulge in brand switching. Thus, not just satisfaction, but the emotional response to satisfaction is what customer delight is all about. All companies need to monitor and improve their level of customer satisfaction, as satisfied customers truly constitute the company's relationship capital. Every hotel provides lodging facilities along with food and beverages, but what leads to a customer base is customer delight. The emotional feeling of being attached to a brand results in higher levels of customer loyalty.

Hence, it is important to note that customer satisfaction is a necessary but not sufficient goal. Customer satisfaction only remotely predicts customer retention in highly competitive markets because companies regularly lose some percentage of their satisfied customers. Thus, companies should aim to delight customers, not simply to satisfy them.

'Customer delight is conceptualized as an emotional response, which results from surprising and positive levels of performance. As such, it could provide an explanation for the observed variation in the intentions and subsequent loyalty of customers reporting the same level of satisfaction' (*Journal of Service Research* 2005). Customer delight, thus, is more than just a very high level of satisfaction. It involves surpassing the standards of service that a customer has thought of, and requires focusing on what is currently unknown or unexpected by the customer. A research conducted by the University of Auckland, New Zealand and Vanderbilt University, UK, analysed that delight is a function of three components:

1. Unexpectedly high levels of performance
2. Arousal (for example, surprise, excitement)
3. Positive effect (for example, pleasure, joy, or happiness)

Satisfaction by contrast, proved to be a function of only disconfirmed expectations (better than expected) and positive effect (Lovelock 2001).

There are various ways in which a company can delight its customers—surpassing (not just meeting) the needs of the customers, keeping word for advertising and sales, and providing the best customer experience. In services especially, word-of-mouth promotion is extremely crucial. It is also important that companies that receive high satisfaction scores should advertise it (Kotler 2003). A high rating ensures that the prospective customers trust the brand and its service; for example, handling of crisis situations arising in the travel and hospitality sector. It is important to manage customers in a way that is consistent with the service promises. The delight of customers is beyond the stated needs and the expected offering. For example, Holiday Inn ran a campaign a few years ago that promised 'No Surprises'. Guest complaints were so high that the slogan 'No Surprises' was mocked, and Holiday Inn quickly withdrew the slogan. The 'moment of truth' in a service offering can make or destroy the customer's perception of a service.

The point to note here is that customer delight does not necessarily mean to raise the expectations of the customers to a never-ending level. The trick is to understate, but over deliver. A close relationship does exist between customer loyalty and high levels of customer satisfaction (customer delight). As customer satisfaction becomes customer delight, customer retention and loyalty increase. A delighted customer (as compared to a merely satisfied customer) is more likely to remain loyal in spite of attractive competitive offerings and a small negative experience will be covered up by an extremely positive one previously.

CUSTOMER LOYALTY

Customer loyalty in a business context has been used to describe a customer's willingness to continue patronizing a firm over a long period of time, purchasing and using its goods or services on a repeated and preferably exclusive basis, and voluntarily recommending the firm's products to friends and associates (Lovelock 2001). Reichheld and Sasser (1995) have discussed the relationship of profit per customer, with the number of years the customer has been with the service business. These profits may emanate from—(1) increased purchases; (2) reduced operating costs; (3) referrals to other customers; and (4) price premium.

Dick and Basu (1994) have proposed four conditions related to loyalty, namely, loyalty, latent loyalty, spurious loyalty, and no loyalty. Loyalty signifies relative attitude and repeat patronage. Latent loyalty is associated with high relative attitude and low repeat patronage. Spurious loyalty represents a low relative attitude with high repeat patronage. No loyalty is associated with low relative attitude combined with low repeat patronage.

Categorization of Customer Loyalty

Rowley (2005) has categorized loyal customers into four different categories—(1) captive; (2) convenience seekers; (3) contented; and (4) committed. The customers in each of these categories respond differently to triggers to switching. Their behaviour and attitudes also vary.

Captive   All stores have some customers in this category because they have no real choice. These customers have few opportunities for switching. For example, when markets open up and competition increases, certain consumers continue to remain captive, and remain inert in attitude and behaviour because they perceive decision-making associated with switching to be something in which they do not wish to engage.

These customers could be poached by competition by reducing switching costs and barriers. Bank loans for housing in India is a case in point. Inter-bank transfers and minimal paper-work have made it easier for customers to switch home loans. These customers have neither positive behaviour nor attitude, and have a low involvement with the brand.

Convenience seeker   A range of convenience factors drives this loyalty. Here, convenience on account of location or timings or brands may be a reason. Distribution network becomes important in this case. Where convenience is a significant factor, customers may switch even when they are satisfied with their existing service provider. Convenience is particularly important in the context of low involvement, routine purchases.

Contented   Contented loyals have a positive attitude towards a brand but are inertial in their behaviour. This means that they continue to expand as a customer but do not extend their involvement with the brand by subscribing to additional services. For example, a Citibank card holder may be a loyal credit card user but may not avail of the company's services such as overdraft facility or personal loans. Such customers may be particularly vulnerable to service or product failure and strong recovery strategies may be an opportunity for sustaining the loyalty of this group.

Committed   These customers are positive in both attitude and behaviour. They are delighted with the brand and can be depended upon for repeat purchases. They make a positive contribution to the ambience of the service experience. Such customers are resistant to competitors' attempts to entice them.

Exhibit 4.12 Loyalty gains

Loyalty programmes, such as loyalty cards, free parking, free gifts/coupons, and point redemption schemes, have become commonplace among both service providers as well as manufacturers. All these companies know the importance of a loyal customer. The loyalty programme strategies mentioned previously play a pivotal role in engaging the customer and encouraging him/her to spend on the products and services more often.

Market analysts believe that loyalty programmes are not just about winning over the customers with gifts; they should be built and developed in a way to create affinity and closeness to the brand. Many coalition loyalty programmes, such as the tie-up between the Delhi Metro and Citibank card, and ICICI and Tata group, also help create loyalty and identification. Retail chain Shoppers Stop started its loyalty programme (First Citizens) way back in 1994 and has over 630,000 members. The salespersons indulge in continuous communication with their customers and reward them with points and gifts. Airlines, such as Jet and Kingfisher, have frequent flyer programmes where the loyalists are upgraded to first class with frequent flyer points.

The biggest advantage of loyalty programmes is that they help to retain customers at value and thus, no company wishes to lose an opportunity to make their customers feel special. The question that arises here is, aren't these loyalty schemes a drain on the company's funds? The answer is no, because it is an investment. Redemption of points against a minimum purchase is an advantage as it indicates the fact that more and more customers see value in the programme and are willing to spend more on the brand.

The challenge is not to consider this as a cost and be patient with the results. It is very important to make the customer feel comfortable and important. It is also important to convert invisible customers into active customers.

Source: Adapted from *Business Standard* (2006).

Loyalty, Switchers, and Stayers

Wangenheim and Bayon (2004) have studied the differences between stayers and switchers, and their impact on loyalty. The results of the study confirm that the switchers differ from stayers in their higher levels of active loyalty and lower levels of reactive loyalty, as well as more positive word-of-mouth publicity. Referral switchers differ from other switchers with respect to their higher satisfaction, active loyalty, and more positive word-of-mouth publicity. Exhibit 4.12 discusses customer loyalty initiatives in the Indian context.

CONSUMERISM

This section discusses consumer rights and responsibilities in the Indian context. Exhibit 4.13 gives insights into the nature of complaints and their redressal.

Although the marketer's slogan has long been 'customer is king', it remains a vocal pledge. The concept of 'caveat emptor' or 'let the buyer beware' is still the motto of many. Hence, there was a need to protect the consumers. The consumer movement was started and what we see now is that 'consumers are more powerful than at any other time, and that power is increasing. One survey revealed that a typical business hears only 4 per cent of its dissatisfied customers. The other 96 per cent just quietly go away and 91 per cent will never return' (Groucutt et al. 2004). This indicates how important it is to keep the customers happy and satisfied.

Exhibit 4.13   Numerous complaints and no penalties

In a shocking revelation to the advocates of the Right to Information Act, 2005, while the Central Information Commissioner has received about 3,256 complaints, no one has been penalized yet. In a case where Kuku Devi filed a case against the Delhi Development Authority (DDA) for denial of information, the sympathy of the entire case seemed to be with the bureaucracy rather than with the public. While in some cases the central public information officer (CPIO) does not appear on hearing dates, in other cases they get away by saying that they took action but forgot to inform the appellants. The cases are sometimes transferred to the education department, whereas the CPIO is supposed to have all information.

On the other hand, word has spread among CPIOs that nothing happens whether information is given or not, and as a result, they have stopped responding to applications. A former secretary of expenditure in the Finance Ministry said that penalties are extremely important as without them the Right to Information Act will be ineffective. Penalties also help to wake up these commissioners to the plight of the consumers. The people on the other hand, have a different story to tell. According to Prof. Ansari, a CIO, information commissioners should not be held responsible for the delay in receiving information. It is also believed that sometimes the information requested for can be used for negative purposes. He also says that till now, the record maintenance system is not in place.

This clearly indicates that whatever confusion might exist, the people at a loss are the consumers who trust government Acts such as the RTI.

Source: Adapted from *Business Standard* (2006).

There is no single definition of consumerism. 'It is generally accepted as being any organized group pressure on behalf of customers or users of a product or service. This may be specific to an individual organization such as a "user group" or aimed at protecting consumers in general from organizations with which there can be exchange relationships' (Adcock et al. 2001). As the consumer movement has gained momentum, customers can raise their voice against an injustice and are increasingly able to communicate with organizations.

The real consumerism, as we know today, started in the US. Consumers today have 'consumer rights' to protect them from any exploitation (Exhibit 4.14).

Exhibit 4.14   Consumer rights and responsibilities

Consumer rights have now become an integral part of our lives. They are much talked about and have been properly documented. Consumer rights, market awareness, and influences have shown an upward trend, and agencies such as the government, consumer courts, and other voluntary organizations are working in order to safeguard these rights.

The presence and influence of markets in our lives increased considerably in the twentieth century. As consumers become more and more dependent on the market for their daily needs, dealers and manufactures find good reason to exploit them. It is a fact that many products and services in the market are of inferior quality and do not prescribe to the strict norms provided by quality control agencies. Overpricing and the inability of the service product to provide value for money, lead to severe losses and inconvenience to consumers, while dealers and service providers mint money through this exploitation. Hence, it is extremely important for consumers to be

Contd

Exhibit 4.14 Contd

aware of their rights and responsibilities. Some of the consumer rights are mentioned here:

- Right to safety
- Right to information
- Right to choice
- Right to be heard
- Right to redress
- Right to consumer education

Source: Adapted from *Consumer Voice* (2008).

The first seeds of the consumer movement in India started in 1966, when the Consumer Guidance Society of India was formed to check food shortages and black-marketing. The Monopolies and Restrictive Trade Practices (MRTP) commission was set up under the MRTP Act of 1969. In 1986, the Consumer Protection Act came into force, and was amended in 2002.

SUMMARY

The chapter introduced the concept of consumer behaviour. It is fundamental to understand the behaviour of the consumer before the company launches its products. Consumer behaviour can be understood by understanding the processes at three levels—pre-purchase activities, purchasing activities, and post-purchasing activities. Consumption can also be analysed during different phases—acquisition, consumption, and disposition. There are three different levels of analysis of consumer behaviour—individual, micro, and macroenvironment. To understand consumer behaviour, an understanding of the decision-making process and the factors that can influence the decision, is important. The steps that a consumer follows when arriving at a decision are need/problem recognition, information search, alternative evaluation, choice, and outcome of the decision. The EKB model for consumer decision-making has also been discussed in detail. The framework for understanding consumer behaviour, which includes market stimuli, and buyers' characteristics, decision-making process, and decisions, has also been enumerated.

The chapter also gives insights into the changing dynamics of Indian consumers. Indian shopping habits have been highlighted using

ACNielsen's survey. The convenience factor is the key for consumers in India, followed by promotions and other factors. The chapter also gives insights on online shoppers in India. Travel reservations in India are increasingly being done online. As the penetration of personal computers and the Internet increases, consumers will increasingly go online. The survey on Indian consumers has also been included. The factors influencing consumer behaviour—cultural, social, personal, and psychological—have been discussed in detail.

The concept of relationship marketing has also been discussed. Relationship paradigm looks at the lifetime value of a customer rather than a transaction-based approach. The deployment of relationship requires infusion of IT in various domains and this is a resource-intensive investment.

The chapter also enumerates on the concept of customer loyalty. Customer loyalty has been categorized as captive, convenience seekers, contented, and committed. The reasons why customers switch have also been discussed.

The concept of consumerism has been elaborated on. The section traced the evolution of consumer rights in India and discussed the consumer rights.

KEY TERMS

Attitude   The way in which an individual views and evaluates something or someone. Attitudes determine whether people like or dislike things, and therefore, how they behave towards them. Attitude is traditionally divided into cognitive, behavioural, and affective components, although the main emphasis now tends to fall on defining attitude in terms of affect—the person's feelings towards the object, brand, etc.

Consumer behaviour   The buying behaviour of individuals and households who buy goods and services for personal consumption. A number of different people, playing different roles, have been identified in the decision to make a specific purchase, i.e., initiator, influencer, decider, buyer, and user.

Consumerism   An organized movement of citizens and government agencies to improve the rights and power of buyers in relation to sellers.

Culture   A complex whole, which includes knowledge, belief, art, morals, customers, and any other capabilities and habits acquired by man as a member of society.

Customer delight   This is conceptualized as an emotional response, which results from surprising and positive levels of performance.

Customer loyalty   A customer's willingness to continue patronizing a firm over a long period of time, purchasing and using its goods or services on a repeated and preferably exclusive basis, and voluntarily recommending the firm's products to friends and associates.

Decision-making   The act of deciding between two or more alternative courses of action.

Motivation   The mental processes that arouse, sustain, and direct human behaviour. Motivation may stem from processes taking place within an individual (intrinsic motivation) or from the impact of factors acting on the individual from outside (extrinsic motivation); in most cases these two influences are continually interacting.

Perception   It is the process by which an individual selects, organizes, and interprets information inputs to create a meaningful picture of the world.

Reference groups   Groups to which consumers belong and which influence their behaviour. Reference groups serve as direct (face-to-face) or indirect points of reference, providing comparisons that help to form a person's attitudes or behaviour.

Relationship marketing   Marketing activities aimed at building long-term relationships with parties (especially customers) that contribute to a company's success. The goal is to ensure long-term value to customers, producing enduring customer satisfaction.

Social class   A system for classifying the population according to social status.

CONCEPT REVIEW QUESTIONS

1. Discuss the factors, which influence consumers' buying processes?

2. How does lifestyle affect the service provider's promotion strategy?

3. How do service providers target consumers in different social categories? Enumerate with different examples.

4. Discuss the Indian consumer's orientation towards shopping.

5. Discuss the future of the Indian consumer's spending pattern through online channels.

6. How does the family influence buying decisions? Discuss with appropriate examples.

CRITICAL THINKING QUESTIONS

1. A very reputed cosmetic manufacturer, which retails its brand under the brand name Lakmé, has also started operating its salons under the brand name of Lakmé Salon. Please study the consumer response to Lakmé Salons in the age group 16–25 years. How does the same compare with other beauty salons operating in your region?

2. Please identify the influence of kids on the choice of various services such as cable vs satellite channels, music stores, restaurants, and multiplexes.

PROJECT ASSIGNMENTS

1. Browse through the website of two telecom service providers. Discuss how effective their strategy is on the website, to attract potential customers.

2. Compare the loyalty programmes of Radisson hotels vis-à-vis Marriott hotels by accessing data available on their websites.

3. Compare the online shopping portals of Indiatimes with Yahoo India. Which one is more consumer-friendly?

4. Prepare a short write-up on consumerism practices in India using Internet-based research.

5. Is relationship marketing really practised in India? Discuss critically.

CASE STUDY

Realities of rural market segmentation*

Introduction

There are a number of myths and realities regarding the immense potential of the Indian rural market. There is no doubt that the rural market presents a huge untapped opportunity as nearly 70 per cent of the population lives in rural India. However, marketers need to explore growth indicators and key strategic tools for successful exploitation of this untapped market. The article focuses on segmentation, targeting, and positioning strategies for rural markets with some success stories of MNCs in the background.

Half a dozen religions, 33 languages, 1,650 dialects, and diversity in castes, sub-castes, tribes, culture, and sub-culture characterize rural India. So rural marketers need to have an open mind and sensitize themselves to understand the rural consumer. Apart from this, communicating in the language that the rural consumer comprehends is a challenge most marketers face. Creative approaches to providing a satisfactory offering in terms of adaptation to consumer needs through differentiated product offering and the advertising message used are absolute essentials to achieve success through effective segmentation and implementation.

In the changing business environment, even the rural customer is very active and quality conscious. Companies have been moving from traditional marketing to modern marketing; hence, marketing calls for more than developing a product, pricing, promoting, and making it accessible to target customers. Technology has also played a key role in transforming marketing. These developments have enriched the field of marketing management. Although there is a greater

---

* B. Shivaraj and T.P. Mohan Kumar (2006), 'Realities of Rural Market Segmentation', *Marketing Mastermind*, October, ICFAI University Press. Printed with the permission of the ICFAI Press.

integration of business functions, unfortunately marketers are yet to understand the full impact of these developments.

Urban markets are increasingly becoming competitive and perhaps, getting saturated. Consider the case of toiletries, packaged tea, dry cell batteries, and even entertainment products and services. For most of these products, the demand seems to be increasing. This situation leads to the search for new markets for growth and satisfaction to both organization and consumers.

Rural markets are new markets, which are opening for consumer goods. Companies that have expanded in these areas have found that they have been able to ward off competition, generate a new demand, and in turn, increase their sales or profits. Many companies have already taken a lead in establishing their products in rural markets. Products of Hindustan Lever Limited (soaps, detergents, etc.) are made available in all rural markets through stockists, wholesalers, and retailers. Bisleri mineral water is available in some rural markets. Bournvita and Horlicks are served in small restaurants in prosperous rural areas. Marico's Parachute hair oil has already entered the rural market. Philips and BPL have become household names in the consumer durable market in rural areas. HMT watches are still preferred in rural markets. Mahindra's jeeps and tractors are very popular with farmers. Proctor and Gamble has introduced its shampoos in small sachets. Similarly, coconut hair oil, biscuits, toothpastes, and cosmetics, are all available in small packs and sachets for rural consumers.

Profile of the Indian Rural Market

1. Around 74.6 crore people live in rural areas and 25.4 crore people live in urban areas.

2. The number of young educated people in rural India is increasing. Nearly 40 per cent of the youth graduate from colleges in villages.

3. According to a study done by MART, a consultancy specializing in rural marketing and rural development, 53 per cent of FMCG sales come from rural areas, as do 59 per cent of consumer durable sales.

4. A study conducted by Francis Kanol of Marketing Planning Services, a Chennai-based consultancy, estimates the rural market for FMCG to be worth Rs 65,000 crore, durables market to be worth Rs 5,000 crore, tractors and agricultural products are worth Rs 45,000 crore, and the market for two and four wheelers is worth Rs 8,000 crore.

5. According to NCAER, there are 3,000 households in rural India that earn over Rs 50,00,000 annually.

6. Five lakh people from rural India have gone abroad in 2002–03.

7. There are nearly 42,000 rural supermarkets *(haats)* in India. The number exceeds the total number of retail chain stores in the US (35,000).

8. One-third of the total number of luxury goods is sold in rural India.

9. Two-thirds of the middle-income households are in rural India.

10. If the rural income goes up by 1 per cent, purchasing power of rural India will go up by Rs 10,000 crore.

11. Of the two million BSNL mobile phone connections, 50 per cent are in rural India.

12. Of the 20 million who have signed up for Rediff mail, 60 per cent are from small towns.

13. Twenty-four million Kisan credit cards (KCC) issued in rural areas exceeds the 17.7 million credit and debit cards issued in urban India. A whopping Rs 52,000 crore has been sanctioned under the KCC scheme.

14. The number of middle and higher income families (having Rs 70,000 plus annual income) in rural India is 21.7 million and the number in urban India is 24.2 million, which is nearly the same.

15. Of the six lakh odd villages in the entire country, 5.22 lakh villages had a village public telephone (VPT) as of March 2005.

Out of the total population of India around 70 per cent lives in rural areas; hence, 'rural India is real India'. India is now seeing a dramatic shift towards consumption and prosperity in rural households. The rural people differ from their urban counterparts on a large number of attributes. Their buying behaviour is also bound to differ and that has important implications for marketers. With the increasing consumption and discretionary incomes in rural India, there has been an upward thrust on measures to develop a marketing framework to exploit opportunities in widely scattered rural markets of the country for effective implementation of market segmentation and targeting.

Potentiality of Rural Markets in India

- The size of India's rural market stated as a percentage of the world population is 12.2 per cent. It means that 12.2 per cent of the world's consumers live in rural India.
- The rural market offers a great opportunity for different branded goods and services to target a large number of potential customers. HLL estimates that out of five lakh villages in India, only one lakh have been tapped so far, which goes to indicate the market potential of the rural market.
- Rural consumption of certain durables and non-durables is more than that in urban areas. Some of the products for which the demand in rural areas is more than in urban areas are sewing machines, radios, wristwatches, bicycles, etc. It is estimated that for durables, the annual growth rate is 25 per cent, which is outstanding by any standards.
- There is also an increase in the average number of working days in a year. This has resulted in an increase in rural income in terms of absolute value.
- Accessibility to rural markets has become easy through improved infrastructural facilities such as transportation, communication, TV penetration, and information technology.
- The urban market is getting saturated and many companies are now targeting the rural market.
- Rural lifestyle is changing. Almost every household has at least one member living and working in a city.

Common Marketing Myths about the Rural Market

There are some myths about rural markets and rural consumers.

Rural market penetration is not beneficial Some people feel that rural consumers are not worth bothering about and can be neglected because they tend to buy unbranded products rather than the branded variety.

In reality, the study conducted by MART reveals that there is a high preference for branded products among rural consumers. It indicates that there is a potential for branded products if a company can fulfil the requirement of the consumers through effective market segmentation and targeting strategies.

Rural consumers will take just what's given to them Another myth that marketers believe is that if the company has solid sales in rural areas, its product is safe and secure.

In reality, the rural sales of Iodex and Amrutanjan are high due to lack of choice. It is true that rural consumers are quite loyal to some brands, such as chyavanprash or toothpaste brands such as Colgate, which have made efforts to build their brand names in rural areas. However, as toilet soaps demonstrate, brand building is required because of a wide choice available to customers. Therefore, rural consumers cannot be counted as blindly loyal. Price also plays a vital role; the higher the price, the more cautious rural consumers will be. They will search for new brands. Where the price is low, they are happy to shop on impulse.

Rural consumers will only buy really cheap mass-market brands One of the important misconceptions about rural consumers is that they are more sensitive to price and purchase low-priced products. Low-priced brands, such as Nirma, are obviously in the lead. However, another startling revelation is that penetration of premium products is being reported even among the poorer sections of the masses.

One family one brand Marketers often expect rural households to be homogeneous in consumption. Marketers make the mistake of thinking that the entire household prefers to use only one brand.

In reality, many families prefer multi-brand usage. The fact is that, rural households are not homogeneous especially when it comes to soaps, detergents, and tea. Even when price differences exist, privileged consumers such as the heads of families or favoured sons, insist on a superior brand of soaps, tea, or washing powder for their use.

Distribution drives rural sales Another misconception is that rural marketing is only about distribution. However, in reality, distribution is clearly the key to rural marketing, but it is wrong to imagine that distribution is all that matters. Rural consumers are not cocooned from the urban world as they are increasingly getting access to markets in towns, either directly or indirectly. Whatever the means are, rural consumers are eager to consume. If marketers do not capture the opportunity to satisfy the needs of rural consumers, then rural consumers will search for other alternatives to fulfil their needs.

Rural market is an extension of the urban market One of the misconceptions is that the marketing campaigns in rural areas are akin to those in urban areas. Hence, marketers believe that the same marketing campaigns will embrace the brand and product preference of the rural market too.

In reality, rural markets possess dynamics that are distinct from their urban counterparts by virtue of their genesis, size, and target audience. Brands and products need to be presented and promoted in a manner that caters to local cultural and social sensitivities. It is also important to introduce features in the product that holds significance for rural consumers.

Size of the market The size of the market can be estimated based on an analysis of current product penetration levels and sales volumes. Even limited acceptance of the product translated into a potential market can bring profits. In reality, limited acceptance in a rural area does not imply that the product has market potential. Such an assumption might cause increased product mortality as a greater number of competing firms flood the market with their products while the actual demand may be very low.

Perception and attitude of rural people are the same It is a myth that the attitude, values, and purchasing behaviour of consumers in rural areas in one region is the same as that in another region. Marketers may also adopt a 'one size fits all' approach for promoting a product. In reality, the rural markets in India are a complex montage of cultural and social mindsets, which greatly influence the local lifestyles. Often purchase decisions are made collectively, with people seeking advice from influential members of the village. Despite education, employment, and income levels being major factors in product preferences, the social, and cultural mindset acts as a key to purchase decisions and this mindset differs from one region to another. Hence, it becomes imperative for marketers to use a multi-level approach for product promotion and to keep the distinct regional dynamics in mind before planning a marketing strategy.

Rural Market Segmentation

The above-mentioned myths and misconceptions regarding the rural market indicate that there is a need for effective rural market segmentation. In fact, the rural market satisfies the prerequisites for market segmentation such as measurability, accessibility, differentiability, and substantiability. Marketers should evaluate the segment opportunity with reference to their short-term and long-term objectives. If a company's objective is to achieve long-term sustainable sales volume by expanding its consumer base, then it has to go rural instead of expecting consumers to come to urban markets to purchase products and services. Companies, such as Asian Paints, HLL, and Colgate-Palmolive, which reach rural homes with their products, demonstrate this. Companies should also examine their resources and capabilities for serving rural markets. They should conduct small pilot projects, which will provide an opportunity to evaluate the target segment behaviour towards the product or service being offered. Smart marketers in rural areas, such as HLL and ITC, initiated pilot projects named Shakti and e-Choupal, which were later transformed into mega rural marketing models.

Rural consumers are influenced by rationality, personal experience, the level of utility that is derived from the consumption, etc. The clever, gimmicky advertisements do not work with rural consumers. Their buying behaviour is influenced by the experience of their own friends, relatives, and family members. Above all, quality of the product and its easy availability are the primary and vital determinants of consumer buying behaviour. The techniques of bombarding product messages have a limited influence. Rural consumers are very much attached to and influenced by the touch and feel aspect of any promotional activity. It is imperative that the marketing experts understand the mindset of rural consumers for every product, in any specified region. Hence, it is necessary that more research studies on the rural market, especially on segmentation, targeting, and positioning strategies should be undertaken. The research will help marketers understand the rural consumers better and generate more reliable data with particular attention to product-specific, region-specific, group-specific, and seasonal-specific information, for effectively segmenting the market. It is also important that language and regional behavioural variations should be given due attention while developing the rural communication strategy. In order to taste success, the aim of marketing agencies must be to 'feel the local touch'. Rural distribution of the products automatically paves the way for the next big market revolution in rural areas. The structure of competition in rural market is very complex and is not uniform. The competition dynamics change from one village to another; this is visible in the form of new local or regional brands on the shelf competing with other national brands.

Rural Marketing Strategies

Marketers can make consistent attempts to innovate tools and strategies to overcome the challenges they face in the business arena. Business innovations are broadly classified under two heads—product/service innovation and process innovation.

Marketers need to design creative solutions to overcome challenges typical of the rural environment, such as physical distribution, channel management, and promotion and communication. Corporate India and government bodies alike have made several efforts to bridge the gap between rural and urban India. The urban–rural divide in FMCG consumption is being bridged rapidly. In the case of some high volume consumables, such as toilet soaps, washing powders, packaged tea, biscuits, and detergent cakes, the penetration and usage in urban and rural markets is comparable, because companies now segment their customers into similar clusters in order to market specialized products and services to each group. Initially, marketers in India concentrated on segmenting only the urban market. But with the saturation of urban markets in recent years, and the simultaneous growing demand in rural markets, the need to segment the rural market is increasingly being felt. More and more companies are moving away from the assumption that rural consumers are a homogeneous mass with little or no differences. Firms are beginning to divide the rural market into homogenous segments in order to reach out to each segment more effectively.

Today, rural marketers have become more focused on consumer choice and requirements. This calls for segmenting, targeting, and positioning (STP). Since the rural market in India began to grow rapidly in the post 1990s, marketers needed to evolve different strategies for different customer groups to tap the rural markets effectively. Creative segmentation can help a company get closer to its customers by developing the appropriate differential marketing mix for each segment through changes in one or more of the four Ps of the marketing mix, i.e., product, price, place, and promotion.

Effective Segmentation and Targeting

Success Stories of Rural Market Segmentation

Earlier the rural market in India was considered a homogeneous mass. HLL was the giant and undisputed market leader in detergents (Surf) in India. However, it suffered significant losses at the hands of a new and small organization called Nirma Chemicals. The latter's washing powder, Nirma, very quickly caught the attention of the middle- and lower-income customers, who were finding it difficult to make both ends meet with their limited monthly income.

Nirma was the lowest priced branded washing powder available in grocery and cooperative stores. The middle-class segment was happy as they could now choose a lower priced washing powder against Surf, which was beyond their budget. Nirma also had an impact on upper middle-class and higher-income families, who chose Nirma for washing their inexpensive clothes. In the year 1984, HLL decided to take a fresh look at the market. Research conducted across the country revealed that different income groups of consumers had varying expectations from detergents and washing powders. Thus, to counter the attack from Nirma, HLL launched Sunlight (yellow), Wheel (green), and Rin (blue) detergent powders for different market segments. This strategy of segmenting the market helped HLL win back part of its lost market. Nirma had already won the first round of the battle for market share by introducing a low priced product for the highly price-sensitive Indian market.

Similarly, T-Series introduced audio cassettes at unbelievably low prices and took away a huge share from the then market leader HMV. These initiatives taught the big firms valuable lessons on the importance of segmenting the market.

Market segmentation offers several benefits over mass marketing. Segmentation helps distinguish one customer profile from another within a given market, and it facilitates in understanding the needs of the target buyers. The company can create more fine-tuned product offerings and price them appropriately for the target segment. Seventy-five per cent of people in rural India are engaged in agriculture, but they cannot be clubbed under one category. There are large farmers, medium farmers, small farmers, marginal farmers, and agricultural labourers. Their income levels, lifestyles, and behaviour are different. Therefore, there is a need to classify rural consumers under different segments. Further, the remaining 25 per cent of the rural population is engaged in non-farm activities, which could be segmented as self-employed labourers, daily wage labourers, salaried employees, traders, micro entrepreneurs, etc.

Those families in rural areas with some members residing in urban areas tend to have a different level of exposure to the outside world, which in turn affects their aspirations and lifestyles. Access to mass media (television or radio) also varies widely in rural areas, which affects consumer behaviour. Hence, these factors need to be considered while segmenting rural customers.

Brooke Bond Lipton India Ltd (now part of HLL) decided to expand its branded tea into the largely unbranded loose-tea segment in the rural market. The company explored the buying, consumption, and other habits of all tea consumers in order to identify a cross-section of people united by common behaviour traits. Only after conducting extensive research did HLL conceive the idea of A1, a new brand of tea for the rural market. A bundle of benefits were designed to meet the needs of the rural segment.

HLL began by collecting photographs and video clips of people across the country, who buy loose tea, in order to study their lifestyles in general, and their tea preparation and tea drinking habits in particular. It studied the number of times people drink tea during the day, the time they drink tea, how they serve it, and the family members who are regular tea drinker. Alongside, HLL tracked other items of food and drink that these people consumed, the soaps and detergents that they used, and how they spent their leisure, so as to understand just where tea and its consumption stood in their matrix of needs. The objectives were to understand exactly what bases of segmentation could be used to differentiate consumer groups. It would have been too simplistic to use just price as a factor to define the segment. As a result of this elaborate exercise, HLL found a simple but highly effective idea that it could use to define its segment—all who desire a strong cup of tea. Cutting across geographical, cultural, income, and age groups, this need emerged as a unifier for many tea drinkers. So, HLL used this as the one overriding characteristic that would distinguish its chosen niche from the rest of the market.

Conclusion

Different marketers have attempted multiple segmentation approaches in the rural market. It seems clear that one cannot rely on a specific segmentation approach. Rather, one needs to explore and understand customers through behavioural research or by undertaking pilot projects in rural areas to be able to identify well-defined segments.

Only effective segmentation will help in reaching the target customers by using the appropriate positioning platform. Merely the adoption of urban segmentation, targeting, and positioning (STP) strategies for rural markets cannot be helpful in winning frontiers in the ever-changing and growing rural market.

This is one area where a lot more work needs to be done by research agencies, advertising agencies, and marketers alike, to develop a holistic STP and understanding of the rural market, as there is a huge potential for the Indian rural market to reap maximum benefit. The challenges of rural market segmentation need to be evolutionary and not revolutionary. It has to be considered as an investment today for a better future tomorrow. Organizations should focus on nurturing the rural markets and should have a long-term perspective rather than concentrating on achieving short-term objectives.

The greatest problem is that the rural market is still evolving in efficient dissemination of information and there is no set format for understanding consumer behaviour. A lot of research is still to be conducted in order to understand the rural market. The future is certainly bright for the Indian rural market through its effective implementation of STP strategies, which will create more room for all players including consumers, marketers, investors, and others in the market. As the market matures and deepens further, one can really hope to see the fortune day very soon by providing a benchmark for traders worldwide, especially in fast moving consumer goods (FMCG), where India is the major consumer as well as a producer. As rightly put by C.K. Prahalad, 'The future lies with those companies who **see** the poor as their customers'.

Questions

1. Discuss the role of consumers in the context of rural markets in India.
2. How can service firms tap the rural markets in India? Does it make sense for them to customize the service offerings in light of the profile of the consumers at the bottom of the pyramid?

SELECT REFERENCES

Biwalkar, M. (2006) 'Loyalty gains', *The Strategist, Business Standard*, New Delhi, 17 October.

Business World (2005), 'Kids' pester power', *The Marketing Whitebook 2005*, pp. 140–141.

Business World (2005), 'The evolving Indian family', *The Marketing Whitebook 2005*, pp. 168–170.

Business World (2008), *The Marketing Whitebook 2007–08*, ABP Pvt Ltd, New Delhi.

Carter, M. (2006), 'Growing up', *The Strategist, Business Standard*, New Delhi, 24 October.

Foss, B. and M. Stone (2001), *Successful Customer Relationship Marketing*, Kogan Page, London.

Hach, S.J. and J. Deighton (1989), 'Managing what consumers learn from experience', *Journal of Marketing*, April, vol. 53, p. 3.

'Is majority of India non-vegetarian?', *The Times of India*, New Delhi, 19 October 2006.

Joshi, P. (2006), 'Cinemas as impulse buy', *Business Standard*, New Delhi, 12 October, p. 11.

Kotler, P. (2002), *Marketing Management: The Millennium Edition*, Prentice Hall, New Delhi.

Krech, David, R.S. Crutchfield, and L.B. Egerton (1962), *Individual in Society*, McGraw-Hill, New York.

Lindquist, J.D. and M.J. Sirgy (2005), 'Shopper, buyer, and consumer behaviour', *Biztantra*, New Delhi.

Lovelock, C. (2001), *Services Marketing*, Addison-Wesley Longman, Delhi.

Nichenametla, P. (2006), '3,256 complaints, 0 penalties', *Business Standard*, New Delhi, 12 October.

Reichheld, F.J. and W.E. Sasser Jr (1995), 'Zero defections: Quality comes to services', *Harvard Business Review*, vol. 73, September–October, pp. 59–75.

Rowley, J. (2005), 'The four Cs of customer loyalty', *Marketing Intelligence and Planning*, Bradford, vol. 23, no. 6/7, p. 8.

Sarkar, K. (2006), 'Micro finance now on LIC agenda', *Business Standard*, New Delhi, 25 October.

Schiffman, L.G. and L.L. Kanuk (1997), *Consumer Behaviour*, 6th edn, Prentice Hall, London.

Swami, M.R. (2006), 'High flyers', *The Strategist, Business Standard*, 24 October.

Wells, W.D. and D.J. Tigert (1971), 'Activities, interest and opinions', *Journal of Advertising Research*, vol. 11, no. 4, August, pp. 27–35.

ACNielsen (2006), 'Insights India—Reading the consumer's mind', http://www.acnielsen.co.in/trends/documents/Insights.pdf, accessed on 9 May 2008.

Cherian, C., N. Dasgupta, and A.G. Doreswamy (2007), 'Effect of marketing on society', Paper presented at the International Marketing Conference on Marketing & Society, 8–10 April, Kozhikode, http://dspace.iimk.ac.in/bitstream/2259/320/1/657-663.pdf, accessed on 14 May 2008.

'Consumer protection as a barometer of India's democracy', http://www.consumer-voice.org/independenceday.asp, accessed on 8 May 2008.

'India's coffee consumption seen up 6 pct in 2007', *Reuters*, http://www.flex-news-food.com/pages/12350/Coffee/India/indias-coffee-consumption-seen-pct-2007.html, accessed on 9 May 2008.

'Internet the new pit stop for Indian shoppers?', http://in.nielsen.com/news/20080201.shtml, accessed on 10 May 2008.

Jayashankar, P. (2008), 'In pursuit of youth', *The Hindu Business Line*, http://www.thehindubusinessline.com/catalyst/2004/09/09/stories/2004090900090200.htm, accessed on 10 May 2008.

Shah, G. (2008), 'Branded toys enter the marketing game', *LiveMint.com, The Wall Street Journal*, http://www.livemint.com/2008/01/15225209/Branded-toys-enter-the-marketi.html, accessed on 14 May 2008.

SRI Consulting Business Intelligence (2008), 'The VALS segments', http://www.sric-bi.com/VALS/types.shtml, accessed on 11 May 2008.

'Youth to drive e-commerce growth in India', IAMI summit news, http//www.domain-b.com/ebusiness/general/20060119_commerce.html, accessed on 10 May 2008.

5

Segmentation, Targeting, and Positioning for a Services Firm

OBJECTIVES

After reading this chapter you will be able to understand the:
- impact of segmenting, targeting, and positioning on the marketing mix
- process and bases of targeting, and the different targeting strategies
- various positioning strategies and the importance of competitive advantage in marketing

INTRODUCTION

The market consists of numerous customers who are geographically scattered and have specific needs and buying practices. A company needs to market its products to this vast sea of customers to remain profitable. Segmentation, targeting, and positioning are strategic fundamentals of marketing used to generate competitive advantage, which can be translated into business opportunities that form the success stories of organizations. Defining a market is the basis of segmentation. Originally, a market was defined as a physical place where buyers and sellers gathered. From time to time, different subject/area experts have given different definitions of a market. To a marketing professional, a market constitutes all the actual and potential buyers of a product or service. It is up to the professional to create a competitive advantage and capture the market share.

Service firms vary widely in their abilities of servicing. It would, then, not be wise to compete in an entire market. Instead, organizations should focus on the set of customers they can serve best. In 1974, Sinner defined focus as 'A narrow product mix for a particular market segment'. According to Johnston (1996), 'Focus is to understand the needs of a specific market and to focus all the efforts of the plant on achieving them through the use of proven technologies'. Thus, it can be said that the focus for a service organization should be a group of buyers who exhibit similarity in their needs, purchasing manners, purchasing situations, consumption styles, lifestyles, etc. For a service organization, the company's focus can be described on two dimensions—the service focus and the market focus. Taking the two variables of services offered and the market served, organizations can be grouped into four types—(1) unfocused; (2) service focused; (3) market focused; and (4) fully focused (Fig. 5.1).

An *unfocused organization* is unformulated at the service concept level. Hence, it tends to serve a wide market with a wide range of services. The idea is to provide a range of

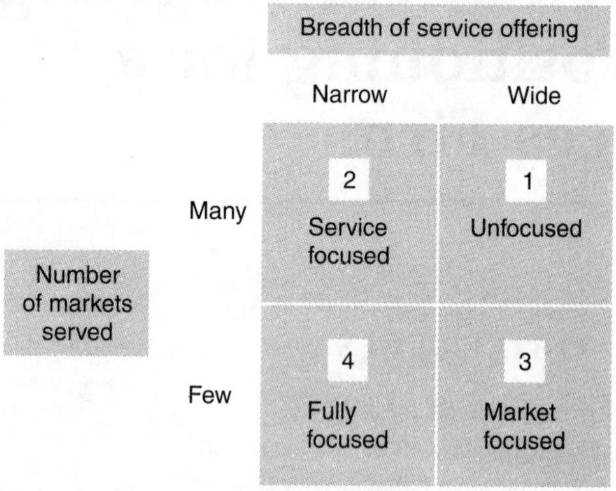

Breadth of service offering

Source: Adapted from Johnston (1996).

Fig. 5.1   Basic focus strategies for service

services so as to cater to any need of a wide variety customers. For example, Tata-AIG General Insurance provides a wide range of commercial, personal, and life insurance products through a variety of distribution channels in approximately 130 countries and jurisdictions throughout the world (Tata 2006).

A *service-focused organization*, on the other hand, provides a narrow range of services to a wide market. For example, Café Coffee Day, India's only vertically integrated coffee company, is the largest café chain. The mission statement, 'To be the best café chain in the country by offering a world-class coffee experience at affordable prices', is thus an example of a service-focused organization, as its focus is providing excellent coffee. Café Coffee Day includes Fresh 'n' Ground (which owns 354 coffee bean and powder retail outlets), Coffee Day Xpress (which owns 341 coffee kiosks), Coffee Day Take-away (which owns 7,000 vending machines), Coffee Day Exports and Coffee Day Perfect (packaged coffee) division (Nanchrichten 2006 and Café Coffee Day 2008). It currently owns 585 cafés in 96 cities around the country. The company has recently opened a café in Vienna, Austria and is planning to open other cafés in the Middle East, Eastern Europe, Eurasia, Egypt, and South East Asia in the coming months. Its menu ranges from hot and cold coffees to several exotic international coffees, food items, desserts, and pastries.

A *market-focused organization*, while concentrating on a narrow market segment, provides a wide range of services. For example, Shahnaz Hussain, a pioneer in herbal beauty care in India, provides a wide range of ayurvedic skin, hair, and body care treatments for women.

This proposition of many services being provided by a single organization may seem convenient for individual customers who want a one-stop shop, but as far as corporate clients are concerned, this might not prove to be a very profitable proposition as purchases

Table 5.1   Advantages and disadvantages of different types of organizations

Organization	Advantages	Disadvantages
Fully focused	▫ Recognizes expertise in a well-defined niche ▫ Since they have expertise in a well-defined niche they can charge a premium ▫ Expertise in a particular niche protects them from would-be competitors	▫ Market too small to generate volume of business needed for financial success ▫ Demand may be displaced by generic competition
Market focused	▫ Can sell multiple services to single purchaser	▫ Managers need to be sure that the organization has the operational capability to deliver the services selected ▫ Managers in B2B markets are disappointed while cross-selling additional services as purchasing practices and preferences in business organizations are different, and purchase decisions are made by different departments/groups within the organization
Service focused	▫ Can create a portfolio of customers	▫ Need expertise in serving each segment—requires broader sales effort and greater investment in market communication
Unfocused	▫ Provides a wide range of services to choose from. Hence, maximum chances of needs being fulfilled ▫ Caters to a wide range of customers so the potential customers are many	▫ Need a lot of expertise in all the services provided ▫ Subject to operational capability

Source: Adapted from Lovelock and Wirtz (2006).

for different services may be made by different people or sometimes different departments altogether.

A *fully-focused organization* provides a very limited range of services to a specific market segment; for example, low-cost carriers work on the premise that a segment of customers needed the core service of quick transportation without the service frills and at reduced fares. The advantages and disadvantages of the different types of organizations are summed up in Table 5.1.

If we consider the traditional MBA programme in India, it is slowly becoming a mass programme with the mushrooming of different business schools, but MBA specialization in retail, hospital management, and agriculture is now catering to a certain segment of professionals and students (Kumar 2006). According to Kotler et al. (2006) marketing has passed through the following different stages—mass marketing, product-variety marketing, target marketing, and micro marketing.

Mass marketing   In this form of marketing, the seller mass produces, mass distributes, and mass promotes one product to all buyers. The idea is to achieve the lowest costs and prices, and create the largest potential market. For example, Haryana Tourism has opened thirty motels in Haryana, which are similar in appearance and have a uniform level of service.

Product-variety marketing In this form of marketing, the seller produces two or more products/services having different features, styles, quality, and size. The argument is that different consumers have different tastes and, therefore, a single product might not satisfy their wants. For example, McDonald's offers different types of burgers, such as hamburgers, chicken burgers, veggie burgers, etc., to cater to a variety of consumer tastes.

Target marketing The seller identifies market segments, selects one or more, and develops products and services tailored to the selected segments in this form of marketing. Today, this concept is well accepted in most industrialized nations. For example, Singapore's population is made up of Chinese, Malay, and Indians, and rice is the staple diet of these three ethnic groups. In order to cater to their palates, McDonald's has added rice burgers and fried beef slices served between two pressed rice cakes to its menu in Singapore. McDonald's was buoyed by the success of its rice burgers in Taiwan (it sold five million rice burgers in six months) and added it to its menu in Singapore (Reuters 2006). Today, more and more companies are looking at target marketing to drive their sales (Exhibit 5.1).

Exhibit 5.1 Global fast food chains think local for growth

Foreign fast food chains such as KFC, McDonald's, and Domino's are realizing that localizing the menu to suit Indian tastes is extremely important. Kentucky Fried Chicken (popularly known as KFC) started its operations in India in the mid-1990s but was forced to shut down. After years, it has re-opened its operations in the country, branding itself as KFC and not reminding customers about Kentucky Fried Chicken. These global companies found that Indians mostly eat out in groups and at least one member of the group is a vegetarian; hence, the vegetarians have definite reservations regarding places such as KFC. To counter this, KFC has included a number of vegetarian options in its menu, although only 15 per cent of the revenues are earned from this.

Domino's, the world leader in the pizza delivery market is positioning itself in several non-metro cities as a dine-in restaurant. It is a fact that in smaller cities, going out to the market and eating out is an integral part of family life; thus, positioning oneself merely as a convenience home delivery store does not make sense. Most Domino's outlets are built bigger and designed to accommodate 25–30 customers. While about 65 per cent of Domino's revenues come from home deliveries, this segment will grow further. But in smaller cities dine-in outlets will drive growth.

McDonald's, the world's fastest fast food chain is immensely popular among children, teenagers, and family alike. The menu is highly localized and it also has low-priced burgers and ice-creams to attract new consumers to the brand. While in metros, McDonald's is seen as a convenience outlet, in smaller cities like Jaipur, it is still an aspirational brand. Hence, McDonald's strategy is to make the brand available to a larger market.

This clearly shows that positioning locally is very important for companies, especially in the food and hospitality sector.

Source: Adapted from Vivek (2006).

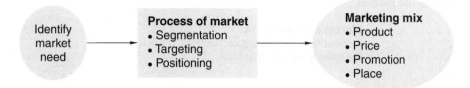

Fig. 5.2 Market need versus segmentation, targeting, and positioning

Micro marketing   The Internet and database technology have helped companies to cater to small segments with distinctive needs. Today, buyers are looking for speciality in the product and service they purchase. Hospitality companies are pursuing this by maintaining databases of regular customers and finding creative ways to serve them with personalized marketing.

The three major steps in focused marketing are—segmentation, targeting, and positioning (Fig. 5.2). Normally, markets are born with a first brand that creates the division. If this category is profitable, another competitor, sensing a good opportunity, enters this category. As more and more competitors enter, it becomes increasingly difficult to capture the attention of the customers. What do marketers do then? They choose a sub-group of persons in the market and address their product directly to them. This is the crux of segmentation.

According to Kotler and Bes (2003), 'Renounce attacking the whole market. Show yourself as the most efficient option for a sub-set of the market and you can become the leader of that segment. It is better to be the head of the mouse than the tail of the lion'.

It is not realistic for a firm to appeal to all the potential buyers in a market. Marketing professionals can, therefore, choose a segment of the market and then direct all their marketing efforts towards them in order to get the maximum benefit. How they choose the segment to be served forms the basis of targeting. Hence, targeting measures the attractiveness of the segment and then selects the segments to be served. Once these segments are chosen, the next step is to tell this segment audience that you are the best choice for them. This is done by highlighting those qualities in the product, which are important to the target customers, and this is known as positioning. Positioning consists of choosing how the company wants its products to be regarded by the customers. These aspects of segmentation, targeting, and positioning are shown in Fig. 5.3. According to Kotler and Bes (2003), the advantages of segmentation, targeting, and positioning are:

1. It fragments the market and at the same time makes it bigger, because once the customers find their needs better covered they tend to increase their consumption.
2. A new player can generate a competitive advantage for itself by following this strategy.
3. By segmenting the market and taking out products for each segment, a market leader can create barriers to competition by discouraging the entry of new competitors.

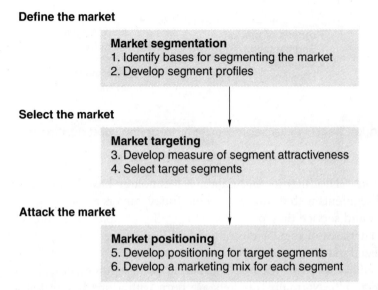

Define the market

> **Market segmentation**
> 1. Identify bases for segmenting the market
> 2. Develop segment profiles

Select the market

> **Market targeting**
> 3. Develop measure of segment attractiveness
> 4. Select target segments

Attack the market

> **Market positioning**
> 5. Develop positioning for target segments
> 6. Develop a marketing mix for each segment

Source: Adapted from Kotler et al. (2006).

Fig. 5.3 Process of market segmentation, targeting, and positioning

SEGMENTATION

Market segmentation is defined as the process of dividing the market into distinct groups that share common characteristics, needs, purchasing behaviour, or consumption patterns. These groups may react to the marketing mix in a similar manner. Market segmentation is a marketing strategy that recognizes the need for 'specialization' to suit the needs of a segment of the market rather than trying to be 'all things to all people'. For example, English news channels in India, such as NDTV, NDTV Profit, Headlines Today, Times Now, CNN-IBN, and CNBC, are devoted to business news targeted at businesspersons, corporate business executives, stock-market traders, and money market dealers (Kumar 2006). Market segmentation is important because it leads to efficient and effective utilization of resources, improves manageability of the market by dividing the markets into smaller parts, and helps to improve the company's ability to satisfy customers. According to Cadeaux (2004), market segmentation has both strategic and operational dimensions.

The strategic decision involves the determination of characteristics and the number of segments to be served, and the development of distinct marketing programmes for a product market entry. The operational decision involves allocation of resources across the segments chosen, so as to optimize some objective such as profit or sales.

Market segmentation helps the firm to more effectively and/or efficiently use its resources. It also helps to design the marketing strategies around the target segments. Thus, there is a closer alignment between the customer needs and the organization's product or service offering. This also leads to enhanced customer satisfaction and loyalty, and hence a stronger competitive advantage leading to superior financial performance (Hunt and Arnett 2004). We can summarize the objectives of segmentation as follows:

1. Identify the similarity of needs of potential buyers within a segment and pursue them with tailored products or services supported by appropriate market mix strategies.
2. Identify the difference between needs of buyers among segments and try to cater to these different needs. For example, the Taj group of hotels, while catering to the luxury and leisure segment, has opened Ginger Hotels (formerly called IndiOne) to cater to business budget travellers.
3. Once the specific segment has been chosen for the marketing efforts, the organization is more focused in its efforts and there is potential for increased return on investment.
4. Even before the marketing efforts are carried out marketers can study the feasibility of their actions, which saves a lot on operational costs and time later.
5. It is simpler for the marketers to assign the buyers to different segments on the basis of a number of parameters and is highly cost-effective.

Market Segmentation

Different segmentation variables can be used to segment a market. There is no single way and a marketer has to try different variables. Some principal segmentation variables can either be based on the consumer or the buying situation. Consumer-based segmentation can be further segmented by geographic, demographic, or psychographic means. The different ways of segmentation are summed up in Fig. 5.4.

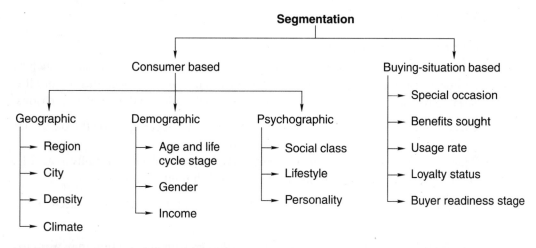

Source: Adapted from Kotler et al. (2006).

Fig. 5.4 Means of market segmentation

Geographic Segmentation

In this type of segmentation, the marketer divides the market into different geographic units such as regions, nations, states, countries, cities, and neighbourhoods. For example, India can be divided into different regions such as north, south, east, west, and central. Each region has its own staple diet; for example, in the north, wheat and pulses form an integral part of the diet, in south India rice forms a vital part of the different dishes, and in east India sea food is more prevalent. Hindustan Unilever Ltd (formerly Hindustan Lever Limited), keeping these local preferences in mind, launched its Annapurna Aata in some select markets in the south where it charged a premium owing to subdued competition.

Geographic segmentation permeates knowledge of customer preferences endorsing companies to modify the product offering accordingly. For example, in India, fast food brands such as Domino's, Pizza Hut, and Café Coffee Day are all looking at Tier-II cities for their next growth phase. According to Ajay Kaul, CEO, Domino's India, eating out in cities such as Bhubaneswar and Baroda is considered in a more integral way, so Domino's plans to have a larger format in these cities, with dine-in arrangements. Café Coffee Day, with a number of stores in India, has presence on highways and temple towns. According to Sandeep Kohli, MD India, Yum! Restaurants International, Pizza Hut, which completes ten years in India, has city-specific promotions, which has helped the brand to gain popularity. All these chains also consider reducing the prices by 5 to 10 per cent as compared to metros and customizing their menus, which are suited to the diner in the different cities they plan to target (Vyas 2006). Banks are also using geographic segmentation; for example, the Gramin Bank concept is intended to give credit and other services to people living in villages in India. ITC has targeted rural farmers with its e-choupal, enabling farmers in the rural hinterland to get the best price for their produce.

Demographic Segmentation

This consists of dividing markets into groups based on demographic variables such as age, life cycle, gender, income, occupation, education, religion, race, and nationality. This variable is most commonly used for segmentation because of the following reasons:

- Customer preference and the number of times they are going to use the particular service product varies closely with this variable.
- These variables are easy to measure and lots of secondary data is usually available.
- It helps to assess the size of the market and reach it efficiently.

Some demographic factors that can be used to segment the markets are discussed in this section.

Age and life cycle stage Consumer preferences change with age. A child may want toy cars, a cricket bat, and candies at the age of five, but at the age of ten the same child may want a cycle, and at the age of eighteen a two-wheeler, mobile, iPod, laptop, etc. Thus, targeting the customers according to their age is a strategy followed by marketers. In India, marketers are increasingly targeting their goods at children keeping in mind the pester power of children. The term *pester power* is increasingly being used in marketing to denote a child's influence on the buying process of parents and relatives (Catlin 2004). Children are becoming increasingly sophisticated consumers in their own right and mobilized by advertising, promotional materials, and peer pressure, seek to influence their parents' spending power and household purchases. The scenario of both working parents, who treat their children to non-obligatory items to compensate for having less time to spend with them, further facilitates this. As per the *Business World* (2005), surveys in fourteen cities indicating the amount of pocket money children get and the frequency with which they receive it provides an insight into the kids' spending power (Table 5.2). The pocket money given city-wise indicates that 39 per cent of all seven to fourteen-year old children in India get pocket money. If we see the percentage distribution of population in India age group-wise, we find that children up to fourteen years of age constitute 32.3 per cent of the total population. Thus, we can conclude that kids are influencing the purchasing decisions and it is increasingly making more sense for the marketers to target them.

Children are an active segment of the market. A high exposure to media and the ever-increasing purchase ability have resulted in children moving up the value chain. This category of consumers plays a very strong role in households relating to purchases such as apparel, footwear, accessories, etc. The parents' role in decision making on brands, outlets, or any other aspect related to the purchase is diminishing (*The Marketing*

Table 5.2 Kids' spending power in India

How much?	
Amount of pocket money (in rupees)	**Numbers (in %)**
1–49	24
50–99	23
100–49	20
150–99	11
200–99	9
300 and above	13
How often?	
Frequency of receipt of pocket money	**Numbers (in %)**
Less often	3
Monthly	10
Every 2 weeks	4
Once a week	20
2–3 times a week	23
Daily	32

Contd

Table 5.2 Contd

Segregated by city	
Name of the city	**% of 7–14 year olds receiving pocket money (base: all mothers)**
Ludhiana	69
Delhi	67
Mumbai	57
Jaipur	54
Hyderabad	47
Guwahati	40
All 14 cities	39
Ahmedabad	35
Madurai	33
Kochi	31
Chennai	30
Bangalore	26
Lucknow	24
Nashik	23
Kolkata	10

Source: Adapted from *The Marketing Whitebook 2005.*

Whitebook 2007–08). 'The average annual expenditure by this age group is approximately Rs 10,360 ($225). It is observed that girls at this stage allocate a higher amount to clothes, while a majority of boys spend on computers' (*The Marketing Whitebook 2007–08*).

An example of how marketers are developing their marketing communication keeping this segment of kids in mind is McDonald's. It added a coupon in the shape of a ball with the Disney Adventures Magazine (a children's magazine) offering a free Soft Serve with every Happy Meal. Thus, when the children buy this magazine and get the coupon they are bound to influence their parents to take them there. This is an example of how kids are being considered as major influencers of buying decisions across various service categories such as fast food chains.

Many banks and financial institutions are using the age and life cycle stage to cater to customer needs. ICICI is catering to the need of a better shopping experience by getting strategic tie-ups with Visa, MasterCard, and with leading retailers such as Big Bazaar and Spencer's for its debit card. It has also launched services such as kid-e-bank for children, bank@campus for students, PowerPay for salaried employees, ICICI select for high net worth individuals, and business multipliers for businesspeople (Raj 2006). If we consider the population distribution of different ASEAN countries, we see why developed nations are targeting India and China in Asia (Table 5.3).

Table 5.4 shows the age group-wise per cent distribution of population.

Table 5.3 Population of different ASEAN countries*

| Country | Age structure | | | | | | Total |
| | 0–14 yrs | | 15–64 yrs | | 65 yrs and over | | |
	Male	Female	Male	Female	Male	Female	
China	142,085,665	125,300,391	491,513,378	465,020,030	50,652,480	55,472,661	1,330,044,605
India	189,238,487	172,168,306	374,157,581	352,868,003	28,285,796	31,277,725	1,147,995,898
Pakistan	31,316,803	29,567,622	51,000,863	48,648,480	3,409,246	3,819,026	167,762,040
Bangladesh	26,364,370	24,859,792	49,412,903	47,468,013	2,912,321	2,529,502	153,546,901
Nepal	5,792,042	5,427,370	8,832,488	8,345,724	542,192	579,298	29,519,114

* as per July 2008 est.

Source: Adapted from World Fact book.

> ***Gender segmentation*** Marketers of products such as clothing, cosmetics, personal care items, jewellery, and footwear commonly segment markets by gender. However, gender segmentation is now being increasingly used in the hospitality business. The marketing implication is to choose characteristics that can appeal across rigid gender roles. As the number of women travellers has increased, hotels have added hair dryers, fitness facilities,

Table 5.4 Age group-wise per cent distribution of population

| Age group | Marital status | | | | | | | | |
| | Total | | | Males | | | Females | | |
	Never married	Married	W/D/S	Never married	Married	W/D/S	Never married	Married	W/D/S
< 10 yrs	22.4	0.0	0.0	22.7	0.0	0.0	22.1	0.0	0.0
10–14	11.2	0.0	0.0	11.4	0.0	0.0	10.9	0.0	0.0
15–19	9.1	1.3	0.0	10.3	0.5	0.0	7.9	2.1	0.0
20–4	4.3	4.7	0.1	6.0	2.8	0.0	2.5	6.6	0.1
25–9	1.6	6.9	0.1	2.4	5.9	0.1	0.6	8.0	0.2
30–4	0.4	6.5	0.2	0.7	6.2	0.1	0.2	6.9	0.3
35–9	0.2	6.4	0.3	0.2	6.4	0.2	0.1	6.4	0.4
40–4	0.1	5.0	0.3	0.1	5.3	0.2	0.1	4.8	0.5
45–9	0.1	3.9	0.4	0.1	4.5	0.2	0.0	3.3	0.5
50–4	0.0	3.7	0.5	0.0	3.4	0.2	0.0	4.0	0.9
55–9	0.0	2.6	0.5	0.0	3.0	0.2	0.0	2.2	0.8
60–4	0.0	1.9	0.7	0.0	2.2	0.3	0.0	1.5	1.2
65–9	0.0	1.3	0.7	0.0	1.5	0.3	0.0	1.0	1.1
70–4	0.0	0.7	0.6	0.0	1.0	0.3	0.0	0.4	1.0
75–9	0.0	0.3	0.3	0.0	0.5	0.2	0.0	0.2	0.5
80–4	0.0	0.2	0.2	0.0	0.2	0.1	0.0	0.1	0.4
85+	0.0	0.1	0.2	0.0	0.1	0.1	0.0	0.0	0.2
All ages	49.4	45.4	5.2	54.0	43.5	2.5	44.5	47.5	8.0

Source: Adapted from Indiastats (2005).

baby-sitting service, and safe deposit boxes. In India, five-star hotels offer a range of services to make women guests feel welcome and secure. With facilities such as women butlers, exclusive fitness centres, customized diets, spa therapists flown in from abroad, designer room appurtenances, and whole floors crafted specially for lady travellers, the Indian hospitality industry is doing its utmost to pamper women guests. This trend is bound to pick up pace because nearly 20 per cent of the urban female population is working (Lal 2005).

The twenty-third floor of New Delhi's ITC Maurya Sheraton has been christened Eva and reserved exclusively for women guests. ITC Grand Central Sheraton in Mumbai, unveiled 15 women's-only rooms. The Taj group offers a special butler service. Women guests can use their assistance for making dinner reservations, booking appointments at the parlour or spa, arranging shopping expeditions, or procuring reading material. The hotel's kitchen occasionally customizes dishes to suit a woman guest's diet plan— Atkins, low-carb, no-sugar, or high-fibre. According to the 2001 census, the gender-wise population of the top 20 districts is given in Table 5.5.

Income Marketers have long used segmentation on the basis of income and class. Exhibit 5.2 illustrates the broad demographics of India on the basis of income and class.

Table 5.5 Gender-wise population of top 20 districts of India

District	Population 2001		
	Persons	**Males**	**Females**
Medinipur	9,638,473	4,929,000	4,709,473
North twenty-four parganas	8,930,295	4,635,262	4,295,033
Mumbai (Suburban)	8,587,561	4,702,761	3,884,800
Thane	8,128,833	4,377,806	3,751,027
Pune	7,224,224	3,768,001	3,456,223
Barddhaman	6,919,698	3,602,675	3,317,023
South twenty-four parganas	6,909,015	3,564,241	3,344,774
Bangalore	6,523,110	3,422,797	3,100,313
Murshidabad	5,863,717	3,004,385	2,859,332
Ahmedabad	5,808,378	3,069,861	2,738,517
Jaipur	5,252,388	2,769,096	2,483,292
Hugli	5,040,047	2,588,322	2,451,725
Surat	4,996,391	2,722,675	2,273,716
Nashik	4,987,923	2,591,980	2,395,943
Allahabad	4,941,510	2,625,872	2,315,638
East Godavari	4,872,622	2,445,811	2,426,811
Patna	4,709,851	2,514,949	2,194,902
Nadia	4,603,756	2,365,054	2,238,702
Kolkata	4,580,544	2,506,029	2,074,515
Guntur	4,405,521	2,220,305	2,185,216
Haora	4,274,010	2,242,395	2,031,615

Source: Indiastats (2005).

Exhibit 5.2 Major income classes in India

India consists of 5,161 cities and towns including major metros such as Delhi and Mumbai. In 2005, these cities and towns included about 318 million people or nearly 30 per cent of the population. It also accounts for 52 per cent of India's net domestic product and one-quarter of India's population. Rural India on the other hand, is home to the bulk of the population. As per the statistics more than 70 per cent of Indians today live in over 600,000 villages of various sizes all around the country.

India is witnessing a high income growth and both urban and rural sectors will benefit from it. India has witnessed an upward trend in the income growth, while in 1985–95 the increase was 5.7 per cent per year, it was 6 per cent in 1995–2005. It is estimated that in 2005–15 the growth will continue at 6.4 per cent.

McKinsey Global Institute has divided Indian households into five economic classes based on real annual disposable income.

1. Deprived (Less than Rs 90,000; less than $1969)

   This is the poorest group, the people living under the poverty line. These people earn their livelihoods by engaging in unskilled- or low-skilled activities, they struggle to find employment, and often engage in seasonal or part-time employment.

2. Aspirers (Rs 90,000–200,000; $1,969–$4,376)

   People belonging to this group are small shopkeepers, small farmers, or low-skilled factory/service workers. Although they cannot be termed deprived, they struggle to live a comfortable life, and spend mostly on basic necessities.

3. Seekers (Rs 200,000–500,000; $4376–$10,941)

   People belonging to this stratum are the most varied in terms of attitudes, age, employment, and other factors. These include young college graduates who have just started to work, mid-level government officials, and medium-level traders and business people.

4. Strivers (Rs 500,000–1,000,000; $10,941–$21,882)

   People belonging to this group are regarded as successful in the Indian society. They work as successful businesspeople, established professionals, senior government officials, and rich farmers, among others. They have done well financially, and have stable sources of income and a reasonable wealth base.

5. Global Indians (>Rs 1,000,000; >$21,882)

   This is the cream of the country and comprises of senior corporate executives, politicians, agricultural landowners, and top professionals. More recently, this group also includes graduates from India's top colleges and B-schools who demand high salaries from their respective companies. This bracket of people enjoys a high standard of living and is truly global in its tastes and preferences.

Source: Adapted from *Business World* (2008).

The hospitality industry has long used income segmentation. The high bracket income group serves as a target for luxury hotels. When Taj's first hotel, the Taj Mahal Palace and Tower, Mumbai, was inaugurated in 1903, it was perhaps the only place where a British viceroy could rub shoulders with an Indian maharajah. Keeping an eye on the growing segment of the business budget travellers, the Indian Hotels Company launched IndiOne (now re-named as Ginger), in Bangalore in June 2004 (Ray 2006). ITC also had Fortune hotel properties spread throughout India to cater to the same segment. Keeping this income segmentation in mind, Air Deccan launched its low-cost, no frills airline carriers in India. Paramount Airlines offers business class experience at higher-end economy fares. It targets the corporate travel segment; customers who are not eligible for business class on full service carriers and do not have time to shop for cheap fares, and the higher end of the leisure market (Kumar 2006). Vijay Mallya of Kingfisher Airlines targeted customers who were willing to pay a slightly higher fare, in comparison to low-cost carriers, for premium in-flight services.

Psychographic Segmentation

This segmentation variable divides buyers on the basis of social class, lifestyle, and personality. Café Coffee Day has tied up with WorldSpace Inc. to offer satellite radio to consumers in more than 130 countries. According to Andy Ras-Work, WorldSpace COO, 'WorldSpace's relationship with Café Coffee Day is intended to reach music lovers in India and create an appreciation of the unique value that WorldSpace offers its subscribers'. Hence, Café Coffee Day is trying to please customers in different age and income brackets but having a common taste for coffee and music. The psychographics of Indian consumers is given in Table 5.6.

Social class Almost every society is made up of social class structure. These social classes are relatively ordered divisions and are of importance to marketers as people from a social class exhibit similar behaviour. They show distinct similarities in product and brand behaviour in areas such as travelling, leisure activities, and food habits. A hotel targeting a social class is more successful than a hotel where different social classes are present, as it breeds dissatisfaction among the consumers. Marketers also use both social class and income to segment the market.

Lifestyle Companies are now trying to understand the customer's lifestyle in a comprehensive manner to design their service to suit their needs. NDTV's website is a classic example. The company has understood the lifestyle of the customers and designed

Table 5.6 Psychographics of the Indian consumer in the urban areas

	Category	Age	Influencing trends	Population spread	Average annual consumption (in Rs)	Major consumption areas (in descending order)
1.	School goers	12–16 years	High exposure to media, lifestyle trends	13.9 million (51.7% Boys and 48.3% girls)	10,360	Apparel, eating out/ ordering in, books, footwear, computers, etc.
2.	Corporate climbers	21–5 years	High disposable incomes, limited responsibility, independence	11.8 million (58% men and 42% women)	17,310	Eating out/ordering in, apparel, financial products, and services, entertainment, footwear, etc.
3.	Cautious planners	31–45 years	Stable incomes, well settled, growing children, securing future	7.9 million (83.2% men and 16.8% women)	19,489	Financial products/ services, eating out/ ordering in, apparel, loans, entertainment, etc.
4.	The home makers	26–60 years	Household's spending pattern	15.1 million	14,326	Financial products/ services, apparel, eating out/ordering in, loans, footwear, etc.

Source: Adapted from *Business World* (2008).

Table 5.7   Segmenting the youth

Name	Characteristics	Percentage spread
Cultural misfit	Have lost idealism, think that they can make no change for the better, have hence changed themselves. They adapt to the system rather than show dissent.	17
Style bhais	Concerned about one's looks, spend most of the time outside the house, partying. Still hold some conservative values.	21
Middle-class Manjus	Girls who spend most of their time at home, cooking or visiting places of worship. Conservative values but liberal. Attitudes towards opposite sex are different from others.	21
Main bhi NRI	Young, experimental with new trends and derive affirmation from peers.	16
Rich brats	Hold opposite values from their parents, sometimes even from their peers.	13
Nerdy Nandus	Time constrained, watch TV to spend time, always behind the trend, work hard to be successful and focused on climbing the ladder.	12

Source: Adapted from *Business World* (2005).

its services for them. If viewers log on to the site to look at the share prices, and want to look at the past financial history of various companies, they can do so at the same site. If they want to book tickets for a vacation abroad, they can use the same site to book air tickets in a link called, Travel. Hotel reservations can also be made from the same site. Apart from this, they can also book movie tickets and do some shopping from the same site (Raj 2006). *The Marketing Whitebook 2005* classifies the Indian youth into six segments (Table 5.7).

Personality   It is the unique psychological characteristic that leads to unvarying and lifelong responses to the environment. Personality is an important segmentation variable as people tend to make purchases according to their personality. Thus, Southwest Airlines has been specializing in humour for a long time and the airline's growing army of flight attendants—now numbering 7,000—includes a few actors, a stand-up comic, and hundreds of skilled amateurs. Thus, people who apart from seeking a low airfare, are fun-loving opt for this airline (Exhibit 5.3). It has achieved a growth rate of 8 per cent over the last decade, making it the only profitable major airline (Suskind 2003).

Behavioural Segmentation

In this type of segmentation buyers are grouped on the basis of their awareness, approach, and use of a service. On the basis of this, buyers can be segmented on the basis of—special occasion, benefits, usage, loyalty, and buyer readiness.

Special occasion segmentation   Buyers are divided into groups on the basis of circumstances when they make a purchase or use a service. This helps firms to build the service use. For example, for a weekend dinner a person might take his/her family to a neighbourhood restaurant, but if the occasion is a birthday or an anniversary celebration

Exhibit 5.3 Southwest Airlines

'Ok people, it's open seating, just like at church—saints up front, sinners in back', Yvonne LeMaster said into the flight attendant's microphone, as chuckling passengers filed from the ramp past the cockpit and tiny galley kitchen. 'Remember, this isn't a furniture store. You're only renting this seat for an hour.'

On Southwest Airlines Flight 639 from Baltimore/Washington International airport to Cleveland, Ms LeMaster's shtick marks a small milestone. Southwest's flight attendants, famous for their airborne stand-up routines, are cracking jokes again.

Co-founded 31 years ago by Herbert Kelleher, a Harley-Davidson-riding iconoclast, Southwest has been specializing in humour for a long time. Over the past decade, as the airline has experienced 8 per cent annual growth and has come to employ 35,000 people, generating laughs has become an official corporate goal, even a part of recruitment. 'Have you ever used humour to solve a workplace problem?' is a question asked in job interviews.

All of this corporate levity worked beautifully through the devil-may-care 1990s, as Southwest—a 'people mover' discount carrier that is now one of the only profitable major airlines—mined and enriched deposits of humour.

Then came 9/11. The laughter stopped on Southwest. No memo from headquarters was needed, though some were sent. 'It is evident that the usual Southwest humour should temporarily play a lesser role in our lives', said a memo dated 18 September 2001. The memo also included a list of cancelled activities, such as Halloween costumes on flight attendants and some regular gags played with passengers. In other words, humour was out of the question until further notice.

Last Spring, letters started to trickle in to the carrier's Dallas headquarters. Passengers said they missed the jokes. Southwest President Colleen Barrett decided the airline should wade in slowly. A memo distributed in late May last year read that, 'based on customer feedback and our take on the national mood, we think it is appropriate to resume the optional use of humour'. Beneath were listed guidelines, such as 'know your audience'—a 'friday night planeload to Las Vegas' compared with a 'weekday morning between business centres'. She also urged the crew to 'use common sense and good judgment', such as 'avoid references to politics, religion, bodily functions, and changes in the airline business since 9/11'. But it wasn't until after Thanksgiving that Southwest got back its groove.

In 16 A, Mark Rafferty, a 45-year old architect and fellow frequent flier, talked about how, on one recent Southwest flight, everyone laughed at a couple of good ones and then just started talking to each other. 'You could see it, row by row', he says. 'The plane was positively noisy, and it wasn't from the engines'.

Then the two men, both converts to Southwest, swapped in-flight favourites across the seat back. 'Oh yeah, there was a great one a few years ago', Mr Rafferty said, a bit later, 'They told everyone on the plane's left side, toward the terminal, to put their faces in the window and smile so our competitors can see what a full flight looks like.'

Source: Adapted from Suskind (2003).

they might go to a fine-dining restaurant such as 360°, Travertino, Bukhara, etc. to celebrate. Airline advertisements aimed at the business traveller often highlight discounts on the spouse's tickets, convenience, and on-time departure. Umaid Bhavan Palace, Jodhpur, a hotel managed by the Taj group, has used the special occasion of Holi festival to target prospective clients. People specially come to Umaid Bhavan Palace to celebrate the festival of Holi here with the present Maharaja, Gaj Singh and his family. This was highlighted during Bill Clinton's first visit to India in 2000, when he along with his daughter Chelsea, celebrated Holi at the hotel (Cherian 2000).

Benefits sought Marketers having an idea of the benefits the customers seek in the service can develop service features that match the benefits their customers are seeking and can communicate the same more effectively to the consumers. Keeping this in mind, various banks, insurance companies, and financial institutions are providing a complete set of financial solutions to cater to different financial needs of the customers. Banks are offering different types of services such as loans for higher studies, housing, computer, and automobile; insurance; pension schemes; kiddy bank (small) savings, etc. (Raj 2006).

Usage rate Customers can be grouped into light, medium, and heavy users. For example, mobile service providers, such as Vodafone and Airtel, provide different plans according to the usage rate of their service. They also provide corporate connections where, at a minimum number of connections they provide free incoming calls among the group and reduced rental plans. Many airlines provide frequent flyer programmes to ensure the continued patronage of their clients.

Loyalty status Segmenting on the basis of loyalty is very useful for organizations as they can then specifically target these customers to make them their brand advocates, i.e., people who are loyal and recommend the brand to friends. Also, if they know about the loyalty status of the customer they can specifically target the marketing strategies to move them up the loyalty ladder. Thus, customers who are brand loyal to Taj hotels will try to stay in a Taj hotel in the cities they visit.

Buyer readiness stage This implies the readiness of the customer to purchase a particular service. A customer might be unaware of the service, some are informed but are not in need of the service at a particular point of time, some want the service, and some are willing to buy it. It is the task of the marketer to move the consumers up this ladder to ultimately purchase the service. For example, at Pragati Maidan, Delhi, different fairs such as book fairs, job fairs, and financial fairs are organized. Various banks and financial institutions market different loans and financial services during such fairs. The idea is to inform customers about their presence and to move the prospective customer up the buyer readiness stage.

Effective Segmentation

The market is replete with great ideas turning into failures. For example, a few years ago, Videocon launched its picture-in-picture (PIP) concept, targeting it at the higher-end television segment in India. This allowed viewers to watch multiple channels at the same time. However, it did not take into account the limitations of the human brain, i.e., registering only one message at a time, and failed (Kumar 2006).

As is evident from the above discussion, there are many ways to segment a market but all are not equally effective for different services provided by different service owners. For a market segment to be useful it should have the following characteristics:

1. Measurable: This implies the degree to which the segment's size and purchasing power can be measured. The segmentation variable chosen should be easy to measure. For example, we have a lot of data available on demographics (see Tables 5.2, 5.3, and 5.4) and for a marketer targeting say, the women segment, it is easy to determine the segment size.

2. Accessible: It implies the degree to which the segment can be reached and served. Thus, a market, which can be easily accessed, is more lucrative for a marketer to target.

3. Sustainable: The segments should be large and profitable enough to serve as a market. For example, Pizza Hut planning to open its chains in Tier-II cities of India intends to reduce the price by 5–10 per cent as compared to its prices in metropolitan cities of India. This is because it knows that smaller cities have the required consumers with the spending capacity in a particular range and hence, wants to cash in on this segment.

4. Actionable: The segment should be large enough and feasible for the company to design programmes to attract and serve it. If the segment is small, then the cost dynamics involved will not make the action profitable.

Keeping the discussion on segmentation in mind it can be concluded that there is no single way to segment the market. A marketer can also use a combination of more than two ways to segment the market.

TARGETING

Once the market has been segmented, the marketers need to decide which segment they are going to focus their activities on. Thus, targeting is the choice of a single segment or group of segments that the organization wishes to select. Thus, it is actually a target sub-market or target segment (Masterson and Pickton 2004). Companies can evaluate and select market segments on the basis of—segment size and growth, segment structural attractiveness, or company objectives and resources. Once the segments have been evaluated the market to be targeted can be selected on the basis of—undifferentiated marketing, differentiated marketing, or concentrated marketing. For companies, the next step is to decide the market coverage strategy for the markets to be targeted.

Evaluating Market Segments

The study of segment size and growth, segment structural attractiveness, and company objectives and resources help us to evaluate market segments.

Segment size and growth   Before entering a segment, a company must first collect information on the current segment sales, growth rate, and expected profitability of various segments. So, if a firm has the skill and the resources it can target a segment which has a higher sales, growth rate, and profitability.

Segment structural attractiveness   A segment having a desirable size and growth may still not offer attractive profits. This depends upon a number of factors. Applying Porter's five-forces model, we can say the segment structural attractiveness depends upon:

Nature and number of competitors present   If the competitors are strong and aggressive, the segment is less attractive.

Substitute products   The presence of a number of substitute products may limit prices and profits, say, the presence of a number of motels may reduce the room rate of a hotel.

Bargaining power of buyers If the buyers in a segment have a strong bargaining power relative to suppliers they may demand more quality services at a lower price and set competitors against each other.

Bargaining power of suppliers If the suppliers are powerful, i.e., they are large and concentrated with few substitutes available, or the supplied product is an important ingredient of a dish, then the market is less attractive.

Threat of new entrants If a segment size and growth is attractive there is always the potential threat of new entrants.

Company objectives and resources After collecting the information on the different segments, a company must match it with its own objectives and resources. Segments may be tempting, but if they do not match with the long-term objectives of the firm they must be discarded straight away, otherwise they may divert the company's attention and resources from the main goal. If the segment fits the company's objectives but the company lacks the resources to compete effectively in the segment, it should not enter the segment. The company should enter a segment only if it can gain a sustainable advantage over its competitors.

Selecting Market Segments

After evaluating different segments the next step is for the company to select the target market, i.e., decide which and how many segments to serve. There are three types of market coverage strategies.

Undifferentiated or mass marketing This concentrates on the common needs of the buyers rather than the differences. Hence, it ignores the market segmentation differences and goes for the entire market with a single offer. For example, in the early 1990s Airtel and Essar promoted mobile services for the entire market without coming up with the different plans that are prevalent today.

Differentiated or segmentation marketing In differentiated marketing, a company targets several market segments while designing separate offers for each. For example, ITC has a chain of luxury hotels such as Maurya Sheraton and Towers on the one hand, and a chain of business budget hotels on the other, with a different marketing mix for each group.

Concentrated or niche marketing In this type of marketing a company goes for a large share of a small market instead of going for a small share of a large market. It is specifically appropriate for companies with limited resources and has proved beneficial for hospitality companies, as they have gained a strong marketing position due to a greater knowledge of the segments' needs. For example, Mahanagar Telephone Nigam Limited launched a mobile promotional plan called 'Trump Vidyarthi Plan' in 2007 to cater to the needs of students.

Customized or micro marketing In this type of marketing, the individual customer preference is important as the marketer specifically focuses on the needs of the individual customer and how to best satisfy these needs. For example, the business process

Table 5.8   Advantages and disadvantages of different targeting strategies

Targeting strategy	Advantages	Disadvantages
Undifferentiated targeting	▫ Cost economies and so potential savings on production/marketing costs ▫ Low market research and product development cost	▫ Unimaginative product offering ▫ Chances of failure high in today's competitive environment ▫ Heavy competition
Differentiated targeting	▫ Greater financial success as compared to undifferentiated targeting ▫ Economies of scale in production/marketing	▫ High costs for marketing, marketing research, forecasting, sales analysis, promotion planning, and advertising ▫ Cannibalization
Concentrated targeting	▫ Concentration of resources ▫ Can better meet the needs of a narrowly defined segment ▫ Allows some small firms to better compete with larger firms ▫ Strong positioning	▫ Segments too small or changing ▫ Large competitors may more effectively market to niche segment

Source: Adapted from Lamb et al. (2004) and Kotler et al. (2006).

outsourcing (BPO) industry caters to the specific requirements of different clients by deputing a specialized workforce. The advantages and disadvantages of the different market coverage strategies are summed up in Table 5.8.

Market Coverage Strategy

The target market selection involves the dynamic process of matching the changing variety of products and services with the changing variety of customer wants (Cadeaux 2004). According to Cadeaux (1997) the selection of target markets is a strategic and entrepreneurial process. Companies need to consider several factors while choosing a market coverage strategy. Some of these are described in this section.

Company's resources   When a company has limited resources, concentrated marketing makes the most sense.

Degree of product homogeneity   Products that can vary in design are more suited to differentiation or concentration whereas undifferentiated marketing is more suited to homogeneous products.

Product life cycle stages   When a firm introduces a new product it may be practical to launch only one version and then undifferentiated or concentrated marketing makes more sense, whereas in the mature stage, differentiated marketing is more feasible.

Market homogeneity   If buyers have the same taste, buy a product in the same quantity, and react similarly to marketing efforts, undifferentiated marketing is an appropriate strategy.

Competitor's marketing strategies When a competitor uses segmentation, undifferentiated marketing can be suicidal. Conversely, when competitors are pursuing undifferentiated marketing a firm can gain advantage by using differentiated or concentrated marketing.

POSITIONING

The concept of positioning coined by Jack Trout and Al Ries in 1969, came into prominence when they elaborated on it in 1972. In their famous treatise, *The Positioning Era Cometh,* the authors emphasized that positioning is the battle for a place in the consumer's mind. According to Ries and Trout (1981), positioning should not be confused with strategy, even though the two are inextricably related.

'Positioning starts with a product. A piece of merchandise, a service, a company, and institution, or even a person ... Positioning is not what you do to a product. It is what you do to the mind of the prospect. That is, you position the product in the mind of the prospect.'

Theodore Levitt (1980) argued that all goods and services are differentiable and there is no such thing as a commodity. All marketing strategies involve a search for a competitive advantage (Hunt and Arnett 2004). Rosser Reeves has defined positioning as 'The art of selecting, out of a number of unique selling propositions, the one which will get you maximum sales.'

Scanlon (1994) defined positioning as, 'The act of defining the product's image and value offer so that the segment's customers understand and appreciate what the product stands for in relation to its competitors.' Kotler (1984) defined positioning as, 'Arranging for a product to occupy a clear, distinctive, and desirable place in the market, and in the minds of target consumers'. Thus, we see that all the experts treat positioning as the image of the product in the mind of the consumers as well as how they are unique or different from the competitors.

Consumers are overloaded with information about products and services. A product's position is the way it is defined by consumers on important attributes—the place the product occupies in consumer's minds relative to competing products. Marketers do not want to leave their product's position to chance. They plan positions that will give their products the greatest advantage in selected target markets and then design marketing mixes to create the planned positions. According to Kotler and Bes (2003), positioning creates differentiated brand personality even within the same market and also allows the brand to be positioned differently in different markets. Positioning can be related to logical, functional, symbolic, and experiential aspects of the service provided. There are three steps to effective positioning:

1. Identify a set of potential competitive advantages to exploit.
2. Select, define, and refine the most appropriate set of product attributes.
3. Effectively communicate the product's position to the desired market.

Positioning Strategies

A brand manager has an entire range of differentiating strategies to decide on the position of his/her service. He/she must choose a strategy, which holds a niche in the market and serves a competitive advantage. These strategies revolve around different aspects of the brand and according to Sengupta (2003), this can be expressed as four strategic questions.

1. Who am I?
2. What am I?
3. For whom am I?
4. Why me?

Who am I? This concerns the corporate credentials of the brand. The prospect thinks of the brand in terms of the stable from which it comes, which can give the brand a competitive advantage. For example, the UB group extended the name of its best-selling beer Kingfisher to its airline and got a competitive advantage.

What am I? The functional capabilities of the service are related to in this aspect. The strategies in this can be grouped as follows:

Category-related positioning When an existing category is crowded, the same service can be positioned in another category. For example, Haryana Tourism offers a set of hotels in Haryana and has categorized them based on adventure, pilgrimage, and golf. Adventure tourism has been further classified as parasailing, rock climbing, canoeing, etc.

Benefit-related positioning A service, which offers more than one benefit, is bound to attract more customers. Thus, we have business hotels that offer conferencing and banqueting facilities too. But if the benefits are large it might leave a vague and diffused imprint on the customer's mind.

Positioning by usage, occasion and time of use A good usage positioning has accounted for the success of many services. Banking firms have come up with different types of loans keeping this in mind. For example, State Bank of India (SBI) offers different types of loans for different household items. SBI organizes loan melas for farmers at the time of purchase of seeds for sowing. The bank thus uses a positioning strategy based on occasion. The time of use has resulted in banks setting up special counters for deposits of income tax during the last dates of filing of returns.

Price–quality positioning This concept occupies great importance in developing economies such as India. Within the last few years a number of low-cost carriers have positioned themselves on the basis of price–quality.

For whom am I? This involves positioning the service according to the target segment. Thus, it would apply to all the consumer-based segmentation variables discussed.

Why me? This tells the consumer why he/she should choose a particular service over the other alternatives present in the market. This allows a company to tell the consumers how they are best suited for them.

Physical attribute differentiation The heritage hotels in Rajasthan, which are conversions of old forts into hotels, differentiate themselves on the basis of their physical attributes. Taj Lake Palace at Udaipur, built in the seventeenth century and run by the Taj group of hotels, is an example of physical attribute differentiation wherein an elegant fantasy in white marble rises out of the turquoise waters of the Pichola Lake.

Service differentiation Providing services that benefit the target market can also provide a competitive advantage. Unwanted differentiation occurs when a company consistently provides terrible service. Many commodity companies are also realizing the importance of service differentiation. For example, Maruti Suzuki has lately positioned itself as having the largest number of service stations in India. Exhibit 5.4 shows how a number of pre-school educational centres brand toddler education.

Personnel differentiation Hiring and retaining better people than the competitors can provide a strong competitive advantage. This also includes training the staff so that they are polite, forthcoming, and respectful. They must understand the customer needs and respond quickly to them.

Location differentiation Location can provide a strong competitive advantage. Hotels located on the main road on any hill station are at a competitive advantage but Green Breeze Resort, Barlowganj, Mussoorie presents its location of being away from the crowded mall, as a competitive advantage. For example, Taj Exotica and Cidade De Goa (facing the Arabian Sea) use their location as a competitive advantage.

Exhibit 5.4 Branding toddler education

Today's competitive times are witnessing the emergence of a number of branded pre-school educational centres. This is also due to the availability of huge incomes and parents looking at pre-school education more seriously. As more and more organized chains enter the market, the focus on branding and positioning is bound to gain importance. Eurokids has 450 playschools and will add another 200 by next year. Kidzee, a Zee Network venture, has 418 operational and 120 signed-up playschools. Apart from these national big players, there are regional players such as Kangaroo Kids in Mumbai, Shamrock in Delhi, and Apple Kids in Tamil Nadu.

According to the managing director of one of the national chains, since this is a service industry, branding is vital as it creates and builds confidence. Today, the choice of a pre-school is a detailed and well thought out selection by parents, which makes competitive positioning all the more important. Since there is no prescribed syllabus for pre-school education there exists a huge opportunity for these chains to differentiate themselves. It is also true that

they basically offer the same thing and end up copying each other. But Kidzee and Eurokids insist that they have uniquely positioned themselves in the market. Eurokids positions itself as 'the pre-school specialist' and Kidzee claims to 'identify and nurture the unique potential in the child'.

These pre-school chains have to advertise in order to create differentiated competitive positioning in the market. Eurokids spends about 10 per cent of its revenues on marketing, and usually uses women's publications such as Femina, Woman's Era, and Good Housekeeping for its print advertisements. The advertising takes place at a national (to promote the brand) and local level (to promote the branch or admissions). Association with shows, such as Sa Re Ga Ma Pa Little Champs, also gives them huge visibility. The fees range from Rs 300 per month for lower-end to Rs 3,000 per month for the higher-end segment. There is no doubt that this sector is going to become more intense as the expectations of parents increase and competition reaches a higher level.

Source: Adapted from Turakhia (2008).

Image differentiation   Image provides a competitive advantage for a product or a service by creating a unique image in the mind of the consumer. The image builds a distinct perception of the product/service in the consumer's mind. For example, there are a number of hotels built in old palaces in Rajasthan, but Umaid Bhavan Palace, Jodhpur, run by the Taj group, differentiates itself as the largest residential palace wherein the present maharaja still resides, and if the guests are lucky they can interact with him, making their experience an interesting one.

Selecting the Right Competitive Advantage

An organization may have several competitive advantages. For example, Taj Exotica, Goa may have a location advantage, personnel advantage, and service advantage, but it has to select the one on which to build the positioning strategy. However, a company can choose more than one competitive advantage too. Rosser Reeves was of the opinion that companies should identify only one unique selling proposition and project itself as number one on that attribute. It is very important that a company also delivers what it proclaims. If it is able to do this, it will get good word-of-mouth recommendations and repeat patronage. Some companies may opt for more than one competitive advantage for their positioning, the advantage being that they can attract customers for each category. However, the disadvantage can be that it may confuse the customers. In general, there are some positioning errors a company must avoid. These are:

Under-positioning   When companies fail to position their services it is referred to as under-positioning. For example, stand-alone restaurants in India never position themselves.

Over-positioning   When companies project a very narrow picture to the buyers it is referred to as over-positioning.

Confused positioning   When a company tries many ways to position its services leaving the customer confused as to what ultimately it stands for, it results in confused positioning.

Distinguishing a Brand from its Competitors

Hunt and Arnett (2004) have grounded the market segmentation strategy and the competitive advantage in the resource–advantage theory. The theory maintains that competitive advantage leads to superior financial performance and this competitive advantage can be obtained by providing more value in the market offering at a lower cost (Fig. 5.5).

According to Hunt and Arnett (2004), competition is the constant struggle among firms for comparative advantage in resources that will yield competitive positions in the marketplace, and hence, superior financial performance. Considering the competitive matrix for segment A in Fig. 5.5, a firm will have an advantage in the marketplace if the market offering has:

1. Superior perceived value as compared to rivals' marketing offer at a cost lower than the competitors (Cell 3A).

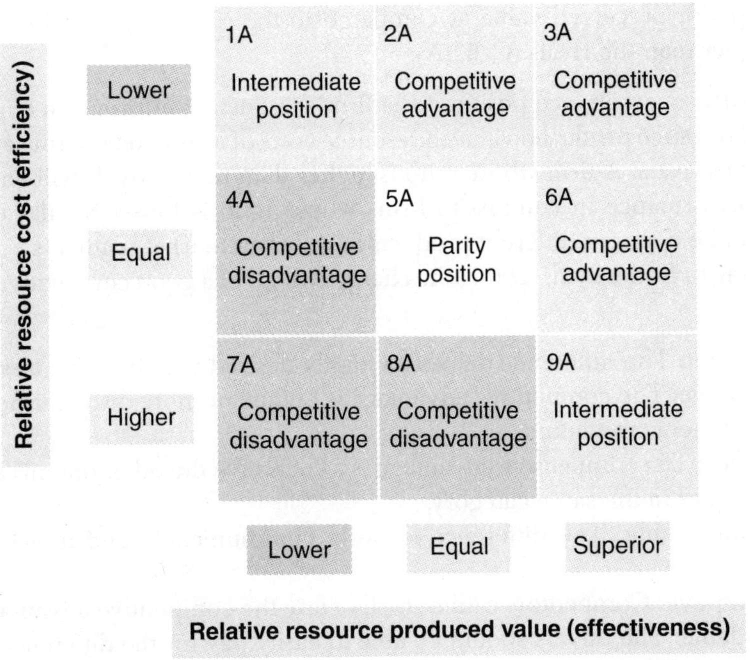

Source: Adapted from Hunt and Arnett (2004).

Fig. 5.5 Competitive position matrix

2. Superior perceived value as compared to rivals' marketing offer at the same cost as rivals (Cell 6A).
3. Perceived value equal to rivals' marketing offer at a price lower than the rivals (Cell 2A).

These positions of competitive advantage lead to enhanced financial performance. A firm is at a disadvantage if it produces a market offering that has:

1. Lower perceived value as compared to the rivals' marketing offer at the same cost as rivals (Cell 4A).
2. Lower perceived value as compared to the rivals' marketing offer at a cost higher than the rivals (Cell 7A).
3. Value equal to the rivals' marketing offer but at a cost higher than the rivals (Cell 8A).

At these positions the firm is at a disadvantage and this leads to inferior financial performance. Apart from these positions of advantage and disadvantage two further positions are possible. These are when the firm produces a market offering, which has:

1. Lower perceived value compared to the rivals' market offerings at a cost lower than the rivals (Cell 1A).

2. Superior perceived value as compared to the rivals' market offering at a cost higher than the rivals (Cell 9A).

In these two marketplace positions the firm's financial performance depends upon the ratio of resource produced value to resource costs of its market offering as compared to those of its rivals. A firm whose ratio is higher than that of rivals will have superior financial performance in contrast to firms whose ratio is lower. Similar competitive analysis can be done for different products in different market segments.

According to Kotler et al. (2006), the characteristics of a good competitive advantage can be:

- Important: The difference delivers a highly desired benefit to the target buyers.
- Distinctive: The competitive advantage is unique or more distinguished than that of the other competitors.
- Superior: The competitive advantage is a cut above the other options available to a customer in the same category.
- Communicable: The difference is easily communicable and noticeable to the buyers.
- Pre-emptive: Competitors cannot easily copy the competitive advantage.
- Affordable: The buyers should be able to easily pay for the difference.
- Profitable: The company should be able to introduce the difference and still be profitable.

Some competitive advantages may be too insignificant, too costly, or not in agreement with the company profile. Thus, the competitive advantage must be chosen with great care. If the company keeps the above points in mind vis-à-vis the objectives and goals of the company, it can choose a competitive advantage that makes the most sense.

Perceptual Mapping

Each brand has a set of competitive advantages, the effective communication of which helps the consumers form a mental image of the product and is thought of as occupying a certain position in the consumer's 'perceptual space'. The favourite means of describing this image is perceptual mapping.

Perceptual mapping is a means of exhibiting in two or more dimensions, the place the product or brand occupies in the consumer's mind. It generally refers to techniques used to represent this product space graphically. We can create a number of maps from the same data, using a different pair of dimensions. Hence, each such map will represent a different context (Semon 1994). In general, marketers have two broad objectives in mind when undertaking perceptual mapping. These are to:

- determine where a target brand is positioned versus the competition.
- help identify product attributes, which are the key determinants in influencing customer choice for the product class.

Determinant attributes are those that are important to customers, and also exhibit differences across brands. Even if a product attribute is very important, if brands are not

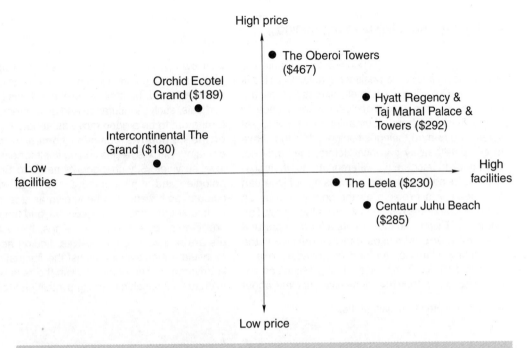

Fig. 5.6 Perceptual map of five-star deluxe hotels in Mumbai, India*

* The information on rates and facilities available were collected from the websites of the various hotels in May 2008.

perceived to differ on that attribute, then the attribute will not be influential in customers' choice decisions. Often, the determining aspects of a product are latent, unobservable constructs, which include a number of manifest, observable attributes. Perceptual mapping techniques can be very useful in uncovering these latent dimensions (Kohli and Leuthesser 1993).

The perceptual mapping of the five-star deluxe hotels in Mumbai has been illustrated in Fig. 5.6. On this map, the positions are essentially neutral. Hence, one location on the map does not necessarily have to be better or worse than another position (Kotler et at. 2006). Increased competition can make a re-positioning strategy necessary. Changing situations also warrant a re-positioning strategy by firms (Exhibit 5.5).

Another example of re-positioning is McDonald's restaurants in Europe. To counter the fast food, drive-through image and create a more sit-down eating experience, McDonald's conducted an experiment in a German hamlet 15 miles south of Munich. The sales of this two-storey restaurant, where the makeover finished, have grown 22 per cent. According to Michael Heinritzi, owner and operator of 30 McDonald's franchises in southern Germany including this one, the customers like the new concept and clients now include businesspeople who drop by in the morning for a coffee. McDonald's has revamped 2,000 of its 6,400 eateries across Europe, which is the second biggest market outside North America. According to Denis Hennequin, 'Re-imaging is important in the fast-moving competitive world of retail' (Sekhri 2007).

Exhibit 5.5   Meaningful re-positioning

Information technology (IT) companies in India are experiencing a lot of re-positioning activities. This is mainly due to falling dollar rates, increased pressure on prices, and the impact of globalization. Hence, to stay ahead of others, companies will have to re-invent and re-map their positioning. While they have to compete heavily on price factors, they may not want price to become the differentiator for their customers. Being typecast as addressing a niche can also become a problem as the company may be seeking to address new industries as they grow. The domestic IT sector in India offers a lot of opportunities and new businesses can be reached if the clients have clarity on the service provider's expertise and offerings. The problem that growing companies face is that they are themselves unclear about

their own positioning strategies and end up giving varied internal communication that reflects on to the external world. Mastek re-positioned itself around verticals, such as insurance and government, which turned out to be a good move as about 70 per cent of the company's business comes from these domains. Citrix is re-positioning itself for enterprise-level services. Sify changed its name to Sify Technologies and implemented a new logo with new colours, as it wanted to be known as a technology company providing IT services, beyond the Internet and e-commerce capabilities. Thus, these IT players are re-inventing themselves, finding new ways to insulate themselves against the fluctuating market dynamics. The ones who win the race will have to create sustainable brand and intellectual property.

Source: Adapted from Jain (2008).

SUMMARY

To be successful, an organization should focus on the target market's needs and requirements. It should shape the product offering based on this analysis. Segmentation, targeting, and positioning helps to focus on the needs of the market and align the company's resources to get the competitive advantage in the market. For a firm to have a longer and profitable innings in the market, the marketing mix should be based on the above mentioned strategies. If marketers

indulge in this activity at the inception level, then the whole marketing plan is clear and leads to profitable courses of action. However, this needs to be reviewed at periodic intervals to cater to changing customer preferences, new competitions in the market, and new opportunities available. Segmentation, targeting, and positioning are extremely important for a company to become profitable.

KEY TERMS

Differentiated marketing   This refers to a marketing exercise in which the marketer selects more than one target market and then develops a separate marketing mix for that segment.

Mass marketing/undifferentiated marketing The type of marketing where the producer produces in bulk, distributes in bulk, and promotes the same to all consumers.

Micro marketing   Databases and the Internet have allowed sellers to target small needs of individual customers. The marketing for these small segments with distinctive needs is known as micro marketing.

Positioning   After targeting a segment, the marketer needs to position the product or service in customers' minds. It refers to the battle for the target consumer's mind space.

Product variety marketing In this type of marketing, the seller produces two or more products or services having different features, style, quality, etc.

Segmentation The process of dividing the market into distinct groups having similar characteristics, needs, purchasing behaviour, geography,

psychographics, etc. These people tend to react to the marketing mix in a similar manner.

Target marketing In this type of marketing the seller segments the market, targets a particular segment, and develops products and services for this segment.

Targeting This step follows the segmentation strategy and means choosing a single segment or group of segments, towards whom the marketing mix will be targeted.

CONCEPT REVIEW QUESTIONS

1. List and define the three stages of target marketing.

2. Discuss the different levels of market segmentation.

3. Explain how companies identify attractive market segments and choose a market coverage strategy.

4. Differentiate between segmentation and positioning.

5. What is positioning? Discuss its importance in the success of a firm.

6. In the competitive position matrix, when is a firm at an advantage in the marketplace?

7. Discuss perceptual mapping and its role in marketing strategies.

CRITICAL THINKING QUESTIONS

1. You have to market a low-cost air carrier in India. Choose your market segmentation criteria giving reasons for the same.

2. You have to market car loans in India. Which targeting strategies are you going to use and why?

3. You are launching a new budget hotel chain in India. What will be your target market and how will you position the hotel vis-à-vis the competitors present in the market?

4. You are in the insurance sector. How will you segment the Indian market for the sales of children's policies?

INTERNET EXERCISES

1. Collect information from the Internet and conduct a demographic segmentation for selling insurance policies in China. (You may choose the type of insurance policy you want to market.)

2. Download details of a business budget hotel's chain in India. Do the perceptual mapping for

the same. What conclusions can you draw from it?

3. Visit the websites of two banking organizations. Compare how they have positioned themselves. What suggestions can you give them to improve their market performance?

CASE STUDY

The Rising Baroda Sun: Reaching the Global Customers*

Bank of Baroda, in an effort to reach global customers and increase its customer base, is repositioning itself with a new logo and a celebrity brand ambassador—Rahul Dravid. The article discusses the journey of the transformation and its effects.

When Maharaja Sayajirao Gaikwad III established the Bank of Baroda in 1908, he could not have known that a hundred years down the line the logo he chose with such care would be changed in the blink of an eye. And the reason stated would be that the old logo was not in sync with the market conditions. The question one may ask is how can a hundred-year old logo be out of place in an industry that is just as old. When the Bank's top management in 2002 sought the answer to this question, the answer was an eye-opener to say the least.

Since its inception the Bank of Baroda has been one of the most prominent banks in the India banking industry. Restricted to the Baroda region in the pre-independence days, the bank expanded rapidly once Baroda was merged with the Indian Union. Its blue-coloured logo depicted an ear of corn and a cogwheel (symbolizing agriculture and industry), and an upraised hand, which blessed the populace stating 'akshayyam te bhavishyati' ('thou shall forever be prosperous' with Bank of Baroda) (Exhibit 5.6). During the phase of nationalization that the Indian banking industry experienced after the 1960s, the Bank of Baroda remained one of the premier banks of the country.

When India liberalized its economy in 1991, the banking sector was opened to private as well as foreign participation. The industry witnessed an influx of new players; amongst them were some of the leaders of our current times, namely, ICICI bank and HDFC bank. Others were renewed foreign banks. Public sector banks (PSBs) like Bank

Exhibit 5.6 Bank of Baroda's old logo

Source: The Economic Times (Brand Equity), 2006.

of Baroda, which until liberalization had operated in an environment of 'symbiotic existence', suddenly found themselves in the midst of a cut-throat market where each player was trying to grab the largest piece of the consumer pie. The new banks leveraged technology and customer-centric practices to boost their market share while, public sector banks, burdened by NPAs (non-performing assets), powerful employee unions that prevented layoffs, and obsolete technology, were unable to keep pace with the changes. The government-owned banks are estimated to have lost 12 to 15 per cent of their customers to private players during the late 1990s. But the one unreplicable advantage that public sector banks continue to have over the Indian private banks is the large network of branches that they established during the 1970s and 80s. Try as they may, banks like ICICI, HDFC, and ABN Amro have found themselves at a loss in their attempts (not the least of which was the signing of Amitabh Bachchan as ICICI's brand ambassador) to overcome this disadvantage. But today, the PSBs have finally awoken. At least that is the message being sent out by the new top management at Bank of

---

* N.J. and R.S. Rathore (2006), 'The rising Baroda sun: Reaching the global customers', *Effective Executive*, July, ICFAI University Press 2006. Reprinted with permission.

Exhibit 5.7 Bank of Baroda's market share (%)

Year Ended March	Deposits	Advances
2000	5.07	5.10
2001	4.69	4.80
2002	4.58	5.00
2003	4.60	4.19
2004	4.03	3.65
2005	4.07	3.26

Source: Bank of Baroda

Baroda. After realizing that the Bank's market share had declined by almost 20 per cent over a six-year period from 2000 to 2005 (Exhibit 5.7), Bank of Baroda commissioned research consultants IMRB and ORG-MARG to conduct market studies.

Both the firms confirmed the growing suspicion that Bank of Baroda was no longer a part of the 'consideration set' among the young and upcoming Indian consumer segment. Its 'mind share' was declining. The Bank's clientele was ageing and its logo, which may have been relevant in the early years of independence, had no salience, no recall value, and weak brand equity (Exhibit 5.10).

In a 'best banks' ranking published by Business Today, Bank of Baroda was ranked 32nd and in India's 'top service brands' ranking published by The Economic Times, it was ranked at 22nd in 2004. Dipankar Mookerjee, Head of Marketing at Band of Baroda, says, 'one very startling thing in our research was that the guys who were with us were very happy. In fact, we were perceived to be one of the friendliest public sector banks. If that was the case why were the accounts not growing? Why was the business not growing? We believe the answer lies in the fact that new accounts were not coming to us because we were not visible; we were not making enough noise in the marketplace. Something about us didn't allow us to break out of this public sector

clutter'. The Bank's management believed that the answer to this dilemma was an organization-wide re-branding exercise.

Dr Anil K. Khandelwal, CMD of Bank of Baroda and the brain behind the history-making re-branding exercise said, 'I think the timing was very ripe. This has been one of the prime banks in the public sector space. At that time, analysts and equity researchers were writing a lot of concerns about the bank; that the bank is not IT savvy because our IT project was delayed, the bank's advances growth was quite slow compared to other banks, and the bank's image was one of the government banks. Even one of the Gartner marketing experts, who had undertaken a study, revealed that the bank could do a lot in terms of marketing efforts. So I think that the timing was absolutely right'.

An Arthur Andersen study, which affirmed the growing importance of intangibles (part of which comprised a brand) in the market valuations of a company, also reiterated this line of thought. Once the proactive board of Bank of Baroda was convinced of the necessity for re-branding, the proposal received the green signal.

Bangalore-based brand consultants Ray+Keshavan were roped in to design a new logo. They came up with the vermilion coloured Baroda sun. Says Sujatha Keshavan, 'Our mandate was to make the process of transformation that the bank was going through, real, tangible, and visible to all stakeholders; customers, investors, and employees. As a symbol the sun is immensely powerful; it enables life and sustains it. It is universally understood, from small villages in India to countries across the globe. It is also timeless. Its integration with the letterform "B" makes it unique to Bank of Baroda, the Baroda sun' (Exhibit 5.8).

Next, the positioning dilemma of the bank was addressed. In an age when marketing gurus were clamouring for the importance of brand differentiation, Bank of Baroda was a bank for 'all purpose, all reason, all people, all times'. To remedy the situation, the bank's management approached Percept/H, a well-known Mumbai based

---

Exhibit 5.8   The new logo

o The intended significance of the sun.
o The sun is one of the most recognizable symbols the world over and it enables and nurtures life.
o The morning sun is symbolic of change—a change from night to day.
o The sun's five rays symbolize the global presence of the Bank of Baroda, in the sense that the rays fall across the five continents where Bank of Baroda operates.
o The vermillion colour symbolizes loyalty in India where married Hindu women wear it as a mark of loyalty to their husbands.
o The new logo is at an angle, to represent the dynamic nature of the bank.

Source: Bank of Baroda

Exhibit 5.9   Reaching new milestones

Performance highlights: 2005–06

Net profit: Rs 827 crore -Up from Rs 677 crore	Total business: Rs 153,574 crore -Up by 2312%
Gross NPA: 3.90% -Down from 7.30%	Net NPA: 0.87% Down from 1.45%
Business per employee: Rs 3.96 crore -Up from Rs 3.16 crore	Capital adequacy ratio: 13.65% -Up from 12.61%
Book value per share: Rs 209.18 -Up from Rs 183.83	Return on Average Net Worth: 15.25% -Up from 13.18%
No. of customers: 27 million -Up from 25 million	□ 8 am to 8 pm banking (over 500 branches) □ 24-hour human banking (select branches) □ More than 650 interconnected ATMs □ Over 125 branches under core banking □ Over 110 Baroda MoneyPlex outlets for retail loans □ Multicity cheque facility across 15 centres

---

advertising firm, to create a distinct positioning statement. At a time when its competitors were trying to establish an emotive connect with the Indian consumer by branding themselves as a friendly neighbourhood bank or good people to bank with, Percept/H capitalized on the idea to use Bank of Baroda's superior international network to differentiate it from its peers. And the result was that Bank of Baroda beat two distinguished competitors (State Bank of India and Bank of India) to stake a claim to the title, 'India's international bank' (Exhibit 5.9).

Rejuvenated from having completed a re-branding initiative at a smaller PSB called the Dena Bank (part of which was using actor Juhi Chawla as the bank's brand ambassador), Dr Khandelwal also proposed a brand ambassador for Bank of Baroda. Likely candidates for the job were suggested in-house. The two shortlisted candidates were from the fields of India's two most popular pastimes—movies and cricket, former Miss Universe and Bollywood actress Sushmita Sen, and cricketing maestro Rahul Dravid, whose international status and popularity with the average Indian consumer almost guaranteed him the Baroda job. Says Dr Khandelwal, 'The public trust, faith about the bank, its solidity, and its consistency, is very important. In Rahul Dravid we found

a complete match. Rahul Dravid is a very stable, dependable man of crisis in Indian cricket. We found that Bank of Baroda too has been consistent in giving profits ever since inception. Rahul Dravid has not been in any controversy, he is a very straight person, he has not been in any scam or match fixing. And the Bank of Baroda is also a scam-free bank. Rahul Dravid is an international star. He is known as much in India as abroad. Bank of Baroda is also an international bank and we were branding it as India's international bank. Finally, Rahul Dravid plays both one-day and test cricket with the same élan and we believe BoB

Exhibit 5.10 Brand equity pyramid

BOB	North Del+Jal+Inc	South Chennai	East Kolkata	West Mum+Baroda
Bonding	4%	2%	3%	5%
Advantage	19%	4%	14%	22%
Performance	36%	8%	33%	33%
Relevance	38%	8%	36%	34%
Presence	47%	13%	49%	38%
SBI				
Bonding	29%	20%	32%	1%
Advantage	80%	61%	60%	65%
Performance	84%	72%	83%	67%
Relevance	87%	74%	86%	68%
Presence	92%	81%	98%	72%
Base: Total sample	**(1186)**	**(216)**	**(550)**	**(1101)**

BoB-Weak Pyramid, Particularly in South

Bonding-Can any other Bank beat it?

Advantage-Does the bank have any advantage?

Performance-Is the performance of the bank satisfactory.

Relevance-Does the bank cater to the respondent?

Presence-Does the respondent know about the bank?

also undertakes rural banking and international banking with the same excellence. We found that the personality fit between the brand ambassador and the institution was complete'. The bank offered him a contract worth Rs 5 crore.

With plans of going in for a public issue in July 2005, Dr Khandelwal proposed (and Mookerjee agreed to) 6 June 2005 as the date of the new logo launch. Dr Khandelwal says, 'I don't know but one day I just decided that on 6 June, we are going to launch the new logo. I don't know where I thought of 6 June, but my experience about the public sector told me that there has to be a certain degree of positive restlessness. You give clear deadlines and everyone runs after that. The moment you only show the intent to do a thing Parkinson's Law applies and you are only chasing people'. The rest, as they say, is history. With 53 days until D-day, the seven-member marketing team of Mookerjee swung into action. The entire re-branding exercise was coordinated from the Baroda corporate centre at Mumbai.

But the path of organizational transformation is never easy; nor is changing a 97-year old logo. Protests from both within and outside the organization were inevitable. Letters were sent to the CMD and even a suit was filed in court objecting to the changes being brought about at the bank, specifically with reference to the logo change. Local press, especially in Baroda, expressed apprehensions about the old values being replaced and things at the bank changing for the worse. There was also widespread resistance from within the organization. Forty-seven being the average age of the bank's employees, many of them had nurtured the logo for at least 25 years. Milind Nadkarni, General Secretary of All India Bank of Baroda Employees' Federation, said, 'When this new logo came, my first reaction was "sacrilege"...just as somebody tarnishing the "Gita"...or may be somebody playing foul with the "Quran". I think many of us, people who have put in more than three decades of service, felt that kind of emotion'.

To address these issues, Dr Khandelwal dispatched letters to each one of the bank's 40,000 employees explaining the 'why, what, when, where, and how' of re-branding. Simultaneously, the marketing department conducted various seminars across the organization. Mookerjee himself visited all of the bank's major zones and regions counselling the managers and trainers, and addressing their points of concern. These managers were in turn asked to explain the idea and need for re-branding to their subordinates and address their misgivings.

Meanwhile, preparations for the brand launch were underway at the bank. The work required to be completed was extensive and the time allotted for completion was impossibly short. Both the external as well as the internal image of the bank required an overhaul. This included changing the external signages at more than 2700 of the bank's branches, corporate applications (business cards, business forms, letterheads, envelopes, memos, files, and folders, etc.), and transaction-related applications (forms, pass book, cheque book, DD format, etc.). The mandate from the CMD's office was clear—the old logo should never resurface after the brand launch, especially in dealings with the customers.

Each member of the marketing department was assigned a specific task. While some were made responsible for changing everything associated with the old logo, others were put in charge of communicating the changing face of the bank to as large an audience as possible. The biggest and costliest job of all was ensuring signage conversion at every branch before the deadline. To coordinate the work, brand champions were appointed at the regional level. 3M, arguably the world's largest and best material supplier, was selected to provide the material for the signages, and eleven converters across the country were chosen to manufacture them. Once these were affixed at the bank branches, they were covered so as to be unveiled across the country on the day of the launch. Meanwhile, print and television ads were developed. Financial, educational, and regional dailies, magazines with large circulations, most visible and prominent centres to display hoardings, and high traffic websites were identified. Three television spots featuring Rahul Dravid, to be aired after the brand launch, were picturized.

The brand launch itself was held in the ballroom at the Hilton Towers hotel in Mumbai. Dignitaries like the grandson of Maharaja Sayajirao Gaikwad III, film producer Yash Chopra and Rahul Dravid himself, apart from the Baroda crowd attended the function.

The brand launch is not the 'be all and end all' of the re-branding at the Bank of Baroda. Dr Khandelwal says, 'BoB had tremendous strength. Its exceptional overseas presence, its human resources, and its strong standing, had not been leveraged because somewhere the ignition was missing. Branding provided that ignition, the point, that could create tremendous amount of motivation in staff, tremendous amount of expectations from customers, and also a certain degree of curiosity in the people as to what is happening in the Bank of Baroda'. Soon after the brand was launched, then the Finance Minister of India, P. Chidambaram, inaugurated 201 new ATMs of the bank. Within a year (March 2005–February 2006), the bank's ATM network had increased from 160 to 600. The bank is also ahead amongst its peers in terms of the number of '8 am to 8 pm branches' and 24-hour banking. Keeping in line with the tagline, 'India's international bank', Dr Khandelwal plans on expanding the Bank's international network to 30-plus countries from the present 21 countries.

Accolades have been pouring in, in the form of appreciation letters from customers and media coverage. ONGC Chairman Subir Raha and noted journalist Sucheta Dalal are known to have appreciated Bank of Baroda's new logo. Undoubtedly, re-branding has boosted the bank's visibility by ten-fold, and infused vibrancy and vigour among the bank's employees. Chidambaram has not only publicly praised Khandelwal's leadership but has also named Bank of Baroda as one of the five strong PSBs shortlisted for leading consolidation in the Indian banking industry.

But has the re-branding been as successful as the Bank would want us to believe? Scepticism abounds. A former Andhra Bank employee was of the opinion that the Indian consumer would not be fooled by Bank of Baroda's new positioning. Some customers also complained that nothing except the external décor had changed at their respective branches.

Meanwhile, Dr Khandelwal does not appear too worried. He says, 'Leadership is the key; leaders have to be grounded in reality. They may have a ninth cloud vision but their feet should be on ground. That's what makes all the difference'.

SELECT REFERENCES

Business World, 'The Income Pyramid', *The Marketing Whitebook 2007–08*, pp. 31–33.

Business World, *The Marketing Whitebook 2005*.

Cadeaux, J.M. (1997), 'Counter-revolutionary forces in the information revolution: Entrepreneurial action, information intensity, and market transformation', *European Journal of Marketing*, vol. 31, no. 11/12, pp. 768–785.

Cadeaux, J.M. (2004), 'A commentary on Hunt and Arnett's Paper—Market segmentation strategy, competitive advantage, and public policy: Grounding segmentation strategy in resource-advantage theory', *Australian Marketing Journal*, vol. 12, no. 1, pp. 26–29.

Catlin, Jenny (2004), 'Marketing to children', *Marketing Mastermind*, February 2005, pp. 45–51.

Lamb, Charles, Joseph Hair, and Carl McDaniel (2004), *Marketing*, Thomson South-Western, Singapore.

Cherian, John (2000), 'The red carpet all the way', *Frontline*, New Delhi, vol. 17, no. 7.

Disney Adventures (2007), 'Promotional offer insert McDonald's', *Disney Adventures*, vol. 1, no. 4.

Festervand, Troy A. (2004), 'Industrial recruitment and economic development: A comparative analysis of competing South-eastern cities using perceptual mapping', *Journal of Business and Industrial Marketing*, vol. 9, no. 7, p. 460.

FH&RA India, 'Indian hotel industry survey, 2004–2005', *HVS International*, New Delhi.

Ganguly, Dibyendu (2006), 'Makeover mania', *Economic Times,* New Delhi, 10 November 2006.

Hunt, Shelby D. and Dennis B. Arnett (2004), 'Market segmentation strategy, competitive advantage, and public policy: Grounding segmentation strategy in resource-advantage Theory', *Australian Marketing Journal*, vol. 12, no. 1, pp. 7–21.

Jain, S. (2008), 'Meaningful re-positioning', *Hindustan Times*, New Delhi, 1 May 2008, p. 30.

Johnston, Robert (1996), 'Achieving focus in service organizations', *The Service Industries Journal*, January, vol. 16, no. 1, pp. 10–20.

Kohli, C.S. and L. Leuthesser (1993), 'Product positioning: A comparison of perceptual mapping techniques', *The Journal of Product and Brand Management*, vol. 2, no. 4, pp. 10–19.

Kotler, Philip and Fernando Trias de Bes (2003), *Lateral Thinking*, John Wiley and Sons, New Jersey.

Kotler, Philip, John T. Bowen, and J.C. Makens (2006), *Marketing for Hospitality and Tourism*, Chapter 8, Pearson Education Inc., New Jersey.

Kumar, V.V. Ravi (2006), 'The niche marketer', *Marketing Mastermind*, May, pp. 29–32.

Lovelock, Christopher and Jochen Wirtz (2006), *Services Marketing*, 5th edn, Pearson Education, New Delhi, Chapter 3.

Masterson, Rosalind and David Pickton (2004), *Marketing: An Introduction*, The McGraw-Hill Companies, Berkshire, Chapter 4, p. 110.

Mehra, Puja and Sandeep Unnithan (2005), 'Airborne Indians', *India Today*, 11 July.

Mohnot, S.R. (2002), 'Market forecasts and indicators 2002–2012: Emerging market in India 2002–2012, The explosive decade', Industrial Techno-Economic Services Pvt Ltd (INTECOS), in association with the Centre for Industrial and Economic Research, New Delhi.

Porter, M.E. and V.E. Millar (1985), 'How information gives you competitive advantage', *Harvard Business Review*, vol. 63, no. 4, July–August 1985.

Raj, T.V. Ram (2006), 'Brand indispensability—An innovative branding strategy', *Marketing Mastermind*, May, pp. 15–20.

Ray, Nayantara (2006,) 'On the Ginger Trail', *Business Standard*, 22 March.

Reuters, *Economic Times*, New Delhi, 3 January 2006.

School Goers: Playful Pretenders, Corporate Climbers, Cautious Planners, The Home Makers, *Business World*, *The Marketing Whitebook 2007–2008*, pp. 195–223.

Sekhri, Ravi (2007), 'McDonald's makeover in Europe increases sales', *The Economic Times*, New Delhi, 28 June, p. 13.

Semon, Thomas T. (1994), 'Classification and perceptual mapping are different tasks', *Marketing News*, 6 June, vol. 28, no. 12.

Sengupta, Subroto (2003), *Brand Positioning: Strategies for Competitive Advantage*, Tata McGraw-Hill Publishing Company Ltd, New Delhi.

Suskind, Ron (2003), 'Humour has returned to Southwest airlines after 9/11 hiatus—Flight attendants try hard to amuse the passengers', *Wall Street Journal*, 13 January.

Turakhia, S. (2008), 'Branding toddler education', *Hindustan Times*, 2 May, p. 28.

Vivek (2006), 'Global fast food chains think local for growth', *The Economic Times*, New Delhi.

Vyas, Suchi (2006), 'Hungry kya? Idli-pizza vie for plate space', *The Economic Times*, 15 May, p. 4.

http://www.asiahotels.com/hotelinfo/InterContinental_The_Grand_Mumbai_Hotel/, accessed on 27 May 2006.

http://www.asiahotels.com/hotelinfo/Orchid_Ecotel_Hotel_Mumbai, accessed on 27 May 2006.

http://www.cafecoffeeday.com/aboutus.htm, accessed on 19 July 2007.

http://www.cia.gov/cia/publications/factbook, accessed on 3 May 2006.

http://www.finanznachrichten.de/nachrichten-2006-01/artikel-5806353.asp, accessed on 28 April 2008.

http://haryanatourism.com/adventure/rock_climbing.asp, accessed on 3 May 2006.

http://www.indiastat.com/india/ShowData.asp? secid=391136&ptid=12977&level=3, accessed on 15 May 2006.

http://www.laterooms.com/de/hotel-reservations/4300_centaur-hotel-juhu-beach.aspx, accessed on 20 May 2006.

http://www.mumbairegency.hyatt.com, accessed on 27 May 2006.

http://www.shahnaz-husain.com/treatments.asp, accessed on 17 May 2006.

http://www.tajhotels.com, accessed on 31 May 2006.

http://www.tajhotels.com/Palace/Umaid% 20Bhawan %20Palace,JODHPUR/default.htm, accessed on 13 May 2006.

http://www.tajhotels.com/Resevation/default.aspx? disprooms=H00073IIndiaIMumbaiIThe%20Taj% 20Mahal%20Palace%20%26%20Tower,Mumbai, accessed on 27 May 2006.

http://www.tata.com/indian_hotels/media/20060322_ginger.htm#, accessed on 12 May 2006.

http://www.tata.com/tata_aig_general/index.htm, accessed on 20 May 2006.

http://www.theleela.com/mumbai/room_only.asp? resident=no, accessed on 20 May 2006.

http://www.tourismofindia.com, accessed on 1 May 2006.

http://www.travelmasti.com/oberoi_mumbai.htm, accessed on 27 May 2006.

http://www.utdallas.edu/~tskim/Lecture%20Note% 206.pdf, accessed on 1 May 2006.

Kotler, Armstrong, http://www.armstrong/Kotler, Marketing, accessed on 15 September 2006.

Lal, Neeta (2005), 'Making room for the ladies', *The Week*, 21 August, http://www.the-week.com/25aug21/lifestyle_article5.htm, accessed on 18 May 2006.

6

Customer Perceptions of Service

OBJECTIVES

After reading this chapter you will be able to understand the:

- perception of customers with respect to services
- concept of customer satisfaction
- different parameters of service quality, which affect service consumers
- influence of perception on consumer buying behaviour
- reasons behind the Gap model of service quality

INTRODUCTION

In the current business environment, the customer is the focus of all marketing activities. Organizations can provide the best services to their utmost capabilities but if the customer does not perceive them to be of quality, all is in vain. Thus, it is very essential for the service provider to understand how customers can perceive the service as a quality service and carry a euphoric feeling. However, not all customers are alike and what might be pleasing to one may not be so to others. It is the task of the marketing team to understand the factors affecting customer perception, service quality, and satisfaction to have a competitive edge, and to create a perceptual difference. If all these are considered and the service provider targets the customers with a total service experience, the customer perceives the service as quality service, spreads positive word-of-mouth, and will reconsider the service provider when he/she next makes a purchase.

CUSTOMER PERCEPTION

'Perception is defined as the process by which an individual selects, organizes, and interprets stimuli into a meaningful and coherent picture of the world. This is a highly individual process based on each person's needs, values, and expectations' (Schiffman and Kanuk 2002). According to them, individuals exercise selectivity in the perception of the environment to which they are exposed and this selection depends upon two major factors:

1. Expectations in cases of first experience with the service and previous experience in case of repeat purchases as it affects expectations, and
2. The motives (needs, desires, etc.) at that particular point of time

Expectations are a pre-conditioned set of notions or ideas that individuals have regarding any activity. If service providers build hype around a product or service, people have high expectations, and if these are not met it leads to disillusionment and ultimately dissatisfaction with the service. Thus, at the time of market entry it is always better to create few expectations so that they are easily met and surpassed.

Motives are the needs or wants of a person at a point of time. Thus, motives change from time to time. If an individual is very hungry he/she would probably notice the amount of time taken to serve the meal, leading to dissatisfaction if the time taken is long. However, if the urgency of food is not great, the same person would notice the way the meal was served and then the outcomes of perception would be completely different. The concept of fast dining and fine-dining restaurants came up to cater to these different motives. Similarly, insurance companies have developed different types of policies and banks have devised different ways of cash dispersal.

Perceptions can be related to the service (as in the service product), or the service delivery and the service provider (as in the organization). It is important to note that perceptions are not fixed but change with time. However, it takes a number of experiences to change quality judgments. In services marketing it is the perception regarding the service provider that is important whenever a new service is launched. All organizations have two types of customers—internal and external. Perceptions and further approaches are related to both sets of customers. Exhibit 6.1 studies the customers' and investors' perceptions of public and private sector banks.

Exhibit 6.1   PSBs score in traditional products

According to an Assocham survey, 'Growth and emergence of public and private sector banks in India: Customer's and investor's perceptions', a comparison of private and public sector banks reveals that the salaried class prefers the public sector banks (PSBs) for traditional products such as insurance, personal loans, and educational loans. However, private banks are preferred for modern facility, such as ATMs, credit cards, debit cards, phone banking, Internet banking, etc.

This survey had a sample size of more than 250 salaried employees, businesspeople, and lawyers. The overall shift seems to be towards the private sector. The 60 per cent businesspeople, who prefer private banks, feel that these banks are professional, quick, and efficient as well as have good infrastructure and appearances. These banks are not preferred when it comes to traditional items, such as loans, as their offers are difficult to comprehend, perceived rate of interests are high, and they appear to be very clever with customers. The PSBs are perceived to have lower rates of interest and are considered more reliable. The private banks seem to have a persuasive banking approach that becomes irritating for the customers.

It is also perceived that PSBs are not profit-oriented; the public sector is preferred for bonds and the private sector is preferred for mutual funds. A very high percentage of all the three categories surveyed have preferred private banks for credit cards, debit cards, ATMs, phone banking, and Internet banking. The popular PSBs are Indian Overseas Bank (IOB), Corporation Bank, Punjab National Bank (PNB), State Bank of India (SBI), and Syndicate Bank, while the popular private banks are HDFC, Citibank, ICICI, and Kotak Mahindra.

Source: Adapted from *The Economic Times* (2006).

SATISFACTION VERSUS SERVICE QUALITY

Customer satisfaction can be attained not only by providing the best possible product and services but also by creating a whole experience, which satisfies the customer. If this experience is satisfactory, customers may even overlook minor details. For example, if an upscale beauty salon provides a beautiful ambience, has attentive attendants, and serves refreshments to waiting clients, then even if the styling outcome is not to the customer's satisfaction, the whole experience is so exhilarating that the client feels cosseted and wants to return. If on the other hand, in a beauty salon with highly-trained staff who would do a good job of styling, but are busy talking to each other and do not focus on the client, the client may feel neglected and not want to return (Schiffman and Kanuk 2002). Thus, satisfaction is a broader concept that includes perceptions of service quality, price, situational factors, and personal factors.

CUSTOMER SATISFACTION

Customer satisfaction is the affable notion of customers if they perceive the service experience to be in line with their expectations. Generally, if a service satisfies the needs and wants of customers, it results in customer satisfaction. The higher the level of fulfilment, the higher is the satisfaction. Since marketing focuses on the needs and wants of customers, one of the prime marketing objectives should be to maximize customer satisfaction. Zeithaml and Bitner (2003) enumerate the following factors that affect customer satisfaction.

Product and service features The service features are the prime determinants of customer satisfaction and cause high levels of satisfaction if they satisfy the customer's needs and wants.

Customer emotions Emotions are a state of the mind and depend upon the customer's feelings at a point of time. They are reflected in the customer's attitude. If the customer is in a happy state of mind he/she will look at things positively, and is not easily irritated or excited.

Attributions for service success or failure This includes the perception of the sequence of events that lead to the success or failure of the service. If the customer perceives the sequence to be one-off and out of control of the service provider, say, a computer error, it leads to less dissatisfaction in comparison to an error, which is repetitive and can easily be controlled.

Perceptions of equity or fairness If the customer feels she has been treated at par with other customers, or that she has received her money's worth, it leads to positive perceptions towards satisfaction.

Customer satisfaction is important because a customer is the one and only judge of service quality. Customers have a set of expectations, and on experiencing a service they examine the service on the basis of the service features, and draw favourable or unfavourable conclusions about the service provided. The conclusion drawn is of prime importance to the service provider as it can provide important insights on how to improve their service processes (Swaddling and Miller 2002).

SERVICE QUALITY

Kasper et al. (1999) defined quality as 'The extent to which the service, service process, and the service organization can satisfy the expectations of the user'. Since services are a series of activities and the 'product' is 'missing' (Grönroos 1998), the service quality forms an important aspect in the perception of services. It can be used as a tool for differentiation and can provide a competitive edge. It is important to study service quality as it impacts organizational profits because it is directly related to customer satisfaction, customer retention, and hence customer loyalty (Mohsin 2005). Kandampully (2000) states that the service quality is crucial for the success of any service organization. At the time of service delivery, customers interact closely with the service providers and get an inside knowledge of the service organization. This knowledge gives them an opportunity to critically assess the service provided and the service provider. Thus, service quality plays an important role in adding value to the overall service experience.

Perceived Service Quality

Grönroos (1988) described how service quality and perception were linked and the factors that constitute service quality (Fig. 6.1). This section discusses perceived service quality on the basis of experienced quality and expected quality.

Experienced quality Due to its innate characteristics, services can also be defined as an experience. Intangibility of services leads the customer to perceive the quality on the basis of the image of the company, which can either be the corporate image, local image, or both. Further, this image is the result of technical quality and functional quality.

- Technical quality is the 'outcome dimension'. It relates to 'what' the customers receive on interacting with the firm and is an important dimension in quality assessment. This quality reflects the basic design of service, namely, its blueprinting and execution. This forms the first impression of customers and this can be

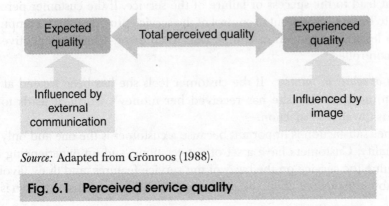

Source: Adapted from Grönroos (1988).

Fig. 6.1 Perceived service quality

controlled to some extent by focusing on the basic product and standardizing the service manufacturing procedures.

- Functional quality is a 'process-related dimension'. It comes into play only when the customer has a positive impression of the technical quality and comes for product trial or re-purchase. It relates to 'how' the service is meted out to the customer at the time of service delivery. This is highly subjective and can depend upon a number of factors such as appearance and behaviour of employees, what they say, and how they say it.

If the organization has a positive image the customers are willing to overlook minor mistakes, but if its image is negative then even minor mistakes can prove fatal for the organization.

Expected quality This is related to customer expectations when they purchase any service. Customer expectations may be based on market communication, organization's image, word-of-mouth referral, and customer needs as described below:

- Market communication: The information provided by organizations regarding their products and services. It is directly controlled by the organization.
- Image of the organization: Image of proven skills, innovativeness, ability to handle problems, performance, etc. It can only be controlled partly by the organization.
- Word-of-mouth: This is an informal, influential communication done voluntarily by the consumers based on their own knowledge and experience with the service. A positive word-of-mouth communication is favourable for the organization, but if the customer is dissatisfied he/she can adversely affect the image of the organization by creating negative word-of-mouth communication. Due to the intangibility associated with services, customers tend to attach more significance to word-of-mouth communication in the purchase of services.
- Customer needs: Customer needs at a particular point of time influence the quality perceptions. Customers who are hard-pressed for time will expect a prompt response in a beauty salon, but if they have ample time they will expect to be pampered and indulged.

If the customer experience is not as per his/her expectations it will result in dissatisfaction and a negative word-of-mouth communication. Thus, while communicating the image of the organization to the market, it is important not to unduly create impressions about the services, which the organization may ultimately not be able to fulfil. If the expected quality matches the experienced quality, it will result in customer satisfaction. However, if the customer experience exceeds the customer expectations, it leads to customer delight. The idea is to move from customer satisfaction towards customer delight. There are different models for measuring service quality, such as SERVQUAL, Gap model, and service encounters.

Dimensions of Service Quality—the SERVQUAL Instrument

The most eminent instrument in attempting to systematize the service quality is the 'gap model' of service or SERVQUAL that was developed by Parasuraman et al. (1985).

This conceptual framework was developed initially to measure customer perception of service quality for the financial service sector, but was later deployed to measure customer satisfaction in other service sectors such as hospitality, telecommunications, and healthcare.

SERVQUAL assumes that service quality is crucially determined by inconsistency between expectations and perceptions of customers (Gupta et al. 2005). According to Parasuraman et al. (1988), service quality includes dimensions of service such as reliability, responsiveness, assurance, empathy, and tangibles. These five elements are explained in detail in this section.

Reliability   This is the consistent ability to perform the promised service both steadfastly and accurately. This means that the service provider provides the service in the same manner, without making errors, and on time. Reliability is very important to consumers' decision-making process, as they need to be confident that the promise the service organization is making will be fulfilled. For example, if an organization has to send an important consignment, which has to reach its destination in a particular time period, then it is bound to choose an organization which scores highest in reliability. Thus, it is a criterion on which the purchase decision is based.

Responsiveness   This is the willingness to help and to provide timely service to consumers. All the employees who are dealing with customers need to be sensitive to the customers' needs and should contribute to creating a 'memorable' experience for them. If a customer is kept waiting for the service he/she requires, it creates inevitable negative perceptions of quality which could otherwise have been avoided. Say, for example, if a person's car repair is taking longer than expected, serving complementary drinks or providing some form of entertainment to the customer can turn a potentially poor customer experience into a favourable one.

Assurance   This is based on communication, trustworthiness, capability, courtesy, and security. In other words, the organization is keeping the customer informed; they are creating feelings of credibility and honesty, and are showing that they have the knowledge and the skills to perform the services well. During this whole process the service providers have to give due courtesy and respect to the customer, and generate feelings of security that his/her interests are safe in their hands. For example, financial companies, such as banks and insurance providers, need to consistently assure their customers that their best interests are being looked into. Punjab National Bank uses the tag line of 'the name you can bank upon'; ICICI uses the tag line '*hum hain na*'.

The Life Insurance Corporation (LIC) of India links its advertisements to the 50 years it has been in business and says, 'Fifty years of insuring lives, fifty years of ensuring smiles'. Union Bank of India claims to be 'Good people to bank with'. In e-business, where the customers are not sure about the credibility of the organizations, the organizations' assurance by providing a consumer rating point can be used to generate feelings of trust and credibility. For example, www.bizrate.com provides ratings for the organizations, which use BizRate to carry on their business. BizRate carries out these ratings by collecting customer reviews (a minimum of twenty reviews in the past ninety days) and conducting statistical analysis on the same. This gives a significant rating of a store's performance and not just the opinion of a handful of customers (BizRate 2006). Similar ratings are given for all the stores present at the BizRate site.

Empathy This involves the provision of caring, individualized attention to the customers. The employees should be approachable, sensitive to the needs of the customers, and make an attempt to understand their needs. The aim is to make the customers feel unique and special. In industrial selling, smaller organizations can provide more personalized service and are hence preferred in comparison to larger organizations. For example, in the airline transportation business it is not uncommon to see a customer's baggage missing in transit. If at that point, the airline staff is able to show empathy and make the customer feel that his/her needs are being given utmost importance, it could take the sting out of a bad experience.

Tangibles These include the appearance of the physical facilities, equipment, personnel, and communication materials. These provide evidence of the care and attention to detail that is exhibited by the service provider. Service companies, especially in the hospitality sector, focus on the tangibles to show their differential advantages. For example, the ITC ad focuses on the environment and sends across the message that to experience the environment, which soothes the five senses, visit an ITC Hotel and experience how it feels to sleep like a baby again. The advertisement of The Grand Hyatt, Mumbai, coaxes you to 'feel the Hyatt touch' and shows the different tangibles such as the room, conference hall, etc.

This SERVQUAL model is used to measure service quality and there is general agreement that it is a good predictor of service quality. However, Sureshchandar et al.

Table 6.1 Critical factors of customer-perceived service quality

S.No.	Critical factors	Description of critical factors
1.	Core service or service product	□ Portrays the content of the service □ What features are offered in the service
2.	Human element of service delivery	□ Aspects such as reliability, responsiveness, assurance, empathy, moments of truth, critical incident, and recovery
3.	Systematization of service delivery: Non-human element	□ Processes, procedures, systems, and technology that will ensure the service delivery process is standardized, streamlined, and simplified
4.	Tangibles of service: Servicescape	□ Tangibles of service facility such as equipment, machinery, signage, employee appearance, and physical environment
5.	Social responsibility	□ Encouraging ethical behaviour improves image and goodwill, positively affecting customer perceptions about service quality and building loyalty

Source: Adapted from Sureshchandar et al. (2003).

(2003) argue that all the factors deal only with the element of human interaction in service delivery; however, other factors such as service product or the core service, standardization of service delivery, the non-human element, and social responsibility, are equally important. Table 6.1 briefly summarizes the critical factors of service quality.

SERVICE ENCOUNTERS AND MOMENTS OF TRUTH

Service encounter is the situation when the customer or consumer is experiencing the service and the service providers are fulfilling all they promised through their different advertisements, and on direct contact with the customers. This concept was introduced by Normann (1983) and literally means 'the time and place, when and where, the service provider has its opportunity to demonstrate to the customer the quality of its services. In the next moment, the situation is over, the customer is gone, and there are no easy ways of adding value to the perceived quality. If a quality problem has occurred it is too late to take corrective action and to do so a new moment of truth has to be created' (Grönroos 1988). If in these service encounters the service providers are able to keep or surpass the services promised, it leads to positive perceptions by the customers. These are referred to as 'moments of truths' because at these points customers are able to differentiate between promises and performances, get a view of the service quality of the service provider, and make judgments about use of that service again in the future. Zeithaml and Bitner (2003) identified three types of service encounters.

Remote encounters   This occurs when there is no direct human contact with the service provider. Examples of remote encounters are cash transactions through ATMs; communication through mail (billing statements); new schemes and incentives, or any form of corporate communication; use of the Internet to order for services, gain information regarding service product, or price; etc. For example, after finding that opening an ATM at railway stations was very profitable, SBI is planning to install 681 ATMs, which will also have an Internet kiosk alongside to book railway tickets (Exhibit 6.2).

Phone encounters   The most convenient and frequent type of customer interaction occurs through the telephone. Since most of the customers make inquiries through the telephone, the service personnel handling the call can, by showing the appropriate knowledge and skills, convert an enquiry into a confirmed order. However, service organizations, which outsource their tele-services, cannot control the quality of the services and most of the time this leads to customer queries not being resolved, thus leading to customer dissatisfaction. This causes a detrimental effect towards the perception of service organizations. For example, to get a billing correction made on the bill received for mobile services used, a customer had to make several calls to the service provider's customer care number, but the issue was not resolved in spite of continual reminders.

Face-to-face encounters   This occurs when a customer is in direct contact with the employees. When a person is in direct contact with the service provider, both verbal and non-verbal forms of communication are important, and understanding service quality becomes more complex. It is at this point that all the tangible cues become important.

Exhibit 6.2   SBI to open ATMs at railway stations

The SBI has entered into a deal with the railways to install 681 automated teller machines (ATM) at railway stations across the country. The majority of these will have an Internet kiosk to book railway tickets. The railway property has been a prized location eyed by banks, as these are places with maximum traffic. Some years ago, the railways allowed banks with the highest bid to the most to set up ATMs at suburban stations in Mumbai. In addition to this, banks have also witnessed transactions from third-party banks, thus generating additional income. Banks have been lobbying for ticket issuing facilities at the ATMs, which was resisted by the railways in order to avoid outsourcing of ticket issuance.

The State Bank group has the largest ATM network in the country with about 5,600 ATMs covering 1,907 centres, with many machines in rural and semi-urban areas. The group is also the largest debit card issuer in South Asia with more than 17 million ATM-cum-debit cards on the Maestro platform of MasterCard International. Apart from the standard facilities of cash withdrawal, balance enquiry, and mini-statement, the bank's ATMs facilitate temple trust donations, tuition fee payments, payments of JMET and GATE fees, utility bill payments, and mobile top-up.

Source: Adapted from *The Economic Times* (2006).

CUSTOMER PERCEPTION, SERVICE QUALITY, CUSTOMER SATISFACTION, AND PURCHASE DECISIONS

Customer perception is dynamic. It is influenced by a number of factors and changes with each interaction with the service provider. For a marketer, this is a cyclical phenomenon, which affects the purchase decision each time the customer purchases the services (Fig. 6.2).

When consumers purchase a service product for the first time they are influenced by the following factors.

- Internal values: The needs and desires of individuals are fulfilled on the basis of their internal values which are influenced by a number of factors such as culture, social group, etc.
- Perception: Their perception of the organization based on the different communications by the organization affect customer perception.
- Disposition at the point of time: This includes the money which they can afford to spend at that point of time and who are they experiencing the service with (for example, a person may eat at any restaurant when he/she is alone but may choose the eating place differently depending upon the company he/she is dining with and the level of impression he/she wants to create). This also includes the mental disposition of the person at the time of purchase. For instance, a person who is not in a mood to venture out will like the meal to be home-delivered, and so he/she would consider only those restaurants, which provide such a facility.
- Word-of-mouth communication: One of the main factors affecting customer perception is the feedback they get from their peer groups or relatives who have experienced the service, or have some information on the service.

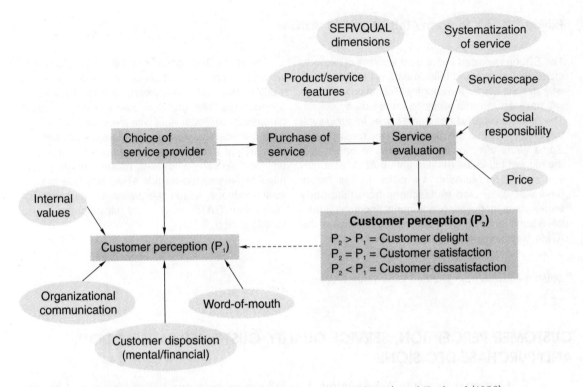

Source: Adapted from Parasuraman et al. (1985), Sureshchandar et al. (2003), and Zeithaml (1988).

Fig. 6.2 Customer perception, service quality, and customer satisfaction affecting service purchase decision

Based on all these considerations consumers perceive different service providers and then choose the service provider they would like to consider for the current purchase. When they purchase the service and experience it themselves, a mental evaluation is made about the services rendered. This depends upon a number of features.

Product/service features Do the features of the service match the requirements of the customers at the point of time? Are they what the customer was looking for? Say, a customer wants good food but he/she realizes that the food is not to his/her taste.

Systematization of service This includes the non-human dimensions, such as processes, procedures, systems, and technology, used by the service providers.

Servicescape This includes the tangible facets of service quality such as machines, equipments, employee appearance, and the ambience of the organization.

Social responsibility The ethical practices observed by the service provider build the image of the organization as a good corporate citizen. It also affects the customers' evaluation of the company.

Price The price of the service in comparison to other service providers is important versus the service product. If a customer feels that he/she is not getting value for money in spite of spending more on the service than he/she would otherwise have spent, it affects the customer's evaluation of the service.

Based on the customer's evaluation of the service, customer perceptions are formed about the service provider and the service rendered. If this perception matches with the perception the consumer had when he/she set out to make the purchase, it leads to customer satisfaction. If this is below the customer's expectations, it leads to customer dissatisfaction. However, if the customer experiences a service, which is more than what he/she had expected, it results in customer delight. This experience of the customer affects the purchase decision when he/she has to purchase the service at a later date. Thus, the customer perception is a cyclic ongoing phenomenon, which affects the service purchase and is influenced by each purchase he/she makes. Thus, it is the task of the service provider to deliver good quality service each and every time a customer is making a purchase.

GAP MODEL OF SERVICE QUALITY

Zeithaml et al. (1988) developed the Gap model to analyse quality problems and to help managers understand the ways of improving service quality (Table 6.2). The model is divided into two parts—one relates to customers and the other relates to service providers.*

Gap 1 (Management Perception Gap)

The first gap occurs due to a difference between customer expectations and the management's perceptions of consumer expectation. Thus, we can say that the management's perception of the customer expectations was inaccurate. This gap is more

Table 6.2 The Gap Model

Gap	Description
1	The gap between *management perceptions of consumer expectations* and *expected service* by the consumer
2	The gap between *translation of perceptions into quality specifications* and *management perceptions of consumer expectations*
3	The gap between *service delivery* and *translation of perceptions into quality specifications*
4	The gap between *external communication to consumers* and *service delivery*
5	The gap between *expected service* and *perceived service* by the consumer

Source: Adapted from Zeithaml and Parasuraman (1988).

Source: * Adapted from Ham et al. 2003, Zeithaml et al. 1988, Zeithaml and Bitner 2003, and Grönroos 2000.

prominent in service organizations than in firms producing tangible goods, and can be caused by marketing research orientation, communication, levels of management, relationship marketing, and service recovery.

Marketing research orientation Marketing research involves collecting information from customers regarding their expectations in this particular instance. It is the key vehicle for understanding consumer expectations and perceptions. The following points are some of the important considerations leading to misconceptions by the organization as far as customer expectation is concerned.

- Market research focus: The organization is conducting market research but is not focusing on the customer expectations.
- Qualitative and quantitative issues in data collection: The organization focuses on customer expectations for conducting marketing research, but the information collected is insufficient or inaccurate.
- Data interpretation: The organization collects sufficient data, which is appropriate to the task at hand, but this data was not interpreted extensively or accurately.
- Management orientation: The information collected is appropriate and is interpreted correctly, but is not used by the service firm. The firm believes that the operational aspect is more important and does not pay due importance to the marketing aspect or the customers.

Communication This is the exchange of ideas between service providers and customers. The degree of communication facilitates the transfer of opinions and feelings of the customers to the service providers and hence, helps them in reducing the gap between the customer perceptions and the expected service. Factors, such as external communication, internal communication, quality of communication, and medium of communication, are considered to provide superior customer service.

- External communication: This is the communication flow between service organizations and customers. This involves all communications with any of the staff of the service provider, say, from the bell porter to the manager in a hotel. The conduct of all the personnel who are in direct contact with the frontline staff is responsible for widening or reducing the gap. Since the top management is responsible for the policy formulations, it is very important for them to get feedback about customer expectations and perceptions. However, the more the number of layers in the organization, or the bigger the organization, the further the top management is from their target customers. Thus, it is advisable for them to interact with the customers on a continual basis and experience the service.
- Upward (internal) communication: Instead of, or, in addition to interacting with the staff, many top managers also get the desired information in the form of regular feedback from the frontline staff. This information can be obtained by going through formal reports or by informal interaction with the staff.
- Quality of communication: The extent to which the inputs are sought at the time of communication constitutes the quality. Only when there is quality interaction can the management get a clear perspective of what the customers want.

- Medium of communication: The medium of communication is important. Direct contact is preferred over written media, as complex and ambiguous messages can also be communicated.

Levels of management Even when the top management makes extra efforts to understand the customers, it is generally seen that the more the layers or tiers of management in an organization, the larger the size of this gap. This occurs because of the communication gap that occurs when the information flows through the layers of the organization.

Relationship marketing This involves building strong relations with the customers instead of just treating them as one-time shoppers. The stronger the relations the lesser the gap, and the customer becomes more loyal in the process. Along with focusing on attracting new customers, the organizations should focus on the changing needs of the existing customers so as to build customer loyalty.

Service recovery Often, when customer services are not up to customer expectations, customers complain. The handling of this complaint is crucial for organizations as this is the moment they can make up for their flaws and satisfy the customer. At the time of service recovery, the service provider gets an insight into the customer perceptions and this helps in reducing the gap. Implementation of these service recovery strategies helps to minimize the gap.

Customer satisfaction is important to create positive perceptions about the organization. Lack of proper understanding of consumer expectations can result in company decisions that are not as per the customer needs. Service recovery strategies are the last resort and are possible only if the customers complain. Instances are observed when a customer experienced a service failure but did not complain about it. Thus, at this instance service recovery is not possible and the customer carries these notions, which can negatively impact the organization.

Gap 2 (Service Quality Specification Gap)

The second gap is the service quality specification gap between the company perceptions of consumer expectations and the customer-driven service designs and standards. The organization has an understanding of what it thinks the customer expects, but is not able to translate this into specifications for the employees to adhere to. These factors are the standards the customer expects in the service delivery that are visible to and measured by the customers. They confirm to the customers priorities rather than to the company requirements of productivity or efficiency. Thus, service design (as per the customer expectations) and its excellent execution are critical for customer satisfaction. The different reasons contributing to this gap are management commitment, internal quality programmes, service design, and perception of feasibility.

Management commitment The policies and organizational culture flow from top to bottom. If the top management is committed towards customers and cherishes them, they make policies and plan the service experience around customers. Managers just have to follow these policies to create customer delight. However, Gap 2 occurs if the top management lacks commitment, which can be due to any of the following factors.

- Resource commitment to quality: If the management shows indifference to the needs of the customers, this results in less or no resource allocation towards improvement of quality that the customers consider vital.
- Management orientation: If the management is profit-oriented it will be interested in maximizing profits and will be unwilling to spend money on something that does not contribute towards improving the efficiency. These organizations have a product-based approach to quality rather than a user-based approach.
- Internal quality programmes: The personnel have to follow an internal quality programme and the customer expectations might not fit into them.

Service design　A poor service design can result in Gap 2 because:

- New service development is unsystematic.
- Service designs developed are ambiguous and unidentified, leading to confusion among the employees, which reflects in their delivery of the service.
- Service design does not confirm to the overall positioning.

Perception of feasibility　Often, organizations feel that what the customers expect is not feasible and do not make an effort in that direction. This lack of feasibility can be due to lack of funds on the part of the service provider or due to some physical constraints such as unavailability of trained personnel. Thus, the greater the management perception that the gap cannot be fulfilled, the larger the gap.

Customer defined standards　In organizations the personnel performance is measured over a period of time for different purposes, such as increments, rewards, bonuses, etc. The organization can have any of the following:

- Lack of properly defined standards: If the management does not incorporate customer expectations in its defined standards it will also not be incorporated in measuring the staff performance. Thus, even if an employee makes an effort to meet customer expectations, it will not be measured in his performance appraisal and thus, de-motivate him from making the extra effort. This will affect the service delivery, and hence, the perception of the quality by the customers.
- Absence of process management to focus on customer requirements: If the process managers are not giving due importance to quality as perceived by customers, it will reflect in their performance, and to create a differential advantage it is important to focus on what the customer feels is important rather than on what the organization feels is important.
- Formal process of setting service quality goals: It is of prime importance that the frontline staff also gives due importance to customers' needs. The staff should be made aware of this and a formal service quality goal should be set by the planners and the management, by taking the staff into confidence. The staff will then realize the importance of customer satisfaction, feel the importance of his role, and be committed to creating a better experience for the customers. However, if the management just lays down rigid specifications for the staff to follow, employees will feel stifled and may not feel motivated to take initiatives to develop customer satisfaction (which is also reflected in Gap 3).

Physical evidence and servicescape These include the tangible elements of service. The servicescape includes the physical setting where the service is delivered. It includes all the tangibles such as business cards, reports, presentations in hard or soft form (say, the use of a laptop in making the presentations), equipment, materials used for service delivery, the appearance of service staff, the uniforms, etc.

The service personnel use the service quality design and standards as benchmarks for service delivery. A flaw in the service design is bound to affect the customer satisfaction, as it would be mirrored in the performance of the personnel. Thus, the management should be very careful in designing the standards for service quality. Organizations can use service blueprinting for reducing this gap.

Gap 3 (Service Delivery Gap)

This gap occurs due to the difference in the service delivery standards and the actual service delivery by the employees. This means that the quality specifications laid down for the staff to follow were not met at the time of service production and delivery process. This can be due to:

Problems in specifications The specifications were too complicated or rigid and hence, could not be followed by the staff.

Employees not fulfilling the roles It is the role of the employees to cater to the effective and efficient delivery of service. An employee not delivering a service to the customer requirement can be doing so due to:

- Inability to perform the job, which would be a reflection on the human resource policies of the organization.
- Technology–job fit, that is, the tools and technologies used for performing the job are wanting or inappropriate.
- The extent to which an employee works as a team is important. If the personal disposition of the employee hinders this, he/she will not get along well with his/her colleagues and superiors, which again, will affect the service delivery of the employee.

Customers not fulfilling the roles Customers are an intrinsic part of service delivery and play an important role in the service quality delivery. Gap 3 can result if the customers are not aware of the roles and responsibilities they play in the service delivery.

Failure to match demand and supply The gap in service delivery can occur if the service providers are not able to match the demand and supply. Services cannot be inventoried and so, if there is an under-demand for their service it results in a loss, as these cannot be stored for later use. On the other hand, if there is an over-demand for the service, the service organizations again lose sales, and hence revenue.

Deficiencies in human resource policies The human resource policies are ineffective or not clear and these result in either choosing the wrong person for the wrong job, or affecting the motivation level of the employees by creating inappropriate policies. The HR policies can show the following deficiencies:

- Ineffective recruitment: The person recruited is not appropriate for the job specifications demanded.
- Role ambiguity: The job description is not clear and this results in confusing the employees about what is expected from them.
- Perceived job control: Employees should not feel restrained by rules and regulations. They should have the leverage to modify their job roles to suit the customer's needs. This is also important at the time of service recovery.
- Inappropriate evaluation and compensation: If employees feel that the evaluation of service rendered and hence, compensation offered is not as per or close to their expectations, or is not at par with what the other employees are offered, it will create feelings of resentment.

Problem with service intermediaries Service intermediaries refers to the retailers, franchisees, agents, and brokers responsible for the delivery of the service. The service organization has only a limited control over them and cannot control the service delivery of these intermediaries who represent them and interact with the customers on their behalf. These service intermediaries have their own goals and in times of conflict they are bound to safeguard their own interests. As they are the first point of contact for the customers, and represent the organization itself, customers are bound to evaluate the service quality on the basis of their interaction with these intermediaries. It is thus, up to the service organizations to motivate the intermediaries to meet the company goals and provide a satisfying experience to the customers.

Services are the product in themselves. If the delivery of service is not as per customer expectations, needs, or wants, it will turn away customers. The strategies to manage the role of employees, intermediaries, and the demand and supply, are covered in the subsequent chapters.

Gap 4 (Market Communication Gap)

The market communication gap occurs when the service delivered is not as per the expectations created by the communication made by the organization. The communication includes sales force interaction, and advertising and promotions of the organization. When the communication strategy does not match the services provided, it creates feelings of dissatisfaction. The gap can occur when there is:

Planning problem or lack of integrated services marketing communication When the operations people are not involved with the marketing communication campaigns, then the promises made by the communication tend not to be realistic or accurate, but can be exaggerated. The customer who forms his expectations on the basis of these promises may be in for a rude shock when he visits the service organization, leading to a gap. This can occur when:

- There is a tendency to view each external communication as independent and not integrating it with service operations.

- The communication is not based on interactive marketing. The service product is delivered by the people and so it is not consistent in behaviour. Customers should be made aware of this fact so that they can form realistic assumptions.
- A strong internal marketing programme is absent.

Execution problem or ineffective management of customer expectations   This occurs due to the following reasons:

- Service organizations are not able to manage the customer expectations through communications.
- They are not able to adequately educate the customers.

Over-promising   In order to sell the services, marketing people can get carried away and promise more than they can execute. Over-promising can be done through:

- advertisements
- personal selling
- physical evidence cues.

The extent to which firms are pressurized to create new business or meet the business of competitors, also affects the extent to which they over-promise. The second reason to over-promise is the industry norm or the extent to which they think the competitors are over-promising.

Inadequate horizontal communications within the organization can increase this gap. These communication gaps can be between:

- sales and operations
- advertising and operations
- differences in policies and procedures across branches and units.

These communication gaps can cause the sales and advertising people to promise more services than the operations people can deliver. The sales people may even price the service inaccurately due to failure in understanding the factors involved in the service delivery. Also, different branches and units of the same service organization may be pursuing different policies due to lack of communication with each other. A customer who visits one facility may expect the same service level from the other, which can again result in a gap.

All the activities of marketing, sales, operations, and communications should be integrated. When the operations people are involved in the communication strategy it results in realistic communication. This leads to higher levels of motivation and commitment among the operations staff. They can also give ideas for services, which may not have occurred to the marketing staff. The strategies for overcoming this gap are discussed later in Chapter 14.

Gap 5 (Perceived Service Quality Gap)

This gap results when the perceived or experienced service is not as per the expectations of the customers. This results in:

- negative quality perceptions
- bad publicity and reputation
- a negative impact on the organization's image
- lost business due to all the negative perceptions.

All the gaps studied are with the assumption that the gap always occurs negatively. The gap can be positive too; for example, when the service quality designs are more than what is expected by the customers, or the service delivered is better than what was promised in the communication and the perceived service quality is more than the customer expectations.

The gap analysis is used to:

- identify inconsistencies between the quality of service provider and customer expectations
- identify the reasons for creation of these quality problems
- develop processes to close these gaps
- inprove the perception of the service quality in the customers and create a quality image for customer satisfaction.

Customer perception is very important in the customer decision-making process for services. If the service provider can understand how the customer is going to perceive the service, he can channellize the energy and the resources to match these customer perceptions, and create a better service quality impact on the customers.

SUMMARY

Customer perception is very important for customer decision-making in the services sector. If the customer does not perceive the services to be good, then all the efforts and the money spent by the service provider will be futile. The marketers thus need to understand what customer perception is and how best to influence this. This has been discussed in this chapter. The chapter further gives an overview what customer satisfaction is and how the service quality can impact customer satisfaction. The service quality has been discussed in the light of the SERVQUAL instrument. It is discussed that the customer is influenced by the service encounters and how these 'moments of truth' can be managed for a better customer experience.

The next section focuses on how customer perception is linked to service quality, which impacts customer satisfaction and hence, their purchase decision. To further help the marketers in influencing the customer perception, the next section talks about the Gap model. This model delineates the various gaps that can occur in the customer expectation and the service provider's delivery of service. The section emphasizes the reasons for the occurrence of the gaps and the implications of the various levels of these gaps. If the service provider can understand how the customer is going to perceive the service, he/she can channelize the energy and the resources to match the customer perceptions, and synergize to create a better service quality impact on the customers.

KEY TERMS

Customer perception A cyclical phenomenon, which affects the purchase decision each time the customer purchases the services.

Customer satisfaction The degree of satisfaction provided by the goods or services of a firm as measured by the number of repeat customers.

Gap model This is a model to analyse the quality problems and to help managers to understand how the service quality can be improved.

Purchase decision A plan to purchase a particular product or service in the future.

Service encounter This is the situation when the customer or consumer is experiencing the service and the service providers are fulfilling all they promised through their different advertisements, and by direct contact with the customers.

Service quality The extent to which the service, service process, and the service organization can satisfy the expectations of the user.

SERVQUAL This model supports the assumption that service quality is crucially determined by inconsistency between the expectations and perceptions of customers.

CONCEPT REVIEW QUESTIONS

1. What is perception and why is it important for an organization to know the customer's perception?

2. What is customer satisfaction and how is it different from customer's perception of service quality?

3. What is service quality? Discuss the various factors affecting service quality.

4. Discuss critically the relationship between customer satisfaction and service quality.

5. What is the Gap model? Critically discuss the various gaps in service delivery.

6. How does the Gap model contribute to effective service delivery?

CRITICAL THINKING QUESTIONS

1. Identify a recent visit to a restaurant. What were your expectations prior to the visit, your experience of the services rendered by the restaurant, and your perception after the visit?

2. During a visit to a bank did you feel any of the gaps in services discussed in the Gap model? How would you like the organization to overcome the gap?

3. Discuss the quality of the service rendered to you during your last visit to get your car serviced or your last visit to a beauty salon.

4. Pick any two well-known restaurants in your locality. Discuss the perceptions about these restaurants and identify points of similarities and differences. What service quality improvements would you recommend to them?

INTERNET EXERCISES

1. Visit the website of your bank. Try to make an online transaction. Identify the factors that lead to your satisfaction/dissatisfaction. How is this different from your experience at the local branch you generally visit?

2. You have to plan your vacation to a hill-station in India. Identify two hotels on the Internet in the same geographic region. Visit their websites and identify your perceptions about the hotels on the basis of information available. Which hotel would you prefer and why?

3. Visit the websites of two hospitals and try to identify how they have addressed the various aspects of service quality and customer satisfaction.

CASE STUDY

Indian Beauty Business: A Focus on Shahnaz Husain*

The Beauty Industry in India

The beauty services industry in India, largely unorganized, and pegged at over Rs 12,000 crore by some observers (others peg it as low as Rs 2,000 crore), is slowly but steadily taking the organized route to do business. The emergence of players such as Marico's Kaya Skin Clinic, Lakmé Beauty Salon, VLCC, Shahnaz Husain Herbals, CavinKare's Limelite and Green Trends, Keune, and Jawed Habib Hair and Beauty, can be attributed to this trend, say observers. According to industry estimates, the organized and semi-organized beauty services industry in the country is about Rs 1,500–Rs 1,600 crore (some peg it as high as Rs 6,000 crore). Clearly, the scope for conversion from unorganized to organized is high, say observers. The organized beauty segment is growing at about 25–30 per cent per annum, which only highlights how fast the rate of transformation is, say analysts. According to Vineet Gupta, Chief Executive Officer, Jawed Habib Hair and Beauty, 'In the next five years, there will be a marked shift from the unorganized to organized segments in the industry. This implies a turnaround for the business' (*Financial Express* 2006).

Pricing

At the moment the prices of services rendered depend on the type of treatment and the provider offering the service, though the accent these days is on high quality at a reasonable price. For instance, the average consumer spend in a Kaya Skin Clinic, Shahnaz Husain Herbal Salon, Lakmé Beauty Salon, or Limelite, works out to about Rs 1,000 per month (Green Trends in comparison, is CavinKare's budget parlour targeted at the family, where the spend is about Rs 300 per month per person). Hair specialists, such as Jawed Habib's, on the other hand, may price their hair

solutions higher to that of its beauty services (Jawed Habib's haircuts and styles, for instances, have a premium price tag, though beauty services are moderately priced).

In contrast, Keune, which is a hair care brand from Holland, marketed by Brushman India through exclusive, company-owned, branded salons and retail outlets, has services modestly priced at about Rs 300–450 for men's and women's haircuts, while applying hair colour costs about Rs 600–1250 per person, according to Brushman MD, Kapil Kumar. Given the burgeoning beauty market, international salon chains are eyeing the Indian marketplace keenly, with the French player Jean-Claude Biguine (JCB), for instance, looking to set up operations in the country shortly.

Distribution

Pantaloon Retail has also taken its first tentative steps in the beauty services segment with the launch of its budget parlour, Star and Sitara in Bangalore, in May 2006. 'We are targeting Big Bazaar and Central malls for the launch of our parlours', says Kishore Biyani, Managing Director, Pantaloon Retail. 'A second parlour is due to be launched in Ahmedabad in the next few days', he added. All this action implies more competition for existing players, who are ramping up operations quickly. Kaya Skin Clinic, for instance, which closed the last financial year with a turnover of Rs 44 crore on the back of 43 company-owned outlets in 15 locations in the country, will increase the overall number to 50 this fiscal. In the Middle East, where it has three clinics in Dubai and Abu Dhabi, the company will add a few more centres, says Rakesh Pandey, Chief Executive Officer, Kaya Skin Clinic. The plan is to achieve a turnover of about Rs 60 crore this fiscal by pitching

---

* Adapted from Dutta, Kirti (2009), 'Case study on Shahnaz Husain', in Vinnie Jauhari and Charla Griffy Brown (eds), *Women, Technology and Entrepreneurship: Global Case Studies*, Reference Press, New Delhi. Printed with the permission of Reference Press.

its flagship skin solutions to customers, though the company does not rule out an entry into the hair care segment too. 'We are currently test marketing a hair loss treatment in Bangalore', he said.

Meanwhile, close rival Lakmé Beauty Salons, which has over 85 franchisee controlled outlets in over 34 cities, is keeping its focus on a select few metros and mini-metros. These include Mumbai, Delhi, Baroda, Kolkata, Jaipur, Ahmedabad, and Kochi among others, says a company spokesperson.

According to S. Jagdish, the business head of CavinKare, the number of Limelite and Green Trends outlets will go up to about 100 in the next two to three years from the current 22 properties located at Bangalore, Chennai, and Delhi (*The Financial Express* 2006).

Service Standardization and Training

VLCC, Keune, Shahnaz Husain (barring some seven to eight outlets in Delhi, all Shahnaz Husain parlours in India are franchisee owned), and Jawed Habib's, are all ramping fast, though the pressure of maintaining a standard format and level of service goes up significantly as outlets increase, especially the franchisee run ones. 'Yes, the pressure of standardization is there', says Shahnaz Husain, proprietor of Shahnaz Husain Herbals, 'but we handle this by providing regular inputs on products and services to our partners'. Lakmé, on the other hand, has a franchisee model, where five company-owned salons act as centres of excellence and training for its associates. 'The aim is to not only to provide brand saliency, but also equip our partners with the latest trends and techniques', says a company spokesperson (*The Financial Express* 2006).

Training, in fact, is a need stressed by all players in the organized beauty segment given the dearth of quality professionals in the industry. 'That is the most important element of the business', says Sandeep Ahuja, Chief Executive Officer, personal care, VLCC, which has five professional training academies in the country apart from 100 slimming-cum-beauty-cum-fitness centres, and a division catering to the manufacture of herbal skincare and body care products.

Modus Operandi

The format or mode of operation is another area critical to a player, with VLCC, for instance, embedding its beauty regimen within its weight loss and fitness programme. Lakmé, in contrast, plays on its exclusive beauty and hair services; Kaya boasts of its scientific approach to skin problems; while Green Trends is all about affordable hair and skin solutions using natural products. 'Limelite is an upmarket salon-cum-day spa targeting a well-heeled audience', says Jagdish. 'Green Trends, however, is your neighbourhood salon', he adds (*The Financial Express* 2006).

The Future Competition

The US-based Regis Corp, the dominant group in the international hair salon segment with some 11,000 outlets in North America and allied locations, also has its sights on India. Not surprisingly then, its entry is being monitored closely by its nearest rival Toni & Guy with some 3,000 salons across the world, who is also believed to be studying the Indian marketplace (*The Financial Express* 2006).

Shahnaz Husain

Of all the players in the beauty industry, Shahnaz Husain in one of the oldest, most acclaimed players who can be credited with a number of firsts. She is a pioneer in herbal cosmetics and has won more accolades, awards, and mentions in the international press than any other Indian women. *The Esprit* magazine of Germany has dubbed her as Asia's Helena Rubenstein, *Good Housekeeping* calls her Estee Lauder, and *The Daily Telegraph* has named her 'the uncrowned queen of Indian beauty therapy'. Today, she heads the largest organization of its kind in the world, with more than 400 franchise salons worldwide and ranges of natural formulations for skin, hair, and body care. Indeed, hers is the story of a truly successful entrepreneur who transcends geographical boundaries to reign over the world.

Shahnaz has launched thousands of beauty products and trained hundreds of housewives in India to set up beauty salons in their own homes just as she had started decades ago. The multi-million dollar business started in 1971 with a capital of Rs 35,000 borrowed from her father. The first Shahnaz Herbal Salon, a small shop in her verandah, has now spread across 104 countries and has six factories and 4,200 employees (Bhardwaj 2006). Her training schools have created entrepreneurs out of housewives and have given a better life opportunity to the speech and hearing impaired girls who have passed out from her Shamute training school. Apart from being the first to start beauty training schools in India, the credit of pioneering franchises of beauty salons in India, and being the number one beautician in the world, as she currently owns the largest franchise chain in the world, also goes to Shahnaz (Rangoonwala 2001). She has also authored books on beauty (Rediff Books 2006).

Early Days

Shahnaz Husain was born in a conservative Muslim family. She received her basic education at an Irish convent, Queen Mary's in Allahabad. Shahnaz was engaged at fourteen, married at fifteen, and on her sixteenth birthday had a two-month old daughter. After her marriage she travelled to Tehran, UK, France, and Germany. Her father was keen that she should study further. So he collected numerous brochures for various courses ranging from engineering to beauty care (Kurian 2003). She selected beauty care and studied as an herbalist by day, wrote by night, did odd typing jobs and ran a magazine in Tehran, in order to earn the extra money required for her course as a chemist (Singh 2002). She studied beauty therapy in Germany, London, and New York. She completed her course in cosmetic chemistry and cosmetology, and was all set to become a beauty care specialist using chemical products like the rest.

Reasons for Starting Business

During her stay abroad, while Shahnaz was studying cosmetic chemistry, she was horrified to witness the havoc caused by the use of chemical treatments. She began to question the use of chemical ingredients in beauty care. 'From my family I had inherited a faith in traditional remedies', she said. Realizing that her mother had used creams and cosmetics made from herbs,

Shahnaz rejected the existing salon treatments and upheld the use of natural ingredients. After studying these age old, time-tested Indian herbal remedies, she came up with concoctions of herbs and oils of plants which aimed to create a perfect balance of body, mind, and spirit (Cunningham 2005). Thus, her famous quote, 'I sell civilization in a jar'. In 1970, she received her license to practice and opened her first store with a loan taken from her father.

Obstacles Encountered

It could not have been easy for a girl who from a child bride went on to become a successful entrepreneur, to be ambitious in a conservative society, blend her own range of creams and potions, and build an empire on it (Singh 2002). However, she says that the support and understanding of her family helped her to retain her belief in herself, and keep trying relentlessly. Her father extended a loan of Rs 35,000 with which she turned her verandah into a beauty salon and later pumped all her revenues into research and development, and eventually bought a 35-acre flower farm. When she started her own exclusive beauty clinic, skin and hair treatments were relatively unknown in India. Superficial beauty treatments or hair styling were special treats women went in for. Shahnaz showed them that beauty is the outcome of long-term and lifelong care (Lane 2000). She devised her own clinical treatments for modern demands; but combining ancient systems with the latest techniques was not the only challenge. Shahnaz also had to create awareness about the goodness of herbs and the dangers of chemical treatments. Thus, to popularize this concept she started writing articles for news papers and magazines.

Entering the international market against great odds of financial constraints and closed doors did not deter her. In 1980, when Shahnaz participated in the Festival of India in London, she was given a counter in the perfumery section at Selfridges. There, rubbing shoulders with the biggest international brands, without financial resources and advertising (compared to the billions of dollars spent on advertising and packaging by the others), and having only her 'India and ayurvedic' image to help her, Shahnaz sold out her consignment in three days, breaking the stores existing cosmetic sales records. *The London Daily* carried the headline 'Herbal hell breaks loose in Selfridges' the next day, heralding the arrival of the diva (*The Times* 2003).

When she participated in the Festival of India in Paris and wanted a permanent counter at Galleries Lafayette, the famous Paris department store, she was informed that in order to have a permanent counter, she had to achieve a certain sales figure. However, realizing that she was running short of the sales target, she knew she had to think of an ingenious idea to push up the sales. So she called her Delhi office and asked her secretary to fly to Paris with four Kashmiri carpets. She offered this carpet as a gift for purchases worth 20,000 francs and over. This resulted in a stampede, something the store had never witnessed before. She actually sold products worth much more than the targeted amount, earning a permanent counter at Galleries Lafayette, the world's most prestigious cosmetic store (Shahnaz press folder).

Since then, there has been no looking back. Shahnaz went on breaking sales records internationally. At the Kuwait Beauty Fair at Mishrif, the world's largest cosmetic bazaar, she sold cosmetics worth 37,000 dinars (Rs 37 lakh) in three days, working only eight hours a day. She actually received a letter from the Guinness Book of World Records, verifying this (Sinha 2006).

More than 40 per cent of Shahnaz's sales come from Japan (CNN 2004). According to Shahnaz, the Japanese prefer well-known brands but when it comes to cosmetics they prefer natural products. Also, Japanese women spend 16 per cent of their income on cosmetics. But gaining an entry there was not easy. The country's drug department cleared all the lotions and potions before they could be launched in the country (Singh 2002).

Shahnaz has used the power of the press to gain entry into other countries. Holding press conferences and talking about the ill effects of chemicals and synthetics, gives her a platform to discuss the benefits of her herbal products. She followed this by providing free consultation. Each paper carried her story, and not her advertisement, along with the address where she could be contacted, for free consultation. Shahnaz has never advertised her products, but has used her larger-than-life personality to sell her brand through personal promotion—a rare instance when a woman entrepreneur has become a brand herself (*Success* 1996). However, in 2005, she planned to advertise extensively both in print and electronic media, for the first time (Majumdar 2005).

Ranges of Specialized Products

As leaders in product innovation, the Shahnaz Husain group has evolved more than 350 formulations for general care, treatment of skin and scalp disorders, health, and fitness. In fact, a characteristic feature of the group has been its dynamism, introducing unique concepts from time to time, and keeping abreast of the latest techniques in ayurvedic and herbal products cosmetology.

The products have grown out of clinical usage, based on massive client feedback, as an answer to precise and individual needs. Based on 'care and cure', the product ranges include entire lines of therapeutic formulations, which perform high level multiple tasks and reflect a deep understanding of the demands of protective, preventive, and corrective care. They have no exact equivalents in the market. Apart from the legendary Shahnaz Herbal Range, there are ranges for precise needs, as well as those based on specific extracts, such as Flower Power (of floral extracts), Neem Range, Honey Health, Himalayan Herb, Sun Range (sun-block products), Man Power, Kids Collection, Colour Magic (range of make-up cosmetics), Aromatherapy bar, and Shapet (ayurvedic formulations for pets). A line of ayurvedic health tonics, medicinal formulations (such as pain relieving balm, blood purifiers, cough syrup, Isabgol), food supplements, herbal drinks, herbal teas, immunity enhancers, medicines, ayurvedic slimming capsules, aromatherapy essential oils, as well as the medicines used in the ayurvedic centres, have also been launched, along with innovative accessories and gift items (Mahajan). The group has recently launched some revolutionary products in modern skin care, which include the 24-carat gold range, pearl cream and mask, oxygen cream, astro-gem therapy range, diamond collection, and a signature spa collection. Shahnaz also entered the mass market with Fair One, a natural fairness cream and plans to launch Shahnaz Forever this year, an entire range at affordable prices for all segments of the market (Shahnaz 2006).

Reasons for Success

The undisputed queen of the world of beauty presented an exciting new level of botanical energy with her flower power collection. Rejecting the synthetic artificiality of the west, she portrayed the innocence of nature in her products. She started this herbal crusade single-handedly. As the saying goes, 'imitation is the best form of flattery', and the number of other people entering this niche segment was a compliment to her. But still, she is a force to reckon with and has earned the sobriquet of 'India's beauty ambassador' from none other than Barbara Cartland, for her tremendous contribution towards popularizing Indian products in the west.

One of the main reasons for her success is that since beauty care is an image-based business, she has become the brand ambassador herself. Basing her customized beauty care on the adage that 'external body condition is a barometer of internal health', Shahnaz came up with beauty care of the level of paramedical care, complete with diagnosis and prescriptions. It was this holistic trend that set the terms for her long innings as the 'Herbal Queen' (Bakshi 2005).

Another reason for her success is that she just did not concentrate only on make-up and doing hair, but proposed total skin care. Her company, showing an annual growth rate of 19.4 per cent is not finance driven but emotion driven.

Current Stage of Business

Health and Beauty Products

Today, Shahnaz is described as Asia's Helena Rubenstein, exporting more than 400 'nature care and cure' products to 104 countries and having over 650 salons globally (Bhardwaj 2006).

Shahnaz has 400 formulations for general care, and treatment of skin and scalp disorders already on the shelves. She has outlets at prestigious stores such as Galleries Lafayette in Paris, Harrods and Selfridges in London, and Seibu Chain in Japan. Her products also sell at Bloomingdales in New York, La Rinascente in Milan, and El Certe Inglis in Spain, as well as in exclusive outlets and clinics worldwide. In fact, Shahnaz was the first Asian to enter Galleries Lafayette in Paris in herbal care, and the first Asian to be featured in the 18-foot shop window of the store. Hers is the first Indian herbal cosmetic company to have featured in Harrods and Selfridges (Shahnaz 2006).

Today, her products are selling globally from US to Japan, in Europe, Russia, Middle East, Africa, South-east Asia, Australia, and even in Iceland. Her empire is estimated to be worth 200 million dollars with a growth rate of 19.4 per cent (CNN 2004, Choong 2004).

After creating a presence in the premium product range, Shahnaz has entered the mass market in India with Shahnaz Forever, which she will be marketing with Elder Pharmaceuticals, starting from Rs 150.

Spas

Shahnaz Husain ventured in to the spa business by setting up the Medispa in the US island of Saipan, off the pacific coast, in collaboration with Hyakumata group of Japan to open a spa at their 24-hour golf course. This is now called Shahnaz Husain Ayurvedic Spa. She has incorporated holistic healing techniques such as yoga and meditation along with the spa experience. The spa has traditional ayurvedic treatments and soothing massages, anti-stress treatments, aromatherapy, specialized body packs, skin and hair treatments, supervised diets, yoga, meditation, etc. This spa received much success and was followed by spas in Toronto and Greece. Based on this success, Shahnaz is planning to launch a spa collection (Bakshi 2005). She is planning to set up a health resort at Dhauj (Haryana), just 45 km from Delhi. It is targeted at foreign tourists and city-dwellers who wish to get a healthy weekend getaway (Mahajan). Currently, the group is considering spa proposals for countries such as Saudi Arabia, Spain, Italy, and Australia.

Beauty Training Schools

Shahnaz is also the pioneer of vocational training in beauty in India. More than three decades ago, when only apprenticeship training was available, Shahnaz started her beauty institute, Woman's World International, to provide comprehensive training in beauty.

All the courses offered at these various institutes are in tune with international standards and students are taught the latest techniques in skin and hair care. These schools were the basis of the franchise-based enterprise (*Hindustan Times* 2006).

The Franchisees

In 1979, Shahnaz started her first franchise clinic in Calcutta. This was the beginning of the worldwide chain. Shahnaz began to encourage ordinary housewives to open salons in their own homes. She had already shown them the way by opening her very first salon in her own house. Shahnaz trained them and offered the Shahnaz Herbal franchise (Rangoonwala 2001).

Shahnaz also adopted a highly successful method to promote the new franchise salons. She made it a point to attend their opening. She addressed press conferences, where she spoke on the benefits of herbal care and also gave free consultations. This not only attracted crowds to the inauguration of the salons, but also gave the new venture a real impetus. It was based on a personal interaction, where she would meet people, listen to their problems, and provide beauty solutions. Apart from training all the franchisees and therapists, refresher courses are also provided from time to time. An excellent feedback system is maintained and all new developments and techniques are communicated to the franchisees from time to time.

Shahnaz Husain Forever Beautiful Shops and Ayurvedic Centres

The success of the franchise system prompted the opening of Shahnaz Husain Forever Beautiful shops, based on a concept of lifestyle marketing. The wide and varied ranges, along with accessories, are housed under one roof, with exclusive shop design and efficient customer information system. Specially trained sales staff provide guidance and information regarding products. Shahnaz Husain ayurvedic centres, carrying out traditional treatments of panchkarma, dhara, and Kerala massage, have also been set up for the cure of various ailments. The centre employs ayurvedic physicians and professionally trained personnel to conduct the various treatments. An individualized approach, along with all necessary facilities have been made available, to provide a perfect environment for treatment (*The Times* 2003).

Research and Development

Research and development have always received high priority in the group's two R&D units. To ensure the purity of raw material, a herb and flower farm has also been set up near Delhi. Thus, quality control is exercised right from the raw material stage. This is done through rigorous testing and research. The extraction of essential oils, infusions, decoctions, tinctures and other extracts is carried out by the group itself. Various methods of soil culture and cultivation are followed, using superior natural composts and fertilizers, which actually contribute not only towards the purity and quality of the raw material, but towards actually creating a superior product. Various preparations are obtained from the herbs and flowers for use in the formulations, such as infusions, decoctions, distillates, essences, powders, tinctures, and so on, in keeping with the ayurvedic system. These are made under strict supervision, using the latest technology. Stringent quality control tests are carried out for various dilutions. Thus, by exercising control at each stage, high quality is ensured (Shahnaz press folder).

Shahnaz Husain Herbal has a large network of over 400 franchise and associate clinics in India and abroad, operating under the franchise system. The franchise clinics have extended not only to the cities, but even small towns all over India. Today, a countrywide zonal distribution network exists, with 40 distributors and more than

600 sub-distributors all over India. There are more than 500 outlets in India, which include the franchise clinics, Shahnaz Husain shops, and counters in leading stores, shops, and cottage industries emporia. Thus, the brand is ideally positioned in the herbal cure and care market. The year 2005 has been a remarkable year of global branding, setting up franchise clinics, shops, and spas, as well as launching products in Russia, Scotland, London, Manchester, Australia, Malaysia, and Indonesia.

Awards and Accolades

Shahnaz has been conferred several national and international awards apart from the Greatest Woman Entrepreneur Award from *Success* magazine. She has received Arch of Europe International Gold Star in Madrid, Spain, the Quality Excellence Award in Geneva, Cannes and London, Golden America Award in New York (*The Times* 2003), the Outstanding Woman Entrepreneur Award in London, Woman of the Millenium Award in USA, Woman of the Year Award from the Governor of California, USA, and the Outstanding Entrepreneur of the Millennium by Dame Barbara Cartland, in London. Shahnaz was the only woman among eighteen leading Indian entrepreneurs, who was invited to attend the recently held Forbes Global CEO Conference in Sydney, Australia (Shahnaz press folder).

In 2006, she received the Padma Shri Award. The prestigious Padma awards are the highest civilian awards and Shahnaz Husain who has single-handedly put India on the world beauty map, and kept the Indian flag flying high at the cosmetic capitals of the world, has truly earned it. She has also been awarded the Udyog Ratan Award for export excellence (won three times), the Rajiv Gandhi Gold Medal for propagating the Indian herbal heritage, and the Export Excellence Award (thrice) from the Delhi government. (*The Financial Express* 2006).

Conclusion and Lessons Learnt

'What really matters in life is not what you want but how badly you want it. You can achieve any level of success if you want it that much', has been one of Shahnaz's guiding principles. She also says that, 'If I am walking towards the goal and if I feel the door is closed, I don't walk away, but open my own doors' (CNN 2004). Thus, having a vision, being passionate and focused about it, and trying to achieve it with a crusader's zeal, no matter what the obstacles, have been the reasons Shahnaz could find success in spite of coming from a conservative family and trying to sell a new concept to the world. The 61-year old entrepreneur says, 'you never fail until you stop trying. I never stop, so I never fail'.

Questions

1. What were Shahnaz's reasons for starting business? Relate it to customer perceptions prevalent at that time.

2. How did Shahnaz use customer perceptions to design her marketing strategies?

3. Critically relate Shahnaz's current businesses with the customer perceptions she has based them on.

SELECT REFERENCES

Bakshi, Veeshal (2005), 'Remaking the beauty business', *The Financial Express*, 5 February, p. 4.

Bhardwaj, Manali (2006), 'Padma Sundari Shahnaz Husain', *City Limits*, 15 February, p. 79.

Business Today (2006), 'The 25 most powerful women in Indian business', *Business Today*, 12 March.

Choong, Renee (2004), 'Herbal products to enhance natural beauty', *The Star*, 10 March.

Cunningham, Jennifer (2005), 'Shahnaz Husain: Ayurvedic cosmetics manufacturer', *The Herald*, 20 June, p. 19.

'Estee Lauder of India', *Global Indian*, Middle East Edition, vol. 2, no. 11, p. 18.

Grönroos, C. (1988), 'Service quality: The six criteria of good perceived service quality', *Review of Business*, vol. 9, no. 3, pp. 10–13.

Grönroos, C. (1998), 'Marketing services: The case of the missing product', *The Journal of Business and Industrial Marketing*, vol. 13, no. 4/5, pp. 322–336.

Grönroos, C. (2000), *Service Management and Marketing: A Customer Relationship Management Approach*, 2nd edn, Chapters 4 and 5, John Wiley and Sons, Chichester.

Gupta, Atul, J.C. McDaniel, and S.K. Herath (2005), 'Quality management in service firms: Sustaining structures of total quality service', *Managing Service Quality*, vol. 15, no. 4, pp. 389–402.

Ham, C.L., W. Johnson, R. Plank, A. Weinstein, and P.L. Johnson (2003), 'Gaining competitive advantage: Analysing the gap between expectations and perceptions of service quality', *International Journal of Value-Based Management*, vol. 12, no. 2, pp. 197–203.

Kandampully, J. (2000), 'The impact of demand fluctuation on the quality of service: A tourism industry example', *Managing Service Quality*, vol. 10, no. 1, pp. 10–18.

Kasper, Hans, P.V. Helsdingen, and W. De Vries (1999), *Services Marketing Management: An International Perspective*, Chapter 5, John Wiley and Sons, England.

Kurian, Anupa (2003), 'A truly beautiful woman must have inner beauty', *Gulf News Tabloid*, 8 May, pp. 1–2.

Lane, Winsome (2000) 'Secrets of eternal beauty', *Standard*, Hong Kong, 27 February, pp. 6–8.

Mahajan, Prarthana, 'India is naaz of Shahnaaz', *Inside Fashion*, vol. 2, no. 7, p. 18.

Majumdar, Pallavi (2005), 'Shahnaz Hussain goes mass market', *Business Standard*, 19 January, p. 22.

Mohsin, Asad (2005), 'Service quality perceptions: An assessment of restaurant and café visitors in Hamilton, New Zealand', *The Business Review*, Cambridge, vol. 3, no. 2, pp. 51–57.

Normann, R. (1983), *Service Management*, John Wiley, New York.

Parasuraman A., V.A. Zeithaml, and L.L. Berry (1985), 'A conceptual model of service quality and its implications for future research', *Journal of Marketing*, vol. 49, no. 4, p. 47.

Parasuraman A., V.A. Zeithaml, and L.L. Berry (1988), 'SERVQUAL: A multiple-item scale for measuring consumer perceptions of service quality', *Journal of Retailing*, vol. 64, no. 1, pp. 12–37.

'PSBs score in traditional products', *The Economic Times*, New Delhi, 4 September.

Rangoonwala, Yousuf (2001), 'Herbal queen', *The Telegraph in Schools*, 19 July–1 August, p. 11.

Sakhuja, Latika (2005), 'Herbal beauty care franchising pioneer', *The Franchising World*, vol. 6, pp. 48–50.

Schiffman, G. Leon and Leslie L. Kanuk (2002), *Consumer Behaviour*, Chapters 6 and 7, Prentice Hall, New Delhi.

Sengupta, Hindol (2003) 'From bloody fingers to hands decked with diamonds', *Mid Day*, Delhi, May 6.

Sherman, Elizabeth (1990), 'India's queen of beauty', *Harpers and Queen*, September, pp. 274–277.

Singh, Kishore (2002), 'In the parlour of the diva of potions', *Business Standard*, 13 February, p. 14.

Sinha, Vimmy (2006), 'Guts and glory', Delhi Times, *The Times of India*, 14 April, p. 11.

Success (1996), 'India's beauty queen', *Success*, June, pp. 37–38.

Sureshchandar, G.S., C. Rajendran, and R.N. Anantharaman (2003), 'Customer perceptions of service quality in the banking sector of a developing economy: A critical analysis', *The International Journal of Bank Marketing*, vol. 21, no. 4/5, pp. 233–241.

Swaddling, David C. and Charles Miller (2002), 'Don't measure customer satisfaction', *Quality Progress*, vol. 35, no. 5, pp. 62–67.

The Times (2003), 'Amazing success story of Shahnaz Husain', *The Times*, Kuwait, 15–31 August.

Zeithaml, Valarie A. (1988), 'Consumer perceptions of price, quality and value: A means-end model and synthesis of evidence', *Journal of Marketing*, vol. 52, no. 3, pp. 2–20.

Zeithaml, Valarie A. and M.J. Bitner (2003), *Services Marketing*, Tata McGraw-Hill Publishing Company Limited, New Delhi.

Zeithaml, Valarie A., Leonard L. Berry, and A. Parasuraman (1988), 'Communication and control processes in the delivery of service quality', *Journal of Marketing*, vol. 52, no. 2.

Financial Express (2006), 'Armed for the beauty market', http://www.financialexpress.com/inc/index.html, accessed on 2 September 2006.

http://www.financialexpress.com/fe_full_story.php? content_id=115954, accessed on 1 September 2006.

http://www.shahnaz-husain.com, accessed on 1 September 2006.

Rangaraj, R. (2005) 'Shahnaz Husain launches Fair One', *Chennai Online*, http://www.chennaionline.com/fashion-lifestyle/Fashiontips/2005/05elder.asp, accessed on 20 September 2006.

Rediff Books (2006), http://books.rediff.com/bookstore/, accessed on 2 September 2006.

'SBI to open ATMs at railway stations', *The Economic Times*, 5 August 2006, http://economictimes.indiatimes.com/articleshow/1855597.cms, accessed on 19 September 2006.

7

Customer Expectations

OBJECTIVES

After reading this chapter you will be able to understand the:

- concept of customer expectation
- classification of consumer expectations
- factors that influence customer expectations
- various steps involved in managing customer expectations

INTRODUCTION

Service providers exist because of customers who are the ultimate judges of the services rendered by an organization. It is important for service providers to know the level of customer expectations in order to meet and even excel them to gain maximum customer satisfaction. As customer expectation is an important criterion for post-consumption evaluation, it is also important for the service providers to manage the customer expectations so that customers do not develop expectations that are difficult for the service providers to satisfy.

The term 'expectation' is used differently in the service quality literature and consumer satisfaction literature. In the consumer satisfaction literature, expectations are predictions about what is likely to happen in a forthcoming transaction. In the service quality literature, expectations are what customers ideally want. They are customers' expressions of what they believe the service provider should offer, rather than would offer (Parasuraman et al. 1988). The service provider's time and effort are both wasted if the customer's expectations are different, as expectations influence the customer satisfaction at the time of service delivery (Coye 2004). According to Zeithaml et al. (1993), 'Expectations are viewed as predictions made by customers about what is likely to happen during an impending transaction or exchange'.

Expectations can be defined as, 'The preconceived set of ideas consumers have, that function as a point of reference against which performance is evaluated or judged'. Parasuraman et al. (1985) studied the different expectations a customer might have related to a service and gave the 'determinants of service quality' (Chapter 6 has already elaborated on customer perception). Kandampully (1998, 2000) stated that service quality is crucial for developing loyal customers and is hence responsible for the success of any service organization. At the time of service delivery the customers interact closely with the service providers and get an inside knowledge of the service organization. This knowledge gives them an opportunity to critically assess the service provided and the service provider. Thus, service quality plays an important role in adding value to the overall service experience. Also, customers seek organizations that are service loyal, that is, aim to provide consistent and superior quality of service for the present and in the long-term, and organizations aiming for this are bound to get customers' loyalty (Kandampully 1998).

A survey of the Indian banking sector in Delhi and National Capital Region (NCR) showed that there was a difference between the customer expectations and perceptions about the service quality offered by the different banks (Fig. 7.1). It was observed that there was a significant difference between customer expectations and perceptions in the public sector banks, while the foreign banks fared well with a low difference.

CUSTOMER EXPECTATIONS

Zeithaml et al. (1993) specified three different types of customer expectations of service—desired service, adequate service, and predicted service. *Desired service* is the service customers want or 'hope to receive'. For example, if a person signs on to www.naukri.com he/she expects to find a job as per his/her specifications, with a desired salary, in a particular locality. It is a combination of what the customer believes 'can be' and 'should be'. *Adequate service* is the standard of service the customers are willing to accept. For example, the customer knows that he may not find a job to suit his profile, or that he may have to compromise on salary, or, if both the profile and salary meet his expectations he may have to relocate. Thus, adequate service is the lowest level of service that the customer is willing to accommodate (Zeithaml et al. 1993). *Predicted service* is the level of service customers believe is likely to occur in a given situation. Predicted service expectations are lower than desired expectations and are the 'will' expectations of the customers (Boulding et al. 1993). These services can lie anywhere between the adequate and desired service levels for the customer to have a positive opinion about the service provider, so as to motivate the customer to try their services. However, predicted and desired services can be equal if the customer feels that the service provider is excellent (Hamer 2006) (Fig. 7.2). A zone of tolerance separates desired service from adequate service, and considerable variation has been found in customers' tolerance zone, which was likely to be different in different situations, and also differed from customer to customer.

Factors Influencing Customer Expectations

Expectations can be formed by a variety of reasons*. Some of these have been elaborated in this section.

---

* Adapted from Zeithaml (1993) and Boulding et al. (1993).

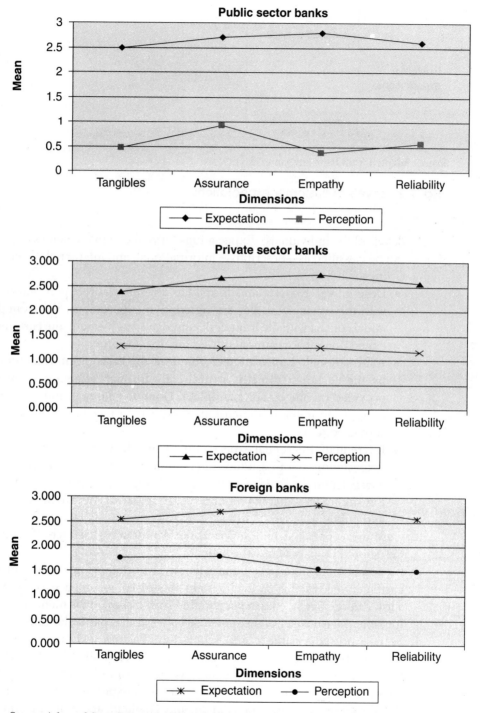

Source: Adapted from Dutta and Dutta (2007).

Fig. 7.1 Customer expectations vs perception of service quality—public, private, and foreign banks

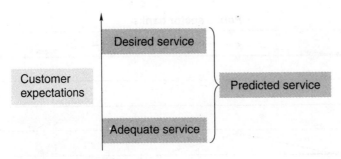

Source: Adapted from Parasuraman et al. (1991).

Fig. 7.2   Levels of customer expectations

1. Beliefs of the individuals: Expectations formed due to the beliefs of individuals can be classified as—descriptive, informational, and inferential (Coye 2004 and Grönroos 1988).
   - Descriptive: Expectations formed as a result of direct personal experience with the service provider are descriptive expectations. For example, if an initial contact with the front desk employee was pleasant, the customer would expect a similar treatment during the next visit too.
   - Informational: Expectations formed on the basis of information collected by the customer directly or indirectly through attention to information provided by others. For example, if Domino's Pizza promises to deliver its pizza in 30 minutes, the customer expects to receive the pizza within the stipulated time.
   - Inferential: Inferential expectation is when the customer draws an inference (expectation) about a future interaction on the basis of a prior belief. For example, on the basis of a pleasant exchange with the front desk employee, a customer feels that the room service staff is also going to be well-mannered and polite.
2. Customer's personal philosophy about a product or service: This influences the 'should be' aspect of expectations.
3. Customer's personal needs and wishes: Expectations are based on what the customer needs at that particular point of time. For example, if a customer needs a low calorie diet, he/she expects to find such dishes on the menu irrespective of the other lavish cuisines the outlet can offer at that particular time.
4. Service provider's image and reputation: Factors such as image of proven skills, performance, etc. which can be partly controlled by the organization also influence customer expectations. For example, the Shangri-La hotel advertisement carefully builds the customer's expectation by telling him/her that the cuisine is from China, Japan, and Thailand, and indicating the cost and the time he/she can expect to spend to dine at 19 Oriental Avenue.
5. Service provider's promises: The promises due to staff interaction, advertising, and other marketing communications can create problems when service providers

Exhibit 7.1   Jalandhar topping for Mac

The city of Jalandhar in Punjab boasts of the highest number of imported vehicles in the country. It is also far ahead of major metros as far as eating out is concerned. The McDonald's restaurant here is the highest selling outlet in the country. This is the major reason why the American fast food chain plans to open up more outlets in Punjab, as well as in other states such as Uttaranchal, Haryana, Himachal Pradesh, and Rajasthan among others. An investment of about Rs 400 crore is planned in India in the near future. The company recorded a CAGR of 40 per cent in the last few years and has had more sales via its drive-through restaurants than the normal ones. This clearly points to the fact that the Indian consumer is also particular about time, like their American counterparts. McDonald's is also having talks with Indian Railways to set up outlets at important railway stations. The talks seem positive and soon we may have travellers queuing up for a McBurger as in other countries, before catching their train.

Source: Adapted from Parameswaran (2006).

over-promise at the time of sale. If the service provider's promises, through staff interaction and advertisements, create expectations that are easily met, it leads to repeat patronage. Exhibit 7.1 illustrates how McDonald's has had a compounded average growth rate of 40 per cent in India in the last few years, and plans to open around 100 outlets in the country in the next two years.

6. Implicit service promises, such as price and tangibles, associated with the service: It is generally observed that people associate a higher price with a higher quality, and hence, their expectations are going to rise if the price is high in comparison to other service providers.

7. Word-of-mouth communication: Positive word-of-mouth communication from other customers, family, and friends, etc. raise customer expectations and due to the intangible characteristic of services, this aspect holds more significance in the purchase of services.

8. Prior experience with the service provider: The perceived service quality delivered by a service organization forms an important basis for the customers to revise their expectations when they next visit the service organization.

9. Perception of service alternatives: Alternatives include the other service providers for the same service category from whom the customer can obtain services. If there are a number of service alternatives customer expectations for the services are bound to be higher than when there are few alternatives available. For example, when only Indian Airlines and Air India were operating in India, and customers did not have any other option, their expectations were different; but with the advent of other players the customer expectations for air travel services are more varied. Similarly, in the UK, Travelodge faced a problem when it felt that four hotel groups Hilton, Marriott, Swallow, and Macdonald advertised their room rates on the basis of price per person. In the January 2006 issue of *The Times*, it made a full-page accusation against the hotels, claiming that the ads quoted indicated price per person, and were based on two people sharing a room, for a minimum of two nights. Hence, the advertised rate of £49.95 was

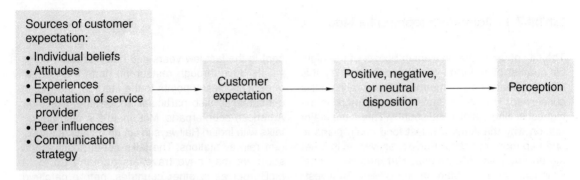

Source: Adapted from Robledo (2001).

Fig. 7.3   Managing customer expectations

likely to cost almost £200 for the stay. Though all the hotels refuted the claim, Travelodge registered its complaint with the advertising standards watchdog, and compiled a dossier of ads it felt were misleading, to present to the Consumer Association (Frewin 2006).

Managing Customer Expectations

Once the service provider is aware of the customer expectations, the next step is to manage the customer expectations. Customer expectations can be managed by controlling the different factors that influence them (Fig. 7.3).

Consumer education   The expectations of consumers can be managed by educating them about the services that the service providers offer. This can be done by different contact methods.

- through call centres, when customer care executives call to provide information about a service that is to be offered
- educating the customer when he/she makes an inquiry prior to a purchase
- using publicity to promote the products.

A case in point is when many service providers offer loyalty points for spending money on their services, but customers realize that after spending so much, the return was negligible. I-mint, India's first coalition loyalty programme has been launched to counter this, so that customers get a better deal for the same money spent (Exhibit 7.2).

By providing customer education, companies can manage individual beliefs and philosophy of the customer. Also, by providing this education at the time of service delivery, they can mould the expectations for the next service interaction with the customer.

Corporate communication   Through their various communication tools, organizations can provide cues to the customers about their service quality and thus help them to build realistic expectations. These expectations are based on the service provider's image and reputation, which can be partly controlled by the service organization.

Exhibit 7.2 How to get more for your loyalty

Loyalty programmes have become commonplace among huge retail chains, such as Shoppers Stop, Lifestyle, and Pantaloons, as well as airlines, restaurants, etc. But the fact remains, that the rewards one gets, even with a loyalty card are minuscule. For example, getting a discount of Rs 100 after spending Rs 10,000 is no motivation at all. To change this, coalition loyalty programmes are being introduced, in which different companies get together to offer a single loyalty programme and collectively reward their customers.

The Nectar Card, one such coalition loyalty card in the UK, has about 55 per cent of Britons as its members. The benefit is that the customer gets an advantage of various stores through a single card and the points accumulated are higher, thus leading to higher rewards. In India, I-mint has introduced coalition loyalty, the first of its kind in India. It currently has six companies partnering it—ICICI Bank, HPCL, Airtel, Lifestyle, makemytrip.com, and Indian. Con-sider the supreme advantage; if one pays one's Airtel bill via an ICICI credit card and fills petrol from HPCL, one gets rewarded by all these companies. Also, the customer is able to redeem the points at any of these six companies within a timeframe of six months.

Other companies such as Big Bazaar have tied up with ICICI to offer rewards to their customers, but only on credit card transactions. This rules out cash and debit card as modes of payment. The coalition loyalty card I-mint on the other hand, allows payment by cash or debit cards as well. Many critics of these cards believe that this process does not develop loyalty and is purely transactional in nature. It surely suits mid-size companies who are not able to undertake technology programmes of this scale. But the truth is that these next generation coalition loyalty cards seem to be the best way for a company to reward its customers.

Source: Adapted from Daftari (2006).

Service delivery Managing customer expectations at the time of service delivery is easier said than done. The delivery of services is a crucial aspect due to the different characteristics of services and the presence of the customers as part of the delivery process. If customer expectations are not met, they can be managed only if the customer complains to the service provider. Chapter 10 provides a more elaborate discussion on service recovery. The delivery of the service in the initial experience of the customer should focus on individual beliefs and try to align them with the service organization's service delivery. They will also form an input for the service quality expectations formed by the customer for subsequent re-purchases. If the service delivery matches or exceeds customer expectations, it results in positive word-of-mouth feedback by the customers and vice-versa.

Service guarantees It can be provided to manage customer expectations as the customer feels that if the expectations are not met there is some compensation attached, and it also gives him/her an added reason to complain to the service provider about any unmet expectation. In the pre-purchase stage, they also act as a reassurance to the customer that if their needs and wishes are not met, there is some compensation attached. Service guarantees also provide a differential advantage to organizations when other competitors in the industry are not following them, and may influence the customer to purchase from the service provider who is offering such guarantees.

Price policy One of the factors affecting the customer's perception of the service quality is the price. Thus, organizations should choose their pricing policy with great care so as to affect the customer expectation in a manner that meets the quality to be delivered by the service organization.

Positioning Another way of managing customer expectations is by positioning the services in the mind of the customers to give a realistic direction to the service expectation. Positioning can create a differential advantage for the firm vis-à-vis other service providers. The positioning strategy should be in line with the pricing strategy so that there is complete harmony in the marketing communications.

Mission statement This gives the customers the long-term vision and values of the organization. Mission statement can be used as a tool to inform customers about the organization's strategy and reason for existence, so that they can form realistic expectations. They help the customer to form the image of the organization and hence, their expectations from the organization.

Service quality Customer expectations can be met and managed by managing the service quality and training, and motivating the staff to follow the best practices.

Related concepts On the basis of all the cues discussed earlier, we can manage customer expectations. As discussed in the Gap model in Chapter 6, a gap occurs when customer expectations and perception of service delivery do not match. We can say that the experience of the delivery of services causes expectations to be as follows (Afthinos et al. 2005 and Hamer 2006):

- Confirmed: When the performance of the service organization is as per expectation, then expectations are said to be confirmed.
- Disconfirmed: When the perceived performance of the service organization is not as per customer expectations, services are said to be disconfirmed. Services can be:
  - Negatively disconfirmed: When the customer's perception of service delivery by the service organization is below expectation, disconfirmation is said to be negative.
  - Positively disconfirmed: When the customer's perception of service delivery by the service organization is better or exceeds expectations, disconfirmation is said to be positive.

Consumers who perceive a positive disconfirmation will perceive the service provider as being higher in quality than a consumer who experiences negative disconfirmation. Thus, exceeding expectations is preferable to failing to meet, or meeting expectations. According to Hamer (2006), exceeding low expectations results in the same level of quality perceptions as exceeding high expectations. As discussed in the section on factors affecting customer perception, the prior experience of customers with the service provider affects their expectations when they next visit the organization. If a firm delivers services that show positive disconfirmation, that is, exceed the customers' initial expectations, they tend to revise their expectations upwards. These revised expectations form the basis of customer perception of service quality when he/she next visits the service organization, who will then have to deliver a higher level of service to keep up with the expectations and this cycle is repeated every time the customer comes to it for a re-purchase.

If the organization under-promises but over-delivers, this will create a problem where the customers form an initial low perception of service quality and may not even want to try the services initially. Thus Hamer (2006) expounded that the best option is to create 'realistic expectation setting' (as proposed by Bitner et al. 1997) by promising realistically and delivering consistently. Rust et al. (1999) by their longitudinal experiment showed that if the customer expectations are exactly met, it results in a positive preference shift. Even not quite meeting customer expectations may still increase the preference for the service provider, as the customer has experienced the service and so there is shrinkage in the variance of predictive service delivery in the next transaction. Thus, the experience leads to decreased risk and this leads to greater preference for the service provider.

If we consider the Gap model as discussed in Chapter 6, we see that the service quality delivery gaps occur initially due to the difference between the customer expectations and the management's perception of the customer expectations. Thus, the first step to managing customer expectations is to conduct market research and analyse what customers actually expect from the service organization. Managers should not only make an effort to understand the customers' needs and expectations, but also communicate this information to all the front-level employees so that they can manage better and cater to those customer expectations.

Customer expectations affect the perceived quality of services. If the communication tools of the company raises the customer expectations then even if the quality of service delivered is high, it may not match with the raised customer expectations and lead to a lower perception by the customers. The importance of managing expectations is further supported by the study that if the perceptions are held as fixed, it is observed that higher the expectations, the lower is the perceived quality (Boulding et al. 1993).

A PROCESS MODEL OF CUSTOMER SERVICE EXPECTATION MANAGEMENT

Managing customer expectations is crucial for an organization's success. As discussed earlier, we have different strategies proposed for managing expectations. Since services involve continuous interaction between the customers and service providers, we can manage expectations at two levels:

- When the customer is not in direct contact with the service provider—pre- and post-service encounters.
- When the customer is in direct contact with the service provider—during the service delivery process.

We have studied that customers have their set of expectations when they enter the process of service delivery. These expectations are affected by the controllable cues (which are directly controllable by the service organization such as price, marketing communication, etc.) and uncontrollable cues (which are not under direct control of the organization such as publicity, word-of-mouth communication, etc.). All these have

Delivery

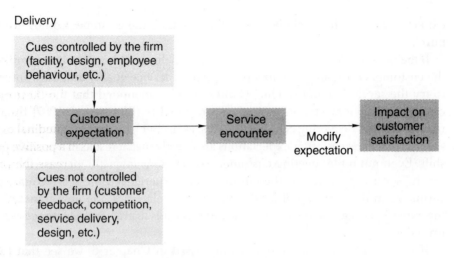

Source: Adapted from Coye (2004).

Fig. 7.4 Expectation management during service

been discussed in detail in the section on managing customer expectations. When the customer enters the service delivery process with such expectations, it is the role of the service provider to manage the customer expectations while providing the services, so that it results in a positive service quality perception by the customer. These can be provided in the form of planned cues and by responding to the unplanned cues. Planned cues are provided with the deliberate intention of raising, lowering, or making relevant initial expectations. They include the planning of tangibles such as facility, design, employee behaviour, delivery of services, client-to-client interaction, etc. If the service provider believes that the initial expectations are unrealistically high, then it is important to modify these expectations to fit closely to what it can deliver. This can be identified by the nature of service request, which if unrealistic can trigger service providers to clarify these unrealistic expectations. For example, if a medical practitioner faces an unrealistic expectation from a client, she can provide standardized responses, and if they do not suffice she can then provide customer specific responses to modify the customer expectations realistically. In the practitioner's office, the display of her various certificates of degrees and achievements are all cues that she is providing to the customers, to form or modify their expectations (Fig. 7.4).

Unplanned cues are the environmental cues provided to the customers within the service delivery scenario and can be in the form of interaction with other customers, observing the service delivery to other clients present, etc. For example, if while waiting for a dental treatment the patient hears other clients complaining about the pain, he may be de-motivated. The service provider's role here is then more of damage control. She will have to reassure the patient that his treatment will be different and hence less painful than that of other patients. It is thus important for the service provider to be aware of the types of cues the customers may react to and try to overcome them, either

---

Exhibit 7.3 Soon, blog from your cell phones

It will soon be easy for people to share photographs, music, etc. via their mobiles, as telephone operators will soon start m-blogging. Imagine sending a photograph of the Taj Mahal instantly to somebody you know. A mobile web log refers to putting something on the net using a mobile phone or PDA. Reliance Communications Ltd (RCL) is the first telecom operator to host a blogging site in India. RCL will charge Rs 5 per MMS for customers who have MMS and video capability on their phones. All other customers will be able to send only text blogs. A return SMS specifies the user's password and the website URL for their blog. It has been recognized that the blogging community is on a rise and other companies, such as Tata Teleservices and Idea Cellular, are offering m-blogging by hosting various URLs.

But, at the same time the thinking of these telecom companies points to the fact that m-blog is not considered a huge revenue generator for the company. It is, in fact, being considered as a service offered in order to serve the needs of the ever-increasing bloggers' community.

Source: Adapted from Pratap (2006).

---

explicitly or covertly. By managing both the planned and unplanned cues, the aim is to modify the customer expectations and make them more realistic. In case the customer does not respond to the cues and expects to experience the same service he had anticipated initially, it is up to the service provider to try and provide cues so that there is minimum gap between the expected and the desired services. One way can be to manage the services product. Keeping in mind the customer expectations, service providers should try to modify the service 'product' the best they can, so that some of the customer's requirements are met. Exhibit 7.3 illustrates how telecom operators provided blogging services on cell phones. Reliance Communications Ltd is the first operator to provide such services and meet the customer expectations.

Influenced by the cues, the customer experiences the service provided and may feel that the expectations are either met or unmet, or a combination of both. Based on the levels of expectations met by the service provider, customers form their perception of the service quality, which ultimately impacts the satisfaction level of the customer with the service provider. If the cues at the time of service delivery are managed well, the chances are that the customer forms realistic expectations, which are most likely to be met at the time of service delivery, leading to a favourable perception of the service provided and hence higher level of satisfaction with the service provider (Coye 2004).

However, it is sometimes observed that the customers are themselves not clear about their expectations. They may have fuzzy, implicit, or unrealistic expectations (Table 7.1). Fuzzy expectations refer to expectations by customers when they are not clear about what they want from the service provider. They may feel that something is wrong or lacking but are themselves not clear about what the change should be. When customers experience the service, fuzzy expectations remain fuzzy and so they do not feel satisfied. The task of the service provider is to focus on the fuzzy expectations and by initiating a dialogue with the customer, try to make the expectations more precise and the customer more convinced of the type of change they are looking for so that on experiencing the service they are clear about their expectations, and hence there is a higher probability of trying to satisfy them.

Table 7.1	A framework for managing expectations	
Input (Customer expectations)	**Process** (Expectations management)	**Output** (Managed expectations)
Fuzzy expectations	Focusing	Precise expectations
Implicit expectations	Revealing	Explicit expectations
Unrealistic expectations	Calibrating	Realistic expectations

Source: Adapted from Ojasalo (2001).

Implicit expectations refer to those elements of the service that are so evident that customers do not think about them consciously and so do not take into account the probability of them not materializing, and are more common when the service provider and the customer have a long history of mutual dealing. However, the problem arises when these expectations are not met. Hence, it is the task of the management to reveal the implicit expectations of the customers in order to make them explicit. If the customers do not make them explicit then the expectations are not met, and hence will be self-evident in the next transaction, as implicit services cause a negative surprise when they are not met but do not cause any positive surprise when they are met. When the service provider does not meet such expectations, it gives the customers reason to complain and be unhappy about the service provided.

Unrealistic expectations are expectations that are highly unlikely to be met by any service provider; for example, an organization wants a recruitment agency to find a type of person who is difficult to find. The customers themselves cannot meet such unrealistic expectations. Such expectations can be managed by calibrating the unrealistic expectation. Defining the problem, and executing the solution and the effects of the solution can often achieve this. By calibrating the expectations, customers are made aware at the onset of the service process that their expectations are unreal and hence cannot be met. This also creates dissatisfaction in the customers but the degree is less than it would have been if the customers had been made to realize this later in the service delivery process, when more time and money had been invested. Fuzzy, implicit, and unrealistic expectations are more common in professional services such as consultancy, recruitment services, etc. (Ojasalo 2001).

SUMMARY

At the time of purchase of services, customers have a perception about what the service providers 'should' offer rather than 'would' offer. This expectation further helps the customer in evaluating the purchase decision leading to customer satisfaction (if expectations are met) or dissatisfaction (if expectations are not met). Expectations that are in line with the delivery of services require the least effort to deliver a satisfactory experience for the customer. The marketers

Contd

Summary Contd

should thus be aware of the various types of customer expectations—desired, adequate, and predicted. If they are aware of the various factors influencing the customer expectation, they can influence and manage them better.

The chapter thus discusses this issue first and then delineates the various factors influencing customer expectations and how to manage them, so that they are as realistic as possible. This is done holistically by not only focusing on customer education but also on other factors such as service guarantees, promotional campaigns, corporate communication, price policy, etc. A model has been proposed to manage customer expectations during the service delivery process so that the customers perceive the service quality positively. Thus managing customer expectations is important as the perceptions of service quality are measured against these. Perception of service quality is the basis of customer satisfaction and, in turn, builds strong customer relationships.

KEY TERMS

Customer expectations   The pre-conceived set of ideas consumers have, that function as a point of reference against which performance is evaluated.

Fuzzy expectations   These expectations are when the customers are not clear about what they want from the service provider.

Implicit expectations   They are elements of the service that are so evident that customers do not think about them consciously and so do not take into account the probability of them not materializing.

Unrealistic expectations   Those expectations that are highly unlikely to be met by any service provider.

CONCEPT REVIEW QUESTIONS

1. Critically discuss the importance of customer expectations in the role of service delivery.

2. Discuss the different types of customer expectations and their relative importance to a service marketer.

3. Critically discuss five factors influencing customer expectations, which according to you are most important.

4. Discuss any three marketing strategies, which can be most effective in managing customer expectations.

5. Explain fuzzy and unrealistic expectations and how the services marketer can overcome them.

CRITICAL THINKING QUESTIONS

1. Consider your recent services purchase, and identify your expectations for the purchase and the factors responsible for forming these expectations.

2. Discuss instances in your service purchases when your expectations were not met. Try and evaluate the reasons for your unmet service expectations.

3. Discuss instances when your service expectations were surpassed. How did this affect your future expectations and interactions with the service organization?

================ **INTERNET EXERCISES** ================

1. Visit the website of an organization in the aviation sector and try to form your expectations based on the information available.

2. If given an opportunity to make changes to the website of your favourite hospitality firm,

what changes would you recommend to influence the expectations of the customers, and why?

CASE STUDY

Distance Learning Programmes

Introduction

The world is witnessing strong winds of change. Global boundaries are vanishing giving rise to the concept of the 'global village'. Rapid transformation in business and industry has revolutionized the executive mindset and education is emerging as the most powerful platform to progress in this world without boundaries. The concept of education is itself changing. It is no longer a static, regimented process confined to the formative years of childhood or adolescence, but is a dynamic, continuous, and ongoing process that extends throughout an individual's professional career. To provide the opportunity of learning along with maintaining a professional career, many institutes have come up with the concept of distance learning programmes. These programmes not only provide higher education without the constraints of location and time, but also give professionals the opportunity of academic enhancement, which reflects in their professional recognition.

Distance learning is being propagated as the education of the twenty-first century. Moving with the e-business, the education sector also plans to accomplish more by changing focus from 'brick-and-mortar' to 'click-and-mortar'. A number of institutes in India are providing distance learning programmes along with regular options of classroom teaching. Some of them are Symbiosis Centre for Distance Learning, Narsee Monjee Institute of Management Studies, HughesNet Global Education, and IMT Distance and Open Learning Institute.

The impact of the rapid pace of transformation in business and industry has triggered a metamorphosis in executive mindsets. This has made it imperative for graduates, aspiring businesspersons, and professionals to equip themselves with the latest know-how and best practices. Versatile management training is indispensable as it provides the requisite skill sets to withstand the emerging challenges of the corporate world and successfully leverage career opportunities.

Higher and Technical Education

The importance of education, especially higher education, has been constantly growing and knowledge-based industries are now occupying centre stage in development. Though the modern higher education system in India is almost 135 years old, its growth has been much faster after India became independent.

Over the past 50 years, there has been a significant growth in the number of new universities and institutions of higher learning in specialized areas. There are now 273 universities/deemed to be universities (including 18 medical universities and 40 agricultural universities) and 12,300 colleges (of which 4,683 are in the rural areas) (Table 7.2).

Ninth Plan

The Ninth Plan reiterates the objectives/policy directions of the National Policy for Education, 1986, and the Programme of Action, 1992.

Table 7.2 Number of institutions of higher education, enrolment, and faculty

Year	Number of colleges	Number of universities*	Students (in 000)	Teachers (in 000)
1950–51	750	30	2,63,000	24,000
1990–91	7,346	177	49,25,000	2,72,000
1996–97	9,703	214	67,55,000	3,21,000
1998–99	11,089	238	74,17,000	3,42,000

Note: * includes institutions that are deemed to be universities, but excludes other institutions.
Source: UGC Annual Report 1996–97 and 1998–99 and selected educational statistics, Ministry of HRD.

Broadly, the Ninth Plan emphasizes the following strategies to improve the higher education system:

o consolidation and expansion of institutions

o development of autonomous colleges and departments

o redesigning of courses

o training of teachers

o strengthening of research

o improvements in efficiency

o review and monitoring, etc.

The Ninth Plan period saw the emergence of separate universities for science and technology, and health sciences; autonomous colleges with the freedom to design curricula; evolution of new methods of teaching and research; framing of admission rules and conducting of examinations; as well as the creation of centres of excellence and the National Assessment and Accreditation Council (NAAC). There are also institutions of higher learning recognized as deemed to be universities with their own sources of funding, in addition to government grants. The major emphasis in strategies relating to higher education during this period has been on an integrated approach, with an emphasis on excellence and equity, relevance, promotion of value education, and strengthening the management systems. Autonomous centres have been set up within the university system to provide common facilities, services, and programmes to universities, and for the promotion of quality.

It is increasingly recognized that in the context of major economic and technological changes, the system of higher education should equip students with adequate skills to enable their full participation in the emerging social, economic, and cultural environment. Universities are thus witnessing a sea change in their outlook and perspective. Also, information and communication technology is leading to fundamental changes in the structure, management, and mode of delivery of the entire educational system.

Many universities have already recognized the strategic significance of open and distance learning and offer correspondence courses. At the beginning of the decade, there were 64 universities offering courses through correspondence. The developments in the field of information technology and expansion of infrastructure for communication all over the country has created an unprecedented opportunity to serve the needs of continuing education, and also to meet the demands for equal opportunity for higher education. The Indira Gandhi National Open University (IGNOU), established in 1985, has 1.2 million students on its rolls and offers 72 programmes. The university has created a countrywide network of student support structures, with 46 regional centres and 765 study centres. It has also created a media network and teleconferencing system to electronically link all distance teaching institutions in the country. Many departments of correspondence courses in various universities were converted into independent open universities during the Ninth Plan period. There are, at present, nine open universities in the country, all started by different states during the 1990s.

Tenth Plan—Objectives, Key Issues, and Focus

The main objective in the Tenth Plan is to raise the enrolment in higher education of the 18–23 year age group from the present 6 per cent to 10 per cent by the end of the plan period. The strategies would focus on increasing access, quality, adoption of state-specific strategies, and the liberalization of the higher education system. Emphasis would also be laid on the relevance of the curriculum, vocationalization, and networking on the use of information technology. The Plan would focus on distance education; convergence of formal, non-formal, distance, and IT education institutions; increased private participation in the management of colleges and deemed to be universities; research in frontier areas of knowledge; and meeting the challenges in the area of internationalization of Indian education.

The issues of access and equity are central to the university/higher education system. Only about 6 per cent of the estimated population in the 18–23 age group is currently in the university system. Measures to increase enrolment, including that of the disadvantaged sections, will thus be given attention during the Plan.

Quality Improvement/Academic Reforms/ Relevance of Curriculum

The basic issue of quality improvement will be addressed through the modernization of syllabi, increased research, networking of universities and departments, and increased allocation of funds. Networking through local area network (LAN), wide area network (WAN), information and library network (INFLIBNET) will also lead to increased academic activities and research. The university system will be expected to utilize the autonomy it enjoys for innovations in teaching and for pursuing high-quality research. The emphasis will be on conferring autonomous status on more colleges, provision of the means to interact across geographical boundaries of institutions, improving the infrastructure, more rationalized funding of research, integration of teaching, research and evaluation, and mutual collaboration and cooperation among universities for optimum utilization of available resources. There is a pressing need

to improve the management and governance of universities to better enforce financial and administrative discipline. Decentralization of the university system, greater powers to faculty departments and nomination of students to university bodies on the basis of merit/excellence are therefore, issues, which will receive attention. The accreditation process should be made more transparent, time-bound, and be progressively freed of government regulations and control, leading to a situation when the whole procedure would be based on a system of public appraisal/acceptance.

Under the ongoing scheme of strengthening scientific research, the UGC will continue to assist university departments, which have achieved excellence in research in different disciplines of science, especially in the emerging areas of biotechnology, biomedicine, genetic engineering, nuclear medicine, social science, humanities, etc.

In view of the resource crunch faced by the UGC and the higher education system, it is proposed to give incentives to universities/colleges, which make efforts to increase/raise internal resources.

Distance Education and IGNOU

The non-formal system (distance and open learning) accounts for only 13 per cent of the total enrolment in higher education. Out of 7.7 million students enrolled in universities and colleges, the distance education/correspondence courses cover only one million students. The distance and open learning system provides flexibility in terms of combination of courses, age of entry, pace of learning, and methods of evaluation. The coverage of open universities will, therefore, need to be extended to the backward regions, remote inaccessible tribal areas of the northeast and some of the eastern states. At present, there are nine state open universities and 64 institutes of correspondence courses and Directorates of Distance Education in conventional universities. The enrolment of distance learners in the open and distance education system is expected to rise significantly in the Tenth Plan period. IGNOU has expanded its regional centres and network of study centres in the Ninth Plan period. It now has 46 regional centres and 691 study centres. It has been vested with the twin responsibilities of acting as an open university and offering need-based education, training, and extension programmes, with special focus on the disadvantaged sections of the society, and acting as the national nodal agency to determine and maintain standards in distance education.

IGNOU has established the Distance Education Council (DEC) to act as the nodal agency for the distance education system at the tertiary level. The university has adopted an integrated multimedia instructions strategy consisting of print material and audio–video programmes, supported by counselling sessions at study centres. It manages a dedicated 24-hour satellite TV channel, Gyan Darshan, which beams educational programmes from school to tertiary level, 24 hours a day. Preparations are on to launch 40 FM educational radio channels (known as Gyan Vani) under a memorandum of understanding with Prasar Bharati. During the Tenth Plan, IGNOU will set up open universities in states where none exist at present, and expand the activities of Gyan Darshan and Gyan Vani. The target is to extend the coverage of the open learning system to the backward regions, remote inaccessible areas of the northeast, and low female literacy blocks in some of the eastern states.

In April 2002, the government constituted the Committee on Promotion of Indian Education Abroad (COPIEA) under the chairmanship of Secretary, Department of Secondary & Higher Education. With globalization of the Indian economy, student mobility across national boundaries has increased phenomenally in the higher, technical, and management sectors. A large number of foreign educational institutes have also established their presence in India and there is immense potential for Indian educational institutions to set up campuses abroad. The COPIEA will monitor all activities aimed at promoting Indian education abroad and will regulate the operation of foreign educational institutions to safeguard the interests of the students and the larger national interest as well. To this end, a system of registration will be introduced under which institutions will have to furnish information on operations and adhere to certain guidelines relating to publicity, maintenance of standards, charging of fees, granting of degrees, etc. The COPIEA will, over a period of time, develop a sectoral policy on foreign direct investment in the education sector.

Symbiosis

Symbiosis Centre for Distance Learning (SCDL) started in 1994, as a 'correspondence section' of Symbiosis Institute of Management Studies (SIMS) for defence personnel and their dependents. In the year 2001, SCDL was established as a separate institute offering courses through the medium of distance education, providing an opportunity to thousands of students to enhance their careers and lives. The vision of SCDL is to create a 'world campus' where any one is able to learn and achieve their dreams for higher education and enhanced career. The mission of SCDL is to provide every student with a means for 'self-paced, self-styled learning' anywhere, anytime.

SCDL has grown exponentially in the last four years, attracting students from all states of India and from more than 20 foreign countries. Today, SCDL has an active student strength of over 60,000. It has introduced new courses each year and established facilities, services, and technologies to assist the student community. In the past three years, SCDL has gained tremendous popularity not only amongst fresh graduates seeking higher education, but also among working professionals from the corporate and administrative sectors. The emphasis on improving the quality of education and students services has been the main reason for this popularity. SCDL diplomas are widely recognized and accepted by the industry, and in fact, SCDL has become the 'preferred education provider' for several top companies nationwide such as IBM, Cognizant, Wipro, Spectramind, Sahara Group, Reliance Infostreams, CSC India, etc.

Learning Methodology

Symbiosis follows blended learning, i.e., combining various forms of learning.

- Customized study material books for self-study.
- Online learning/e-learning to enhance understanding of key concepts through interactive e-learning modules.
- Monthly classroom lectures at the corporate premises—faculty based learning to promote peer-interaction.
- Students address their specific academic queries via e-mail to SCDL, to which an in-depth reply is sent by an expert faculty within 2–3 days e-mentoring.

Narsee Monjee Institute of Management Studies

In order to meet the growing demand for management education, Narsee Monjee Institute of Management and Higher Studies (NMIMS) was established in 1981. The institute commenced its activities with a master's degree programme in management studies. It later started the distance learning programme under the Department of Distance Learning and offers various courses.

Learning Methodology

The programmes include study material, self-evaluatory quizzes, discussion questions and personal contact programmes (PCPs). Students can interact with designated NMIMS faculty via e-mail for clarification of doubts.

HughesNet Global Education

HughesNet is a premier, satellite-based education and training service for corporates and working professionals. The HughesNet Global Education platform seeks to re-define the next generation of education—real time interactive onsite learning (IOL). The platform seamlessly integrates the strengths and advantages of the traditional method of education with the latest in technology. Using a very powerful interface, HughesNet Global Education enables a student to have highly interactive sessions with students and instructors all over the country, using video, voice, and data.

Over the last two years, over 4,750 students have successfully completed a programme on this platform, thus demonstrating its efficacy and effectiveness. Best of all, these programmes are convenient, accessible, and targeted to suit the continuing education needs. With 50 classrooms in 34 different cities in the country, HughesNet Global Education has made higher education simpler than ever before. It has tied-up with premier institutes in India (and abroad), which include names such as the IIMs, XLRI, NMIMS, etc.

IIM Kozhikode

In May 2002, IIM Kozhikode became the first management institute in India to offer a management programme (Executive Management Education Programme—e-MEP) over the Hughes DirecWay platform. Over 500 professionals have taken up the 10-month programme.

IIM Calcutta

In November 1961, the Government of India established the Indian Institute of Management, Calcutta (IIMC) as the first national institute for post-graduate studies and research in management. It has been playing a pioneering role in professionalizing Indian management through its post graduate and doctoral level programmes, executive training programmes, and research and consulting activities.

For example, if you log on to IIMC for a general management programme for IT professionals, the programme delivery is shown as follows. The sessions will be delivered on HughesNet Global Education's Interactive Onsite Learning platform. The heart of the platform is a powerful user interface that enables a large number of geographically distributed students to have a highly interactive 'one-to-one'/'one-to-many' exchange with a central faculty. The system incorporates live broadcast video, and two-way audio and data interactivity to enable students to watch and interact with the faculty live on their PCs.

IIM Bangalore

The Indian Institute of Management, Bangalore (IIMB) was established in 1973. Today, IIMB is recognized as India's best business school. Its world-class infrastructure provides the foundation for its programmes of teaching, research, consulting, and other professional services.

XLRI Jamshedpur

XLRI Jamshedpur, one of India's premier management institutes, announced the launch of a Post Graduate Certificate in Business Management (PGCBM) in August 2002. This programme is designed for high potential, mid-career managers moving up to the next level in business management.

IIFT Delhi

One of the top 10 management institutes in India, IIFT Delhi offers working executives one of its most sought-after programmes on the HughesNet Global Education Interactive Onsite Learning platform, namely, Executive Masters in International Business or EMIB.

Manipal University

This, the largest private education initiative in India, will offer a one-year executive MBA programme on the HughesNet Global Education platform. Other Courses offered are MBA-FS and PGDBM.

Narsee Monjee Institute of Management Studies (Deemed University)

Better known as NMIMS (Deemed University), it is one of the top ten business schools in India with excellent brand value, intellectual capital, infrastructure, and focus towards growth (*Business India* 2002). PGDGM offered by NMIMS is a 14-month programme designed specifically for working executives and is tailor-made for all those who want an edge without quitting their current job and without compromising on the faculty or the institute from which they would like to acquire the necessary knowledge.

Apollo University

Apollo International, in cooperation with Hughes Escorts Communication Limited (HECL), is making US-accredited Western International Universities (WIU) degrees accessible to Indian students supported by HECL satellite technology. Students go through a 14-month course in international business, and are enrolled directly with the Apollo University.

Loyola Institute of Business Administration

Loyola Institute of Business Administration (LIBA) had its origin in the year 1979. Located in the sprawling campus of scenic and idyllic Loyola College (established in 1925), LIBA is one of the most prestigious management institutes in south India. It has attained an enviable ninth position among management schools in India. To retain its status as a premier business school, LIBA relies heavily on a two-way interaction with business and industry.

Conclusion

Thus, we see that a number of institutes are offering distance learning programmes by adopting a variety of standardized programme delivery methods. The question arises that with these standardized programmes being offered to a vast majority of students in different parts of the country, with varied academic standings, and hence, requirements, how do these universities cater to the expectations and needs of the different customers. How do they make sure that the needs of the students for the academic quest are being fulfilled? To what extent are the customer expectations being achieved and what are the customer expectations from such institutes? These are some of the issues that need to be discussed.

Questions

1. What according to you are the customer expectations in the distance learning programmes?

2. What are the ways in which the distance learning programmes are imparting knowledge to the students in the different institutes covered?

3. Critically discuss the programme delivery methodology adopted by the different institutes and give suggestions for future delivery of courses.

SELECT REFERENCES

Afthinos, Yanni, Nicholas Theodorakis, and Nassis Pantelis (2005), 'Customers' expectations of service in Greek fitness centres', *Managing Service Quality*, vol. 15, no. 3, pp. 245–258.

Bitner, Mary Jo, William T. Faranda, Amy R. Hubbert, and Valarie A. Zeithaml (1997), 'Customer contributions and roles in service delivery', *International Journal of Service Industry Management* vol. 8, no. 3, pp. 193–202.

Boulding, William, Ajay Kalra, Richard Staelin, and Valarie A. Zeithaml (1993), 'A dynamic process model of service quality: From expectations to behavioural intentions', *Journal of Marketing Research*, vol. 30, no. 1, pp. 7–27.

Coye, Ray W. (2004), 'Managing customer expectations in the service encounter', *International Journal of Service Industry Management*, vol. 15, no. 1, pp. 54–71.

Daftari, Irshad (2006), 'How to get more for your loyalty', *The Economic Times*, 4 September, p. 13.

Dutta, Kirti and Anil Dutta (2007), 'Customer expectations and perceptions of service quality in the banking sector: A study of India', 3rd International conference on Services Management, Pennsylvania State University.

Frewin, Angela (2006), 'Travelodge hits out at "misleading" ads', *Caterer & Hotelkeeper*, vol. 196, no. 4408.

Grönroos, C. (1988), 'Service quality: The six criteria of good perceived service quality', *Review of Business*, vol. 9, no. 3, pp. 10–13.

Hamer, Lawrence (2006), 'A confirmation perspective on perceived service quality', *Journal of Services Marketing*, vol. 20, no. 4, pp. 219–232.

Kandampully, Jay (1998), 'Service quality to service loyalty: A relationship which goes beyond customer services', *Total Quality Management*, vol. 9, no. 6, pp. 431–444.

Kandampully, Jay (2000), 'The impact of demand fluctuation on the quality of service: A tourism industry example', *Managing Service Quality*, vol. 10, no. 1, pp. 10–18.

Kangis, Peter and Vassilis Voukelatos (1997), 'Private and public banks: A comparison of customer expectations and perceptions', *International Journal of Bank Marketing*, vol. 15, no. 7, pp. 279–287.

Ojasalo, Jukka (2001), 'Managing customer expectations in professional services', *Managing Service Quality*, vol. 11, no. 3, pp. 200–212.

Parameswaran, Maheswaran (2006), 'Jalandhar topping for Mac', *The Economic Times*, 18 September, p. 4.

Parasuraman, A., V.A. Zeithaml, and L.L. Berry (1985), 'A conceptual model of service quality and its implications for future research', *Journal of Marketing*, vol. 49, no. 4, p. 47.

Parasuraman, A., V.A. Zeithaml, and L.L. Berry (1988), 'SERVQUAL: A multiple-item scale for measuring consumer perceptions of service quality', *Journal of Retailing*, vol. 64, no. 1, pp. 12–37.

Parasuraman, A., V.A. Zeithaml, and L.L. Berry (1991), 'Understanding customer expectations of service', *Sloan Management Review*, vol. 32, no. 3, pp. 39–48.

Pratap, Rashmi (2006), 'Soon, blog from your cell phones: Reliance first operator to launch moblogging', *The Economic Times*, 10 October.

Robledo, Marco Antonio (2001), 'Measuring and managing service quality: Integrating customer expectations', *Managing Service Quality*, vol. 11, no. 1, pp. 22–31.

Rust, Roland T., Jeffery J. Inman, Jianmin Jia, and Anthony Zahorik (1999), 'What you don't know about customer perceived quality: The role of customer expectation distributions', *Marketing Science*, vol. 18, no. 1, pp. 77–92.

Shangri-La advertisement (2006), *The Economic Times*, 3 November.

Zeithaml, Valarie A. and Mary Jo Bitner (2003), *Services Marketing*, Tata McGraw-Hill Publishing Company Limited, New Delhi.

Zeithaml, V.A., L.L. Berry, and A. Parasuraman (1993), 'The nature and determinants of customer expectations of service', *Journal of the Academy of Marketing Service*, vol. 21, no. 1, pp. 1–12.

http://www.cityofahmedabad.com/nmims/, accessed on 7 November 2006.

Hughes (2006), http://www.hughes-ecomm.com/services/global_services.htm, accessed on 6 November 2006.

Narsee Monjee Institute for Management Studies (2006), www.nmims.edu, accessed on 7 November 2006.

Planning Commission (2006), Vision 2020, Planning Commission, Government of India, http://planning commission.nic.in/plans/planrel/fiveyr/10th/volume2/v2_ch2_5.pdf, accessed on 6 November 2006.

Symbiosis Centre for Distance Learning (2006), http://www.scdl.net, accessed on 6 November 2006.

8

Physical Evidence

OBJECTIVES

After reading this chapter you will be able to understand the:
- concept of physical evidence
- importance of physical evidence in the management of services
- management of different elements of physical evidence

INTRODUCTION

Convincing customers about the quality of the service prior to purchase can be a tricky affair for service providers due to the intangible nature of services. This difficulty is directly proportionate to the intangibility of the services. However, by supplying cues service providers can make it more tangible for the customer and hence easier to evaluate. Tangibility can be incorporated by managing the physical environment of services. Another characteristic of services that affects the physical environment of services is inseparability, or the simultaneous production and consumption of services. This aspect makes it inevitable for the customer to be present at the time of production and delivery of services. The physical evidence can affect the perception of the customer at the time of service delivery, especially for leisure and entertainment services such as upscale restaurants, theatres, resorts, leisure parks, etc. (Wakefield and Blodgett 1994). This implies that physical evidence also communicates with the customers along with the other aspects of marketing mix and needs to be managed carefully by the services organizations.

PHYSICAL EVIDENCE

According to Shostack (1977), customers are frequently searching for 'surrogates' or 'cues' to help determine the firm's capabilities to overcome the 'intangibility' of firms. On the basis of this reasoning, Booms and Bitner (1981) broadened the traditional four Ps into the seven Ps of services. Physical evidence was one of the Ps added for all the tangible cues along with the physical surroundings. According to Zeithaml and Bitner (2003), physical evidence is 'The environment in which the service is delivered and where the firm and customer interact, and any tangible components that facilitate performance or communication of the service'. Bitner (1992) introduced the nomenclature of 'servicescape' to the physical facility where the services are delivered or offered/performed.

Importance of Physical Evidence

'Environment is vivid because the stimulus a person receives from one source can generate multiple and unexpected sensations, images and ideas' (Greenland and McGoldrick 2005). In Chapter 6, we have already seen how physical evidence or servicescape affects the evaluation of services by the customers, and ultimately has an affect on the customer's perception of the service quality of the service provider. The servicescape can be managed to get the following benefits:

1. It helps to package the service offering for the customers.
2. Servicescape can appeal to the emotions of a person and educe a favourable response from the customers.
3. It can act as a facilitator to shape customer behaviour and enable effective flow of activities.
4. It can act as a differentiator to distinguish a service provider from its competitors. For example, fast food restaurants, such as McDonald's and KFC, differentiate their services on the basis of their standard designed servicescapes. Differentiation also allows the service provider to charge different prices for different services targeted at different customer segments (Exhibit 8.1).
5. It influences a customer's subjective perception of waiting time. Baker and Cameron (1996) identified how different physical evidences can be controlled to influence the customer's subjective perception of waiting time. They defined subjective time as 'How individuals perceive and feel about the length of a time duration'. This is important considering the fact that 'As the waiting time increases the customer satisfaction tends to decrease' (Baker and Cameron 1996).

Servicescapes

According to Bitner (1992) there are two types of servicescapes—lean and elaborate. Services requiring a simple structure, relatively few elements, and few spaces to deliver

---

Exhibit 8.1 The super-rich spice up their Jumbo Jet voyages

Recent trends of premium segment consumers show that the extremely rich have a very different lifestyle, even from the merely rich. Some of them own big, long-haul airliners that are converted to private jets. These private jets not only pamper their owners and their entourages, but also their cars and racehorses. The interiors of these jets, which can normally carry 300–400 passengers, are re-configured for the enjoyment of a few people. Lufthansa has recently introduced a Boeing 787 with 36 seats, most of which can be used as single lie-flat seats, queen-size beds, or double beds. These are exclusively configured for VIP use. There are about 39 Boeing 747s, and many 757s and 767s. Lufthansa's subsidiary, Lufthansa Technik designs and builds new and used airliners for corporate and individual use.

Source: Adapted from Sharkey (2006).

the service are referred to as *lean* servicescapes. For example, a post office kiosk requires a simple structure for the delivery of service. The design of the physical evidence for a lean servicescape is simple, especially where there is no interaction between customers and employees. Services requiring an ornate structure, with many elements and forms, is referred to as an *elaborate* servicescapes. For example, a heart specialist will require an elaborate set up with proper machinery for conducting different tests, an operation theatre, rooms, etc. when deciding upon the physical evidence.

MANAGING PHYSICAL EVIDENCE

The physical evidence comprises of a number of factors each of which has a bearing on the customer perception of the service provider. Services are intangible but they are accompanied by 'physical objects' that cannot be categorized as true product elements. The benefit of these objects is that they verify the existence or completion of a service, whereas a true product never requires evidence. For example, when travelling by any airline, the ticket confirms the service that the airline is going to provide and serves as an evidence of the service. This evidence is of two types—peripheral evidence and essential evidence. *Peripheral evidence* is actually possessed as part of purchase and has little or no independent value; for example, a debit card is useless without the funds it represents. On the other hand, the customer cannot possess the *essential evidence*, but it is so dominant in its impact on service purchase and use that it is considered an element on its own. For example, if a person purchases a credit contract (which in itself is a peripheral evidence), the bank that facilitates this has a strong impact on the service perception and is an essential element.

Whether essential or peripheral, service evidence forms the heart of the service image, and must be carefully designed and managed as a service in itself. This evidence provides clues and confirmations, and influences customer perceptions and expectations about the service (Danciu 2007). For example, try and remember the last time you walked out of a servicescape without availing the services of the service provider just because you felt the services provided would not be as per your expectations. The physical evidence has the power to turn away or generate an emotional appeal with the customers. According to Turley and Fugate (1992), the different broad categories to be considered while designing the physical evidence for a service are the:

- locational perspective
- atmospheric and image perspective
- operational perspective
- consumer use perspective
- contact personnel perspective.

Locational Perspective

One of the most important physical evidence affecting services is the location of the service provider (when there is direct contact with the service provider) or the facility from which the service is to be provided (for example, ATMs, drop boxes, etc.). A good strategic location does most of the work for the service provider, especially in the hospitality sector, retail outlets, banking services, etc. It has generally been observed that for day-to-day services, customers prefer services which are available conveniently; therefore, firms that are located close to where people work or live have an added advantage. However, if a person is going on a holiday they would prefer a location with scenic beauty and one that is away from the chaos of daily life. Whatever be the case, we see that location is an important factor, comes at a prime cost, and cannot be easily renovated or changed.

Atmospheric and Image Perspective

This includes the controllable factors of the internal and external environment that influence the customers. Customers use whatever cues are available in the servicescape to draw their perceptions of the service to be provided, and hence the atmosphere plays an important role in influencing customer's initial perceptions. Some of these factors are discussed in this section.

Layout/decor The layout or decor of the servicescape can affect the customer's perception of the service to be provided. This includes the layout of the service delivery, the parking, waiting area, etc. The layout and decor in an upscale restaurant would be more important than that of a roadside inn (*dhaba*). The furniture, colour concept, and central theme of the restaurant, will all be a part of the decisions to be considered while finalizing the decor.

Signage The signage includes the signs, logos, style of decor, and personal artefacts used by the service provider. All these signs communicate the style statement of the service provider and influence the perception of the customers. These include signs for direction, communications of rules such as no smoking, etc., and the certificates displayed by a medical practitioner in the servicescape. Signs are important in forming the initial impression of the servicescape.

Ambience It includes both the internal and external ambience of the servicescape. The external ambience includes landscaping, cleanliness of the external environment, scenic beauty, etc. Internal ambience includes factors such as air quality, temperature, noise, music, odour, etc. For example, if you go to a fair the brightly coloured tents, the bright, colourful, and jovial appearances of the performers, etc. all bring forth the fact that the customers are going to have a fun-filled experience. Oakes (2000) carried out a detailed study to see how the musicscape influences customers and found that music affects customer expectations, generates emotions by stimulating original memories with the music being played, and encourages behavioural response of repeat patronage.

The internal atmosphere of an organization can be altered by renovations, which is time-consuming and expensive (keeping in mind the actual cost involved in the renovations and opportunity cost of the customers who would have otherwise patronized the place). Thus, it is important to place initial close attention while planning the environment.

Operational Perspective

This includes both the production and delivery of services. Services are experiences and, therefore, require the customers to be present at the time of service delivery. The servicescape in such a scenario involves various factors.

Equipment   Use of technology to deliver a consistent service helps the service providers to reduce the heterogeneous characteristic of services. Technology also ensures that the service quality delivered across different locations is fairly uniform.

Signs for use of technology   Allocation of equipment is in itself not effective until it is used properly. Thus, at ATMs detailed instructions are provided for customers about the process for using the facility. The customers must be made to feel comfortable, and the technology should be easy to follow and use, for mass acceptance of the same.

Cleanliness   The other important factor to consider in the operations is the cleanliness of the servicescape. This also acquires importance depending upon the type of service delivered. For example, in the hospitality and healthcare industry a lot of importance is attached to cleanliness, whereas a not so clean banking servicescape may still be acceptable to the customers.

Consumer Use Perspective

This aspect focuses on the degree to which a servicescape is designed around the customer rather than the operations. This includes factors as explained in this section.

Billing statement   This involves the ease of understanding; for example, a mobile services bill has a number of sections, such as SMS charges, incoming calls, outgoing calls, and roaming charges, for the customer's information. Telecom service providers have the facility of call centres where customers can call and get clarifications for any queries.

Stationery   This includes business cards, brochures, menus, etc. designed for the customer's use and easy referral.

Internet/web page   Customers are increasingly using the Internet for information search. Thus, the Internet or web page should be such that it provides the information that customers may require regarding the services such as pricing, availability, booking option, etc.

Tickets   Tickets are a part of the physical evidence and affect customer perceptions. Indian Railways through its Internet site allows customers to book tickets online and follows it up by delivering the tickets within 24 hours. IndiGo, a low cost, no frills airline has the facility of providing tickets online, which customers could print from their own computer terminals and produce at the time of boarding, along with an identity proof. Facilities like these, which provide customer convenience, add favourably to customer perceptions (Exhibit 8.2).

Contact Personnel Perspective

The contact personnel are a part of the servicescape and also form a part of the services product. The appearance of the contact personnel—their cleanliness, dress code,

---

Exhibit 8.2   Spice up your life with bar-coded mobile tickets

Spice Telecom, a popular telecom provider in North India, has recently launched the service of bar-coded mobile tickets in Punjab, to coincide with the Spice Heartline Concert. It would enable subscribers to book tickets for commercially sponsored theatre and music shows organized by Spice. The telecom provider also plans tie-ups with cinema halls, cricket matches, parking lots, etc. Providing details about the service, Spice Telecom's AGM (Marketing) said that after a Spice subscriber sends an SMS, he would receive a mobile ticket in the form of a barcode. This bar-coded mobile ticket can be scanned under a barcode scanner for authenticity. Exclusively available for Spice subscribers, the SMS will cost Rs 3.

Source: Adapted from *The Economic Times* (2006).

---

demeanour, friendly, and smiling countenance—forms an initial and lasting impact on the customer's perception of the services.*

There are a number of factors affecting the customer's perception of the servicescape. All the factors are equally important and service managers have to make a trade-off depending upon the situational factors and the type of response they want to elicit from the customer.

MANAGING PHYSICAL EVIDENCE AS A STRATEGY

We have seen how physical strategy acts as a motivator to influence people for repeat purchases. It also affects the customer's initial purchase decision. Thus, strategic management of the physical evidence by organizations can influence their profitability (Fig. 8.1).

Corporate Vision, Mission, and Goal

The corporate vision, mission, and goal direct the organization in the type of service they want to deliver within a service industry. For example, within the hospitality industry, organizations may decide to open an upscale restaurant with a specific vision and mission for the same (Exhibit 8.3).

Corporate strategy   This includes the strategic layout of the services keeping in mind the vision, mission, and goal of the service organization. This aspect is cross-functional and involves finance, marketing, HR, etc.

Clarify roles of servicescapes   Once the corporate strategy for services delivery has been worked out, it is easier for the organization to work out the role servicescape plays in the delivery of the service (for example, lean or elaborate). This can further be classified according to servicescape usage such as self-service, interpersonal service, or remote service.

Planning the servicescape   On the basis of the role of servicescape, the management can now plan (map) the different elements of the servicescape such as operational,

---

* Based on Turley and Fugate (1992), Zeithaml and Bitner (2003), Vignali and Davies (1994), and Vignali (2001).

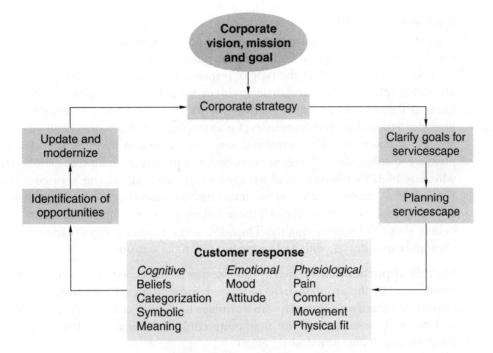

Source: Adapted from Bitner (1992), Zeithaml and Bitner (2003), and Turley and Fugate (1992).

Fig. 8.1 Strategic management of physical evidence

locational, atmospheric, etc. The brand name and logo can be planned in accordance with the image the service organization wants to portray. A detailed blueprint of the servicescape should be formed and all decisions thought out after much deliberation, as any oversight here will cost more later on, in the form of renovations, etc.

Exhibit 8.3 Metros warming up to boutique hotels

Hotelier Vikram Chatwal, who owns Hampshire Hotels and Resorts, believes that Indian metros are not only ready for Manhattan style boutique hotels but also Hautel Couture. Chatwal, who has nine hotel brands in his portfolio, has recently opened one in Manhattan. He believes that the style conscious guests frequenting the city have an eye for design and detail. His core customers are business executives from media, finance, and technology industries, including celebrities who form 10 per cent of the clientele. The Hautel Couture takes care of aspects such as location, design, logo, graphics, food, music, art, staff, and so on. The trend, which started with Morgan in Manhattan, has spread around the world. With extreme detailing for architecture and unusual designs, the aim is to provide a richer, unique, and more intimate experience. The concept in India is already quite popular in Rajasthan where many hotels offer a unique product and service mix. This concept is surely gaining a lot of popularity among the rich and famous, and is all set to be another innovative hospitality wave.

Source: Adapted from Duttagupta and Awasthi (2006).

Customer response Servicescape communicates with the customers and elicits a response from them. It is for the organization to monitor the customer response and check for gaps. This can be done with the help of various market research techniques. According to Bitner (1992), the type of response generated is cognitive, emotional, and physiological. Cognitive response involves influencing the beliefs of the customers towards the service provider. This also helps the customers to categorize the service provider within that service industry; for example, restaurants are classified as fast food, elegant sit-down, etc. The emotional response generated involves two dimensions—pleasure–displeasure and degree of arousal. Customers are bound to go to a restaurant, which is high in pleasure and arouses excitement about the service experience. Physiological comfort is affected by factors such as noise, degree of temperature, lighting, floor space for movement, etc. All these factors act as 'surrogate indicators' in forming beliefs about the service quality. Thus, the service organization management should constantly monitor the effect of servicescape on the customers.

Identify opportunities Based upon customer feedback and research, the organization should identify the problem areas or missed opportunities. For example, the marketing communication may not match with the image being portrayed by the physical evidence and so needs a revision in the marketing communication, which will be more cost-effective and deliver the desired effect.

Update and modernize Once the different opportunities have been identified, the management needs to update and modernize the physical evidence. Also, time and fashion changes, and the depreciation of assets affect the decision to modernize or update the servicescape. The management should identify what needs to be done and the cycle is again repeated, starting from the corporate strategy.

SUMMARY

Services being intangible, create problems for both customers—who are consistently looking for cues to overcome this, and service providers—who want to elicit a favourable response from the customers. The service providers can overcome this by managing the servicescape. The process of strategic management of servicescape is a continuous process and needs to be updated constantly. Customers are present at the time of delivery of services. Physical evidence is thus an important aspect of the seven Ps of marketing. It communicates with the customers along with the other elements of the marketing mix and helps them evaluate the services, both 'prior to' and 'after' the service delivery.

The importance of physical evidence is further highlighted by the fact that it affects customer satisfaction too. The chapter brings forth the importance of managing physical evidence. It delineates the location, atmosphere and image, operations, consumer use, and the contact personnel perspectives for designing physical evidence. A model, which links the physical evidence with the corporate vision and strategy, and customer response, has been designed to manage physical evidence as a strategy. This is a cyclical process and allows the management to upgrade and modernize the facility with time. Thus, by effectively managing the servicescape, an organization can subtly influence customer perception, decision, and satisfaction while purchasing the services.

KEY TERMS

Atmospheric and image perspective It includes controllable factors of the internal and external environment that influence the customers.

Consumer use perspective This aspect focuses on the degree to which a servicescape is designed around the customer rather than the operation of the service.

Contact personnel perspective This includes the appearance of the contact personnel, their cleanliness, dress code, demeanour, and friendliness, among others.

Locational perspective The location of the service provider or the facility from which the service is to be provided.

Operational perspective This includes both the production and delivery of services.

Physical evidence This is the environment in which the service is delivered, and the firm and customer interact, and include any tangible components that facilitate performance or communication of the service.

Servicescape This includes the tangible facets of service such as machines, equipment, employee appearance, and the ambience of the organization.

CONCEPT REVIEW QUESTIONS

1. Critically evaluate the role of physical evidence in delivery of services.
2. Discuss the different ways in which a service provider can use physical evidence in affecting customer perceptions.
3. How can a service provider manage the atmospheric physical evidence? Explain by taking the example of any service provider.
4. Critically discuss the importance of managing the physical evidence by a service organization.

CRITICAL THINKING QUESTIONS

1. Identify a recent visit to a restaurant. How did the physical evidence affect your perceptions? Give reasons.
2. What are the different physical evidences that a service provider of life insurance can plan?
3. Choose any service organization. Identify the current physical evidence they are using and suggest recommendations to enhance customer perception.

INTERNET EXERCISES

1. Visit the website of a travel service organization. Identify the different physical evidences that have been used to influence the customers.
2. Visit the website of your bank. How is it similar/dissimilar to the other forms of physical evidence provided by the bank?

CASE STUDY

Physical Evidence—A Case of KFC

KFC Corporation

'KFC Corporation, based in Louisville, United States, is the world's most popular chicken restaurant chain. Since Colonel Harland Sanders founded it in 1952, KFC has been serving customers delicious, already-prepared, complete family meals. There are over 13,000 KFC outlets in more than 80 countries and territories around the world. KFC is part of Yum! Brands, Inc., which is the world's largest restaurant system with over 32,500 KFC, A&W All-American Food™, Taco Bell, Long John Silver's, and Pizza Hut restaurants in more than 100 countries and territories.

Colonel Sanders, an early developer of the quick-service food business and a pioneer of the restaurant franchise concept founded KFC in Corbin. He began franchising his chicken business at the age of 65. Building on a foundation of family-orientation, quick service, high-quality food, and affordable prices, the Colonel signed up his first franchisee, Pete Harman, in 1952. Soon after, Colonel Sanders created the restaurant franchise concept and quickly expanded throughout the United States.

By 1964, Colonel Sanders had more than 600 franchised outlets for his chicken in the United States and Canada. That year, a group of investors bought KFC and is credited with growing the chain to its segment dominance. PepsiCo Inc. acquired the company in 1986 and in 1991 Kentucky Fried Chicken switched to KFC as its official identifier.

In October 1997, PepsiCo spun-off KFC, Pizza Hut, and Taco Bell thereby forming Tricon Global Restaurants Inc., the world's largest restaurant company in terms of system units. In May 2002, Tricon Global Restaurants, Inc. acquired Long John Silver's and A&W Restaurants to accelerate the company's multi-branding strategy and drive global growth by offering consumers two brands and more choice in one restaurant. The company changed its name to Yum! Brands, Inc. from Tricon Global Restaurants, Inc., to reflect its expanding portfolio of brands and its ticker symbol on the New York Stock Exchange (Yum 2006).

Colonel Harland Sanders

'Colonel Harland Sanders, born on 9 September 1890, actively began franchising his chicken business at the age of 65. He used his $105 social security cheque to start a business and has become a symbol of entrepreneurial spirit.

When the Colonel was six, his father died. His mother was forced to go to work, and young Harland had to take care of his three-year old brother and baby sister. This meant doing much of the family cooking. By the age of seven, he was a master of several regional dishes.

At age 10, he got his first job working on a nearby farm for $2 a month. When he was 12, his mother remarried and he left his home for a job on a farm. He held a series of jobs over the next few years, first as a 15-year old streetcar conductor in New Albany, and then as a 16-year old private, soldiering for six months in Cuba.

After that he was a railroad fireman, studied law by correspondence, practised in justice of the peace courts, sold insurance, operated an Ohio River steamboat ferry, sold tyres, and operated service stations. When he was 40, the Colonel began cooking for hungry travellers who stopped at his service station in Corbin. He did not have a restaurant then, but served folks on his own dining table in the living quarters of his service station.

As more people started coming just for food, he moved across the street to a motel and restaurant that seated 142 people. Over the next nine years, he perfected his secret blend of 11 herbs and spices, and the basic cooking technique that is still used today.

Sander's fame grew. Governor Ruby Laffoon made him a Kentucky Colonel in 1935 in recognition of his contributions to the state's cuisine, and in 1939, his establishment was first listed in Duncan Hines' *Adventures in Good Eating*.

In the early 1950s, a new interstate highway was planned to bypass the town of Corbin. Seeing an end to his business, the Colonel auctioned off his operations. After paying his bills, he was reduced to living on his $105 social security checks.

Confident of the quality of his fried chicken, he devoted himself to the chicken franchising business that he started in 1952. He travelled across the country by car from restaurant to restaurant, cooking batches of chicken for restaurant owners and their employees. If the reaction was favourable, he entered into a handshake agreement on a deal that stipulated a payment to him, of a nickel for each chicken the restaurant sold. In 1957, Kentucky Fried Chicken was first sold in buckets (which are still in use today). By 1964, Colonel Sanders had more than 600 franchised outlets for his chicken in the United States and Canada. That year, he sold his interest in the company for $2 million to a group of investors including John Y. Brown Jr., who later became governor of Kentucky from 1980 to 1984. The Colonel remained a public spokesman for the company. In 1976, an independent survey ranked him as the world's second most recognizable celebrity'.

Pressure Cooker

'Colonel Sanders was always experimenting with food at his restaurant in Corbin, in those early days of the 1930s. He kept adding things to the flour for frying chicken and came out with a pretty good-tasting product. But customers still had to wait 30 minutes for it while he fried it up in an iron skillet. That was just too long to wait, he thought. Most other restaurants serving what they called 'Southern' fried chicken fried it in deep fat. That was quicker, but the taste wasn't the same.

Then the Colonel went to a demonstration of a 'new-fangled gizmo' called a pressure cooker, sometime in the late 1930s. During the demonstration, green beans turned out tasty and were done just right in only a few minutes. This set his

mind to thinking. He wondered how it might work on chicken.

He bought one of the pressure cookers and made a few adjustments. After a lot of experimenting with cooking time, pressure, shortening temperature and level, he found a way to fry chicken quickly, under pressure, and come out with the best chicken he'd ever tasted.

Today, there are several different kinds of cookers used to make Original Recipe® chicken. But every one of them fries under pressure, the principle established by this now-famous Kentuckian. The Colonel's first pressure cooker is still around. It holds a place of honour at KFC's Restaurant Support Centre in Louisville' (KFC 2006).

The New Logo of KFC

Recently KFC changed its logo and the new logo depicts Colonel Sanders with his signature string tie, but for the first time, replaces his classic white, double-breasted suit with a red apron. The apron symbolizes the home-style culinary heritage of the brand and reminds customers that KFC is always in the kitchen cooking delicious, high quality, freshly prepared chicken by hand, just the way Colonel Sanders did 50 years ago. This is only the fourth time in more than 50 years that the logo has changed.

The Colonel's Top Secret Mission

The giant Colonel Sanders logo was built off the world's only extraterrestrial highway in Rachel, Nevada, also known as the 'UFO capital of the world', and the epicentre of inter-galactic communication. The massive logo, which was referred to as the 'Face from Space' by the project team, is so large it dwarfs one of America's largest and most famous landmarks, Mt Rushmore. The huge carved faces of Presidents Washington, Jefferson, Roosevelt, and Lincoln would all fit easily in to the 'Face from Space'. There would even be enough room left over for a *fifth* presidential face in the Colonel Sanders logo! 'If there are extraterrestrials in outer space, KFC wants to become their restaurant of choice. For now, we'll be very content satisfying the entire human population with our Finger Lickin' Good Chicken. If we hear back from a life form in space today—whether NASA astronauts or a signal from some life form on Mars—we'll send up some Original Recipe Chicken', said Gregg Dedrick, President of KFC Corp.

KFC Restaurant of the Future

After three years of testing different restaurant designs in the US and international markets, KFC is today revealing its restaurant look of the future. KFC's new global image is in the process of rolling out in restaurants around the world and will be implemented in newly constructed stores within the next 12 months.

The new global restaurant design is refreshing, contemporary, highly-differentiated, and helps keep KFC relevant with customers by giving them a higher quality, overall dining experience. The new design is based on thoughtful strategic tenets, which provide a strong brand image foundation, while being flexible for different international market needs. It communicates a progressive and energetic spirit for KFC and prepares the brand for future global growth.

Design features for the US include:

○ Bright, and bold graphics on the restaurant exterior and interior that incorporate the Kentucky Fried Chicken name as well as KFC, communicate a fresh sense of brand pride. African American artist Charly (Carlos) Palmer took KFC's historical icons and gave them an updated, cool, and modern look.

○ Graphics and pub signs that showcase the company's icons: '11 Secret Herbs and Spices', 'Finger Lickin' Good', and 'Sunday Dinner, 7 Days a Week'.

○ Signature symbols (the Colonel, the bucket, Kentucky Fried Chicken) create distinctly KFC retail style shop front designs that invite customers inside with open glass.

○ Heroic use of the signature red colour in a bold architectural way, and crisp white design accents to keep the brand youthful and fresh.

○ Warm and contemporary interior designs with spacious and innovative seating help customers feel welcome and comfortable in groups or alone.

○ Thoughtful interior and exterior lighting enhances the customer experience.

○ A digital jukebox that is free of charge for customers to play the music they enjoy most.

○ Southern-inspired brand new menu items, slow-cooked, and served fast to star alongside KFC's core products.

Since the first Kentucky Fried Chicken restaurant opened its doors in Utah in 1952, the brand continues to enjoy growing popularity around the world. The company's top markets outside the United States are China, the UK, Australia, South Korea, Mexico, and Europe, including France, Germany, the Netherlands, and Holland. KFC is also tapping growth in important emerging markets such as India, Russia, and Brazil. Each new restaurant opening brings jobs and career opportunities along with economic vitality for that community.

KFC's enduring success and popularity is attributed to a relentless focus on great taste, high quality, and the nearly 500,000 talented employees focused on providing great service to the 4.5 billion guests who visit their restaurants around the world each year (*Businesswire* 2006).

Questions

1. Discuss the different physical evidence factors being used by KFC.

2. Discuss the new logo of KFC. What are the different changes made and why? As a customer, compare your perceptions about the new versus the old logo.

3. Critically discuss the physical evidence features KFC is going to use in the upcoming outlets.

SELECT REFERENCES

Baker, Julie and Michaelle Cameron (1996), 'The effects of the service environment on affect and consumer perception of waiting time: An integrative review and research propositions', *Journal of Academy of Marketing Science*, vol. 24, no. 4, pp. 338–349.

Bitner, M.J. (1990), 'Evaluating the service encounters: The effects of physical surroundings and employee responses', *Journal of Marketing*, April, vol. 54, no. 2, pp. 69–82.

Bitner, M.J. (1992), 'Servicescapes: The impact of physical surroundings on customers and employees', *Journal of Marketing*, vol. 56, no. 2, pp. 57–71.

Danciu, Victor (2007), 'Performance in service marketing from philosophy to customer relationship management', http://www.ectap.ro/articole/237.pdf, accessed on 2 July 2008.

Duttagupta, Ishani and Raja Awasthi (2006), 'Metros warming up to boutique hotels', *The Economic Times*, New Delhi, 6 July 2006, p. 4.

Greenland, Steve and Peter McGoldrick (2005), 'Evaluating the design of retail financial service environments', *The International Journal of Bank Marketing*, vol. 23, no. 2/3, pp. 132–152.

Lovelock, Christopher and Evert Gummesson (2004), 'Whither services marketing? In search of a new paradigm and fresh perspectives', *Journal of Services Research*, vol. 7, no. 1, pp. 20–41.

Oakes, Steve (2000), 'The influence of the musicscape within service environments', *The Journal of Services Marketing*, vol. 14, no. 7, pp. 539–554.

Sharkey (2006), 'The super-rich spice up their jumbo jet voyages', *The Times of India*, New Delhi, 19 October, p. 38.

Shostack, Lynn G. (1977), 'Breaking free from product marketing', *Journal of Marketing*, vol. 41, no. 2, pp. 73–80.

'Spice up your life with bar-coded mobile ticket', *The Economic Times*, New Delhi, 13 October 2006, p. 5.

Turley, Lou W. and Douglas L. Fugate (1992), 'The multidimensional nature of service facilities: Viewpoints and recommendations', *The Journal of Services Marketing*, vol. 6, no. 3, pp. 37–46.

Vignali, Claudio (2001), 'McDonald's: Think global, act local—the marketing mix', *British Food Journal*, vol. 103, no. 2, pp. 97–108.

Vignali, Claudio and B.J. Davies (1994), 'The marketing mix redefined and mapped: Introducing the MIXMAP model', *Management Decision*, London, vol. 32, no. 8, pp. 11–16.

Wakefield, Kirk L. and Jeffery G. Blodgett (1994), 'The importance of servicescapes in leisure service settings', *The Journal of Services Marketing*, vol. 8, no. 3, pp. 66–76.

Zeithaml, V.A. and Bitner, M.J. (2003), *Services Marketing*, Tata McGraw-Hill Publishing Company Limited, New Delhi.

http://home.businesswire.com/portal/site/google/index.jsp?ndmViewId=news_view&newsId=20061114005428&newsLang=en, accessed on 15 December 2006.

http://www.kfc.ca/home/en/news.html>, accessed on 17 December 2006.

http://www.kfc.com/about/colonel.htm, accessed on 17 December 2006.

http://www.yum.com/about/brands.asp, accessed on 20 December 2006.

9 Managing Service Operations and Processes

OBJECTIVES

After reading this chapter you will be able to understand the:

- concept of service processes
- relationship between profitability and service process
- essentials of a service blueprint
- importance of a customer's role in service delivery
- characteristics of a service guarantee
- dimensions of service process matrix

INTRODUCTION

Managing service processes has a very special significance in the service industry as it offers a process for delivery of the services. Efficient service offering creates unique customer experiences, which would make the consumers use the services. Consumers do believe in a moment-of-truth, which is a point in service delivery where customers interact with service employees or self-serve equipment, and the outcome may affect perceptions of service quality (Lovelock and Wright 1999). So, the service providers must ensure that the front- and back-end processes are aligned in such a manner that they demonstrate a positive moment-of-truth for the customer.

This chapter gives an overview of service processes and explores the relationship between profitability and service blue printing. It also provides an insight into managing the dynamics of demand and supply. It assesses various waiting line strategies and assesses the role of customers in service delivery. The concept of service guarantees has also been explained.

SERVICE PROCESS

The choice of a service process depends on numerous factors. There is a need to understand the service context and the nature of the service offering. Lovelock and Wright (1999) have provided an insight into the classification process of service, which affects the nature of the operation chosen. The contextual elements that are factored which deciding on a service process are discussed in detail in this section.

Table 9.1   Direct recipients of service

Nature of service act	People	Possession
Tangible action	Service directed at people's bodies/ healthcare services	Service directed at people's possessions/ car repair
Intangible action	Service directed at people's minds (Art performance and religion)	Service directed at intangible assets (Religion and counselling)

Degree of tangibility   The degree of tangibility has an impact on the way the service process is structured. A highly intangible service, such as consulting, will need to create tangibility around its offering. This may be in terms of reports or other evidence, which may evoke a feeling of trust in the minds of the consumer.

Direct recipient   Depending upon whether the recipient of the service is a person or a thing, or both, the process of service delivery will vary. For example, a hair salon will target its offering on a person; whereas a service centre offering repair services for equipment, may offer pick up and drop services and give guarantees on the quality of the service offering. Table 9.1 gives an idea of various factors that may be considered while deciding a service process.

Place and time   The place and time of offering of services will also determine how the service processes are structured. For instance, in many developed economies, such as Japan, food is available through vending machines on account of high labour costs and convenience factors. Some hotels, which do not have restaurant facilities and student canteens in universities in Japan, offer food vending machines where different combinations of food are displayed and one can choose from a variety of options.

Customization vs standardization   The service firm also has to make a key decision as to whether it will have a standardized offering for customers or will opt for customization. Many large service firms, especially restaurants and hotels, prefer a standardized offering and offer standardized services across various outlets, globally. On the other hand, some automobile firms offer customization services, such as special designing of interiors and moulding the external body of the cars.

Consumer relationship   The nature of the relationship in terms of a firm looking for spending a large amount of time with the customer versus a scenario wherein the processes are largely automated, also determine the nature of service process. A salon would prefer to offer personalized service, while a banking outlet would prefer to automate its offerings wherever possible.

Demand and supply   In the case of the supply being balanced with demand and there existing a fair amount of competition, service firms are careful of their offering and the way they treat customers, as the switch over threshold may not be very high. Such firms have to be very careful of how they manage their processes.

Service Process and Profitability

Certain services rely heavily on consumers' word-of-mouth for new business generation. Earlier research has established the importance of word-of-mouth with regards to obtaining lawyers, travel agents, hotels, financial planning, tax accountants, insurance agents, banks, automobile mechanics, etc. (File et al. 1992). The research conducted by File et al., points out that the variety of intensity of client participation during the service delivery process is predictive of positive word-of-mouth and referrals. The study conducted on 331 service recipients indicates that four dimensions of client participation are highly predictive of both positive word-of-mouth and new client referrals. The four salient participation factors are tangibility, empathy, attendance, and meaningful interaction. These findings support interactive marketing management for providers of complex services and form the basis of a specific delivery system.

A customer service can be regarded as a process that consists of actual steps to satisfy customer requirements. A customer service process model is required for analysing customer expectations and designing customer service. A better service design provides the key to market success and growth (Shostack 1984). In the service industry, there is still a gap in the rigorous process design standards prior to introducing new services. Before implementing or initiating any changes in the service processes, it is essential to identify bottlenecks and rationalize them. Kim & Kim (2001) suggest a service process rationalization method to minimize the risk inherent in a service change project. For this, a customer service process model is suggested, which can be used for understanding customer expectations by incorporating customer viewpoints and their actions in the model. Based on the service process model, a performance test on current expectations and alternatives could be undertaken. Thereafter, on the basis of identified bottlenecks from performance simulation, the service process could be rationalized. Exhibit 9.1 illustrates how service processes help in precipitating sales. Service blueprinting is one such model.

Service Process and Productivity

Byus and Lomerson (2004) have discussed that the primary strength of a consumer-derived, value-based performance measure, is its ability to reconcile many of the differences which exist when considering performance analysis among the business and economics description. They have proposed a consumer value model, which supports the fundamental promises inherent in the marketing concept. Customer focus, integrated organizational effort, and long-term profitability are some of the factors. Improving value as perceived by the customer will enhance long-term profitability of the firm. Consumer value, when used as an integral part of the strategic performance measurement process, is a useful tool for deciding which processes and activities produce the greatest value. Consumer value can provide a substantive proof for allocation of resources of the firm.

Exhibit 9.1 Service process as facilitation to product sales

Some services help to precipitate product sales. A unique example is wine production, a service experience, which may have an impact on wine sales. O'Neil et al. (2002) have discussed wine tourism and have given an insight on how winery operators invite customers to their wineries and this has a positive impact on future wine sales. Wine tourism involves customers visiting a vineyard where experience of tangible and service production processes are an essential part of the service benefit. The tasting of a tangible product (the wine) is an important element of the benefit from a visit. This latter benefit is one that many vineyard operators focus on, and many see cellar door visits as a means of promoting their product and introducing new customers to it. This research was conducted in Australia.

They suggest that high levels of service can encourage the development of relationship marketing strategies, as currently interpreted, (for example, through the use of mailing lists and targeted incentives) as well as a relationship to a brand in a more traditional sense (Fig. 9.1).

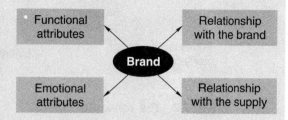

Fig. 9.1 Elements in a successful relationship

The research identified the importance of service related cues to the sale of the tangible product of wine. The research indicates that service process factors were more closely linked to wine purchase than tangible elements.

Source: Adapted from O'Neil et al. (2002)

SERVICE BLUEPRINTING

The concept of service blueprint and deploying the same in the service industry has been explained in this section.

Building a Service Blueprint

To have an effective service process, it is necessary to document the flow of activities and map them carefully. A service blueprint offers this facility. Zeithaml and Bitner (2000) have elaborated on the service blueprint. Blueprinting is a device that addresses the challenges of designing and specifying intangible service processes (Shostack 1984). According to Zeithaml and Bitner (2000), a service blueprint visually displays the service by simultaneously depicting the process of service delivery, the points of consumer contact, the role of customers and employees, and the visible element of services (Fig. 9.2).

They have outlined the following steps to build a service blueprint.

1. Identify the process to be blueprinted.
2. Identify the customer or segment targeted.
3. Map the process from the customer's point of view.
4. Map contact employee actions, onstage and backstage.
5. Link customer and contact person activities needed to support functions.
6. Ask for evidence of service at each customer action step.

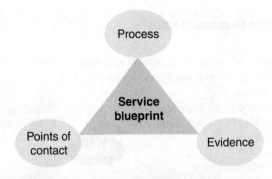

Fig. 9.2 The service blueprint

The blueprinting process in case of a fine dining Indian restaurant is illustrated in Table 9.2.

Advantages of blueprinting The blueprinting process offers numerous advantages, such as, it:

- brings clarity to the service delivery process
- enables identification of critical incidents, which contribute or damage the consumer experience
- provides insights on areas where employees need to be trained
- enables further improvement of the process
- helps to put coordination activities in perspective

Table 9.2 Blueprinting for restaurant services

Process name	Start	End	Critical incident
Greeting and seating	Customer arrives and escorted, preference sought	Customer is seated	✓
Menu delivery	Customer is seated	Customer receives the menu	
Order taking for dinner	Customer receives the menu	Customer orders drinks	✓
Drinks are delivered	Drinks are ordered	Drinks are delivered	✓
Order taking for food	Customer receives the dinner menu	Customer orders the meal	✓
Meal delivery	The table is laid	The food is served	✓
Clearing of table	Checks for additional requirement	Clears plates	
Finger bowls	Served	Cleared	
Billing	Customer asks for the bill	Customer receives the bill	
Payment	Customer is handed the bill	Customer pays	✓
Bill settling	Customer makes the payment	Change is brought back	✓
Leave-taking	Customer leaves the table	Customer departs	✓
Problem	Problems are identified	Problems are resolved	

- can be used to assess and control costs
- facilitates external and internal marketing and can be a source of competitive advantages.

MANAGING DEMAND AND SUPPLY

Managing demand is critical in providing a better service experience. The excess demand may lead to chaos and long queues in a service operation wherein the consumers experience may suffer. Demand and supply mismatch could manifest by:

- demand exceeding supply
- supply exceeding demand
- matching demand and supply.

Lovelock (2001) provides an insight into understanding the patterns of demand, raising the following issues.

- Do they follow a predictable cycle?
- What are the causes of cyclical variation?

There may be day-to-day strategies for shifting demand to match capacity. If the demand is too high, then some of the following strategies may be initiated.

1. Use signage to communicate busy days for reservations; this could be reflected in advertisements as well.
2. Provide incentives to consumers to use non-peak times. For example, restaurants and hotels offer seasonal discounts.
3. Take care of loyal consumers first. For example, AmEx gives priority to its own credit card users by designating separate queues for them.
4. Charge full price. When the demand is high, service marketers are likely to enhance revenue by deploying premium pricing to contribute to their profitability. For example, hotels in Delhi charge a higher price on account of higher number of tourists visiting India during the peak seasons (winter/spring).

If the demand is too low then some of the following strategies may be initiated.

1. Use sales and adverting to increase the demand.
2. Modify the service offering and appeal to new marketing segments.
3. Offer discounts.
4. Modify hours of operation.
5. Remove the obstacles for consumption.

Waiting Line Strategies

There are numerous strategies to manage the waiting time. Dickson et al. (2005) have placed them in the three following categories.

1. Manage the reality of the actual wait through use of techniques that help match capacity with the customer.

2. Manage the perception of wait by responding to how customers perceive the wait.
3. Make the wait invisible by developing virtual queues, which allow the customer to participate in other activities. Dickson et al. have highlighted the major limiting factor with a reservation system when there is a fixed and predictable capacity. When the capacity is variable and demand is unpredictable, such as fast food or an attraction in a theme park, the reservation does not yield the required solution.

For example, FASTPASS^{TM} system installed at Walt Disney World in 1999 helps to manage virtual queues. More than 50 million guests each year use this system. When guests insert their park admission ticket into a specially designated FASTPASS turnstile, it places them in a virtual queue. Based on the number of guests in the virtual queue and the current processing capacity, the computer estimates the time it will take for their position in the virtual queue to get to the front of the line. There are some possible applications of virtual queuing. On cruise lines or at resorts, there are numerous activities, such as shooting, dinner shows, games, excursions, etc.

Some of the waiting line strategies that can be adopted are outlined ahead:

1. Introduce a token system
2. Establish reservation system
3. Segment different waiting customers into loyal customers, premium customers, etc.
4. Make waiting a fun for the consumers
5. Bring clarity about the waiting time
6. Offer value to the service
7. Solo waits feel longer than group waits, so a method that takes care of this aspect may be devised.

Queuing Strategies

Capacity management is about maintaining a good balance between the costs of capacity and demand, in relation to the demand. 'The capacity of a facility is the maximum load that can be handled by it during a given period' (Bedi 2007). If there is a discrepancy in demand and supply, and there is no option but to reserve in advance, such as in the services sector, the customers have to wait in a queue. This increases the risk that many customers may switch loyalties. However, the advantage is that the service personnel can be kept busy and facilities can be fully utilized.

In the services sector, as the rate of arrivals approaches the service rate, the average length of the queue increases. Thus, an imbalance of supply and demand will have a different impact on the front and back stages of a service system. Capacity in service operations is generally divided into fixed and variable capacity*.

Fixed capacity   This is determined by physical sources such as facilities, computers, and beds among others. It is generally represented by significant strategy choices and investments, and takes time to acquire and deploy. These largely determine the maximum capacity of the service; for example, hotel rooms, seats on airplanes, telephone lines, etc.

Source: * Adapted from http://courses.ischool.berkeley.edu/i210/f07/lectures/210-20070919.pdf.

Variable capacity   Scheduling of equipment and deliveries is a critical issue in service design. If facilities (trains, buses) and equipment can be easily relocated, rescheduled, or re-configured for different tasks or functions, they can be viewed as variable capacity. The following rules can be used to manage back-stage service operations:

1. Shortest processing time: Perform the service that will take the least amount of work to complete.
2. Promised completion of date and time: Perform the service that has the first due date.
3. Start date: Perform the service that has the earliest start date.
4. Slack time remaining: Perform the service on the job for which the amount of slack is the lowest (slack is the difference between the due date and the amount of work left).
5. Idle capacity: Manage the amount of idle capacity.

CUSTOMERS' ROLE IN SERVICE DELIVERY

The changing business dynamics has re-defined the role of consumers in the service process. Customers can increasingly participate in the service delivery. They can actually control or contribute to their own satisfaction (Schneider and Bowen 1995).

Martin and Pranter (1989) have defined compatibility management as, 'A process of first attracting homogeneous consumers to the service environment; then, actively managing both the physical environment and customer-to-customer encounters so as to enhance satisfying encounters and minimize dissatisfying encounters; for example, health clubs, hospitals, public transportation'. The level of participation may be different across different service areas (Hubbert 1995). It could be low, moderate, or high.

1. Low: Consumer presence required during service delivery; for example, fast food delivery or online payment.
2. Moderate: Consumer inputs required for service creation; for example, haircut or full-service restaurant.
3. High: Customer co-creates the service product; for example, counselling, consulting, gym, or insurance plan.

Customer Role in Service Processes

Customers play different roles in different service segments. Customer role is defined as a set of behaviour patterns learned through experience and communication, performed by an individual in a certain social interaction, in order to attain maximum effectiveness in goal accomplishment (Bateson 1989). There is still a lot of room for research on the customer role in service processes. The customer behaviour in services in usually perceived as volatile and unpredictable. Chervonnaya (2003) has identified 10 major customer roles in services and has tried to relate them to specific service processes.

Depending on the specific requirements of the role, customers can be expected to possess different types of skills. 'The ten roles which a customer can perform can be identified with the help of existing academic studies and can fit into the eight categories listed below. The roles "inert" and "idle" can be coupled together with the first item and "decision-maker" and "hunter" can be coupled together in the eighth item' (Chervonnaya 2003). These eight categories are discussed as under.

Passive consumer   A customer could act as a passive consumer of service benefits; for example, a passive patient or an 'inert' patient. They have low motivation or it could by virtue of their socio-economic or demographic background. It could also depend on the category of service that is being accessed and by the demand–supply situation. In India, for example, given the large number of patients who frequent out-patient departments in government hospitals, or even private hospitals, many patients even if they would want information on line of treatment, do not get satisfactory answers. This is on account of demand–supply mismatch, and long queues, which doctors have to manage.

Learning   A customer can be a source of producer learning. These are referred to as 'instructor customers'. In an educational set up, the experience with various cohorts of students is an immense source of learning.

Resource   Customers often serve as resource by contributing information input. Such customers are referred to as 'ingredient customers'. The decisions of service employees is linked to their ability to clarify the problem (Mills and Margulies 1980).

Co-producers   These are customers who have to participate in the service process; for example, students taking up full-time courses, patients undergoing medical treatment, consultancy, wherein the attitude and the nature of process impacts the delivery process.

Auditor customer   Here, the customer evaluates service quality not only on outcomes but also in the process of service delivery itself.

Competitor   He/she is a self-service consumer who is competing with the companies that supply the same service (Zeithaml and Bitner 2000).

Marketing   Here the customer recommends the services to others.

Decision-maker   The customer often engages in the decision-making process. He/she decides whether to produce service on his/her own or which producer to choose.

Models of Service Process

Mayer et al. (2003) have proposed a model of service process, which consists of an interactive hierarchy with two primary dimensions—the process of service assembly (PSA) and the process of service delivery (PSD). During a service encounter, customers' perceptual filters modify both PSA and PSD. The model is based on the premise that the result of service process assembly and delivery is encounter satisfaction, which is the customers' perception of his/her discrete experience with a service. Thus, encounter satisfaction is posited to be the outcome of the service process model. Bitner and Hubbert (1994) have concluded that encounter satisfaction is a separate construct from overall satisfaction and service quality, as it relates it to a discrete service experience. Mayer et al. (2003) state that the process of service assembly is composed of steps, tasks, procedures, mechanisms, and activities necessary to the rendering of a service. They have proposed the following eight descriptors (parameters) in the model.

1. Technology
2. Visibility
3. Customization
4. Physical appearance
5. Accessibility
6. Employee costume
7. Amount of interaction
8. Delivery method

Model for process of service delivery As in the process of service assembly, the process of service delivery is composed of various steps, tasks, and mechanisms. Mayer et al. (2003) outlined eight situational descriptors of service delivery. They are as follows:

1. Duration
2. Work area appearance
3. Employee appearance
4. Empathy
5. Assurance
6. Employee effort
7. Reliability
8. Customer participation

Apart from the service process model, the customer's perceptual filters, such as brand image, mood, and perceived risk also have an impact on encounter satisfaction.

SERVICE GUARANTEES

Service guarantees help service firms to infuse greater confidence among consumers for their service offering. Many services require immense human involvement and hence, consumers expect a degree of assurance that these will be delivered to their expectations, or the standards set by the firm.

For instance, IT firms, which sell big servers for banking and airline reservation systems assure extensive service guarantees. The service has to be flawless as the damage caused by failure can result in a completely chaotic situation. Real estate firms, which build apartments/houses, offer guarantees in terms of time of delivery and specification of materials used. If projects get delayed, compensation at a pre-determined rate is offered to the consumers. Many mobile firms offer lifetime cards to ensure a lasting relationship with the consumers. Domino's offers a guarantee on time of delivery. If the pizza is delivered late, no charges are made for home delivery. The challenge for the service firms thus is to heighten the service reliability and implementation of service guarantee (Exhibit 9.2).

Exhibit 9.2   Customer complaining behaviour in technology-based service encounters

A study conducted by Snellman and Vihtkari (2003) compared the complaining behaviour of consumers in traditional and technology-based service encounters. In the study, 160 critical incidents were analysed. Finnish retail banking has witnessed a major shift to technology-based service encounters during the past decade. Finnish bank customers now have the option to use self-service technologies including ATMs, bill payment machines, Internet banking, and mobile banking services. Recent statistics indicate that 88 per cent of Finnish payment transactions are electronic, and that the use of bank services via the Internet and mobile phones continues to increase (The Finnish Bankers Association 2001).

The study, however, showed that there were no significant differences in the complaining rates between the two types of service encounters. That was attributed to the high reliance on traditional complaining methods in both types of service encounters. It pointed out that complaints about technology-based service encounters had significantly higher response rates than complaints about traditional service encounters. It also found that customers who actually considered themselves guilty for the outcome were the most frequent complainers, while the ones attributing the outcome to technology failure on service process failures complained less often.

Source: Adapted from Snellman and Vihtkari (2003).

Characteristics

Marmorstein et al. (2001) have raised the issues related to service guarantee. They suggest that for a guarantee to be effective it needs to be credible, simple, and meaningful to the consumer. It must be the centrepiece of an organization's commitment to quality, and not just a marketing campaign (Hart 1988). The study conducted by Marmorstein reveals that a service guarantee is more credible among companies, which explains why their services have improved.

The study also points out that the customer's main interest is to receive a reliable service. Being awarded compensation for problems is of only secondary importance. Firms should, therefore, concentrate first on improving their service levels and only subsequently, introduce a compensation policy. Exhibit 9.3 provides an insight into service improvement processes. Service guarantees have been discussed in detail in Chapter 10.

SERVICE PROCESS MATRIX

Schmenner (2004) has suggested an evolved service process matrix based on a matrix developed earlier and the gaps therein. He has based his approach on the 'theory of swift, even flow'. He suggests that from an operations standpoint, the 'degree of interaction with and customization for the consumer translates into variation in the provision of a service. The services could be mapped on a two-dimensional scale. The X-axis could be titled the degree of variation, and the Y-axis could be labelled as relative throughput time.

Interaction and customization are common sources of variation and they are unquestioned drags on service productivity. A service may call for much variation in

Exhibit 9.3 Service process improvement: Ten lessons from Japanese manufacturing

Kannan (2005) has pointed out ten service process lessons that can be drawn from Japanese manufacturing firms. These are as follows.

Lesson 1 Service process quality improvement increases revenues and at the same time reduces costs. Japanese manufacturing techniques have proven that you can increase quality and, at the same time, cut costs.

Lesson 2 Service process improvement is a continuous and never-ending effort.

Lesson 3 Reducing *muda (*wasteful activity).

Lesson 4 Reducing *mura* (inconsistencies).

Lessons 5 Reducing *muri* (physical strain).

Lessons 6 *Genchi gembutsu*—In Japanese, this means going to the actual scene (*genchi*) and confirming the actual happenings or things (*gembutsu*).

Lesson 7 Multi-skill development and job rotation.

Lesson 8 *Poka Yoke* methods—In Japanese, it means fool proofing. Mistakes and re-work can be avoided by carefully mistake proofing every step of a service process.

Lesson 9 Fixing root causes rather than symptoms.

Lesson 10 Address non value-adding activities.

Source: Adapted from Mayer and Moulton (2003) and Kannan (2005).

their provision (for example, Subway's sandwich). As illustrated in Fig. 9.3, the critical interval (the throughput time) on the Y-axis is the clock time between—(1) the moment when the service and any facilitating goods are available for use in the 'service encounter', and (2) the moment when that service encounter is completed. The matrix, therefore, examines productivity and not necessarily profitability.

Moving up the diagonal is a move to a greater productivity although not necessarily to greater profitability. Off diagonal location in the matrix can be very profitable.

To deliver flawless service operations, different processes have to be performed. It is not just about the processes visible to the customer, but those invisible to the customer have an immense impact on the overall delivery of the service. A case in point is fast

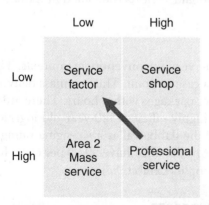

Source: Adapted from Schmenner (2004).

Fig. 9.3 Degree of variation

Exhibit 9.4   McDonald's: Planning supply chain two years ahead of service delivery

One would not be wrong in saying that McDonald's is the world's most popular and largest fast food chain. The American company started operations in India in October 1996 and has now expanded to destinations such as Vadodra, Ahmedabad, Ludhiana, Jaipur, Noida, and Doraha, apart from the popular cities and metros.

McDonald's local suppliers in India provide the ingredients of the best quality. There is complete adherence to the government's regulations on food, health, and hygiene, as well as international food standards. Their quick, friendly service is the worldwide mantra and the stringent cleaning standards ensure that all tables, seats, and high chairs are sanitized.

Efficient supply chain management is also a cornerstone of McDonald's success over the years. This means helping poultry farmers and farmers to improve yields on the crop. The suppliers are made to upgrade their systems, minimize waste, and speed up production. Prior to production, McDonald's looked at 250 ingredients that went into making their Indian offerings. The Indian management zeroed in on five products, which account for 80 per cent of McDonald's ingredient costs. These include the patty, iceberg lettuce, buns, potatoes, and cheese. Until 1996, iceberg lettuce was nowhere on its supplier Trikaya's crop menu. Since, lettuce is highly vulnerable to weather changes and McDonald's accepts only good quality material, the crop has to be harvested at the right time. To avoid calamities, McDonald's suggested that the lettuce seeds be planted on raised beds or moved to non-flood areas. A lettuce crop has a 3-month cycle. Once the seed is planted, it lies in the nursery for 30 days. For the next 60 days it is in the fields. Once harvested, its shelf life can be 15 days depending on how quickly the temperature is lowered to two degrees centigrade.

McDonald's planning of the supply chain is so intense that it begins the journey two years prior to the product hitting the market. This gives the suppliers enough time to upgrade their technology.

Source: Adapted from http://www.mcdonaldsindia.com.

---

food chain McDonald's operations in India. In order to standardize its offering and to make a pleasant experience for its customers, the organization makes huge investment in the supply chain management control and the quality of the delivered food products. It is an impressive investment in numerous firms, and immense amount of support and standardization efforts. The case of McDonald's efforts is detailed in Exhibit 9.4.

MASS PRODUCTION AND DELIVERY

Service processes can work even in some very unconventional contexts. The case of 'Mumbai dabbawallas' (tiffin carriers) is a case in point. This is a mass delivery system run by *dabbawallas* who collect and deliver packages within hours. There are lessons to be learnt from this unique, simple, and highly efficient 120-year old logistics system. The efficiency of the process has earned the dabbawallas a six-sigma rating from the *Forbes* magazine. The six-sigma rating means that they have 99.99 per cent efficiency in delivering the lunch boxes to the right people (Exhibit 9.5).

SERVICES PROFITABILITY AND SERVICE PROCESSES

There is a relationship between service processes and profitability. Efficient service processes help to reduce the time of delivery to the final consumer by expediting the

Exhibit 9.5 Mumbai dabbawallas: A lesson in managing service

The Nutan Tiffin Box Supply Charity Trust, better known as the Mumbai dabbawallas, are a supreme example of flawless service operations being managed in the food delivery segment in Mumbai. This case is a mass delivery system run by 3,000 semi-literate dabbawallas who collect and deliver 1,75,000 packages within hours. Such is the efficiency of their supply chain management that Forbes gave them a six-sigma performance rating; this indicates 99.999999 per cent correctness, i.e., one error in six million transactions.

About 5,000 dabbawallas work everyday through a system of multiple relays to deliver tiffin boxes in Mumbai. This exercise begins at nine in the morning and lasts till five in the evening. So, wherever you may be in Mumbai, a metropolis with a population of more than 16 million, you never fail to receive home food in time for lunch. The dabbawallas have been functioning for about 100 years and are rightly recognized as the best network management system in the world.

The history of dabbawallas runs parallel to the history of Mumbai's development. As the population started growing, people started to settle further from the original fort complex. Residential colonies started to move further away and a lot of office goers found it difficult to get home for lunch. Also, carrying lunch boxes from home was not that fashionable. In 1890, a Parsi broker hired a young man to fetch his lunch every afternoon. Business picked up and more and more people had to be hired. A charitable trust called Nutan Mumbai Tiffin Box Suppliers Trust was registered in 1956.

Although most tiffin carriers are illiterate, they are the ultimate practitioners of logistics management. The recruitment usually happens by word-of-mouth and a majority of them hail from neighbouring towns and villages in western Maharashtra. The recruitment policy is such that even before a new recruit leaves his hometown for Mumbai, his area of operation and remuneration are decided. While one set of tiffin-carriers collect the tiffins from homes and take them to stations such as Borivili or Kandivili, another set unloads them at Andheri, Dadar, or Churchgate. A third set waiting at the respective stations sorts out and assembles their respective sets of tiffins, and each carrier then sets out for the delivery.

As per the dabbawallas, their USPs are:

- They rely on low capital and use cycles, wooden carriages, and local trains to achieve their target.
- There are several groups that work independently and network with each other to achieve one goal.
- They meet once a month where all the groups gather and thrash out issues.
- There is no retirement age.
- They have a simple lifestyle and their job involves a lot of physical exercise; thus, they rarely suffer from illnesses.
- The dabbawallas have a credit society, which helps them during credit crunches.
- They are respected as they are considered *annadattas* or food providers.

Source: Adapted from Rajesh Vora (Dinodia Photo Library) and Ajay J. Thokal's project report on 'Logistics and customer's satisfaction of Nutan Mumbai Tiffin-Box Suppliers Association', http://www.bpic.co.uk/articles/dabawallas.htm, and http://www.mid-day.com/news/city/2003/october/66240.htm.

service delivery, with minimal interventions. The case of HDFC illustrates this relationship (Exhibit 9.6). The processes for loan disbursement have been so restructured by the bank that it leads to faster disbursement of loans. This helped enhance the efficiency and made the bank a market leader thanks to the service processes, which were driven by customer needs.

Exhibit 9.6   HDFC's loan servicing model: Cashing in on client's needs

The Housing Development Finance Corporation Limited (HDFC) was amongst the first to receive an 'in principle' approval from the Reserve Bank of India (RBI) to set up a bank in the private sector, as part of the country's liberalization of the banking sector. HDFC Band Ltd was thus was incorporated in August 1994 with its registered office in Mumbai. It commenced operations as a scheduled commercial bank in January 1995. HDFC Bank is highly automated in terms of information technology and communication systems. All the bank's branches have online connectivity, enabling it to offer speedy funds transfer facilities to its customers. Multi-branch access is also provided to retail customers through the branch network and automated teller machines (ATMs).

The bank made a lot of effort and investments to acquire the best technology available internationally and build the infrastructure of a world-class bank. Engagement in technology is a high priority and the Internet as one of the key goals has already made significant progress in web-enabling its core businesses. In each of its businesses, the bank has succeeded in leveraging its market position, expertise, and technology to create a competitive advantage and build market share.

HDFC has been improving its processes over years. Since no local role model was available, HDFC evolved its own business model. The goal was to make it simpler for individuals to take loans. They have created a service triangle with the customer in the centre and HDFC's services, systems, and empowered people at its three apexes. Cutting down cycle-time has enhanced process quality, completely decentralizing the loan appraisal system, and investing in information management systems. HDFC constantly tinkers with every form a customer has to fill during the period of his/her relationship with the company to make each one more user-friendly.

HDFC noticed that many of its loan applicants were young professionals eligible for small loans on the basis of their current income, but who would earn many times more in the future. It, therefore, introduced a step-up repayment facility that allows instalments to keep pace with urban professionals' upwardly mobile pay packets. A step-down facility for father-and-son teams whose repayment capacity came down when the father retired, was created.

To further enhance its process quality, HDFC delineated its service standards into tangible and intangible parameters. The former includes the number of times a customer visits an HDFC office to get a loan, the number of minutes she has to wait in the reception area, and the amount of information available to her on the various schemes while she waits. The intangible element was staff attitudes—behaving not like a moneylender but as a facilitator of the most important purchase a middle-class Indian makes in his/her life.

HDFC's loan granting cycle became two to four weeks. The next improvement was: a customer submits his/her papers, is interviewed immediately, and, if everything is in order, receives an offer letter the same day, and the cheque in the next two to three days. Managing this is, of course, impossible without a motivated team. In recruiting employees, HDFC believes in hiring the young and the inexperienced. The logic is that, they do not carry the baggage of unhealthy values, work practices, and assumptions from previous jobs. The mantra they believe in is training. Satish Mehta, a General Manager at HDFC, has been regularly conducting one-day workshops on customer service as an induction programme for every new employee, and repeat programmes for those who come into direct contact with the customers.

Source: Adapted from http://www.hdfcbank.com/aboutus/general/default.htm.

SUMMARY

Managing services is a complex task, which requires a lot of planning for front as well as back office operations. Various categories of services are offered, which can be classified in numerous ways. Marketers have to plan their strategies appropriately so that they address issues

Contd

of demand management. Service experience is a critical element and the service encounters have to be managed well. The role of the customer in a service process has to be assessed carefully. Also, service guarantees have to be looked into. The chapter has discussed the roles that service providers will have to manage. It has also examined the case of a leading multinational fast food chain, which has maintained global standards to provide quality service to consumers. The company manages its supply chain to maintain quality standards. Another case of service operation, which meets the six-sigma rating in spite of a semi-literate workforce, is also cited to emphasize the significance of designing and managing the service process. The case study of HDFC Bank provides an insight into how processes can be realigned to catapult the firm to a market leadership status.

KEY TERMS

Blueprinting   The detailed modelling of the production process for a new product or service.

Customer roles   The re-defined role of customers in the service process, indicating the fact that customers can increasingly participate in the service delivery.

Demand–supply   Synchronization of demand–supply is critical to service experience. Excess demand may lead to chaos and long queues and the experience may suffer.

Mass production   A type of process in which high volumes of identical, or very similar products are made in a set sequence of operations.

Service delivery   The process of offering service, including the place and time. Service delivery determines how service processes are structured.

Service guarantees   The process of offering a guarantee on the service delivery in order to make the service credible, simple, and meaningful to the customer.

Service processes   The various processes involved in the delivery of services to the customer. Efficient service processes create unique customer experiences, which help customers make use of the services.

Service profitability   The fact that efficient service helps to reduce the time of delivery to the final customer and hence makes it profitable.

Waiting-line strategies   Numerous strategies adopted by companies to manage the waiting time of customers.

CONCEPT REVIEW QUESTIONS

1. Discuss the relationship between profitability and service processes.

2. What is the significance of managing the blueprinting process in a service firm?

3. What are the roles played by the consumers in the service processes?

4. How can the service processes be managed to create profits?

5. Does the workforce always need to be educated in order to provide good quality service?

6. What are the lessons, which can be learnt from McDonald's supply chain interventions? How are they related to service process management?

7. What lessons can be learnt from the Mumbai dabbawallas case study?

8. What are the service process dimensions highlighted in the case study on HDFC Bank?

CRITICAL THINKING QUESTIONS

1. An entrepreneur is setting up a new restaurant, which offers multi-cuisine in a modern ambience in Gurgaon, a suburb of Delhi. The area has lot of malls and footfalls (visitors) are high as many of these malls have multiplexes as well. What are the service process issues that the entrepreneur must keep in mind?

2. A multinational bank claims that it provides 24 × 7 services on online banking facilities. A person visits a branch and asks for half-yearly statements. The staff at the counter is rude

and tells her to come back later. The consumer files a complaint by calling customer services but she does not get any response from the bank for six months. What kind of service issues would you like to raise here with the bank?

3. Evaluate the service guarantees of five service firms. Which are the common elements in these? Where are the common gaps? What are your recommendations about an ideal service guarantee? What dimensions should be incorporated in a service guarantee?

INTERNET EXERCISES

1. Go to the website of Haldiram's. What would be your comments on the service processes adopted by the food chain?

2. Critically analyse the service process adopted by Domino's and Pizza Corner in the Indian market by collecting information from Indian websites.

CASE STUDY

Ferns 'n' Petals

Ferns 'n' Petals, established in 1994, is the country's only branded chain of retail flower shops and provides a one-stop solution for everybody's floral needs. It caters to the:

- ○ online purchase of flowers for any occasion
- ○ online purchase of floral decor for weddings/parties/events
- ○ fresh flower delivery across India and abroad for offices/corporates.

Offices

The retail offices of Ferns 'n' Petals are located across all metros and major cities, such as Bangalore, Mangalore, Jalandhar, Pune, Hyderabad, Bhopal, Nagpur, Ahmadabad, Kolkata, Bhubaneswar, Ranchi, and Varanasi, among others.

Aim

The company feels that customer satisfaction is the keyword to success. Catering to exquisite

tastes and an exclusive list of clientele, Ferns 'n' Petals aims to offer the customer the privilege of buying flowers and deftly crafted floral arrangements online and through retail flowers shops, and service the customer with a never-before experience. Ferns 'n' Petals aims to be a premium online florist offering fresh flower delivery services to almost any location in India.

Vision

From aiming to make flower showrooms as common as friendly neighbourhood grocery stores, Ferns 'n' Petals, a premium place from where one can get fresh flowers delivered anywhere in India, endeavours to expand the chain manifold to become a household name not only in India but all over the world.

Operations

The operations of the floral chain span across various segments, such as:

○ Growing many varieties of flowers at the company's own horticulture farm in Bangalore, using state-of-the-art technology.

○ Wholesaling and retailing of fresh flowers to various florists and institutions around Delhi, India, apart from its own outlets.

○ Importing tulips, orchids, and other exotic flowers. The Delhi Florists Association has awarded FNP for bringing these exotic flowers to the capital.

○ Handcrafting all kinds of flower arrangements, including fresh flowers, dried flowers, and artificial flowers.

○ Renting of gas heaters, balloon lights, silent gensets, and exclusive furniture and party accessories.

○ Wedding decor arrangements

○ Venue selection

○ Catering and bartending

○ Trousseau and gift packing

○ Invitation cards

○ Photography

○ Other allied services for marriages.

Online Business

Ferns 'n' Petals offer a convenient and safe online mode of payment, which can also be tracked. It offers opportunities to place orders online for flowers and gifts (200 products) with delivery possibilities in 65 cities in the country and 156 cities worldwide. Each gift chosen includes a description of the gift and the arrangement of flowers. The sending process is convenient with the earliest date of delivery being shown along with the gift chosen. It is extremely easy to customize a booking on the basis of minimum price, maximum price, and the city of delivery. Customers have more than 90 cities to choose from.

Price Options

The website offers convenience as the products or their combinations are available in various price categories. The combination includes flower arrangements to flowers bundled with chocolates, soft toys, or cakes. The large varieties of arrangements are a perfect gift for any occasion.

Aids to Decision-making

The options help customers make instant choices and aids their decision-making process. It offers categories from which a customer can choose flowers and gifts. These are the best sellers (The most popular categories), price, and occasions.

There are various options of delivery such as international delivery, mid-night delivery, same day delivery, fixed time delivery, and delivery in remote locations and towns.

International Designers

Ferns 'n' Petals has the following designers on their panel—Mr Pao from Bangkok, Mr Daniel Ost from Belgium, and Mr Role Van Helden from United Kingdom.

Strategic Alliances

In addition to 36 outlets of their own, the group has a network of 65 strategic alliances in India for national deliveries, and 156 vendor partners outside of India for global deliveries. FNP believes that flowers alone do not add to the beauty of a decor. The way flowers are arranged is equally important. FNP's team of floral design specialists breathes life into any occasion using a variety of flowers, foliage, fabric, and other accessories.

Customer Help Desk

Customer support is available via telephone or e-mail till 20.00 hrs.

Official Florists

Ferns 'n' Petals currently has exclusive tie-ups with hotels such as Taj Palace, Grand Hyatt, and the Park Royal for providing all their floral requirements. It is the preferred florist for the Maurya Sheraton, the Oberoi, the Hyatt Regency, and official florists for several reputed designers and companies.

Wholesale Business

FNP Marketing is one of India's leading flower wholesale organizations. The roots of the company date back to 2001, when the company was established with the objective to provide rare domestic and exotic flowers to Indian consumers. Dealing in the widest and freshest range of Indian and imported flowers, FNP Marketing is a division of Ferns 'n' Petals group, the country's only branded retail chain of lifestyle floral boutiques established by Mr Vikas Gutgutia.

As a wholesale organization, FNP functions as a bridge between growers and the market. FNP's strategy is to support the growers' produce by developing a route to market and at the same time sustaining market growth by making quality flowers readily available at cost-effective prices.

Operating from a 10,000 sq. ft area the company has a considerably big packing facility. FNP has a dedicated team present round-the-clock that ensure that the flowers are sourced directly from growers and their timely deliveries. Upon arrival there is a quality check to ensure that they meet the stringent quality standards. The flowers are then immediately dispatched to retailers throughout India. Thus, FNP ensures that its customers get good quality, fresh flowers, with a long shelf life.

FNP keeps itself abreast with the latest trends on flowers and is credited with being the pioneer to introduce imported exotic flowers to India. The testimony to its impeccable functioning, product quality, cost-effectiveness, and wide range of expertise, is its ever-growing client list.

FNP Marketing has expanded to all major cities in the country and plays a significant role in the growth of the Indian flower business. Fast emerging as a powerful national platform for bringing together the growers and the retailers, the company contributes immensely to promoting and organizing the still unorganized Indian floriculture industry.

FNP Marketing is actively involved in the day-to-day operations of wholesale business of flowers. It caters to varying tastes and requirements of the traders and customers, keeping particular variables in mind, namely, type of flower and foliage, colour, quantity, and competitive price.

Import

FNP Marketing also imports exotic flowers and was one of the first companies to introduce them in India. Currently, it imports flowers and foliage from Thailand, Nepal, South Africa, Australia, and Sri Lanka.

Training

FNP plays a significant role in educating growers on the latest methods of quality produce and quantity maintenance and thus, helps them to get better results from their produce. Through the simple act of service, FNP Marketing has given the flower world a fine example in ways of loving and caring for flowers. Through the network of dedicated growers and its team, FNP Marketing reflects the uncompromising commitment towards marketing flowers, which exemplifies the perfection that results from services.

Recently, the company has decided to foray into the overseas market by opening its outlet in Dubai, besides scaling up its domestic presence by rolling out 35 new outlets, this fiscal. The company hopes to fulfil the requirement of wedding decor with this launch. The retail chain has also embarked upon an aggressive expansion plan and will open 35 new outlets targeting Tier II and Tier III cities across the country, on a franchise model.

'Yes, we have plans to go public but it will happen in 2009–10 for our two to three new ventures', FNP, General Manager, Lalita Raghav said. Post expansion, the company is looking at a turnover of Rs 100–10 crore by end of 2008–09 compared to a turnover of Rs 80 crore achieved in the last fiscal. 'We are expecting sales of Rs 110 crore in 2008–09', she said. The company has diversified into various flower-related fields including weddings, event management, marketing, and the rentals business.

Questions

1. Discuss the structuring of the service process by Ferns 'n' Petals.

2. Which of the processes listed by Ferns 'n' Petals adds value to the customer?

SELECT REFERENCES

Bedi, K. (2007), *Production and Operations Management*, 2nd edn, Oxford University Press, New Delhi.

Byus, K. and W.L. Lomerson (2004), 'Consumer or originated value: A framework for performance analysis', *Journal of Intellectual Capital*, vol. 5, no. 3, p. 464.

Chervonnaya, O. (2003), 'Customer role and skill trajectories in services', *International Journal of Service Industry Management*, vol. 14, no. 3/4, p. 347.

Dickson, D., R.C. Ford, and B. Laval (2005), 'Managing real and virtual waits in hospitality and service organizations', *Cornell Hotel and Administration Quarterly*, February, vol. 46, no. 10.

File, K.M., B.B. Judd, and R.A. Prince (1992), 'Interactive marketing: The influence of participation positive word-of-mouth and referrals', *The Journal of Service Marketing*, vol. 6, no. 4, p. 5.

Hubbert, A.R. (1995), 'Customer-co-creation of service outcomes: Effects of locus of causality attributions', Doctoral dissertation, Arizona State University, Arizona.

India Committee of the Netherlands (1997), 'No roses without a thorn', *India Committee of the Netherlands*, Utrecht, Netherlands.

Lakshman, N. (2003), 'From supply chain to customer value: The McDonalds' way', *Indian Management*, August.

Lovelock, C. (2001), *Services Marketing*, Pearson Education, Asia, Delhi.

Lovelock, C. and L. Wright (1999), *Principles of Service Marketing and Management*, Prentice Hall, New Jersey.

Marmorstein, H.O. Sarel, and W.M. Lassor (2001), 'Increasing the persuasiveness of a service guarantee: The role of service process evidence', *The Journal of Service Marketing*, vol. 15, no. 2, p. 147.

Martin, C.I. and C.A. Pranter (1989), 'Compatibility management: Customer-to-customer relationship in service environments', *Journal of Services Marketing*, vol. 3, no. 3, summer, pp. 5–15.

O'Neil, M., A. Palmer, and S. Charters (2002), 'Wine production as a service experience: The effects of service quality on wine sales', *The Journal of Service Marketing*, vol. 16, no. 4, p. 342.

Schmenner, R.W. (2004), 'Service businesses and productivity', *Decision Sciences*, vol. 35, no. 3, p. 333.

Schneider, B. and D.E. Bowen (1995), *Winning the Service Game*, Harvard Business School Press, Boston.

Shostack, G.L. (1984), 'Designing services that deliver', *Harvard Business Review*, Jan–Feb, pp. 13–39, 133–139.

Zeithaml, V.A. and M.J. Bitner (2000), *Service Marketing Integrating Customer Focus Across the Firm*, Irwin McGraw-Hill, Boston.

http://courses.ischool.berkeley.edu/i210/f07/lectures/210-20070919.pdf, accessed on 4 December 2008

http://www.bpic.co.uk/articles/dabawallas.htm, accessed on 23 June 2008.

http://www.business-standard.com/common/story page_c_online.php?leftnm=10&bKeyFlag=IN&autono=40629, accessed on 23 June 2008.

http://www.fnp.in, accessed on 23 June 2008.

http://www.hdfcbank.com/aboutus/general/default.htm, accessed on 23 June 2008.

http://www.mcdonaldsindia.com, accessed on 23 June 2008.

http://www.mid-day.com/news/city/2003/october/66240.htm, accessed on 23 June 2008.

10 Customer Feedback and Service Recovery

OBJECTIVES

After reading this chapter you will be able to understand the:
- concept of service recovery
- importance of service recovery
- strategies for an effective service recovery
- design and implementation process of service guarantees

INTRODUCTION

In the preceding chapters we have discussed customer expectations, service quality, and customer perceptions about services. We have studied the gap model and have seen that what the customers want and what is delivered to them is often not at par. Providing a 'zero-defect' service should be the objective of all service providers but problems arise when gaps are left in the service delivery (Weun et al. 2004). The importance of customers is highlighted by the fact that it costs a lot more to attract a new client than to retain an old one (Oliver 1999). However, it is estimated that businesses typically lose 50 per cent of their customers every five years (Mack et al. 2000).

SERVICE FAILURE AND RECOVERY

The inability of the services organization to deliver as per customer expectations constitutes service failure. The multi-dimensional nature of the service encounter creates an environment where failure may often be the norm, not the exception (Mack et al. 2000). According to Palmer et al. (2000), service customers perceive failure when something goes wrong, irrespective of responsibility. We can define service failure as 'during the course of a service experience by the customer, when the customer perceives services quality to fall below the customer expectations and invokes feelings of mistrust in the customer's perception about the service provider, it is called as service failure'.

Failure can occur if the service is unavailable when promised, is delivered late or too slowly, the outcome is not as per expectations, or the employees are indifferent and uncaring (Zeithaml and Bitner 2000). The problem of service failure is further compounded by the fact that there is increased competition in most service industries

(Lee et al. 2003). Also, few companies can claim to offer a product so unique that competitors cannot offer it (La and Kandampully 2004). Thus, the customer has many options to choose from. Hence, in an era of increased competition and perceptual differences between customers and the service providers leading to service failures, service recovery becomes an important strategy to reduce dissonance among customers.

A failure to deliver a service as per his/her expectations creates depredation in the customer's psychology, which if left unattended can ring the death knell for the organization. Grönroos (1988), in his six criteria of good perceived services quality gives due importance to service recovery saying that 'If the customers realize that whenever something goes wrong or something unpredictable happens, the service provider will immediately and actively take action to keep them in control of the situation and find a new, acceptable solution then they are bound to have a better perception of the organization'. Thus, service recovery involves what a service provider does in response to service failures (Weun et al. 2004).

It has also been defined as 'Service recovery is a service employee's performance resulting from a customer's perception of initial service delivery falling below the customer's zone of tolerance' Zeithaml et al. (1993). Keaveney (1995) stated that if organizations do not adopt recovery strategies it could lead to customers switching over to another service provider. Bitner et al. (1990) and Chung and Hoffman (1998) identified three categories of failure.

SERVICE SYSTEM FAILURE

This occurs in a core service, such as hotels, and includes product defects, such as cold food, slow or unavailable service, facility problems; cleanliness issues such as dirty silverware, insect, or rodent problems; unfriendly guest policies such as not accepting cheques or credit cards; and out-of-stock conditions such as inadequate supply of menu items. When a customer experiences a problem in the core service delivery, the employee's response determines the customer's perceived satisfaction or dissatisfaction. For example, if there is a core service failure such as slow service, then an unsatisfactory handling of the situation could be either to give no information, or wrong information and make a one hour delay turn into a five- or six-hour wait. On the other hand, a satisfactory handling of the situation could entail explaining the flight delay, giving the correct reply for the time required, and offering refreshments on the house, or some activities to make the wait bearable. On getting a home delivery of the special Navratra *thali* from Nirula's, a customer found that the food was not cooked properly. On calling Nirula's and lodging a complaint, he found that not only were they apologetic, but also offered to send their special sundaes, which could be consumed during the *Navratra* fast. Thus, the customer who was not happy with the service delivery initially, became a satisfied one due to service recovery by the provider.

Failure in Implicit or Explicit Customer Requests

This occurs chiefly when employees are unable to comply with the customer's individual needs such as food not cooked as per the order, seating problems such as seating smokers in non-smoking section, or lost reservations. Consider this instance. A person travelling with a child who gets airsick will need to take care of the child. If the flight attendant helps that passenger it will create a satisfactory experience for him.

Unprompted and Unsolicited Employee Actions

This includes behaviour of employees that is unacceptable to guests such as rudeness, poor attitude, wrong order delivered, or order misplaced or not fulfilled. It would also include incorrect charges such as charging customers for items not ordered or giving incorrect change. According to Bitner et al. (1990), a truly out-of-the-ordinary employee behaviour was when a family, travelling with their teddy bears, returned to their hotel room and saw that the maid had arranged the bears, holding hands, comfortably together on a chair.

According to a study on restaurant failures by Chung and Hoffman (1998), it was observed that the incident rate for service system failure was 44.4 per cent, delivery failure due to implicit or explicit customer requests was 18.4 per cent, and unprompted and unsolicited employee action was 37.2 per cent (Fig. 10.1). All the failures rated above six on a scale of 1–10, where one was a minor mistake. After an average time period of 294 days it was observed that 69.6 per cent of customers facing service delivery failure were retained, 80.6 per cent of them facing customer request problems were still loyal, and 78.4 per cent facing employee action service problems were loyal. Thus, we see that the core service delivery affects customers the most and is the prime candidate for managerial intervention.

When a customer experiences a service failure, the type of failure, and the magnitude of the failure prompt the customer to take a follow-up action. Even if the customer decides not to complain to the service provider, he may still not be satisfied with the

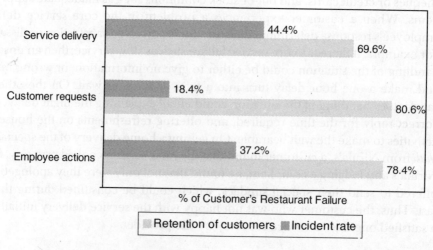

Source: Beth and Hoffman (1998).

Fig. 10.1   Restaurant failures

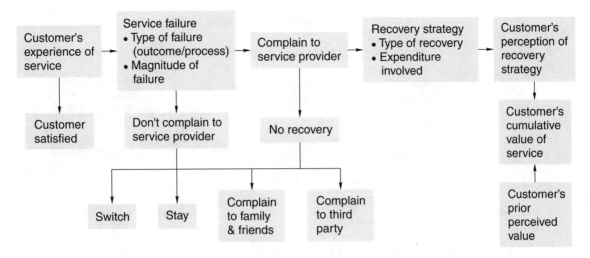

Source: Adapted from Zhu et al. (2004).

Fig. 10.2 Importance of service recovery on value of service

service and may decide to switch over to another service provider, and may also complain to family and friends. Alternatively, he can complain to a third party (Exhibit 10.1). This strategy of the customer is dangerous for the service provider as it does not give him a second chance to rectify the problem. If the consumer complains to the service provider, he gets the opportunity to satisfy the consumer by offering a recovery. The cumulative value of the service provider is the effect of the customer's perception of the recovery strategy along with the initial perception the customer had about the service provider. Figure 10.2 highlights the importance of service recovery for a service provider.

AIMS OF SERVICE RECOVERY

The following points must be kept in mind while organizing a service recovery. They are to:

- satisfy customers who have experienced a service failure
- retain those customers who have experienced a failure
- improve organization-wide processes as a result of information from failures.

Customers' Response to Service Failures

When customers choose a service organization to purchase a service, they have their own perceptions about it. On experiencing the service they develop their perceptions about the quality of the service at the time of delivery. If this is in accordance with their perceived perceptions, it leads to customer satisfaction. However, if the service rendered is below their expectation it leads to service failure.

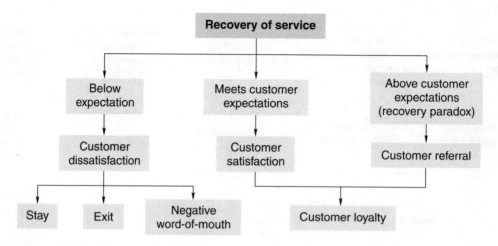

Source: Adapted from Zeithaml and Bitner (2000).

Fig. 10.3   Effect of service recovery

If a service failure occurs the customer has two options—either to complain about it to the provider or to nurture the grievance quietly without telling the service provider about it at that point of time. If the customer complains, it gives the service provider a chance to retrieve the situation. It is the customers who do not complain that are a cause of concern for the service providers as they nurture negative feelings and are the ones who are never likely to return for repurchase of services. Moreover, they can also spread negative word-of-mouth to relatives, friends, and acquaintances. That is more harmful, as then, the service provider faces the danger of losing all potential customers (Fig. 10.2). The effectiveness of the service recovery influences the customer's perceptions about the service provider, which along with their initial perception, form the overall perception of the value of the service provider in the eyes of the customer. This perception can however, have negative implications if the service recovery was below their expectations (Fig. 10.3). If the service recovery has met the expectations of the customers it can lead to customer satisfaction, and if the service recovery was above expectations it would lead to customer delight, and the recovery paradox would come into play. (The concept is discussed in detail later in the chapter).

Types of Complainers

Broadly, there are two types of customers—those who complain and those who do not. Several authors have uncovered the following four reasons why customers are reluctant to complain (Bamford and Xystouri 2005).

- The customers believe that the organization will not be responsive.
- They do not wish to confront the individual responsible for the failure.
- They are uncertain about their rights and the firm's obligations.
- They are concerned about the high cost in time and effort of complaining.

Zeithaml and Bitner (2000) identified four types of complainers—passive, voicers, irates, and activists.

Passives This group of customers is least likely to take any action. They do not say anything to the service provider, are less likely to spread negative word-of-mouth, and are unlikely to complain to a third party. This is because they doubt the effectiveness of complaining, thinking that the consequence will not merit the time and effort they are going to spend on it.

Voicers This group of customers actively complains to the service provider but is less likely to spread negative word-of-mouth, switch patronage, or go to a third party for redressal of their complaints. They are the service providers' true friends, helping them to improve their services by giving them a second chance.

Irates They are most likely to complain to friends and relatives, and switch over to another service provider. They are angry with the service provider, and are about average in their complaint to the service provider. They are less likely to give the service provider a second chance and will switch services, and complain to family and friends.

Activists In comparison to others, they have a higher propensity to complain to the service provider, relatives, friends, and to third parties. This fits in with their personal norms. They are highly optimistic about the positive consequences of all types of complaints.

Table 10.1 provides an insight into the various types of complainers.

Table 10.1   Types of complainers

Types of complainers	Action taken	Belief	Alienation from market
Passives	No action	No point in complaining, as it will not have any positive outcome.	Less alienated than irates and activists.
Voicers	Complain only to service provider and not to anyone else.	Complaining has social benefits. Consequence is positive and gives the service provider a second chance to improve their service.	Also less alienated than irates and activists.
Irates	Complaint to service provider is average and more likely to spread negative word-of-mouth, and switch service providers. Unlikely to complain to third parties.	Complaining to service provider can have social benefits but less likely to give service providers a second chance.	Feel alienated from the marketplace.
Activists	Above-average propensity to complain to all parties and most likely than others to complain to a third party.	Optimistic about the potential positive consequence of all types of complaining.	Feel alienated from the marketplace.

Source: Adapted from Zeithaml and Bitner (2000).

We see that when customers complain they believe it is a social obligation to do so—to bring about a change for the better so that others do not face the same problem, and/or to punish the service provider.

Customer's Expectations on Complaint Handling

When customers complain there can be only two outcomes (Berry 1990). They are either satisfied or not satisfied with the company's response. As a service provider, the focus is to create more of the former than the latter outcomes. What customers expect when they voice their grievances is of primary importance. There are three specific types of justice that customers look for following their complaints (Berry 1990).

Outcome fairness   Customers expect the compensation or the service recovery strategy to match the level of dissatisfaction. They expect objectivity in that, they want to be compensated no more or less than the mistake the service provider has committed, and equality in getting the same compensation that any other customer would get.

Procedural fairness   In addition to compensation, customers expect the policies, rules, and the timeliness of the complaint process to be fair. The complaint process should be easy and hassle free, handled quickly, and by the first person the complainant contacts. The service recovery procedures should be adaptable and should match individual circumstances.

Interactional fairness   Along with the outcome and procedural fairness, customers expect the recovery process to be carried out politely, with care and honesty. If customers feel the employees are uncaring and have done little to resolve the problem, it can hamper the recovery process. The skills and demeanour of employees influence the customer's evaluation of service quality. On their part, employees, due to lack of training and empowerment, may feel frustrated and show an indifferent attitude, especially if the customers are irate, it would adversely affect the recovery process.

If the customers feel that the problem faced is not handled properly they can file a complaint under the Consumer Protection Act, 1986. For banking grievances customers can also file a complaint under the Banking Ombudsman Scheme that has been revised by the Reserve Bank of India (RBI) with effect from 2006 (Exhibit 10.1).

Recovery Paradox

A good recovery can turn angry, frustrated customers into loyal ones and may create more goodwill than if things had gone on smoothly in the first place (Hart et al. 1990). For example, if a person orders a meal and finds that what he has received is not as per quality, and the restaurant manager immediately gets him another meal along with drinks at no extra cost, the customer is thrilled. The manager's gesture also affects the customer's purchase decision in the future. Some authors have suggested that companies should plan to disappoint customers so that they can recover and gain a higher level of loyalty from them than they would have gained in the first place. This idea is termed as the *recovery paradox*.

In their study, Weun et al. (2004) have offered mixed views concerning service recovery paradox. They argued that post-recovery satisfaction can be higher than pre-failure

Exhibit 10.1 Thinking out of the drop box

Imagine a situation where a customer deposits a cheque in the drop box but later finds this payment is not reflected in her account, or that no credit is reflected in the future bills, or the bank denies having received the cheque in the first place. In this case, the unfortunate part is that the customer has no substantiating evidence that she indeed deposited the cheque in the drop box before the due date.

In such a scenario where no foolproof system of accounting exists in the case of deposits through the drop box, the Committee on Procedures and Performance Audit on Public Services recommended that an acknowledgement at collection counters should exist, and that no branch should refuse an acknowledgement to the customer. RBI has even advised the banks to send reminders to all customers around the due date, or if no payment has been received. Any late payment charges levied without sending reminders will amount to deficiency in service.

Another fact is that in cases where a cheque is lost due to the bank's negligence or late pick-up of the cheque from the drop box, the consumer can file a complaint under the Consumer Protection Act, 1986. In case of a belated collection, a photocopy would suffice, whereas in case of a loss of cheque the consumer will have to produce sufficient evidence that the cheque was indeed deposited; the photocopy and pay-in slip would not be helpful as there is no endorsement from the bank on these.

Some ways in which customer litigation can be prevented are:

- Customers who have online viewing and transaction facilities can see whether the amount is reflected in the statements or not. The amount is ideally reflected as soon as the cheque is sent for clearing.
- Most of these collection machines have automatic systems to scan the cheque and issue a pay-in slip. A person deputed at the collection counter can endorse the pay-in slip, which can act as a proof of deposit and provide relief to the customer in case of a lost cheque.

Source: Adapted from Goel (2006).

satisfaction for minor failures provided they are handled exceptionally well. As these failures become more severe they are unlikely to generate positive feelings towards the service provider regardless of how they are handled. Mack et al. have also researched that the customers who perceived their service failures as minor, rated the recovery efforts as very good (over 78 per cent of the customers felt so), but the customers who had faced a major service failure were more likely to judge the recovery effort as poor (approximately 58 per cent). Thus, if the management has to derive value from the recovery paradox it should not focus on the core services for doing this.

RECOVERY STRATEGIES

Service recovery strategies describe the actions of service providers in response to defects or failures (Grönroos 1988). A service provider can either do nothing, or do whatever it takes to fix the problem. The commonly used actions are apology and compensation (Bitner et al. 1990, Hoffman et al. 1995, and McDougall and Levesque 1999).

Apology   Service providers apologize for the service failure.

Assistance   This includes the actions taken to rectify the problem. This is the single most effective recovery strategy as it brings the customer back to the original purpose of buying the service. For example, if the customer has to wait for a service even with a reservation, the recovery strategy could include a reduction in the time that he waits for it.

Compensation   This includes monetary payments to the customers for the inconvenience experienced. It is generally resorted to when customers feel that assistance alone cannot offset the trouble 'cost' of the problem. Compensation can be in the form of free food, discounts, or a coupon for a drink or meal at a restaurant.

The effectiveness of recovery strategies is situational and is influenced by the type of service. According to McDougall and Levesque (1999), effectiveness of a recovery strategy depends on the following factors:

- What is done? This includes the recovery action taken by the service provider.
- How it is done? This includes the way in which the service provider has handled the problem, that is, responsiveness, empathy, and understanding. Even if the best of service recovery strategy is offered, but its delivery process is done grudgingly, the customer can see through it and the impact or effectiveness of service recovery stands diluted. Service providers should thus show sincerity in the process of fixing the problem and try to add value beyond the fix.

Types of Service Recovery Strategies

This section elaborates on the various strategies for handling service recovery.*

Encourage customers to complain   The service provider should see the process of service recovery as an opportunity and encourage the customers to complain. For example, British Airways analysed its datamine of consumer complaints and transformed it into meaningful information pointing to persistent service problems. They analysed the information and found ways to improve customer satisfaction (Exhibit 10.2). The customers can be encouraged to complain if they find that the service provider has clear procedures for complaint handling, and these are easily accessible and user-friendly. Also, showing the customers that the organization is serious about the complaints received and acts on them, further motivates them to state the service failures that they have encountered.

Timely action   This is the most obvious service strategy and focuses on getting the service recovery right the first time. Service providers should create a culture where the staff is encouraged to acknowledge and deal with service failures, and bring it to the notice of the management. If justice is delayed to customers who are already facing a service failure it will just add fuel to the fire. The staff should thus be efficient and understand the need of the hour.

Staff empowerment and training   It is very essential to empower the frontline staff so that they know the extent to which they can go in solving issues. Doing this also gives the staff the added confidence that they have the power to deal with the service failures to some extent. Moreover, if the staff is empowered to take some decisions they do not need to contact higher authorities for approval at the time of service failure. This also

---

Source: * Adapted from Berry et al. (1990), Zeithaml and Bitner (2000), and Cranage (2004).

Exhibit 10.2 Service recovery strategy of British Airways

Once dubbed 'bloody awful', British Airways is today one of the most profitable and respected airlines in the world. In the 1980s, the BA management knew something was very wrong. Many customers were complaining about flight delays and food problems. The customers who complained were just one-third of the customers who had actually faced a problem in service delivery. The company estimates that unresolved customer service problems cost it as much as $600 million in lost revenue. The airline's management was determined to 'melt the complainant iceberg'. Its approach was first to change the culture via extensive employee training. The next move was to revise performance measures. Instead of emphasizing on complaint reduction, new steps such as rewarding employees who helped bring hidden problems to the surface, were introduced.

The five-step process This redesigned process was supported by investments in a database engine and workstations capable of simultaneously displaying a customer's scanned-in letter, and relevant data

in other systems such as frequent-flier status. The airline's employees were taught to use their judgement to determine how best to respond to customer problems.

Previously, when customers wrote to complain about flight delays or food, service representatives consulted a two-inch thick manual and followed a 13-step investigation process. It sometimes took them as long as twelve weeks to respond. This long method was condensed into five important steps:

- listen
- apologize
- express concern
- make amends
- record the event.

One manager observed, 'We have nothing to gain by squabbling with customers'. However, BA has everything to gain by turning dissatisfied customers into loyalists.

Source: Cash (1995).

helps provide the customers timely service recovery, thus enhancing their view of service recovery further. The management should include service recovery aspects in the responsibilities chart of the employees so that they have a clear understanding of what is expected of them. This should also be reiterated to them from time to time during training sessions. The staff should be trained on how to deal with angry customers and how to help them solve problems. For example, American Express customer service representatives handling cardholders' monthly statements are trained and empowered to solve 85 per cent of the problems on the spot (Berry et al. 1990).

Creating the right employee behaviour Apart from the 'what' aspect, the 'how' aspect of the service recovery should also be highlighted to the employees. The importance of dealing with customers with empathy and compassion should be highlighted so that when they are resolving service failures they can be highly effective, and in the process create a recovery paradox. Employees, by creating 'warmth' in service delivery, are found to positively precipitate the relationship experience (Lemmink and Mattsson 2002). Similarly, we can say that at the time of service recovery this will create a short-term emotional judgment, which will have a long-term effect on the customers' perception.

Empower customers Some service firms have a recovery strategy that empowers the customers too. This means that they allow the customers to solve their own problems and come up with solutions they seem fit for the service failures.

Follow up with timely personal communication with customers   Companies should undertake a follow up with the customers who have complained about service failures. This would help the service provider in various ways as illustrated here:

- Make sure that the customer is satisfied and is not holding a grudge.
- Communicate to the customer that his/her satisfaction is important to the organization.
- Create an opportunity for a dialogue—to listen, ask questions, explain, apologize, and seek suggestions from the customer.
- Regain the customer's favour.

Document the service failure   This is an important aspect of service recovery strategy. The purpose is to ensure that the service failures are understood by the staff at all levels so that the same failures are not repeated. It can also be referred to when a similar failure occurs, to understand the recovery strategy used and the impact of the same (that is, did the customer return or not).

Recovery Strategies for Managers

We see that service failures occur as a norm, but it is the way the employee handles the failure that creates a lasting impression on the customers (Fig. 10.2). The knowledge of the service process, service delivery, and its operation, and the system standards enables employees to inform customers about what can and cannot be done to address their problem. In many cases, information alone can create satisfaction. For many encounters, action of some kind is needed to create satisfaction. These responses can be standardized or tailored to the situation. In either case, when information has to be given or some action has to be taken, if the employee is in the know and empowered then he/she can fix situations and respond to requests in effective ways. Thus, managers should undertake the following measures in this direction.

- Identify what information customers consider important and disseminate that information to the employees.
- Identify the range of action alternatives the employees can exercise.
- Train the employees to practice a range of action alternatives, which they can use at the time of service recovery.
- Develop a set of 'Plan B' actions with the employees and incorporate them as 'fail-safes' in the service system.
- Along with this, the employees must be empowered, that is, given discretion to take whatever action they deem necessary to retrieve the given situation (Weun et al. 2004).
- Unprompted and unsolicited employee action is, however, less subject to management control. To overcome this, an organization can, through the recruitment and selection procedures, hire employees with a strong service orientation. According to Chris Dunn, Regional Director of Talent Management, Marriott Hotels International Ltd, most of the employees working at Marriott are Indians who are doing quite well for themselves because the Indian culture of

hospitality is quite close to the Marriott culture of serving the associates, the customer, and the community.

Effectiveness of Recovery Strategies

Many studies have been conducted to gauge the effectiveness of the recovery strategies. Researchers have found that a good service recovery is a key factor in building ongoing relationships with customers who were initially unhappy with the service delivery (Bitner 1990; Maxham 2001; and Smith et al. 1999). According to Weun et al. (2004), it is the severity of the service failure or the perceived intensity of the problem that influences the evaluation of a service provider after a service failure. If the service failure is severe, then despite adequate service recovery the customers will still perceive the loss to be greater. This will also affect the customers' trust, their commitment, and word-of-mouth publicity. A customer who reports satisfaction with the service recovery may not necessarily possess an equally high level of commitment to the service organization. Thus, managers should engage in additional efforts after the service recovery to attempt to build customer commitment. Satisfaction is a major driver of customer commitment and if service managers continue to satisfy customers after a service failure, then customer commitment can still be developed. McDougall and Levesque (1999), in a study on the effectiveness of recovery strategy on customers who had to wait for services even after making reservations, found that irrespective of the recovery strategy taken, the customers showed a negative future intention towards the service provider. Thus, the customer is not willing to forgive and forget. The service provider has to do it right the first time to ensure customer loyalty. Alternatively, we can manage the whole recovery process and create a value enhancement for the organization.

Value Enhancement through Service Recovery

La and Kandampully (2004) proposed a model of value enhancement that is inspired by service failure and recovery. They proposed that service recovery that leads to value enhancement takes the firm through three stages of service orientation—operational, strategic, and service vision.

Operational

This stage of service orientation includes measures that are primarily aimed towards recovering from service failure. These would include the following:

- provide alternatives of recovery so that the customer's needs are met
- acknowledge the understanding of the service failure
- provide immediate rewards for employees involved in successful recovery
- provide further training to employees who contributed to the initial failure.

Strategic

Once the recovery process is in place, the organization graduates to the next level of value enhancement, which entails strategy planning on the basis of learning and realignment as a result of the damage control systems in place. It entails the following measures:

- Align the firm's external orientation with internal orientation to create right customer perception and minimize service failures.
- Conduct a systematic analysis of the entire service delivery system to create a foolproof method and do it 'right the first time'.
- Learn from the service failure and recovery to realign the inner mechanism so that the same mistake is not repeated in the future.
- Create a culture of learning by assimilating and disseminating information.
- Effect improvements that will reflect on the firm's competency and market performance.

Service Vision

Once the two stages are achieved, steps can be taken to initiate innovative value enhancement that progresses through the operation, strategy, and vision of the firm for the ultimate benefit of customers, employees, and the firm itself.

Although the service recovery is often regarded as an operational concern, if integrated with strategic and conceptual issues, it can contribute to the firm's business orientation immensely and continually, thus creating a competitive advantage. Moreover, the organization-wide realignment and reorientation will create superior customer value.

SERVICE GUARANTEES

Due to the characteristics of services, the customers cannot be sure of the quality of a service until they experience it themselves. As costs are involved and the process cannot be undone, in order to generate a feeling of trust and commitment, the service providers try to give guarantees in a bid to ensure that the service delivery is going to satisfy the customers. A service guarantee is a commitment the service provider gives to the customer concerning all or part of the service process and may also include a compensation for the customer if the commitment is not honoured (Kashyap 2001). Guarantees are common in manufactured products and have recently been applied to the service sector. According to Wirtz (1996) guarantees can be used as a quality tool, marketing tool, and customer service tool. The different types of service guarantees are illustrated in this section.

Unconditional service guarantee An unconditional service guarantee, guarantees cent per cent customer satisfaction irrespective of any terms and conditions. This applies to the customer's overall satisfaction.

Conditional service guarantee A conditional guarantee is when the service provider intends to promote a certain element of the service offering. For example, Bharti group is giving guarantees on the Touchtel (fixed line telephone) service in Chennai. In the service level agreement, Touchtel mentions issues such as down time (how long a telephone connection will be out of service in case of a fault), billing errors, and in the

Exhibit 10.3	Introduction of loan back guarantee by GE Money

GE Money, India has decided to introduce a 15-day loan back guarantee to bring in transparency while approving mortgages, loans against property, and personal loans.

This guarantee will give its customers, an option of returning a loan within 15 days if they find a gap in delivery in key terms and services versus the promise made to them while applying for the loan. No processing fee or penalty on loan will be levied on the customer. Also, even before the customer has availed the loan, he/she will be provided with a document called the 'most important document', which will contain the paperwork on the important terms of the loan and the simplified tariff card.

This campaign seems to be an attempt by GE Money to provide small-ticket loans to customers with inadequate ability to pay. The size of this business seems to be anywhere around Rs 31,440 crore. Some competitors feel that this step only provides a warranty and does not improve product quality.

Source: Adapted from Banerjee (2007).

case of the DSL service, speed of the Internet connection. The service is provided in key cities, such as Hyderabad, where the business segment is viewed as a potential area that the service provider can tap (Ramakrishna 2004). Exhibit 10.3 elaborates the concept further.

Designing the Service Guarantee

Fabien (2005) gave a model to support the decision of service guarantee development. The proposed model advocated five steps, namely, preliminary analysis, service quality signalling, guarantee design, implementation and communication, and performance analysis.

Preliminary Analysis

A preliminary analysis on taking a decision on service guarantee is undertaken at the outset. It can be done by analysing the external and the internal factors (Fig. 10.4).

External factors   The following external factors are taken into account while conducting a preliminary analysis.

Industry standards   An industry that has few acknowledged standards or where service supply variability is high can be recommended to give guarantees.

Competition   Being the first firm to offer guarantees, always provides a competitive advantage to the firm. For example, Standard Chartered Bank became the first bank in Singapore to offer service guarantees (Exhibit 10.4).

Legal aspects   The regulations that govern the transactions must be considered in detail. Legally, a commitment constitutes a type of contract, and failure to honour the same can have negative implications.

Customer expectations   This is of utmost importance as what the customers expect and what they want is vital and the organization providing service guarantees should be aware of this. It will also help them spend the money in the right direction.

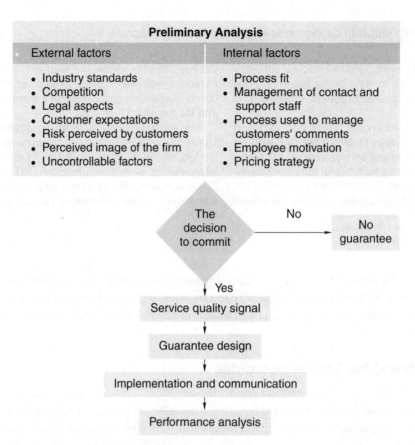

Source: Adapted from Fabien (2005).

Fig. 10.4 Designing the service guarantee

Risk perceived by customers Service guarantees assume special significance when customers feel that the risk associated with the purchase of service is high, or they do

Exhibit 10.4 StanChart innovates with service guarantee

Standard Chartered Bank will offer a new service guarantee, known as the overnight document checking service, to its Singapore customers. As a result of this commitment, trade customers will have a quicker turnaround time, which in turn, will help the company's cash flows and reduce interest costs. This service will help customers to submit export letters of credit documents to the bank till 6.00 pm, along with a commitment that any notice of discrepancy will be delivered by the next working day. In case this deadline is not met, the service guarantee offers customers the ability to claim a credit note of up to SG$100 in commission fees of their next trade transaction. This is a value-added service that will allow the trade customers to speed up their trade capabilities and further strengthen the company's position in the market.

Source: Adapted from *Trade Finance* (2006).

not feel qualified to assess the service, or where they feel emotionally involved in the service. In such cases if a service guarantee is offered by the service provider it can positively influence the purchase decision of the customer.

Perceived image of the firm A firm with a low perceived image is bound to benefit from providing service guarantees as it will reassure the potential customers about the service quality. On the other hand, for a well-known organization, the strong corporate image is a guarantee in itself. If such firms provide guarantees it will create doubts in the minds of the customers.

Uncontrollable factors These are the factors beyond the firm's control. For example, an airline cannot guarantee flight departure times because of a number of external factors, such as weather condition, air traffic, etc.

Internal factors The following internal factors should be considered during a preliminary analysis on service guarantees.

Process fit This is one of the most important internal factors that should be taken into account because if the process is lacking or not fit enough, then the firms should not provide the guarantees. For instance, if a bank promises a financing proposal within 72 hours of receiving an application, then they must make adequate provisions for the human resources and processes to achieve success in the service guarantees.

Management of contact and support staff The cooperation of the contact and support staff is a must when providing service guarantees. The contact and support staff should be made aware that if they do not perform within the stipulated time, it is going to cost the firm monetarily as well as create negative perceptions about the organization.

Process used to manage customer's comments A firm that clearly informs its customers about the standards they are entitled to expect and compensation they will receive if the same is not met, actually motivates the clients to express service dissatisfaction. Once a firm offers guarantees, there is bound to be a surge in customer complaints. The firm should have a process in place to manage these complaints so that they can recover the customers they would have otherwise lost due to service failures. Service guarantees thus help to retain the customers who would otherwise have been lost and also help the firm to make improvements in their service delivery process.

Employee motivation It is important for the employees to be motivated so that they can perform and honour the service guarantees. An employee who is aware of, and comfortable with the service guarantees can concentrate on meeting the commitments and improving processes in case of service failures. The guarantees provide a 'framework' for the employees and give 'meaning' to their work. However, if the guarantees are unrealistic they can de-motivate the staff, as they cannot meet the unrealistic promises made by the company.

Pricing strategy The final, but not the least important, point to consider is compatibility of the service guarantee with the pricing strategy. Service guarantees have cost implications in the form of retribution to customers, training to employees, introduction of new systems, and upgradation of existing systems. Firms offering service guarantees are found to charge more than their competitors not following this policy. It has been observed that customers are often willing to pay more to prevent poor service delivery.

Service Quality Signal

Service guarantees help the organization to send signals of their service quality to potential and existing customers, competitors, and partners (subcontractors, distributors, suppliers, etc.). If customers who have different options to choose from, base their purchase decisions on the quality of the service, they are influenced by the service guarantees, which in turn can motivate them in favour of the service provider.

Guarantee Design

The guarantee design is successful if a firm takes into consideration the following aspects:

- It bases the design on customer expectations on a regular basis and adopts a customer-oriented approach when designing its service.
- It defines a service standard, and reviews the efficiency and effectiveness of its service process on a regular basis to ensure that promises are honoured every time.

The service guarantee is not only a 'persuasive focus of communication' to attract new customers, but also helps the employees to understand better their respective roles in the 'service chain'.

Implementation and Communication

A service guarantee once designed should first be pre-tested within a group of customers from the target market. After the necessary amendments are made, the service guarantee needs to be communicated to the customers for its implementation. This communication should be done in a phased manner, spread over six months to two years, to allow the firm to perfect the applications of the guarantees. While launching service guarantees, a media offensive strategy helps maximize the effect.

Performance Analysis

It is important for a firm to know the effectiveness of a service guarantee for a given period and in a given commercial environment for it to continue to provide the same effectively and profitably. The costs involved in service guarantees should be evaluated. The costs include the money and resources spent on the following:

- market research required for the preliminary analysis
- pre-testing the guarantee
- measurement of performance indicators
- time spent on designing guarantees
- communication campaign
- compensation for dissatisfied customers
- cost of process triggered by request for compensation
- legal options required in case of failure to fulfil a guarantee
- costs involved if the service guarantee is withdrawn prematurely.

It is not easy to isolate the impact of a given marketing strategy. A number of factors, such as price wars, counter-attack by competitors, or changes in economic environment, all add to the complexities. Another way to ensure the effectiveness of a service guarantee is to study certain performance indicators before and (six months) after its launch even though the marketing communication is spread over a period of many months. Some of the relevant indicators that can be studied are as follows:

- customer retention rate
- net margins
- net profit
- number of new customers
- gross revenue generated before and during the service guarantee period
- number of applications for compensation
- value of compensation offered
- value of transaction entered into by a customer after compensation.

A study of these indicators provides information about the immediate or short-term benefits of guarantees. It is also important to consider the medium- and long-term benefits of the guarantees. A higher customer retention rate points towards customer loyalty which will prove beneficial in the medium and long-run, when the loyalists turn advocates for the service organization, providing them service satisfaction through guarantees. The senior management's determination and commitment to provide customer satisfaction creates a positive culture where all the employees learn about the importance of a happy customer. This results in lower employee turnover, and higher employee loyalty and commitment towards the organization. Subsequently, this gets reflected in their service quality, and ultimately in customer satisfaction.

An ideal service guarantee should be:

- transparent
- offered unconditionally
- credible and realistic
- focused on the key service features
- supported by significant compensation to the customers
- easy to understand and communicate
- easy to invoke
- easy to implement.

An unconditional guarantee offers to provide full customer satisfaction. However, it is found that unconditional guarantees are viewed as 'blank cheques' where the customers do not have to give reasons for their dissatisfaction. Thus, organizations can balance an unconditional guarantee with promises concerning the performance of certain elements of the service.

Disadvantages of Service Guarantees

Service guarantees pressurize employees to meet the guarantees, which can be difficult if systems are not in place. This causes disillusionment and frustration among them when they cannot meet the customer expectations, and results in confrontations (quarrels, foul language, etc.) with them. The result is not only a high rate of customer loss, but higher employee turnover too. So, for a service guarantee to be successful it is not only important to keep the customer expectations in mind but also to have an internal focus, and get the processes in order, and ensure that the workforce is also in tune with the guarantees.

SUMMARY

Service failures are not an exception in an organization that focuses on services delivery. Failures are bound to happen in service organizations. It is thus imperative that an organization be aware of the different service failures and how the customers respond to the same. A model has been highlighted wherein the importance of service recovery on the value of the service has been delineated. It is, therefore, important for an organization to salvage the situation by providing recovery strategies. If good recovery strategies are adopted and if the initial failure is not severe, it is possible to create a higher satisfaction in the customers. This can only happen if the customers bring the service failures to the notice of the organization. Recovery strategies not only provide satisfaction to customers encountering a service failure (recovery paradox) but also help in retaining the customers and when tied strategically with the business orientation can lead to creating a competitive advantage. Service guarantees are used as a tool to help the organization to coax the customers to bring the failure points to the notice of the organization. This then gives the organization a chance to recover the customer's trust. The various service guarantees that can be used by an organization and the guidelines to help an organization design its own service guarantees have been discussed.

KEY TERMS

Complaint handling The process of dealing with customer grievances.

Complaints An after-effect of service failure, when the customer nurtures negative perceptions about the same. A complaint gives the service provider a second chance to retrieve the situation.

Customer dissatisfaction This arises when the service rendered to the customer does not meet his/her expectation. This can lead to a customer complaint or a silent customer who does not complain about the service problem.

Feedback Customers are an important source of feedback; they can provide information or opinions about the performance of a product, system, intervention, or employee.

Service failure When the service rendered to the customer is below his/her expectation, it leads to service failure.

Service guarantee A promise made by a third party who is not party to a contract between two others, to accept liability if one of the parties fails to fulfil the contractual obligations.

Service recovery A strategy devised to reverse the decline in profitability of a firm or subsidiary, enabling it to achieve a viable and sustainable future.

Value enhancement The logical flow of service failure leading to service recovery and finally, enhancement of value of service.

CONCEPT REVIEW QUESTIONS

1. Critically discuss the importance of the concept of service recovery.

2. What is 'recovery paradox'? Do you agree with the concept? In what situations will the recovery paradox fail? Give examples to support your answer.

3. Discuss any two recovery strategies that you think are best suited for a fast food

restaurant. Give reasons to support your chosen strategies.

4. What are service guarantees? Discuss the circumstances under which an organization should adopt or stay away from offering service guarantees.

5. Critically discuss the importance of service guarantees in the process of service recovery.

CRITICAL THINKING QUESTIONS

1. Describe the last service failure you experienced. Discuss your response to the service failure. Give reasons for the same. In retrospect do you think it was the right action to take? Why?

2. Discuss an incident in which you faced a service failure and complained to the service provider. What was the response of the

service provider? What recovery strategy did he/she choose and what was the effect of the same on your overall perception of the service provider value.

3. Identify a service organization you patronize regularly. Design a service guarantee for the same.

INTERNET EXERCISES

1. Visit the website of any two hospitality chains that provide service guarantees. Compare the guarantees provided. As a customer what would your response be to both the organizations and why?

2. Visit the website of your insurance agent. Is there any provision for customer complaint? If yes, try and file a complaint and wait for the response. How would you have handled the same situation if given a chance?

CASE STUDY

Service Failure and Recovery Strategies in the Restaurant Sector: An Indo-US Comparative Study*

Introduction

It is of prime importance both to academicians and practitioners to zero in on the factors that constitute service quality so as to provide customer satisfaction with the aim of developing loyal customers. The importance of customers is further highlighted by the fact that it costs a lot more to attract a new customer than to retain an old one (Oliver 1999). However, it is estimated that businesses typically lose 50 per cent of their

customers every five years. The multi-dimensional nature of the service encounter creates an environment where failure may often be the norm, not the exception (Mack et al. 2000).

In an era of increased competition and perceptual differences between the customers and the service providers leading to service failures, service recovery becomes an important strategy to reduce the dissonance among customers.

---

* Dutta, Kirti , Umashankar Venkatesh, and H.G. Parsa (2007).

In light of the above discussion, a comparative study of service recovery in India and US was undertaken. The idea was to see that in a developed market like US where consumers have high disposable incomes, compared to a developing market like India where disposable income is growing, eating out, rather than being a luxury is becoming part and parcel of urban life. The data collection instrument used was a structured and non-disguised questionnaire. The customer responses collected were for the service failures experienced and the recovery strategy offered by the restaurants, and the after-effects of various recovery strategies were elicited in the form of customer response on repeat visits and recommendations to family and acquaintances.

Degree and Extent of Customer Complaint

The data indicates that there is a very high degree of service failure for a wide variety of reasons in both societies (India and the US) covered in this study. Overall, 98 per cent restaurant goers reported having experienced service failures of one kind or the other while being served in a restaurant. The difference between Indian and US customers is that whereas almost everyone experiencing a service failure in India orally communicated their complaint in one way or the other, only 75 per cent of the customers in US chose to register their complaint. This may be explained by the possibility that recovery may have been initiated by an alert team member in the US context before a complaint can be registered, whereas in India there may be a belief among the customers that unless communicated, no recovery action may be initiated; or, that the perceived or actual severity of the failure is proportionately of a higher order in India than in the US, which is actually borne out in a later finding in this section. In the US, 25 per cent of the dissatisfied customers do not register their complaint, which is serious, as they are possibly not going to be repeat clients and may also spread negative word-of-mouth. In the Indian context, the almost 100 per cent incidence of customers verbalizing/registering their complaints arising out of service failure, also indicates a more serious deficit in the 'trust' factor that customers could have in the 'system', with a belief that the system will, or is designed to deliver customer satisfaction and serve customer interest by default. This obviously is a cause for greater worry and needs long-term strategies on the part of companies in India to enhance the feeling of security and trust among their clients, through proper and timely communication along with delivery.

Categories of Service Failure

The study has found generic resemblance across the two markets as far as causes for dissatisfactions are concerned. It has elicited responses across five categories of service failure, namely, operations, hygiene, behaviour, quality of food and beverages, and physical evidence. In both the markets, operations-related service failures have been ranked first followed by quality of F&B, hygiene, and physical evidence, in that order. Within operations, slow service is cited as the top reason for customer complaints across both the markets. The specific causes for service failure across India and the US have been highlighted in Table 10.2.

Table 10.2   Categories of service failure

Specific complaint	India		US	
	%	Rank	%	Rank
I. Operations				
Slow service	66.3	1	60.8	1
Inefficient staff	17.9	4	21.6	3
Incorrect billing	20.0	3	18.6	4
Reservation missing	0.0	–	4.9	7
Advertisement promises not met	4.2	8	3.9	8
II. Food and beverage				
Food and beverage quality problem	36.8	2	29.4	2
III. Hygiene				
Poor cleanliness	15.8	5	9.8	6
Untidy/unkempt staff	5.3	7	0.0	–
IV. Behaviour				
Unfriendly and unhelpful staff	15.8	5	16.7	5
V. Physical evidence				
Lacking in ambience	7.4	6	0.0	–

Seemingly, slow service, below par F&B quality, improper billing, inefficient and unfriendly staff, and cleanliness, are the top five complaints across both the markets. More than 60 per cent respondents have complained about the slow service across both the markets studied. 37 per cent Indian respondents and about 29 per cent US respondents have complained about poor F&B (product) quality. Reduction in cycle-time is an obvious area of improvement, along with improving the quality of F&B as per the promise directly/indirectly conveyed.

Perceptions of staff inefficiency in general, and incorrect billing in particular, are both indicative of poor staff training on the one hand and/or lack of appropriate systems and processes on the other. Almost 20 per cent respondents have complained of incorrect billing across the two markets, which is slightly more difficult to explain in the US context as most restaurants there use automated systems. This obviously is, therefore, more due to employee failure in terms of incorrect customer orders/KOTs being generated in the first place, or incorrect punching-in of data on the system at a later stage.

Finally, almost equal complaints have been raised about inefficient, unfriendly, or unhelpful staff across both markets, indicating a lack of the right attitude and/or aptitude on the part of the staff. This obviously has implications on the various stages of human resource management—right from the job design, job description/specification phase to recruitment, selection, induction, training, and compensation of team members, scheduling of shifts, and team design and management.

Customer Perceptions about Intensity of Service Failure

Based on gradation of customer perception of seriousness of the complaint into high, medium, and low, across both markets the trends are similar. About 48 per cent of the respondents in India feel that the intensity of the problem they encountered in the restaurant is extremely serious, whereas for US customers this has been around 41 per cent. This disparity is most probably the reason why only 75 per cent of US customers

who experience service failures actually verbalize/register their complaints vis-à-vis almost 100 per cent in India. Managing customer perception and making them feel that as service providers we have their interests close to our heart, is our main intent, and this is a higher priority for Indian restaurant companies as compared to US companies. A higher percentage of respondents in the US have medium to low anxiety levels as compared to Indian customers. In India, major cities such as New Delhi, Kolkata, Mumbai, or Chennai, are among other things, characterized by a rapidly burgeoning population, ever-increasing cost of living, cramped spaces (literally as well as figuratively), stretched public utilities and services, over-crowded public spaces, and spiralling aspirations of an inquisitive and acquisitive middle-class. This has created a very high sense of insecurity leading to tension and stress in personal and relational existences of common people and a misguided sense of competition, which is cut throat in a 'dog-eat-dog' kind of atmosphere. People are becoming very aggressive in these urban societies and are seemingly on a very short fuse, and that too, almost perpetually. Service providers bear the brunt of this and restaurants in India are no exceptions. It is, therefore, common to see restaurant staff in India being completely defensive and overtly servile all the time, while they may be feeling diametrically opposite inside. This also leads to a state where fear of confronting an irate client makes them more delayed in their reactions, adding fuel to the fire. Motivational training and support, team structures, and team-leaders, who lead from the front may be some of the steps that may help to alleviate this problem.

Strategies Employed for Service Failure Recovery by Restaurants

There is a major departure in this area between Indian and US restaurants. In India, almost 60 per cent of the complaints are dealt with by extending an apology and offering assistance short of compensation, whereas in the US, extending an apology along with an offer of assistance and compensation is the chosen strategy for service recovery in almost 68 per cent of the cases. This reflects a clear abhorrence amongst the management of Indian restaurant companies to offer compensation to aggrieved clients. It is significant to relate this to the lower percentage of complainants in the US compared to almost 100 per cent in India. And secondly, later on in this discussion it is also going to be clear that almost double the percentage of aggrieved (and compensated) clients in the US are ready to return to the same outlet and more than double are willing to recommend the said outlet to their acquaintances as compared to Indian respondents. This clearly indicates the effectiveness of offering compensation as a service recovery strategy vis-à-vis offering apologies or assistance. This also points towards the aspect of poor empowerment environment in Indian restaurants, and a distinct lack of laid down (formal and documented) system of handling customer complaints based on which the staff are trained and are obligated to respond in a specific manner.

Customer Perceptions about Recovery Strategies

About 58 per cent of Indian customers reported that recovery step taken by the staff was prompt as compared to 55 per cent of US respondents. But this needs to be tempered with the fact that in Indian restaurants usually an apology or offer of assistance was the only outcome of a service failure, compared to almost double this percentage in the US, where compensation was offered. Obviously, the higher percentage of promptness in Indian restaurants is due to the fact that mostly it does not entail any financial/in-kind compensation, and an apology does not 'cost' anything. Again, if a higher degree of Indian customers felt that recovery was prompt, then why are such a majority of them either not willing to recommend the outlet to their friends or family, or themselves not wanting to return? The answer is simple; most probably the customers also understand these apologies as mere 'lip-service' and no more, and worse, so does the staff member responsible for this.

At 43 per cent, a larger chunk of the US respondents have reported delayed response. This obviously can be connected to the fact that

most of the time they offer a compensation of some kind to their aggrieved clients, and hence, this may require an approval/decision-making process, which may take a bit longer than offering apologies/assistance.

The conclusion is, therefore, that compensation works better than an apology or offer for assistance in case of a service failure as it denotes seriousness on the part of the service provider towards valuing (the franchise of) their clients and their eagerness to have them back as repeat customers. Secondly, the need is to have simpler and quicker processes for offering these compensations, and laying down and communicating formal procedures to handle such eventualities, based on a philosophy of 'compensate first and then discuss the reasons thereof'. And finally, the employees need to be trained in these recovery strategies, enabling them to face irate customers with confidence and empathy, rather than being defensive and antagonistic.

Outcome of Recovery Action

Significantly, in the case of Indian restaurants, in almost 51 per cent of the cases the result of recovery action has been characterized as one of helplessness (on part of the staffer), inappropriate communication, or worse, a feeling of 'could have been handled better', whereas in the US context this constitutes only about 26 per cent. Almost 47 per cent of US respondents said that they had to speak to the manager for a solution, whereas in India this was only about 23 per cent. This harks back to the point made earlier, that a defensive mindset leads to the manager not coming to the fore and letting the staff bear the brunt of the customers' ire in Indian restaurants. It also indicates that most probably the Indian manager was not empowered to take a compensation decision and hence felt no reason (or use) to go in and intervene in the altercation. Significantly, in both the markets an equal percentage of respondents—26 per cent—felt that the team displayed adequate flexibility.

Customer Reaction to the Whole Episode

A majority of 44 per cent of the Indian and 62 per cent of US respondents had a negative memory.

of the service failure (and ensuing aftermath) they encountered. This is a serious indicator of losing a large percentage of valuable clientele due to ineffective handling of customer complaints. Significantly, 24 per cent of Indian, and 21 per cent US clients remembered this positively.

A majority (60 per cent) of Indian clients decided definitely not to return to the said outlet again compared to 36 per cent in the US. Obviously, the compensation aspect of recovery is the key to this relatively lower attrition in the US. This is further accentuated by the fact that about 41 per cent of US clients are willing to return to the same outlet, whereas only 21 per cent of Indian clients are willing to do so. This leads to the conclusion that because of the relative openness and flexibility with which a US staffer approaches such an event as compared to the Indian team, US customers actually get to trust the outlet more and probably look at the service failure as a one-off mishap rather than a systemic (or worse deliberate) failure, and is hence forgiving enough

to come back. The Indian customer, however, looks at this as having been 'cheated' and takes it as a personal affront, and decides not to return. This obviously has dire consequences because in the latter case, a negative word-of-mouth is the only logical outcome. As an indicator of this, data reveals that 71 per cent Indian respondents decided definitely not to recommend the outlet to anyone else compared to 35 per cent US clients. More importantly, as a positive outcome of recovery action, almost 44 per cent of US clients give a positive recommendation compared to only 17 per cent Indian customers. This basically bears out the hypothesis that an effective recovery strategy at the right time has the ability to actually turn a negative situation around for the organization.

Looking at the discussion above, on an overall basis, the fishbone diagram, adapted from Lovelock (1993), has been described to summarize the cause and effect relationships between various service delivery attributes, and customer expectations and perceptions (Fig. 10.5).

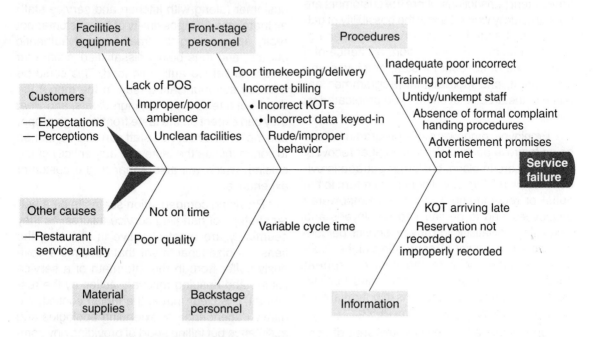

Source: Adapted from Lovelock (1993).

Fig. 10.5 Cause and effect fishbone diagram

Conclusion

Past research indicates that when organizations offer similar levels of product and service quality, the delivery of relationship benefits becomes an important means of gaining competitive advantage (Berry 1995; Gwinner et al. 1998; and Juttner et al. 1994). Relationship-related efforts and the creation of trust based on positive customer experience takes on greater significance in the 'servicescape'. The extent to which a service-provider makes relationship efforts is what proves to the customer that he/she is believable, cares for the relationship, and is willing to make sacrifices (Doney and Cannon 1997). Increased levels of communication between buyers and sellers enhances feelings of trust among customers (Bendapudi and Berry 1997 and Doney and Cannon 1997) and, therefore, needs to be planned for and practised, particularly in Indian restaurants, where there clearly is a trust deficit that exists between clients and the firm. The environment needs to be one of openness, and transparent transactions where the customers are not perpetually worried about the possibility of getting short-changed by the service provider. For this to happen, team orientation, existence of a formal code of conduct for staff, employee empowerment, and motivational programmes are some of the areas that seem to be predicated by the data.

Employee empowerment programmes are going to prove beneficial, as even after recovery strategies are in place, customer outrage is evident in their relative unwillingness to return to the outlet or recommend it to others. Empowered employees tend to be satisfied employees and increasing job satisfaction among service personnel has the potential of generating higher customer satisfaction with the service, repeat purchases by current customers, and positive word-of-mouth communications to potential customers (Venkatesh and Kulkarni 2002).

Operational efficiency is a key area of concern, and the way out is to create, communicate, and implement formal and documented procedures, and systems, which also lay down the policies and procedures for handling customer complaints. This should clearly state the recovery actions to be taken, assign responsibilities for the same, and define the way in which the 'action taken' report is to be documented.

Improving cycle time is of clear concern across markets and demands that restaurant companies re-look at their process design, and rationalize the order taking and delivery cycle so that customer wait time is minimized. Informing the customer of the approximate wait time at the time of confirming the order can also alleviate customer anxiety. Another variation on this could be to print the wait time in front of the entrée on the menu, provided one is sure of being able to deliver within that time.

Quality of F&B is seemingly a 'grey' area as it relates to customer tastes and perceptions on one hand, and how the restaurant has defined their cuisine/recipe as well as the resources available in terms of skills and raw material/ingredients, on the other. Authenticity needs to be defined for the customer (along with kitchen and service staff) as there may be a possibility of the customer not really appreciating the 'real' taste of authentic cuisine, and thus being 'dissatisfied' even after he/she is served authentic food. This could be done by communicating (say, in the menu) the details of a recipe and the ingredients, and what they can expect on the taste front through proper description. The service staff can also be trained to communicate the taste and authenticity of the cuisine, which will also enhance the customer experience.

Providing compensation seems to be a better strategy of handling service failures, as they seemingly are most effective in reducing the sense of disenchantment that customers obviously suffer from in the aftermath of a service failure, and ensuing recovery action by the restaurant. It is clear that in the Indian context, the heavy dependence of extending apologies and assistance but falling short of providing any compensation vis-à-vis the US markets where there is much a higher propensity to provide for immediate compensation, is working to the detriment of the industry.

Finally, there is a need to manage the dissonance that seemingly still remains once the recovery action has been implemented, especially in the context of Indian restaurants. This could be done by co-opting these clients in the new promotional schemes and giving them overtly preferential offers as 'valued customers'. It is imperative that effort is made to win these clients back to the outlet's fold as the negative word-of-mouth that may be generated can severely damage the reputation of the outlet.

Questions

1. Discuss the different reasons for service failure in India and the US. Give your observations about the customers in the two countries.

2. Discuss alternative recovery strategies that restaurants can follow for effective customer recovery.

SELECT REFERENCES

Bendapudi, N. and L.L. Berry (1997), 'Customers' motivations for maintaining relationships with service providers', *Journal of Retailing*, vol. 73, no. 1, pp. 15–37.

Berry, L.L. (1995), 'Relationship marketing of services: Growing interest, emerging perspectives', *Journal of the Academy of Marketing Science*, vol. 23, no. 4, pp. 236–245.

Berry, L.L., Valarie A. Zeithaml, and A. Parasuraman (1990), 'Five imperatives for improving service quality', *Sloan Management Review*, vol. 31, no. 4, pp. 29–38.

Bitner, M.J., B.H. Booms, and Tetreault M. Stanfield (1990), 'The service encounter: Diagnosing favourable and unfavourable incidents', *Journal of Marketing*, vol. 54, no. 1, pp. 71–84.

Bramford, David and Tatiana Xystouri (2005), 'A case study of service failure and recovery within an international airline', *Managing Service Quality*, vol. 15, no. 3, pp. 306–315.

Cash Jr, James I. (1995), 'British Air gets on course: Airline uses information technology to support service recovery strategy', *Information Week*, 1 May.

Chung, Beth and Douglas K. Hoffman (1998), 'Critical incidents', *Cornell Hotel and Restaurant Administration Quarterly*, vol. 39, no. 3, pp. 66–71.

Doney, P.M. and J.P. Cannon (1997), 'An examination of the nature of trust in buyer-seller relationships', *Journal of Marketing*, vol. 51, no. 2, pp. 11–27.

Dutta, Kirti, Umashankar Venkatesh, and H.G. Parsa (2007), 'Service failure and recovery strategies in the restaurant sector: An Indo-US comparative study', *International Journal of Contemporary Hospitality Management*, vol. 19, no. 5, pp. 351–363.

Fabien, Louis (2005), 'Design and implementation of a service guarantee', *The Journal of Services Marketing*, vol. 19, no. 1, pp. 33–38.

Goel, Sumit (2006), 'Thinking out of the drop box', *The Economic Times*, 13 October, p. 9.

Grönroos, C. (1988), 'Service quality: The six criteria of good perceived service quality', *Review of Business*, vol. 9, no. 3, pp. 10–13.

Gwinner, K.P., D.G. Dwayne, and M.J. Bitner (1998), 'Relational benefits in service industries: The customers' perspective', *Journal of the Academy of Marketing Science*, vol. 26, no. 2, pp. 101–114.

Hart, C.W.L., W.E. Sasser Jr, and J.L. Heskett (1990), 'The profitable art of service recovery', *Harvard Business Review*, July–August, pp. 148–156.

Hoffman, K.D., S.W. Kelly, and H.M. Rotasky (1995), 'Tracking service failures and employee recovery efforts', *Journal of Marketing*, vol. 9, no. 2, pp. 49–61.

Juttner, U. and H.P. Wehrli (1994), 'Relationship marketing from a value system perspective', *International Journal of Service Industry Management*, vol. 5, no. 5, pp. 54–73.

Kashyap, R. (2001), 'The effects of service guarantees on external and internal markets', *Journal of Academy of Marketing Science*, vol. 1, no. 10.

Keaveney, S.M. (1995), 'Customer switching behaviour in service industries: An exploratory study', *Journal of Marketing*, vol. 59, April, pp. 71–81.

La, Kahn V. and J. Kandampully (2004), 'Market oriented learning and customer value enhancement through service recovery management', *Managing Service Quality*, vol. 14, no. 5, pp. 390–401.

Lee, S.C., S. Barker, and J. Kandampully (2003), 'Technology, service quality and customer loyalty in hotels: Australian managerial perspective', *Managing Service Quality*, vol. 13, no. 5, pp. 423–432.

Lemmink, Jos and Jan Mattsson (2002), 'Employee behaviour, feelings of warmth, and customers' perceptions in service encounters', *International Journal of Retail and Distribution Management*, vol. 30, no. 1, pp. 18–33.

Lovelock (1993), *Product Plus*, McGraw-Hill, New York.

Mack, R., R. Mueller, J. Crotts, and A. Broderick (2000), 'Perceptions, corrections, and defections: Implications for service recovery in the restaurant industry', *Managing Service Quality*, vol. 10, no. 6, pp. 339–346.

Mack, Rhonda, Rene Mueller, John Crotts, and Amanda Broderick (2000), 'Perceptions, corrections, and defections: Implications for service recovery in the restaurant industry', *Managing Service Quality*, Bedford, vol. 10, no. 6, pp. 339–346.

Maxham, J.G. (2001), 'Service recovery's influence on consumer satisfaction, positive word-of-mouth, and purchase intentions', *Journal of Business Research*, vol. 54, pp. 11–24.

McDougall, Gordon H.G. and T.J. Levesque (1999), 'Waiting for service: The effectiveness of recovery strategies', *International Journal of Contemporary Hospitality Management*, vol. 11, no. 1, pp. 6–16.

Oliver, R. (1999), 'Whence consumer loyalty', *Journal of Marketing*, vol. 68, pp. 33–44.

Palmer, A., R. Beggs, and C. Keown-McMullan (2000), 'Equity and repurchase intention following service failure', *Journal of Services Marketing*, vol. 14, no. 6, pp. 512–528.

Ramakrishna, N. (2004), 'Touchtel to guarantee service levels to users', *Businessline*, 20 March, p. 1.

Smith, A.K., R.N. Bolton, and J. Wagner (1999), 'A model of customer satisfaction with service encounters involving failure and recovery', *Journal of Marketing Research*, vol. 36, no. 3, pp. 356–372.

Trade Finance, London, September 2006, p. 1.

Venkatesh, U. and A. Kulkarni (2002), 'Employee motivation and empowerment in hospitality, rhetoric or reality: Some observations from India', *Journal of Services Research*, vol. 2, no. 1, pp. 31–53.

Weun, Seungoog, Sharon E. Beatty, and Michael Jones (2004), 'The impact of service failure severity on service recovery evaluations and post-recovery relationships', *The Journal of Services Marketing*, vol. 18, no. 2/3, pp. 133–146.

Wirtz, J. (1996), 'Development of a model on the impacts of service guarantees', Paper presented at the fourth International Research Seminar on Services Management.

Zeithaml, V.A., L.L. Berry, and A. Parasuraman (1993), 'The nature and determinants of customer expectations of service', *Journal of the Academy of Marketing Science*, vol. 21, no. 1, pp. 1–12.

Zeithaml, V.A. and M.J. Bitner (2000), *Services Marketing*, 2nd edn, Tata McGraw-Hill Publishing Company Limited, New Delhi.

Zhu, Zhen, K. Sivakumar, and A. Parasuraman (2004), 'A mathematical model of service failure and recovery strategies', *Decision Sciences*, vol. 35, no. 3, pp. 493–525.

Banerjee, G. (2007), 'GE Money introduces loan-back guarantee', http://www.livemint.com/2007/11/07221434/GE-Money-introduces-loanback.html, accessed on 7 November 2007.

http://airtelbroadband.in/experience6.htm, accessed on 19 October 2006.

11 Managing Distribution Channels in Service Industry

OBJECTIVES

After reading this chapter you will be able to understand the:
- importance of distribution in services
- relevance of different channels in the distribution of services
- concept of distribution channels
- dimensions of a global distribution system

INTRODUCTION

In marketing, the distribution of services holds an important place. Services are inseparable, i.e., there is simultaneous production and consumption of services. Due to increased competition in the marketplace, there are a number of options available to customers. Thus, the distribution or place element of the services marketing mix is strategically important as the service providers need to be present at convenient locations when customers require them.

DISTRIBUTION

Distribution includes the flow of services from service provider to customer and can be performed by service providers themselves or by a service intermediary, such as a travel agent booking tickets on major airlines for customers. In services, the customer has to be brought to the service provider rather than the service product being delivered to the customers. Thus, location is of prime importance; by occupying strategic locations the service provider can draw the customers. The different characteristics of services make the distribution of services more direct than distribution for physical goods. The network through which distribution takes place is known as the distribution channel and consists of independent organizations involved in the process of making a service available for consumption by customers. In Chapter 1, we studied the classification of services in relation to place and time. Accordingly, services can be of the following types (Lovelock 1983):

- Customer goes to the service organization: This includes services such as hospitals, hospitality industry, and transportation services (such as bus, rail, and air).

- Service organization comes to the customer: This includes personal services such as cleaning and laundry and repair services such as plumbing and electrical repairs.
- Customer and the service organization transact at arms length (mail or electronic communications): This includes broadcast services, communications services such as telephones and mobiles, etc.

FACTORS AFFECTING CHOICE OF DISTRIBUTION CHANNELS

Distribution holds an important position in the purchase of all the three types of services. The distribution factors affecting their choice can be divided into:

- factors affecting the choice of service provider by customers
- factors affecting the choice of distribution channels by service providers.

Factors Affecting the Choice of Service Provider by Customers

The various factors are discussed in this section.

Outlet type   The type of service provided and its requirement by customers at the time of purchase, decides the selection of the service provider. For example, in medical services, if a person has a heart problem he/she will choose a hospital providing a cardiac specialist but if he/she is suffering from a common cold the choice of service provider will be different. The same is the case with the hospitality industry where a person wanting a Chinese meal will visit a service provider selling this instead of say an Italian cuisine provider. The distribution of these services requires their presence at convenient locations, which are easily accessible by the customers. The timing of the availability of the services is also equally important.

Outlet numbers   The number of outlets operated by the service provider also has an implication on the distribution because the more the number of outlets the better distributed the service provider is, and so the chances of customers availing the services are also more. For example, McDonald's, one of the leading global food service retailers, has more than 30,000 local restaurants serving nearly 50 million people in more than 119 countries each day (McDonald's Corporation 2006). In India, McDonald's is opening its outlets at railway stations and petrol pumps (Exhibit 11.1). Kentucky Fried Chicken has more than 11,000 restaurants in more than 80 countries and territories around the world (Kentucky Fried Chicken 2006). Jet Airways has an offering in the low-cost segment known as Jet Lite, which connects big cities with smaller towns. Mobile users in Delhi are facing a crunch of mobile towers or base transceiver station (BTS), as a result of which mobile signals get weak. According to a TRAI report, posh areas of Lutyens bungalow zone in New Delhi had only 18 cell sites in 2005, as compared to actual requirements of 153 cell sites. These weak networks not only cause inconvenience to customers but also adversely affect the handsets by severely reducing the life of the battery, affecting the chip on the service circuit board, LCD screen, etc. (Singh 2006). Thus, we see the importance of the number of outlets in services delivery.

Accessibility   There are a number of service providers in the market and so there are unlimited choices for the customers. Thus, to be the first choice of the customer the

McDonald's the major American fast food joint is all set to open outlets at railway stations and airports. It has already opened outlets at petrol pumps. Agreements have been signed with the Airports Authority of India (AAI) to open outlets at the domestic airports in New Delhi. Several other formats of expansion have been planned that will include a limited menu and will be known as McDonald's Express. According to sources at McDonald's, there are various expansion plans in the pipeline that include investing Rs 400 crore within the next three years. The outlets at railway stations will include just 70 per cent of the menu with a space of about 500–1,000 square feet, while a usual McDonald's restaurant with the complete menu has about 2000 square feet of space.

A kiosk format that will sell only desserts is also being planned. In smaller towns, where a lot of people go out to eat, the American major plans to open larger stores with 100 seats. The attractive price menu attached to the McDonald's tag is also one of the major reasons for attracting consumers. Other experiments include introducing healthier options such as baked paneer (cheese) and chicken wrap.

Source: Monga and Verma (2006).

service provider has to be easily available to the customers. For example, a number of banks are forming ATM sharing arrangements wherein the customer has the option of using ATMs of other banks for money transactions. Currently, there are 16 banks who are members of the National Financial Switch (NFS)—Allahabad Bank, Andhra Bank, Bank of Baroda, Corporation Bank, ICICI Bank, IDBI Bank, J&K Bank, Karnataka Bank, Punjab National Bank, United Western Bank, Dhanalakshmi Bank, Tamilnadu Mercantile Bank, South Indian Bank, Oriental Bank of Commerce, Karur Vysya Bank, and Yes Bank. The NFS allows the customers of these banks to use ATMs of other member banks for money transactions (*Times* 2006).

Location   The location of the service provider determines the type of services they are going to provide. For example, in the hospitality sector, a service offer targeting adventurous customers will be located in the mountainous region. This allows the service provider to offer options of trekking, paragliding, etc., and customers visiting hill stations can avail of these opportunities.

Factors Affecting the Choice of Distribution Channels by Service Providers

The various factors are explained in this section.

Resource considerations   When the distribution of the services is made directly to the customer, the number of outlets is important in order to capture a wider customer base. If the service provider has sufficient resources (financial, human resource, etc.) to monitor and supply quality services at multiple sites they can directly open their branches at different locations. However, another option is adopting the franchisee route. In franchising, the service provider (franchiser) charges fees from the franchisee, and in return, allows the franchisee to sell the services under a fixed format (decided by the franchiser) and use the brand name. McDonald's has a strength of over 2,400 franchisees and along with the use of the trademarks, it provides support in areas of operations, human resource and training, marketing, etc. (McDonald's Corporation 2006). Choice Hotels International markets more than 5,000 hotels across 40 countries. In India, the company is represented by four brands—Quality Inn, Comfort Inn, Clarion Hotels, and Sleep Inn. They franchise the Quality Inn and Comfort Inn brand hotels throughout India with hotels in Ahmedabad, Aurangabad, Corbett, Chennai, Delhi, Hyderabad, Lucknow, Mumbai, Mussoorie, Panchgani, Pune, Shimla and Thiruvananthapuram (*Times* 2006).

The major benefit to the franchiser is that it increases distribution of their services, expands the brand, and gets revenues from sales; but the disadvantages are that they have to manage the channels in the form of monitoring the franchisees to ensure consistency in delivery as per their standards, managing channel conflicts, etc. The benefit to the franchisee is that they get consultation and support from the franchisers in the form of operations, marketing support, etc., which helps them to set up the business faster. However, the disadvantages are that they have to pay fees and royalty to the franchiser, face restrictions in terms of products offered and services delivered, and the poor service delivery of a sister franchisee can adversely affect the reputation of the entire chain (Kotler et al. 2006).

Choice of intermediaries   There are different choices available to the service provider. These are shown in Fig. 11.1.

The service provider can directly supply the services to the customers without going through a channel intermediary. All the nationalized banks open their offices to directly cater to the needs of the customers.

The second option available is going through a channel intermediary—a wholesaler, who in turn sells to customers. An example is the different tour wholesalers offering assembled packages. The third option is again through an intermediary—a retailer. Most of the retail chains supply the products from the manufacturer to the customers. For example, Reliance retail chains and Subhiksha retail chains in India. Reliance is setting up rural business hubs in Punjab, Haryana, Himachal Pradesh, Uttaranchal, and West Bengal. These hubs will act as procurement centres for grains and milk, which will give Reliance a cost advantage. Thus, Reliance plans not only to sell these through its retail chains, but also to supply to other retail players such as Big Bazaar (Monga and Philip 2006). In such a situation, Reliance is acting as a wholesaler and Big Bazaar is a

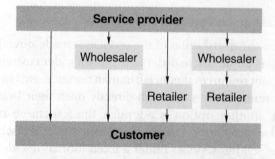

Fig. 11.1   Distribution channels in services

retailer selling the products directly to the customers—the fourth option in Fig. 11.1. Service providers can also use a combination of different channels. For example, Hutch and Airtel are selling through retailers and also providing services directly to customers through company-owned outlets such as Hindustan Petroleum fuel stations, and travel agents of which 200 agents are grocery sellers, small vendors, etc.

National and state tourist agencies are an excellent way to promote services related to tourism in a particular nation or state. For example, the Ministry of Tourism in India releases the 'Incredible India' advertisements promoting tourism to different states in India and the advertisements promoting tourism to Kerala sponsored by Department of Tourism, Government of Kerala (Kerala Tourism 2006).

Market need An organization decides on the number of distribution outlets keeping in mind the need of the market. A case in point is discount grocery store Subhiksha, which is targeting to open 1,000 stores by end 2007. Categories, such as fruit, vegetables, and food and beverages, have to be easily available for consumers in cities such as Delhi and Mumbai, and to cater to this need Subhiksha has adopted a cluster strategy—it has 100 stores in and around Delhi. This cluster strategy allows them to be present in areas with high density of consumers, ensuring cannibalization of sales within the network of stores rather than other chains (Banerjee 2006).

STRATEGIES FOR DISTRIBUTION

Distribution of services can be achieved in a number of ways as discussed in the earlier section. Keeping in mind the nature of the product, kind of image an organization wants to portray, and the coverage area, the organization can go for intensive, selective, and exclusive distribution.

Intensive distribution This strategy enables the service provider to make available its services through as many service providers or outlets as possible. For example, if we look at the banking industry, the unique selling proposition of public sector banks is the number of branches present throughout the country. The postal system still has a number of branches in remote areas too. The services of Indian Oil, Bharat Petroleum, etc., can be availed through a number of petrol pumps located throughout the length and breadth of the country. Indian Railways, apart from its online presence, has a number of booking counters from where railway tickets can be booked. It has also tied up with the postal department and Indian Oil Corporation, so that a customer can also book railway tickets through these outlets.

Selective distribution In this type of distribution, the service provider chooses some intermediaries to make available its services to the consumers. In this case, the organization does not have to worry about managing a number of service outlets and can have a greater control over the distribution system. For example, an airline can choose travel agents to sell its services from a number of travel agents present in a city.

Exclusive distribution In exclusive distribution the number of intermediaries is limited and as the name suggests it involves sole dealing arrangements between the service producer and the intermediary/retailer. This is generally done to create an image of exclusivity and class. For example, Lladro, the Spanish luxury porcelain brand, has entered into exclusive shop-in-shop arrangements with Ethos Swiss Watch Studio in Chandigarh. It plans to open exclusive outlets in Indian metros. According to Anisha Gaur, Manager (Retail Operations), Lladro, 'The exclusive stores are flagship stores, which create a complete brand experience, including the perfect merchandise, music, and customer service. Our three-year plan for India will focus mainly on metros and mini metros and we will have our exclusive stores only in metros' (*Retailer* 2008).

Another strategy for distribution of services is *franchising*. The word is derived from the French meaning 'to be free from servitude'. The rapid development of franchising is attributed to the growth of service-sector activities. Franchising involves selling a business service to an independent investor who has working capital, but little or no prior experience. Services generally require business format 'package' franchising in which the franchiser transfers most elements necessary for the local entity to establish a business and run it profitably. This may include 'managerial assistance in setting up and running local operations', advertising and marketing support, research and development, etc. Companies such as McDonald's, Pizza Hut, and Starbucks, follow this model (Hollensen 1998). Depending upon the intensive, selective, and exclusive distribution an organization is going for, it can choose the number of franchisees in a particular geographic area.

MANAGING DISTRIBUTION CHANNELS

Management of the channels lies with the service organization. Jobber (2001) gave the following issues to be addressed while managing channels:

Selection This consists of the choice of channel members. The different candidates must be identified and selection criteria should be drawn so that all the channel members are at par. When distributing its products in Russia, Panasonic failed to take this into consideration and faced a major problem as is evident from Exhibit 11.2.

Motivation Service organizations can motivate channel members to act as franchisees. For example, Mother's Pride advertisements motivate people to be a master franchisee and individual franchisees by focusing on love, respect, and trust.

Exhibit 11.2 Russian retailers threaten boycott of Panasonic

Major Russian electronic retailers have threatened to boycott products from Japan's Panasonic recently. They have accused the Japanese company of selling goods to intermediaries who often paid no import duties, or lacked certification. A German retailer was found selling Panasonic flat televisions at hefty discounts to its competitors. The Russian office of Panasonic denies all charges, but the situation does not seem easy to handle. According to them, the 'grey' imports charges are baseless. The retailers aim to solve the issue as a joint effort and also seem to be ready to sacrifice immediate profits to set rules that are in line with Russian practices.

Source: Reuters (2006).

They further motivate people to act as master and individual franchisees by highlighting the fact that by creating a unique educational landmark they would be known and respected in their town, i.e., they would get name, fame, fortune, and goodwill.

Training Most of the organizations train their franchisee to maintain the standards expected of them. McDonald's and KFC both focus on the training they provide to their franchisees. In KFC, which is a part of Yum! Brands, each brand has a franchise business coach (FBC) and/or franchise business leader (FBL) to provide business insight and instruction to the franchisees. As the franchisees move into steady-state operations, the FBC or FBL keeps them abreast of important business initiatives, organizes key regional training activity, and acts as the primary point of contact (KFC 2006). By providing training, organizations instil product knowledge in franchisees giving them the confidence to market their services (Jobber 2001).

Evaluation Evaluation of the distribution channel members at regular intervals is necessary to provide an insight into the functioning of the channel intermediary. The idea is to check for standard deviations in supply of service, identify the reasons for the same, and try to remove these so that the level of service is maintained. However, if after repeated efforts the channel intermediary shows no signs of improving it is best to drop that channel member. Different criteria for evaluation can be sales performance, profitability, quality of service provided, etc.

Managing conflict The distribution process consists of a number of independent organizations working together for a common goal. Ideally, they should all work together keeping the best interest of all concerned in mind. However, individual members rarely take this view. They all try to maximize their own gain and then channel conflicts are bound to occur. Broadly, two types of channel conflicts are observed—horizontal conflict and vertical conflict.

Horizontal conflict This is the difference in opinion between channel members at the same level. For example, a McDonald's franchisee in Delhi might compromise on the personnel employed for delivery of service to increase his/her profits, but this would in turn affect the quality of service and may dissatisfy the customers. This dissatisfaction would be against McDonald's and so would affect the perception of the customers towards all the McDonald's outlets. This would result in conflict among the franchisees and cause horizontal conflict.

Vertical conflict This is the result of disagreement between different levels of the same channel. For example, Reliance (wholesaler) might have a disagreement with Big Bazaar (a retailer) regarding delivery of products. This would result in a vertical conflict (Kotler et al. 2006).

As a service provider the onus for the amicable resolution of the conflict lies with them. They should think in terms of trying to create win-win situations for all. They can also try and avoid conflicts by organizing regular meetings with channel partners so as to create environment of mutual trust and understanding. To avoid horizontal conflict, market partitioning can be done or areas may be allotted to different members for providing services. Jobber (2001) also lists coercion or use of force to garner compliance from channel members and the effective but expensive way of buying out the channel member (channel ownership).

EFFECT OF THE INTERNET—GLOBAL DISTRIBUTION SYSTEM

According to Kotler et al. (2006), the Internet is an effective marketing tool for hospitality and travel companies. The Internet is an effective distribution system allowing for the purchase of services from any corner without visiting the store or service provider. The online payment system further facilitates the purchase of services. (For more details on Internet marketing, see Chapter 14 on Services Promotion). The distribution of services such as travel, airline reservation, hotel/rail/cruise/reservation, car rentals, etc., via the Internet deserves a mention of the global distribution system (GDS). In the 1960s, GDS was first developed by the airline industry to keep track of flight schedules, availability, and prices. The conceptualization of the Sabre system began in 1953 with a chance meeting between American Airlines President C.R. Smith and R. Blair Smith, a senior sales representative for IBM, on an American Airlines flight from Los Angeles to New York. Their conversation about the travel industry sparked the idea of a data processing system that would create a complete airline seat reservation and make all the data instantly available electronically to any agent, at any place. This idea became a reality six years later when American Airlines and IBM jointly announced a plan to develop a semi-automatic business research environment, better known as Sabre. 'The revolutionary system was the first real time business application of computer technology. It enabled American Airlines to leapfrog from handwritten passenger reservation information in the 1950s, to an automated system. In 1960, the first Sabre reservations system was installed in Briarcliff Manor, New York. The mainframe system was state-of-the-art technology and processed 84,000 telephone calls per day. When the network was completed in 1964, it became the largest, private, real-time data processing system, second only to the US government's system. It became an integral part of AMR Corporation, saving American Airlines 30 per cent on its investments in staff alone (Sabre Travel Network 2006).

However, the travel agents were spending excessive time in manually entering reservation. To facilitate them, Sabre (owned by American Airlines) and Apollo (United) installed their proprietary internal reservation systems in travel agencies in the mid-1970s; they were among the first e-commerce companies facilitating B2B e-commerce. The automation of the reservation process for travel agents increased their productivity and made them an extension of the airline's sales force. There are currently four major GDS systems—Amadeus, Galileo, Sabre, and Worldspan. In addition, there are several smaller or regional GDSs, including SITA's Sahara, Infini (Japan), Axess (Japan), Tapas (Korea), Fantasia (South Pacific), and Abacus (Asia/Pacific) that serve the interests of specific regions or countries (Das 2002). Out of these, Abacus, Infini, and Axess are joint ventures with Sabre (Sabre Travel Network 2006). Exhibit 11.3 illustrates how Indian (formerly Indian Airlines) is using the GDS platform to compete against the low-cost carriers in India.

Exhibit 11.3   Indian goes agro on ticket sales

Now it is time for Indian to sign up for more global distribution system (GDS) platforms to take on increasing competition from low-cost carriers. According to analysts, this will help Indian to increase its distribution reach by adding another 15,000–18,000 booking terminals. This will also help Indian to bring more high yielding passengers from business class. Other domestic airlines such as Jet Airways and Kingfisher are already on various GDS platforms. In fact, airlines have been using the Internet extensively to sell tickets, giving them cost advantages.

Although the incremental cost of distribution and acquisition of new customers will be high for Indian, the new GDS platforms will help travel agents book Indian flights on the same system as other airlines, making it easier to compare and offer the best prices to the customers.

Source: Dey (2006).

SUMMARY

Distribution stands for place in the seven Ps and is one of the vital aspects of marketing. Services involve simultaneous production and consumption and they cannot be inventoried. Successful marketing of services is not possible unless it is made easily available to the customers for purchase. This chapter defines distribution and delineates factors affecting the choice of service outlet by the customer and also the factors affecting the choice of distribution channel by the service provider. Keeping in mind the factors affecting the choice of the customer the service provider can choose their own distribution channel vis-à-vis their organizational strategy. Here the different channels available for distribution have been highlighted. The strategies for distribution—intensive, selective, and exclusive have been discussed. The section on managing distribution channel further talks about how the different distribution channels can be managed to distribute the services effectively and efficiently. Conflict management along with the various types of conflicts have also been distinguished. The Internet revolution has impacted the delivery of services. The last section in the chapter therefore talks about the same and discusses the global distribution system and the impact of e-commerce on the delivery of services.

Services require the customer to be present in the servicescape. Thus, if the service outlet is not located at a convenient place then the whole process of designing and producing the services product is futile due to the absence of customers. Products on the other hand can be distributed from the factory (production unit) to the store where the customers can purchase them (retail outlet).

KEY TERMS

Distribution   The allocation of goods to consumers by means of wholesalers and retailers.

Distribution channel   The network of firms necessary to distribute goods or services from the manufacturers to the consumers.

Franchisee   A license given to a manufacturer, distributor, trader, etc., to enable them to manufacture or sell a named product or service in a particular area for a stated period.

Retailer   A distributor selling goods or services to consumers.

Wholesaler   A distributor selling goods in large quantities, usually to other distributors.

CONCEPT REVIEW QUESTIONS

1. Critically discuss the importance of distribution in the marketing of services.

2. Discuss the different types of distribution channels and their relative importance to a service marketer in the insurance sector.

3. What is channel conflict? Discuss giving different types of channel conflicts.

4. In the light of channel conflicts, which type of distribution channel is most effective in the marketing of services, and why?

5. Discuss the relevance of GDS in the distribution of travel industry services.

CRITICAL THINKING QUESTIONS

1. Consider the recent purchase of mobile services by you or your family. Identify the different alternatives available for purchase of this service from a service provider. Which channel did you choose and why?

2. Identify two dissimilar services such as hospitality and mobile network services. Discuss the distribution channels for these and how they are similar or dissimilar.

3. Consider an instance when you faced unsatisfactory service delivery in a franchisee restaurant. How did this affect your perception about the restaurant chain? Discuss strategies you can suggest to the franchiser for managing such a situation.

INTERNET EXERCISES

- Visit the website of any two no-frills, low-cost airline service providers. What are the different options available for booking their services? Compare the sites and evaluate which site delivers the service in a better manner and why?

- You have to open an account in a bank (online). Of the different options available on the net identify any two to three service providers. Which service provider would you choose and why? (Focus the evaluation on the basis of delivery of services by the service provider).

CASE STUDY

Challenges for Distribution Strategy for Fast Food Segment in India*

Fast Food Sector in India

The Indian food sector is teeming with activity. It has seen many Indian and foreign brand names emerging—a post-liberalization effect. The advent of foreign chains, such as McDonald's, Domino's, Pizza Hut, and TGIF, has given the local entrepreneurs a run for their money. Indian chains, such as Nirula's, have woken up to the challenge and

are aggressively on an expansion drive. They have also altered their business strategies. Then there are chains, such as Haldiram's in Delhi, which also offer huge competition to the well-known fast food outlets. The market has still not matured and is in a stage of infancy. There is really no Indian food chain, which has a national presence; although there are well-known chains, which

* Adapted from Jauhari, Vinnie (2004), 'Challenges for distribution strategy for the fast food segment in India', *Journal of Services Research*, vol. 3, no. 2, October 2003–March 2004. Printed with permission.

have a regional presence. However, there is a drive by some established brands to have a national presence.

Nirula's

Established in 1934, Nirula's is a diversified group having a chain of elegant business hotels, waiter service restaurants, family style restaurants, ice cream parlours, pastry shops, and food processing plants in India. The chain caters to over 50,000 guests every day. Very recently, Nirula's also launched a complete range of sauces, jams, and syrups. All of these are the blanket brands of Nirula's.

Nirula's was India's first fast food chain. As a case study by Dana (1999) indicates:

'This company was started by Mr L.C. Nirula and his brother Mr M. Nirula, both originally from Lahore, when the city was still in India, prior to the creation of Pakistan. The brothers moved to New Delhi and in 1934 they created Nirula's, a restaurant with a 12-room hotel. In the 1950s, Nirula's introduced fast food burgers and chips (fries). Lalit and Deepak Nirula, the sons of the founding brothers, left India to study in New York. They attended the Cornell University School of Hotel Administration and upon their return, they elaborated the restaurant's menu, adding Indian food and 21 flavours of ice cream. They trademarked a logo with pink and white—almost identical to that of Baskin Robbins.' Nirula's was sold to the Malaysian firm Navis Capital Partners in 2006 and promoter Samir Kuckreja also has some minority stake in the venture. Navis Capital Partners is a eight-year-old private equity fund based in Malaysia. Navis currently manages 500 million dollar in capital commitments and has interests in various sectors including hospitality, food processing, car rental, outdoor media, and others in eight countries across Asia.

Nirula's Expansion Drive

In light of competition, Nirula's is reorganizing its organization structure. From only four general managers in 2001 for engineering, finance, human resources, and purchase, the company intends to have 12 general managers by the end of the year 2002 for all core functions such as sales,

marketing, new projects, operations, and even training. From a mid-sized company a few years ago, it now needs each area to be manned by a professional to help surge forward and combat the competition.

Nirula's has also launched its '21' range of ice cream cafes to attract the younger generation. The advantage for the Indian chains is that they know the tastes of the Indian market while foreign chains such as Pizza Hut are still trying to understand the consumer dynamics. However, Pizza Hut has Indianized its pizzas and has opened the world's first 100 per cent vegetarian outlet in India. Domino's has also customized its offering to suit Indian taste buds, launching among others, a 'paneer pizza' to cater to Indian taste.

In order to expand, Nirula's has also tied up with Delhi Tourism & Transport Development Corporation (DTTDC) and has opened up two ice cream parlours at the three coffee houses in Delhi, managed by DTTDC. These outlets have been opened in central areas of Delhi. Especially meant for ice cream lovers, these parlours remain open from 11 a.m. to 11 p.m. on all weekdays. Other than ice creams, one can also indulge in other delicious food delights such as pastries, Pronto Pizzas (a 6-inch pizza with five varieties to choose from), sundaes, and milk shakes. This is the first time that Nirula's has tied up with any government body for running a food parlour and caters to residential areas, business houses, and offices.

Nirula's also operates Byte cyber bars. This is a modern friendly cyber bar with multiple Internet terminal posts and a well-stocked bar serving premium liquors, wines, beers, and cocktails. It is open on all days from 11 a.m. to midnight. There is only one such bar that is operational in the heart of Delhi.

The multinationals have changed the dynamics of the industry by investing in product development, sourcing practices, quality standards, service levels, and standardizing operating procedures, which they have developed from years of experience.

Each chain has a unique positioning strategy. McDonald's is primarily seen as a children and family fun place. Nirula's is seen as more of a place for the college-going crowd. Of late, it has put in a play corner to attract kids. It has invested in chic furniture and ambience with bright vibrant colours, which exude youthfulness. The menu is a mix of continental, Indian, South Indian, and Chinese options along with ice creams, desserts, and bakery products.

Production Facilities at Nirula's

The chain has over 60 outlets in more than five states and is estimated to cater to over 50,000 customers every day. The production facility of Nirula's is among the oldest present in the restaurant business in India. There are two production units in India—one in Noida near Delhi, and another in the industrial area of Delhi.

The logistics are staggering—6,50,000 kg of flour, 20,00,000 litres of milk, 1,20,00,000 eggs, 180 tonnes of meat, 100 tonnes of chicken, 200 tonnes of cream, 230 tonnes of sugar, 27 tonnes of milk powder, 55 tonnes of butter, and 2,00,000 litres of oil are used in a year at Nirula's. Despite such huge quantities, the quality has never been compromised. Working round the clock are 20 food and dairy technologists and other personnel managers, who ensure that only the best reaches the consumers. The Noida production facility includes the food processing unit, cheese processing unit, and a bakery.

Food Processing Unit

This division produces 60–70 products ranging from a variety of ketchups to jams, fruit toppings, and syrups. These are sealed in airtight pouches and dispatched to Nirula's' outlets for consumption.

Cheese processing unit Nirula's is one of the largest manufacturers of cheese in India, processing at least 10 varieties of cheese such as processed cheese, mozzarella, cream cheese, cottage cheese, Monterey Jack, feta, cheese spreads, etc. The company's cheese factory has a capacity to process 10,000 litres of milk per shift. In winter, the unit produces 17–18 tonnes of cheese and in summer the production is about 8–10 tonnes, per month. Special stretching and moulding machines have been imported from Italy for production.

Bakery Spread across 10,000 square feet, the bakery unit at Nirula's produces 35–40 items every day. The unit produces three varieties of pizza bases, 15 types of breads, waffle cones, and bread cones. The bakery division uses high-speed mixing machines, which prepare the dough in just three minutes. Nirula's also makes 50 types of pastries with 16–17 different flavours, from 1,000 types of cakes to 15 types of cookies, chocolates, mint sticks, and stick jaws. The Okhla facility contains the central commissary, butchery, ice cream manufacturing unit, confectionery, and central control unit.

Central kitchen The central kitchen produces a whole range of semi-processed and finished products ranging from curries, soups, and vegetable burgers, to patties and South Indian dishes.

Ice cream manufacturing unit Nirula's is one of the pioneers in the ice cream industry in India, manufacturing five thousand litres of ice cream on a daily basis. The ice cream is stored in cold storage rooms with temperatures as low as −28 degrees Celsius, before being dispatched to various outlets. At any given point of time, 21 flavours are available to customers.

The butchery Non-vegetarian specialities, such as tandoori chicken, seekh kebabs, frankfurters, hamburgers, patties, chops, etc., are processed at the butchery in the manufacturing unit in Delhi. Quality control measures are strictly adhered to at every point—from processing to storing at sub-zero temperatures, and later transportation in special refrigerated vans.

Confectionery Nirula's has a well-organized confectionery at its manufacturing plant, endowed with experienced chefs who can whip up a variety of cakes, pastries, cookies, savouries, caramels, and chocolates.

Quality Assurance Department

The quality assurance department (QAD) has 18 qualified and experienced food technologists, chemists, and microbiologists for monitoring the quality systems at Nirula's. The QAD reports to the managing director for his personal review. The department has a well-established laboratory with modern testing facilities at each production centre.

Various tests of raw materials, under process material, and finished products, on the lines of ISO 9000 and HACCP, are carried out to ensure that all the products fulfil the desired standards.

Raw Material Specifications

Nirula's QAD has formulated stringent quality standards for all raw materials conforming to the regulatory requirements. The products are checked at every stage for analysis of:

- raw material
- under-process material
- finished product.

Nirula's has charted out an aggressive plan to go national. Starting from the northern part of the country, the company has already identified different locations in Punjab, and will soon open restaurants in Jalandhar, Ludhiana, and Chandigarh. Besides Punjab, Nirula's is also looking at Haryana, Uttaranchal, Shimla, and Jaipur as potential markets, and is currently in the process of finalizing a few locations for setting up new restaurants there. The company will spend approximately Rs 10 crore in the venture. As far as investment is concerned, it will not be too high for the company as its focus is primarily only on taking over the management of the outlets (Kaul 2002).

Nirula's is planning a nation-wide expansion with an investment of Rs 100 crore starting 2007. Their target is to become India's largest player by 2012 and open about 150 outlets in the next three years. Nirula's plans to have a presence in Mumbai by early 2008. Post 2008 the chains will open about 35 outlets in North and Central India and thereby move to States such as Rajasthan and Madhya Pradesh. Currently, Nirula's has a total of 44 outlets. Nirula's is also looking to explore cities such as Jaipur, Agra, Lucknow, Jalandhar, and Chandigarh for opening budget hotels, and expand into Himachal Pradesh, Uttaranchal, and Punjab for family style restaurants. The hotel in Panipat was Nirula's first highway hotel and restaurant in the region. Despite the coming of foreign companies, the chain has maintained its growth of around 20 per cent.

Three new formats will be introduced by Nirula's, they are namely Nirula's Express, Food Court unit and Ice Cream kiosks, though the main aim will be to maximize reach to the high traffic locations. The first Express outlet recently opened at the Delhi Airport, while the first Food Court Unit started operations at a mall in Delhi NCR.

Competitive Scenario

In a market predominated by small operators, international chains such as McDonald's and Domino's have entered the Indian market. The local brands developed in India are also gaining a lot of ground such as Barista and Pizza Corner. Chains such as Pizza Hut are also on an expansion spree.

McDonald's

McDonald's, built by a visionary, the late Ray Kroc, has become a very successful international company with outlets in nearly 120 countries. Its products are popular with large numbers of customers and certainly not just children.

The multinational companies have given the domestic competition a run for their money. While McDonald's sells more than Nirula's, Pizza Hut and Domino's are doing more business than Pizza Corner. In the year 2001, while McDonald's clocked a turnover of about Rs 125 crore, Nirula's, which has been present in the country since 1934, could garner only Rs 100 crore as turnover. Also, both Domino's and Pizza Hut clocked a turnover of about Rs 60 crore, but Pizza Corner lagged behind with a turnover of Rs 25–30 crore (Gupta 2002).

A Global Phenomenon

Internationally, the first McDonald's restaurant opened in 1955 in Des Plaines, Illinois, USA. The company is the world's largest food service system with more than 30,000 restaurants in 121 countries across six continents serving nearly 45 million customers every day (McDonald's 2003a).

McDonald's has been adjudged the best employer in the retail industry in Brazil by a leading business magazine. McDonald's focus on training, employee development, and opportunities for advancement, were key factors in receiving this award especially since McDonald's is a first job for 67 per cent of the crew in Brazil (McDonald's 2003b). McDonald's is also the largest employer in the retail industry in Brazil.

A leading Swedish university recently named McDonald's Sweden the best competence company. The judges studied over one hundred companies' commitment to employee training and career development. The culture of enthusiasm and commitment at McDonald's, which provides real opportunity to all employees, was a key factor in their unanimous vote.

The Australia National Training Association named McDonald's Australia, as 1999 employer of the year. It was the third consecutive year that McDonald's was so honoured.

Vision It wishes to 'Be the best employer and lead the community around the world' (McDonald's 2003c).

Indian Operations

McDonald's opened its first restaurant in India on 13 October 1996. In the year 2007, the company in India planned to expand from 105 restaurants to 155 (Domain-b.com). McDonald's has aggressive plans to target 30–35 per cent per annum are likely to be actualised by opening 60 more restaurants currently and investing $93.41 million in the next three years. This would bring the total count of McDonald's restaurants in India to 220 in 2008.

In India, McDonald's entered the market without the brands flagship product, the Big Mac. Keeping in mind the religious sentiments of the local population, no beef or pork products are listed on the menu. A product similar to Big Mac was created with mutton and chicken patties and was christened Maharaja Mac and Chicken Maharaja Mac, respectively. For the vegetarian population, an entire vegetarian range was introduced. Eggless mayonnaise was used in vegetarian burgers.

Supply Chain

Every year, Rs 50,000 worth of food produced is wasted in India on account of lack of infrastructure for storage and transportation (McDonald's 2003). McDonald's has its own cold chain. It is necessary to maintain the integrity of food products and retain their freshness and nutritional value. It refers to procurement, warehousing, transportation, and retailing of food products under controlled temperatures. Setting up the cold chain has involved the transfer of state-of-the-art food processing technology by McDonald's and its international suppliers to pioneering Indian entrepreneurs who have become an integral part of the cold chain. McDonald's quality inspection programme carries out the quality checks at over 20 different points in the cold chain system.

They have, for example, identified Trikaya Agriculture to successfully grow specialty crops such as iceberg lettuce, special herbs, and many oriental vegetables. The farm infrastructure features:

o specialized nursery with a team of agricultural experts
o drip and sprinkler irrigation in raised farm beds with fertilizer mixing plant
o pre-cooling room and a large cold room for post harvest handling
o refrigerated tank for transportation.

Vista Processed Foods supplies McDonald's with chicken and vegetable products. They have world-class infrastructure at their plant at Taloja, Maharashtra. Dynamix supplies the company with cheese. They have a fully automated international standard processing facility, which has the capacity to convert milk into cheese, butter/ghee, skimmed milk powder, lactose, casein, whey protein, and humanized baby food.

Amrit Food supplies items with a long life—ultra high temperature (UHT) milk and milk products for frozen deserts. It is an ISO 9000 company, which manufactures brands such as Gagan Milk and Nandan Ghee at its factory in Ghaziabad, located close to Delhi. It has an installed capacity of 6,000 litres/hour for producing homogenized UHT processed milk and milk products.

It has identified Radhakrishna Food Land, which runs distribution centres for Delhi and Mumbai. It specializes in handling large volumes, providing the entire range of services including procurement, quality, inspection, storage, inventory management, deliveries, data collection, recording, and reporting. The salient strength is that it is a one-stop shop for all distribution management services. There is a dry and cold storage facility to store and transport perishable products at temperatures up to –22 degrees Celsius. There is also an effective process control for minimum distribution cost.

Expansion Strategy

McDonald's has always been a franchising company and has relied on its franchisees to play a major role in its success. McDonald's remains committed to franchising as a predominant way of doing business. Approximately, 70 per cent of McDonald's worldwide restaurant businesses are owned and operated by independent businesspersons. McDonald's continues to be recognized as a premier franchising company around the world. Success for McDonald's corporation flows from the success of its business partners. The selection of prospective candidates is based on an assessment of overall business experience and personal qualification. Franchises are given only to individuals and not to corporations.

When McDonald's expanded, Kroc's major innovation lay in the way he franchised McDonald's. He did not permit regional franchises in which a single franchisee received control over all the outlets to be opened in a given area. McDonald's avoided the problems faced by other franchisers that had become very powerful and conflicted with the basic tenets of the respective organization. McDonald's maximized central control and thereby, uniformity throughout the system, by granting franchises one at a time and rarely granting more than one franchise to a specific individual. The franchise fee was fixed at $950, which was a rock-bottom fee but made money on store sales at the rate of 1.9 per cent of store sales. The success of McDonald's was thus linked with the success of the franchisee, many of whom then became millionaires (Ritzer 2000).

McDonald's is selective while expanding at various locations. Internationally, there are now McDonald's branches in American hospitals,

military bases, and zoos; worldwide they can be found in airport terminals, motorway service stations, supermarkets (Tesco), on-board cruise ships, and Swiss trains. McDonald's has been received with a lot of enthusiasm in the Indian industry. When a new outlet was launched at Jaipur in early March 2003, there were 12,000 customers who tramped through the restaurant on the opening day (Gupta 2003). McDonald's has more than 31,000 restaurants in 118 countries serving 50 million customers each day. Some figures give an interesting insight into the market dynamics:

According to a report by Gupta (2003) in *The Business Standard*, 'McDonald's has been growing at a compounded rate of 40 per cent every year. McDonald's outlets are company-owned but McDonald's is looking for an expansion strategy through franchising in non-metros. It would also be tying up with the petrol companies, especially on the highways. There are 3,000 customers who drop in each day at every McDonald's outlet in the country. Nirula's gets about 60,000 people daily at 64 outlets compared to 1.44 lakh at 48 outlets of McDonald's. Indian McDonald's are among the top 10 worldwide for the high number of transactions that take place.' McDonald's India is planning to increase its restaurants from 105 to 155 in 2007.

McDonald's stays ahead of its competitors by being innovative and looking for new opportunities. It relies heavily on its suppliers for fresh food; again, arrangements are carefully planned, monitored, and controlled. To enhance its image of food value, and to compete in a very dynamic industry, McDonald's offers 'extra-value meals', special combinations at low prices. The company is an industry leader and contends there are six main reasons behind this:

1. Visibility: To this end substantial resources are devoted to marketing. The golden arches symbol is instantly recognizable.

2. Ownership or control of real estate sites: McDonald's argues that this factor differentiates it from its competitors who lease more.

3. Its commitment to franchising and supplier partnerships.

4. It is worldwide, with restaurants in some 118 countries, and uses local managers and employees.

5. The structure is very decentralized but lines of responsibility and accountability are clear.

6. It is a growth company.

In India, McDonald's has done an immense amount of customization. The menu is Indianized and it also respects the local traditions. During a Hindu festival week, Navratris, only vegetarian menu is offered. Also, local sauces are used and burgers contain fillings, which gel with the local Indian market.

Domino's

Domino's has also done good business in India. As Arvind Singhal, Managing Director of retail consultancy firm KSA Technopak observes, 'The reasons for Domino's success in India are customization, consistent quality, and the company's strength in supply chain and logistics management, which have created a unique brand equity for Domino's'.

Domino's entered India when McDonald's and Pizza Hut were already in the market and several strong players, such as Nirula's, were snapping at its heels. It was not just competition that Domino's had to deal with, but also logistics to deliver the pizza in precisely 30 minutes, and ensure that taste and quality at affordable prices were made available. Bhartiyas in India got the mandate from Domino's USA to sell pizzas to one-fifth of the world's population (the entire South east Asian region).

To get the logistics in place, Domino's built central kitchens and cold chains, and set up new outlets. Today, the company's enviable cold chain helps it store and process its ingredients and manage time efficiently. If the food industry has to develop, efficient cold chains have to be laid out. Domino's made investments in the same. The progress was promising and venture capital firm Chase bought a 26 per cent stake in the company in the year 2000 (*The Economic Times* 2000).

Domino's looked at an aggressive pricing strategy to reach out to the mass market. The company could have gone the franchising way but this did not seem attractive and it put a professional management team in place. Top managers were sourced in the areas of HR, logistics, and finance from firms such as General Electric, Pepsi, and Hyatt Hotel. Pricing was still an issue and it wanted to bring down the prices further. The product had to be affordable for the masses. Domino's hopped onto the fast track and put up 20–30 stores. This gave it the economies of scale and the benefits were passed on to the consumers. Over time, the main triggers for buying pizza were the freebies. Domino's stopped offering any deals and the growth was still good. The price and the menu grid were still in place, establishing all the elements of proposition. Domino's gave the consumers the freedom to pick their own toppings. They came up with the punch line, '*Hungry Kya?*' (translates as, are you hungry?) and the branding was put in place.

Competitors such as Pizza Hut reacted by saying that they prefer not to be compared with Domino's, as it is more into delivery and take-away options.

Pizza Corner

Pizza Corner was created in 1996 by Global Franchise Architects (GFA). This winning idea is one among several supported by GFA, a builder of specialty retail franchisees since 1996. Its current portfolio consists of four self-created brands: Pizza Corner, Coffee World, New York Deli, and The Cream and Fudge Factory. The mission of Pizza Corner has been to wow every guest.

The venture was launched from Chennai in India. Pizza Corner today is present in Chennai, Bangalore, Mysore, Hyderabad, Puducherry, Kochi, and New Delhi. It was set up with active consultation with American and European food consultants. The aim was to establish 100 restaurants in the next four years. Pizza Corner has restaurants in the following categories (Pizza Corner 2008):

o dine-in restaurants with an area of 1200–2500 sq. ft.

o delivery outlets that will take care of only deliveries with an area of 700–800 sq. ft.

The company uses the best software in the world developed for the pizza business, which supports its operation (Pizza Corner 2003). The Pizza Corner delivery system and outlets accept all major credit cards and allow flexibility for the guests. It is the first firm to offer 'credit' on delivery in India.

Pizza Corner is also gearing up and has set an expansion plan for itself. It had adopted franchising as the route for growth.

Barista

Barista is another example of success. Barista Coffee Company started its operations in 1999 with the aim of identifying growth opportunities in the coffee business. As on September 2002, Barista operated 110 espresso bars spread across major cities in India (EH&C 2002). It is positioned as an experiential lifestyle brand. It is a part of the $9 billion Tata group. The outlets are swanky, with smart employees offering the wares, which are predominantly options in coffee, other beverages, cookies, cakes, and desserts. The merchandise basically reflects the Italian spirit although the chain has an Indian origin. To deliver an authentic Italian experience, Barista has outsourced 100 per cent Arabica beans, which are roasted. It offers fast food such as wraps, sandwiches, and a new range of desserts at its outlets. It is looking for international expansion by setting up outlets in Sri Lanka at an investment of Rs 30,000,000. The second phase may see a new concept bar, a pavement bar at Taj Samudra, in Colombo. The alliance will provide a strong coffee platform for Barista in the coffee retail segment in Sri Lanka.

Developing Barista as a lifestyle brand meant that it focused on the consumer experiences. As Ravi Deol, Managing Director of the Barista coffee company, remarked, 'Orienting the company in this manner did not really require a great deal of technology. Instead, it was important for the frontline staff to live and breath the customer' (Sethi 2002). To do this meant greeting regular customers by name, knowing their preferences, creating the right ambience, making the place safe for women to visit, providing clean toilets, etc. The

press reports do contain some accounts that do not match with the expectations of the top management. Barista has around 206 outlets, including 17 in the overseas market. There are plans to increase the total count of outlets to 300 in 2008 and 80 new stores with an investment of about 32 crores. The company is also focusing on opening stores following three models the *corporate ones*, in which it opens outlets near offices, the *high-street area* of high footfalls such as malls and shopping complexes, and *company-owned exclusive* stores.

The company has an invaluable first mover advantage. But entry barriers to this business are low and there are new players entering the market all the time.

Ahmedabad	Dehradun	Jaipur	Mumbai
Amritsar	Delhi	Jalandhar	Mussoorie
Bangalore	Ghaziabad	Kanpur	Mysore
Baroda	Goa	Kolkata	Nasik
Chandigarh	Gurgaon	Lucknow	Noida
Chennai	Guwahati	Ludhiana	Pune
Kochi	Hyderabad	Manipal	Shimla
Coimbatore	Indore	Meerut	

In the UAE, Barista is present in the cities of Dubai and Abu Dhabi.

Source: Barista 2008.

Barista has a presence in the following cities:

Barista coffee is not restricted to the espresso bars alone; it can be taken anywhere—club lawn, malls, theatres, restaurants, hotels, airlines, etc.

Growth Plans

The company believes that the prime factor, which facilitates the success, is location. It has adopted a top-down approach where the cities have been identified first.

The selection of cities is based on:

- sizeable population of executives, students, and families, SEC A and B category
- high disposable incomes
- high level of organized retail activity
- rapid socio-economic development

○ level of commercial importance (industrial cities, state capital, etc.).

Barista is working on 50 overseas locations. They have already done the groundwork in terms of getting the brand and name registrations in over 30 locations. It has also tied up with the prestigious Taj group to offer its products in India. Barista outlets also sell several kinds of merchandise such as various varieties of coffee, books, music, gift certificates, etc. It would conduct interviews at the country's premier management institutes, such as the prestigious IIMs at Ahmedabad and Calcutta, to recruit management graduates. Out of a class of 200 at IIM Kolkata, as many as 134 students applied to Barista. Similarly, at IIM Ahmedabad, out of 140 students, 104 applied for an interview with the company. This essentially reflects the positive image that the company nurtures with prospective employees.

Barista was bought by the Lavazza group in 2007.

Café Coffee Day

Café Coffee Day is a leading, Bangalore-based coffee chain owned by Amalgamated Bean Coffee Trading Company Limited. It entered into a partnership with Bharat Petroleum Corporation Limited to open Café Coffee Day outlets in select BPCL filling stations across the country. The outlets will be standalone café or kiosks/coffee counters within BPCL's chain of convenience centres, 'In and Out', which are located within the petrol pump. Café Coffee Day (CCD), being one of India's largest retail chain of coffee cafes, is in the process of launching new formats to stretch its horizon and expand its target group. Café Coffee Day's expansion plans will be made keeping in mind the factors of accessibility, affordability, and acceptability. Café Coffee Day (till August 2008) had 620 cafés across 103 cities in the country, with 172 outlets in the northern region alone. It is also mulling over opening its outlets in multiplexes, based on a sports theme, i.e., a Sports Café. Coffee Day is also planning to expand in overseas markets and is planning to launch at least 50 outlets in Austria, Pakistan, and eastern Europe in 2008. The chain also aims at opening 1,000 cafés by 2009 (Live Mint 2007).

Mumbai has seen the advent of many food chains of late. Specialized outlets such as Only Parathas, Just Biryani, Just Kababs, Noodle Bar, and Dosas, have established their presence in Mumbai and are looking for increasing their market share. Analysts estimate the market to be worth $3 billion and the market is still growing (Kothari 2002). There are many entrepreneurs in the fray but only those with reasonable pricing and quality food in a hygienic environment will be able to survive.

Just Corns

Another case, which illustrates this activity, is Just Corns. The concept consists of offering corn-based food options. Approximately Rs 2,500,000 was spent as an investment in the project. The first outlet was started in Mumbai in Kandivili, with investments in property, interiors, furniture, furnishings, crockery, labour, and specially-designed movable trolleys. There is also a tie-up with Indian Oil to place trolleys at petrol pumps in all the prime locations. Efforts are also being made to tie up with restaurants just as cola companies do. They may have a counter in the restaurants or can be offered as additional items in the menu. The pricing of the corn items served at the outlet is between Rs 25–50 and with three outlets in Mumbai, the sales touch Rs 2.5 lakh per month. The chain operates at a very low profit margin and the portion of the food served is also very low.

Fries 'N' Brown

Fries 'n' Brown is an international company, which entered the Indian market with a pioneering concept of serving ready to eat hot and fresh snacks through a chain of snack outlets under the brand name Fries 'n' Browns. These outlets have been set up through franchising. The chain felt that there is a tremendous opportunity in the quick food service industry. This format of snack outlets is a well-accepted format worldwide and there are chains having their outlets at high traffic locations such as airports, railway stations, theatres, cinema halls, family entertainment centres, etc. Priced at Rs 24 with a choice of three dips and two exotic drinks, priced at Rs 12 each, these snacks are being served in the city at places such as shopping malls, theatres, and so on. The company also has franchised outlets at railway stations, amusement parks, airports, cafeterias, clubs, and colleges. The snack products served at these outlets are sourced from their international partner McCain Foods Ltd, Canada, which supplies to food companies such as McDonald's, Pizza Hut, and Burger King. Each snack outlet is a self-contained retail outlet that includes an instant heating machine, freezer unit for pre-cooked frozen food, kiosk, drink dispensing machine, electronic cash register, and a cabinet to house peripherals such as garnishing, packaging, etc. This outlet occupies a floor space of 100 sq. ft, and apart from snacks, also serves food varieties such as samosas, vadas, kachoris, mini cheese rolls, vegetable nuggets, etc.

Conclusion

The above analysis indicates that the Indian market has still not matured and there are very few chains. The market is flooded with small operators and most businesses are run on a gut feel. In this scenario, there is a huge potential for chains such as McDonald's, Nirula's, Barista, and others. The numbers flooding McDonald's is enormous and, therefore, there are important lessons to be drawn from the same. The cases presented can provide an insight into what the strategies for growth for an Indian chain such as Nirula's can be. It may also be important to reflect on the alternative routes of growth available for Nirula's and can also be used for competitive analysis.

Questions

1. Compare and contrast the distribution strategies being followed by the different fast food chains in India.

2. What distribution strategy should Nirula's adopt to tackle the growing competition from foreign chains?

3. Comment on the distribution strategy adopted by McDonald's for market expansion.

SELECT REFERENCES

Banerjee, Rajiv (2006), 'Subhiksha draws up carpet bombing plan', *The Economic Times*, 6 December, p. 4.

Business Standard (2002), 'Barista appoints new head for local operations', 5 August 2002.

Dey, Sudipto (2006), 'Indian goes agro on ticket sales', *The Economic Times*, 14 November, p. 4.

EH&C (2002), 'Barista coffee sets up new company in Sri Lanka', *Express Hotelier & Caterer*, 23 September.

Gooptu, Pradeep (2002), 'Barista coffee brews South Asian thrust, *Business Standard*, 3 December.

Gupta, Parul (2002), 'Multinational fast food majors outpace local peers', *Business Standard*, 4 October.

Gupta, Sanjeet Das (2002), 'Barista Coffee Company grabs IIM graduates' fancy in New Delhi', *Business Standard*, 22 February.

Hollensen, Svend (1998), *Global Marketing*, Prentice Hall, London, Chapter 9, pp. 235–263.

Jobber, David (2001), *Principles and Practices of Marketing*, Berkshire, McGraw-Hill Publishing Company, Chapters 11–15.

Kaul, J. (2002), 'Nirula's plans to go national', *Express Hotelier & Caterer*, 26 August.

Kaul, P. (2003), 'Pizza Corner to take franchising route', *Express Hotelier & Caterer*, 20 January.

Kothari, D. (2002), 'The fast food boom', *Express Hotelier & Caterer*, 23 September, p. 11.

Kotler, Philip, John T. Bowen, and J.C. Makens (2006), *Marketing for Hospitality and Tourism*, Pearson Education Inc., New Jersey, Chapter 13.

Lovelock, Christopher H. (1983), 'Classifying services to gain strategic marketing insights', *Journal of Marketing*, vol. 47, Summer, pp. 9–20.

Monga, Deepshikha and Joji Thomas Philip (2006), 'RIL wants to play big in supply chain', *The Economic Times*, 26 September, p. 4.

Monga, Deepshikha and Meenakshi Verma (2006), 'Now Mac Express at stations and airports', *The Economic Times*, 8 December, p. 5.

Retailer (2008), 'Lladro plans to expand in tier-II cities', *Retailer*, New Delhi, vol. 3, no. 5, p. 14.

Reuters (2006), 'Russian retailers threaten boycott of Panasonic', *The Economic Times*, New Delhi, 8 December, p. 25.

Ritzer, G. (2000), *The McDonaldization of Society*, Pine Forge, New Delhi.

Scanlon, N.L. (1998), Quality Restaurant Service Guaranteed, John Wiley, New York.

Singh, Harsimran (2006), 'Battery glitch? Blame it on your mobile operator: Weak network stresses cell phone, reduces handsets life say experts', *The Economic Times*, 11 December 2006.

Times News Network (2006), 'Choice Hotels charts Rs 750 crore expansion', *The Times of India*, 4 December.

Das, Samipatra 'Global distribution system in present times', http://www.hotel-online.com/News/PR2002_4th/Oct02_GDS.html, accessed on 14 December 2006.

http//www.mcdonalds.com/corporate/promise/vision/index.html, accessed in 2003.

http//www.pizzacorner.com/aboutus/, accessed on 3 October 2008.

http://economictimes.indiatimes.com/articleshow/1232731.cms, accessed on 14 December 2006.

http://www.barista.co.in, accessed on 7 October 2008.

http://www.domain-b.com/companies/companies_m/mcDonald/20070222_franchise.html). accessed on 27 February 2007.

http://www.expresshospitality.com/20080831/market21.shtml, accessed on 7 October 2008.

http://www.financialexpress.com/old/latest_full_story.php?content_id=132468, accessed on 7 October 2008.

http://www.ibef.org/artdisplay.aspx?tdy=1&art_id=19321&cat_id=60 accessed on 6 October 2008.

http://www.keralatourism.org/index.php, accessed on 13 December 2006.

http://www.kfc.com/about/, accessed on 13 December 2006.

http://www.livemint.com/2007/11/28235623/Caf%C3%A9-Coffee-Day-eyes-overseas.html, accessed 7 October 2008.

http://www.mcdonalds.com/corp/about.html, accessed on 14 December 2006.

http://www.mcdonaldsindia.com/supchain.htm, accessed in 2003.

http://www.sabretravelnetwork.com/about/history.htm, accessed on 14 December 2006.

http://www.thehindubusinessline.com/2007/01/23/stories/2007012302712300.htm> accessed on 6 October 2008.

http://www.thehindubusinessline.com/2007/03/02/stories/2007030203260500.htm, accessed on 6 October 2008.

http://www.thehindubusinessline.com/2007/03/02/stories/2007030203260500.htm accessed on 7 October 2008.

Sethi, Sunil (2002), 'CEO-Speak vs employee per cent', *Business Standard*, 22 November, www.business-standard.com/archives/2002/nov 30th.

12 Managing People in Service Industry

OBJECTIVES

After reading this chapter you will be able to understand the:

- concept of internal and external labour markets and how do they impact people management issues in a service firm
- importance of service culture and its impact on customer satisfaction
- people-related factors that contribute towards creating excellence in service culture in a firm
- relationship between customer satisfaction, employee satisfaction, and profitability of the firm

INTRODUCTION

This chapter deals with the human perspective on services, i.e., the effect people have on management of services. An overview of the labour market and how it affects people has also been discussed. The chapter also discusses service culture and its impact on customer satisfaction. The factors contributing to service excellence are examined along with an overview on the relationship between employee satisfaction, customer satisfaction, and the overall profitability of the firm.

The services industry is very strongly driven by the human factor. The nature of services industry is such that people become a very important component in the delivery of the services. The experience factor in consumption of a service contributes immensely to consumer loyalty.

For instance, good experiences while dining, travelling, and education stay with you forever and you will want to come back to re-live the same experience. Brands such as McDonald's, Disney Theme Parks, Domino's, Pizza Hut, Four Seasons, and Malaysian Airlines, have won laurels on account of their unique experience and being able to live up to people's expectations.

In recent times, technology has acted as a driver to enhance the experience for the consumer, but the human factor cannot be eliminated. There are service sectors wherein the human element plays an important role in delivery of the experience such as education, consulting, beauty services, telecommunication, and insurance among other sectors. Human resources are the efforts, skills, and capabilities that people contribute to an employing organization (Leopold et al. 1999). Strategic human resource management helps to achieve competitive advantage through the development of a highly committed and capable workforce (Storey 1995). Culture and leadership styles become the important focus in the strategic human resource management approach (Towers 1994). Culture and human resources provides a distinctive edge to the services firm. It is human capability and commitment that distinguish successful organizations from the rest (Storey 1989). Jones (1997) agrees and argues that people and the way they are managed and deployed are the single-most sustainable source of competitive advantage.

Employees are the face of the firm. Hence, it is important that they are treated like internal customers. If employees are not treated well, they will not treat the customers of the firm well and that is very dangerous for the firm. Every unpleasant experience can lead to negative word-of-mouth, which will drive customers away from the firm. In the light of creating positive experiences for the customers, it is important to care for the employees in a firm just as one would treat customers. To understand people issues in a service firm, it is important to understand the following questions. This chapter tries to address these issues.

1. How does the external supply of manpower impact people management issues in a firm?
2. What constitutes the culture of a firm?
3. How can a service culture of firms across various cultures be compared? What impact will it have on the management of people in cross-cultural firms?
4. How can a service culture of excellence be created in a firm?
5. How does teamwork help to improve the service offering?
6. How can training and development contribute to a positive consumer experience?
7. How can the employees in service firms be motivated?
8. How can the employees in service firms be empowered?
9. How can employees in a service firm be made to feel secure?

CHALLENGES OF MANAGING PEOPLE IN A SERVICE FIRM

Services is a dynamic sector, which is growing worldwide. Since the sector is growing and the foreign direct investment is increasing because of the opening of economies, globally there is a demand for professionals in the service sector. Sectors such as software, information technology enabled services (ITES), hospitality, tourism, and healthcare, are all areas where there is a dearth of professionals. This raises issues on the supply side, which means there are implications for the education side as well as the industry. Some of the challenges are as follows:

- dealing with high rates of attrition
- high level of stress
- high degree of customer interface
- challenges for retaining employees and motivating them
- ensuring adequate supply of professionals into a service stream
- training the people
- managing cultural diversity issues
- performance measurement and rewards.

People Management

The concept of people management is very generic and cannot have a panacea for all the challenges that confront a particular industry. Each industry, which operates in the domain of services, has certain unique challenges before it. The concept of labour markets is extremely vital to understand the dynamics of HR in a particular cultural and industry context. Labour markets are the pool of people available for taking up work assignments. As Riley (1996) points out, at any given point of time, labour markets exist at both the factual and perceptual level. There are people who are looking out for a change and employers who are seeking people for assignments for their firms. According to conventional economic theory, supply and demand is brought into equilibrium by the price of the labour, and it is brought about by the independent and unconnected decisions of thousands of people. The external labour market skills are distributed by the price of labour, yet the internal labour market (within the organization) follows different dynamics. The concept of internal labour markets is based on the idea that sets of rules and conventions within organizations, which act as allocative mechanisms, govern the movement of people and the pricing of jobs. These rules are related to growth opportunities, investments in training, pay differentials, and evaluation of jobs. It is also about openness to external labour markets, which represents the interface between what goes inside the firm and what goes outside.

CHARACTERISTICS OF STRONG AND WEAK LABOUR MARKETS

The characteristics of strong internal labour markets according to Riley (1996) are as follows:

- structural features
- specified hiring standards
- single point of entry
- high skill specificity
- continuous on job training
- fixed criteria for promotion and transfer
- strong workplace customs
- pay differentials remain fixed over time.

Weak labour markets have the following characteristics:

- unspecified hiring standards
- multiple points of entry
- low skill specificity
- no on the job training
- no fixed criteria for promotion and transfer
- weak workplace customs
- pay differentials vary over time.

We would expect to find low rates of labour turnover associated with strong internal labour markets. The labour turnover is high with weak internal labour markets. This is, however, a rough indication. Organizations can initiate various measures for improving the internal labour market scenario:

- alter pay and working conditions
- alter training practices
- alter growth opportunities for people in the firm
- use overtime and other forms of increased form of labour supply, which could happen by introducing shifts or may be part time options as well bringing larger number of people in the work domain
- alter points of entry into the firm
- alter job design and structure of the firm.

The Hospitality Sector in India

The Indian hospitality industry is characterized by a weak internal labour market. There is a stream of 10,000 hospitality students graduating every year (Ministry of HRD, Government of India) from various public and private institutions. However, the management trainee positions are merely restricted to about 100–150. Most graduates join as operations trainees and then wait for another few years to become management trainees. The work conditions in most hotels in India, apart from the top luxury brands, leaves a lot to be desired. The attrition rates are high. Long work hours with low compensation motivates employees to look for greener pastures. Many of the multinational brands act as a training ground for interns who later take up more lucrative assignments elsewhere. The reason for shifting jobs are slight increments in salary, the work environment lacks openness, and sharing of concerns by employees is seldom the norm. The employee to room ratio is extremely high.

Hotels deploy more people rather than investing in a multi-skilled task force. These issues can be attributed to the supply side of the labour in this industry. The education system needs to change. Incorporation of management-related modules in the curriculum could be helpful and give insights into management of brands and sensitivity to issues related to strategy, financial management, and people as an important resource.

RELEVANCE OF PEOPLE MANAGEMENT ISSUES

In a service firm, service encounter in many situations involves human interface. At such times, the competence and attitude of an employee determines the outcome of an interaction. There may be instances wherein the features offered by a service are outstanding, yet the employee attitude can completely put off a consumer. There may be a case of an average attribute offering, yet an enthusiastic delivery can be a unique experience for the consumer. There is a need for creating memorable experiences during service encounters, which could result in generating loyal customers for the firm. If the employee is a strong link between the firm and the consumer then it becomes pertinent that the employee truly represents the philosophy the firm stands for.

How well this philosophy is conveyed in spirit and deed is determined by numerous factors. These are as follows:

Competence level of an employee It is important that the person performing the job is well informed and knows his responsibilities. In a restaurant, if a waiter is unaware about the menu and is unable to make recommendations when asked, it indicates lack of detailing and customer orientation. For example, in case of an educational institution, the person who counsels students for possible recruitments into the various programmes should be able to guide them into the accreditation process; provide comparative insights with other similar offerings and details about placement opportunities.

Vision of the firm The orientation of the employees is a reflection of the vision of the firm in many situations. A firm that wants to be a lead player will care both for its customers and its employees. It will also inform the people about its vision and commitment to various concerns. For instance, Hewlett-Packard has been known for the 'HP way of life'. This is a reflection on care for its employees and customers. It means creating an environment of openness and trust, and making life easier for employees so that they give their best to the job in hand.

Institutionalization of core values of the firm Firms with outstanding service cultures make sure that values are communicated across the firm and shared with employees. The signages, specific communication training, and artefacts, all reinforce the values of the firm. Internal newsletters and communication are all reflections of institutionalizing of values. The performance measurement and appraisal systems can be used as powerful systems to ensure that all employees work towards fulfilment of the core values. For instance, Xerox ascribes to four values, namely, employee satisfaction, customer satisfaction, return on investment, and return on assets. People's performance was measured on these dimensions in the firm.

Investment in training Training helps to make people perform at the desired level of expectation. It helps the service firm to provide uniform service across all outlets. The banking experience at Citibank is uniform across all branches. The experience at any Hilton or Marriott will be identical. This emanates on account of similar vision and similar training imparted at various outlets and properties. Walt Disney makes massive investments in training to ensure an unforgettable experience.

Well-defined processes and structure This helps to minimize confusion in service delivery. To minimize human error, the flow of activities and processes helps to attain standardization and uniformity of delivery. The process of delineating the workflow is called blueprinting.

Empowerment on certain decisions The employees with a customer interface help to deal with difficult customer situations. If a person handling customers does not have the authority to deviate from prescribed rules, situations sometimes become difficult to handle. A certain amount of responsibility must accompany the job. However, the recruitment strategy needs to be appropriate so that employees who are performing these roles are adequately mature. Let's take the case of a travel firm that organizes tours. Suppose on a tour the bus breaks down and the guide is not empowered to take instantaneous decisions, it will have a negative impact on the overall experience. The domain of empowerment of employees should be clearly defined. More of this is discussed in the section on service recovery.

Rewards and reinforcement of certain kinds of behaviour There is sufficient evidence in literature that links profitability in a firm to customer satisfaction. Customer satisfaction is not just dependent on the attributes of the service offering; the entire experience and employees contribute distinctly to the whole experience. If, for instance, we take the case of a restaurant, it may offer great food and ambience but if the staff who takes care of the service is rude or unconcerned, it will ruin the whole experience.

The research in human resource management has shown a connection between employee-oriented practices, employee behaviour, and organizational effectiveness. Service employees provide service to customers commensurate with the treatment they receive from their employers (Schneider and Bowen 1985).

The service quality measures in literature are clear pointers towards the importance of people management. The SERVQUAL instrument to measure the service quality clearly delineates the following dimensions, which contribute to the overall experience:

- Assurance: This is defined as the knowledge and courtesy of the employees and their ability to convey trust and confidence.
- Empathy: Caring, individualized attention, which the firm provides to its customers.
- Reliability: The ability to perform the promised service dependably and accurately.
- Responsiveness: The willingness to help customers and provide prompt service.
- Tangibles: The appearance of physical facilities, equipment, personnel, and communication materials.

The above elements clearly indicate that the employees need to be managed effectively, and in order to maintain quality it is pertinent that the employees are trained and treated well.

The Deming's quality paradigm suggests that the following initiatives have a bearing on institutionalizing quality:

- create constancy of purpose for improvement of product and service
- adopt the new philosophy
- cease dependence on mass production
- end the practice of awarding business on price tag alone
- improve constantly and forever the system of production and service
- institute training
- institute leadership
- drive out fear
- break down barriers between staff areas
- eliminate slogans, exhortations, and targets for the workforce
- eliminate numerical quotas
- remove barriers to pride of workmanship
- institute a vigorous programme of education and re-training
- take action to accomplish the transformation.

The above points clearly indicate the importance of investment in people in the services industry.

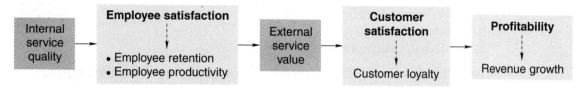

Source: Adapted from Heskett et al. (1994).

Fig. 12.1 Link between employee satisfaction, customer satisfaction, and profitability

FRAMEWORK LINKING EMPLOYEE SATISFACTION, CUSTOMER SATISFACTION, AND PROFITABILITY

The framework as postulated by Heskett et al. (1994) lists the relationship between employee satisfaction, customer satisfaction, and profitability. This is depicted in Fig. 12.1. The framework postulates that in a firm profitability and revenue growth is driven by customer loyalty. Customer loyalty can only emanate if the customers are happy with the firm and the customers will be happy if their experience with the firm has been good. As employees are an integral part of the whole experience in a service firm, their behaviour will contribute to making the entire experience enjoyable. If the employee is happy with the work, and has the right attitude and training, he/she will be productive and will drive the profitability through repeat business. The internal service culture will, therefore, have a huge impact on the employee satisfaction and orientation.

SERVICES INDUSTRY AND CULTURE

All successful organizations have a distinct service culture. It contributes to people's orientation towards customers, treating each other with respect, and upholding the values as cherished by the firm. Service culture has a bearing on employees' attitudes and work ethics. It is, therefore, important to understand the dynamics of service culture. The roots of the service culture lie in the culture itself. It is also interesting to see how different cultures shape the communication and employee dynamics globally. This section gives insights into culture and service culture and suggests how this can be embedded into the day-to-day lives of employees in a firm.

Culture

Culture is an umbrella word that encompasses a whole set of implicit, widely-shared beliefs, traditions, values, and expectations that characterize a particular group of people. It identifies the uniqueness of a social unit, its values, and beliefs (Leavitt and Bahrami 1988). Hofstede (1980) defined culture as 'The collective programming of the mind which distinguishes the members of one human group from another...the interactive aggregate of common characteristics that influence a human group's response to the environment'. Schein (1990) distinguishes between three levels of culture:

1. Behaviour and artefacts (buildings, art, and literature)
2. Beliefs and values
3. Underlying assumptions

Culture exerts a lot of influence on the employees in a firm (Webster 1992). It:

- provides the central theme around which employees' behaviour can converge
- is the critical key strategic managers may use to direct the course of their firm
- provides a pattern of shared values and beliefs, the norms for behaviour, and a form of control of employees
- influences productivity, the manner in which the firm copes with the various aspects of the external environment, and newcomer socialization
- aids in hiring practices, i.e., helps in understanding the characteristics of people who would do well in the firm
- establishes the rationale for 'dos and don'ts' of behaviour.

Culture exists at various levels such as country, industry, and corporate (Pizam 1993). It is interesting to see that different nations and firms can be compared on certain parameters, which help to understand cultures. Each country can be categorized on cultural dimensions as in Hofstede's typology. Each industry also has certain unique characteristics. Similarly, local and multinational firms also have their unique cultures, which are influenced by the national and the industry cultures.

Hofstede (1980) identified the following dimensions of culture that can have an impact on work values in an organizational context:

1. Power distance
2. Individualism
3. Masculinity
4. Uncertainty avoidance

Power distance   Power distance defines the extent to which societies accept inequality in power and consider it as normal. This dimension does not deal with mere existence of power distance, which is universal, but the magnitude that is tolerated. The extent to which power is distributed among people, equally or unequally, is reflected in superior–subordinate relationship such as parent–child, teacher–pupil, manager–employee, or sovereign–subject. In societies with large power gaps, the superior exerts more power over the junior partner. Austria and Israel have been categorized as low power distance societies, whereas India and Philippines are high power distance societies.

Individualism   This is the degree to which cultures encourage individual concerns as opposed to collectivist concerns. The driving urge in case of individualist cultures is 'me first'. In a collectivist society, the group concerns take precedence over individual concerns; the conformance to group norms is perceived to be important. Japan is an example of a collectivist society, whereas US is seen to be a highly individualistic society. In an individualistic culture, it is important for individuals to have control over their personal and private life, to stand on their own feet, to make decisions that affect their lives, and to look after themselves and their immediate family members. In a collectivist culture, people are more dependent on others in a group, both financially and morally (Tayeb 1997).

Masculinity This is a characteristic that opposes feminity. In masculine cultures, the social sex roles are clearly differentiated. Men should be assertive while women are clearly caring and nurturing. Japan is high on masculinity (Tayeb 1997). This trait is reflected in the great emphasis that Japanese parents place on competitiveness and excellence at every stage of their children's education, from kindergarten to the firm for which they end up working.

Uncertainty avoidance This defines the extent to which people within a culture are encouraged to take risks and can tolerate uncertainty. Cultures high on uncertainty avoidance adhere to rules, work hard, and feel compelled to devise means to beat the future. People weak in uncertainty avoidance tend to accept each day as it comes, take risks easily, and do not work too hard. There are fewer rules, and they can be easily broken and changed.

To institutionalize a service culture, especially in a global context, it is important to understand the cultural context both for dealing with customers as well as employees. In a global workplace, there is a need for understanding the values cherished by a local culture.

Tayeb (1995) has tried to establish links between the culture and the competitive advantage of firms in various countries. The local culture influences institutions in a country, which reflects in the national competitiveness of a nation. We, therefore, have instances wherein workforces from different countries are labelled as hardworking, achievement driven, or laid back. This reflects in work dynamics at the workplace as well.

The difference between Indian and English cultural values and attitudes is indicated below (Tayeb 1987).

Indian people are	English people are
more emotional	less emotional
fearful of people in power	respectful of people in power
more obedient to seniors	less obedient to seniors
more fatalistic	less fatalistic
submissive	aggressive
more open to bribery	less open to bribery
less willing to accept responsibility	more willing to accept responsibility
less disciplined	more disciplined
friendlier	less friendly
more clan-oriented	less clan-oriented
less willing to take into account other people's views.	more willing to take into account other people's views.

Service Culture and Excellence

Research into service culture has largely been positioned within the latter (variable) perspective. The prescriptions have often been based on case studies focusing on so-called 'excellent' service firms (Berry 1999; Berry and Bendapudi 2003; Muldrow et al. 2002; Schneider and Bowen 1995). Berry (1999) for example, based his study on award-winning organizations such as Bergstrom Hotels, Midwest Express Airlines, and Dana Commercial Credit. He found that the organizations studied were all driven by seven values:

1. Innovation
2. Joy
3. Respect
4. Teamwork
5. Social profit
6. Integrity
7. Excellence

Excellence in a firm can be achieved through employees (Hesselink and Assem 2002). They have the following observations:

- Excellent leadership will be achieved through clear vision and mission statements, and the distinct role model behaviour of managers who are proud of their organization and know what is expected of them.
- Excellent employees will be created through excellent leadership, good recruitment and selection procedures, good education and training facilities, and clear guidelines about what is expected of them.
- Satisfied candidates will be created through excellent employees who see every candidate as a VIP (very individual person), for whom every little detail is covered and for whom the employees carefully assess what the best service is in each specific situation.
- Satisfied customers will be created through satisfied candidates and excellent employees who treat their customers as individuals, for whom every little detail is covered, and for whom the employees carefully assess what the best service will be in each specific situation.
- Satisfied customers will spread the word to others and return again and thus ensure good financial results.

Exhibit 12.1 is a clear example of how a global service culture can be instituted.

HUMAN RESOURCE STRATEGY AND SERVICE OPERATIONS

It is important to match the human resource strategy with the service operations of a firm. The services offered by a firm range from being customized to being mass-produced. For example, in case of TGIF restaurants the services are customized, whereas, in the case of McDonald's they are standardized. The human resource strategy must fit the product offering. In a customer service situation, the employee works within the controls

Exhibit 12.1   Global service culture at walt disney

Walt Disney is undoubtedly one of the most success-ful 'children' brands in the world. It has been very successfully running theme parks for children at numerous cities such as Tokyo, Paris, and at loca-tions in US. As a firm, the following values are an integral part of the Disney culture:

□ **Innovation**   The firm strongly supports innova-tion.

□ **Quality**   The firm is committed to achieving ex-cellence in all its products and operations.

□ **Community**   The firm is committed to including the entire family in its product offering.

□ **Storytelling**   Every Disney product tells a story and the firm believes that timeless and engaging stories delight and inspire.

□ **Optimism**   At The Walt Disney Company, enter-tainment is about hope, aspiration, and positive resolutions.

□ **Decency**   The firm honours and respects the trust people place in it.

Source: Adapted from Walt Disney (2006).

set by the organization. In these circumstances, control and commitment are variables of equal importance. To consider all these dimensions of standardization, customization, control, and commitment, Lashley postulated a theory to evolve a human resource strategic framework.

Lashley (1998) has delved upon the approaches to management of human resources in service organizations. The framework is proposed in Fig. 12.2.

He postulates that there are four styles of management. The professional style of management is located in the top right quadrant. The offer to the customers is highly customized with a high degree of internal control by employees. Examples of these services are medicine, consultants, accountants, etc. The human resource strategy is likely to be based around employees exercising a high degree of discretion over their tasks with high autonomy over the organization of work. This strategy places a lot of importance on recruitment strategy and selection processes as well.

The command and control style is characterized by a highly standardized service offering such as McDonald's and Pizza Hut. They organize the human resource management through traditional approaches using external control processes to monitor employee performance. The human resource strategy calls for low discretion to employees and emphasis on systems is very strong. Its selection procedures are simplified. Service interactions are trained and in some cases scripted. The standards are well defined. Employee empowerment in these situations is quite limited.

The involvement style is located in the top left quadrant of the figure. This service style is such that it is customized in the intangible component of the customer offer but is highly standardized in the tangible element. Employee performance is controlled through external processes as means of ensuring the totality of the customer experience. An experience in the luxury hotel segment may fall in this category. The processes are system driven and through manuals. This approach includes gaining employee involvement and commitment to service objectives, with little power to influence decisions beyond this. Managers place a lot of emphasis on motivating employees but remain in control of employees' actions.

	The Involvement Style	The Professional Style
Customized offer	• Brand identity: tangibles/intangibles • Moderate predictability/market change • Moderate/high volume • Simple/expanding tasks • Low discretion • Ask permission, share information • Task specific power • Calculative commitment • Moderate control culture	• Brand identity: intangible/dominant • Low predictability • Low volume • Complex tasks • High discretion • Responsible autonomy • Power to shape objectives • Moral involvement, psychological needs • Trust culture
	The Command and Control Style	The Participative Style
Standardized offer	• Brand identity: tangible/dominant • High predictability • High volume • Simple routine tasks • Low discretion • Asks permission • Task specific power • Calculative involvement • Control culture	• Brand identity: tangibles/intangibles • High predictability • Moderate volume • Simple routine tasks • High discretion in intangibles • Autonomy within limits • Role-specific power • Moral involvement • Moderate trust culture
	External control	Internal control

Source: Adapted from Lashley (1998).

Fig. 12.2   Approaches to the management of human resources in a service organization

The participative style falls in the bottom right quadrant. It is characterized by highly standardized offers, but banks more on the internal commitment of people. There is a high degree of predictability of the service offering. This can be in the case of banking, which follows both online and real-time banking options. The services are standardized, yet each service experience may be different and unique in terms of experience. The autonomy is well defined and the powers allocated to employees are outlined. The system works on the moral involvement of employees and there is a moderate trust culture.

So, to conclude, there is no one best way of structuring the human resource strategy, but depending on the service offering and uniqueness of experience which one creates, a different human resource strategy can be initiated.

CREATING THE RIGHT SERVICE CULTURE

To create the right culture in a service organization, the following aspects need to be looked into (Redman and Mathews 1998):

- recruitment
- retention

- teamwork
- training and development
- rewarding quality
- job security

Recruitment

Every organization needs to make efforts to recruit the right kind of people into the firm. The service culture is greatly influenced by the kind of people who work in an organization. If one assesses the role theory as practiced by Disney, it assumes that the service firm is like a stage wherein each participant has a role to play. So, the role needs to be played perfectly. But the pursuit of perfection can be achieved only if the people have the right attitude and invest in inducting the right people into the system. As an example, well-known firms such as Southwest Airlines (an airlines firm in USA), Infosys (a software firm in India), and Four Seasons (an international luxury hotel chain) have well-known recruitment processes in place, which follow the basic values. Hiring people with the wrong attitude can be disastrous and impinge negatively on a firm's service culture.

Job descriptions, expectations from the employees, and mapping their career are some essential pre-requisites, which are needed to attract the right candidates for the service firms.

Zeithaml and Bitner (2003) have postulated that there are three aspects related to hiring that need to be kept in mind. These are:

- compete for the best people
- hire for service competencies and service inclinations
- be the preferred employer.

Exhibit 12.2   The case of hiring and attracting global talent at Infosys

Infosys, a world leader in consulting and information technology services, partners with Global 2,000 companies to provide business consulting, systems integration, application development, and product engineering services. It was started in 1981 by seven people with $250 and is today a global leader in IT and consulting, with revenues of more than $4 billion. Through these services, Infosys enables its clients to fully exploit technology for business transformation. Clients leverage Infosys' global delivery model, which is based on the system of taking the work to the location where the best talent is available in order to achieve higher quality, rapid time-to-market, and cost-effective solutions. Infosys has more than 91,000 employees in over 40 offices worldwide.

As economies expand their global presence, developing human capital has become a top priority. Organizations are realizing that companies can go as far as the workforce can take them. The quality of the workforce has a bearing on the performance of the firm. In 2005, over 1.3 million people applied for a job at Infosys. Only 1 per cent of them were hired. In comparison, Harvard University took in 9 per cent of candidates. Infosys has always focused on inducting and educating the best and the brightest, and they have global hiring practices coupled with ever-expanding university programmes such as campus connect and development centres. 'Infosys U' trains over 15,000 new recruits every year and is well prepared to win the battle for top-notch talent. This

Contd

Exhibit 12.2 Contd

education programme is supported with a fully equipped $120 million facility in Mysore, which is about 90 miles from Bangalore. In 2005, *Computerworld* magazine, while ranking Infosys among the 100 best IT places to work in, placed it at the very top of the list of best places for education and training. *Fortune* magazine, in its March 2006 issue, stepped inside the gates of 'Infosys U' and emerged with the impression that gaining admission to the 'Taj Mahal of training centres' is harder than getting into Harvard.

In 2006, Infosys Technologies Ltd announced its first large-scale plan to recruit 300 college graduates from universities in the United States and 25 graduates from the United Kingdom in 2007. This was a step towards an ongoing commitment to create a diversified, global workforce. Infosys has recruited people of about 25 different nationalities.

Under this global recruitment initiative, US brought more than 100 American college graduates to India in August 2006. These new employees developed their engineering skills at Infosys development centres across India for six months, before returning to Infosys' office in the US. 'This represents a very important landmark in the evolution of Infosys'. Chairman and chief mentor, Mr N.R. Narayana Murthy, Infosys Technologies Ltd says, 'Through the breadth of understanding and cross-cultural adaptability that can only be found in a diverse workforce, Infosys will play an even more strategic role for its clients.'

Ten young Americans came to work in Bangalore as part of a pilot programme; the success of this programme started the recruitment of young Americans from US campuses. Applications were admitted from all majors, including liberal arts majors, for the software engineering position. In August 2006, more than 100 new employees from American universities began their careers at the Infosys global education centre in Mysore, India, one of the largest corporate education centres of its kind in the world.

'As we expand our global presence, we need to attract bright talent from the local economies. It was with this in mind that we launched university-level recruiting programmes in the US,' said Mr T.V. Mohandas Pai, member of the board, human resources and education & research, Infosys Technologies Ltd. 'We plan to run a pilot programme at top universities in UK this year for 25 positions. We feel college graduates from the US and UK offer unique skills and perspectives that will blend with the skills of our Indian employees, to expand our capabilities in all areas,' he added.

This will be the first instance of Infosys recruiting graduates abroad for permanent positions from schools such as Stanford Graduate School of Business, MIT Sloan School of Management, Harvard Business School, and the Said Business School of Oxford. These institutions have been competing to visit Infosys' Bangalore campus for InStep, the Infosys internship programme. InStep received over 11,000 applications for 100 positions in 2006. InStep recruits students from 82 universities in 18 countries to come to India for 8–24 weeks to intern at Infosys.

Infosys Consulting Inc., the consulting arm of Infosys Technologies Ltd, which primarily recruits in the United States, will reach 500 employees in the next two years while Infosys China hopes to reach 6,000 employees by 2010.

Source: Adapted from Infosys (2006).

Exhibit 12.2 on Infosys, which is one of the leading software development firms in India, has identified numerous methods to attract global talent that can be groomed. It attracts talent from across the globe, and some of the finest universities in the world compete to get an entry into the firm.

Retention

Service firms have a great challenge before them to hire the right kind of employees and retain them as well. In India, ITES is an emerging area in which many call centres operate, handling jobs that are very elementary, to those that are highly complex. The attrition rate at some of the well-known firms is extremely high. This could vary from 30 per cent to 50 per cent in some firms. This is a serious concern as it has financial implications in inducting and re-training new employees. Schlesinger and Heskett (1991) describe a 'cycle of failure' where high employee turnover results in low productivity, poor service, angry customers, and even more discontented workers, and thus continuing high turnover. Organizations with strategies of high customer service such as Walt Disney (Miller 1992) and British Airways (Robson 1993) also have programmes aimed at high nurturing of a loyal workforce, in order to achieve the former.

The newspapers in India are almost always full of recruitment advertisements for ITES services. The reasons are manifold—working on night shifts, lack of clarity of future growth, low levels of maturity, and lack of clear career path. Though the work life offers advantages such as good compensation, transport facilities from home to work and back, and bonuses, lack of a normal work life becomes stressful and also hampers their social life.

Hotel firms in India also face a huge challenge for retaining the staff at entry level. The industry struggles desperately to retain good people. With the sector expanding rapidly, there are newer opportunities coming in, hence creating opportunities for attrition. Organizations therefore have to make investments in employee development, benchmark compensation, and provide a culture that cares for its employees and provides opportunities for growth. The adverse work conditions such as long hours, low levels of compensation, lack of compensation for extra hours put at work, a bureaucratic work culture, power distance from the top, and lack of culture for voicing and addressing concerns of employees are all triggers which make people look at greener pastures in other industries. The solution is not just at the firm level, the industry as a whole needs to have a different mindset. The education segment also needs a complete revamp and more growth opportunities need to be provided for people, rather than looking at the growth opportunities with an archaic mindset.

Exhibit 12.3 indicates the range of Tata Consultancy Services (TCS) operations globally. It is India's largest software development firm. With its employees posted all over the world, TCS offers opportunities for fostering a sense of belonging in the community through its initiative named Maitree. It provides an opportunity for the spouses to channelize their talents and brings the employees closer.

Teamwork

Most service firms require an extraordinary effort and synchronization to deliver a flawless service. The inter-departmental co-ordination requires people to have an understanding and sympathetic attitude towards the firm's internal customers. For instance, development of software requires inputs by various people. There are people who understand the flow of work and processes such as programmers and systems administrators, and each person has to work as a team to deliver the whole project effectively. The restaurant industry also depends heavily on the effectiveness of teams for the complete delivery of a unified experience. To achieve a level of synchronization and to make the experience uniform for all team members, it is essential that all team members are trained in the systems and processes.

Exhibit 12.3 Tata Consultancy Services

Tata Consultancy Services (TCS) is among the leading global information technology consulting, services, and business process outsourcing organizations. It offers services to clients across 55 countries and is a pioneer of the flexible global delivery model for IT services. TCS has a focus to deliver technology-led business solutions to its international customers across varied industries. The company's vision is to be a global top 10 IT services company by 2010.

TCS offers a comprehensive range of IT services to clients in diverse industries such as banking and financial services, insurance, manufacturing, telecommunications, retail, and transportation. It has offices in 33 countries, with over 35,000 consultants from 30 nationalities, and more than 1,00,000 person years of experience. The fact is that six of the top 10 corporations in the Fortune 500 list of the largest corporations in the United States are among TCS' clients.

Headquartered in Mumbai, India, TCS has operations in more than 45 countries. It has a training centre in Thiruvananthapuram, India, and the Tata Research Development and Design Centre at Pune, India. The company has developed IT solutions for over 800 customers all over the world and has clients such as AT&T, Boeing, British Airways, British Telecom, Canadian Depository for Securities, Citibank, Compaq, Dell Computer Corporation, Eaton Corporation, Fidelity Investment, Ford, HSBC, General Motors, General Electric, ING America, Lucent Technologies, Microsoft, Nike, Nortel Networks, Prudential Insurance USA, Qwest, SAAB, Swisscom, Singapore Airlines, Texas Instruments, and SIS (SegaInterSettle).

The company has about 2,20,000 members in its diverse and widespread family. The group's many pioneering initiatives to benefit and empower employees have few parallels anywhere in the world and it has blended its traditional benevolence with evolving human resource methodologies to deliver a lot more than mere jobs.

Maitree is a 60,000 friendship and support network for TCS employees who are working at various locations around the world. This constitutes more than 36,000 employees, including some 1500 foreign nationals, working in offices spread across 32 countries on five continents. Binding these people from Asia's largest software company together is Maitree. Maitree means 'friendship' in a host of Indian languages and acts as friend, guide, and counsellor for the families of TCS employees. It started in February 2002, when Mala Ramadorai, an educationist with long years of experience, decided to start an organization to connect and support the spouses of many TCSers who had to adjust to an entirely different culture at short notice. Ms Ramadorai felt that many ladies just wanted to talk to someone and share their experiences and problems.

Maitree started as a forum where the wives of TCSers on foreign postings could get together for social gatherings and share their concerns such as finding good schools for their children, the best place to shop for Indian groceries, and understanding the local language. It has now blossomed into a 60,000-strong network and plays an integral part in the lives of TCSers and their spouses.

The activities of Maitree fulfil needs at different levels and cut across various age groups, involving employees, their spouses, children, and even parents. TCSers, who work long hours and whose hobbies have to take a backseat owing to work demands, love these extra-curricular initiatives. Yoga classes, theatre workshops, flower-arrangement sessions, ballroom dancing classes, computer workshops— Maitree offers something for everyone. TCS helps in providing relocation assistance and foreign language courses, besides conducting classes in Maths and Hindi for employees posted overseas. 'At the India day we conducted at the Amsterdam office, we presented sarees to the wives of our clients. This helped to break the cultural divide and we now have a Yahoo! Group, which links all the overseas TCS community. Recently, we brought the US and Latin American office into the fold,' adds Mala Ramadorai.

It is said that the family that plays together stays together. Maitree is striving to ensure that the unusually large TCS family stays in touch through sharing of experiences, dissemination of information, and most importantly, friendship.

Source: Adapted from Pandey (2004).

Managing Teams

The globalization of firms and tendencies towards outsourcing offers new challenges for firms. There is a need to manage multi-cultural teams and also manage the expectations of virtual teams. As the firms are expanding global operations, they have employees from different countries who have to work with each other. The managers should be sensitive to cultural differences. Having more teams in an organization will lead to a flatter organization structure.

Teams can be defined as small groups of people committed to a common purpose, who possess complimentary skills, and who have agreed on specific performance goals for which the teams holds itself mutually accountable (Katznebach and Smith 1994).

Gordon (2002) quotes Birch (2001) on enumerating the factors contributing to the success of the team. These are:

- clear goals
- defined roles for each member
- open and clear communication
- effective decision-making
- balanced participation
- valued diversity
- managed conflict
- atmosphere
- cooperative relationships
- participative leadership.

Benefits of teamworking West (2004) enumerates on the benefits of working as a team:

- Teams enable organizations to learn more effectively. When one member leaves, the learning of the team is not lost.
- The diverse range of skills and knowledge of team members can be deployed for creating more effective organizations.
- Teamwork can lead to financial benefits. A synchronized team effort contributes to efficiency and quality, which can impact the bottom line of a firm.
- Change can be easier to implement in an organization where teams work efficiently.

Employees who work in effective teams report lower levels of stress. A sense of support is generated within teams, as members share their struggle. Stress is reduced because team members share their struggles and successes. There is greater clarity on roles as team colleagues help in clarifying what those roles are. Team workers have commented on the satisfaction gained by each one learning from the other.

There can be different types of teams such as:

- production and service teams
- project and development teams
- advise and involvement teams
- crews
- action and negotiation teams.

Jassawalla and Sashittal (1999) in their work on cross-functional teams indicate that though some teams have improved new product processes, in many organizations not all work equally well nor are they collaborative. In a study they conducted of 40 managers across areas such as R&D, production, and marketing functions in 10 firms, there were certain challenges, which they faced such as:

- functional–hierarchical designs
- rigid perceptual and spatial boundaries among the functional group
- differences in priorities and agendas resulting in turf protection behaviours
- errors and re-work
- chronic cost escalations
- missed deadlines.

Globally, virtual teams (teams located across different geographical locations) are playing an increasingly important role in international business by offering organizations the opportunity for reaching beyond traditional boundaries (Pauleen and Yoong 2001). While information and communication technologies present real and compelling challenges to facilitators, they also present teams with unparalleled opportunities for expanding on new approaches and ideas. There is, however little research on the effects of crossing organizational, cultural, and time and distance boundaries on relationship building in virtual teams.

As outsourcing becomes important, there may be cultural issues and coordination issues involving teamwork. As indicated in Table 12.1, Pauleen and Yoong (2001) have summed up the issues in managing boundary-crossing (crossing barriers of time and space) virtual teams:

To ensure success in team-based designs such as software, hospitality, and other project-based service firms, certain aspects need to be kept in mind. For example, Callanan (2004) has suggested certain recommendations to ensure success in organizations using team-based designs. These are:

1. Adopt an empowerment philosophy in leadership. The organizational leaders must disallow the Machiavellian philosophy that rewards the hoarding of power and information, and instead adopt an empowerment philosophy. This has implications on the recruitment, selection, and development process of the competencies that support the empowerment. To be empowered, employees should have sufficient amount of maturity, experience, and knowledge. For this, the recruitment strategy of the firm should be appropriate. Power in the wrong hands can be disastrous for a service firm.

2. Help leaders overcome the 'fear of irrelevance'. Major impediments to empowerment and success of team-based designs are leaders who fear loss of power. Training imparted to leaders helps them to overcome these fears.

3. Build on successes but see failure as a learning opportunity. Establishing an empowerment philosophy does not happen without conscious efforts. Organizations need to avoid the temptation to view failures as discrediting empowerment in total. Instead, failure should be viewed as future opportunities.

Table 12.1 Summary of boundary-crossing issues and facilitator responses when building relationships

Boundary	Issues	Organizational and facilitator responses	Effect on facilitating relationships
Organization	Differing organizational cultures and policies	Recognize differences and harmonize them whenever possible	The greater the differences, the greater the complexity in relationship-building processes, and more the time needed
	Availability of appropriate communication options	See time and distance below	
Cultural/ Language	Different cultures and languages leading to misunderstandings, distortions, attribution bias, etc.	Offer relevant training, create explicit understanding of processes and protocols, build shared contexts and trust	As above, plus may need upfront and regular face-to-face contact and use of richer media in general
Time and distance	Dealing with technology breakdowns and incompatibilities	Use universal systems, support cross-platform solutions, encourage back-up systems	Must skilfully choose and use available communication channels for crossing organizational, cultural, and technological boundaries
	Arranging times for synchronous meetings	Share 'inconveniences'	
	Pacing asynchronous exchanges	Set expectations and communication protocols	

Source: Adapted from Pauleen and Yoong (2001).

4. Foster initiative and the acceptance of responsibility. Organizations often fail to recognize that empowerment and a team-based structure will work only if members of the organization are willing to be empowered and to participate in teams and workgroups.

Training and Development

Training is a strategic activity in the services industry as it can be deployed as a tool to create relevant skill sets in people and can contribute towards creating a distinct experience for the people. The availability of required quality and quantity of human resource and maintenance of such employment through training would be HR's strategic response to the worldwide changes that are taking place. In today's world, there is a need to follow the principle 'innovation-training-development-action-sustainable-growth' with true concern for the meaningful development of human society as a whole (Jain and Agrawal 2005).

Jain and Agrawal (2005) have quoted the Buckley and Caple (2000) approach to training and development (Fig. 12.3).

In their analysis of training practices in Indian firms, Jain and Agrawal (2005) indicate that though focus is on the analysis and design, the 'evaluation of training' has been

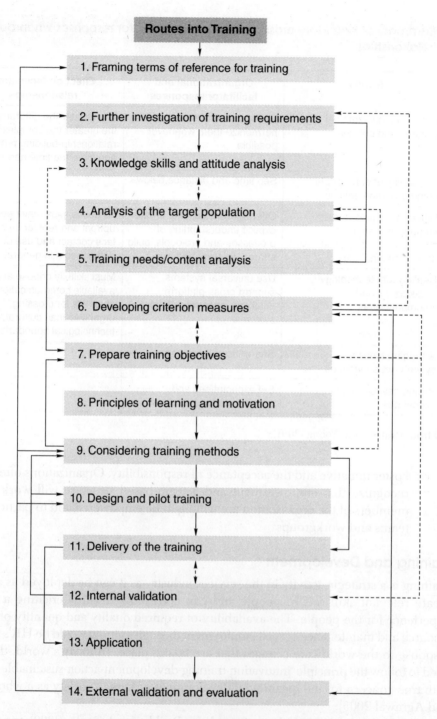

Routes into Training

1. Framing terms of reference for training

2. Further investigation of training requirements

3. Knowledge skills and attitude analysis

4. Analysis of the target population

5. Training needs/content analysis

6. Developing criterion measures

7. Prepare training objectives

8. Principles of learning and motivation

9. Considering training methods

10. Design and pilot training

11. Delivery of the training

12. Internal validation

13. Application

14. External validation and evaluation

Source: Adapted from Buckley and Caple (2000).

Fig. 12.3   A systematic approach to training

largely ignored. The internal evaluation by professionals and practitioners should be predominant over the ritual type evaluation by system administrators from outside. According to ASTD, in 1997, only 52 per cent of organizations used self-directed data and most organizations train their teams, training only 1 per cent of their employees. Only a very small proportion of employees actually get trained. The actual numbers may be large but in percentage terms this number would be a small proportion of the total number of employees. See Appendix 1 for a detailed view on the evaluation of training programmes.

Experiential learning through internships helps to train the upcoming workforce to better understand the organization and industry. Internships also immensely facilitate students to mature from academic knowledge to applied working knowledge. 'The internship experience provides students with meaningful experiences applying theories and practices discussed and sometimes applied in the classroom. The implications and influences of workplace are far more extensive than the limits and boundaries imposed by the classroom, peers, and instructors. The environmental, social, and cultural conditions of the workplace can help the students identify their own strengths, interests, and abilities' (Tovey 2001). It can also be inferred that an internship experience is meaningful for both the students as well as for the industry, as they can benefit from the skills, strategies, and innovative approaches that students carry from their experience. Training with an organization can add to the hiring process, as the trainee is already aware of the work ethics, culture, and capabilities that exist in the organization.

It is important to ensure that training and development activities initiated in a firm are relevant to a service firm. Training is a resource extensive exercise and if training is not relevant to employees and the firm's needs, then the desired objective of an enhanced service delivery will not be achievable. The training conducted in a firm should be addressed appropriately. Kirkpatrick (1967, 1987, 1994) suggests the following framework for evaluation of training.

1. Reaction (Level 1)
   - What was the trainees' response to the programme?
   - Did the trainees find it useful?
   - Seeking a reaction from trainees is not enough.
2. Learning (Level 2)
   - Did the trainees learn what they should have learnt? This is important and any effect HRD programme should be assessed on this parameter.
3. Job Behaviour (Level 3)
   - Does the trainee use what was learned in training back on the job? Measuring whether training has transferred to the job requires observation of the trainee's on-the-job behaviour.
4. Results
   - Has the training or HRD effort improved the organization's effectiveness?
   - Is the organization more efficient and profitable? This is the most challenging level to assess, given that many things beyond employee performance can affect organizational performance.

Zeithaml and Bitner (2003) have argued that people have to be developed to deliver service quality. There is a need for taking initiatives such as:

- train for technical and interactive skills
- empower employees
- promote teamwork.

These various issues raise the question of how firms should develop an optimal education and training programme. It appears that educational institutions such as universities or professional training institutes are the most appropriate source for providing generic knowledge. This does not mean that the delivery of this training is dependent on these institutions. Firms, for example, could arrange for staff to complete distance based or e-learning programmes.

Exhibit 12.4 indicates some of the training initiatives undertaken by some well-known corporate firms. The ideas range from instituting corporate universities to simulations.

Exhibit 12.5 gives an idea about the scope of operations of training activities in the world's second largest railway, which is Indian Railways. Over 2,00,000 people are trained every year in their training facilities. Service firms should develop the capabilities to train their employees to ensure a distinct experience.

Exhibit 12.6 enumerates the training experiences at Walt Disney. To create memorable service experiences for its customers a lot of investment is made in training the employees. (Exhibit 12.6) documents the initiatives at Walt Disney.

Exhibit 12.7 documents training initiatives at TCS.

Exhibit 12.4 Training initiatives across corporations

Burton–Jones (2001) have enumerated on the framework for developing education and training in the new economy.

Tacit and firm specific knowledge cannot be completely provided by external learning institutions. For this type of training, other methods need to be investigated. One option is for firms to develop collaborative relationships with educational institutions that would enable the institutions to provide, if not fully firm-specific, at least more industry-specific training. Ford, GM, and Chrysler, for example, in conjunction with industry and union representatives and a local university, have established the Michigan Virtual Automotive College, to raise levels of industry-specific education among automotive industry workers (Probst et al. 2000).

Other methods available are to implement their own internal learning programmes designed to foster the transfer and development of specialized tacit knowledge. Such initiatives may include formal mentoring, coaching, storytelling, simulation of on-the-job tasks, and encouraging the development of communities of interest and practice. Firms can designate each member of the core group as mentors for one or more members of the associate group. They can also establish storytelling sessions where experienced staff members discuss assignments and lessons learned 'on-the-job'. Management consulting firm McKinsey, formed internal groups of experts called 'practices' to collect and distill experience gained in particular fields such as manufacturing and energy, and to communicate industry and project specific knowledge to others in the firm. Xerox Corporation, having discovered its representatives' habit of exchanging information about issues while maintaining photocopiers, facilitated the practice by providing network infrastructure and tools for recording and disseminating their experiences. The payback from nurturing these informal exchanges of tacit, on-the-job knowledge across the corporation has reportedly saved Xerox $100 million a year in maintenance costs (Brown and Duguid 2000).

Source: Adapted from Jones (2001).

Exhibit 12.5 Training initiatives at Indian Railways

The Indian railway system is the second largest railway system in the world under a single management. Indian Railways has 1,08,706 track kms (63,028 route kms), 7,500 locomotives, 2,22,147 units of freight cars, 42,750 passenger cars, 6,853 stations, and 15,45,300 staff. It operates 8,520 passenger trains every day.

Apart from having its own facilities for production of automotives and other rolling stock and a research design and standard wing to carry out research work in railway technology, standardization, and application to self-sufficiency, Indian Railways has the best training facilities, in Asia and Africa, to train people in rail transport.

Training is considered the most common mechanism in human resource development. It is actually a process that attempts to fill the gap by way of what the employee has to offer. This is done by way of honing the skills, experience, and knowledge that is required on the job. Following are a few institutes to train executives responsible for maintenance, operation, planning, development of infrastructure, and assets at the Indian Railways:

- Railway Staff College, Vadodara
- Indian Railway Institute of Civil Engineering, Pune
- Indian Railway Institute of Signal Engineering and Telecommunications, Secunderabad
- Indian Railway Institute of Mechanical and Electrical Engineering, Jabalpur

Besides these, there are another 200 training schools located over zonal railways to provide training to supervisors and staff engaged in operations and management.

Source: http://www.rites.com/web/images/stories/guide.pdf#s.

Exhibit 12.6 Learning initiatives at Walt Disney

The Walt Disney Company was founded in 1923 and has remained faithful in its commitment to produce unparalleled entertainment experiences based on its rich legacy of quality creative content and exceptional storytelling. Disney is divided into four major business segments—Studio Entertainment, Parks and Resorts, Consumer Products, and Media Networks. Each segment consists of integrated, well-connected businesses that operate in order to maximize exposure and growth worldwide.

Walt Disney Parks and Resorts, opened in a lot of cities worldwide, are where the magic lives and are home to Disney's beloved characters. The segment traces its roots to 1952, when Walt Disney formed what is now known as Walt Disney Imagineering to build Disneyland in Anaheim, California. Today, Walt Disney Parks and Resorts operates or licenses 10 theme parks on three continents. The eleventh park is currently under construction in Hong Kong, along with 35 resort hotels, two luxury cruise ships, and a wide variety of other entertainment offerings at various destinations across the state. The locations of the five Disney destinations around the world, all dedicated to the best in innovative entertainment are as follows:

- Disneyland Resort, Anaheim, California
- Walt Disney World Resort, Lake Buena Vista, Florida
- Tokyo Disney Resort, Urayasu, Chiba
- Disneyland Resort Paris, Marne La Valle, France
- Hong Kong Disneyland, Penny's Bay, Lantau Island

The Walt Disney Company knows that their employees and cast members make the magic happen. Their brands are innovative, entertaining, and inviting, and create a similar learning environment that encourages employees to learn and develop themselves in engaging and empowering ways.

The Walt Disney Company has a number of training programmes and learning opportunities for

Contd

Exhibit 12.6 Contd

its imaginative and bright employees and these are designed to build the capabilities of its employees and cast members around the world. These include:

- Disney programmes
- new hire orientation
- Disney Dimensions, an executive development programme
- Disney Way 1, designed to showcase the various Disney businesses to managers and above
- Disney ethics, integrity, and diversity programmes

- professional development
- management/leadership development
- computer skills.

In addition to the above, the company provides educational reimbursement for full-time employees and cast members. They are also in the process of developing an exciting e-learning programme, which will allow their employees and cast members around the world to access learning opportunities at their convenience.

Source: Walt Disney (2006), http://corporate.disney.go.com/ accessed on 5 December 2006.

Exhibit 12.7   Training initiatives at TCS

Working with TCS is an experience in itself. Apart from being enlightening and enriching, the organization is now making it better than ever before for its worldwide family of employees.

Currently, about 6,000 people, many of them local recruits, work for TCS in foreign countries. This is a great change from the late 1990s, when the workforce, although globally mobile, was still largely Indian.

Generally, TCS employs local people with 15–20 years of experience at senior positions. As part of the training, the foreign talent is brought to India and taught the values that TCS stands for. The employees are also imparted knowledge of industries such as banking, insurance, manufacturing, and healthcare, so that they can get a feel of the organization.

Most of the work of TCS is done in India, as this is where its largest team is based. This translates into very good cost advantages for clients. Sometimes, the work is executed at the client's site. This is done when the client has to be directly involved in matters such as specifications, requirements, design validation, or implementation.

TCS encourages the people in charge of the development to take over the implementation. This way, the knowledge that the teams gain can be put back into the implementation. Therefore, movement of people becomes extremely important. But in countries where English isn't the main language,

it is important to have people who have an IT background, understand the value proposition, and can express it in the local language.

As far as marketing is concerned, it makes sense to have technologists who can conceive a situation and market it, rather than front-end marketing people who can only create the initial opening in a given environment.

TCS had created a marketing stream with senior people to size up large projects. The focus was on big clients. This enabled the organization to make a real difference and offer end-to-end services. One of the ways in which this has been achieved is through the establishment of offshore and onsite centres. Offshore work is popular as clients can get their work done without having to worry about space or communication links. Besides, it does not require local employees. TCS has 10 offshore centres across the globe with about 50 people in each. There are six each in Canada and the United States and one in Britain.

Developers are given the necessary training, while new recruits are sent to Thiruvananthapuram for a four-month course, before being transferred to a work location—Chennai for IBM mainframes, Delhi for open systems, and Mumbai for e-business. A month's training in the relevant technology area follows this.

Foreign recruits are put through the same kind of training. The only difference is that instead of four

Contd

Exhibit 12.7 Contd

months in Thiruvananthapuram, they spend only six weeks there. Sometimes, the training is conducted in the new recruit's home country. Part of the training consists of soft skills and information on how to work in a global environment. Also, foreign recruits are taught to be India-sensitive.

A movement called 'Propel' has now been initiated at TCS. This initiative comprises of conferences and camps that help people conduct group meetings, transfer their learning as a best practice, and make a difference to the company in a better and smarter way.

In addition to the above, every experienced employee is encouraged to spend at least 20 days each year in TCS's continuing education programme, which mainly focuses on developing technical and managerial skills, as each role has clearly defined competencies. Therefore, any person moving to a new role has to go through the relevant training programmes.

The first-level management education teaches people how to manage in a TCS environment, through the framework of the Tata business excellence model. They then go through all the seven categories and learn about customer relationship models, managing by data, process orientation, and the way the company motivates and energizes people.

Management education beyond the project-leader level, attempts to provide an MBA type of education

to people. Link-ups with select management institutes that provide an executive MBA programme can be customized for senior people. These technical and management education programmes are critical for an employees' overall growth.

The growth prospects of foreign and local recruits are exactly the same. Typically, at TCS one begins as a team member, becomes a specialist, a project leader, and then a manager. From here, people can move to higher levels in managing various practices. The culture of the organization is oriented towards competence and skills, and towards satisfying clients.

The appraisal happens on the basis of performance. For example, SPEED is an internet-based performance management system, which allows employees to adopt practices that they can retain. This is necessary as TCS is a flat organization where people move from one place to another.

Total incentives at TCS are distributed in such a way that 50 per cent goes towards improvement in corporate performance, 30 per cent for business unit performances, and 20 per cent for individual performances.

Today, TCS has truly become a global organization. It encourages people to believe in themselves, set their own goals, and drive themselves. What it promises them is the right environment to enhance their abilities and make a difference to the organization.

Source: Adapted from Tata Sons. http:// www.tatasons.com/tcs, accessed on 10 December 2006.

Rewards

The best people need to be retained and rewarded. They should set up pace and also the role models for others to emulate. Employees should also be treated as internal customers and should be incorporated in the vision of the firm. It is essential that an adequate reward system be in place.

To institute the right reward system in an organization, it is essential to have the right measurement systems in place in the organization. If the performance measurement systems are not appropriate then the rewards will not be fair, and cannot discriminate between performers and non-performers. Also, the system and the top management must handle the appraisal fairly. It is important not only to be fair, but also to be perceived as being fair. It is of great importance that the systems and processes are in place, if the people have to be retained and rewarded appropriately. For instance, in many start-up corporations, multi-tasking is done and interdepartmental teams are quite common. At the time of attributing rewards it becomes difficult to attribute and recognize individual effort. In certain corporations, team rewards are instituted to encourage team effort and to motivate the employees.

There are numerous instances where organizations have instituted numerous awards for retaining and attracting better talent. However, it is important that individual effort is recognized, as individual identity is important to each person.

Exhibit 12.8 documents the employee benefits that are offered at one of the most innovative airlines in the world, which has been profitable year after year since its inception.

Exhibit 12.8   Training initiatives at Southwest Airlines

An excellent and effective employee training programme is the key to the success of an organization. Examples of such effective training programmes can be witnessed in the case of Southwest Airlines. This airline company is committed to providing its employees a stable work environment, with equal opportunity for learning and personal growth. Employees are encouraged to be creative and innovative and are an important factor in improving the effectiveness of Southwest Airlines. The website states that, 'Above all, employees will be provided the same concern, respect, and caring attitude within the organization that they are expected to share externally with every Southwest customer.'

The employees of Southwest Airlines have access to the following privileges. This also creates a sense of ownership among employees.

Passes/Travel Privileges
Employees can travel for free. This privilege is effective from the first day of employment. Employees, their spouses, eligible dependent children, and parents have unlimited space-available travel privileges on Southwest. They also have discounted travel arrangements with other carriers through the Southwest Airlines Pass Bureau, subject to eligibility requirements and other restrictions.

Profit Sharing and 401(k) Plan
Participation in the profit sharing plan is offered to all eligible employees. Company contributions to profit sharing accounts, which are made when the company meets profitability goals set each year, funds the plan.

The 401(k) plan is designed to help employees to prepare for the future. Eligible employees may contribute up to 50 per cent of their pay to the plan,

on a pre-tax basis. A company match is offered based on employee groups. Rollovers are accepted from the employee's former employer's qualified plan.

Stock Purchase Plan
This plan is specially designed to allow employees to share in the success of the company. Through this plan, employees may invest in Southwest Airlines stock through payroll deductions. Employees pay only 90 per cent of the market value for the stock, while the company pays broker commissions on stock purchases.

Medical Insurance
Employees may choose from several different medical plan options depending on their lifestyle, needs, and priorities. Most medical plan options are available to employees at no cost, with family coverage available at minimal cost.

Dental Insurance
Dental coverage is also offered through several dental plan options and basic dental coverage is available to employees at no cost. Optional additions and family coverage are available at minimal cost.

Vision
Vision coverage is offered to provide affordable vision care for employees and their families. Coverage under the vision plan includes complete eye examinations and lenses and frames, or contact lenses. Under some plans, vision coverage is available only to certain workgroups.

Life Insurance
Southwest Airlines employees are provided with a basic life insurance at no cost. Coverage is based on annual salary.

Contd

Exhibit 12.8 Contd

Sick Leave, Vacation, and Holidays

Depending on employment classifications, employees are able to accrue time off for personal illness and vacation. Employees celebrate several paid holidays throughout the calendar, based on their employment classifications.

Other Benefits

Other benefits such as long-term disability insurance, dependant care spending account, healthcare spending account, adoption assistance reimbursement benefit, child and elder care resource and referral programme, mental health chemical dependency employee assistance programme are provided to employees.

Source: Adapted from Southwest Airlines (2006).

Stars of the Month

Each month Southwest Airlines selects an outstanding employee to be the star of the month, in Southwest Airlines Spirit Magazine. Their 31,000 employees have a special quality—Southwest Spirit—which has helped Southwest Airlines to earn five consecutive Triple Crowns in 1992, 1993, 1994, 1995, and 1996, for the best baggage handling, fewest customer complaints, and best on-time performance, according to statistics published in the Department of Transportation (DOT) air travel consumer reports.

Job Security

Providing a climate of trust is essential for a firm. It is even more important in case of a service firm, as there is a huge amount of interdepartmental coordination, which is required. A feeling of trust can be evoked if the organization has a specific direction and owns up to its commitments. The employees have to be truly treated as stakeholders in the organization. Lack of trust at the workplace, triggers the desire to look for alternative assignments. This leads to poor performance and non-commitment to tasks at hand. Hence, it is essential that open systems be created for employees to share their feelings and be able to contribute and take up feedback positively. In the Indian hotel industry, attrition rates are high for certain brands as the management feels that there is no need for sharing the profitability status, and there are no forums for employees to discuss job-related stresses and issues with their managers. When discussion is perceived as being judgmental, then employees' perception about the system is that it is close, and hence, they would not want to be a part of it, if given a choice.

The public explanation as to why Starbucks is so successful, as suggested by Howard Schultz, who with David Olsen acquired Starbucks in 1987 from its founders, is that the company is absolutely dedicated to brewing the best cup of coffee in the world. It acquires its own coffee beans, roasts and grinds them, and has strict controls on temperatures at which each specialty drink is mixed and served. It also enjoys tremendous publicity for the way it treats employees, backing up its idea that happy employees treat customers well. It offers stock options to full-time employees and medical benefits even to part-timers. It ranks third on the *Fortune 2005* list of 100 best companies to work for (*Fortune* 2005).

SUMMARY

People management is an important part of management in the services industry. It is essential that people are cared for and are treated as internal customers. Managing people component is challenging as, to provide similar level of experiences people have to be trained well in systems, processes, and responses. The success of the firm to a large extent depends on the quality of people the firm has. The availability of labour or external manpower determines the kind of people that get hired by the firm. An overview of the labour market and how it affects availability of manpower is discussed. This chapter also discusses service culture and its impact on customer satisfaction. The factors contributing to service excellence are discussed along with an overview on the relationship between employee satisfaction, customer satisfaction, and the overall profitability of the firm.

The following factors play an important role in creating the right service culture in the organization: recruitment, retention, team work, training and development, rewards, and job security.

All these processes have to be managed judiciously to have the right people in the jobs. They have to be trained well so that there is a uniformity of service experience. Caring for employees and investing in their development will lead to higher retention, saving costs for the firm and hiring for replacement. Fostering team work is a pre-requisite for a successful service firm. The rewards and recognition keep the employees motivated. Investments will have to be made in recruitment, training, and development, team building, and creating a sense of trust in employees, for lasting success.

KEY TERMS

Customer satisfaction When the service delivery by an organization matches with the customer's expectation, it leads to customer satisfaction.

Job security Providing a climate of trust to the employees, treating employees as true stakeholders in the firm, and owning up to its commitments provides a sense of job security to the employees.

Labour market An informal market where workers find paying work, employers find willing workers, and where wage rates are determined. Labour markets may be local or national (even international) in their scope and are made up of smaller, interacting labour markets for different qualifications, skills, and geographical locations.

Recruitment Process of identifying and hiring the best-qualified candidate (from within or outside an organization) for a job vacancy, in a most timely and cost-effective manner.

Rewards Something that is offered or given in return for some service or attainment.

Teamwork Cooperative or coordinated effort on the part of a group of persons acting together as a team or in the interests of a common cause.

Training and development The field concerned with workplace learning to improve performance. Such training can be generally categorized as on-the-job or off-the-job.

CONCEPT REVIEW QUESTIONS

1. Evaluate the role of employees in service delivery.

2. Discuss critically the relationship between employee satisfaction, customer satisfaction, and profitability of the firm.

3. How can training and development contribute to effective service delivery?
4. How can teamwork be instituted in a service firm?
5. Evaluate service culture of a firm with examples.
6. How does the labour market have an impact on the people management issues in a service firm?
7. What are the characteristics of weak labour markets?
8. How can rewards be instituted as motivators in a service firm?

CRITICAL THINKING QUESTIONS

1. There is a restaurant with 20 tables with as many as 10 staff allocated for these tables. There are just about four tables that are occupied during lunch, which is served as a buffet arrangement. However, during service, there is little eye contact with the staff. The guests have to wait for 10 minutes to have a refill of water. Food is not replenished in the buffet without asking.

   a. Analyse the service culture of the restaurant.

   b. What interventions can be initiated to change the attitude of the staff?

2. A woman boards an aircraft with hand baggage. She tries to stack it on the luggage bin but is unable to do so independently. Aircraft crew standing close by do not help her. The woman requests the crew. The lady crew responds, 'Stand up on the chair and then keep the baggage.' Bewildered by the response, the guest just stares at her. Then she remarks, 'I will never fly this airline again.'

   What is the HR issue in this context? How can the airline avoid such encounters?

3. A tourist takes a boat ride as part of an itinerary and at one of the destinations the boat starts leaking and passengers are advised to get off. The tourist is stranded with no response from the captain or the firm.

   Discuss the critical people management issues related to this episode.

4. In an aircraft, the crew is serving the meals and the staff is clumsy. While the meal is being served, the coffee spills over one of the guests. There is little apology on the part of the crew. Will the guest want a future association with the airline?

INTERNET EXERCISES

1. Identify any two firms operating in a similar service industry. Browse through their website. Critically compare the HR concerns and compare employee orientation in the two firms.

2. Search for firms that have received global appreciation for service excellence. (Hint: You may look at firms that have international awards such as Malcolm Baldridge or European Award for Quality Management.)

3. Identify two firms in India and China that have been identified as the 'Best places to work'. What are the similarities and dissimilarities?

4. Evaluate the leadership in two firms in India and Europe in service industries such as banks, hotels, and airlines. Compare and contrast them on HR aspects.

CASE STUDY

Relationship between employee satisfaction, customer satisfaction, and market share—the case of Hewlett–Packard*

HP's operations in India started in the year 1988 under the leadership of Suresh Rajpal. According to him, the making of an excellent organization consists of two very important aspects—employee satisfaction and customer satisfaction. Traditionally, literature has pointed very strongly towards customer satisfaction. However, in HP, it has been a belief that customer satisfaction is not possible without employee satisfaction. The following paradigm indicated in Fig. 12.4, is proposed for a growth in the market share.

For an employee to be satisfied, job satisfaction is extremely important. To achieve job satisfaction one must have the right skills and the other factor that becomes important is the satisfaction with the job. If the score on satisfaction with the job and satisfaction with the right skills is high, it will contribute to enhanced employee satisfaction. When employee satisfaction is high, productivity is high and the cost of quality is low. A high satisfaction level leads to an enhanced market share, which further reinforces employee satisfaction.

Fig. 12.5 indicates the trend in the growth of the market share, employee satisfaction, and customer satisfaction in Hewlett-Packard over a period of five years. The graph indicates a similar trend in all the three cases. The data taken for this graph is only for the medical equipment division.

Initiatives for Employee Satisfaction

HP has taken a number of steps to satisfy their employees. There is a proactive HR department, which treats all the other departments as its internal customers. The HR division has identified for itself a mission statement to promote innovation and a feeling of competitiveness in its employees in order to enhance their performance, while contributing to organization goals. There are five values that are considered to be sacrosanct. These are trust, teamwork, integrity, innovation, and high achievement. The desirable objectives are profitability, employee care, and customer care. Not only are these values treasured, but also

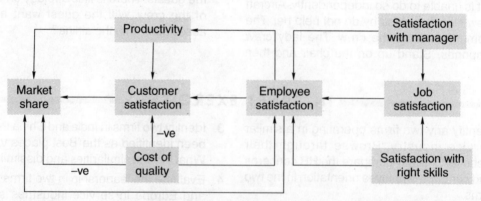

Source: Jauhari (2000).

Fig. 12.4   Relationship between employee satisfaction, customer satisfaction, and market share

---

*Jauhari, Vinnie, *Journal of Services Research*, vol. 1, no. 1, April–September 2001. Published with the permission of *Journal of Services Research*.

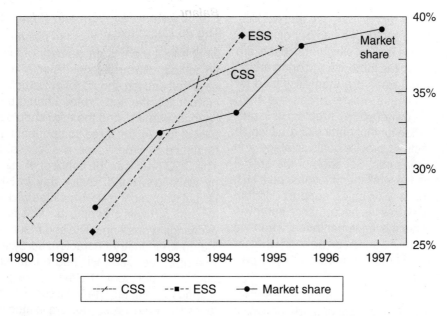

Source: Jauhari (2000).

Fig. 12.5 Relationship between customer satisfaction, employee satisfaction, and market share

the element of institutionalization is very high through the deployment of different strategies in different areas. This is achieved by communication of these values to the employees and demonstration of these values in their day-to-day behaviour.

When the new CEO, Carly Fiorina took charge of HP in July 1999, she drove the new HP Invent global campaign. This consists of a charter called 'The rules of the garage', which has been circulated to every employee and is in front of them all the time, so that there is a constant drive towards achievement, and a culture of entrepreneurship is created in an organization. The behaviour is reinforced by linking the performance of an individual to his growth in the organization. Every employee has to demonstrate these key values and the performance measurement system tracks down all these aspects. The culture in the organization is very open. The communication systems are open, the sitting spaces are open, there are only glass panels; and there are instances when call escalations have reached

the CEO, Carly, herself. That is the extent of the reach to the top.

Whenever a new employee joins the organization, the values are communicated to him at the time of induction within the organization. The HR manager views each of the business areas as an account. He maintains an ongoing dialogue with the different accounts, and identifies their needs and reverts back to them after getting the expert's advice. The vision of the HR department is to achieve a higher level of employee satisfaction, higher level of satisfaction with the HR department, and a decline in the attrition rate of the organization.

A de-motivated, unenthusiastic, and unhappy employee will never care for the customers. Also, organizations willing to spend money when they are doing well should spend on employees more, rather than less, when things get bad. An employee satisfaction survey is carried out regularly on an ongoing basis. In the employee satisfaction survey, input is taken on a number of parameters such as management, supervision, communication job, recognition, pay, and worklife, among other factors. Out of a number of issues, the top three to five issues, which are critical are identified, and also the three least scoring areas. The least scoring areas are then assessed for their criticality. These critical areas are then passed on to the owners of the problem who prepare a Hoshin Plan for that particular area which consists of objectives, precise goals, strategy, and performance measures. So, each of the critical areas is addressed in all the functions, be it HR, finance, production, or sales support. Hoshin plans are made so that the performance improves considerably. After the implementation, when the survey is again carried out, it can be seen whether there is an improvement in the score on a particular parameter.

Training needs are continuously assessed for every employee. Assessment is made on which training programmes are essential to do the current job well, which programmes are essential to grow to the next level, and to determine the unique strengths of an individual which can be deployed usefully by the organization. Every six months, an employee survey is conducted that is kept confidential. The questionnaires are filled and sent to the corporate HQ directly. Regular feedback is also given to the employees regarding the steps that are being taken to check the discrepancies, if any.

Some of the initiatives taken by the top management are as follows.

Right Genetic Code

It is an organization whose genetic code is right. This means that the value system is in place and there is a shared vision. Even the mailroom boy knows about his operational objectives. Every employee's performance is measured and synchronized with the organization's performance. The yardstick for performance measurement is absolutely fixed and one knows how one's performance is going to be measured at the end of the year. Every individual within the organization knows about his growth path at a particular level. He is even aware of skills and knowledgebase required to move to the next level.

Balance Between Work and Private Life

The workplace has to be a fun place. One enjoys work only if there is an element of fun. Drawing an analogy of a three-legged stool, Suresh Rajpal says that one leg should reflect excellence in the current job, the second leg should be the continuous learning, and the third should be having a lot of fun. All the three components need to be balanced in order to be a successful person. The CEO practices the concept of management by walking around. Every day in HP, Suresh Rajpal would spend 40–5 minutes walking around the office, calling people by first names, and exchanging greetings. The end result was amazing. In an industry characterized by an attrition rate of 25 per cent, HP had an attrition rate of about 3.8 per cent. It even has a programme named Alumni, targeted at people who have left for greener pastures. They are invited over at HP parties and informed about the current achievements of HP. Eighty per cent of people want to come back. They are still considered to be a part of the HP family.

Doing the Right Things

One should know what to say at the appropriate time. One should not tell people to do right things, but to find people doing the right things, thank them, and congratulate them. The bottleneck in most organizations is not people, but the leadership.

Making the Workplace a Fun Place

One needs to re-invent things to make the workplace a fun place. One way of getting a lot of ideas is to reward people who generate these ideas. HP capitalizes on these ideas and rewards employees who make useful contributions.

Creating Positive Surprises for the Customers

To create special surprises for the employees, every engineer, manager, and functional manager is given a certain budget every month to surprise others. For instance, Suresh Rajpal volunteered to surprise his employees by booking the entire theatre screening of the film, Titanic, for the weekend and handed out four tickets to each employee. The result was that everyone in the HP family was overwhelmed by the gesture and the CEO was flooded with thank-you mails and compliments.

Life Made Easy

Another aspect that is very unique is learning from one's mistakes and not looking at things in a conventional manner. One should not just be satisfied with one good answer, but continue with the quest for the next, best answer. Most people stop thinking when they arrive at the first best answer. Employees are given the flexibility to work at the hours of their choice, but are required to put in a requisite number of hours at the workplace. Productivity is not measured by the number of hours that one puts in, but by the actual contributions made by the employee. To ensure that the employee does not feel harassed about having to pay bills or undertake other personal chores, the organization has arranged for all these services to be taken care of on payment of a nominal amount of money. All the bills can be paid, repairs can be done, food can be ordered, and clothes laundered, just by picking up a phone and assigning the responsibility to an individual.

CII Excellence Award

HP India got the CII Business Excellence Award for the year 1997. The employee satisfaction in HP was 82 per cent whereas the norm in Asia was 50 per cent. The award is given after tracking the performance of the organization for five years, on different parameters, each of which carries a certain number of points. These parameters are divided into enablers and results.

Enablers comprise:

o leadership
o people policy deployment
o resources and partnership
o processes.

Results include parameters such as:

o employee satisfaction
o customer satisfaction
o society
o business results.

The measures indicated in the above paradigms clearly point out the importance of people management in achieving the service quality. It is necessary that people in the organization be committed to the service values. Excellent companies have seven core values in common—excellence, innovation, joy, teamwork, respect, integrity, and social profit (Berry 1992). The right culture instilled in an organization brings out an environment that helps people to unleash their creativity and potential. The culture is also reflected in the degree of empowerment.

Questions

1. In HP's context what has been the relationship between people orientation and profitability?

2. What are the lessons that other service firms can learn from the philosophy on people management?

SELECT REFERENCES

Beich, E. (2001), *The Pfeiffer Book of Successful Team Building*, Jose V-Bass/Pfeiffer, San Francisco.

Berry, L.L. (1999), *Discovering the Soul of Service: The Nine Drivers of Sustainable Business Success*, The Free Press, New York.

Berry, L.L. and N. Bendapudi (2003), 'Glueing-in customers', *Harvard Business Review*, vol. 81, no. 2, pp. 2–7.

Brinkerhoff, R.O. (1987), *Achieving Results from Training*, Jossey-Bass, San Francisco.

Buckley, R. and Jim Caple (2000), *A Systematic Approach to Training: The Theory and Practice of Training*, Kogan, Stylus Publishing Co., 4th edn, pp. 17–26, pp. 269–274.

Bushnell, D.S. (1990), 'Input, process, output: A model for evaluating training', *Training and Development Journal*, vol. 44, no. 3, pp. 41–43.

Callanan, G.A. (2004), 'What would Machiavelli think? An overview of the leadership challenges in team-based structures', *Team Performance Management*, Bradford, vol. 10, no. 3/4, p. 77.

Desimone, R.L., J.M. Werner, and D.M. Harris (2002), *Human Resource Development*, Thomson, Singapore.

Desimone, R.L., J.M. Werner, and D.M. Harris (2002), *Human Resource Development*, Thomson South Western, Bangalore.

Galvin, J.C. (1983), 'What trainers can learn from educators about evaluating management training', *Training and Development Journal*, vol. 37, no. 8, pp. 52–57.

Gordon, J. (2002), 'A perspective on team-building', *Journal of American Academy of Business*, Cambridge, Hollywood, vol. 2, no. 1.

Heskett, J.L. et al. (1994), 'Putting the service–profit chain to work', *Harvard Business Review*, March–April, p. 166.

Hesselink, M. and F. Van den Assem (2002), 'Building people and organizational excellence: The start service excellence programme', *Managing Service Quality*, vol. 12, no. 3, p. 139.

Hofstede, G. (1980), *Culture Consequences: International Differences in Work-related Values*, Sage, Beverly Hills, California.

Holton, E.F. III (1996), 'The flawed four-level evaluation model', *Human Resource Development Quarterly*, vol. 7, pp. 5–21.

Hoque, K. (1999), 'Human resource management and performance in the UK hotel industry', *British Journal of Industrial Relations*, vol. 37, no. 3, pp. 419–443.

Jain, R.K. and R. Agrawal (2005), 'Indian and international perspectives on employee training practices: A trend report', *South Asian Journal of Management*, New Delhi.

Jassawalla, A.R. and H.C. Sashittal (1999), 'Building collaborative cross-functional new product teams', *The Academy of Management Executive*, vol. 13, no. 3, p. 50.

Jones, G. (1997), 'Conference presentation', *Institute of Personnel and Development Conference*, Harrogate, October.

Katznebach, J.R. and D.K. Smith (1994), *The Wisdom of Teams: Creating the High Performance Organization*, Harper Business Book, US.

Kaufman, R. and J.M. Keller (1994), 'Levels of evaluation: Beyond Kirkpatrick', *Human Resource Development Quarterly*, vol. 5, pp. 371–380.

Kirkpatrick, D.L. (1967), 'Evaluation' in R.L. Craig and L.R. Bittel (eds), *Training and Development Handbook*, McGraw-Hill, New York, pp. 87–112.

Kirkpatrick, D.L. (1987), 'Evaluation', in R.L. Craig (ed), *Training and Development Handbook*, 3rd edn, McGraw-Hill, New York, pp. 301–319.

Kirkpatrick, D.L. (1994), *Evaluating Training Programmes: The Four Levels*, Berrett-Kochles, Warr, San Francisco.

Kirkpatrick, D.L. (1996), 'Invited reaction: Reaction to Holton article', *Human Resource Development Quarterly*, vol. 7, pp. 23–25.

Kraiger, K., J.K. Ford, and E. Salas (1993), 'Application of cognitive, skill based, and affective theories of learning outcomes to new methods of training evaluation', *Journal of Applied Psychology*, vol. 78, pp. 311–328.

Lashley, C. (1998), 'Matching the management of human resources to service operations', *International Journal of Contemporary Hospitality Management*, vol. 10, no. 1, pp. 24–33.

Leavitt, H.J. and H. Bahrami (1988), *Managerial Psychology*, University of Chicago Press, Chicago.

Leopold, J., L. Harris, and T. Watson (1999), 'Strategic human resourcing principles, perspectives and practices', *Financial Times*, Pitman Publishing, London.

Lucas, R. (2002), 'Fragments of HRM in hospitality? Evidence from the 1998 workplace employee relations survey', *International Journal of Contemporary Hospitality Management*, vol. 14, no. 5, pp. 207–212.

Miller, B.W. (1992), 'It's a kind of magic', *Managing Service Quality*, vol. 2, no. 4, pp. 191–193.

Muldrow, T.W., T. Buckley, and B.W. Schay (2002), 'Creating high-performance organizations in the public sector', *Human Resource Management*, vol. 41, no. 3, pp. 341–354.

Pauleen, D.J. and P. Yoong (2001), 'Relationship building and the use of ICT in boundary crossing virtual teams: A facilitated perspective', *Journal of Information Technology*, vol. 16, pp. 205–220.

Phillips, J.J. (1996), 'ROI: The search for the best practices', *Training and Development*, vol. 50, no. 2, pp. 43–47.

Pizam, J. (1993), 'Managing cross cultural hospitality enterprises', in Peter Jones and Pizam Abraham (eds), *International Hospitality Industry—Organizational and Operational Issues*, Longman Group, Essex, England.

Probst, G., S. Raub, and K. Romhardt (2000), *Managing Knowledge: Building Blocks for Success*, John Wiley & Sons, Chichester.

Redman, T. and Brian P. Mathews (1998), Service quality and human resource management: A review and research agenda', *Personnel Review*, vol. 27, no. 1, p. 57.

Riley, M. (1996), *Human Resource Management in the Hospitality and Tourism Industry*, Butterworth–Heinemann, Oxford.

Robson, J. (1993), 'Soaring to new heights', *Managing Service Quality*, January, pp. 465–468.

Schein, E. (1990), *Organizational Culture and Leadership*, Jossey Bass, San Francisco, California.

Schlesinger, L.J. and J.L. Heskett (1991), 'Breaking the cycle of failures in services', *Sloan Management Review*, vol. 32, no. 3, pp. 17–28.

Schneider, B. and D.E. Bowen (1985), 'Employee and customer perception of service in banks: Republication and extension', *Journal of Applied Psychology*, vol. 70, pp. 423–433.

Schneider, B. and D.E. Bowen (1995), *Winning the Service Game*, Harvard Business School Press, Boston, Massachusetts.

Seely, Brown J. and P. Duguid (2000), *The Social Life of Information*, Harvard Business School Press, Boston, Massachusetts.

Storey, J. (1989) (ed), *New Perspectives on HRM*, Routledge, London.

Storey, J. (1995), *Human Resource Management: A Critical Text*, Routledge, London.

Tayeb, M.H. (1987), 'Contingency theory and culture: A study of matched English and Indian manufacturing firms', *Organization Studies*, vol. 8, pp. 241–262.

Tayeb, M.H. (1995), 'The competitive advantage of nations: The role of HRM and its socio-cultural context', *International Journal of Human Resource Management*, vol. 6, pp. 588–605.

Tayeb, M.H. (1997), *The Management of Multicultural Work Force*, John Wiley and Sons, New York.

Tovey, J. (2001), 'Building connections between industry and university: Implementing an internship programme at a regional university', *Technical Communication Quarterly*, Spring 2001, vol. 10, no. 2, ABI/INFORM Global, p. 225.

Towers, T. (1994), *The Handbook of Human Resource Management*, Blackwell, Oxford.

Warr, P., M. Bird, and N. Rackham (1970), *Evaluation of Management Training*, Gower Press, London.

Watson, S. and N. D'Annunzio-Green (1996), 'Implementing cultural change through human resources: The elusive organizational alchemy', *International Journal of Contemporary Hospitality Management*, vol. 8, no. 2, pp. 25–30.

Webster, Cynthia (1992), '*What kind of marketing culture exists in your service firm? An audit*', The Journal of Services Marketing, Santa Barbara, Spring, vol. 6, no. 2, p. 54.

West, M. (2004), *The Secrets of Successful Team Management*, Duncan Baird, London.

Worsfold, P. (1999), 'HRM, performance, commitment, and service quality in the hotel industry', *International Journal of Contemporary Hospitality Management*, vol. 11, no. 7, pp. 340–348.

Zeithaml, V.A. and M.J. Bitner (2003), *Services Marketing: Integrating Customer Focus across the Firm*, 3rd edn, McGraw-Hill, New York.

http://corporate.disney.go.com/careers/culture.html.

APPENDIX 1

Models and Framework of Evaluation of Training Programmes

Desimone et al. (2002) have consolidated the framework for evaluating training initiatives in an organization. These are listed in Table 12.2.

Table 12.2   Training evaluation criteria

Model/framework	Training evaluation criteria
1. Kirkpatrick (1967, 1987, 1994)	Four levels: Reaction, learning, job behaviour, and results
2. CIPP (Galvin 1983)	Four levels: Context, input, process, and product
3. CIRO (Warr et al. 1970)	Context, input, reaction, and outcome
4. Brinkerhoff (1987)	Six stages: Goal setting, programme design, programme implementation, immediate outcomes, intermediate or usage outcomes, and impacts and worth.
5. Systems approach (Bushnell 1990)	Four sets of activities: Inputs, process, outputs, and outcomes
6. Kraiger, Ford and Salas (1993)	A classification scheme that specifies three categories of learning outcomes (cognitive, skill-based, affective) suggested by the literature and proposes evaluation measures appropriate for each category of outcomes
7. Kaufman and Keller (1994)	Five levels: Enabling and reaction, acquisition, application, organizational outputs, and societal outcomes
8. Holton (1996)	Identifies five categories of variables and the relationships among them: Secondary influences, motivation elements, environmental elements, outcomes, ability/enabling elements
9. Phillips (1996)	Five levels: Reaction and planned action, learning, applied learning on the job, business results, and return on investment

Source: Adapted from Desimone et al. (2002).

13 Pricing Strategies for Services

OBJECTIVES

After reading this chapter you will be able to understand the:
- factors influencing pricing concerns of a firm
- various pricing objectives
- various methods of pricing services
- explain the factors involved in marketing-oriented pricing

INTRODUCTION

This chapter gives an overview of the pricing concerns of a firm. It also gives an overview of alternate pricing strategies adopted by service firms. The categorization of service strategies is done in three broad areas—cost-oriented pricing, competitor-oriented pricing, and marketing-oriented pricing.

Pricing the services is an immensely challenging task. The attributes of services are very different as compared to manufactured products. The attributes of intangibility, inseparability, perishability, and heterogeneity make the task complicated. Services also vary on the experience and credence attributes, which create psychological costs such as anxiety, and mental and physical effort (Lovelock 2001). Lovelock indicates the following four non-financial costs:

1. Time expenditures (time spent on finding out about prices and attributes of a service offering)
2. Physical effort (such as fatigue and discomfort)
3. Psychological burdens (such as mental effort and negative feelings)
4. Negative sensory burdens (unpleasant sensations affecting any of the five senses).

There may be numerous considerations for pricing services. These can be listed as follows:

- Revenue oriented—the concept of costs and profits may be important.
- Capacity oriented—this is to meet the available supply.
- Demand oriented—this is to maximize demand
  - recognize the paying potential
  - offer different modes of payment.

Pricing decisions can have a great impact on profitability, assuming that the service, which is being delivered, meets the customer needs. Pricing is one of the elements of the service mix and needs to complement the other elements of the service mix.

Demand plays an important role in an economist's approach to pricing. In certain cases, the pricing pattern may depend on the demand. However, the regulatory framework and market conditions may determine the pricing strategies of a firm.

PRICING OBJECTIVES

There may be numerous objectives, which a service firm may deploy before choosing a pricing strategy (Avlonitis and Indounas 2005):

- maintenance of existing customers
- attraction of new customers
- customers' need satisfaction
- cost coverage
- creation of prestige for the firm
- long-term survival
- service quality leadership
- achievement of satisfactory profits
- sales maximization
- market development
- achievement of satisfactory market share
- determination of fair prices by customers
- profit maximization
- sales stability in the market.

For instance, power supply is the domain of state governments and the government sets the tariffs. Similarly, the concerned ministry sets railway fares in India. The government regulates the supply and prices of LPG. The fee charged by government schools is regulated. Market conditions such as monopoly, monopolistic, or oligopoly market structures may influence pricing decisions. In a monopoly environment, a single player holds a major market share. He may or may not be free to set prices if the market is regulated. For instance, when the telecom sector in India was not de-regulated, the government decided the STD/ISD tariffs. With de-regulation, private players have a higher degree of autonomy to decide the pricing strategies.

METHODS OF PRICING SERVICES

Shapiro and Jackson (1978) have identified three methods used by managers to set prices:

1. Cost-oriented pricing
2. Competitor-oriented pricing
3. Marketing-oriented pricing

Cost-oriented strategy is an internally driven strategy. Competitor-oriented pricing is driven more by competitors, strategies. Marketing-oriented pricing focuses on the value that the customer places on the service being driven.

Cost-oriented Pricing

This strategy aims to recover some of the costs incurred in offering the services to the consumer. There are four methods, which reflect this ideology:

1. Full cost pricing
2. Marginal cost pricing
3. Target return pricing
4. Contribution analysis

Full cost pricing This method prices the services after taking into account the fixed as well as the variable costs (direct costs). The issue with this approach is that it is not market driven. The sale may be determined by the demand and the paying capacity of the market.

Marginal cost pricing This strategy aims at pricing the service in a manner that direct costs can be recovered and the full costs may be recovered after a certain period of time. The price is set below total and variable costs so as to cover marginal cost (Palmes 1994). This strategy is adopted specially in the service sector, as they are perishable. When occupancy levels in a hotel are low and when an aircraft is flying with unoccupied seats, prices are lowered so that some costs may be recovered, rather than losing the entire cost.

This strategy has a bearing on reducing the impact of excess capacity. Also, in certain service sectors like telecom, where private players are operating, the breakeven timeframe is larger, but the service provider looks in at larger volumes to achieve the profitability scenario.

Target return pricing Here, the price is determined at the point that yields the firms' target rate of return on investment (McIver and Naylor 1986; Meidan 1996).

Contribution analysis This is the deviation from the breakeven analysis where only the direct costs of a product or service are taken into consideration (Bateson 1995).

Empirical research indicates that many service companies in the US have followed the cost plus method. This takes care of all the costs and also includes a profit margin. Zeithaml et al. (1985) in their study of the pricing behaviour of 323 service companies in 13 different sectors in the US, found that 63 per cent of these companies had adopted the cost plus method.

Competitor-oriented Pricing

There are two forms, which service providers may adopt:

1. Going rate pricing
2. Competitive bidding

Exhibit 13.1   Penetrating the market through aggressive pricing

With the telecom boom in India, users of companies like BSNL will have a bonanza. They will be able to enjoy STD calls at just about Re 1 per minute, which is actually a reduction of about 60 per cent. According to analysts, this strategy is indeed a masterstroke, as users will lap up the plan since the rentals will remain constant. BSNL aims to increase the STD traffic by about 65–68 per cent. According to sources, this strategy is two pronged—the first is to rope in more landline subscribers, and the second to boost the communications minister's project, OneIndia, allowing local as well as national calls at Re 1 per minute. The OneIndia plan had failed to take off despite various attempts by BSNL, as the rentals were high. The figures are—under 0.5 million OneIndia users, just 1.14 per cent of the total landline base of 37 million.

Source: Adapted from Philip and Pratap (2006).

Going Rate Pricing

In this scenario, the pricing is done as per the competition in the market. However, marketers may like to use price differentials to differentiate their service offering to the consumers. The prices may, however, be similar to that of the competition (Palmar 1994; Zeithaml and Bitner 1996).

- The pricing may be below that of competitors (Payne 1993; Zeithaml and Bitner 1996). Exhibit 13.1 explains penetrating the market through aggressive pricing, and Exhibit 13.2 explains pricing competition between public (MTNL) and private sector (Bharti) telecom firms.
- Pricing according to dominant price in the market—the leader's price that is adopted by the rest of the companies (Kurtz and Clow 1998).
- The pricing may be above that of the competition. Exhibit 13.3 explains pricing above the competition.

Competitive Bidding

In this particular case, the bid is offered to the lowest bidder. Bidding is a complex task, especially in the case of large service firms and contracts. For instance, building of

---

Exhibit 13.2   Pricing competition between MTNL and Bharti

Bharti Airtel's profits went up while MTNL's reduced by 25.53 per cent. The situation was very different earlier. Bharti Airtel asked everyone to focus on EBITDA (earnings before interest, tax, depreciation, and amortization), as its share price had fallen with the initial public offering. MTNL, at this point in time, was mainly focused on the biggest markets, such as Delhi and Mumbai. The situation now has reversed. Bharti Airtel is driven by Sunil Bharti Mittal's entrepreneurial spirit and increased FDI and Airtel has been adding circles after circles to its existing network base. MTNL's biggest problem lies in the fact that it has only focused on two markets—Delhi and Mumbai. MTNL also needs innovative and aggressive marketing strategies to counter private players like Bharti Airtel.

Source: Adapted from *The Economic Times* (2006).

Exhibit 13.3   Hotel rates sky high at Delhi and National Capital Region (NCR)

Room rates in India are at an all-time high. The rates in Delhi and NCR will rise by 30–40 per cent in the future, making India one of the most expensive destinations in Asia. The hike in Delhi and Mumbai has overtaken Bangalore. The rates of an average five-star hotel room was about Rs 10,000–12,000, but has now reached about Rs 16,000. As India suffers from a lack of rooms, 150 hotel projects are under active development. A factor for this rise is attributed to the increase in inbound business travellers. A major disadvantage of this rise in rates is that India might lose a lot of its inbound tourists due to very expensive costs. They may end up choosing alternate destinations for travel.

Source: Adapted from Awasthi and Dey (2006).

flyovers or privatization of airports, require complex pricing procedures with complex documentation. The building of power plants, offering telecom services, and privatization of railways, etc. are all complex cases where bidding is used to allocate business. The most usual process is the drawing up of a detailed specification for a process and putting the papers up for tender.

Many service firms also offer bidding prices on products. For instance, India Times shopping invites bidding for airline tickets. These may be to invite new price conscious consumers into the ambit of the service provider.

Marketing-oriented Pricing

This strategy takes into account a much wider range of factors. Jobber (2001) has discussed 10 factors, which could influence marketing-oriented pricing strategy:

1. Marketing strategy
2. Price–quality relationships
3. Product line pricing
4. Negotiating margins
5. Political factors
6. Costs
7. Effect on distributors/retailers
8. Competition
9. Explicability
10. Value to the customer

Please see Exhibit 13.4 on how accommodation sector in India needs to adopt a marketing oriented approach to pricing.

Marketing Strategy

The marketing strategy has a considerable influence on the pricing strategy of the firm. The target market and its characteristics, demand, positioning, strategy, and nature of competition, all have a bearing on the marketing strategy.

Exhibit 13.4   Pricing vis-à-vis a competing tourist destination

The Indian tourism sector needs to mend its ways; otherwise smaller destinations such as Tunisia, Reunion Island, and Uzbekistan, among others, will start pinching the huge number of European travellers that India gets. France is India's second largest market and contributes about 28 per cent to India's total inbound tourists figure. The latest travel market show, TopResa in France, displayed a few realities of the tourism market in India. The Indian Tourism Board at TopResa was bland and lacked life, as compared to those of Sri Lanka and Mauritius. According to one tour operator present at the show, a big reason was that India has become too overpriced.

Reservations at a luxury hotel like Maurya Sheraton are at about $500 for a standard room. This in fact is more expensive than a 304-day trip at Reunion Island or Tunisia. The operators also feel that the hotels in India try and up sell the hotel rooms. They try to sell the premium category rooms even when the regular rooms are available. Some close observers feel that increase in the number of inbound tourists is mainly due to the business travellers, because the number of leisure travellers has actually gone down. It is not wrong to say that rooms in New York are cheaper than those in India!

Source: Adapted from Sharma (2006).

The service provider may opt for different pricing strategies. It may be penetration pricing (low pricing strategy) or may be 'skimming-the-cream' strategy (charging premium for the service offering). The penetration-pricing strategy aims at generating volumes, whereas the premium-pricing strategy looks at higher profits from smaller numbers. Some service providers offer multiple service brands to map the complete market.

For example, Fruchter and Rao (2001) in their research have discussed the 'optimal-pricing strategy' for a provider of network services. The researchers propose that the optimal-strategy consists of penetration strategy for a membership fee, low at the beginning, increasing with network size, and a skimming strategy for the usage price, starting high and declining later.

Other examples of such a pricing strategy include Internet access, web-based services such as financial and other business services, telecommunication services, and other growing membership-based services. For example, for Internet services, if usage demand is decreasing in the network size, the optimal policy is one of penetration in membership fee and skimming in usage price. If on the other hand, the usage demand is increasing in the network size, the optimal policy is one of penetration not only in membership fee, but also in usage price.

Price changes   With regard to demand, Rathmell (1974) observed that the demand for professional services is usually price inelastic on the downward size. Reducing the price of a professional service is not likely to increase primary demand or expand the size of the market served by 'small' service businesses. The search, credence, and experience characteristics of the service product influence consumer demand (Darby and Karni 1973).

Rhymer (2001) has raised the issues of price raise and its timing. She remarks that many service providers fear losing customers when prices are raised. The secret is to explain to the customers the reason behind the price change. The timing of the price

Exhibit 13.5 Service upgrades

Service providers operating in sectors such as airlines, train services, hotels, sports stadiums, and performing art companies, typically offer different service classes (e.g., first class, business class, and economy class). Biyalogorsky et al. (2005) have suggested a model that considers the use of upgrades as a contingent mechanism to ameliorate situations in which the realized demand for upper-class service is lower than allocated capacity. Providers typically struggle between two alternative strategies—advance selling first class units at a reduced price, or reserving them for sale at a full price. The first strategy eliminates the opportunity to sell first class units at the full price if such a demand occurs later, but the second strategy is risky because demand uncertainty may lead to valuable units not being used.

The managers could issue upgradeable tickets. These tickets provide a way to ensure that first class capacity can always be used, allowing the provider to capture more potential value. Compared with advance selling first class units at discounted prices, employing upgradeable tickets allows a service provider to sell first class units at a full price whenever feasible.

The managerial guidelines to improve allocation of upper class capacity include the following:

- Use upgradeable tickets to increase profits, if the probability of obtaining full price for first class is sufficiently high.
- When using upgradeable tickets, reserve more first class units for sale at full price compared to the units reserved without upgradeable tickets.
- Advance selling is the most profitable policy and reserving is the least profitable, if the probability of selling first class at full price is very small.
- Offering upgradeable tickets is the most profitable policy and reserving is the least profitable, if the probability of selling first class at full price is intermediate.
- Offering upgradeable tickets is the most profitable policy and advance selling is the least profitable, if the probability of selling first class at full price is sufficiently high.

Source: Adapted from Biyalogorsky et al. (2005).

change also may matter. For example, parking lots in Gurgaon (NCR) charge much more on weekends than on weekdays.

In order to target various consumer segments simultaneously and to save loss of revenue, the demand of the service across various segments is also taken into consideration. For instance, service upgrades illustrates the concept further (Exhibit 13.5).

Exhibit 13.6 gives an insight into managing variable demand.

Price changes over the service life cycle Avlonitis et al. (2005) have discussed the pricing objectives over the service life cycle. They have pointed out that a comprehensive review of literature on services marketing reveals that the model of the life cycle has not been examined as thoroughly as in the case of physical products. In their research on 170 companies operating in six different sectors in Greece, they have pointed out the following:

'The service firms have a hierarchy of pricing objectives. They aim at sustaining customer relations along with attracting new customers in order to achieve satisfactory rather than maximum financial results, and ensuring the firms' long-term position in the market. It was found that transportation and shipping companies emphasize on managing capacity and assets, while insurance companies are interested in satisfying their customers' and distributors' needs and developing the market. Information

---

Exhibit 13.6 Option-based approach for pricing perishable service assets

Option pricing is used to develop an alternative model for pricing services that have fixed availability and expiration. Pricing of hotel rooms is used to demonstrate this in a marketing context.

The use of the option model approach
The model is based on a binomial option model for discrete time. Finch et al. (1998) have proposed a method of price cut option, allowing us to predict and manage revenues in a more dynamic way. Such a calculation assumes an appreciation of market price elasticity (wherein price change affects sales), information about consumer price sensitivity, and sufficient margin to make the price cut option

practical. Finch et al. (1998) propose that the option to cut prices works best where a high priced service is involved. High prices and key margins allow greater flexibility in pricing.

Availability of service has a bearing on choosing the option pricing strategy. Option to cut prices is a strong one where alternatives are far off. There should also be a means of informing consumers about the price changes. Internet and other multimedia equipment provide greater opportunities for such communication. Effective revenue tracking and accounting systems enable the option-pricing strategy to work for the firm.

Source: Adapted from Finch et al. (1998).

---

technology companies focus on high quality service, while airlines are interested in maintaining and expanding their customer base.'

According to a research conducted by Avlonitis and Indounas (2005), it is pointed out that service firms in the sample, paid very little attention to adopting customer-oriented methods, perhaps due to the difficulty in determining their customers' demand and needs. The sample of the research includes 170 service firms operating in Greece. Their research covers banks, insurance companies, transportation and shipping firms, airlines, information technology business, and medical services.

Exhibit 13.7 elaborates the concept of transfer pricing (TP).

Price–Quality Relationships

Consumers consider price as an indicator of quality; for example, first class or business class options advertised by Kingfisher Airlines in India. Exhibit 13.8 provides an

---

Exhibit 13.7 Transfer pricing

Car makers Maruti and Toyota along with companies such as Samsung, Sony, a host of BPOs, and foreign banks have been slapped with additional income tax demands. This has happened due to alleged violation of income tax laws in the country. For example, Maruti's enhanced profits due to TP has been about Rs 180 crore; the same has been about Rs 197 crore for Toyota. Both the companies have filed an appeal with the income tax authority against

the order. Both also feel that they have suffered the order due to overpricing of components and lower scale realization of exports. TP is actually described as the price charged by one group company to an associated enterprise for an international transaction relating to the supply of goods, services, and property. Countries trying to protect their tax base and earn a reasonable share of their tax price, look aggressively at TP to get extra revenues.

Source: Adapted from Gupta and Ramakrishnan (2006).

Exhibit 13.8 Pricing strategies for alternate technologies

An interesting fact that has emerged is, if one assumes usage time to be the sole criterion, then CDMA operators should be making more money than GSM operators. The reason is that on an average a CDMA phone user makes 284 min of calls and receives 266 min of calls every month, as compared to 163 min of outgoing and 232 min of incoming calls for GSM users. Also, GSM subscribers pay Rs 100 more. As per the latest data from TRAI (Telecom Regulatory Authority of India), GSM operators hold the edge in both pre-paid and post-paid categories. Industry analysts attribute the difference in revenues to two major factors—first, that GSM has double blended revenue per minute; and second, that GSM telecom operators' rope in much more through roaming.

Source: Adapted from Philip (2006).

additional perspective on the price–quality relationship. In this particular case, the pricing strategy for two alternate technologies is compared. So, price comparisons are used as a basis for helping consumers to make choices.

The case of Lufthansa is different. Here the firm mentions categorically that 'there is no better way to fly'. The firm also mentions prices to attract consumers to international destinations.

Product Line Pricing

This pricing strategy offers different levels of services at different prices. There may be different offerings to the consumer based on differentials in pricing; for example, economy and business class rooms offered by a hotel. Some service firms offer different brands in order to offer services at different price ranges; for example, Carlson offers Radisson, Country Inns and Suites, and Park Plaza to map consumers who are willing to pay different prices for different service categories.

Differential pricing is a widespread strategy in the service sector. The method is widely accepted in almost every sector of the economy. The basic concept of differential pricing involves charging different prices to different consumer segments for the same service. A simple example can be medical services, where the healthcare fee is subsidized for poor people, while other patients are required to pay a standardized fee. Also, some services such as transportation, airlines, and railways are subsidized for senior citizens. This general fact of differential pricing has been accepted and customers do not complain when senior citizens are being charged less. People understand that many senior citizens are on fixed incomes and may not be able to afford the services at the standard rate. Providing differential advantage may ensure higher profits for the company in general, as it ensures that the services are available to the maximum number of people.

Negotiating Margins

In some firms, customers expect a price reduction. The price paid by the customer is very different from the list price. The difference may be on account of order size discounted, competitive discounts, or fast case payment discounts. For example, for institutional usage of Internet or travel services, firms may offer special rates.

Exhibit 13.9	Taxation in FMCG firms

Large FMCG companies have been making use of tax holidays in places such as Uttaranchal and Himachal Pradesh to become more competitive. The introduction of Value Added Tax (VAT) has been very helpful, as it made evasion more difficult for the unorganized sector. As many FMCG factories are being set up in excise-free locations, the differential has come down. The tax on unbranded goods should help FMCGs in the long run.

Source: Adapted from *The Economic Times* (2006).

Political Factors

When pricing policy acts against public interest, the government may intervene. For example, the railways in India are not privatized, and government decides the pricing, which is not based on market factors. Similarly, the prices of LPG and basic telephony or Internet services are influenced by government policy. Please see Exhibit 13.9.

Costs

The strategies have already been discussed in the previous section under cost-based pricing.

Effect on Distributors

Distribution systems play a key role in certain service categories such as travel and hotel reservations. Their margins must be adequate for them to push the production. However, online bookings directly with the service providers are changing the dynamics of interaction with the distributor network. Many airlines in India such as Deccan, IndiGo, Kingfisher, and Jet Airlines offer online bookings and charge much lower fees if the consumer books directly, ahead of the date of travel. The booking of tickets through travel agents is more expensive. Hence, the online options are redefining the role of distributors. Today, online portals such as Indiatimes, Yahoo, and Google offer more attractive options for booking travel through them.

Competition

The service firm may make comparisons on product features. Refer to the discussion under competition-based pricing in an earlier section, where examples have been provided.

Explicability

The service provider in this case should be able to explain the price differentials on its service offerings logically. For example, SOTC and Thomas Cook holiday advertisements in India. These tour operators offer various family tours to different locations in Europe. Depending on the number of destinations covered, number of nights, food, and entry fees to different destinations, different prices are charged for different tours to similar destinations.

Value to the Customer

This pricing strategy assesses the pricing decisions from a consumer's perspective. The target market, demand, and economic factors in a market, may influence the decision to price service. For example, India is a price conscious market. Variables operating in India have budget airlines, such as GoAir and IndiGo, which offer apex fares and compete with rail travel over long distances. The air travel by domestic consumers has greatly increased.

The second aspect is that the consumer has become solution oriented. She does not look at individual services but a combination of services, which offers her convenience. Guiltinan (1987) has elaborated on some of the strategies, which marketers have adopted in offering bundled services. Bundling is the practice of marketing two or more products/services in a single 'package' for a special price:

- Some banks offer special programs in which customers with large deposits are offered locker facilities, overdraft, and credit cards at no annual fees.
- Hotels offer special packages with complimentary nights and sightseeing.
- Hospitals build in complementary tests with some packages for medical check-ups.

Jobber (2001) has discussed four methods of estimating value to the consumers.

Buy response method This estimates directly the value that customers place on a product by asking them if they are willing to buy at various price levels.

Trade-off analysis It measures the trade-off between price and other product features so that their effects on product preference can be established.

Experimentation This pricing strategy attempts to place a service at scale, at different locations at varying prices. Test marketing may be used here initially to test the effect of services offered at varying levels. The customer satisfaction level may be monitored at various levels. After test marketing, changes may be made in the service offering. For example, when the Oberoi Group launched Trident as a brand, it was supposed to be a budget brand. When the demand started to increase and Oberoi's service was considered exceptional, the company raised the prices of its rooms and Trident is no longer a budget brand, but an upmarket brand. Testing helps the firm to calibrate its offering.

Analysis of the economic value to the customer If a firm can provide higher economic value to the customer, it can charge a higher price. This helps in building up revenues for more services provided.

Exhibit 13.10 explains value-to-customer pricing. Exhibit 13.11 explains the price dumping in compact disc (CD) business.

Exhibit 13.10 Value-to-customer pricing

Big hotel chains such as Radisson, Taj, and Royal Orchid among others are planning to enter the budget hotel segment, thus making things even more complicated for their smaller counterparts. The bigger hotels can afford and, hence, plan to acquire strategically located properties, or tie up with

Contd

Exhibit 13.10 Contd

existing hotels and upgrade them. In the Rs 10,200 crore hotel industry, small and medium enterprise (SME) hotels account for a turnover of Rs 350 crore. These hotels are primarily one- and two-star hotels, with about 9,500 rooms and account for at least 260 hotels in the country. Most of them are in cities such as Haridwar and Jaipur.

The budget hotels are also known as 'no frills' hotels and about 2,000–5,000 rooms are expected to come up in the next few years. The disadvantage remains that the ever-increasing real estate prices may force the budget hotels to either increase prices or face a margin squeeze. Another roadblock for SMEs is funding, and as interest and land prices are going up, banks should be allowed to extend the term loan tenure to fund such projects. Such hotels have a high inflow of domestic travellers, unlike deluxe or five-star hotels with a large proportion of foreign travellers. An important factor in favour of budget hotels is that these hotels can operate at 50 per cent occupancy and still make profits. The main reason for this is that these hotels have lower fixed costs as compared to deluxe or mid-segment hotels.

Source: Adapted from *The Economic Times* (2006).

Exhibit 13.11   Dumping price

The government has imposed anti-dumping duty ranging from Rs 2.24 per unit to Rs 4.20 per unit on import of CDs, i.e., recordable CD-R from China, Singapore, and Taiwan. This move is expected to set the stage for investments towards the expansion of CD-R capacities. There may perhaps, be a temporary respite, as CD manufacturers are facing stiff competition from newer technologies such as flash memory and huge online storage spaces. The department of commerce has reaffirmed its preliminary investigation findings that while the demand of the subject good in the domestic market increased by 200 per cent, the share of dumped imports increased by 17 per cent. The current demand in India is about 800 million units, of which Indian manufacturers account for about 50 per cent. While 20–25 per cent is driven by IT applications, music and films account for the balance.

Source: Adapted from *The Economic Times* (2006).

SUMMARY

This chapter gives an overview of the pricing concerns for service firms. It provides information on detailed strategies deployed by firms and also categorizes the strategies under three broad areas—cost oriented, competitor oriented, and marketing oriented. Ethical issues in pricing are also discussed along with inputs on differential pricing methodology.

This chapter delineates the pricing objectives. These could be—maintenance of existing customers; attraction of new customers; customers' need satisfaction; cost coverage; creation of prestige for the firm; long-term survival; service quality leadership; and achievement of satisfactory profits among others.

There are numerous strategies that service firms adopt. These can be broadly classified in three categories—cost-oriented pricing, competitor-oriented pricing, and marketing-oriented pricing. Under each of these categories, there are numerous strategies that the firm can deploy. The examples of the firms give an insight into how these strategies may be adopted, either in combination or isolation. The service firms

Contd

Summary Contd

should be able to judge the impact of business environment changes, which are occurring and adopt appropriate strategies. The emerging economies offer immense opportunities for services that the mass market can adopt. Focusing on volumes while offering good value can be a very strong strategy for long-term sustenance of the firm. However, premium pricing strategies are used by firms to target niche markets. Their product design and communication strategies should resonate with the pricing strategy.

KEY TERMS

Cost plus pricing An approach to establishing the selling price of a product or service is estimated, and a percentage mark-up is added in order to obtain a profitable selling price. A variation to this approach is to estimate the costs to a particular stage, say, the costs of production only, and then add a percentage mark-up to cover both, the other overheads (including administration, selling, and distribution costs), and the profit margin.

Full cost pricing An approach to setting selling prices ensuring that the price of a good or service is based on all the costs incurred in its supply, including overheads. It usually involves an absorption approach to the costing of units.

Marginal cost pricing The setting of product selling prices based on charging only marginal costs to the product. The approach is only likely to be used in exceptional circumstances, such as when competition is intense, as its application to a complete range of products is likely to cause the business to make losses by its failure to cover its fixed costs.

Mark-up The amount by which the cost of a service or product has been increased to arrive at the selling price. It is calculated by expressing the profit as a percentage of the cost of the good or service. The mark-up is used in retailing, both for setting prices and as a ratio for control and decision-making.

Price discrimination The sale of the same product at different prices to different buyers. Usually practised by monopolists, it requires that a market can be sub-divided to exploit different sets of consumers and that these divisions can be sustained.

Pricing The setting of selling prices for products and services supplied by an organization. In many cases, selling prices will be based on market prices but in other circumstances pricing will be based on costs using information provided by the management accounting system.

CONCEPT REVIEW QUESTIONS

1. What role does pricing policy play in forming an opinion about the service offering?

2. Which method should the marketers deploy for pricing their services?

3. How do service upgrades take care of the limitations of demand supply mismatch?

4. Is the life cycle concept applicable for pricing services? What role does it play in deciding a pricing strategy?

CRITICAL THINKING QUESTIONS

1. The hotels offer a specific price if bookings are made online. When a customer approaches the desk for extension of her stay in the hotel she is offered the rack rate. The customer

requests for an online rate, but the staff does not agree. She goes to a business centre and books the hotel online, and gets a confirmed reservation at a lower price. Please examine the pricing strategy of the hotel critically.

2. Should the service firm opt for cost plus pricing or value for money pricing? Please evaluate the statement and support with examples.

3. Compare the online prices offered for a hotel through various search engines. What is your advice to the consumer on the choices he should make for online reservation for a hotel?

INTERNET EXERCISES

1. Choose two website firms in India, which deploy the mechanism of auction pricing. Compare and contrast their offering for an airline reservation.

2. Select two tour operators. Compare a tour option between Delhi and Switzerland for the tours offered by them. Are there price differences? Are the differences in pricing strategy explained by the tour operators? Browse through their websites to arrive at logical conclusions.

CASE STUDY

Why Differential Pricing Helps the Poor?*

When consumers find out that a restaurant gives senior citizens a 10 per cent discount off their tabs, the under-65 customers do not complain that they are 'subsidizing' seniors—being charged more so that seniors can be charged less. Nor do they complain that if the restaurant can charge seniors less, it can afford to charge everyone less. People seem to understand that many seniors are on fixed incomes and may not be able to afford as much as those under age 65. And, when parents taking their children to an amusement park pay half the adult price for a child's ticket, those patrons buying adult tickets do not demand the same discount, claiming it is unfair to charge adults more so that children can be charged less. Indeed, they seem to sympathize with the parents.

This is called 'differential pricing', and it is widely accepted in just about every sector of the economy—except in the market for prescription drugs.

What is Differential Pricing?

Differential pricing is the practice of charging some customers or clients more, while charging others less, for the same product or service. Virtually every industry and most companies engage in some form of differential pricing. For example, the airlines have a range of fares they charge customers, based on when and how they make their reservation, whether they want to fly first, business class, or coach, or whether they are willing to stay over a Saturday night. And many passengers fly free by using frequent flier miles. Historically, healthcare providers have also engaged in differential pricing. Doctors charge most patients their standard fee, but poor patients often pay a reduced amount—if they pay anything at all. Such doctors are not criticized, but commended for their charity and public service because they—not the patients paying full price—were perceived as bearing the loss.

---

* Matthews Jr, M. (2003), 'Why differential pricing helps the poor?', *Insider Online,* http://www.insideronline.org/archives/2003/may03/pricing.pdf, accessed on 12 August 2008. Printed with permission.

Why do Companies Practise Differential Pricing?

Economists argue that companies engage in differential pricing in order to maximize sales and thus, profits. First, a company establishes a business model that anticipates a standard price for the product or service that should result in a profit if sales goals are met. The question then arises, 'Are there those outside the business model who may purchase the product if it costs less?' The answer is almost always yes, and so the company begins to look for ways to reach those individuals. It is the market's way of ensuring that more consumers get products and services at lower prices, and companies make higher profits—a win–win for both companies and consumers—unless, of course, you manufacture and sell a product that is politically sensitive, such as brand-name prescription drugs. For instance, the media, many politicians, and special interest groups have come to believe that differential pricing helps the drug companies while hurting the poor. In fact, eliminating differential pricing in prescription drugs will only hurt the poor.

Differential Pricing as a Social Benefit

Differential pricing permits companies and individuals to make their products or services available to people in a wider range of incomes. Take, for example, airlines. The airlines want to sell as many tickets to as many people as possible. Their most lucrative business model is to sell expensive tickets to business travellers who expense the costs to their company and so, are less sensitive to the price. But many people without such expense accounts are not willing to pay that price. Since the aircraft is making the trip anyway, and the 'marginal cost' of adding more passengers is virtually zero, the airlines devised a way to identify pleasure travellers by requiring a Saturday night stay—which many business travellers do not want—thus allowing millions of people with lower incomes or no expense account to travel to see family and friends.

Pharmaceuticals and Differential Pricing

Like most industries, pharmaceutical manufacturers too engage in differential pricing. And like most industries, differential pricing has allowed lower income people, both here and abroad, to have access to drugs they never would have had otherwise. In US, drug manufacturers provide billions of dollars in free or drastically discounted brand-name drugs to states and programmes that seek to provide care to the poor and indigent. In addition, several drug companies have implemented discount cards for qualified low-income seniors. Pfizer and Eli Lilly went a step further by allowing all qualified low-income seniors to purchase any drug they sell for $15 and $12 per month, respectively. By identifying low-income seniors, drug companies are able to segment those who need help the most.

Differential Pricing and Other Countries

Drug companies are often criticized for selling bulk quantities of prescription drugs to foreign governments, especially Canada and Mexico, for prices lower than many Americans can purchase them. However, such practices are common and well accepted in other industries, and make sense from an economic standpoint. Canada's per capita GDP is about two-thirds that of the US—$19,170 vs $29,240 (1998, US dollars). Mexico's is a mere $3,840. Even automakers sometimes sell their cars for less in Canada, and some Americans have been crossing the border to buy those cheaper cars—spurring a backlash from US auto dealers, who lose sales as a result. But when drug companies discount their products or give them to impoverished countries, critics claim that such practices prove the companies are charging Americans too much and so they clamour for price controls.

They ignore the fact that the only reason doctors can afford to provide free services to some low-income people is that many others are willing to pay the full price. If no one pays the full price, no one can get a deeply discounted price.

Who does Differential Pricing Help?

If a company that sells a product for several different prices were told by the government that it could only sell at one price, the company likely would no longer be able to sell the product for the current lowest price. Higher income people who are willing and able to pay more would pay lower prices. And lower income people would be forced to pay more—precisely the opposite of what lawmakers intend by single-price legislation. Differential pricing helps low-income people get a product they could not otherwise afford. If Congress were to do away with differential pricing in the market for prescription drugs—for example, by forcing a drug company to sell to every purchaser at the lowest price paid by any purchaser—it would ensure that low-income

people all over the world would pay more or could no longer get the drugs they need.

Conclusion

Providing the widest possible access to a product means permitting—even encouraging—differential pricing. Eliminating differential pricing ensures that low-income people will have little or no access to the newest, life-saving drugs. It's a death warrant masquerading as social do-goodism.

Questions

1. What is differential pricing? Discuss with help of examples from various sectors.

2. How can differential pricing be used as a strategic tool to enhance consumerism?

SELECT REFERENCES

Avlonitis, G.J. and K.A. Indounas (2005), 'Pricing objectives and pricing methods in the services sector', *The Journal of Services Marketing*, vol. 19, no. 1, p. 47.

Avlonitis, G.J. and K.A. Indounas (2004), 'Pricing strategy and practice: The impact of market structure on pricing', *The Journal of Product and Brand Management*, vol. 13, no. 4/5, p. 343.

Avlonitis, G.J., K.A. Indounas, and S.P. Gounaris (2005), 'Pricing objectives over the service life cycle: Some empirical evidence', *European Journal of Marketing*, vol. 39, no. 5/6.

Awasthi, R. and S. Dey (2006), 'Hotel rates in Delhi & NCR move skyward', *The Economic Times*, 8 September, p. 4.

Baterson, J.E.G. (1995), *Managing Services Marketing Texts and Readings*, 3rd edn, The Dryden Press, Orlando.

Biyalogorsky, E.E. Gerstner, D. Weirs, and J. Xie (2005), 'The economics of service upgrades', *Journal of Service Research*, February, vol. 7, no. 3.

'Budget hotels offer rooms with a view', *The Economic Times*, 22 August 2006.

Darby, M.R. and Edi Karni (1973), 'Free competition and the optimal amount of fraud', *Journal of Law and Economics*, 16 April.

Finch, J.H., R.C. Becherer, and R. Casavant (1998), 'An option based approach for pricing perishable service assets', *The Journal of Services Marketing*, vol. 12, no. 6, p. 473.

Fruchter, G.E. and R.C. Rao (2001), 'Optimal membership fee and usage price over time for a network service', *Journal of Service Research*, vol. 4, no. 1, August, pp. 3–14.

'Government slaps anti-dumping duty on recordable discs', *The Economic Times*, 10 October 2006, p. 10.

Guiltinan, J.P. (1987), 'The price bundling of services: A normative framework', *Journal of Marketing*, vol. 51, April, pp. 74–85.

Gupta, N.S. and H. Ramakrishnan (2006), 'Maruti and MNCs face transfer pricing rap', *The Economic Times*, 15 May, New Delhi.

Jobber, D. (2001), *Principles and Practice of Marketing*, McGraw-Hill, London.

Kurtz, D.L. and K.E. Clow (1998), *Services Marketing*, John Wiley, New York.

Lovelock, C. (2001), *Service Marketing: People, Technology, Strategy*, Addison Wesley Longman, New Delhi.

McIver, C. and G. Naylor (1986), *Marketing Financial Services*, 2nd edn, The Institute of Bankers, Canterbury.

Meidan, A. (1996), *Marketing Financial Services*, Macmillan Business Press, London.

Palmer, A. (1994), *Principles of Services Marketing*, McGraw-Hill, London.

Payne, A. (1993), *The Essence of Services Marketing*, Prentice-Hall, London.

Philip and Pratap (2006), 'BSNL cuts STD rates to Re 1/ min', *The Economic Times*, 12 October, p. 5.

Philip, J.T. (2006), 'Cellcos need quality time', *The Economic Times*, 3 July.

Rathmell, John M. (1974), *Marketing in the Service Sector*, Winthrop Publishers, Cambridge.

Rhymer, J. (2001), 'Avoiding the pricing trap: Customers care up to a point', *Franchising World*, vol. 33, no. 8, p. 30.

Shapiro, B.P. and B.B. Jackson (1978), 'Industrial pricing to meet customer needs', *Harvard Business Review*, Nov–Dec, pp. 119–127.

Sharma, R. (2006), 'Incredibly overpriced India', *The Economic Times*.

'Bharti Airtel gives MTNL blues', *The Economic Times*, 27 October 2006.

'Jet set fly', *The Economic Times*, 21 September 2006.

'Tax on unbranded goods to help FMCGs in long run', *The Economic Times*, 2006.

Zeithaml, V.A. and M.J. Bitner (1996), *Services Marketing*, McGraw-Hill, Singapore.

Zeithaml, V.A., A. Parasuraman, and L.L. Berry (1985), 'Problems and strategies in services marketing', *Journal of Marketing*, vol. 49, no. 4, pp. 33–46.

14 Strategies for Promotion for Service Sector

OBJECTIVES

After reading this chapter you will be able to understand the:
- ingredients of marketing communication
- need for marketing communication
- process of communication
- nuances of promotion planning and strategy
- different elements of the promotion mix and when are they selected
- importance of advertising
- dimension of sales promotion, personal selling, and direct marketing
- essentials of public relations and e-marketing
- importance of an integrated marketing communication

INTRODUCTION

Today, with liberalization, the world has become a marketplace where local products rub shoulders with the best of national and international brands. The customer is treated as a king and has a number of options to choose from. In the consumer buying process we saw that the customer purchases a product or service from the awareness set, i.e., the brands the customer is aware of, out of the total number of brands (total set) available to him/her. If the service meets the initial buying requirements of the customer they form the consideration set and as the customer gathers more information, the strong contenders form the choice set from which the customer makes the final choice (Kotler and Keller 2006). If the customer is not aware of the service it will not fall in the awareness set and consequently, will not form the final choice for purchase of services. Hence, it is of utmost importance to communicate to the customer the service that is offered by the organization and influence the customer so that the service organization is the final choice for purchase. Once the communication has been initiated, it is important for the organization to continue the communication with the current and potential customers in different ways to cover pre-purchase, purchase and consumption, and post-purchase stages.

MARKETING COMMUNICATION AND PROMOTION

Promotion is the communication function of marketing and is defined as (Engel et al. 1987):

'Controlled, integrated programme of communication methods and materials designed to present an organization and its products to prospective customers; to communicate need-satisfying attributes of products to facilitate sales and thus contribute to long-run profit performance.'

Promotion includes all forms of marketing communication, which is the manner in which an organization communicates with other organizations and customers to facilitate exchange processes. However, an organization also needs to communicate with other organizations for procurement, distribution, and even sale of services. Deolozier (1976) gave the following definition of marketing communication:

'The process of presenting an integrated set of stimuli to a market with the intent of evoking a desired set of responses within that market set and setting up channels to receive, interpret, and act upon messages from the market, for the purposes of modifying present company messages and identifying new communication opportunities.'

This definition is important as it focuses on an 'integrated' approach and talks about 'setting up channels...from the market', i.e., a feedback approach from the market. Fill (2002) gave a definition, as follows:

'Marketing communication is a management process through which an organization enters into a dialogue with its various audiences. Based upon an understanding of the audiences' communications environment, an organization develops and presents messages for its identified stakeholder groups, and evaluates and acts upon the responses received. The objective of the process is to (re)position the organization and/or its products and services, in the minds of members of the target market, by influencing their perception and understanding. The goal is to generate attitudinal and behavioural responses.'

This definition focuses on three aspects—dialogue, positioning, and cognitive response. *Dialogue* is the communication between the organization and the target audience. *Positioning* comes into play when there is more than one organization providing the same service in the given category. The marketing communication should focus on the perceptive position the organization wants to create about their service in the consumer's mind in relation to other services. *Cognitive response* is the response of the consumers to the marketing communication, which is revealed in the form of influencing the purchasing or organization related activities. Marketing communication promotes both the organization and its service offering, and effective communication is critical for the success of an organization. Marketing communication is generally taken as communication with the external audience, but good communication with the internal audience like employees is also vital for the success of an organization.

In light of the above discussion we can define promotion as, 'The managerial process of communication an organization has with its target audience to generate attitudinal and behavioural responses and facilitate exchanges for mutual benefit.'

The promotion mix consists of the following five modes of communication—advertising, personal selling, sales promotion, direct marketing, and publicity (Kotler 2006):

1. 'Advertising: Any paid form of non-personal presentation and promotion of ideas, goods, or services by an identified sponsor.
2. Personal selling: Face-to-face interaction with one or more prospective purchasers for the purpose of making presentations, answering questions, and procuring orders.
3. Sales promotion: A variety of short-term incentives to encourage trial or purchase of a product or service.
4. Direct marketing: Use of mail, telephone, fax, e-mail, or Internet to communicate directly with, or solicit response or dialogue, from specific customers and prospects.
5. Publicity: A variety of programmes designed to promote or protect a company's image or its individual products.'

In the service sector we can also talk about the following two factors, which play an important role in the promotion of services:

Word-of-mouth These include recommendations from other customers and are not directly under the control of the organization. Indirectly, the organization can control these communications by providing an experience that meets, or is above the consumer expectations, so that the word-of-mouth is always positive. This aspect is more important in view of the fact that less knowledgeable customers rely more on word-of-mouth to guide their decision-making (Lovelock and Wirtz 2006). A study by ACNielsen shows that it is word-of-mouth that affects the purchase choice of Indians the most. In developed countries, it is advertising that affects the purchase choice, but in developing countries, such as India and Indonesia, it is word-of-mouth that affects the purchase decision the most. Indians are a closely-knit society and are easily influenced by their peers, relatives, etc. This effect is most obvious in purchase of services such as holidays and loans, with the loan market being dominated by word-of-mouth rather than advertising. Even though the use of the Internet is widespread in India, the reliance on blogs for making buying decisions, though on the rise in the West, has not been greatly accepted in India (Vivek 2006).

Internet marketing or e-marketing Distribution of services information and promotion through electronic media is known as e-marketing or Internet marketing (Jobber 2001).

Need for Marketing Communication

The need to promote the product has been explained in this section.

Differentiate Marketing communication aims to differentiate the services, especially when there is no perceptible difference available. For example, not much differentiation is possible in the services provided by the banking sector—where Allahabad Bank, State Bank of Hyderabad (SBH), and Union Bank are all advertising their education loan. They all provide loans up to Rs 7.5 lakh (for studies in India) and Rs 15 lakh (for studies abroad), but Allahabad Bank focuses on a better career; SBH focuses on the right support; and Union Bank talks about the good future, education, and the right bank to bank upon. Thus, with the help of advertising they have tried to differentiate their products to appear as unique in the minds of customers.

Remind Marketing communication involves promotion of the service, which reminds the consumers of the need they may have so that they can enter into a similar exchange. It also tries to reassure the consumers about the services being provided by the service provider, and is important, as it helps in retaining current customers.

Inform The communication about the services product helps in informing the target market about the services being offered, so that the same can be incorporated in the awareness set. When the objective is to inform, the advertising copy contains the details of the services being provided, for example, Jet Airways informing consumers about its e-ticketing facility and trying to build confidence about the same by informing about payment protection being used (VeriSign and Thawte) that is in line with the industry standard.

Persuade Communication attempts to persuade current and potential customers about the desirability of entering into an exchange relationship.

THE COMMUNICATION PROCESS

The communication process consists of a source, or the organization that intends to send a message to its audience (Fig. 14.1). The organization decides what message it wants to convey to the customers, through which medium it intends to send the message, and how it wants to deliver (encode) the message. This message then reaches the target audience, which deciphers (decodes) the message and gives a feedback to the source in the form of either verbal communication or indirect communication, in the form of purchase of goods. The target audience deciphers the message in accordance with a number of factors such as beliefs, attitudes, needs, etc. In reality, there can be a difference in the message perceived by the audience and the message that was originally intended

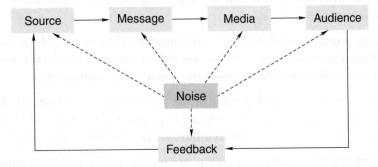

Source: Adapted from Kotler et al. (2006).

Fig. 14.1 The communication process

by the communicator. For example, the advertisement by United Colors of Benetton showing the hands of a white man handcuffed to those of a black man was accepted variably across different parts of the globe. In New York, for instance, there were a lot of complaints as people deciphered it as a black man under arrest (*Time* 1989). However, it was awarded the 16th Grand Prix for Best Poster (*Advertising History* 2006). A goal-oriented communicator begins with the target audience and codes the message in coordination with their needs and perceptions so that the message deciphered is what was intended by the source.

PROMOTION PLANNING AND STRATEGY

Promotion planning and strategy is a sequential process and involves careful planning for an effective impact. The different steps involved in promotion planning are shown in Fig. 14.2.

Situational Analysis

Situational analysis is the current analysis of both the internal and external factors affecting the organization. The internal factors consist of all the factors internal to an organization and the external factors consist of market segment analysis, environmental analysis, and competitor analysis.

Internal analysis   Some of the factors to be considered while performing the internal analysis are:

Strengths and weaknesses   The company should list out the strengths and weaknesses of the organization. The idea is to cash in on the strength by focusing on it and conveying the same to the target audience and to work on the weakness and try to overcome them, and not highlight the weak areas in the marketing communication. The strengths and weaknesses of all the strategic business units/departments such as operations, finance, marketing, etc. must be carried out.

Service specifications   The service specifications or the services product must be worked out in detail so that there is no ambiguity regarding the communication of the offering to be made.

Price   Pricing is one of the four Ps of marketing and the price at which the service is offered is of utmost importance. It is also one of the considerations on the basis of which the customer sets his expectations about the quality of service offering.

Company's past experience with the promotion mix   If the service organization has already worked on the promotion mix, the previous experience of the same (difficulties faced, outcome assessments, etc.) is bound to influence the mix to be selected.

Service recovery feedback   Service recovery occurs due to a number of reasons one of them being marketing communications (see Chapter 10). If the marketing communication creates expectations that cannot be fulfilled, and if any such issues are highlighted during recovery feedback, then they should also be taken into consideration.

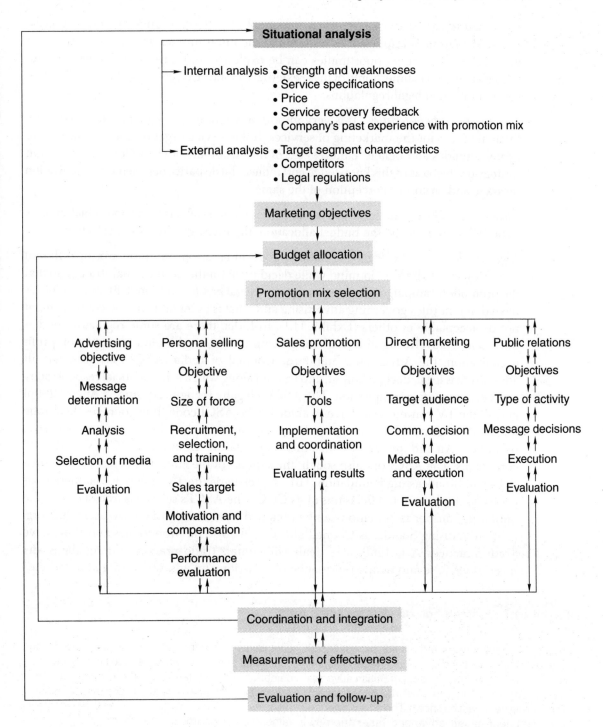

Situational analysis

→ Internal analysis • Strength and weaknesses
• Service specifications
• Price
• Service recovery feedback
• Company's past experience with promotion mix

→ External analysis • Target segment characteristics
• Competitors
• Legal regulations

Marketing objectives

Budget allocation

Promotion mix selection

Advertising objective	Personal selling	Sales promotion	Direct marketing	Public relations
Message determination	Objective	Objectives	Objectives	Objectives
Analysis	Size of force	Tools	Target audience	Type of activity
Selection of media	Recruitment, selection, and training	Implementation and coordination	Comm. decision	Message decisions
Evaluation	Sales target	Evaluating results	Media selection and execution	Execution
	Motivation and compensation		Evaluation	Evaluation
	Performance evaluation			

Coordination and integration

Measurement of effectiveness

Evaluation and follow-up

Source: Adapted from Michael Ray (1973); Engel et al. (1987); Kotler et al. (2006); and Jobber (2001).

Fig. 14.2 Promotion planning strategy

External analysis External factors are important while designing the promotion strategy. External analysis is important to understand the opportunities and threats existing in the market so that the opportunities can be exploited and threats can be worked out strategically, well in time. Some of these external factors are target segment characteristics, competitors, and legal regulations.

Target segment characteristics It is very important to study the segment identified to be the main focus for the marketing of services. If the service organization is aware of the needs, attitudes and beliefs, culture, etc., of the customers, it can tailor the promotion strategy on the basis of this knowledge and reduce the disparity between the organization message and customer perception of the same.

Competitors The promotional activity of the competitors affects the promotional strategy to be followed, namely, the budget allocation, the message, the media selection, etc.

Legal regulations The legal regulations governing the promotion mix in different countries have to be kept in mind while deciding upon the promotional strategy so that the promotion campaign does not run into any legal hassles later on. Different countries have different rules governing advertising and what is acceptable in one country might not be acceptable in others (Exhibit 14.1). In India, there are some regulatory bodies that control advertising and marketing communication. A voluntary and non-profit organization, the Advertising Standards Council of India (ASCI), ensures that all advertising is legal, decent, honest, and truthful along with a sense of social responsibility and encourages fair competition. The ASCI is legally recognized (since 2 August 2006) and all the TV commercials have to abide by the ASCI code. It encourages the public to complain against advertisements, which they consider to be false, misleading, offensive, or unfair. An independent Consumer Complaints Council (CCC) evaluates all complaints. The ASCI has also sought the support of the concerned associations, such as Indian Broadcasting Foundation (IBF), to persuade the TV channels to adhere to its code and implement the decisions of its CCC. The ASCI's service is free of cost to the public and further information can be obtained from the website www.ascionline.org. (The Advertising Standards Council of India, 2006). The Monopolies and Restrictive Trade Practices Act, 1969, also deals with unfair trade practices. It regulates any misleading, false and wrong representation in writing (in ads, warranty guarantee, etc.)

Exhibit 14.1 Warne's hair ad violates British rules

A hair loss treatment advertisement by Advanced Hair Studio features Australian cricket legend Shane Warne. This ad was found to breach British advertising industry rules since a celebrity endorsement using medicine cannot be shown. The advert referred to a treatment called advanced laser therapy, which uses a medicine called noxidil. After probing complaints about the ad, the standards watchdog concluded that the ad breached the code by using a celebrity endorsement involving a medicine. The Advanced Hair Studio wants to appeal against the ruling as it feels that Warne promotes their company rather than any particular treatment.

Source: Adapted from *The Times of India* (2006).

or oral (at the time of sale) even if no actual injury is caused. It also considers all business promotion schemes announcing 'free gifts', 'contests', etc., where an element of deception is involved. The department of consumer affairs is also working on legislation to curb misleading ads and communications. Under the new norms, if the advertised service or product fails to deliver as per its promise, it will attract a penalty. Also, the companies will now be responsible for any misuse of brands by fake marketers (Jha and Philip 2006).

Marketing objectives

The marketing objectives to be achieved in the communication campaign should be clear from the outset. The ultimate aim of communication is to stimulate sales and increase profits, but the objectives have operational value, and can be related to sales (the buyer knowledge and buyer readiness stage) (Kotler et al. 2006) and distribution of the service. Some of the marketing objectives are as follows:

Brand awareness When a service organization enters a market it needs to make the consumers aware of their presence and the services they offer. Thus, when HDFC advertised its home loan, it had to inform the consumers that it was providing both the options of floating and fixed interest rate in one. Also, with the passage of time, to have a top-of-the-mind awareness recall, the service organization needs to constantly keep the customers aware of the services being offered. Thus, creating brand awareness is a never-ending process. For example, the advertisement encouraging tourists and making them aware of Goa as a tourism destination promoting adventure; beach; medical meetings, incentives, conference, and exhibitions (MICE); etc. Central Bank of India is creating awareness of the fact that, in spite of being in the market for generations, they still provide value service without a generation gap.

Brand knowledge The purpose of awareness is to build brand recall and recognition, but often customers might not be aware of the different services being provided by a service provider. Thus, organizations frequently communicate with the target audience to make them aware of the services being provided. Radisson informs customers of the wedding services it provides. Similarly, IDBI informs customers about the various services IDBI Bank offers, be it corporate banking, retail banking, SME products, or agro products.

Brand attitude Organizations can communicate with their various audiences to create a favourable attitude towards the brand. An attitude is developed when the customers assess the brand with the perceived ability of the service to meet the need under consideration. Depending upon the need at hand the customers can develop a liking or a preference for the service.

Liking It is important for the service provider to have a favourable attitude towards the brand. If not, the organization must try to identify the factors responsible for a negative attitude and try to remove these feelings. Bank of India is trying to develop a positive attitude in the customers' mind by stressing in their print, as well as TV and radio advertisements, that they value relationships and in their bank, along with banking services, relations are also developed.

Preference If a customer likes a particular brand the next step is to create a preference for the brand over other service providers. An organization can create preferences by trying to identify what they are good at and then try to promote these features to try to build preference in the target audience. For example, BSNL's advertisement highlights the 15-second pulse rate offer and builds customer preference by trying to highlight the need for charging calls at a pulse rate of 15 seconds. The message, 'why pay for the whole when you just need a part of it' drives the benefit clearly to the customers.

Conviction Another aspect of communication is trying to instil confidence in the customers in order to motivate them to make the purchase. Favourable attitudes can be converted into conviction by marketing communication. The marketing communication of BSNL's Dataone broadband informs customers that it is India's number one Internet service provider and highlights the various features of its broadband service. UCO Bank's advertisement tries to convince the customers that it is the right option for carrying out business in the twenty-first century. It also ends with the tagline, 'Honours your trust'.

Sales There can be a time lag between convincing the customers about the purchase and the actual act of purchase by the customer. To remove this time lag, the service provider can motivate customers to make purchases by offering schemes for a limited period. For example, the advertisement of CellOne tries to convince customers to purchase the CellOne connection by providing free talk time worth Rs 600 for six months, provided they make the purchase between 1st and 15th August, and informing them that there is no hidden cost and they should not miss this 'golden opportunity'.

Distribution The service organization can also communicate with its audience to search for franchisees or distributors for their services. For example, when Jay Retailing and Merchandizing Pvt. Ltd wanted to expand its retail chain 'The Loot', it placed double-paged advertisements in magazines highlighting the requirements the franchisee has to fulfil.

Budget Allocation

The following four methods for allocating the budget for marketing communication are generally used (Kotler and Keller 2006; Kotler et al. 2006; and Jobber 2001):

Affordable method This is a simple method of identifying the amount of money the organization can afford to spend in a particular financial year. It is not related to the objective of marketing communication or the amount of money required to perform effective marketing communications.

Percentage of sales method Some organizations fix a particular percentage of sales as the amount allocated for marketing communications.

Supporters of this method find the following advantages related to it:

- Companies spend as much as they can afford.
- It encourages managers to correlate selling price, promotion cost, and profit per unit.
- Encourages stability, especially when the industry spends the same percentage.

However this method has its limitations. These are:

- It views sales as a cause of promotion rather than the result.
- Budget allocation is on the basis of availability rather than based on opportunities.
- If sales fall then the communications also are limited, whereas more communication may be required to boost the flagging sales.
- As the sales vary from year to year, the budget for communication also varies and makes long-term planning difficult.
- There is no logical basis for choosing the percentage other than what competitors are doing or what the organization has already been doing.

Competitive parity method This method allocates the budget for marketing communication on the basis of competitor's outlay. This method advocates that:

- Competitor's budget represents the industry wisdom.
- Spending what competitors spend prevents promotion war.

However, it is seen that neither of the cases is necessarily applicable.

The objective and task method Setting the budget on the basis of costs involved in performing specific tasks for achieving specified objectives is known as allocating budget on objective and task method. In this method the management decides beforehand what they want to achieve from their marketing communication, plans the tasks involved, and sets the budget accordingly, thus focusing on the objectives to be achieved rather than on what competitors are doing.

Promotion Mix Selection

The next step is to select the promotion mix based on the communication objectives and budget allocated. An organization can opt for a combination of mixes, say, advertising, sales promotion, and personal selling, or only sales promotion and personal selling, etc. All the different promotion mixes are studied in more detail in the communication mix. A summary of the advantages and disadvantages of the different communication mixes can be drawn here to give a comprehensive view (Table 14.1). A detailed discussion of the promotion mix follows in the subsequent portions of the chapter.

The following factors influence the choice of promotional mix (Jobber 2001; Kotler and Keller 2006):

Resource available and cost of promotional tool The different communication mixes have varying costs associated with them. Advertising may require more money, whereas sales promotion and publicity might cost a lot less. Thus, resources available for the communication mix will affect the choice of promotion.

Market size and concentration Advertising is seen to be most effective when a mass market is present and if the market is also geographically dispersed. Internet marketing is also gaining prominence with more consumers getting online and the cost associated is also less compared to some of the other methods of promotion. If the target audience is small, reaching them through personal selling will be more feasible.

Table 14.1	Advantages and disadvantages of different elements of the promotional mix		

S. no.	Promotional tool	Advantages	Disadvantages
1	Advertising	□ Informs customers about the services □ Reaches mass audience □ It reminds and reinforces the services offered □ Can be used both for long-term image building and quick sales □ Reaches geographically dispersed customers at low cost per exposure	□ One way communication □ Impersonal and not as persuasive as some of the other promotion mixes □ TV advertising requires a large budget and is faced by multiple channel options and channel switching □ Advertising copy needs to be changed after regular intervals to continue generating consumer's interest
2	Sales promotion	□ Gain attention for the service □ Offers strong incentives to customers to purchase the service	□ Effects are short-lived □ Do not contribute to long-term brand value
3	Personal selling	□ Most effective in building buyer preference, conviction, and purchase □ Is interactive and can tailor presentations according to buyers' needs □ Two-way communication can take place, where service providers also get insights into the customer's requirements for the services product □ At the time of re-purchase, it provides service providers an opportunity for service recovery (if any) □ The information provided is current □ Helps in building customer relationships	□ Is the organizations' most expensive promotional tool □ Other promotional tools like advertising and sales promotion can be stopped after a period of time but personal selling requires more commitment and cannot be varied easily
4	Direct marketing	□ Can customize the message to individual requirements □ The message will be more current as regards service details as the time period required for flow of information from service provider to customer is less in comparison to advertising	□ The reach is limited and cannot reach mass audience with this method (except through Internet marketing)
5	Publicity	□ Consumers believe publicity material more in comparison to advertisements □ Can reach those customers also who avoid advertisements and sales force □ Can reach a wider audience at negligible or low cost to the organization	□ Often negative publicity can also be created

Source: Adapted from Kotler et al. (2006); Pickton and Broderick (2001).

Customer information needs Personal selling is used if the service involved requires technical discussions or discussions of different options available, e.g., in the sale of insurance policies—a cover can range from Rs 30,000 to Rs 25 lakh, and the advertisement encourages consumers to call and ask for more options. If not much technical information is required customers can be satisfied by advertisements.

Table 14.2 Effect of product life cycle on choice of promotion mix

	Introduction	Growth	Maturity	Decline
Advertising	Build product awareness among early adopters and dealers	Build awareness and interest in the mass market	Stress brand differences and benefits	Reduce to level needed to retain hardcore loyals
Sales promotion	Use heavy sales promotion to entice trial	Reduce to take advantage of heavy customer demand	Increase to encourage brand switching	Reduce to minimal level

Source: Adapted from Wasson (1978); Weber (1976); and Doyle (1976, 2002).

Push versus pull If the service provider is focusing on the channel intermediaries it focuses on push strategy, which can be achieved through personal selling and sales incentives, but if the consumers are the focus then service providers engage in pull strategies, which can be achieved by advertising and consumer promotion.

Product life cycle The stage of the life cycle the service is in affects the choice of promotion mix. For example, in the introductory stage, the organization will invest in both advertising and sales promotion, whereas in the decline stage the investment in both the activities is reduced (Table 14.2). For a detailed discussion on the effect of product life cycle in promotion mix, refer to Chapter 2.

Buyer readiness stage The stage of the buyer in the purchase process affects the choice of the promotion mix. It is seen that in the awareness, interest, desire, action (AIDA) model of consumer purchase, advertising and publicity help to raise awareness and create interest in the consumers, but are not very effective in encouraging consumers to take action. Sales promotion and personal selling are known to affect desire and inspire customers to take action and purchase the product.

Coordination and Integration

The whole marketing plan needs to be coordinated and the message displayed should be uniform so as not to confuse the customers about the services provided. It should also be in line with the services provided so that the customer expectations can be met easily and surpassed, as the case may be. Moreover, since a combination of promotion mix is used, which different departments handle (advertising by advertising department or agency, personal selling by the sales department, etc.), there can be issues when the message delivered may not be consistent. Say, the advertising department may position the service as premium, whereas the sales force may offer discounts giving a contrary notion.

Measuring Effectiveness

Measuring effectiveness of the communication helps the management to know about the outcome of the effort and the money spent on the communication strategy.

Effectiveness can be measured by conducting communication (advertising) research. Measuring recall and recognition of the services by the target audience, what features they recall, their perceptions about the service provided based on the marketing communication, and attitude formation or change (for a first time consumer or a re-purchaser of the service provided), all provide interesting knowledge and information to the managerial staff. Generally, what is targeted should be measured. Thus, if the objective of communication is sales, then the sales department should be the focus of research to measure the impact of advertisement on sales. The New York American Marketing Association has in affiliation with Advertising Club Bombay started the EFFIE Awards in India (Advertising Club Bombay 2006). These awards measure the success of an agency in increasing the clients business across a variety of parameters. In 2006, Lowe won the trophy for the Effie Agency of the year. O&M won a golden Effie for its 'Surprisingly SBI' advertisement (*The Economic Times* 2006).

COMMUNICATION MIX

Advertising

Advertising is a paid form of communication by the service provider with its target audience to facilitate exchanges (of services or information) with its stakeholders. An organization can either design the advertisement in-house (by creating a department) or it can outsource it from an advertising agency. In India, the advertising industry stood at Rs 9,600 crore in 2003 (*Business World* 2005) and currently stands at Rs 13,200 crore (Razdan 2006). There are many advertising agencies, the most prominent being Ogilvy and Mather (O&M), Lowe, McCann-Erickson, Contract Advertising, FCB-Ulka, etc. In deciding the advertising programme, an organization has to look into the following five Ms of advertising (Kotler and Keller 2006):

1. **Mission** The mission is the objective the organization wants to achieve from the advertisement. The advertisers can have different missions such as to inform, to persuade, or to remind the customers, and hence the advertisement copy will defer depending upon which objective the advertiser wants to achieve.
2. **Money** This includes the money allotted for the advertisement (budget allocation).
3. **Message** This relates to the objective and positioning strategy, organizations spend a lot of time and effort in finalizing the message they want to convey to the consumers. For example, the Hutch network advertisement campaign showing a boy being followed by his dog was a very simple way of showing the area coverage of the Hutch service providers, and made a complete connection with the consumers.
4. **Media** Based on the reach of the target audience and costs involved, a number of media options are available for the service organization to choose from.
5. **Measurement** The measurement of the effectiveness of the advertisement can be done in the form of communication impact and sales impact.

Advertising objective
↓↑
Message determination
↓↑
Analysis
↓↑
Selection of media
↓↑
Evaluation

Fig. 14.3   The advertising process

The Advertising Process

The advertising process consists of the steps shown in Fig. 14.3.

Advertising Objective

Advertisements are most effective when they flow from a particular objective to be achieved. These objectives can be as follows (Jobber 2001):

Create awareness   Advertisements are used to create awareness about the service provider among the consumers. For example, the Airtel advertisement where the purpose is to create awareness about the Internet connection and details have been provided about the charges, speed, etc. Another example is Indian Overseas Bank's Tax Saver plan, the details of which have been communicated in their ad.

Stimulate trial   Advertisements can stimulate trial of the service, considering the fact that once the consumers try the service and are satisfied they are bound to return. For example, the ad of www.apollosindhoor.com, which offers free account opening for a limited period of time to stimulate trial. Also, the advertisement of Windsor Club, Indirapuram, tries to stimulate trial by positioning itself as a family club with recreational and sports facilities, restaurants, bar, fitness centre, spa, etc. It further tries to initiate trial by urging consumers to avail pre-launch membership benefits.

Position services   Product positioning is very important, as it is how the customers perceive the service that determines their consumption of the same. The services can be positioned on the basis of the following:

Service characteristics and customer benefits   This is generally used in the hospitality industry where hotels are classified as luxury, budget, etc. on the basis of services being provided. For example, the advertisement of Air Sahara, which talks about great fares even during peak seasons and customer benefits in terms of great timing, great food, great fares, and being on time, every time. Another example is the co-branding by Indian Oil with Air Sahara, and yet another example is that of Central Bank of India, which advertises its Cent Tax Saver scheme as having the dual benefit of earning interest and saving tax.

Price   Positioning services on the basis of price, signifies value for money and quality services at low prices.

Service user   Services can be positioned on the basis of the target audience for whom they are meant. For example, the advertisement of Indraprastha Apollo hospitals positions the service—advanced heart check—on the basis of service user, i.e., smokers.

Service use   Services can be positioned on the basis of how they are going to be used by the consumer. Banking services use this for loan advertisements; for example, State Bank of Bikaner and Jaipur advertises different types of retail loans, and Canara Bank highlights corporate finance, personal finance, export finance, infrastructure finance, etc.

Symbols   Symbols can be used to position services; for example, the golden arches of McDonald's, the logo of Punjab National Bank, currently Deutsche Bank is using the symbol depicted as inserted in the pocket/purse of famous personalities like Sunil Gavaskar and Sania Mirza.

Competition   Positioning against well-known competitors increases effectiveness as they can be used as reference points. For example, Maruti released full-page advertisements in *The Times of India*, New Delhi, 14 August 2006, showing how Maruti provides unmatched value whether you buy it, run it, or sell it. The advertisement then went on to compare the mileage of various models of Maruti (800, Alto, Omni, etc.) with that of Tata Indica and Hyundai Santro. It also compared the maintenance cost and resale value. However, Maruti was forced to stop this ad when Hyundai lodged a complaint with MRTP saying that the ad was 'misleading and disparaging' and was a fit case of 'unfair trade practice' (*The Economic Times* 2006). Another example of positioning against well-known competitors is that of CNN-IBN proclaiming that it is the most watched English news channel, and providing comparative results with NDTV, another well-known Indian channel. Another very interesting advertisement of positioning against competitors is that of *Dainik Jagran*, which considers news channels as its competitors and has tried to position itself in relation to them.

Social context   Positioning the service provider as a socially conscious organization is becoming relevant, especially in the current century. For example, see advertisements of ICICI Bank.

Correcting misconceptions   Advertisements can be used to correct misconceptions that exist about the services. For example, if at the time of service recovery, a service provider finds that certain misconceptions exist about the services that are creating expectations, which the service provider cannot fulfil, it should try to correct the same with the help of advertisements.

Remind and reinforce   Hutch and Airtel advertise constantly just to remind the customers about their presence and create top-of-the-mind recall so as to maintain their market share. Advertisements meant for reminding the customers are generally targeted at sales, so that the market share is retained.

Provide support to sales force   Advertisements have a wide reach and make the consumers aware about the service provider, thus giving the sales force an edge when they make their sales call. An aware consumer is bound to be more receptive towards the sales force than a consumer who is not aware about the service provider. Also, contact numbers and e-mail addresses are given in the advertisements so that interested consumers can call. It then becomes easy for the sales force, as they need call on interested parties only. For example, see the ad of MTNL targeted at business clients; it states a contact number where interested parties can call and also provides an e-mail address.

When the promotion mix is being selected, the budget is allocated for the different promotion mixes to be selected. This defines the budget allocated for advertising, which can again depend upon the stage in the product life cycle—competition, frequency of advertisements, and differentiation of services product.

Message Determination

The message to be conveyed to the consumers should be important for the consumers and should communicate the advantages that the service is going to provide to the customer. The message should be:

Simple So that it can be recalled easily like, 'Punjab National Bank—The name you can bank upon', or 'BSNL—Connecting India'.

Focus on differential advantage Ads should highlight how the service provider is different and how it can satisfy the needs and wants of the customers. For example, Finnair's advertisement highlights the lie-flat seat consumers can enjoy while travelling between Delhi and Europe.

Lifestyle The advertisement can target a particular lifestyle and relate the service to it. For example, Punjab National Bank uses lifestyle to put forth the idea of its e-banking facilities by showing a couple eating fast food and working on a laptop. They also highlight facilities like tele-banking, Internet banking, and debit/credit cards.

Fantasy This implies creating a wonder around the service provided. For example, the advertisement of Kerala Tourism tries to create fantasy by giving it a heavenly feel and the tag line, 'God's own country'.

Testimonials They can also be used when a known celebrity endorses a service. For example, cellular phone service providers use four celebrities to endorse their products, while Rahul Dravid features prominently in ads of Bank of Baroda and Abhishek Bachchan endorses American Express. Table 14.3 provides a snapshot on celebrity endorsements. However, there is a trend of employing celebrity endorsers too. These are experts in their sphere of professional careers like chef Sanjeev Kapoor, beauticians such as Coleen Khan, Naina Balsavar, Jawed Habib, etc. (Vyas 2006). Number of Advertisers in 2007 with top celebrities are listed in Table 14.4.

Many service providers also use customers to endorse their services, such as advertisement of Air Deccan featuring Nitin Jain, an HR consultant.

Once the advertisement message has been decided, it is very important to put it forth in an attractive manner so that it grabs the viewers' attention. The following points must be given careful consideration before finalizing the advertisement:

- illustration
- headline
- copy.

Table 14.3 Celebrity endorsements on TV during 2007

Category	Personality	% Share of overall Celebrity endorsement
Film industry [81%]	Film actor	50
	Film actress	31
TV industry [5%]	TV actor	3
	TV actress	2
Sports [14%]	Sportsmen	14

Source: Adapted from AdEx India online (2008).

For example, the advertisement of Presidium, Proposed Secondary School, though illustrated in black and white and does not use any celebrity, draws attention because the message has been portrayed in such a manner. The headline is enticing as it makes the consumer want to read further and the copy or the main text is simple, yet strong and convincing.

Analysis and Selection of Media

The advertising message can be presented before the audience through a number of media. The major ones for advertising can be categorized into print, electronic, and outdoor (also referred to as out-of-home).

- Print: newspaper, magazine, letters
- Electronic: radio, TV, cinema, e-mail
- Outdoor: kiosks, billboards, street furniture, transport (neon lit high-tech mobile trucks, etc.)

Factors affecting selection of media The major factors affecting the choice of media are as follows:

Media reach The task of the manager is to select the media that has maximum reach for the target audience. Reach denotes the number of people that are being exposed to that medium. The media reach in Indian states is given in Table 14.5.

Table 14.4 Top celebrities with the maximum number of advertisers in 2007

Celebrity	Number of advertisers
Shah Rukh Khan	21
Amitabh Bachchan	20
Shweta Tiwari	19
Sachin Tendulkar	17
Rahul Dravid	16

Source: Adapted from AdEx India online (2008).

Table 14.5 Media reach in Indian states

Media	Reach (%)
Press	23.7
TV	55
Satellite	27
Radio	20.7
Cinema	11.4

Source: Adapted from *The Marketing Whitebook* (2008).

In India, TV has the maximum media reach; even more than press. This holds true for all the states, except Kerala (*The Marketing Whitebook* 2005).

Type of service The type of service being advertised also affects the choice of media. For example, hotel and restaurant ads are better shown in colour magazines and as coloured ads in newspapers. The glossy Brand Equity supplement of *The Economic Times* carries coloured ads of Four Seasons, Emirates, etc. The advertisement of VLCC's 80–90 health movement, offering a 50 per cent discount on all packages from 26–28 November 2006 and free health check-ups on 26 November—anti-obesity day—was promoted heavily in radio (and some newspapers) during the period the offer was valid.

Cost involved The cost involved in the particular media and its fit with the budget is also a major consideration. Even though television has high initial cost, the cost per thousand exposures is considerably less.

A study of the money spent in global advertising across different media, shows that the Internet is growing at the highest CAGR (8.6 per cent), followed by radio (5.6 per cent) (see Table 14.6).

Media The different media, such as television, print, and radio, are discussed in detail in this section.

Television Globally, TV accounts for more than 40 per cent of advertising expenditure and contributed 41 per cent to the total media ad market in India in the year 2006 (*Business World* 2008). Also, year on year the time spent on watching TV ads is growing. Television has a distinct advantage over the other media as it uses both audio and visuals to create a dramatic effect, and is highly persuasive. The physical evidence of services can be brought about better with the help of this media. Moreover, it has broad acceptability and high believability. In India, it has a broader reach than even the newspapers. TV can also target the illiterate masses in rural areas.

Advertisements of products and services can be linked to events like cricket matches, or FIFA World Cup when there are opportunities of targeting maximum viewers. A lot of money is spent in advertisements during the match intervals, both on ground and on-screen, where viewers are exposed to the brand messages (see Exhibit 14.2). For example, BSNL sponsors all the fours and sixes in cricket matches, and as soon as a four or a six is scored it is announced as, 'BSNL four (or six)'.

Table 14.6 Global advertising in different media types

Segment	Global advertising (in $ millions)									
	1998	1999	2000	2001	2002P	2003	2004	2005	2006	2007
Television	1,02,480	1,07,029	1,20,523	1,15,082	1,20,275	1,22,869	1,31,337	1,35,323	1,43,834	1,49,680
% Change	8.3	4.4	12.6	-4.5	4.5	2.2	6.9	3.0	6.3	4.1
Internet	2,214	5,255	9,972	9,089	8,376	8,917	9,588	10,668	11,712	12,628
% Change	116.1	147.4	89.8	-8.9	-7.8	6.5	7.5	11.3	9.8	7.8
Magazines	39,922	41,631	45,261	41,386	39,416	39,854	40,873	42,291	44,488	47,089
% Change	4.8	4.3	8.7	8.6	-4.8	1.1	2.6	3.5	5.2	5.8
Newspapers	90,109	94,206	1,01,607	94,939	93,930	94,848	97,002	1,00,073	1,03,527	1,07,524
% Change	3.8	4.5	7.9	-6.6	-1.1	1.0	2.3	3.2	3.5	3.9
Radio	22,960	25,561	28,504	26,777	27,953	29,337	31,032	32,838	34,727	36,652
% Change	8.9	11.3	11.5	-6.1	4.4	5.0	5.8	5.8	5.8	5.5
Out-of-Home	15,329	15,931	17,154	17,091	17,551	18,021	18,795	19,698	20,684	21,716
% Change	2.4	3.9	7.7	-0.4	2.7	2.7	4.3	4.8	5.0	5.0
Total	2,72,924	2,89,613	3,23,021	3,04,364	3,07,501	3,13,846	3,28,627	3,40,891	3,58,972	3,75,289
% Change	6.4	6.1	11.5	-5.8	1.0	2.1	4.7	3.7	5.3	4.5

Source: Adapted from *The Marketing Whitebook (2008)*.

Exhibit 14.2 Indian Premier League's Ad spend

The extremely popular Indian Premier League (IPL) Twenty20 Tournament is estimated to have generated ad revenues of Rs 600 crore in its first season itself. Each of the 8 teams plans to spend around Rs 25 crore on marketing and promotion. The advertising market in India including the below-the-line activities is around Rs 22,000 crore per year. The Board of Cricket Control of India (BCCI) had put aside approximately Rs 100 crore as its advertising budget while Sony Entertainment Television, which owns the rights to telecast the matches, will earn around Rs 300 crore. IPL clearly becomes a new contribution to the ad industry.

Source: Adapted from Sheikh (2008).

Prime time charges are always higher in comparison to late night or other non-prime time slots. However, there are certain drawbacks associated with TV; the first being that the number of ads have increased from 86,000 in 2001 to 2,60,000 in 2005, and 200 channels have been added. Thus, along with the fragmentation of the media there has been an increase in the number of adverts leading to ad clutter. Globally, the ad clutter is increasing and stands at 484 (TV ads every week). India ranks at number 32 with a clutter of 311 compared to US, which has a clutter of 789 (Krishna and Soneji 2006). With the launch of numerous channels, consumers have many options and channel switching is very common; hence, to capture the viewers' attention service organizations have to invest in many channels. Alternatively, organizations can segment the target audience and choose the channel accordingly. For example, to reach business people advertisements can be aired on Aaj Tak (No. 1 channel for Hindi news viewership) or Zee News (No. 2 channel for viewership of Hindi news) (*The Marketing Whitebook 2005*). Table 14.7 shows the top 10 growing television channel genres across India for the year 2005–06.

Viewers get bored watching the same ad repeatedly. Thus, to generate interest companies have to change ad copy at regular intervals, which also involves costs. Getting

Table 14.7 Top 10 growing channel genres in India

	Growth (%)
Regional News	172
Business	105
English News	68
English Entertainment	51
Sports	50
English Movies	42
Hindi News	40
Regional Music	37
Hindi Movies	32
Infotainment	29

Source: Adapted from *The Marketing Whitebook (2008).*

Language	Newspaper	Readership (in lakh)
English	The Times of India	136
	Hindustan Times	61
	The Hindu	53
	The Telegraph	30
	Deccan Chronicle	30
Hindi	Dainik Jagran	536
	Dainik Bhaskar	306
	Amar Ujala	282
	Hindustan	235
	Rajsthan Patrika	132
	Punjab Kesari	109
	Aaj	76

Source: Adapted from Indian Readership Survey (IRS) (2007).

viewers' attention is very difficult due to channel switching; thus, even if the ad is aired at prime time there is no guarantee of audience viewership. Surprisingly, even though regional language channels enjoy maximum viewership it is the mass entertainment channels that draw the maximum advertising revenue (Table 14.8).

Another decision regarding ads on TV is the time duration of the ads. It was seen that 20-, 30-, and 50-second ads form 60 per cent of the ads in 2003 (*The Marketing Whitebook* 2005), but the current trend is towards long playing ads.

Press This includes both newspapers and magazines at national and regional level. With the onslaught of TV and now the Internet, consumers have many distractions and press has to compete very hard. This is combined with the fact that press can use only visuals, audio and motion appeal are both lacking; and only 45.8 per cent of the population is literate (*The Marketing Whitebook* 2005). The circulation figures of top dailies (in both Hindi and English) are provided in Table 14.8.

A look at the adspend distribution by year from 1990 to 2004 shows that print constituted 70 per cent of adspend in 1990, which reduced to 51 per cent in 2004 (*The Marketing Whitebook 2005*). Most of the cellular service providers and credit card companies mail promotional material of new schemes and services launched directly to existing customers.

Press offers opportunities to segment market demographically and psychographically, and gives credibility and prestige. The ads in the magazines or newspaper can be reviewed at leisure and referring back to an ad for information (say, phone number or address of the service organization) is easier. There is a good pass along readership. The quality of reproduction is also good in most of the magazines, e.g., the ad for Singapore Airlines.

However, there are some weaknesses too, as readers can just gloss over advertisements (selective attention) thus ignoring the campaigns. If ads have been targeted in, say, auto magazines then there is high competitive clutter. Moreover, there is a long ad purchase lead-time and the position is also not guaranteed in magazines.

Newspapers have the added advantage of immediacy and information on discounts and sales offers are best passed on by newspapers. However, it faces the issues of low quality reproduction and lacks colour quality. Moreover, doubling the size of the ad does not double readership but definitely doubles the cost.

Radio Radio, being cheaper than TV still lags behind in penetration in India. In 2003, it contributed just 2 per cent to the overall advertising revenue and is way behind the share of 6–7 per cent in developing countries and 14 per cent in US (*The Marketing Whitebook* 2005). In China, radio advertising is growing at an average rate of 39 per cent annually and is expected to reach $38 million in 2006 (Madden 2006). With the private sector allowed to enter, there are now a number of players in the urban areas, with 22 radio stations in 2003. However, with the government giving due consideration to spread of radio in the Tenth Five Year Plan (2002–07), the revenue is expected to reach Rs 688 crore by 2008. Radio has the advantage of geographic localization and has the distinct advantage of being mobile. Radio is preferred by organizations as here you can give audio effects to the advertisement, the ad is cheaper to produce, and during traffic rush hours there is bound to be wider coverage. However, the drawback associated with radio is that there are no visuals and it has to rely on the audience's imagination.

Outdoor Outdoor advertising is getting a new look with newer technology upgrading the quality of the hoardings and availability of newer options such as bus shelters, kiosks, and mobile trucks.

In India, outdoor advertising has a long history and other than hoardings, ads painted on walls are a common sight especially on the highways. Outdoor spending on ads has increased from 2000 when it was 8 per cent of ad expenditure to 8.5 per cent in 2003. The expected top spenders across three major media categories are given in Table 14.9.

The cost of hoardings indicated in Table 14.10 provides an idea of the costs involved.

However, the guidelines and policies set for roadside advertisements were formulated in 1972, but the traffic population has faced a drastic change since then. The Delhi Police have filed an affidavit in the Supreme Court against the same (Exhibit 14.3). However, outdoor advertisements have limitations and they can serve as additional (reminder) ads but not as the sole medium of advertising. They suffer from short exposure time, maybe a couple of seconds, are expensive, and are affected by environmental conditions (Table 14.10).

Cinema Cinema was a weak medium of advertising with the ads placed during the start of the movie or during the interval when the audience viewership fell drastically. However, now innovative ways of placing products or services in the movies has opened up new vistas. It has been studied that consumers recognize a product more if they have seen it placed in a movie or a TV programme. Film placements, associative marketing, cross-branding, and integrated promotion with movie and TV serials, are increasingly becoming a part of the media budget. According to Navin Shah, CEO, P9 Integrated, an

Table 14.9 Top spenders by category

	Television		Radio		Print	
	Top 10 advertisers	**Spends (Rs millions)**	**Top 10 advertisers**	**Spends (Rs millions)**	**Top 10 advertisers**	**Spends (Rs millions)**
1	Hindustan Lever Ltd	6,377	Hindustan Lever Ltd	161	Hewlett-Packard India Ltd	828
2	Reckitt Benckiser (India) Ltd	1,952	MTNL	60	Maruti Udyog Ltd	711
3	Paras Pharmaceuticals Ltd	1,633	GTM Builders & Promoters	47	Pantaloons Retail India Ltd	594
4	Procter & Gamble	1,190	Reliance Communications	45	Bajaj Auto	513
5	L'Oreal India Pvt. Ltd	1,166	Bharti Airtel Ltd	45	LG Electronics India Ltd	458
6	Colgate Palmolive India Ltd	1,132	LIC	33	Tata Motors Ltd	440
7	Coca-Cola India Ltd	1,082	Maruti Udyog Ltd	26	Hero Honda Motors Ltd	433
8	Johnson & Johnson Ltd	1,016	Prince Pharma	25	Reliance Communications	417
9	Dabur India Ltd	1,008	Hutchison Essar Telecom Ltd	24	Samsung India Electronics Ltd	365
10	Brooke Bond Lipton	947	Tata Sky Ltd	23	Nokia Corporation	356

Source: Adapted from *The Marketing Whitebook (2008).*

arm of Percept India, associative marketing attracted Rs 55–60 crore and has increased to Rs 150 crore by the end of 2006 (Exhibit 14.4). The mega blockbuster *Kkrish* is a successful example of how Singapore tied up with the movie to promote tourism in Singapore.

Exhibit 14.3 Cops want key roads cleared of hoardings

The cops in Delhi want certain roadside areas to be clear of advertising hoardings, which can prove to be hazardous for commuters. According to police officials, the civil agencies allow these hoardings since it is a source of revenue for them. Since the city has undergone a lot of changes as far as the traffic scenario is concerned, there is a need to formulate new strategies for the same. The nature of hoardings is dependent on the location, size, distance, colour, and object. The location, colour scheme, content, and pictorial representation are responsible for drawing the attention of the drivers. Hazardous hoardings that distract drivers can prove fatal.

Source: Adapted from Singh (2006).

Table 14.10 Cost of top hoardings in India

City	Location	Size	Approx (net/month) (in Rs lakh)
Mumbai	Patel Bridge	136×16	15.00
	Mahim overhead	160×10	12.00
Chennai	Gemini Flyover	90×30	4.00
	Airport Road	100×40	5.00
	Anna Nagar	67×40	4.00
Bangalore	M G Road	25×12	2.00
	Residency Road	25×12	2.00
	Airport Road	60×25	5.00
Hyderabad	Khairatabad Unipole	50×40	3.25
	Nagarjuna Circle	140×40	4.00
	Begumpet Flyover	50×25	1.30
Kolkata	In front of Science City (Boat City)	60×40	1.90
	Gariahat Flyover	40×20	0.65
	Ultadanga Bridge—to airport	60×30	1.60
	Ultadanga Bridge—from airport	30×30	1.50
Ahmedabad	CG Road, Stadium Circle	30×15	0.85
	Ashram Road	30×15	0.30
	Fun Republic Circle	60×40	1.30

Source: Adapted from *The Marketing Whitebook (2005).*

Internet Advertising on the Internet is rising in India as more and more consumers are going online for their needs. Internet advertising is at $0.6 billion and is projected to grow at a CAGR of 40.1 per cent (Exhibit 14.5). There are a number of models available for advertising on the net, such as intromercials, ultramercials, and contextual advertising. With brick and mortar companies opting to advertise online, a number of dot com companies are using the traditional media of press and hoardings to reach the target audience. Naukri.com's famous Hari Sadu ad comes to mind, and see the screenshot from Shaadi.com to understand how the company is investing in a combination of media choices to build its presence in the market.

Internet advertising gains more importance considering the fact that consumers give up the time on TV to offset time spent on the Internet. Moreover, the Internet is eating into the prime time viewership as over half of all home Internet users log in between 6.00 p.m., and midnight (Table 14.11).

With the launch of the Internet protocol television (IPTV) by MTNL (BSNL, Bharti, and Reliance are conducting trials for the same) wherein an individual can watch TV

Exhibit 14.4 Happily married: Brands, show biz

There is a new trend of associative marketing, cross-branding, integrated promotions, and brand tie-ups among brand marketers and entertainment industry. Brands are spending as much as five crore to capture the entertainment market. Brands are increasingly being looked at as more than just wallpapers in movies and other entertainment forms. Associative marketing is an effective way of leveraging from a movie, as there is no gestation period required while the movie is under production. Another trend is that of brands associating themselves with movies that star their brand ambassadors. One can recall Coke's activities around *Rang de Basanti* since Aamir Khan endorsed the brand. These trends point to the fact that brands are looking for attentive viewing, which movies can offer in an uncluttered environment.

Source: Adapted from *The Economic Times* (2006).

channels, surf on the net, and talk on the phone with Triple-play, the future of Internet appears brighter (Anand 2006). See Table 14.12.

Evaluation According to John Philip Jones, renowned advertising icon, 'Any advertising that does not deliver sales in the first seven days is completely ineffectual' (*The Economic Times* 2006). To gauge the effect of advertising programmes they need to be evaluated constantly. The effect of advertising can be measured by measuring the ad recall or by measuring the sales effect. Ad recall can be measured by taking recall tests wherein consumers are asked to recall everything related to advertisers—the advertising message, brand name, etc. Sales effect of advertising is more difficult to measure than the ad recall as the sales are affected by a number of factors such as individual preferences, service features, and price. However, one way to measure the affect of advertising is to compare the sales vis-à-vis the advertising budget.

Exhibit 14.5 Value Ad net gain

Even though India is behind Taiwan and Thailand in the size of Internet advertising, India's market is poised to grow. By 2010, India is set to reach the fourth position from the current sixth. While China continues to grow at a modest 25 per cent, South Korea—supposed to be one of the most wired nations in the world—will grow only in low single digits. The following table clarifies the situation.

Country	By 2010	Percentage growth
China	64.0	25.4
Japan	16.7	7.7
South Korea	8.6	3.8
Taiwan	1.7	8.0
Thailand	1.1	17.0
India	2.2	40.1

Source: Adapted from PwC Entertainment & Media Outlook, (2006–10).

Table 14.11   Prime time

Duration of usage per day (from home)	Less than 30 minutes	30 minutes to 2 hours	2 hours to 5 hours
Internet	17%	66%	13%
Television	14%	71%	14%

Preferred time of Internet usage (from home)	
Before 9.00 a.m.	5%
9.00 a.m. to 6.00 p.m.	28%
6.00 p.m. to midnight	52%
After midnight/throughout the day	15%

Source: Adapted from Dobhal (2006).

The short-term impact of advertising can be influenced by a 'good creative', whereas the medium (one year) impact can be affected by a combination of creative, ad spend, and media choice. Long-term effects of advertising can be measured by studying the penetration, purchase frequency, advertising intensiveness, advertising elasticity, etc.

It is seen that organizations often opt for a combination of media to get their message across. A case in point is Shaaditimes.com, which has chosen different media to convey its messages.

There are different advertising companies offering advertising solutions in India. A ranking of them is given in Table 14.13.

Personal Selling

Personal selling involves selling the product of the service organization through the sales force. This involves maintaining a sales force and hence a sales department, the personnel of which are involved in direct contact with the customers. The maintenance of the sales people, their travelling cost while on sales calls, etc., all cost the organization a great deal. Thus, in the overall communication budget they are responsible for a major chunk of the money allocation. The sales force performs the following functions (Kotler et al. 2006):

Prospecting   This involves search for identification of prospective new customers.

Table 14.12   Forecast for growth of Internet

Type of User	2005–06	2006–07	2007–08	2008–09
Ever Users (in millions)	32.2	42.5	53.5	64.6
Active Users (in millions)	21.1	28.7	35.7	43.5

Source: Adapted from *The Marketing Whitebook (2008)*.

Table 14.13   Overall ranking of top 25 ad agencies in India

Rank	Agency	Score
1	O&M	7.47
2	McCann Erickson	6.76
3	Lowe Lintas	6.71
4	JWT	6.59
5	Leo Burnett	6.58
6	Mudra	6.29
7	Grey Worldwide	6.26
8	FCB-Ulka	6.03
9	Contract	5.92
10	Rediffusion DY&R	5.86
11	RK Swamy BBDO	5.82
12	Saatchi & Saatchi	5.79
13	iB&W	5.77
14	Euro RSCG	5.63
15	Bates Enterprise	5.61
16	Ambience Publicis	5.56
17	SSC&B Lintas	5.51
18	Everest	5.48
19	Dentsu	5.46
20	Interface	5.45
21	Publicis India	5.33
22	Triton	5.21
23	Percept H	5.13
24	Equus Red Cell	5.09
24	TBWA	5.09

Source: Adapted from Brand Equity, *The Economic Times* (2006).

Targeting   This involves allocation of time (fixing appointments) with the prospective customers and at the same time allocating time to servicing current customers.

Communicating   The sales employees communicate about the service organization's 'product' offering and try to answer all their queries.

Selling   After communicating about the services the sales personnel approach their main goal—closing the sale. To achieve this, they may make commitments, promises, offer discounts, and try to mould the service offering in the best possible manner.

Servicing Certain services; e.g., the sale of insurance, require the sales representatives to constantly assist the customers by getting all the forms filled, collecting the cheques and depositing them with the service organization, and delivering the documents to the customer.

Information gathering Since the sales people interact continuously with the customers they can get the customers' feedback regarding service requirements, service delivery gaps, and how they can make improvements. The organization should decide what information they want from the customers and direct the sales people accordingly.

Allocating During scarce delivery it is the task of the sales personnel to decide whom to allocate the resources to. For example, during the season when there is requirement for banqueting or conferencing from different sources, the sales people decide whom to allocate the same to.

Personal selling can be a challenging job as Akshara, the Kerala IT mission's e-literacy and enterprise programme implemented in association with local bodies, realized. When they had to market the idea of computer learning to fishermen, they realized that the fishermen never had the time, as they were mostly offshore. So Akshara hit upon an innovative idea of going on fibre boats to groups of fishing boats at sea. When the fishermen had cast their nets and were waiting for their catch, the Akshara team utilized this opportunity to inform them about e-learning, and the encouraging results speak for themselves (Exhibit 14.6).

Sales Force Management

The management of the sales force requires the following functions—objectives; the size of the force; recruitment, selection, and training; allocation of sales targets; motivation and compensation; and performance evaluation (Fig. 14.4).

Objectives This involves the specific objectives for the sales force, that is, to achieve a market share of 15 per cent from 12 per cent, or to achieve a certain average rate of return (ARR). These targets can then be divided geographically or region-wise and further targets can be allocated to the sales personnel. This helps the management to also decide the number of personnel required in the department in a particular territory.

Exhibit 14.6   Kerala fisherfolk finally discover how to use net

The fisherfolk in Kerala have something more interesting than their fish catch. The Kerala IT mission's e-literacy and enterprise programme implemented in association with local bodies, has led the fishermen community to undergo computer literacy programmes. The e-literacy classes cost Rs 40 each while the local body contributes Rs 80 for each of the beneficiaries. Those who have finished the course use net telephony to chat with their kids abroad. Officials also point out that these fishing communities are now ready to enjoy the benefits of the state's e-governance initiatives.

Source: Adapted from *The Scaria* (2006).

Personal selling

Objective

Size of force

Recruitment, selection, and training

Sales target

Motivation and compensation

Performance evaluation

Fig. 14.4 Personal selling process

Size   The sales force can follow a geographic structure, product structure, or a customer-based structure. In the geographic structure, geographic areas are allotted to the sales force, and they are responsible for the sales of all the service products and the customer satisfaction in that particular area. In the product structure, the sales force is allotted specific service products and are responsible for the sale of that service product. For example, in the insurance sector, products, such as life insurance, general insurance, vehicle, or event insurance, can be allotted to different sales personnel. In a customer-based structure, the sales force is allotted customers on the basis of market segmentation, say, for booking rooms in hotels. The sales force can also be assigned as exhibition and fairs event managers, managers to handle different corporate accounts, etc. Once this is decided, specific requirements of the sales force are drawn for recruitment.

Recruitment, selection, and training   Once the job description is drawn the next step is to identify sources from where the sales force is to be recruited. The human resource department can place an advertisement in the newspapers, place requirements with consultants, or draw from their network, etc. The list of prospective candidates are drawn and interviewed. The short-listed candidates are then enrolled and passed through a training programme where knowledge about the organization, its services, its competitor organization and their services, selling procedures, etc., is imparted to them.

Sales target allocation   Once the training is over the sales personnel are informed about their sales areas (geographic, product-wise, etc.) and the targets (in line with the objectives set) they have to achieve.

Motivation and compensation   Once the sales force has been allocated targets, motivation is provided to them in the form of incentives, either monetary or otherwise. In some organizations the compensation or remuneration offered is itself linked to the sales in the form of commission.

Performance evaluation   At regular intervals (weekly, monthly, etc.) the performance of the sales force is reviewed. This helps the organization to keep a check on them. If a person has performed well, they reward him/her (e.g., employee of the month), or if the performance is not as per expectations they try to find reasons for this—service product failure, sales force drawback—and try to overcome them. If at subsequent performance evaluations the employee is still not performing, he/she may be replaced.

The evaluation and control of the total sales force is done at the coordination and integration level. This is also required to make sure that the advertising and other promotion mixes are in tune with the promises and communications made by the sales personnel.

Sales Promotion

'Sales promotion consists of short-term incentives to encourage the purchase or sale of services', (Kotler et al. 2006). The potential of sales promotion can be derived from the fact that the promotional marketing industry in India (not including the marketing of movies) is Rs 500 crore and has shown a growth of about 50 per cent in the past couple of years, and is expected to grow to Rs 1,500 crore by 2008. FMCG companies have used this since long, but services industry such as insurance, financial services, healthcare, telecom, hotels, etc., are also using it increasingly. In the services industry, promotions are used to increase customer loyalty and to generate a buzz or excitement about their services (Kaushik 2003). Sales promotion can include coupons, rebates, price off, contests, demonstrations, etc.; it is most effective when used along with other promotion techniques. A good sales promotion can also result in publicity when it is talked about in the media; the vice versa also holds true. For example, major domestic airlines in India, such as Jet Airways (Jet Privilege scheme), Indian (Flying Returns), and Kingfisher (King Club), provide frequent flyer schemes. A person can join the programme anytime by filling up a form for that particular airline. However, for Kingfisher, to become a permanent member of the club you have to take at least three flights. Kingfisher gives 500 free miles after the first three flights, and for accrual of points—the higher the membership status, class travelled, and distance—the greater is the number of points accrued (Exhibit 14.7). Thus, for a successful promotion, ideation and implementation should be worked out in detail so that it achieves the desired results. The timeframe for running a promotion is also an important consideration in sales promotion. If a sales promotion runs for too long or too often, it becomes part of customer expectations and if it is then discontinued, it builds resentment in the minds of the customers, who even stop using that service provider. It is argued that promotion benefits customers who would have bought the product anyway and so a proportion of the money spent is wasted anyway.

There are different tools available for achieving the sales promotion, but first the objective has to be clear as to what has to be achieved from it. Sales promotion steps are shown in Fig. 14.5.

Setting Objectives

Sales promotion is part of marketing communication and hence, the objectives would flow from the objectives set out for the same. In general, the objective of sales promotion is to increase short-term sales by attracting customers from competitors by providing

---

Exhibit 14.7 Frequent flyer? Miles to go before you can redeem points

Various airlines in India offer frequent flyer schemes. But the fact is that many flyers do not know the details of the programme and how the redemption and accrual system works. It becomes important then to understand the fine print of various schemes to see which one is the most value for money. The popular frequent flyer programmes are Jet Privilege (Jet Airways), Kingfisher Club (Kingfisher Airlines), and Fly- ing Returns (Indian). With some airlines, becoming a privileged member is as easy as filling up a form, while with others one has to fly a few times with the airline. Each time a person flies, mileage points are added, based on the distance travelled, class flown, frequency of travel, membership status, etc. The following table provides an overview of the various plans and privileges of selected airlines.

Feature	Jet Airways	Indian	Kingfisher
Additional bonus earned in first class	50%	150%	50%
Threshold miles/points needed for redemption	10,000	20,000	10,000
Value of one mile/point	Rs 1.25	Re 1	—
Validity of miles/points	Till 13th quarter	3 yrs from date of enrolment	3 yrs from date of accrual
Penalty for ticket cancellation	500 JPMiles	500 Mileage Points	500 King miles

Source: Adapted from *The Israni* (2006).

---

them with some incentives. They can also be used for rewarding loyal customers or trying to hold on to new customers. It is important to note that the promotional objective should fit in with the brand values and the market segment being targeted should desire the offering.

Selecting the Promotional Tool

There are different tools that can be used for promoting sales. Some of them are elaborated in this section.

Coupons Coupons allow a customer to gain some discounts on purchase of specified products or services. Coupons can be mailed to customers or they can be placed in ads

Fig. 14.5 Sales promotion process

in newspapers or magazines. They can even be inserted in newspapers, or as in the case of Domino's they can be attached to the menu pamphlet and offer discounts on the next purchase (within a specific time period). As a case of joint promotion, Reliance distributed coupons (with discounts valid in specific places of other service providers) on the purchase of Reliance mobile services. Coupons can be used either at the introductory stage (as in the case of Reliance) or at a mature stage to boost the sagging sales.

Packages   Packaged tours are very much on the rise in India. There are a number of options for customers to choose from. Club Mahindra offers packages for different destinations. A visit to the company's website provides the details of the tariffs for complete holiday packages at different locations. The tariffs for vacations in Goa are given in the screenshot. The tariffs are different from 1 October to 19 December and 6 January to 30 April (Rs 3,500 for superior rooms) as compared to the rates for the period from 20 December to 5 January where the same room (superior room) costs Rs 10,000. On becoming a lifetime member Club Mahindra also offered a Sony Handycam, 4 nights domestic holiday, and dining vouchers worth Rs 2,000.

Reward points and premiums   Most companies provide reward points as an incentive to use their services more often. Most of the airline companies provide frequent flier programmes for their clients so that the next time they fly they can use their services and gain points, which they can redeem by opting for the various promotional offers. For example, see the advertisement of Emirates, which states, 'Fly Emirates and earn up to 15,000 bonus skyward miles' (Exhibit 14.7). Credit card companies also offer reward points to encourage customers to use their cards more often. Every time they use their cards to make purchases, points are accrued which are collected and can be redeemed later when they can exchange points for merchandise.

Premiums are merchandise offered to customers as an incentive to purchase or use their service. The merchandise offered can be:

Free in the mail offers   Credit card companies are using this sales promotion technique clubbing reward points with other brands. For example, ICICI Bank credit cards offered Kingston 512 MB pen drive, Jaipan toaster, etc., against certain reward points.

Self-liquidating offers   These are offers wherein along with using reward points customers have to pay some cash also. For example, HDFC Bank offers books, DVDs, etc., against reward points and cash.

Deals   To sell their services, credit card companies also offer certain deals wherein other brands are offered for sale at discounted prices on payment of equated monthly instalments (EMIs). For example, HDFC offers products like Apple iPod; Motorola universal bluetooth handset H500; Motorola PDA phone A760; Sony Ericsson phone T610; Mustek portable DVD player MP72; etc., at discounted prices. To further encourage sales they have also offered Rs 500 off on purchase of two or more products. It also offers zero per cent interest on purchases from select outlets.

Price off   This is a big motivation for people who are ready to make the purchase decision. Advertisers generally make such offers for a limited period so as to influence the customers to purchase the product in a stipulated time. For example, the ad of

MTNL where Rs 1,300 has been waived and urgency has been created by telling customers that the offer closes on 15 November 2006. HDFC bank has clubbed their gold bar offer with the issue of HDFC credit card and are offering 4 per cent discount.

Special offers Organizations take out special offers, sometimes clubbing it with an anniversary celebration, etc., to promote their services. For example, the advertisement of Star Cruises for SuperStar Virgo and SuperStar Libra, wherein they have clubbed discounts (30 per cent) with the anniversary celebration in SuperStar Libra and added fabulous gifts, free cabin upgrades, etc., for their anniversary sailings. Special offers can be offered to boost sales. Taj Holidays came up with a special offer of 50 per cent discount on the third night from 1 to 20 December in order to boost sales.

Live demonstrations and roadshows Roadshows are organized to create awareness about the product and to attract the public some competitions are organized and prizes announced. Aviva Life Insurance, as part of its initiatives to expand the customer base in India and build awareness about the importance of life insurance policies, kicked off a series of roadshows across 14 towns and cities in Kerala. Revolving around the theme of man's desire to predict the future, the roadshow designed several themes and attractions, including gifts for participants (*Business Line* 2006). Standard Chartered Bank held career-counselling sessions for children in Mumbai where they gave students a guided tour on the details of banking. They also organized a Harry Potter party at some of their branches along with games revolving around actual incidents in the Harry Potter story (Kaushik 2003). The roadshow organized by Airtel in Chandigarh for the launch of Airtel Magic I-card was organized to create brand awareness.

Kiosks and free service camps Organizations frequently put up roadside kiosks where they offer information about their products and also offer free service for products purchased previously. For example, Aquaguard follows this practice as part of its customer service programme.

In-store competitions This promotional activity creates a buzz for the service provider and gives the youth an impression that something is happening and they should be a part of it. For example, Barista organized a competition in its Delhi, Mumbai, Bangalore, Pune, and Kolkata outlets where customers filled a five-word form on why they found coffee fashionable. Winners were flown to Delhi to get a makeover by Elite Modelling Agency and wardrobe by H2O Cue! design house. Café Coffee Day and Barista came up with different types of promotions during the football world cup in 2006 (Krishnan 2006). Café Coffe Day tied up with sponsors to award prizes to weekly winners, while Barista tied up with ESPN to offer live feed in major metros and provided instant gratification to customers who predicted the correct outcome of the match (Exhibit 14.8).

Point-of-purchase material Service organizations offer brochures and leaflets to dealers and at their retail outlets providing information about their service products. For example, Tata Indicom and Bajaj Allianz provide brochures to their target customers.

Contests Contests are also used as a sales promotion technique with rewards announced to attract customers. For example, Singapore is a successful example of how it tied up with the movie *Krrish* to promote tourism in the country. Later, Singapore highlighted

Exhibit 14.8   Cash-in on IPL

The new record of success that has been set by the Indian Premiere League (IPL) has inspired many firms in India to replicate the success internally. Companies across various sectors have launched new marketing campaigns around the IPL theme to cash in on the residual popularity of the tournament. Companies such as Frito-Lay have divided the sales team across the country into five and each team has been named after the IPL teams. According to the company, each team has a target of boosting sales in their respective region and expanding growth. Even SET MAX, the films and events channel of Sony Entertainment Television, the official broadcaster of IPL, launched a film festival called GFL or Great Films Lagaatar, immediately after the IPL ended. Broadcaster NDTV Ltd had no IPL rights to boast of, but they still launched two new bulletins titled 'Newsnight 20–20' and 'News 20–20'. These two shows pack in 20 news items in 20 minutes without any ad breaks. Some factors of IPL and the 20–20 concept that made it attractive were its success and its universal appeal. These two factors were enough for a company to sell its products and services.

Source: Adapted from Mehra (2008).

the spots and even ran contests to attend the premier of the movie in Singapore. They also built a special package of four days and three nights and offered free T-shirts autographed by Hrithik Roshan and free tickets for watching the movie in Singapore. They offered tours of all the places where the film was shot (Exhibit 14.9). After the success of its promotional campaign of sunsilkgangofgirls.com, Sunsilk plans to go international as well as rural where it will be re-christened *Sunsilk Saheliyan*. The site features gang games, blogs, parade ground, hot jobs, etc., in addition to advice on hair care, relationships, and astrology. The website has 2,50,000 registrations, 25,000 gangs or user clubs, and the site has registered 200 million hits and gets an average of 12–13 million page views every month (Coutinho 2006).

Scratch cards   Scratch cards are used to provide instant rewards to customers and are generally used by service providers to encourage customers to use their services. An example is of *Loksatta* newspaper whose marketing objective was to increase its circulation before the launch of its new supplement 'Viva'. The paper held Scratch2Win, a contest where readers had to scratch a coupon and if they were lucky, could win anything from

Exhibit 14.9   Towards 360-degree

The time has come for a 360-degree brand experience wherein clever promos tie in branded content with interactive, online, and mainstream media components. The publicity of the movie *Krrish* is an example of this trend. The tourism board of Singapore offered fans a highly discounted tour package of Singapore and a contest to visit a premiere of the film in Singapore. A campaign about Singapore also featured the actors talking about the movie. FMCG majors, such as Unilever and Procter and Gamble, are attempting to build communities and encourage user-related content through websites such as sunsilkgangofgirls.com.

Source: Adapted from Balakrishnan (2006).

a pen to a house. Public response to the communication was overwhelming and *Loksatta* was compelled to extend Scratch2Win by another month. During the campaign, the paper's circulation increased by a whopping 22 per cent.

Implementation and Coordination

Once the promotional technique has been identified, other decisions, such as the scale of implementation (in a city, metros, or all-India basis, etc.), time-duration for running the promotional offer, and management responsibility of the feature, follow. The consumers have to be made aware about the promotional campaign and different outlets/ branches have also to be informed so that they can handle queries. A successful implementation and coordination is equally essential for the success of any promotional programme.

Evaluate the Results

As always, the results achieved have to be measured so as to evaluate the effectiveness of the programme. This can be measured by keeping an eye on the sales figures before, during, and after running the promotional programme. Many times consumers pre-pone/postpone their programmes to avail of the promotional offer, thus accounting for some of the sales, but the long-run increase in sales denotes that new customers are also attracted by promotional offers.

Direct Marketing

Over the years direct marketing has assumed new meanings. Originally, direct marketing attracted customers by contacting them without involving any intermediaries. Thus, salespersons were also a part of direct marketing. However, with the introduction of media, such as telephone, television, and the Internet, the concept was redefined.

The Direct Marketing Association (DMA) defined it as 'An interactive system of marketing that uses one or more advertising media to affect a measurable response and/or transaction at any location' (Kotler et al. 2006).

Direct selling started in India in the year 1995. It is generally defined as a low investment and high returns business. In the last 10 years, it has grown from a $20 million to a $600 million market. The industry is set to cross $100 million by 2010. Key players in India include Amway, Oriflame, Avon, and Modicare, among others (Direct Marketing Association of India 2008).

Jobber (2001) defined it as, 'The distribution of product, information, and promotional benefit to target consumers through interactive communication in a way that allows response to be measured.'

Thus, direct marketing is usually short-term and allows an immediate measure of the programme response. With the growing use of Internet, there are a whole lot of opportunities for direct marketing. The general method adopted in direct marketing (see Fig. 14.6) is as follows:

Objective setting The objective of direct marketing must be set in order to be clear as to what has to be achieved from the activity. The aim must be in line with the

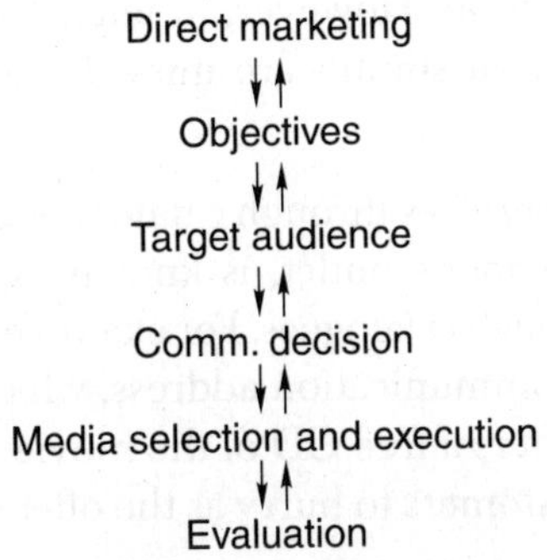

Direct marketing
↓↑
Objectives
↓↑
Target audience
↓↑
Comm. decision
↓↑
Media selection and execution
↓↑
Evaluation

Fig. 14.6 Direct marketing process

communication objective and can be marketing related (to generate enquires, acquire customers, etc.), communication related (to create awareness about the service, about any new service introduced, etc.), and finance related (to increase sales, ROI, etc.). Service providers can also target a combination of objectives such as providing information about a new service and at the same time trying to sell it too.

Identifying target customers Once the objective is decided, the next step is to draw a list of the target or potential customers based on the objective to be achieved. This list can include all the existing customers who are already purchasing from the service provider, customers who purchased in the past, a list of enquirers, and a list of prospective customers that can be drawn from a database (directories, yellow pages, paid databases available in the market, etc.).

Communication decision Based on the objectives, the decision regarding the message to be conveyed is taken. For example, if the objective is communication and sales of a new service product, then what is to be communicated is decided.

Media selection and execution How the message is conveyed is decided in media selection. The different media available for direct marketing are as follows:

Direct mail Communication messages sent via post to prospective customers constitute direct mail. Dell Computers is an organization sending direct mails to corporates in India through brochures on laptops and computers with their specifications, price, etc. Direct mail allows messages to be personalized for customers. The initial cost can be high and the response received is generally 2 per cent (Jobber 2001).

Telemarketing Using telecommunications and information technology to communicate with customers is called telemarketing. With the growing use of telephones and mobile phones, and falling costs of call charges, telemarketing is increasingly being used by organizations to reach their audience. The use of toll-free numbers has also helped to increase inbound calls. Most noticeable are the finance companies offering loan facilities to their customers. Telemarketing also acts as a support to the sales personnel as the customers evincing interest can be asked for appointments so that the sales personnel can visit them. Telemarketing is preferred as it is less time-consuming than personal selling with the facility of a two-way communication. However, in telemarketing it is easier for a person to be negative, the non-verbal stimuli are missed out, and it is considered intrusive.

Catalogue marketing   The sale of products and services through catalogues distributed to agents and customers, or at the service provider's outlet, is known as catalogue marketing. Many agents sell holiday packages through catalogues. For example, catalogue of HDFC Kids Advantage account provides a communication address, which helps in the measurement of responses. The catalogue offers a free CD of the movie Hanuman on opening an account and urges prospective customers to hurry as the offer is valid till 31 December, i.e., for a limited period.

Inserts   Inserts are generally put in newspapers or magazines where they are clubbed with some promotional offer. For example, *Outlook, Reader's Digest,* etc. put inserts in their magazines for subscription to their magazines and offer different gifts for different periods of subscription ordered.

Evaluation   The measure of the effectiveness of the direct selling activities can be achieved by studying the response rate to the campaign, the sales affected as a result of the campaign, the enquiries generated, etc.

Public Relations and Publicity

Management of the relationship with the various stakeholders such as employees, shareholders, and government falls under the management of public relations. Jobber (2001) defines public relations as, 'The management of communication and relationships, to establish goodwill and mutual understanding between an organization and its public'.

The management of public relations consists of the following steps (Fig. 14.7):

Setting objectives   Management of public relations can accomplish many objectives. Some of these are to advance the reputation, which in turn will help them to gain good employees and to sell, etc., overcome misconceptions, create goodwill with employees, customers, government, etc.

Major tools   Public relation activities include corporate advertising, seminars, lobbying, donations, publicity, etc. Publicity constitutes a major portion and involves communicating through news in the media without paying for it. Placement in the news gives the message more credibility and hence is a more delicate situation to be managed, as there is no control over the viewpoint expressed by the news supplier.

For example, Shahnaz Hussain, since the inception of business in 1970s until 2005, relied on publicity to gain media attention. She attended conferences and featured regularly on BBC since 1977, talking about Indian herbs versus chemical treatments. During her launches abroad she made sure that enough buzz was created and was covered by the media (*The Times* 2003).

The most popular way of dissemination of information is through a news release, which pleases editors and stands a greater chance of being used, and can be written using the guidelines given in message decisions. Other publications such as annual

Fig. 14.7   Public relations process

reports, newsletters, and magazines, also help to build company image and communicate news to target markets.

Organizing events (e.g., Lakme fashion week and Kingfisher fashion awards for sports events, fashion events, etc., also gives companies a chance to reach the target audience and draw attention to the company's name and products.

Message decisions   Deciding what has to be said and how it is to be said is a very important decision. Editors can reject press releases if they do not find them appealing. This can be overcome by making the headline factual instead of using ostentatious or grandiose language. The opening paragraph should be a brief summary of the release, content should also be factual, and the less important message should be towards the end as lower paragraphs have a higher probability of being cut. The news release should not be lengthy and the layout should have small paragraphs with lots of white space to show that it is easy to read.

Execution   The execution of the publicity or seminar, or donation should be in line with the other marketing communications made by the organization so that the image being portrayed is uniform and does not create any ambiguity in the mind of the consumers.

Evaluation   Kotler et al. (2006) identified the following three ways of evaluating the effects of public relations. These are:

Exposures   An easy way to measure public relations is to measure the physical space covered in the different media like publications, radio, and TV and the average audience covered by the same. For example, 2,000 column inches of news covered in 100 publications with a circulation of 100 million. However, this is not a very satisfactory method, as presence in a media does not guarantee the audience has read it or paid attention to it, or that they remember it.

Awareness/attitude change   An alternate way is to measure the awareness created or attitude change due to public relations. For example, how many people heard about the news or how many changed their views as a result of the news, etc.

Sales and profit contribution   The change in sales before and after the campaign can be measured to evaluate its effectiveness. However, public relations is never done in isolation, but is always in coordination with other promotional tools hence, it is difficult to measure the individual effect of public relations on sales.

E-MARKETING

Internet is a global medium and the companies using it are potentially addressing global audience (Wymbs 2000). This is because the use of Internet is growing at a fast rate not only in India but also worldwide. What took the radio 38 years and TV 13 years, Internet did in five years, i.e., reach an audience of 50 million users (Lagrosen 2005). The World Wide Web has revolutionized the communication process, be it information search, product purchases, etc. The Internet provides unlimited opportunities—many of them still unexplored—for the marketing of goods and services. The growing use of Internet across the globe adds to the opportunities offered by it. Companies start with a presence on the net—through their website—by providing corporate information; the second stage is the interaction stage where service providers interact with customers online; and in the progressive stages there is transaction of business and services online and further integration with the supply chain (referred to as e-business) (Levy and Powell 2002).

For customers to be attracted to a site it should take a few seconds to download or open, be attractive, user-friendly, and informative. Table 14.14 and Exhibit 14.10 show that after e-mails it is information search that people devote maximum time to, and this pattern has been continuing over the years. The Internet allows organizations to connect to the masses at minimum cost, and remote customers can also be contacted, thus giving the organizations opportunities for direct marketing.

The overall Internet-using population in urban India has grown by 28 per cent between April 2006 and April 2007 to reach 30.32 million currently. The regular Internet users

Table 14.14   Popularity of online activities

Rank	Online activity	2007 (%)	2006 (%)	Increase (%)
1	E-mailing	95	94	1
2	Job search	73	53	20
3	Instant messaging	62	37	25
4	Check news	61	53	8
5	Online music	60	48	12
6	Chatting	59	49	10
7	E-greetings	58	57	1
8	Check sports	57	35	22
9	Online games	54	35	20
10	Dating/friendship	51	27	25

Source: Adapted from Juxt Consult online (2008).

Exhibit 14.10 Data-wise Internet and Metros

Statistics show that Mumbai tops the charts for active Internet users. Different drivers for using Internet exist in various major cities. The following table summarizes the major Internet drivers for various cities.

	Mumbai	Delhi	Kolkata	Chennai
Active users	26	18	11	13
E-mail	31	57	36	63
Information search	33	17	30	12
Chat/telephony	10	11	4	9
Entertainment	9	4	8	7
Business info	10	4	5	2
Job/matrimonial	3	4	9	3

Source: Adapted from *Economic Times* (2006).

(at least once a month) have grown by 15 per cent and the occasional Internet users (less than once a month) by 212 per cent; increasing the total Internet using urban individuals by 28 per cent (Juxt Consult online 2008).

The Internet has a limitation in marketing products, as consumers cannot physically see the product before purchasing. In services marketing, due to the different characteristics of services like intangibility and inseparability, Internet has an added advantage. Better quality of pictures can be placed on the website, giving a feel of the ambience and the services to be provided. For example, Taj View Hotel at Agra has given photos of its exterior, lobby, etc.

In India, various government organizations are also going online. An example is Indian Railways, which has provided train schedules, online reservations and bookings, and train planner, etc. Also see the number of advertisements—ICICI Bank, Citibank, NBC India.com—posted on this site.

Many organizations also send e-mails to prospective buyers to provide information. As this trend is increasing, customers have started treating it as junk mail and are spending less and less time on them. However, some traditional services such as computer programming can be directly delivered online. Some service industries have evolved to becoming virtual organizations where they provide services only through the net. In a more dramatic breakthrough, a heart specialist sitting in a Delhi clinic can perform even delicate surgeries, such as an open heart operation, on a patient in Bangalore.

NEED FOR COORDINATION IN MARKETING COMMUNICATION

It is important for the marketing communication to deliver a uniform message so as to build a consistent brand image. This also enforces the message being sent to the target customers for them to form an opinion about the services provided. Coordination in marketing communication is required at two levels:

- within the different marketing communications
- between the marketing department and rest of the services.

Coordination within the marketing communication means that the different types of communications chosen (advertising, promotion, etc., and within advertising, print media, outdoor, electronic media, etc.) should be delivering a uniform message.

In Chapter 7, we have studied the importance of customer education through marketing communication. It is very easy to sell the services by making promises to lure customers but what happens when these promises are not met? Exhibit 14.11 gives a fair idea of the consequences a service provider may have to face, apart from bad publicity and word-of-mouth by the affected party.

Integration of marketing communication can be managed by focusing on factors such as the service promised, communication message, Internet communication, and guarantees.

Service promised The service promised in marketing communication should be in line with the services being delivered by the service provider and all the personnel in the organization must be aware of what services the customers expect.

Communicated message The message should be focused on educating the customers about the services to be provided so that the customer expectations are more realistic and in line with what is to be delivered to them. Thus, in various communications the service provider should focus on the services to be provided so the customer has a fair idea of what to expect.

Internal communication The flow of information within the organization should be at all levels—horizontal and vertical. For example, the operations department should know what the sales and marketing department has promised (either through advertising or through personal interaction) the customers, so as to manage customer expectations.

Exhibit 14.11   Cruise nightmare

An elderly couple's holiday in Egypt turned into a nightmare. Their travel operator in Delhi failed to provide them with the services he promised and was asked to pay a compensation of Rs 32,500 to the couple. The old couple had complained that the cabin allotted to them on the cruise was dark and dingy and they had to climb four floors to reach it. When these problems were brought to their notice, they were ignored. The complaints of the couple were accepted since, when any service provider adver-tises in a newspaper that the facilities being provided will be of five-star standard, it has to live up to it, without any deficiency. Failure to provide such service, entitles the consumer to receive compensation. While the tour operator continued to claim its international standards, the Court concluded that if the complainants had not suffered the trauma of the trip, they had no reason to approach the district forum at the expense of their time and money.

Source: Adapted from Chhabra (2006).

The operations department in isolation can also work at its best but it would not get the desired results if it is not in line with what the customers are expecting. Thus, the idea is that all the employees are aware of what has been promised by the organization so that they can all work towards the same goal.

Guarantees Guarantees of 100 per cent satisfaction build trust in the customers that the service organization will stand by their promises. For more details on guarantees refer to Chapter 10.

SUMMARY

Marketing communication is an important aspect of marketing and helps the organizations to communicate with their target customers. This chapter delineates the importance of marketing communication There are different ways to develop marketing communication and a mix of promotional tools gives the service provider the opportunity to communicate with a wider target audience. A detailed discussion of the process of advertising gives a perspective on advertising of services and helps to decide which medium or combination of media to choose for advertising different services. An insight into the product placement in movies as an advertising tool is provided. The use of the Internet as an advertising media has been emphasized. It is important to note that with the introduction of subsequent media (say radio, TV, etc., and now the Internet), the previous media tools were not wiped out but each media has its pros and cons, and it is for the marketer to decide which media reaches the target audience best.

The elements of promotion mix are discussed. The promotion planning and strategies are discussed in the context of services industry.

Personal selling process and the functions being performed by the sales force are highlighted in the section on personal selling. The next section on sales promotion defines the same and various options available to manage sales strategically for the benefit of the organization. The section on direct marketing delineates how an organization can interact directly with the target audience and involves the use of a media. The section on public relations discusses how communication and relationships can be managed to establish goodwill between an organization and its public. The next section discusses the growing popularity of online activities and the need for an organization to manage this. The availability of different tools for the marketer highlights the need to have congruent messages. All the personnel of the service organization should be aware of the messages being communicated to provide maximum customer satisfaction.

KEY TERMS

Advertising A communication that is paid for by an identified sponsor with the object of promoting ideas, goods, or services. It is intended to persuade and sometimes to inform. The two basic aspects of advertising are the message and the medium. The media that carry advertising messages range from the press, television, cinema, radio, and posters, to company logos on apparel. Advertising creates awareness of a product, extensive advertising creates confidence in the product, and good advertising creates a desire to buy the product. Advertising is a part of an organization's total marketing communication programme.

Direct marketing Selling by means of dealing directly with consumers rather than through retailers. Traditional methods include mail order, direct mail selling, cold calling, telephone selling, and door-to-door calling. More recently telemarketing, direct radio selling, magazine and TV advertising, and online computer shopping have been developed.

Personal selling Person-to-person interaction between a buyer and a seller in which the seller's purpose is to persuade the buyer of the merits of the product, to convince the buyer of his/her need for it, and to develop with the buyer an ongoing customer relationship.

Promotional mix An organization's total promotional effort, including personal selling, advertising, publicity, public relations, and sales promotion. The promotional mix attempts to attain integrated marketing communications.

Public relations Influencing the public so that they regard an individual, firm, charity, etc., in a favourable light compared to their competitors, as in business a good corporate image is an important asset.

Publicity The technique of attracting the attention of the public to a product, organization, or event by the mass media. Publicity involves a third party, such as a newspaper editor or TV presenter, who determines whether the message is sufficiently newsworthy to publish and what the nature of the message should be.

Sales promotion An activity designed to boost the sales of a product or service. It may include an advertising campaign, increased PR activity, a free-sample campaign, offering free gifts or trading stamps, arranging demonstrations or exhibitions, setting up competitions with attractive prizes, temporary price reductions, door-to-door calling, telephone selling, personal letters, etc.

CONCEPT REVIEW QUESTIONS

1. What is marketing communication? What are the different decisions required to be taken in a marketing communication?

2. Critically discuss the relevance of marketing communication in a services organization.

3. Of the different promotion mix, which would you choose for a hospitality service provider and why.

4. Critically discuss the different media available for advertising. To advertise a restaurant, which media would you choose and why?

5. Differentiate between personal selling and direct marketing.

6. Evaluate the importance of coordinated marketing communications for service organizations.

CRITICAL THINKING QUESTIONS

1. Discuss the need for marketing communication when the audience is well informed about the different services available.

2. Do you think it is important to have an objective of marketing communication at the start of the communication campaign.

3. What would you suggest—advertising or personal selling—for attracting new customers by an insurance provider?

4. What promotional tools can a marketing consultancy firm use to attract and retain customers?

5. Discuss the use of different promotion mixes at the time of launching a new restaurant.

=========================== **INTERNET EXERCISES** ===========================

1. Visit the website of at least two banking service providers. Discuss the different promotional tools being used by them. Which one would you choose as a customer?

2. Visit the website of two renowned hospitality chains. Evaluate the sites in terms of marketing communication. Do these sites help in promoting or selling the services? Give reasons.

3. Enumerate the different sales promotion techniques being used by a travel industry service provider. What can you suggest to enhance their effectiveness?

CASE STUDY

Marketing Communications and Corporate Social Responsibility*

Organizations have long considered profit as the main goal to be achieved and all the strategic actions are directed towards this. Though it is still one of the main drivers for corporate activities it is no longer considered its only 'raison d'être'. Companies consider themselves as an integral part of society and act in a socially responsible way (European Commission 2001) that goes well beyond the performance of a narrowly defined economic function (Khan and Atkinson 1987). Corporate social responsibility (CSR) in the past few decades has intrigued not only scholars but practitioners as well. It is 'essentially a concept whereby companies decide voluntarily to contribute to a better society and a cleaner environment' (EC 2001). High performing businesses show a strong correlation between CSR activities and stronger performance in terms of profitability and productivity (*Women in Management Review* 2004).

Growth of CSR

Corporate social responsibility till very recently was viewed as a philanthropic activity indulged in only when the firms were in jeopardy (Adenekan 2007). Though the earlier decades are referred to as 'false dawns' wherein CSR had a regional, person-centred, philanthropic focus, it is now viewed to be inclusive, broad, and diverse (Silberhorn and Warren 2007). It is not only used for fulfilling legal expectations but also for investing more into human capital, the environment, and relations with stakeholders. Companies facing the challenges of globalization are aware that CSR can be of direct, economic value. They view these activities not as a cost but an investment, as a 'long-term strategy minimizing risks linked to uncertainty'. (EC 2001). According to Sacconi (2007), when firms fulfil their 'fiduciary duties' to their stakeholders, they benefit from reputation and the 'positioning of the firm with respect to social issues is clearly a way to differentiate the firm, and its products and services in ways that create value' (Husted and Allen 2007). Marketing communications of companies are also focusing on the communication of their CSR initiatives (e.g., Sunfeast). It has also been studied that the composition of the board of directors also influences the CSR, as outside directors appear more concerned about CSR and hence, the firm is more likely to engage in socially responsible activities (Ibrahim et al. 2003).

Increased globalization along with increasing the opportunities for business has also brought the businesses under the scrutiny of different audiences, NGOs, and media. It is predicted that in the times to come companies will be 'judged more by their social policies than on their delivery of products and services' (Juholin 2004). Debacles such as Enron and WorldCom did cause a slew of critiques against the CSR initiatives but these were largely ill-founded (Stoll 2007). Many theorists have also argued about the economic impact of CSR, some relating it positively to profit (Adenekan 2007; Joyner and Payne

---

* Kirti Dutta and M. Durgamohan

2002) and some feeling that no such relationship exists (Aupperle et al. 1985). Bird et al. (2007) studied that the market is influenced by independent CSR activities and also by the totality of these activities and the gains can be in terms of economic performance or social performance (Cottrill 1990).

Corporate social responsibility is often understood only from the perspective of business generosity to community projects and charitable donations. This perspective however fails to capture the valuable contributions organizations can otherwise make (Adenekan 2007). In a 1987 empirical study by Khan and Atkinson it was found that a large percentage of the Indian executives studied agreed that CSR was relevant to business and felt that business had responsibility not only to the shareholders and employees but also to customers, suppliers, society, and to the state. Both the Indian and UK respondents felt that CSR eventually promotes 'a better relationship between industry and people, a good work environment, enhanced customer relationships, and enhanced corporate image of the company'.

It is also observed that large firms are more likely to identify relevant stakeholders and meet their CSR requirements through specific and formal CSR strategies (Perrini et al. 2007). Firms with a high value for social responsibility are much more likely to engage in traditional kinds of plans for social strategy. The use of social strategy depends upon the presence of specific configurations of industry environment, resources, and values (Husted and Allen 2007). Since CSR and corporate reputation are the two sides of the same coin, corporate enterprises can use CSR initiatives as a part of their corporate strategy and build it into their marketing communications so as to make the general masses aware about their initiative, and derive long-term sustainability and profitability (Hillenbrand and Money 2007).

Some CSR Initiatives in India

CSR is a multidimensional concept (Stanwick and Stanwick 1998) and is comprised of a number of variables. These variables include a firm's profitability, charitable giving, environmental emissions, women and minority members on the board of directors, women and minority members within the firm, and annual salary and monetary bonus of the chief executive officer.

Kids in Mumbai's Bainganwadi slums are grateful to Surf Excel. The Rs 485 crore brand in turn has to thank them for a feel-good marketing campaign—the Surf Excel 10/10 drive. This saw Excel buyers in the four cities of Mumbai, Delhi, Bangalore, and Kolkata SMSing an amount to HLL (now HUL). The company in turn donated that amount to an NGO that was involved in educating under-privileged children.

Keeping Surf company is the company's Rs 355 crore brand Ponds that has tied up with the United Nations Development Fund for Women. For every flap of Ponds cold cream mailed by the consumer, the company contributes Rs 2 to the fund to fight domestic violence. Even though, the proportion of adspends from its Rs 1,000 crore advertising and promotion budget have been minimal, HLL says that most of its brands will look for long-term strategic linkages with social causes.

The Vice President of the company Ashok Venkatramani told CNBC-TV18, 'If the activity is not housed in brand promise, then it looks like a charitable activity and in my view, those activities are difficult to sustain in the long-run. In our case, specific to Fair and Lovely, or even Ponds, these are strongly housed in what the brand stands for and what brand promise is all about, hence, they are easy to sustain and will reap huge benefits'. Industry watchers say that the company has moved gingerly towards backing this creative tack. Four years ago, it did an on-ground activation on Lifebuoy under the 'Swasth Chetana' campaign, and saw sales go up by 20 per cent in 17,000 villages. With such proof of better sales, the company is set to extend that initiative to urban areas. Further, the soap has extended the idea of social focus to their mainline TV advertising, featuring little Gandhi. Creative gurus think brands walking the social talk are welcome.

Executive Creative Director, Lowe, R. Balakrishnan explains, 'There are so many causes which are so fresh and which have not been tapped, so, they are all potentially great ideas lying there. Only look at it that way, I won't look at this as a tack that'll be the focus of corporates' in the future.'

Here's another difference to note. Corporate social responsibility is being used to build individual brands rather than the corporate brand. A case in point is the Rs 16,000 crore ITC company that ran its CSR campaign about putting India first for its e-choupal initiative two years back. Cut to the present. The company has linked the Sunfeast brand to its social forestry campaign, where the company chips in with 25 paise for every pack of Sunfeast biscuit and pasta sold and consumers who buy the atta brand, Aashirvaad, contribute towards ITC's rain harvesting campaign.

Divisional Chief Executive, ITC, Ravi Naware says, 'Consumers like to connect with the brand. If the brand is seen as a responsible brand, then consumers get an emotional connect that's far beyond just usage of the brand and consuming it. It's this higher level of connect that we are attempting to create through this campaign. So, in an attempt to connect with consumers at several levels, we will run this campaign, parallel to other campaigns, that talk about differentiated innovative products under the Sunfeast brand.'

Back home too, experts say that brand loyalty is passé. For the shopper, both Rin and Tide offer stain-removing benefits at a similar price and soon the retailer's in-store brands will add to that list of me-too brands. Marketing consultant and founder of Nobby, Nabankur Gupta adds, 'Product differentiation is completely drying up, service aspects are narrowed out, so the brand value question will come up in the durables sector as well. It will come up in the auto sector in my view. This will be a very live issue as we move forward in time' (Vaid 2008).

However, some of the services firms like Axis Bank, State Bank of India, and Oberoi Group of Hotels are not communicating about their CSR initiatives (if any). Sri Lanka's Jetwing Hotels Ltd, which is planning to enter the hospitality sector in India, is also trying to differentiate itself with the CSR it is following in Sri Lanka and plans to follow in India. 'In Sri Lanka, Jetwing manages 14 properties, of which it owns 13, and all properties have corporate social responsibility programmes. It works with local communities in Sri Lanka to help train young people for jobs in the tourism industry. This includes teaching them English and skills required in hotels. The company also works with groups such as *tuk-tuk* (autorickshaw) drivers, training them to also work as local guides,' said Mr Hiran Cooray, Deputy Chairman, Jetwing Hotels Ltd (Radhakrishnan 2008).

The Taj uses its competencies in areas such as food production, housekeeping, and laundry to develop and train 'raw' people to enable their earning a livelihood. For example, partnering with NGOs to train underprivileged women/housewives in hospitality, self-grooming, and housekeeping. Globally, the Taj is synonymous with the culture and heritage of India and the 'Building Livelihoods' theme is extended to the artisans and craftsmen of India. The Taj, in association with 'Paramparik Karigar', identifies the artisans and craftsmen across India in areas close to and in and around the location of their hotels, and assigns projects to trainees who identify projects that the hotel can take forward (Taj 2008).

Conclusion

Organizations are increasingly realizing that CSR is no longer a collection of discreet practices or occasional gestures motivated by marketing or public relations. It is rather a comprehensive set of practices and policies that should be integrated into the organizations operations and activities. Drawing from the sustainability programme of Wal-Mart (Lindstrom 2008) wherein all the 1.3 million employees are motivated to work for the same, it can be concluded that for a CSR plan to be effective it has to be supported and rewarded by the top management. To be successful it should be incorporated into the decision-making process, and supported and rewarded by the top management.

'A growing number of companies in many sectors and geographic regions have discovered concrete value and competitive advantage from socially responsible practices in pollution prevention, energy efficiency, environmentally oriented design, supply chain management, and health and sustainable agriculture initiatives, among others. For these firms, CSR has had positive impact on profits' (Adenekan 2007; Joyner and Payne 2002). Also by being socially responsible 'firms can proactively anticipate and deter government regulations, exploit opportunities arising from increasing levels of cultural, environmental, and sexual awareness, and differentiate their products from their less socially responsible competitors' (Jones and Haigh 2007). We can conclude that CSR initiatives should form part of the overall business strategy so that they are taken in earnest by firms and successfully implemented. Further, CSR is increasingly becoming a driver of business growth and is seminal in the success of the organization in the years to come.

Questions

1. Do you think it is pertinent for marketers to discuss their CSR initiative in their marketing communications?

2. What are the various CSR initiatives being practiced by the services firms?

3. Choose one services organization and discuss how you can differentiate it on the basis of CSR. What initiative would you like to choose and why?

SELECT REFERENCES

Adenekan, Samuel Abiola (2007), 'Putting CSR into perspective', *Communication World*, San Francisco, vol. 24, no. 6, p. 48.

'Air Deccan anniversary offer', *The Economic Times*, New Delhi, 24 August 2006, p. 4.

'Amazing success story of Shahnaz Husain', *The Times*, Kuwait, 15–31 August 2003.

Amway India, http://www.amwayindia.com/htmls/Business Opportunity.html, accessed on 29 August 2008.

Amway India, http://www.amwayindia.com/htmls/Business Opportunity.html, accessed on 2 September 2008.

Anand, Sanjay (2006), 'Now, watch TV via MTNL phone lines', *The Times of India*, 13 October, p. 19.

Aupperle, K.D., A.B. Carroll, and J.D. Hatfield (1985), 'An empirical examination of the relationship between corporate social responsibility and profitability', *Academy of Management Journal*, vol. 28, no. 2, pp. 446–463.

'Avoid targeted ad war, MRTPC tells Maruti, Hyundai', *The Economic Times*, New Delhi, 13 October 2006, p. 4.

Balakrishnan, Ravi (2006), 'Out-of-the-box, on the box, towards 360', Brand Equity, *The Economic Times*, 20 September.

Basu, Aparimita (2006), 'Media laws and overview', http://www.legalserviceindia.com/articles/media.htm, accessed on 28 November 2006.

Bird, R., A.D. Hall, F. Momente, and F. Reggiani (2007), 'What corporate social responsibility activities are valued by the market', *Journal of Business Ethics*, vol. 76, pp. 189–206.

Business Line (2006), 'Aviva roadshows across Kerala', http://www.blonnet.com/2006/09/16/stories/2006091601861900.htm, accessed on 1 December 2006.

Business World (2005), *The Marketing Whitebook*, 2005.

Chhabra, Rahul (2006), 'After cruse nightmare, Rs 32,500 compensation', *The Times of India*, November.

Cottrill, M.T. (1990), 'Corporate social responsibility and the marketplace', *Journal of Business Ethics*, vol. 9, no. 9, pp. 723–729.

Coutinho, Ashley (2006), 'Sunsilk's Gang of Girls goes global', *The Economic Times*, 17 November.

Direct Marketing Association of India, http://www.direct-marketing-association-india.org/DM_report_outline.asp, accessed on 18 August 2008.

Dobhal, Shailesh (2006), 'TV fast losing its net worth', *The Economic Times*, p.1.

Doyle, Peter (1976), 'The realities of the product life cycle', *Quarterly Review of Marketing*, Summer.

Doyle, Peter (2002), *Marketing Management and Strategy*, 3rd edn, Pearson Education, Chapter 5, pp. 130–156, Essex.

Economic Times (2006a), www.indiaontop.net, *The Economic Times*, New Delhi, 17 August.

Engel, James F., Martin R. Warshaw, and Thomas C. Kinnear (1987), *Promotional Strategy Managing and Marketing Communications Process*, 6th edn, Irwin, Chapter 1, Homewood, Illinois.

European Commission (2001), 'Promoting a European framework for corporate social responsibility', European Commission.

Hillenbrand, C. and K. Money (2007), 'Corporate responsibility and corporate reputation: Two separate concepts or two sides of the same coin?', *Corporate Reputation Review*, vol. 10, no. 4, pp. 261–277.

Husted, B.W. and D.B. Allen (2007), 'Corporate social strategy in multinational enterprises: Antecedents and value creation', *Journal of Business Ethics*, vol. 74, pp. 345–361.

Ibrahim, N.A., D.P. Howard, and J.P. Angelidis (2003), 'Board members in the service industry: An empirical examination of the relationship between corporate social responsibility orientation and directorial type', *Journal of Business Ethics*, vol. 4.

'Internet and metros', *The Economic Times*, 16 November 2006, p. 4.

Israni, Naveena (2006), 'Infrequent flyer? Miles to go before you can redeem points', *The Economic Times*, New Delhi, 20 October.

Jha, Mayur Shekhar and Joji Thomas Philip (2006), 'Advertisers face penalty for misleading claims', *The Economic Times*, 11 August, p. 5.

Jobber, David (2001), *Principles and Practices of Marketing*, McGraw-Hill Publishing Company, Chapters 11–15, Berkshire.

Jones, Marc T. and M. Haigh (2007), 'The transnational corporation and new corporate citizenship theory: A critical analysis', *The Journal of Corporate Citizenship*, vol. 27, pp. 51–69.

Joyner, B.E. and D. Payne (2002), 'Evolution and implementation: A study of values, business ethics, and corporate social responsibility', *Journal of Business Ethics*, vol. 41, no. 4, pp. 297–311.

Juholin, E. (2004), 'For business or the good of all? A Finnish approach to corporate social responsibility', *Corporate Governance*, vol. 4, no. 3, pp. 20–31.

Kaushik, Neha (2003), 'The promise in promotions', *Businessline*, Chennai, 4 September.

Khan, A.F. and A. Atkinson (1987), 'Managerial attitudes to social responsibility: A comparative study in India and Britain', *Journal of Business Ethics*, vol. 6, pp. 419–432.

Kotler, Philip and Kevin Lane Keller (2006), 'Marketing Management', 12th edn, Prentice Hall of India Private Limited, New Delhi, p. 193.

Kotler, Philip, John T. Bowens, and James C. Makens (2006), *Marketing for Hospitality and Tourism*, 4th edn, Pearson Education Inc., New Jersey, Chapter 9.

Krishna, Sonali and Haresh Soneji (2006), 'TV ad clutter triples in India but not everyone's watching', *The Economic Times*, New Delhi, 5 September, p. 4.

Krishnan, Raghu (2006a), 'Coffee cafes kick off World Cup mood', *The Economic Times*.

Krishnan, Raghu (2006b), 'Innovation wins the day for Coffee Café', *The Economic Times*, 5 September, p. 4.

Lagrosen, Stefan (2005), 'Effects of the Internet on the marketing communication of service companies', *Journal of Services Marketing*, vol. 19, no. 2, pp. 63–69.

Levy, Margi and Philip Powell (2002), 'SME Internet adpotion: Towards a transporter model', presented at 15th Bled Electronic Commerce conference e-Reality: Constructing the e-Economy, Bled, Slovenia, 17–19 June 2002.

Lindstorm, Martin (2008), 'Inside Wal-Mart's sustainability program', http://www.adage.com/brightcover/lineup.php, accessed on 21 February 2008.

Lovelock, Christopher and Jochen Wirtz (2006), *Services Marketing*, 5th edn, Pearson Education, New Delhi, Chapter 5.

'Maruti advertisement', *The Times of India*, 14 August 2006.

'Overall ranking of top 25 ad agencies', Brand Equity, *The Economic Times*, New Delhi, 24 May 2006, p. 4.

Perrini, F., A. Russo, and A. Tencati (2007), 'CSR strategies of SMEs and large firms: Evidence from Italy', *Journal of Business Ethics*, vol. 74, pp. 285–300.

Pickton, David and Amanda Broderick (2001), *Integrated Marketing Communications*, Pearson Education Ltd, Harlow, Essex.

Ray, Michael (1973), 'A decision sequence analysis of developments in marketing', *Journal of Marketing*, vol. 37, no. 1, p. 31.

Razdan, (2006), 'Filmmakers are at advantage in Rs 13,000 crore advertising market', *The Economic Times*, 3 March.

Sacconi, Lorenzo (2007), 'A social contract account for CSR as an extended model of corporate governance (II): Compliance, reputation, and reciprocity', *Journal of Business Ethics*, vol. 75, pp. 77–96.

Scaria, (2006), 'Kerala fisherfolk finally discover how to use net', *The Economic Times*, 11 August, p.18.

Sharma, Samidha (2006), 'FIFA cup: Big boys' ad party', *The Economic Times*, New Delhi, 7 June, p. 4.

Sharma, Samidha (2006), 'Happily married: Brands, show biz', *The Economic Times*, 15 June, p. 4.

Sheikh, Aminah (2008), http://in.rediff.com/money/2008/feb/20ipl.htm, accessed on 20 August 2008.

Silberhorn, D. and R.C. Warren (2007), 'Defining corporate social responsibility: A view from big companies in Germany and the UK', *European Business Review*, vol. 19, no. 5, pp. 352–372.

Singh, Sanjay K. (2006), 'Cops want key roads cleared of hoardings', *The Economic Times*, 10 November, p. 4.

Stanwick, P.A. and S.D. Stanwick (1998), 'The determinants of corporate social performance: An empirical examination', *American Business Review*, vol. 16, no. 1, pp. 86–93.

Stoll, M.L. (2007), 'Backlash hits business ethics: Finding effective strategies for communicating the importance of corporate social responsibility', *Journal of Business Ethics*, vol. 78, pp. 17–24.

'The effectiveness effect', *The Economic Times*, New Delhi, 20 November, p. 4.

The Marketing Whitebook, Business World, 2008.

'Value ad net gain', *The Economic Times*, 31 October 2006, New Delhi, p. 4.

Verma, Meenakshi and Mayur Shekhar Jha (2006), 'Multiplexes the new battlefield for ad wars', *The Economic Times*, 15 June 2006, p. 4.

Vivek, T.R. (2006), 'Nothing beats word-of-mouth in India', *The Economic Times*, 24 October, p. 4.

'Warne's hair ad violates British rules', *The Times of India*, New Delhi, 18 May 2006, p. 32.

Wasson, Chester R. (1968), 'How predictable are fashion and other product life cycles', *Journal of Marketing*, vol. 32, no. 3, pp. 36–43.

Wasson, Chester R. (1978), *Dynamic Competition Strategy and Product Life Cycles*, Austin Press, Austin.

Weber, John A. (1976), 'Planning corporate growth with inverted product life cycles', *Long Range Planning*, October.

Women in Management Review, (2004), 'CSR activities generate higher performance—official', *Women in Management Review*, vol. 19, no. 5–6, pp. 280–281.

Wymbs (2000), 'How e-comerce is transforming and internationalizing service industries', *Journal of Services Marketing*, vol. 14, pp. 463–478.

Zeithaml V.A. and Bitner M. (2000), *Services Marketing*, 2nd edn, Tata McGraw-Hill Publishing Company Limited, New Delhi.

http://www.adclubbombay.com/affiliates.htm, accessed on 12 November 2006.

http://www.indiantelevision.com/tamadex/y2k8/apr/tam.14.php, accessed on 18 August 2008.

http://www.museedelapub.org/pubgb/virt/mp/benettion/pub_benetton.html, accessed on 15 November 2006.

http://www.time.com/time/magazine/article/0,9171,959158,00.html, accessed on 16 November 2006.

http://www.time.com/time/magazine/article/09171955915800.html, accessed on 16 November 2006.

http://www.tribuneindia.com/2003/20030404/chd.htm, accessed on 1 December 2006.

http://www.vgc.in, accessed on 30 October 2006.

Indian Television.com's AdEx India Analysis, http://www.indiantelevision.com/tamadex/y2k8/apr/tam14.php, accessed on 18 August 2008.

Juxt Consult, http://www.juxtconsult.com/syndicated_research/indiaonline2007/internet_report_mail.asp, accessed on 20 August 2008.

Madden, Normandy, 'Radio ad revenue grows 39 per cent', http://adage.com, accessed on 1 December 2006.

Mehra, P. (2008), 'Products, even news bulletins continue to cash in on IPL', http://www.livemint.com/Articles/PrintArticle.aspx, accessed on 22 June 2008.

Radhakrishnan, S. (2008), 'Sri Lanka's Jetwing Hotels plans India foray', http://www.thehindubusinessline.com/2008/03/23/stories/2008032351110300.htm, accessed on 9 September 2008.

Taj (2008), http://www.tajhotels.com/AboutTaj/Careers/Corporate_Social.htm, accessed on 10 September 2008.

Taj Hotels, http://www.tajhotels.com/Leisure/Taj%20View%20Hotel,AGRA/facilities.htm, accessed on 29 August 2008.

The Advertising Standards Council of India, http://www.ascionline.org/five/recentdvpt.htm, accessed on 28 November 2006.

UNESCO report, http://unesdoc.unesco.org/images/0014/001461/146192e.pdf., accessed on 29 August 2008.

United Colors of Benetton, http://www.benettongroup.com/40years-press/img_our_campaigns.html, accessed on 2 September 2008.

United Colors of Benetton, http://www.museedelapub.org/pubgb/virt/mp/benetton/pub_benetton.html, accessed on 15 November 2006.

Vaid (2008), 'Brands that prick the conscience', http://www.moneycontrol.com/india/news/presselease/brands-that-prickconscience/20/34/259806, accessed on 11 September 2008.

15 Impact of Technology on Marketing of Services

OBJECTIVES

After reading this chapter you will be able to understand the:
- various technology issues pertaining to firms
- impact of technology on service firms
- various challenges for managing the use of online technology

INTRODUCTION

This chapter discusses the technology issues that need to be addressed across various service segments. It also discusses the impact of technology on services firms. Businesses are confronted with enormous challenges to perform. Product life cycles are shortening, development in material science and technology is accelerating, customer sophistication is growing, and concern with the environment and its resources is emerging as a key issue since the 1990s (Zairi 1995). The convergence of technologies is giving rise to new businesses. Mobile commerce and broadband technologies are re-defining the domain of entertainment and media businesses. Technology when assessed as an issue, not only impacts the R&D dimension and hence, the development of new products/services, but there are also so many more manifestations of technology at the workplace. These issues are discussed in the following section.

There are numerous aspects that need to be understood in the context of management of technology. Some of these aspects are discussed in this chapter.

Choosing Alternate Technology

This means deciding a particular technology for manufacturing or for providing services. For instance, when telecom firms offer mobile services they have to address complex technology issues.

- Do they need to adhere to the standards set up in the country?
- Do the countries allow alternative technologies to be used in a particular domain? What will be the impact on the customer?
- Will he/she be able to afford the new technology?
- What will be the impact on profitability of the firm?
- Is this technology sustainable over a long period?

Carlson (2004) has discussed the issues of using technology foresight to create business value. He suggests that developing an R&D strategy and identifying new technology-based opportunities is a critical activity today. From incremental maintenance of core technologies to long-term threats and opportunities, such as nanotechnology, a business needs to understand and manage more technology options today than ever before. He suggests that technology foresight is a perspective and a process that can sort the options, identify new technology opportunities, and develop coherence between short- and long-term R&D. He has pointed out some major aspects, which indicate the criticality of technology foresight:

- commoditization of markets, products, and most technologies
- more perfect global markets
- capital availability in second- and third-world countries
- global technology equilibrium (catalyzed by the Internet)
- increasing pace of scientific discovery
- large coherent technology initiatives such as nanotechnology and biotechnology
- relentless productivity increase from information technology.

Exhibit 15.1 gives an insight into how small theatres are using digital technologies which result in cost savings for them.

Assessment of the lifespan of the technology

A very important issue, which needs to be addressed, is related to assessment of the lifespan of the technology. The lifespan of the technology needs to be assessed and also some forecasts are essential. It is a very complex task and needs expert insight into the domain. Many technologies, when developed, become the standard for the industry to follow. For instance, the Pentium configuration developed by Intel and the operating system developed by Microsoft have become accepted global standards. Similarly, the UNIX platform too is an accepted global standard. Worldwide, many software professionals have got together to develop an open software system named Linux. So, when such technology becomes an acceptable standard by the industry, it opens doors for new challenges which need to be addressed. For how long can the competitive

---

Exhibit 15.1   Digital experience at cinemas

Digital technology has entered cinemas in small cities such as Cuttack (Orissa) and Pedapally (Andhra Pradesh). With the distributors' permission, a film that does not run well can be changed. The owner of a cinema hall in Cuttack says that though there is a choice to change the film, the publicity required for a film makes this difficult. Different owners have different takes on this. Also, distributors responsible for distributing the movies to particular locations feel that switching movies entails a huge cost, although some lenient ones do allow the cinema owners to discontinue a movie in case there is no crowd. Further, the regional database for digital films is yet to pick up because of the fact that converting print to digital is costly.

Source: Adapted from *Business Standard* (2006).

advantage be maintained? According to Chesbrough (2003), the concept of 'open innovation' is the key to thriving in today's competitive environment. He further adds that open innovation is all about making greater use of external ideas and technologies in their own businesses, while also allowing their unused ideas to be used by other companies.

SERVICE INNOVATION

Increasingly, firms do not consider themselves to be strictly in the services or manufacturing domain. Instead, they view themselves as offering solutions which deploy both products and services. On one hand, manufacturing firms offer hardware/product and after-sales service. On the other hand, service firms that offer service may need to offer hardware in order to facilitate the delivery of the service. For example, the telecommunication service provider may provide the necessary hardware to access Internet and telephone services at the customer location.

Firms need to continuously change and evolve. Innovation is the successful exploitation of new ideas; this definition applies to all firms in the economy and is equally relevant to services innovation as well.

Innovation, if explained using Schumpeter's approach (1934), can emanate from any of the following areas:

1. New product offering: If applied to the services domain, it would mean offering new services or adding new features.
2. Targeting new markets for the services: As an example, a service firm may target new geographies and align its offering to the local needs.
3. New sources of supply: This particular innovation involves using new modes of supply.
4. New methods of production: This applies in terms of deployment of new methods of production. In the services domain, it means the processes for delivery such as ATMs in banks.
5. Use of new technology: The use of IT has led to the emergence of new product offerings. For example, airline or hotel reservations have witnessed a boom in online reservations.

There can be numerous approaches to understanding the concept of service innovation. Soete and Miozzo (1989) provide a more differentiated picture of the services industry, distinguishing between supplier-dominated, scale-intensive physical networks and information networks, and specialized science-based services. The research literature points outs that services deliver a substantial contribution to the innovation processes. Other than technological elements, non-technological elements, such as people and processes, play an important role in the innovation process.

Hertog and Bilderbeek (1999) have put forward the following framework for understanding the process of service innovation. This is referred to as the Dialogic's four-dimensional model of innovation in services. This particular model helps to understand the process of service innovation. There are four important dimensions that help in describing and analysing service innovation. These are:

1. Dimension 1 (new service concept)
2. Dimension 2 (client interface)
3. Dimension 3 (service delivery system)
4. Dimension 4 (technological options)

New service concept This deals with a new service offering or deployment of new technology for offering the service. For example, call centres offering various kinds of support for back office operation. Another example is, using Internet-based technologies for offering online services. New service development has been dealt with in sufficient detail in the second chapter.

Client interface A second element of service innovation is the client interface. In services delivery, a client is an essential part of the service delivery in many cases. (For example, a student in case of face-to-face teaching in a classroom.) A student's participation as an active learner makes a lot of difference to the overall classroom experience. The calibre of the learner and teacher also impacts the overall learning experience. The deployment of technology facilitates the service delivery more effectively and can be a source of innovation. For example, in airlines, self-operated kiosks, which enable self check-in, make processes less cumbersome and also reduce the waiting time for passengers to check-in. This is particularly helpful when there are long queues due to stringent security measures deployed by the airlines.

Service delivery system This refers to internal delivery mechanisms that have to be managed in order to allow service workers to perform their tasks more effectively. It is closely related to employee empowerment. This theme has been dealt with in detail in Chapter 9 and the cases of the *dabbawallahs* and HDFC Bank are an example of this category of innovation.

Technological options Technology also facilitates service innovation. The offering of value-added services by telecommunication firms is an example. The SMS service and broadband access are some additional features which are offered on the mobile phone.

MAPPING PATTERNS OF SERVICE INNOVATIONS

There are different patterns of service innovation. As innovations can emanate from different sources, the patterns of service innovation can be quite varied. Hertog and Bilderbeek (1999) have postulated the following patterns, which explain service innovation.

Supplier-dominated innovation In this particular case, the service innovation emanates from the hardware industry. These innovations come in from an external supplier, and are disseminated and implemented by service industry users who, in turn, can satisfy the need of their clients. For example, the use of the microwave has greatly extended food preparation possibilities in cafés and restaurants. Cash registers and mobile phones have been assimilated in many small firms that use little new technology otherwise. In transport and logistics operations, the deployment of on-board computers is a case in point. In financial services, these innovations may pertain to new distribution channels based on technical platforms such as SMS alerts, mobile devices, etc.

Innovation within services Here the innovation may arise from both technological and non-technological sources, for example, the use of technology for more effective delivery of content in classroom. The relay of lectures online and simultaneous interaction with speakers from remote location is one example, and franchising in the retailing industry is another.

Client-led innovation In this case, the service firm responds to the needs expressed by the clients. For example, online banking helps save paper and is a more sustainable way for transactions. Organic products delivered at the doorstep is another example of client-led innovation.

Innovation through services This pattern is more complicated. The service firm influences the actual innovation in the client firm by providing R&D services or offering IT solutions for making processes more effective. Shippers offering clients tracking and tracing facilities contribute to the reduction of stocks.

Paradigmatic innovations This pattern affects everyone across the value chain. It is a complex and pervasive innovation, which will affect the usage and consumption patterns of the users. For example, shifting to Dish TV or using set-top boxes for viewing a large number of channels is a case in point. There is a fundamental shift from free viewing of the aired content to paying for viewing different channels. E-commerce also offers a shift in buying and consumption patterns. Online access to research databases, which can be bought online and viewed online, is an illustration of this pattern.

Innovation in a firm's internalized service function Internal services to employees (internal consumers) can also be a source of innovation, impacting their productivity and effectiveness. For example, the deployment of various services such as HR and payroll, travel-related reservations, and IT support through online methods within the organization help to eliminate bureaucracy and to streamline operations, especially where the size of the organization is large.

Innovation in an outsourced service function Many large firms outsource IT solutions or deploy separate departments, which offer solutions to employees within the firm. Security and cleaning services are also often outsourced.

INNOVATION POLICY FRAMEWORK

The innovation policy framework of a country helps to foster innovation in firms. This may vary across various industry segments. For example, in India after de-regulation of the insurance and banking segment, firms have deployed innovative practices to provide better services to consumers. Technology deployment has enabled easy access and online transactions. Stiff competition between the service firms helps consumers and they compete on a better service offering to the consumer.

Government policies play a key role in influencing innovation across various firms. It affects firms as enumerated in this section (DTI 2007).

Creating opportunities The regulatory framework developed by the government helps to create opportunities. Post-liberalization in India, in 2001, service sectors such as telecommunication, finance, and airlines have seen a lot of improvement in service offerings as firms compete with each other for a higher market share.

Enabling framework The government provides a conducive intellectual framework to protect the investments in innovation by the firms. There is also a measurement system for innovation and standards are created to control the processes and protect consumer interests.

Advice and support framework Here, the government offers support for various programmes, access to technology, finance availability, R&D tax benefits, and infrastructure benefits. For example, in India, the creation of science parks has facilitated entrepreneurial growth and exports through software firms operating out of these parks.

Supportive climate for innovation The government provides and works for macroeconomic stability, which ensures investors trust and a climate ripe for investment. A policy of fair competition encourages firms to invest. Sound investments in education policy ensure availability of manpower. The physical and IT infrastructure also become facilitating factors. An effective science policy and trade policy also influences the investments in a particular industry segment.

Exhibit 15.2 provides further insights into the potential of technology.

Deployment of Technology in the Service Firm

The choice of technology has a bearing on the functional relationships between employees, consumers, and markets. The choice of technology determines the nature

---

Exhibit 15.2   PVR Cinemas—Magic of innovation

Priya Village Roadshow (PVR) multiplexes have added a special punch to the cinema experience in India. The technology experience of movie goers starts much before they leave their homes. Besides offering e-tickets and m-tickets, the multiplexes have adopted the latest sound and projection technologies to ensure ultimate viewer satisfaction. Automation technology has reduced the transaction time and the long queues may soon become a thing of the past. The introduction of mobile ticketing at PVR has been a success and the interactive voice response (IVR) mechanism and ticketing kiosks have introduced easier ways of interacting with the customers. The movie schedules are available on the mobile and the user just has to send an SMS. The Intranet boosts the security set-up of PVR Cinemas with a network of close circuit cameras constantly updating the central control rooms. The PVR website has 5 lakh registered users and 11 per cent of ticket sales are through remote channels.

PVR has a presence in about 22 locations in India. They have edge-to-edge screens and are equipped with modern projection and sound systems. Fourteen PVR screens have moved to the electronic format and plan to roll out digital cinema screens soon. The theatres will soon work on the principle of digitized content being distributed through satellite or fibre networks, uploaded to digital cinema servers that will then serve it to a digital projector for screening.

Source: Adapted from *Outlook Business* (2008).

of relationships. However, there is a lot of debate on whether technology should determine relationships, or relationships should determine the choice of technology. The issue is a complex one and does not deserve a simple answer.

The customer expectations should ideally be determinant of the service processes. In order to bring efficiency in the service procedures, some or all of the areas can be automated. Information flow within the organization changes the dynamics of interaction and also shifts the power base in the organization.

The use of ERP, for instance, has had a very positive effect on some organizations whereas some other organizations did not benefit to the extent that they had expected to. In a study conducted by Davenport (1998) and reported in *Harvard Business Review*, a lot of insight is given as to how some organizations had to make massive changes in their organizational structures to integrate the new technologies, which in some cases did not gel well with the customers. So, it is important to assess the use of technology in light of the impact it will have on customers.

Another issue that needs to be addressed here is the category of product/service, which is being discussed. For instance, in high tech areas, the consumer may not even be aware of the consequences and features of the technology and the service. He/She sees the offering and buys it. Very soon technological innovation takes place and the product is rendered obsolete. The case of IT products and the services offered by telecom companies are a demonstration of this issue. So, here the customer is not in a position to dictate the choice of technology. After the service providers have learnt from market experience they can make educated decisions on the shifts in technology that they would like to make.

Trade-off between Cost of Technology versus Returns from Technology

Firms that make investments in technology tend to benefit, especially in the high tech segment. They make a lot of money through patents, royalty, and licensing revenues. They have the first mover advantage and hence they tend to look for global markets. The emerging economies, however, have a technology lag and often find a contemporary technology out of reach. The issue is certainly one of costs involved and the consequent returns thereof. It is important for service firms to understand these issues. Setting up firms with obsolete technologies will surely have issues with long-term sustenance of the firm.

The issues of energy crisis are imminent in the decades to come. Environmental issues will also have to be addressed. The effects of global warming are quite evident. Firms will have to look at sources of technologies and the conduct of business in such a way that resource consumption and ill effects on the environment are minimized. The issue of technologies is so vast that at any given point even a small organization would be using a range of technologies in different domains such as serving markets, communication, and offering services. So, one needs to be clear about whether we are using technology as a supporting device to make a transaction, offer final service to the consumer, or open a door for communication. Understanding the intent is important.

Exhibit 15.3 indicates the change in business format in the healthcare segment.

Exhibit 15.3   New age emergency services in hospitals

More and more medical service providers, government officials, and the public in general, are realizing the importance of emergency medical service (EMS). This movement started in 1999 and has since witnessed steady development in major metros as well as in cities such as Ahmedabad, Vellore, Hyderabad, and Pune, among others. EMS requires well-equipped ambulances and well-trained manpower. The private sector and government are working together to upgrade EMS in the country. Fortis hospitals have set up a number of hospitals in the country with dedicated people and quality ambulances. Those in the business believe that steady growth can be attributed to the increasing awareness of emergency treatment. People in India are becoming aware of international standards and thus demand similar services. A lot of people travel from smaller towns to receive medical services. Air rescues are also gaining importance. EMS is actually a product of quality teamwork. A few steps that are proposed are:

- A common three-digit number needs to be introduced in the country.
- The road transport office should certify ambulances depending on the nature of equipment they carry.
- Paramedical council needs to be established in order to test and dispense licenses to medical service providers.

Source: Adapted from *Business Standard* (2006).

Market Preparedness for Technology

For many service firms, the markets need to be prepared for launch of such services. For instance, in the banking segment in India, there were aspects that needed to be considered when the banks were being automated. What essentially happened was that the nationalized banks such as the State Bank of India (SBI) were not computerized in the 1970s and 1980s and customer transactions were manual. When the move to computerize the bank was initiated, there was at first, a lot of resistance from employees. Massive efforts were made to train the employees. Also, efforts were made to put in ATM machines so that many transactions could be automated. In India, Hindi is a dominant language and when ATM machines were installed, the language concerns of the local population was an important consideration. However, the shift to move to the usage of ATM machines is quite evident, especially in urban areas in India. Service firms have to take these aspects into consideration.

Exhibit 15.4 gives an overview of Apple Corporation and its revolutionary products that have changed the world in a number of ways.

Another case in point is the food industry (Exhibit 15.5).

IMPACT OF TECHNOLOGY ON SERVICE FIRMS

Technology has numerous consequences on the working of service firms. Some of these impacts are detailed as follows:

Productivity

The effective use of technology, especially information technology, has helped to improve the productivity of service firms. A case in point is the banking segment wherein the

Exhibit 15.4   Apple—One of the most innovative companies in the world

Apple Corporation has recently been named America's most respected company based on a poll of US business people. The iPod and Macintosh are attributed as the main drivers in Apple's success. The company has been one of the world's most innovative companies and its unique visual identity, store design, and product designs are truly inspiring. This is a major reason why the products of Apple have become an experience in themselves. Apple's 'Think Different' campaign saluted innovators who were dismissed as crazy. The latest offering by Apple is the iPhone, which has been recently launched in India. Apple has projected worldwide sales of 10 million by the end of 2008. Before this, the iPod had created a revolution that changed the world of music. This revolutionary MP3 player has sold about 119 million pieces and has helped increase the company's market capitalization from $6 billion to $155 billion.

Source: Adapted from *Livemint* (2008).

time for inter-bank transfers from across countries has reduced significantly. Electronic transfers have become an acceptable norm for financial transactions. Similarly, the concept of ATM machines has helped to reduce manpower costs and hence, made processes more efficient for the consumer. Similarly, in the airline and hotel industry, online reservations and tele check-ins have made life much more comfortable for the consumer, with the benefits of saving time and money. Government online portals have really helped, for instance, to systematize the processes for various kinds of licenses such as driving, passport, election I-cards, etc.

Technology also helps save time and costs, as illustrated in Exhibit 15.6.

Offering New Services

The advent of new technologies has enabled service firms to offer new services. Tele-medicine is a case in point. Similarly, software can be downloaded after making a payment. Digital libraries are being created. People can go in for online subscriptions for databases and can access literature online. Gaming and entertainment has been completely re-defined. Microsoft, Nintendo, and Sony are some of the key operators

Exhibit 15.5   Robots as waiters!

The Robot Kitchen in Hong Kong claims to be the first eatery to be staffed by machines. In a flash of light, a robot whizzes to the restaurant table and takes the customers' order, while the second delivers plates of steaming food. These robots do not resemble humans and rather look like boxes on wheels, covered in shiny paper, with an illuminated bulb to represent the head. The computer inside can recognize voice patterns, take meal orders, and send them by infrared to cooks in the kitchen. Being steered by a video camera, it detects objects in its way. Due to their limited abilities, however, new staff had to be hired and thus these robots are not complete labour-saving devices. This also shows that the commercially available robots are still very basic. The problem is that technology is there to do complicated tasks, but people expect robots to do much more than humans do.

Source: Adapted from *Hindustan Times* (2006).

Exhibit 15.6   Changing loyalties towards Web conferencing

Technology upgradations are fast catching up with PC desktop users worldwide. Boardroom video conferencing, which was considered a privilege for *Fortune 500* executives, is becoming commonplace. The video conferencing market touched Rs 65.6 crore in 2005–06 and is likely to grow at a compounded annual growth rate (CAGR) of 24.9 per cent till 2011. This effort is largely to ease the discomfort of jet-lagged executives who are burned out due to extended business travel. Companies are fast installing video conferencing systems that simulate real time face-to-face meetings over long distances. Hewlett–Packard's (HP) Halo technology is an example of this. By 2009, web conferencing and software services will be a $9 billion industry, globally. Factors such as cost of ownership, maintenance of infrastructure, and general perception are some issues that cause trouble for this industry.

Source: Adapted from *Business Standard* (2006).

---

offering services in these areas. Biotechnology and prescriptive medicine on account of developments in the genome project are all the consequences of application of technology to conventional fields of science.

The implications for service firms, however, is that they need to have a clear understanding of training of manpower and present standardized offerings. They need to define the processes for management of these services. There is also a need for understanding the critical success factors.

Exhibit 15.7 illustrates how the market dynamics change. It gives an insight into Wikipedia and its upgradation.

Control Mechanisms

Service firms have devised new ways of imbibing control mechanisms in the organizations. For example, FedEx has a unique tracking system, which it uses for tracking the goods in transit and offers distinct value to its customers. Firms, which have their websites, sometimes install cookies to help to track the usage patterns of the visitors on their websites. This helps them to make suitable modifications in their offering so that customers derive better value from such websites.

Exhibit 15.7   Wikipedia and its upgradation

Wikipedia is the collaborative Internet encyclopaedia and is an example of one of the most visible successes of mass collaboration on the Web. Since this encyclopaedia is available to be written and edited by anyone on the net, it has drawn charges of being unreliable and vulnerable to disputes. This is mostly due to opposing views and happens particularly on politically sensitive topics. Larry Sanger, one of the founders of Wikipedia, plans to bring some order to this chaos by drawing traditional measures. This implies that though the portal will receive submissions by everyone, the power to authorize them will be in the hands of editors and other volunteer constables. He is receiving financial backing from an unidentified foundation while a web-hosting foundation is providing free services. Volunteers will be called 'citizendiums' and will be selected only if they are able to show minimum levels of qualification.

Source: Adapted from *Business Standard* (2006).

The IT systems installed in organizations also enable them to track the time spent by their employees on the IT systems or the usage patterns of the same. Mobile technology has helped to foster increased connectivity but has an impact in terms of invasion of privacy as it makes a person accessible all the time. This impinges on the work–life balance in some cases.

Widening the Reach of Distribution Channels for the Service Firms

Service firms can use technology to widen the horizons of reach for the firm. The website and IT can be used effectively to tap alternate segments of the market. The institution of the online reservation system for hotels or airlines has had a big impact on the distribution strategy adopted by the service firms. The commissions of the intermediaries have greatly decreased as firms are trying to tap the customers directly, doing away with the distribution channels.

Al Bawaba (2006) indicates that the airlines would be the first fully web-enabled industry. Internet protocol (IP) has enabled data transmission from different devices and applications over the same network. Apart from simplifying processes, technology also helps reduce costs. IP traffic is carried across a wide area network (WAN) providing connectivity for geographically distributed hosts, or local area network (LAN). To provide IP-based networking services that meet the customers' growing needs is both an opportunity and a challenge for service providers. Internet protocol is the underlying communication technology that enables many new applications such as online reservation systems; it has brought out a radical change to air travel ever since SITA developed the first Internet booking engine just over 10 years ago. It also drives the self-service business model, which is both convenient for passengers and helps airlines keep ticket prices lower. The airlines are anticipating savings of 13 per cent compared to the traditional processes, up from 10 per cent as pointed out in a survey quoted by *Al Bawaba*. SITA is the world's leading service provider of IT business solutions and communications services to the air transport industry. It manages complex communication solutions for its air transport, government, and global distribution system (GDS) customers over the world's most extensive communication network, complemented by consultancy in design, deployment, and integration of communication services.

Interlocked Relationships

The use of certain technologies leads to long-term relationships between the service firms. For instance, computer firms tie-up with software vendors and sign long-term contracts. Thus, Hewlett–Packard (HP) may sell Microsoft's operating system, or UNIX servers, as a part of such agreements. Similarly, there are relationships between the telecom companies and mobile phone manufacturers. Software manufacturers also have relationships with companies such as Cisco Systems and Oracle for meeting various needs as required by the customers.

Any changes in such relationships can have an impact on the supplier relationships and hence, on the profitability of the firm.

The implication for this is that firms need to make investments in IT very carefully. There is a need to assess the long-term consequences of such partnerships. There is a need to closely monitor such partnerships and ways to explore changes as and when required.

Managing Customer Relationships

The use of information technology has completely re-defined the dynamics of managing customer relationships. Information technology enables creation of databases of consumers, and depending on the categorization of the same service firms can think of appropriate technologies to reach out to these consumers. There is evidence that building of customer relationships can generate business for a lifetime and technology can facilitate this process. However, the use of technology has to be assessed carefully; for example, mobile phone users in India feel abused by the number of telemarketing calls, which they receive for bank loans, credit cards, and promotional SMS messages from a wide variety of suppliers. Firms have been using data mining techniques to foster linkages with customers. Service firms use data mining and data warehousing to know and understand the consumers well in order to customize the strategies. The concepts of data mining and data warehousing have been discussed later in the chapter.

Fostering Linkages with Various Stakeholders

Technology can play a wonderful role in fostering new relationships with various stakeholders in a service firm. These linkages can be created by the use of a website and digital content. Channels of communication can be opened up with academic institutions, which are suppliers of manpower and business ideas, and users of the services namely, society, suppliers, consumers, government, NGOs, and other trade organizations. The links on the website can open doors for potential relationships with various stakeholders in society.

Global Information Technology Sourcing

The global information technology sourcing (GITS) represents a change that has the potential to transform the manner in which companies do business. Globally, many companies have committed the development and maintenance of internationally sourcing portions of their systems to offshore entities. The globalization of talent, trade liberalization in developing countries, quantum improvements in worldwide telecom-munication infrastructure, and cost-cutting pressures on organizations have led to the emergence and acceptance of offshoring as a business model (Legard 2004). Rao et al. (2006) have enumerated the primary drivers of outsourcing by some of the companies:

- lower cost
- quick access to expertise not available in-house
- flexibility to meet capacity needs while maintaining steady domestic head count
- accessing a global skills-base
- access to new markets
- improved quality of product

- developing experience with external collaborations
- assisting domestic IT staff to improve processes.

India is a widely recognized destination for information technology enabled services (ITES) outsourcing. Bangalore, Gurgaon, Hyderabad, Pune, and Mumbai are emerging hubs for ITES outsourcing activities. Please refer to Chapter 19 for a detailed discussion on IT and ITES.

ISSUES IN MANAGING ONLINE TECHNOLOGIES

Online technologies have a deep impact on service firms. There is a need to assess the issues related to online technologies, which service firms need to keep in mind. Some of these issues are detailed in this section.

Service mix Service firms have to decide whether they need to open options for online services as well. The service firms that use online technologies manage the demand better. For example, in India every year there are lakhs of applicants for a US visa. In view of such a huge rush of applications, the US consulate in India has now tried to use online technologies to manage the process. The application forms and appointments are made online and real time information on the status of application is available. This is very different from the cumbersome manual procedures, which used to result in huge delays. Similarly, the airlines industry, as has been explained earlier, is the first fully web-enabled industry.

Costs involved The dynamics of setting up online businesses involves making fixed-cost investments. The business model is such that fixed-cost investments are higher than operational/variable expenses. So, the service operators should realize this and the profit margins in subsequent years could be very high.

Integration issues The service firm, when it uses online technologies for conducting business, needs to put a fool proof process in place. It all depends upon the stakeholders it is targeting and the processes that it wants to automate. There are firms that have used online technologies to address the needs of customers, suppliers, potential and current employees, obtain information about philanthropic activities, and open doors for building communication channels with various stakeholders.

If, for example, a particular retail outlet also offers opportunities for online selling, then there is a massive coordination effort required, both for procurement and delivery of the products. Also, secure payment channels need to be created.

Building relationships with consumers Service firms can exploit online technologies to open doors of communication, both with internal and external customers. This can provide opportunities for improvement of the business. It also reduces the efforts to be made to reach out to the customers.

Website The website, which the service firms use, can be very dynamic and address the needs of various stakeholders. The aspects, which firms need to keep in mind while designing the website, are indicated in Exhibit 15.8.

Exhibit 15.8 Challenges for managing the use of online technology

The different challenges for managing the use of a website can broadly be categorized into—(1) content and (2) design.

Content The issues that should be monitored while designing the content of the website are as follows:

- **Uncomplicated** The basic content of the site should be easy to determine.
- **Current information** The information provided should be updated frequently and the date of revision should be mentioned for the viewer.
- Availability of a contact person or an address for the site viewer to contact for further information about the services.
- Links to other sites, if present, should be current and working properly.
- The quality of information provided should be relevant to the target customers.
- Information should be accurate, well organized, easy to understand, and related to the needs and purposes of the customers.
- The content should be complete and there should be no 'under-construction' signs.
- The content on the site should be free of bias.
- The site should be interactive.
- The privacy policy should be clearly mentioned for the customers to view and understand.

Design of the site The site desigzn gives the first impression of the site and should be attractive for the customers to continue further interaction with the site. The important considerations to be kept in mind are the following:

- The speed of the homepage download should be quick for the customers to be engaged with the site.

- The home page content design should be eye-catching and interesting.
- There should be a table of contents so that the information is easily categorized.
- Multimedia or animation can be used for the site to be interactive and appealing for the users, and should make a significant contribution to the site.
- Directions for using the site should be provided and should be easy to follow.
- The links to other pages within the site should be helpful and appropriate and there should be an option to come back to the main site from these links.
- The site should be compatible with a number of browsers such as Netscape, Internet Explorer, etc.

Finding and retrieving information from the Internet has become common and at the same time lack of formal structure in the natural language narrative makes the text search and processing very difficult. This leads us to the importance of developing efficient and effective text searching, retrieval, and mining techniques for the ever-increasing and essential collection of text data. 'In recent years, data mining has been successfully applied to a number of information retrieval tasks such as statistical inference, machine learning and information retrieval, supervised learning and its application to text classification, unsupervised/semi-supervised learning and its applications to collaborative filtering, and text clustering. In all these applications, data mining models are able to assist the process of information retrieval more efficiently and effectively.'

Source: Adapted from IEEE International Symposium on Data Mining and Information Retrieval, IEEE DMIR-07, 21–23 May 2007.

DATA MINING

Data mining involves the use of sophisticated data analysis tools to discover previously unknown, valid patterns and relationships in large data sets. These tools can include statistical models, mathematical algorithms, and machine learning methods (Adriaans

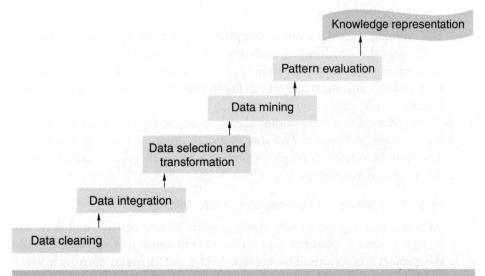

Fig. 15.1   Knowledge discovery process

and Zantinge 1996). Data mining is also known as knowledge discovery in databases (KDD) and refers to non-trivial extraction of implicit, previously unknown, and potentially useful information from data in databases (Zaiane 1999).

Knowledge Discovery Process

Data mining is a part of the knowledge discovery process. The knowledge discovery process is a multi-step process, which consists of the following (see Fig. 15.1):

- **Data cleaning** In this phase the unnecessary details are eliminated.
- **Data integration** Multiple data sources from different sources can be combined together.
- **Data selection** Data relevant to analysis is decided on and retrieved from data collection.
- **Data transformation** This is also known as data consolidation; data is transformed into forms for appropriate mining procedure.
- **Data mining** This is the crucial step in which clever techniques are applied to extract patterns as potentially useful.
- **Pattern evaluation** In this step, knowledge is identified based on given measures.
- **Knowledge representation** This is the final phase in which the discovered knowledge is visually represented to the user.

Data mining is being used in both the private and public sector across a range of manufacturing and service firms. Industries such as insurance, medicine, retailing, hospitality, and healthcare use data mining to reduce costs, enhance research, and increase sales. Data mining includes more than collecting and managing data. It includes analysis and prediction as well.

Uses of Data Mining

Data mining is used for numerous purposes. For example, the insurance and banking sector uses these techniques to detect fraud and assist in risk assessment. Retailers use data mining techniques for collecting information on shopper's club cards, frequent flyer points, contests, etc. Data mining techniques can be used for—(1) descriptive data mining and (2) predictive data mining.

Descriptive data mining studies usually describe the characteristics of a data set using some means of filtering. *Predictive studies* are about predicting trends and forecasting. This may be related to projections for the future based on current characteristics and other defined variables.

Important Issues in Implementing Data Mining

As with other aspects of data mining, while technological capabilities are important, there are other implementation and oversight issues that can influence the success of the project's outcome. The service firm needs to take care of several factors for implementing the data mining solutions (Zaiane 1999).

Data quality Data quality is one of the biggest challenges for data mining. Data quality refers to the accuracy and completeness of the data. It can also be affected by the structure and consistency of the data being analysed (Seifart 2004).

Interoperability This refers to the 'compatibility of the computer system or data with other systems and data using common standard processes or standards' (Seifart 2004). For data mining, inter operability of databases and software is important.

Security and social issues This is an important issue with any database. Data mining can disclose new implicit knowledge about individuals or groups that may be against the privacy issues. For example, in India, mobile phone users get numerous calls from banks and insurance firms to take personal loans or credit cards. Consumers are very upset with such calls and the government is struggling to implement a solution, which respects the privacy of consumers.

User interface issues The knowledge discovered by data mining tools is useful as long as it is useful to the end user. An effective data visualization and depiction helps to absorb information effectively. This depiction needs to be user friendly. For example, there are research databases that provide financial information of the firm to the researcher. However, the access to information, to get appropriate results, is so complicated that the researcher has to spend a lot of time in accessing and interpreting the results. So, firms need to ensure that the interface issues are addressed to ease the access and output for the search process.

Methodology issues There are numerous mining methodology issues such as diversity of data available, dimensionality of the domain, assessment of the knowledge discovered, exploitation of background knowledge and metadata, and control and handling of noise in data. These are all examples that dictate mining methodology choices.

Performance issues There are many statistical methods, which exist for data analysis and interpretation. However, the data sizes that firms are dealing with are very large.

The issues of scalability and efficiency of data mining methods is an important consideration.

Data source issues There are many issues related to data sources. The data sources should be correct, as false data could be a major problem.

DATA WAREHOUSING

Data warehousing technology comprises a set of new concepts and tools, which support the knowledge worker (executive, manager, and analyst) with information material for decision-making. The fundamental reason for building a data warehouse is to improve the quality of information in the organization (Gatziu and Vavouras 1999).

Characteristics of Data Warehouse Data

Data in data warehousing are integrated from various operational systems and further external data sources. Access to historical data is one of the primary reasons for adopting the data warehouse approach.

The potential volume of historical data and the associated storage costs should be important considerations in relation with potential business benefits.

Data Warehouse System Architecture

A data warehouse has three broad aspects, which need to be considered.

1. Acquisition of data
2. Design/storage of data
3. Access to data

A data warehouse system comprises the data warehouse and all components used for building, accessing, and maintaining the data warehouse. The centre of the data warehouse system is the data warehouse itself. A metadata management component is responsible for management, definition, and access of all different types of metadata. In general, a metadata is a 'data about data'. It helps in the classification of data.

The implementation of data warehouse is a two-step process. In the *configuration process*, a conceptual view of a warehouse is first specified according to user requirement. After initial loading, refreshing data at a subsequent stage is the next step.

In the *operation phase*, the data warehouse must be regularly refreshed, i.e., modifications of operational data since the last data warehousing refreshment must be propagated into the warehouse such that data stored in the data warehousing reflect the state of the underlying operational systems. It also includes other tasks such as archiving, purging of data warehousing, refreshment, and monitoring.

A typical data warehouse system architecture is as follows:

Data Warehousing Design

The data warehousing design methods consider the read-oriented character of warehouse data and enable efficient query processing of huge amounts of data. A special type of

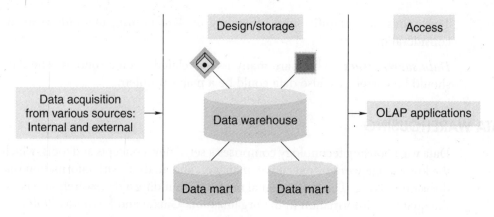

Source: Adapted from Gatziu and Vavouras (1999).

Fig. 15.2   A typical data warehouse system architecture

relational database schemas, referred to as star schema, is often used to model the multiple dimensions of warehouse data. The categories in which data needs to be collected must be chosen carefully so that the output addresses the needs of various users.

Data Storage and Access

Adequate data collection and storage methods have to be considered for query processing and management of the same. Access to data warehouse can be speeded up by settling subsets of the same in the form of data marts. A *data mart* is a selected part of the data warehouse, which supports specific decision support application requirements of a company's department or geographical region.

Developing a data warehouse system is an exceedingly demanding and costly activity with a typical warehousing costing in excess of $1 million (Watson and Haley 1998). Improving access to information and delivering better and more accurate information is a far higher motivation for companies to use the data warehousing technology.

SUMMARY

The use of technologies by service firms is a complex issue and needs to be addressed with a lot of care. There are a range of issues that service firms need to address relating to the forecasting of technology, assessment of technology choices, impact on future returns to technology investments, consequences to the society, and organizational issues. Technologies should be used to offer better experience to consumers and not merely imbibe technology for the sake of using it. Technology solutions are usually resource and capital intensive. Any firm has to trade-off between investments and returns. The technology infusion leads to emergence of new services and a better experience for consumers. In certain cases such as multiplexes and Internet, information is available at the fingertips, whereas automated responses for

Contd

Summary Contd

customer complaints is a nightmare in some cases. The firms need to assure consumers that technology solutions will work when operations are scaled up. Deployment of technology may automate transactions but the human effort cannot be completely eliminated. There is really a need to strike an adequate balance between human interface and automation.

The Internet has also affected and transformed the way consumers access services. Ipod is a case in point; it has transformed the way in which music and video is accessed and bought. The access device has changed the face of the music industry. The MP3 format has also brought down the cost of music CDs.

The data mining and data warehousing concepts have also been discussed. They require a huge investment to address customer issues and have to be considered carefully to map an organization's IT needs. The basic uses and challenges for data mining efforts have been discussed. Data warehousing characteristics have also been delved upon.

KEY TERMS

Customer relationship management systems Computer applications that integrate a company's information about its customers with the knowledge of how best to use this information.

Data mining Involves the use of sophisticated data analysis tools to discover previously unknown valid patterns, and relationships in large datasets.

Data warehousing Computer technology enabling data from multiple operational processing systems to be brought together into a single source, which can then be accessed and interrogated. The data can be both current and historical. Warehousing differs from previous management information systems in that designers do not need to think about what questions might be asked of the system. The data is held in detail, rather than pre-specified categories; it is, therefore, possible to ask questions and to relate variables that may never have seemed relevant before, without having to interrupt ongoing operational processes.

Technological change An increase in the level of output resulting from automation and computerized methods of production. Apart from increasing output, technological change can affect the ratio of capital to labour used in a factory. If it involves reducing the labour force it can lead to technological unemployment in an area or industry.

CONCEPT REVIEW QUESTIONS

1. How are the changes in technology influencing the service firms?

2. Evaluate the technology issues that service firms should consider?

3. Examine the issues, which service firms have to consider when making choices about which technologies to deploy.

4. New technology deployment has led to emergence of new service firms. Please elaborate using some examples and the challenges faced by them (Hint: You could discuss about Internet-based businesses).

5. Elaborate on the application of data mining for service firms and the challenges faced in implementation of data mining.

6. Can all service firms deploy data warehousing? What are the challenges faced by such firms?

7. How can service firms channelize technology to build relationships with customers?

CRITICAL THINKING QUESTIONS

1. A small firm offering real estate consultancy is deploying an agency for reaching out to the consumers in Delhi. It tries to reach them through telecalling to initiate the first contact with the consumer. Please assess the choice of technology medium used by the firm. Also suggest other media that can be chosen, which deploy technology intensively. You may also give an insight into the costs involved in implementing the same. You may make assumptions about the turnover of the firm.

2. Evaluate the use of technology by consumer banks in India.

3. How has the Internet changed the travel choices of Indian consumers? Please carry out a small survey and share the findings in the classroom.

PROJECT ASSIGNMENTS

1. Explore the alternate technologies available for mobile telephony? What are the issues involved for a particular country when choosing a particular technology?

2. Assess the online reservation systems for two international airlines. Which one is better and why?

3. Assess the customer relationship programmes of two service firms in any domain.

How has technology been used to implement the programme? Which programme is better and why?

4. Identify a service firm, which has deployed data mining techniques to manage its customers. What are the strengths and weaknesses of the programme?

CASE STUDY

The Online Advertising Food Chain*

Online advertising is growing by leaps and bounds, but are there opportunities for smaller players?

It is said that during any economic downturn, the first sector to get impacted is advertising as it is the first place where companies like to cut back. However, thanks in part to a small base, the Indian online advertising and marketing sector is growing at a fast pace offering many opportunities for different classes of people.

From around Rs 150–200 crore in the financial year 2007, online ad spends targeting Indians are expected to have jumped to around Rs 500 crore in FY 2008, according to industry estimates. 'In 2008–09, we expect it to hit Rs 900 crore', says Mahesh Murthy, whose firm Pinstorm alone would have bought Rs 115 crore worth of ads by the end of this year (Fig. 15.3).

In other words, Pinstorm, which claims a market share of around 15 per cent in India, will alone oversee ad sales almost 50 per cent higher than the total industry turnover of Rs 80 crore during 2006.

While still accounting for just around 5 per cent of the estimated Rs 15,000 crore spent on advertising in India, online promotions account for between 15 to 20 per cent in places like the US and parts of Europe (Fig. 15.4). Recently, a new media specialist research firm eMarketer, revised down its estimate for online promotion

---

* 'The online advertising food chain', Eluvangal, S. (2008), *The Online Advertising Food Chain*, DARE, 31 August 2008.

Reprinted with the permission of Mr Krishna Kumar, Group Editor, DARE, www.dare.co.in.

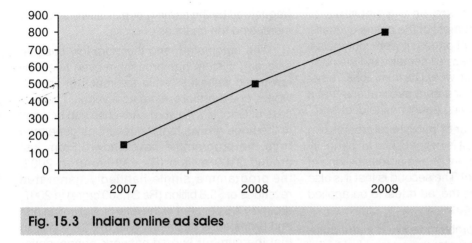

Fig. 15.3   Indian online ad sales

expenditure by US companies due to the economic recession. Yet, the new estimate for 2008 for US companies alone stood at $25.9 billion (Rs 111,000 crore), up 23 per cent from its estimate for 2007.

To understand the opportunities thrown up by the new medium, it is important to understand the 'food chain' of the online ad market.

As in traditional mass media advertising, online marketing has also started throwing up different strata of service providers. Between the advertiser on one end and the website owner or publisher on the other, there are many layers of service providers.

The Network or the Media Agency

The most important intermediary is the ad or affiliate network. This is in effect, what brings the advertiser and the publisher together and is the closest equivalent to the media agency of traditional advertising. The simplest model of the online advertising chain can be formed with just these three participants, with the ad network helping the advertiser and the publisher discover each other. In this respect, an ad network is like the traditional media buying agency, helping big companies to buy ad space on TV and newspapers.

However, the analogy cannot be taken very far due to the fact that unlike in the traditional

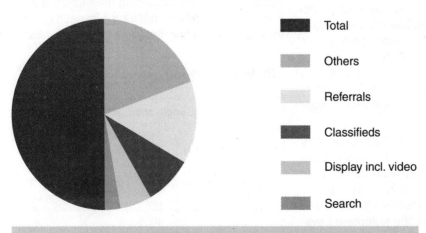

Fig. 15.4   US online ad market (2007)

media world, there are no big networks or websites that attract most of the online eyeballs. Each of the billions of pages of web content is a potential vehicle for advertisement and the number of website owners would be in millions, rather than the tens of TV and print publications that a traditional media buying agent has to deal with.

The huge number of 'publishers' creates two problems. One, that it is not possible to manually manage the placement of ads across billions of pages of web content. The second is that it is also difficult to determine the 'ad rates' to be applied to each of these pages.

While the first problem resulted in the automation of ad placements, the second led to the evolution of alternate standards for measuring the impact and reach of a publication or web page. Thus, most of the ads today are placed by algorithms that 'read' the content of a web page and gauge the potential interests of its readers from the content itself.

As for the second difficulty, as it is not possible to keep track of how many visitors each page of a website has, unlike tracking popularity of the 9 o'clock news, ad networks have evolved the concept of pay-per-click. Under this system, the publisher is paid according to the number of relevant visitors to his or her page as measured by the number of people clicking on the ads.

The shift to a pay-per-click model also simplifies the first problem of intelligent ad placements, as the publisher now has the incentive to make sure that the most relevant ads from the network are displayed on his pages. Many older networks, especially those that pay on the basis of sales or leads instead of clicks, still rely on the publisher to choose the best ads on their networks.

However, their success has been eclipsed by the emergence of Google's automated ad placement mechanism called Adsense Adwords. While preventing the network from being overwhelmed by the sheer scale of manually choosing the right ads for the right page, the automated system has the additional advantage of being able to periodically refresh the ads displayed on pages

frequented by the same group of viewers, further increasing the chances of clicks.

The automated, and therefore low cost, ad selection system has brought in even relatively low-traffic websites within the reach of ad networks, and therefore, extra ad revenue. The success of Google's Adwords Adsense can be seen in the huge growth that the revenues generated from the programme have shown. From just around $100 million (Rs 430 crore) in 2002, the programme single-handedly generated revenues of $5.8 billion (Rs 24,500 crore) in 2007, around 17.5 per cent of the total global online ads and promotions business. With the $2.4 billion that the number two ad network, Yahoo, generated for its publishers, the two net-works together accounted for a quarter of all online advertising and marketing revenues for 2007. Please see Table 15.1 for statistics on Google.

The business of ad networks, therefore, is restricted in its scope for new entrants. However, there are some smaller networks that still rely on the publisher or the website owner choosing the links he/she wants to display. Such networks have survived by specializing in verticals and having a different business model. Unlike the two big networks, which calculate the impact of the ads based on the number of people clicking on them, the specialized networks such as Commission Junction offer much higher commissions to the publisher, but only for getting their readers to fill out forms or purchase online. While each click on the big networks may get you as little as five cents

Table 15.1 Google statistics

Google stats (2007)	
Total revenues	$16.59 bn
From Adv and Mkg	99%
From the US	52%
% given to publishers*	79%
Y-on-Y growth	56.50%

* not applicable to revenues from Google's own pages

Source: Google investors relations (2009).

(Rs 2.30), in these networks, typically called referral networks or cost per action (CPA) or cost per sale (CPS) networks, publishers can expect to make between $10 to $30 (Rs 430 to Rs 1290) per lead.

Unlike the automated click-based networks such as those of Google and Yahoo, CPS or affiliate or referral networks are areas that are yet to see much traction in India. Typical 'actions' on the basis of which publishers get paid include filling up a loan request form or a car enquiry form.

A big plus for referral networks is the ability of the publisher or the site owner to fine-tune the displayed ads. For example, a website on the latest cars can host referral ads for cars, spare parts, car insurance, etc. Many publishers prefer such non-automated networks due to the control that it gives them over the links as well as the chances of higher revenues in case of niche websites. For example, if you have one lakh unique visitors per month and around 300,000 visits or impressions, then a referral network may work better for you. If targeted properly, around 9,000 to 10,000 out of the 100,000 can be converted. 'Each hot lead can fetch $25 to $30,' says Suresh Reddy, Chairman and Managing Director of Ybrant Digital, a Hyderabad-based digital marketing company.

The two big challenges in this space are the recent entry of Google's own referral network, as well as the little headway the business has made in India. Traditional affiliate marketing is expected to generate commissions of $2.27 billion this year in the US alone or about 8.75 per cent of the total online ad spend there, according to eMarketer. In India, however, they 'accounted for less than Rs 10 crore out of the total Rs 600 crore online ad spend last year—around 1.67%,' according to Mahesh Murthy of Pinstorm.

With the recent announcement of the Google Affiliate Network, there are fears that Google may also 'algorithmize' the online affiliate marketing industry, just as it did the CPC industry. Shawn Collins, a long time affiliate-marketing industry observer based in the US, however feels that the higher level of involvement between the brand, the affiliate network, and the publisher will make it unsuitable for automation. Automatic networks are notoriously susceptible to fraud and unscrupulous marketing practices, such as repeatedly clicking on the ads placed on one's own website. 'Affiliate marketing is ultimately about relationships,' he says, 'and companies will not want to expose themselves to liabilities for their brand, can-spam, etc., by automating everything.'

The Optimizers or the Creatives

Most of the smaller companies no longer entertain hopes of growing into big enough ad networks to challenge the hegemony of Google and Yahoo. Many, however, have carved out a niche for themselves, in a role similar to that of a creative agency that makes the ad in the traditional world.

These firms offer their services to advertisers, promising to make their advertising strategy more effective, like a creative agency would. Like a traditional creative agency that is tasked with designing the most effective message within a given TV time slot or newspaper print space, the optimizers set themselves the job of getting the advertisers, value for their money.

Such optimizers owe their emergence and existence to the preponderance of algorithms in determining visibility in the world of online advertising.

Display advertising, whether algorithmized or not, and whether in the form of text links, pictures or video, is usually targeted at static content. However, it suffers from the disadvantage that, like in the traditional media, the viewer or reader is usually trying to focus on something else and the ads turn up as intrusions or distractions. Yet, there is one publisher whose readers are usually receptive to suggestions and advertisements—the search engine.

Thus, notwithstanding the fact that Google and Yahoo operate the largest ad-networks online, they generate more revenues from their roles as publishers of search results than as ad network operators. For example, while Google generated $5.8 billion in 2007 by placing ads on the millions of pages included in its ad network, it generated almost double that, $10.62 billion, by placing ads on its own website—its search result pages

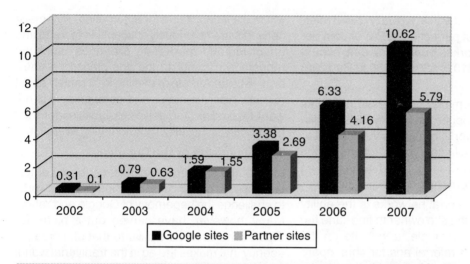

Fig. 15.5   Ad revenues through Google

(Fig. 15.5). Similarly, Yahoo generated $3.67 billion worth of advertisements on its own pages in 2007, compared to $2.4 billion on those of its partners.

According to eMarketer, search pages accounted for ads worth $8.62 billion of adspent in the US last year, comprising 40 per cent of the total US online adspent. Besides this, even display ads including picture and video ads are increasingly being delivered on the basis of search algorithms applied to the target publisher's page. A new crop of companies have made themselves a business by figuring out the most low cost way to put the advertiser's message in front of the surfer.

'In search, the better you are, the more margins you can deliver,' points out Vivek Bhargava, CEO of a contextual marketing company, Communicate2. 'It's about expertise. If I can get him the same amount of display or traffic for Rs 150 for which he is spending Rs 200 now, he saves Rs 50 and we get a share of the savings,' he adds.

Pinstorm too works on similar principles. 'We will deliver the most bang for the advertisers buck,'

says Mahesh. 'In our case, we don't even involve the client in details such as how we are going to use paid listing on search engines, etc. All we say is, let us measure the impact of our campaign, in terms of increased traffic, higher visibility, etc., and pay us for it. Whether we use paid search, or displays, or optimize your website, or write reviews is immaterial.'

Next Is What?

The next step, most people realize, is in selecting the ads not just on the basis of the search term or the content of a website, but on the past behaviour of the viewer. This, however, may create further stumbling blocks for the independent 'creative' experts, as most of the user data is with companies like Google and Yahoo who offer 'logged in' and therefore, traceable, experiences to Internet users. While it is easier for Google or a social networking website like FaceBook to keep a tab on what their users do online while logged in, it will be trickier for third parties. 'We believe that this information will also be made available to third parties, at least by some providers,' says Mahesh.

Questions

1. What is online advertising and how is it different from traditional mass media advertising?

2. Discuss the various forms of online advertising highlighted in the case study.

3. Discuss the difference between automated click-based network and affiliate or referral networks.

SELECT REFERENCES

Adriaans, Pieter and D. Zantinge (1996), *Data Mining*, Addison-Wesley, New York.

Al Bawaba (2006), 'SITA survey finds world's airlines on way to become the first totally web-enabled global industry', *Al Bawaba*, London, 13 November, p. 1.

Business Outlook (2006), 20 November, India, pp. 36–40.

Business Standard (2006), 'Digital wave hits small theaters too', 17 October 2006.

Business Standard (2006), 'Catching up on camera', 22 November, New Delhi.

Business Standard, 'Dial E for emergency', 22 November 2006.

Business Standard (2006), 'Wikipedia founder plans rival', 19 October, New Delhi.

Carlson, L.W. (2004), 'Using technology foresight to create business value', *Research Technology Management*, September/October, vol. 47, no. 5, p. 51.

Chesbrough, H.W. (2003) The Era of Innovation, *MIT Sloan Management Review*, vol. 44, no. 3.

Davenport, T.H. (1998) 'Putting the enterprise into the Enterprise System', *Harvard Business Review*, July–August, vol. 76 no. 4.

DTI (2007), 'Innovation in services', Occasional Paper, 9 June 2007.

Gatziu, S. and A. Vavouras (1999), 'Data warehousing: Concepts and mechanisms', *Informatik Informatique*, vol. 1.

Hertog, Pim den and R. Bilderbeek (1999), 'Conceptualising service innovation and service innovation patterns', Research Programme Strategic Information Provision on Innovation and Services (SIID), for the Ministry of Economic Affairs, Directorate for General Technology Policy.

Hindustan Times (2006), 'Robots as waiters at Hong Kong malls', 24 October, p. 25.

Livemint (2008), http://www.livemint.com/2008/01/14171331/Apple-will-shine-but-not-as-b.html, accessed on 25 August 2008.

Mitsch, R.A. (1992), 'R&D at 3M: Continuing to play a big role', *Research & Technology Management*, September–October.

Rao, M.T., W. Poole, P.V. Raven, and D.L. Lockwood (2006), 'Trends, implications, and responses to global IT sourcing: A field study', *Journal of Global Information Technology Management*, vol. 9, no. 3.

Schumpeter, J.A. (1934), *Theory of Economic Development*, Harvard University Press, Cambridge, Massachusetts.

Seifart, J.W. (2004), 'Data mining: An overview', CRS Report for Congress, Congressional Research Service, The Library of Congress, USA.

Soete, L. and M. Miozzo (1989), 'Trade and development in services: A technological perspective', MERIT 89-031, Maastricht.

Watson, H.J. and B.J. Haley (1998), 'Data warehousing: Managerial considerations', *Communications of the ACM*, vol. 41, no. 9, September.

Zaiane, O.R. (1999), 'Principles of knowledge discovery in databases', University of Alberta, www.exinfm.com/pdffiles/intro_dm.pdf, accessed on 1 December 2008.

Zairi, M. (1995), 'Benchmarking in R&D', *Productivity*, vol. 36, no. 3, October–December.

http://investor.google.com/fin_data.html, accessed on 22 January 2009.

http://www.cis.drexel.edu/faculty/thu/DMIR-07/DMIR07.htm, http://www.cyberbee.com/content.pdf., accessed on 25 August 2008.

16 Managing Quality and Excellence

OBJECTIVES

After reading this chapter you will be able to understand the:

- essentials of service quality
- different models for service excellence
- criteria for choosing TQM framework
- blueprint for service excellence

INTRODUCTION

The need to provide excellent services is important keeping in mind the growing competition in the market and the cost involved in attracting and retaining customers. Grönroos (1998) first described products as outcome consumption and services as process consumption. Products are manufactured and thus can be described as an outcome of a series of activities involved in the planning and production of the products. Services involve simultaneous production and consumption and hence, are more of a process consumption rather than an outcome consumption. Since the customers are present at the time of production, the quality of managing the production holds more importance in the case of services. If satisfied with the quality of services, the customers are bound to return and repeated customer satisfaction leads to customer loyalty. Thus, the development of customer loyalty is affected by the quality of service delivered, which in turn, profoundly impacts the organization's profits (Mohsin 2005).

REGULATORY AND COMPLIANCE ISSUES

The major services industries in India are run partially or entirely by the government. However, both foreign and domestic private firms play a large role in advertising, accounting, consulting services, etc. (USTR 2001). The growing awareness of India's potential in the services sector has resulted in an influx of major players into the Indian market. Industries such as insurance, banking, and foreign securities saw a number of foreign players joining the fray. The Securities and Exchange Board of India (SEBI) was established on 12 April 1992 'To protect the interests of investors in securities, and to promote the development of, and to regulate the securities market' (SEBI 2008). The Insurance Regulatory and Development Authority (IRDA) Bill was passed in 1999 and opened India's insurance market to private participation up to 26 per cent of paid-up capital. Reserve Bank of India (RBI) issued new guidelines in 1993 under which new private sector banks could be established (USTR 2001).

The World Bank (2007) report on 'Regulatory trends in service convergence' discusses the regulatory issues that arise with technological convergence and challenge the traditional framework.

Authorization and licensing Conventionally, authorization and licensing were based on the type of service. However, converging technologies and service providers dealing in multiple domains have made it difficult for regulators to clearly classify them. For example, the licensing of Internet protocol television (IPTV) services offered by MTNL, a telecom service provider.

Competition policy Interconnection, ownership, market access, and access to content and services are important determinants of competition policy.

Interconnection Formerly, interconnection models worked within the same facilities. The complexity created by the overlapping of services and networks have made the conventional approaches to interconnection charging unsuitable. For instance, inter-connection required between broadcasters and telecom providers for IPTV services.

Ownership Traditional regulations include concentration limits and cross-ownership limits to restrict monopoly of one owner on different media and across different media, respectively. Complications arise as these restrictions are dependent on defining the services in the context of multiple play. For example, should Voice over Internet Protocol (VoIP) be regulated under broadcasting or as a substitute for analogue voice services?

Market access Market access has been heavily regulated in the past and governments have been charging heavy licensing fees to traditional service providers. With new entrants in the market due to convergence, available capacity may increase, making the competition more severe.

Access to content and services Different technologies have a fair chance of catering to varied customer choices and hence should be provided through interconnections with their default carriers.

Managing scarce resources Spectrum management and numbering plans and prob-ability are used to manage scarce resources.

Spectrum management As a conceptual model, it focuses on mitigating three types of conflicts—uses, users, and technologies.

Numbering plans and probability Such regulations were introduced to address voice telephony services. The numbering plans established different ranges for voice services and within fixed telephony it was divided into geographical areas.

Service regulation It constitutes the quality of service, privacy and law enforcement, content regulation, and universal service goals and funding.

Quality of service This is vital as the telecom network has a point-to-point nature, where networks allocate and distribute limited resources across multiple subscribers.

Privacy and law enforcement Voice over Internet protocol (VoIP) calls may travel over public Internet, making it possible that their privacy is compromised, which is actually a legal guarantee in most countries. Voice over Internet protocol may even become a security threat in case government or law enforcement agencies want to survey voice conversations.

Content regulation Via converged content delivery mechanism, content that was formerly dedicated to specific networks can be conveyed on different infrastructures and delivery platforms.

Universal service goals and funding Convergence challenges traditional, universal service policies and the means by which universal service objectives are currently met.

Legal frameworks As services converge into the same medium, it might become difficult for traditionally separate regulators dealing with different services to assert their jurisdictions in the converged environment.

Traditionally, different services were regulated differently (Table 16.1). However, as convergence has blurred the lines of demarcation among multiple services, media, and networks, very specific and complex regulatory challenges have emerged.

Technological advancement has been the key driver of convergence. This includes digitization, increase in computing power, and consequently data compression, implying that the carrying capacity of channels increases even when the bandwidth is kept constant. Further, the availability of significant broadband penetration; consolidation in the development and provision of content and services; development and online advertising; and the ability to offer new and possibly bundled services and deliver them over one access network to the consumer, are some of the key market factors encouraging convergence. Table 16.2 takes the example of the information and communications industry to draw attention to the need for regulatory frameworks that are sensitive to convergence.

The breaking down of barriers on corporate activities and strengthening of the market, 'Is supposed to induce or force boards to monitor and work with management in creating more dynamic, efficient, and responsible business structures, which will provide competitively priced, and high-quality goods and services, and produce profits for shareholders. According to this logic, those companies that are well governed will survive and possibly thrive, while those which are not will be taken over or perish' (Reed and Mukherjee 2004). The concept of corporate governance thus came into being and is defined by Nobel Laureate Milton Friedman as, 'The conduct of business in accordance with shareholders' desires, which generally is to make as much money as possible while conforming to the basic rules of the society embodied in law and local customs' (The Institute of Company Secretaries of India 2003). Thus, if companies are practising corporate governance, people feel they will perform better over time. Some feel that

Table 16.1   Regulatory asymmetry across the communications industry

Services/ regulatory features	Data networks	Wireless telephony	Wireline telephony	Cable television	Broadcast radio	Broadcast television
Market entry	Usually open entry is the norm	Difficult due to spectrum constraints	Differs from country to country	Depends on jurisdiction	Difficult due to spectrum constraints	Difficult due to spectrum constraints
Focus of carriage	Quality of service	Spectrum and quality of service	Quality of service	Quality of service	Spectrum	Spectrum
Content regulation	Typically absent	Typically absent	Typically absent	Variable: from mild to strict	Strict	Very strict
Level of competition	Typically competitive	Oligopolies	Monopolies or oligopolies	Monopolies or oligopolies	Monopolies or oligopolies	Monopolies or oligopolies
Numbering issues	IP addresses	Phone numbers, portability	Phone numbers, portability	Channel numbering	—	Channel numbering
Spectrum licensing	Only in case of licensed broadband wireless, market-oriented	Yes, with entry fees and annual charges, often through markets	None	None	Typically administered	Typically administered
Interconnection management	Market-driven	Regulated	Regulated	May be regulated	—	—
Universal service goals	Typically absent	Yes	Yes	Free-to-air channels	Public service broadcasting	Public service broadcasting

Source: Adapted from The World Bank (2007).

corporate governance acts as a 'Means for limiting or reducing the risk to which a company is exposed'. Still others feel that it is a fad and go along with it as so many investors increasingly think it matters (Wallace and Zinkin 2006). Thus, there are various compliance and regulatory issues that guide a firm. However, the best judge of any organization is its customer, and since this book focuses on the services industry it tries to look at service quality and discusses some of the various models of excellence being practised. We thus start with a discussion on service quality.

SERVICE QUALITY

Quality has been defined by a number of people. Some of the definitions are as follows.
According to the British Standard 4778 (1987), quality is 'The totality of features and characteristics of a product or service that bear on its ability to satisfy a stated or implied need', and the stated need here is that of a customer (Lockwood et al. 1996).

Table 16.2　The genesis of the regulatory challenge

Traditional	Convergent
Each type of content had one dedicated network infrastructure. For example, television carried uni-directional video and audio; and print transmitted text-based content.	Possible to use one network for multiple services with digitization, packet switching, and growth of IP-based networking. For example, data communication over the telephone network.
Regulatory approaches depended on the clear division between the different services and a one-to-one mapping of service to network.	Specific regulations for specific content used over dedicated networks are becoming redundant. Regulators need to respond to the challenges posed by accelerated diffusion of services. For example, VoIP and IPTV.
Essential to ensure that policy and regulation enable free and fair competition and supports the full play of market forces.	Even more essential to ensure that policy and regulation enables free and fair competition and supports the full play of market forces.
Services were clearly classified.	For example, VoIP can allow non-telephony operators to offer voice services. European Union is regulating VoIP as an Internet service. Canada is temporarily regulating VoIP as per existing rules for telephones.

Source: Adapted from The World Bank (2007).

According to the German standard DIN 55350, quality is defined as 'The totality of characteristics and features of a product or process, which facilitate realization of given requirements' (Mohanty and Lakhe 2002). Garvin (1984) presented five different approaches to defining quality. These are listed as follows:

Transcendent view　According to this view, quality cannot be analysed or defined precisely. It can only be recognized through experience.

Product-based view　According to this view, quality is a precise and measurable variable, and service can be quantified as a set of tangible attributes.

User-based view　As the title suggests, quality depends upon the user. Thus, it focuses on the ability of the organization to deliver what the customer requires. This takes an external view of the organization and tries to identify the different needs and expectations of the customers.

Manufacturing-based view　This view focuses on the engineering and manufacturing practices, and emphasizes the management and control of the supply side of quality. It takes an internal perspective of the organization and helps them to deliver a standard service to the customers.

Value-based view　This view describes quality in relation to cost and price, i.e., cost to the service provider and price to the customer. According to this view, a quality product or service is one that is available to the customers at an acceptable price or cost.

Kasper et al. (1999) defined quality as, 'The extent to which the service, service process, and the service organization can satisfy the expectations of the user'. Kandampully (2000) concluded that service quality is crucial for the success of any service organization, and Grönroos (1988) linked service quality with customer perception of service quality. This concept has already been elaborated in Chapter 6.

MODEL OF SERVICE QUALITY

The most eminent instrument in attempting to systematize the service quality is the SERVQUAL model that was developed by Parasuraman et al. (1985). This model is discussed in detail in Chapter 6.

MODELS OF EXCELLENCE

The earliest approach to looking for quality was the quality inspection approach, which simply introduces the inspection stage to identify the defects in the product or service before it reaches the customer. However, this approach focused on identifying the occurrence of non-conformance rather than identifying the source of the problem and setting things right. Thus, this method gave way to quality control which focused on the fact that quality checks are important throughout the production process rather than at the end. The drawback of this method was that it focused on mistakes and so the quality assurance approach was practised to entrench quality into the process so that mistakes did not occur and if they did, they were identified and corrected. All the concepts discussed till now focused internally, i.e., within the organization and attempted to rectify the service product before it reached the customer. The main focus in total quality management (TQM) was on the customers and on the satisfaction of their needs by the continuous improvement of the processes (Lockwood et al. 1996). This is an organizational concept and tries to involve all the people for the successful achievement of customer satisfaction, and the ultimate aim is to achieve organizational excellence. Different frameworks for TQM have been given, which are as follows:

- BS En ISO 9000
- Malcolm Baldrige National Quality Award
- EQA
- CII awards.

BS En ISO 9000

The British Standards Institute first published their guidelines in 1979 as BS 5750, based on a series of Ministry of Defence supplier standards. After achieving international success this, with modifications, became the model for international standards published as ISO 9000 and EN 29000. In 1994, it was adopted as ISO 9000 (Lockwood et al. 1996). According to Asher (1996), 'ISO 9000 is a method for guaranteeing consistency of approach through the use of written procedures, systems audit, and review'. ISO 9000 should not be confused with the quality of the product or service, as it only relates to a documented quality management system operated by the supplier. The main aspects of the ISO 9000 system are the following*:

- Its aim is to produce a product/service 'right first time'.
- It has a 'plan-do-check-act' (PDCA) cycle.
- All documentation is in written form.
- A system of independent audits is put into place to check that the procedures in the quality system are fully implemented.
- The company can have ISO certificate in parts.
- It is used to derive continuous improvement.

The main strengths of this model are:

- It is more prescriptive in the way the company must work with its suppliers.
- It ensures that company subcontractors have process capability and control over their processes.
- Training is an important aspect.
- There are regular audits and continuous improvement.
- It enables employees at all levels to suggest improved methods of operation.

The main drawbacks of this system:

- Interpretation of ISO 9000 for a particular industry can often be subjective and auditors form a view based on their experience.
- Achieving certification gives no explicit guarantee of product/service quality.
- The standard only addresses the capability and control of the manufacturing, installation, or servicing process.
- Very often, quality audits are not seen as opportunities for improvement, but as policing activities.

The improvement opportunities in this model:

- Scope of the approach should be broadened to also include customers.
- ISO training should be imparted to the temporary staff as well, especially where they have direct contact with customers.
- The audits must form the basis of improvement action and should encourage the results to be taken in a positive way.

Malcolm Baldrige National Quality Award

The Malcolm Baldrige National Quality Award is one of the best-known quality awards and was used to recognize US companies for business excellence and quality achievement. It was named in remembrance of Malcolm Baldrige who served as the US Secretary of Commerce from 1981 until his tragic death in a rodeo accident in 1987. It was created by public law and was signed by President Reagan on 20 August 1987. This led to a new public–private partnership to promote business excellence. Since then, many countries, such as Australia, Singapore, and Dubai, have adopted the

---

Source: * Adapted from Porter and Tanner (2002).

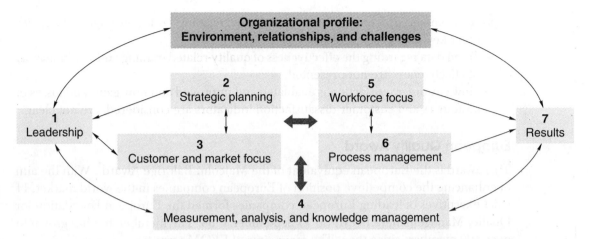

Source: The 2008 Criteria for Performance Excellence National Institute of Standards and Technology.

Fig. 16.1   Baldrige criteria for performance excellence framework: A system's perspective

framework (Fig. 16.1), and run their own award programmes. The main features of this award are as follows:

- It helps improve quality performance practices and capabilities.
- Facilitates communication and sharing of best practices information among and within organizations of all types.
- Serves as a working tool for managing performance, planning, training, and assessment.
- Results in improvement of overall company operational performance and capabilities, thus resulting in marketplace success.

The main strengths of this award are:

- customer focus and satisfaction
- translation of customer requirement into design through use of cross-functional teams
- address quality requirements early in the process and provide for a process control plan
- risk assessment is conducted bi-annually at each production facility and outcomes used as input to the planning process
- focus on corporate responsibility and citizenship.

The main areas for improvement are*:

- Planned benchmarking approach is utilized but how the benchmarking needs and priorities are determined is not clearly detailed.

Source: * Based on Porter and Tanner (2002).

- A systematic process does not exist for aggregating customer-related data with other key data to set priorities.
- Trend data regarding the effectiveness of quality-related training and key indicators of effectiveness are not presented.
- How customer satisfaction is evaluated and improved and how gains and losses of customers and customer dissatisfaction indicators are considered, are not clear.

European Quality Award

This award is the European equivalent of the Malcolm Baldrige Award[*]. With the aim of enhancing the competitive position of European companies in the world market, 14 chief executives of leading European companies formed the European Foundation for Quality Management (EFQM) on 15 September 1988. The membership has grown to over 400 members since then. The main aims of EFQM were to:

- support the European organization in making quality an important aspect in achieving global competitive advantage
- enhance the quality culture in Europe by deploying quality improvement activities.

So far, the following four awards have been developed by EFQM:

1. Thesis award
2. Media award
3. Leadership award
4. Award for companies and public services

The company award will now be referred to as EQA and the main features of this award are that it:

- is based on Malcolm Baldrige Award and Deming Prize model
- focuses attention on TQM as a strategic imperative
- focuses on high level of customer satisfaction, people/employee satisfaction, and sense of social duty
- actively promotes total quality outside the organization also, by presenting papers at quality conference, writing articles, working with local schools and colleges, etc.

The EFQM Excellence Model is a practical tool that can be used in a number of different ways:

- as a tool for *self-assessment*
- as a way to *benchmark* with other organizations
- as a guide to identify areas for *improvement*
- as the basis for a common *vocabulary* and a way of thinking
- as a *structure* for the organization's management system.

The EFQM Excellence Model is a non-prescriptive framework based on nine criteria (Fig. 16.2). Five of these are 'enablers' and four are 'results'. The enabler

---

Source: [*] Adapted from Porter and Tanner (2002).

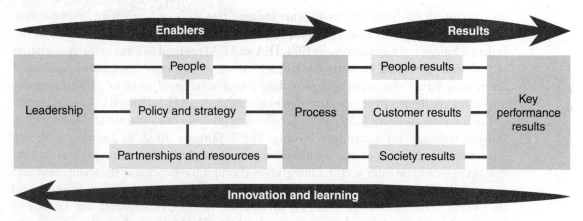

Source: © 1999–2003 EFQM, http://www.efqm.org.
® The EFQM Excellence Model is a registered trademark of EFQM.

Fig. 16.2   EFQM excellence model

criteria cover what an organization does. The results criteria cover what an organization achieves. Enablers lead to results, and are improved using feedback from results (EFQM 2006).

The main strengths of this award are:

- focus on TQM both within and outside the organization
- timely recognition and appreciation of the efforts and success of individuals, and teams
- focus on top-down, bottom-up, and lateral communication.

Areas for improvement are as follows:

- Started in 1991, so insufficient history at this time to show that it is a rigorous model for business effectiveness.
- It is very exhaustive.

CII Awards

The journey of CII began in 1895 when five engineering firms, all members of Bengal Chamber of Commerce and Industry, joined hands to form the Engineering and Iron Trades Association (EITA), with the aim of pressurizing the colonial government to place government orders for iron and steel with companies based in India, instead of in the UK*. The name changed to Indian Engineering Association (IEA) when the association decided to forge a commitment for manufacturing and exclude traders from the membership. Till 1942, IEA was the only All-India Association of Engineering Industries and represented big engineering companies, particularly British firms. Thus,

---

Source: * Adapted from Porter and Tanner (2002) and CII (2006).

the interests of medium- and small-scale Indian firms were not sufficiently represented. The Engineering Association of India (EAI) was formed in 1942, as an affiliate of the Indian Chamber of Commerce. In 1974, IEA and EAI merged to form to the Association of Indian Engineering Industry (AIEI), which was a 'Stronger association capable of harnessing larger resources and providing a wider range of services'. Foreseeing the upcoming challenges of competition due to globalization, AIEI changed to Confederation of Engineering Industry (CEI) in 1974, reflecting greater consolidation and solidarity to put the industry on a stronger footing. On 1 January 1992, in keeping with the government's decision to opt for liberalization of the Indian economy, it was natural that there would be inter-sectoral integration through the process of diversification and expansion, where engineering units could diversify into non-engineering units and vice versa. The name was changed to CII. In 1994, CII adopted the European Quality Award Model and introduced the CII–EXIM Bank Award for business excellence jointly with the Export–Import Bank of India to enhance the competitiveness of India Inc. (Fig. 16.3).

The main features of this award are:

- The CII–EXIM Bank Award for business excellence is the most prestigious award in India that an Indian company can receive.
- It demonstrates excellence in results with respect to its various stakeholders through excellence in processes and people.
- The award is administered by CII with technical support from EFQM.

The CII Excellence Award is one of the most respected and sought-after awards for business excellence, as it recognizes the best company among Indian industry. It incorporates stringent criteria and rigour in the assessment process, as it is based on the European model for business excellence—the US MBNQA, Japan Quality Award, and

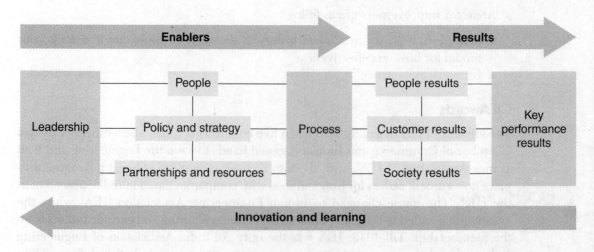

Source: The CII–EXIM Bank Award for Business Excellence. Reprinted with the permission of CII.

Fig. 16.3   The CII–EXIM Bank Award model

Table 16.3   Recipients of CII–EXIM Bank Awards

Organization	Year
Tata Motors	2005
Infosys Technologies Limited	2002
Tata Iron & Steel Co. Ltd	2000
Maruti Udyog Limited	1998
Hewlett-Packard (India) Limited	1997

Source: Adapted from *The Hindu Business Line* (2006).

Australian Quality Award. The companies that receive this award are comparable to the best globally. 'Excellent results with respect to performance, customers, people, and society, are achieved through leadership driving policy and strategy, people, partnerships, and resources and processes. The arrows emphasize the dynamic nature of the model and show that innovation and learning help to improve enablers, which in turn leads to improved results'. Five Indian companies have received this award till now (see Table 16.3), (CII 2006).

The CII–EXIM Bank Award has four levels of recognition starting from the commendation certificate for strong commitment and going up to the award. Thus, organizations at different levels of competitiveness can benefit from participating in the award process (Fig. 16.4).

CRITERIA FOR CHOOSING TQM FRAMEWORK

After discussing the different models for service excellence, how do we decide which model to choose for an organization? According to Porter and Tanner (2002), the different models can be chosen depending upon—(1) basic philosophy; (2) operational logistics; and (3) experience.

The *basic philosophy* can be used to guide the choice of the TQM. The different philosophies can be listed as follows:

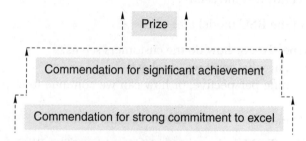

Source: Adapted from CII–EXIM Bank Awards.

Fig. 16.4   The CII–EXIM Bank Award levels of recognition

- If an organization's ultimate goal is excellence in business, then it should choose the EQA model.
- If the basic aim is to provide ever improving value to customers, then the organization should choose the Baldrige award.

On the basis of *operational logistics,* an organization can choose either of the frameworks. Thus, if an organization has European operations it is likely to choose the EQA framework. In the same way, companies based in US and Asia-Pacific are likely to choose the Baldrige framework.

An organization's *experience* is also an important factor in the choice of TQM. An organization relatively new to self-assessment will use EQA or Baldrige depending upon its location, but if its business planning process is integrated, well-established self-assessment systems it will have a system based on the Baldrige model (Porter and Tanner 2002).

BLUEPRINT FOR SERVICE EXCELLENCE

The different frameworks talk about excellence in services, but how organizations work strategically to achieve this excellence is a fundamental question. In early 1992, Robert Kaplan and David Norton developed a new approach to strategic management, which acts not only as a measurement system but also as a management system enabling organizations to clarify their vision and strategy and translate them into action. The *balanced scorecard* (BSC) can 'Motivate the management to make breakthrough improvement in critical areas such as product, process, customer, and market development' (Kaplan and Norton 1993). The main features of this approach are listed as follows:

- It is a set of measures that gives top managers a fast and comprehensive view of the business by putting together, on a single management report, many of the dissimilar elements of the company's agenda.
- It includes financial measures that give the results of actions already taken and complements the financial measures with operational measures on customer satisfaction, internal processes, and organization's innovation and improvement activities, i.e., the operational measures.
- It puts strategy, not control, at the centre.

The four perspectives of the BSC model are:

1. The customer perspective, or how do the customers see us?
2. Internal perspective, or what must we excel at?
3. Innovation and learning perspective, or how can we continue to improve and create value?
4. Financial perspective, or how do we look to our shareholders?

The companies following TQM lack a sense of integration. The BSC acts as the focal point for the organization's efforts, defining and communicating priorities to the different stakeholders (Fig. 16.5). 'The BSC is not a template that can be applied to businesses in general or even industry-wide. Different market situations, product

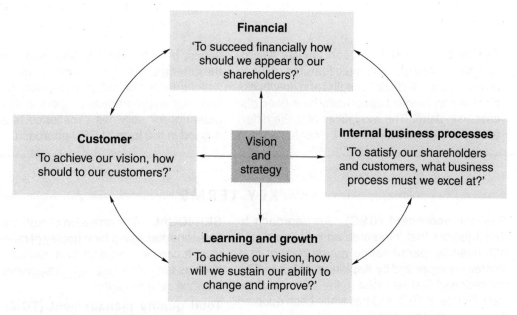

Source: Adapted from Kaplan and Norton (1992).

Fig. 16.5 The balanced scorecard

strategies, and competitive environments require different scorecards. Business units devise customized scorecards to fit their mission, strategy, technology, and culture' (Kaplan and Norton 1993).

Thus, the BSC approach helps companies to become the kind of organization they want to be. It puts vision and strategy, and not control, at the centre assuming that people will adopt necessary behaviours and actions to achieve these goals.

SUMMARY

Customers are the ultimate deciders of an organization's success. However, the service-providing organizations can also script their own success by providing excellent services and meeting the customer needs and requirements, which in turn, make the customers return repeatedly for the services being provided. The prevalence of various regulatory and compliance issues further necessitates this. This chapter highlights the need for an organization to maintain excellence in the production and delivery of services. It starts by discussing the various regulatory and compliance issues and their relevance in the market. The chapter goes on to focus on the need to manage excellence as a strategic tool, the relevance of service quality maintenance by an organization offering services and its importance to the customers. Different models based on service quality have been proposed for attaining excellence in services.

This chapter specifically highlights the BS En ISO 9000 model, Malcolm Baldrige National

Contd

Summary Contd

Quality Award, The European Quality Award, and the CII Awards. The main features of these awards along with their strengths and drawbacks and the improvement opportunity have been discussed in detail. The availability of these different models of excellence can be confusing for a service provider. The next section thus highlights the criteria to help the service-providing organizations to decide which framework to choose from the abovementioned models. Finally, the blueprint for services excellence is also discussed in the form of BSC approach.

KEY TERMS

Balance scorecard (BSC) An approach to management that integrates both financial and non-financial performance measurement in a framework proposed by Kaplan and Norton. The concept was first reported in the *Harvard Business Review* in 1992 and has since been adopted by various organizations.

Convergence The general trend in which computers, telecommunications, and the broadcast media have become increasingly interdependent and have assumed similar functions for many business and other purposes.

SERVQUAL The provision of high-quality products together with a high quality of customer service. It can be identified by a number of factors such as tangibles, reliability, responsiveness, assurance, and empathy.

Total quality management (TQM) An approach to management that seeks to integrate all the elements of an organization in order to meet the needs and expectations of its customers.

CONCEPT REVIEW QUESTIONS

1. Critically evaluate the importance of service quality.
2. Enumerate the different models for service excellence and discuss any one model in detail.
3. Discuss the European Quality Award and Malcolm Baldrige National Quality Award. Highlight the similarities between the two models.
4. Briefly discuss the BSC approach and its relevance in an organization.

CRITICAL THINKING QUESTIONS

1. How will you choose an excellence model for an organization operating in China for the past three years? Give reasons for your answer.
2. You are the service provider in the hospitality sector. Try designing the BSC model for your organization. Make realistic assumptions.

INTERNET EXERCISES

1. Visit the website of Malcolm Baldrige Quality Award and identify the different organizations that have received the award in the services sector.
2. Visit the website of European Quality Award and compare it with the MBNQA website. Which according to you is more informative, and why?

CASE STUDY

Balanced Scorecards in Managing Higher Education Institutions: An Indian Perspective*

Introduction

Organizational failure can usually be traced to deficient strategic planning, poor organization structure, recruitment and retention of staff, ineffective or non-existent internal control, and a lack of communication and feedback. On a more operational level, poor budgeting and inattention to cash flows are also often the cause of organizational failure. Educational institutions of higher learning are no different; it is just that in the Indian context, traditionally, the government has controlled these institutions and, at times, strategic management and its derivative tenets are not so visible in the initiation and operation of such institutions.

Heimerdinger (2002) indicates a need for training perceived by non-profit managers that manifests the traditional concerns of human services professionals who find themselves promoted into managerial positions without the benefit of traditional formal training in management—referring to those tasks usually defined by activities such as planning, organizing, motivating and controlling, and feedback. Sub-tending all of these is the need for leadership. If we juxtapose the above-mentioned comment with the fact that educational institutions of higher learning in India have traditionally been 'administered' (managed) in a way in which academic staff have been given apex positions in the administrative hierarchy, it highlights this need for developing managerial capacity.

Universities worldwide are facing the challenge of being centres of excellence for teaching as well as research. On one hand, universities are increasingly being required to teach ever increasing number of students in multiplying varieties of specializations and disciplines, and on the other, they are being asked to pay more attention to quality of teaching and educational programmes (Smeby 2003). This again indicates the requirement to re-look at the ways institutions of higher learning are to be managed.

This article looks at focusing attention on one of the contemporary tools of management, namely, the BSC, and tries to discuss how it may be beneficial in the strategic management of higher education institutions in India.

Tertiary Education in India

In India, the university system, as we see today, originated about a century and half ago with the establishment of universities at Kolkata, Chennai, Mumbai, Allahabad, and Lahore between 1857 and 1902. These were modelled after the British universities of that period. The Central Advisory Board of Education's (CABE) Committee on Autonomy of Higher Education Institutions (2005) in its report states that currently the Indian higher education system consists of 343 university level institutions and about 16,885 colleges, and that there are many nagging concerns about its role and performance. Many of our reputed universities and colleges have lost their pre-eminent positions. Only a few manage to maintain their status and dignity in an environment of complex socio-economic pressures and worldwide changes in approaches to the educational processes. Under the rapidly expanding situation with multiplicity of expectations from the higher education system it has become necessary to identify those attributes, which distinguish a first-rate institution from a mediocre one. The complex array of associated issues deserves a total re-thinking of our approach to higher education. Serious efforts are now underway to develop the policy perspectives

---

* Umashankar, Venkatesh and Kirti Dutta (2007), 'Balanced scorecards in managing higher education institutions: An Indian perspective', *International Journal of Education Management*, vol. 21, no. 1, Bradford.
Reprinted with the permission of Emerald Group Publishing Limited.

in education involving deeper national introspection and fundamental changes in the structure, content, and delivery mechanisms of our university system.

The report further indicates that the enrolment in the Indian higher education system has increased from 7.42 million in 1999–2000 to about 9.7 million at present, indicating nearly 10 per cent annual growth. The colleges account for about 80 per cent of the enrolment with the rest in the university departments. Thus, the programmes available in the college system largely determine the quality of our higher education. In the past decade, there has been a sharp increase in the number of private colleges as well as universities with the status of either deemed to be universities or state universities. The proportion of the eligible age group wishing to enter higher educational institutions will most likely increase significantly from the present level of about 7 per cent. The regulatory mechanisms will perhaps be liberalized. Higher education is continuing to expand, mostly in an unplanned manner, without even minimum levels of checks and balances. Many universities are burdened with an unmanageable number of affiliated colleges; some have more than 300 colleges affiliated to them. New universities are being carved out of existing ones to reduce the number of affiliated colleges. Under these circumstances, our dependence on autonomy as the means to improve the quality of such a huge higher education system poses serious challenges.

Venkatesha (2003) compares and finds a lot of differences in the work culture between the teachers of post-graduate departments of universities with those of colleges. In degree colleges, teaching is the only mandate and pertaining to this, teachers have to improve their knowledge in teaching by undergoing orientation and refresher courses, summer camps, workshops, and participating in seminars/symposia from time to time. On the basis of these activities, teachers are considered for promotion to the next cadre. Some college teachers who are interested in research may conduct research and publish papers. The research activity of college teachers is invariably out of their natural interest rather than a yardstick for their promotion, unlike in universities. Once a university teacher acquires a Ph.D. degree, many university teachers lapse into routine teaching assignments. Because of this type of dual role of teaching and research without defined guidelines, university teachers can neglect either teaching or research, or sometimes both. In Indian universities, teachers are promoted based on their research publications, books written, papers presented in seminars/symposia, membership of various academic societies, etc., but not much importance has been given to the teachers' contributions towards teaching.

This type of situation in our universities tempts many teachers to neglect teaching and take up some sort of research mostly uneconomical, unproductive, outdated, and repetitive, and venture into the business of publishing substandard research articles. The system normally recognizes quantity, like the number of Ph.D. students guided, number of papers published, etc., rather than quality of the research and publications. Unfortunately, no concrete method has been developed so far to judge the teaching and research aptitude of university teachers. Some academicians argue that both teaching and research cannot be done at the same time. However, it is generally thought that education (even from the undergraduate level) and research should co-exist to complement each other. Special emphasis on assessment-oriented teaching and research will impart a new dimension to the role of a teacher.

Commenting upon the inherent contradictions in higher education and research in sciences, Chidambaram (1999) indicates a peculiar situation existing in the country. Wherein on one hand, a large number of people are being given post-graduate degrees in science disciplines without an appreciation of their possible future careers; on the other hand, there is a considerable reduction in the number of such talented and motivated students seeking admissions to science courses. The dilution of resources that this irrelevant training represents has the consequence of deteriorating the quality of the training for the really talented people.

Staying on with science education, Narlikar (1999) identifies poor methodology of science teaching that encourages rote learning, ill-equipped teachers and labs, lack of inspirational and committed teachers, poorly written textbooks, and peer pressure to join lucrative courses, as some of the causes of the current sickness that has afflicted the science scenario. Our institutions or universities are just not projecting the romance of science and a proper and correct image. In his opinion, this unfortunate trend can be reversed if society displays a will and creates an environment to cure the causes of the deeply entrenched malady.

Altbach (2005) provides an overview of the ailments afflicting the higher education machinery in India when he says that India's colleges and universities, with just a few exceptions, have become 'large, under-funded, ungovernable institutions'. Many of them are infested with politics that has intruded into campus life, influencing academic appointments and decisions across levels. Under-investment in libraries, information technology, laboratories, and classrooms makes it very difficult to provide top-quality instruction or engage in cutting-edge research. A rising number of part-time and ad hoc teachers and the limitation on new full-time appointments in many places have affected morale in the academic profession. The lack of accountability means that teaching and research performance is seldom measured with the system, providing few incentives to perform. He goes on to say that India has survived with an increasingly mediocre higher education system for decades. Now, as India strives to compete in a global economy, in areas that require highly trained professionals, the quality of higher education becomes increasingly important. So far, India's large educated population base and its reservoir of at least moderately well trained university graduates have permitted the country to move ahead. He concludes that the panacea to the ailments of Indian universities is an academic culture based on merit-based norms and competition for advancement and research funds, along with a judicious mix of autonomy to do creative research, and accountability to ensure productivity. He rightly says that

'world-class universities require world-class professors and students—and a culture to sustain and stimulate them'.

He recommends a combination of specific conditions and resources to create outstanding universities in India including:

o sustained financial support, with an appropriate mix of accountability and autonomy

o the development of a clearly differentiated academic system—including private institutions—in which academic institutions have different missions, resources, and purposes

o managerial reforms and the introduction of effective administration

o truly merit-based hiring and promotion policies for the academic profession, and similarly, rigorous and honest recruitment, selection, and instruction of students.

Misra (2002) identifies 'management without objectives' as one of the key reasons for the downfall of the Indian university system. He highlights the need for adopting a functional approach in our universities; periodic academic audits; greater autonomy and accountability in all spheres of operations; open door policy welcoming ideas and people from all over; administrative restructuring, decentralizing university departments and schools; and making education relevant to our people and times; as the basic steps towards improving the Indian universities.

The earlier discussion establishes the need for accountability-based autonomy and being consistently relevant to the context in which the Indian universities (or any other universities anywhere for that matter) may exist. This creates the backdrop for adopting the basic tenets of strategic management in the paradigms of operating our universities. The BSC is one such basic tool that can certainly be of assistance in this rationalization process.

The Balanced Scorecard

Kaplan and Norton (1992) first introduced the concept of the BSC in their *Harvard Business Review* article, 'The Balance Scorecard—Measures that Drive Performance'. Focusing on the fact that managers needed a balanced presentation of both financial and operational measures, they propounded four perspectives as the drivers of future financial performance:

1. Customer perspective: How do customers see us?

2. Internal perspective: What must we excel at?

3. Innovation and learning perspective: Can we continue to improve and create value?

4. Financial perspective: How do we look to our stakeholders?

The scorecard provides executives with a comprehensive framework that translates a company's strategic objectives into a coherent set of performance measures. It represents a fundamental change in the underlying assumptions about performance measurement and helps focus the strategic vision.

According to Kaplan and Norton (1993), local improvement programmes such as process reengineering, total quality, and employee empowerment lack a sense of integration. The BSC can serve as the focal point for the organization's efforts. ISO model for excellence introduced in 1987 aims to produce a product/service 'right first time' by standardizing the functions in different departments and performing regular audits; continuous improvement is observed but it does not take the customers into account. However, the scorecard takes customers as one of the perspectives. It puts strategy and vision, not control, at the centre. It allows people to adopt whatever behaviour and whatever actions are necessary to arrive at these goals (Kaplan and Norton 1992). Thus, the whole arena is open for innovative ideas and action plans.

The BSC is not just a measurement system; it is a management system to motivate breakthrough competitive performance and is most successful when used to drive the process of change (Kaplan and Norton 1993).

According to Kaplan and Norton (1996b), the management shifts from reviewing the past to learning about the future in the BSC application. It retains the measures of financial performance—the lagging outcome indicators—but supplements these with measures and the drivers—the lead indicators—of future financial performance (Kaplan and Norton 2001). This also triggers a double-loop learning process.

The BSC's widespread adoption and use is well documented, for example, Kaplan and Norton (2001) reported that by 2001 about 50 per cent of the Fortune 1000 companies in North America and 40–45 per cent of the companies in Europe were using the BSC (cited in Karathanos and Karathanos, 2005). Kaplan and Norton (2001) formulated a new framework, namely, the 'Strategy Map', a comprehensive architecture for describing strategy. It provides a visual representation of the strategy and is a single-page view of how objectives in the four perspectives integrate and combine to describe the strategy (Kaplan and Norton 2004).

Application of BSC in Education

It is evident that the BSC has been widely adopted in the business sector, but the education sector has not embraced the BSC concept widely as indicated by the dearth of published research on this topic (Karathanos and Karathanos, 2005). Cullen et al. (2003) proposed that BSC be used in educational institutions for reinforcement of the importance of managing rather than just monitoring performance. Sutherland (2000) (cited in Karathanos and Karathanos 2005) reported that the Rossier School of Education at University of Southern California adopted the BSC to assess its academic programme and planning process. Also Chang and Chow (1999) reported in a survey of 69 accounting departments heads that they were generally supportive of the BSC applicability and benefits to accounting education programmes. Ivy (2001) studied how universities in both UK and South Africa use marketing to differentiate their images in the higher education market. At a time when higher educational institutions around the globe face declining student numbers and decreasing funding grants, it becomes imperative for them to determine their images in the eyes of their various publics. Karathanos and Karathanos (2005) describe how the Baldrige education criteria for performance excellence has adapted the concept of the BSC to education, and discuss significant differences as well as similarities between the BSC for business and the BSC for education.

In higher education, as in business, there are acceptable conventions of measuring excellence. Rather than emphasizing financial performance, higher education has emphasized academic measures. As in the case of business, the demands of external accountability and comparability, and measurement in higher education, have generally emphasized those academic variables that are most easily quantifiable (Ruben 1999). These measures usually are built on and around such aspects as faculty/student numbers (ratios), demographics, student pass percentages and dispersion of scores, class rank, percentile scores, graduation rates, percentage of graduates employed on graduation, faculty teaching load, faculty research/publications, statistics on physical resources, such as library and computer laboratories. Ruben (1999) indicates that one area deserving greater attention in this process of measurement is the student, faculty, and staff expectations and satisfaction levels. He opines that in most higher education centres very little attention is paid to systematically measuring students', faculty, and staff satisfaction, despite sharing the widely accepted viewpoint that attracting and retaining the best talent/people is the primary goal and critical success factor for institutions of higher learning.

In a study conducted by Ewell (1994) (cited in Ruben 1999), the measures used in 10 states in the US in performance reports of higher education institutions, were:

○ enrolment/graduation rates by gender, ethnicity, and programme

○ degree completion and time to degree

○ persistence and retention rates by gender, ethnicity, and programme

○ remediation activities and indicators of their effectiveness

○ transfer rates to and from two- and four-year institutions

○ pass rates on professional exams

○ job placement data on graduates and graduates' satisfaction with their jobs

○ faculty workload and productivity in the form of student/faculty ratios and instructional contact hours.

Karanthanos and Karanthanos (2005) have compared the Baldrige Award and BSC criteria in the context of education and have come out with measures closely aligned among both the instruments (see Table 16.4).

Table 16.4 Expected measures in BSC and Baldrige criteria for education and business

	Education	Business
1.	Student learning results: Results should be based on a variety of assessment methods, should reflect overall mission and improvement objectives. Should reflect holistic appraisals of student learning.	Customer-focused results: Customer satisfaction measurements about specific product and service features, delivery, relationships, and transactions that bear upon the customers future actions.
2.	Student and stakeholder focused result: Student and stakeholder satisfaction measurements about specific educational programme and service features. Delivery, interactions and transactions that bear upon student development and learning and the students' and stakeholders' future actions.	Product and service results: Key measures or indicators of product and service performance important to the customers.
3.	Budgetary financial and market results: Instructional and general administration expenditure per student, tuition and fee levels, cost per academic credit, resources redirected to education from other areas, scholarship growth.	Financial and market results: Return on investment, asset use, operating margins, profitability, liquidity, and value added per employee.

Contd

Table 16.4 Contd

4.	Faculty and staff results: Innovation and suggestion rates; courses or educational programmes completed; learning; on-the-job performance improvements; cross-training rates; collaboration and teamwork; knowledge and skill sharing across work functions, units and locations; employee well-being, satisfaction and dissatisfaction.	Human resource results: Innovation and suggestion rates; courses completed; learning; on-the-job performance improvements; cross-training rates; measures and indicators of work system performance and effectiveness; collaboration and teamwork; knowledge and skill sharing across work functions, units, and locations; employee well-being, satisfaction and dissatisfaction.
5.	Organizational effectiveness results (including key internal operations performance measures): Capacity to improve student performance, student development, education climate, indicators of responsiveness to student or stakeholder needs, supplier and partner performance, key measures or indicators of accomplishment of organizational strategy and action plan.	Organizational effectiveness results (including key internal operations performance measures): Productivity, cycle time, supplier and partner performance, key measures or indicators of accomplishment of organizational strategy and action plan.
6.	Governance and social responsibility results: Fiscal accountability, both internal and external; measures or indicators of ethical behaviour and stakeholder trust in the governance of the organization; regulatory and legal compliance; organizational citizenship.	Governance and social responsibility results: Fiscal accountability, both internal and external; measures or indicators of ethical behaviour and of stakeholder trust in the governance of the organization; regulatory and legal compliance; organizational citizenship.

Source: Adapted from Karanthanos and Karanthanos (2005).

Applicability and Design of the BSC in the Indian Environment

Review of extant literature indicates that business organizations, as well as academic institutions, are fundamentally rethinking their strategies and operations because of the changing environment demanding more accountability. The BSC is described as a novel approach to face these challenges (Dorweiler and Yakhou 2005). The strategies for creating value in education need to be based on managing knowledge that creates and deploys an organization's intangible assets. The scorecard defines the theory of the business on which the strategy is based; hence, performance monitoring can take the form of hypothesis testing and double-loop learning. A good BSC should have a mix of outcome measures and performance drivers (Kaplan and Norton 1996b).

Marketing and communication strategies vis-à-vis institutions of higher education assume greater import as the image portrayed by these institutions plays a critical role in shaping the attitudes and perceptions of the institution's public towards that institution (Yavas and Shemwell 1996). In India, for instance, institutions of higher education are becoming increasingly aggressive in their marketing activities. In this increasingly competitive environment, the marketers of higher education should be concerned about their institution's positioning and image.

The marketing of educational programmes has attracted the attention of researchers who have identified research-based planning and programme development, relationship marketing, and non-traditional methods for education delivery as key areas for future focus (Hayes 1996). Some of the reasons that marketing of higher education has gained importance in the management of higher education programmes and institutions are the founding missions being found increasingly ill-suited for the demands of the marketplace; budgets becoming excruciatingly tight while departments and programmes clamour for more support; the recruiting and fund-raising arenas having become extremely competitive as well as hostile; higher education being more and more dominated by many largely undifferentiated colleges and universities offering similar programmes; demographic shifts in the operating environment marked by diminishing numbers of traditional full-time students, fewer full-pay students, and fewer residential students; escalating demand for adult higher education, and continuing and special focus programmes; and last but not the least, the sharp rise in the cost of higher education (Kanis 2000). In India too, recently, as liberalization has progressed, although in fits and starts, governmental support to institutions of higher learning in the form of grants and subsidies is drying up. The movement of self-sustenance is gaining force. This also adds up and forces managers of educational institutions, especially in the public domain, to re-think their mission and strategies (Venkatesh 2001).

Ruben (2004) says that students are affected not only by the teaching environment but also by the learning environment, which includes facilities, accommodation, physical environment, policies, and procedures, and more importantly, interpersonal relations and communication, and from every encounter and experience. Hence, the faculty, staff, and administrators have to set good examples by their deeds and recognize that everyone in an institution is a teacher. Keeping in mind that the continual self-examination by institutions should focus on the institution's contribution to students' intellectual and personal development, we can propose the following model (Table 16.5–16.8) for the BSC approach in the Indian higher education scenario, largely based on the analysis of the findings presented variously by Chang and Chow (1999), Stewart and Hubin (2000), Ivy (2001), Cribb and Hogan (2003), and Karanthanos and Karanthanos (2005):

Table 16.5 Component one: Customer perspective—including students, faculty, staff, alumni, parents, and corporations

Objective	Measures
Students/Parents	
▢ Highly-valued programme	▢ External rankings in press, percentage of enrolment out of applications
▢ Quality academic advising	▢ Student evaluation of advising
	▢ Student satisfaction survey
▢ Flexible course scheduling	▢ Alumni evaluation, graduating student survey
▢ Quality instruction	▢ Accreditation, recruiter evaluation, professional exam passing rate
▢ Effective student placement	▢ Percentage of students with job offers at graduation, number of companies recruiting on campus, average starting salaries
Faculty/Staff	
▢ Growth opportunities	▢ Salary growth over period of time
	▢ Courses or educational programs completed
▢ Learning opportunities	▢ Knowledge and skill sharing across work functions, units, and locations
	▢ Employee well-being
Alumni	
▢ Knowledge updation with passage of time	▢ Alumni feedback
	▢ Alumni satisfaction survey
▢ Knowledge reinforcement	

Contd

Table 16.5 Contd

Corporate	
❑ Hiring quality students	❑ Number of students hired ❑ Number of job offers per student
❑ Knowledge extension, i.e., research, consultancy, training, continuing education-related linkages	❑ Average salaries offered ❑ Number of people benefiting from training programmes conducted by institution ❑ Grants/endowments garnered from industry
Society	
❑ Good citizenship	❑ Number of alumni in public service, community service, NGOs. ❑ Philanthropic record of alumni, faculty, staff ❑ Legally clean record of alumni, faculty, staff

As listed in Tables 16.5–16.8, a wide range of stakeholders and their diverse claims/interests and objectives have to be addressed in the context of the institution of higher education in India. The first component, customer perspective, is supposed to aim at the immediate needs and desires of the students, parents, faculty and staff, alumni, the corporate sector, and the society at large. It is relevant here to state that looking at students solely as customers becomes a sort of a misnomer, as they are also (if not only) the 'throughput' that eventually gets processed in the institution and ends up accepted (or rejected) at the verge of graduation. Hence, the corporation and society at large should be considered as the real customers. The second component involves the internal business or operations perspective. This inherently focuses on the implementation and delivery of the academic, research, and other programmes by the institution and the degree of excellence achieved in the same. The third component, innovation and learning perspective of the organization, looks at the development of faculty and staff as a precursor and foundation to excellence in programme design and delivery. Finally, the fourth component constitutes the financial performance and its measure. It is clear in the Indian context especially, that although the

Table 16.6   Component two: Internal business perspective student/stakeholder focus

Objective	Measures
❑ To achieve continuous improvement of services, facilities, and resources	Meeting service standards, response time to customer, service facilities to staff
❑ To improve new product and service development	Number of new products and services introduced, i.e., new courses, syllabi, programmes, and curriculum changes
❑ Quality assurance	Distribution of grades awarded, exit exam, or student competency evaluation
❑ Internship programme	Number of internships available, number of companies available, student evaluation
❑ Cost-efficiency	Faculty-to-student ratio, educational expenses per student
❑ Unique or specialized curriculum	Number of faculty in specialized area, number of schools offering the same programme

Table 16.7 Component three: Innovation and learning perspective faculty and staff, organizational effectiveness, social responsibility

Objective	Measures
❑ Faculty professional growth	Number of faculty presentations at conferences; number of faculty presentations; number of seminars attended, travel budget for conference attendance
❑ Staff motivation and development	Percentage of budget spent on staff development; staff satisfaction index in staff survey; number of cross-trained or multi-skilled staff
❑ Incorporating technology into teaching	Number of courses incorporating new technology
❑ Innovation in teaching	Number of teaching workshops attended by faculty, number of teaching innovation projects
❑ Curriculum innovation	Number of curriculum revisions in last five years; number of new courses offered in last five years
❑ Partnering with corporations for campus recruitment	Number of firms involved; number of joint activities
❑ Organizational citizenship	Academic excellence; and increased research productivity; increased outreach to community
❑ Resource management	Number of campus partnerships, entrepreneurial initiatives, trends in energy use

government eschews the 'profit' word for educational institutions, it emphasizes more and more on self-sustaining programmes and institutions as a desirable outcome of the strategies and models envisaged and pursued by universities and colleges. Surpluses are important, as only then can institutions look for achieving greater autonomy in designing and delivering ever new courses and programmes that are relevant to the population in context, but expensive to implement. Fig. 16.6 proposes a schematic model of the BSC approach for institutions of higher education in India, based on the model designed by Kaplan and Norton (2001).

Kaplan and Norton (1996a) say that companies are using scorecard to:

o clarify and update vision and strategic direction

Table 16.8 Component four: Financial perspective

Objective	Measures
❑ Prosper	Annual grants; amount of permanent endowment
❑ Succeed	Enrolment trend
❑ Grow	Enhancement in student intake
❑ Survive	Level of student enrolment; funding per student
❑ Maximize asset utilization	More efficient and effective use of facilities, space, services, systems, and resources as measured by various usage studies and statistics

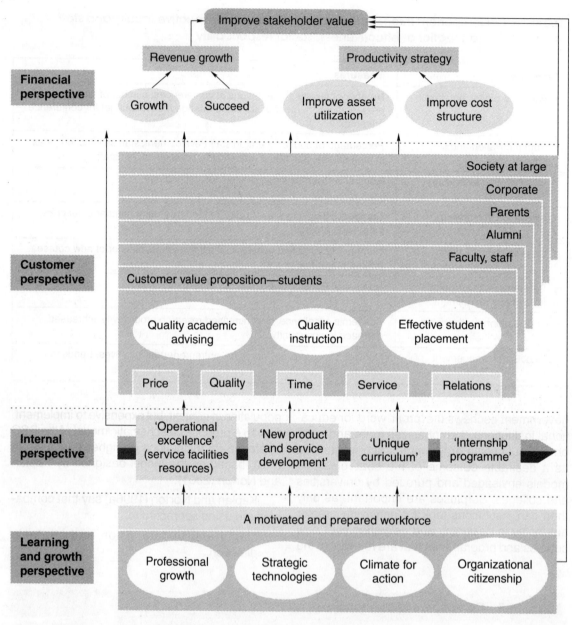

Source: Adapted from Kaplan and Norton (2001).

Fig. 16.6   Proposed balanced scorecard model for institutions of higher education

- ○ communicate strategic objectives and measures throughout the organization
- ○ align department and individual goals with the organization's vision and strategy
- ○ link strategic objectives to long-term targets and annual budgets
- ○ identify and align strategic initiatives

o conduct periodic performance reviews to learn about and improve strategy

o obtain feedback to learn about and improve strategy.

All the above-mentioned benefits are relevant in the context of the institutions higher learning in India. As Pandey (2005), indicates, 'A good aspect of the BSC is that it is a simple, systematic, easy-to-understand approach for performance measurement, review, and evaluation. It is also a convenient mechanism to communicate strategy and strategic objectives to all levels of management'. According to Kaplan and Norton (2001), the most important potential benefit is that the BSC approach aligns with strategy leading to better communication and motivation, which causes better performance. Considering the linkages in service management profit chain (Kaplan and Norton 2001), we can list the potential benefits as follows:

o Investments in faculty and staff training lead to improvements in service quality.

o Better service quality leads to higher customer (stakeholder) satisfaction.

o Higher customer satisfaction leads to increased customer loyalty.

o Increased customer loyalty generates positive word-of-mouth, increased grants/revenues, and surpluses that can be ploughed into the system for further growth and development.

With growing popularity for Indian engineers and graduates in job employment abroad (*The Times of India* 2006) India has to build world-class quality into higher education. In fact, a critical test of a scorecard's success is its transparency: from the 15–20 scorecard measures, an observer is able to see through the organizations corporate strategy (Kaplan and Norton 1993). Thus, if higher education institutions apply the BSC approach to their organization they will be able to position their students and programmes positively in the minds of the international audience.

Conclusion

Universities need to consciously and explicitly manage the processes associated with the creation of their knowledge assets and recognize the value of their intellectual capital to their continuing role in society in a wider global marketplace for higher education (Rowley 2000).

Translating the BSC approach to the complex world of academia is a challenge (Ruben 1999). There are some critical success factors highlighted for higher education institutions in India. These factors are critical because if they are executed properly, the institution will achieve excellence in its chosen field(s). It serves as a driving force to move institutions towards their goals. In the process of reaching these goals, institutions are confronted with many barriers that are difficult to overcome; however, many barriers originate from the institutions organizational members themselves by way of resistance to change, fear of accountability, and its derivative pressure, lack of commitment, and fear of failure. If quality can be nurtured into the senses of all the functionaries in the institutions, then organizational members will engage in the co-operation and commitment required of them (Kanji et al. 1999). The BSC approach offers an institution the opportunity to formulate a cascade of measures to translate the mission of knowledge creation, sharing, and utilization into a comprehensive, coherent, communicable, and mobilizing framework—for external stakeholders, and for one another.

The current state of Indian universities and other institutions of higher learning can benefit through the application of BSCs to cull out areas that they need to urgently focus upon and design appropriate strategies.

Questions

1. Discuss the scenario of tertiary education in India.

2. What is the balanced scorecard and how can it be applied to business?

3. Critically evaluate the application of balanced scorecard in education.

SELECT REFERENCES

Altbach, Philip G. (2005), 'Higher education in India', *The Hindu*, 12 April.

Asher, Mike (1996), *Managing Quality in Service Sector*, Kogan Page Limited, London, Chapter 2.

CABE (2005), 'Autonomy of higher education institutions', New Delhi, Ministry of Human Resource Development, Department of Secondary and Higher Education, Government of India.

Chang, O.H. and C.W. Chow (1999), 'The balanced scorecard: A potential tool for supporting change and continuous improvement in accounting education', *Issues in Accounting Education*, vol. 14, no. 3, pp. 395–412.

Chhaparia, Parul (2006), 'Bahamas come head-hunting to India', *Times of India*, 12 February, p. 7.

Chidambaram, R. (1999), 'Patterns and Priorities in Indian research and development', *Current Science*, vol. 77, no. 7, pp. 859–868.

Cullen, J., J. Joyce, T. Hassall, and M. Broadbent (2003), 'Quality in higher education: From monitoring to management', *Quality Assurance in Higher Education*, vol. 11, no. 1, pp. 30–34.

Dorweiler, V.P. and M. Yakhou (2005), 'Scorecard for academic administration performance on the campus', *Managerial Auditing Journal*, vol. 20, no. 2, pp. 138–144.

Grönroos, Christian (1988), 'Service quality: The six criteria of good perceived service quality', *Review of Business*, vol. 9, no. 3, pp. 10–13.

Grönroos, Christian (1998), 'Marketing services: The case of the missing product', *The Journal of Business and Industrial Marketing*, vol. 13, no. 4/5, pp. 322–336.

Hayes, Tom (1996), 'Higher education marketing symposium wins top grades', *Marketing News*, vol. 30, no. 3, pp. 10–11.

Heimerdinger, John F. (2002), 'Commentary', *Non-profit Management and Leadership*, vol. 13, no. 2, p. 205.

Ivy, Jonathan (2001), 'Higher education institution image: A correspondence analysis approach', *The International Journal of Educational Management*, vol. 15, no. 6/7, pp. 276–282.

Kandampully, J. (2000), 'The impact of demand fluctuation on the quality of service: A tourism industry example', *Managing Service Quality*, vol. 10, no. 1, pp. 10–18.

Kanis, Ed (2000), 'Marketing in higher education is a must today', *Business First*, Louisville, vol. 16, no. 25, p. 55.

Kanji, Gopal K., Abdul M. Bin, A. Tambi, and W. Wallace (1999), 'A comparative study of quality practices in higher education institutions in the US and Malaysia', *Total Quality Management*, vol. 10, no. 3, pp. 357–371.

Kaplan, Robert S. and David P. Norton (1992), 'The balanced scorecard: Measures that drive performance', *Harvard Business Review*, January–February, pp. 71–79.

Kaplan, Robert S. and David P. Norton (1993), 'Putting the balanced scorecard to work', *Harvard Business Review*, September–October, pp. 134–142.

Kaplan, R.S. and D.P. Norton (1996a), 'Using the balanced scorecard as a strategic management system', *Harvard Business Review*, Jan–Feb, pp. 75–85.

Kaplan, R.S. and D.P. Norton (1996b), 'Strategic learning and the balanced scorecard', *Strategy and Leadership*, Sept–Oct, pp. 18–24.

Kaplan, R.S. and D.P. Norton (2001), 'Transforming the balanced scorecard from performance measurement to strategic management: Part I', *Accounting Horizons*, vol. 15, no. 1, pp. 87–104.

Kaplan, R.S. and D.P. Norton (2004), 'How strategy maps frame an organization's objectives', *Financial Executive*, March–April, pp. 40–45.

Karathanos, D. and P. Karathanos (2005), 'Applying the balanced scorecard to education', *Journal of Education for Business*, vol. 80, no. 4, pp. 222–230.

Kasper, Hans, P.V. Helsdingen, and W. de Vries Jr (1999), *Services Marketing Management: An International Perspective*, John Wiley and Sons, England, Chapter 5.

Lockwood, Andrew, Michael Baker, and Andrew Ghillyer (1996), *Quality Management in Hospitality*, Cassel, New York, Chapters 1 and 2.

Misra, R.P. (2002), 'Globalization and Indian universities: Challenges and prospects', unpublished speech at the Third Dr Amarnath Jha Memorial Lecture, delivered at Lalit Narayan Mithila University, Darbhanga, Bihar on 2 September 2002.

Mohanty, R.P. and R.R. Lakhe (2002), *TQM in Service Sector*, Jaico Publishing House, Mumbai, Chapter 1.

Mohsin, Asad (2005), 'Service quality perceptions: An assessment of restaurant and café visitors in Hamilton, New Zealand', *The Business Review*, Cambridge, vol. 3, no. 2, pp. 51–57.

Narlikar, J.V. (1999), 'No fizz and spark—decline in science education', *The Times of India*, 6 May, p. 10.

Pandey, I.M. (2005), 'Balanced scorecard: Myth and reality', *The Vikalpa*, vol. 30, no. 1, pp. 51–66.

Parasuraman A., V.A. Zeithaml, and L.L. Berry (1985), 'A conceptual model of service quality and its implications for future research', *Journal of Marketing*, vol. 49, no. 4, p. 47.

Porter L. and S. Tanner (2002), *Assessing Business Excellence*, Butterworth–Heinemann Publications, Oxford, Chapters 2, 4, and 6.

Reed, Darryl and Sanjoy Mukherjee (2004), *Corporate Governance, Economic Reforms, and Development: The Indian Experience*, Oxford University Press, New Delhi.

Rowley, Jennifer (2000), 'Higher education ready for knowledge management', *The International Journal of Educational Management*, vol. 14, no. 7, p. 325.

Ruben, Brent D. (2004), *Pursuing Excellence in Higher Education: Eight Fundamental Challenges*, Jossey-Bass, San Francisco.

Smeby, Jens Christian (2003), 'The impact of massification of university research', *Tertiary Education and Management*, vol. 9, no. 2, pp. 131–144.

Stewart, A.C. and J. Carpenter-Hubin (2000), 'The balanced scorecard: Beyond reports and rankings', *Planning for Higher Education*, Winter 2000–01, pp. 37–42.

The Institute of Company Secretaries of India (2003), *Corporate Governance (Modules of Best Practices)*, 5th edn, The Institute of Company Secretaries of India, New Delhi.

The World Bank (2007), 'Regulatory trends in service convergence', Policy Division, Global Information and Communication Technologies Department, Washington, D.C., United States.

Venkatesh, Umashankar (2001), 'The importance of managing point-of-marketing in marketing higher education programmes: Some conclusions', *Journal of Services Research*, vol. 1, no. 1, pp. 125–140.

Venkatesha, M.G. (2003), 'Teaching versus research in Indian universities', *Current Science*, vol. 84, no. 11, pp. 1384–1385.

Wallace, Peter and John Zinkin (2006), *Mastering Business in Asia Corporate Governance*, John Wiley & Sons (Asia) Pte Ltd, New Delhi.

Yavas, U. and D.J. Shemwell, (1996), 'Graphical representation of university image: A correspondence analysis', *Journal for Marketing for Higher Education*, vol. 7, no. 2, pp. 75–84.

Cribb, G. and C. Hogan (2003), 'Balanced scorecard: Linking strategic planning to measurement and communication', 24th Annual Conference of the International Association of Technological University Libraries, http://www.iatul.org/conference/proceedings/vol13/papers/CRIBB_fulltext.pdf, accessed on 22 January 2009.

http://www.balancedscorecard.org/images/BSC.jpg, accessed on 19 December 2006.

http://www.ciionline.org/Common/201/images/Business%20Excellence%20Model.pdf, accessed on 19 December 2007.

http://www.cii-iq.in/pdfs/excellence.pdf, accessed on 25 January 2009.

http://www.efqm.org, accessed on 19 December 2007.

http://www.efqm.org/Default.aspx?tabid=35, accessed on 5 September 2008.

http://www.quality.nist.gov/Ambassador/Slides/Criteria%20for%20Performance%20Excellence.ppt#6, accessed on 19 December 2007.

http://www.quality.nist.gov/PDF_files/2008_Business_Nonprofit_Criteria.pdf, accessed on 5 September 2008.

http://www.thehindubusinessline.com/2006/09/01/stories/2006090102460300.htm, accessed on 6 September 2008.

http://www.sebi.gov.in/Index.jsp?contentDisp=AboutSEBI, accessed on 5 September 2008.

http://www.ustr.gov/assets/Document_Library/Reports_Publications/2001/2001_NTE_Report/asset_upload_file786_6575.pdf, accessed on 5 September 2008.

Ruben, Brent D. (1999), 'Towards a balanced scorecard of higher education: Rethinking the college and universities excellence framework', Higher Education Forum, QCI Centre for Organizational Development and Leadership, Rutgers University, http://www.qci.rutgers.edu, accessed on 2 January 2006.

17 Ethics in Service Firms

OBJECTIVES

After reading this chapter you will be able to understand the:
- concept of ethics and values
- various sources of ethics
- importance of ethics in an organization
- guiding principles of ethics
- describe ethics in an organizational context
- myths around organizational ethics
- issues relating to ethics in service firms

INTRODUCTION

The words 'ethics' and 'values' have been in use since ages. However, the aspect and meaning ascribed to these words has been different. This chapter attempts to reconcile some of the views on the subject and analyses them for managerial implications. The Oxford dictionary defines *values* as moral or professional standards of behaviour, principle, artistic, legal, and scientific values, and *ethics* as a science that deals with morals. Chakraborty (1991) elaborates that values serve the process of 'becoming' in the sense of transformation of the level of consciousness, purer higher levels. They help us to distinguish between the 'desired' and the 'desirable', between the 'delectable' and the 'electable', between the 'short-term' and the 'long-term'. While education is more germane to values, training relates more closely to skills.

ROLE OF VALUES IN SKILLS DEVELOPMENT

Datta (1995) has discussed that the skills relating to leadership negotiation, counselling, communication, public relations, and team building would not serve their purpose unless they flow from a value based 'pure mind'. Effective leadership style requires an understanding of three fundamental ingredients that make up each individual (as suggested by Sankhya Philosophy)—*sattwa*, i.e., purity and righteousness: *rajas*, i.e., a strong liking or aversion, and selfishness; and *tamas*, i.e., ignorance and laziness.

ETHICS

Miller (1960) states that ethics is a part of reality. It is the recognition of and responsibility for the realities involved in any relationship. He believes that God's will is done when man relates himself to the task of bringing creation to its fullest expression. Human relationships are of three orders:

1. *With things:* which are below human beings in creation. It signifies dominance.
2. *With persons:* who are alongside. It signifies mutuality.
3. *With God:* who is above human beings. It signifies dependence.

Any attempt to treat a relationship other than as in reality, denies the basic reality of the relationship. Ethics, as elaborated by Miller, is respecting other individuals' dignity and entity. It also gives a direction for formulation of ethics with respect to various entities.

Ethics is about honouring one's word. It is to stand by your commitment and carry conviction in your action. There are no overtones of being right or wrong, for these are subjective words. This can have negative implications also, because if someone stands for something outrageous and stands up with conviction it can have serious repercussions. The guiding spirit for the conviction must come from a well thought out process of self analysis and analysis of the context. It is here that one's sense of judgement becomes important.

Ethics cannot be talked of in an absolute sense since there are a number of elements attached to them, so there are bound to be differences. However, the important thing is that ethics becomes meaningful when supported by analysing the context and applying judgemental power. 'A person will be committed to values only when he sees them to be precious to him. People make such choices that make them feel good' (Shah 1995).

Sources of Values

Steiner (1975) remarks that there are five principal repositories of values that influence a businessperson—religious, philosophical, cultural, legal, and professional. A common bond threaded through these systems binds together the great majority of individuals in a society.

Classification

It is desirable to classify ethics into two categories—(1) professional ethics; and (2) personal ethics.

Professional ethics These reflect the ethics or commitment of word in the worklife. It relates to one's commitment to professionally laid out principles and objectives.

Personal ethics These reflect one's value system and feelings about a number of issues.

Both professional and personal ethics have a common core. There has to be an overlap between the two. Ethics are like habits; they reflect in all circumstances. A person who is committed will maintain commitment in all relationships. A person in the habit of lying will lie even without the circumstances demanding it.

Sources of Ethics

Daft (1988) defines the sources of ethics as indicated in Table 17.1.

Table 17.1   Sources of ethics

Type	Reflect	Source of adoption
Personal	Religion, social consciousness, and personal attitudes toward social responsibility	Values of individual managers
Corporate	The policies and standard industry practice	Organizations' values and culture
Professional	Appropriate behaviour for member individuals and companies	Defined by professional occupational groups, e.g., Indian Medical Association, ICWAI

From another point of view, there could be three sources of ethics:

1. *Classical element:* There are certain values, such as honesty and integrity, which have a timeless appeal. These are appreciated always, in any situation.
2. *Contextual element:* These refer to the collective norms of the society which reflect in an individual's behaviour in a particular society. These will change with geographical boundaries and cultures. So, something considered very normal in one society may have negative overtones in another.
3. *Personal elements:* These are the values inherited through parents. These are acquired by birth. Issues of morality come in here. The morality issues differ from family to family though at a level of a society there is a convergence to a particular trend.

Principles of Personal Ethics

Personal ethics may also be called morality, since they reflect the general expectations of any person, in any society, acting in any capacity. These are the principles we try to instill in our children and expect of one another without needing to articulate the expectation or formalize it in any way.

Principles of personal ethics include:

- concern for the well-being of others
- respect for the autonomy of others
- trustworthiness and honesty
- willing compliance with the law (with the exception of civil disobedience)
- basic justice; being fair
- refusing to take unfair advantage
- benevolence, or doing good
- preventing harm.

Principles of Professional Ethics

In addition to what we should all aspire to, individuals acting in a professional capacity take on an additional burden of ethical responsibility. For example, professional associations have codes of ethics that prescribe required behaviour within the context of a professional practice such as medicine, law, accounting, or engineering. These written codes provide rules of conduct and standards of behaviour based on the principles of professional ethics, which include:

- impartiality; objectivity
- openness; full disclosure
- confidentiality
- due diligence/duty of care
- fidelity to professional responsibilities
- avoiding potential or apparent conflict of interest.

Co-existence of Principles

Each of us influences the world by simply existing; and it is always wise to 'think globally'. An added measure of accountability is placed on globally influential enterprises such as governments and transnational corporations. (Responsibility comes with power whether we accept it or not.)

One of the burdens of leadership is to influence society and world affairs in a positive way. Can a person (or company) truly be 'successful' while causing human suffering or irreparable environmental damage? A more modern and complete model of success also considers impact on humanity and the earth's ecology. Principles of global ethics include:

- global justice (as reflected in international laws)
- society before self/social responsibility
- environmental stewardship
- interdependence and responsibility for the 'whole'
- reverence for place.

Ethics in Business

Although philosophical debates about ethics can be traced back to antiquity (Small 1993), it is only relatively recently that there appears to have been a marked surge in interest in the area of business ethics as a discipline.

Smith and Johnson (1996) point out that, for instance, one orientation is to identify business ethics with application of normative ethical theory to business (for example, Ozar 1979; Davis 1985; Goodpaster and Matthews 1982; and Velasquez 1988).

Velasquez (1988) argues that business ethics is applied ethics. It is the application of our understanding of what is good and right to the assortment of institutions, technologies, transactions, activities, and pursuits which we call 'business'.

This implies that even with the systematic attempt to integrate models of moral problem-solving with practical moral dilemmas in business, there may be no one correct solution to a given problem. There may be different explanations for alternate solutions. This situation raises two issues. Firstly, that of praxis—business ethics is an applied, practical area of investigation. It is not simply the study of ethical thought divorced from the social context of business activities. Its test bed must be business environments with all their complexity, confusion, and uncertainty. Secondly, there is no one set of universally agreed cannon. Instead, any business practitioner is confronted by an array of competing views, derived from moral philosophies, each articulating different prescriptions about what is good or bad for the conduct of business behaviour.

Raphael (1981) puts the issue quite succinctly when he observes that in philosophy, far more than in science, one is left in the end with a number of possible theories, none of them proved, none of them definitely disproved. The individual must then decide for himself which, if any, to accept. So, do not expect moral philosophy to solve the practical problems of life or to be a crutch on which you can lean. A study of philosophy makes it more necessary, not less, to stand on your own feet, to be self critical, and to be obliged to choose for yourself.

As Raphael implies, perhaps the main value of moral philosophy to the business-person is its ability to facilitate critical self-reflection rather than the provision of clear guidelines that enable the construction of optimal solutions. Of the problem, some commentators avoid defining business ethics purely in terms of the application of ethical theory to business affairs. For instance, De George (1986) argues that business ethics is an interdisciplinary field in which the methodologies of the various areas of business education are as applicable as those of ethical and philosophical analysis. McHugh (1988) provides a good induction of this variety of academic influence when he indicates that there are a dozen or so disciplines which can be said to have a claim to providing an input to business ethics. These include philosophy, sociology, psychology, history, law, politics, and economics.

The subject matter of business ethics is more than an individual responsibility and the application of moral beliefs to business practice.

There will be different answers to ethical issues depending on the assumptions or 'mode of engagement', of whoever is proposing the answers. Many commentators (e.g., Buchholz 1989; Stace 1988; and Sumner 1988) have differentiated what may be called 'prescriptive', 'cognitive', or 'absolutist' moral statements from what are termed, 'descriptive', 'non-cognitive', and 'relativist' moral statements. How a person is oriented with regard to this dichotomy determines the extent to which he or she believes it is possible to specify what is good or bad, right or wrong, for people in general and for members of business organizations.

Typically, Hoffman and Moore (1990) observe that 'It is…the study of what is good and right for the human being. It asks what goals people ought to pursue and what actions they ought to perform. Business ethics is a branch of applied ethics; it studies the relationship of what is good and what is right to business.'

CODE OF ETHICS IN THE ORGANIZATIONAL CONTEXT

Code of ethics is a formal statement of the company's values concerning social issues. The purpose of a code of ethics is to communicate to employees in plain language what the company stands for. Codes of ethics are valuable when they explicitly state those behaviours that are expected and those that will not be tolerated, and are backed by management's actions. Without top management support, there is no assurance that the code will be followed. Codes serve to remind employees of existing values and guidelines and to tell the public at large what the company stands for.

Why Must Business Pursue Ethical Practice?

Steiner (1975) writes, 'Businessmen think that practising good ethics will help their business because customers repeat sales, employees like to work for an ethical manager, a good reputation will attract business, a reputation for sharp business practice is not an asset, and consistent behaviour is valued by customers.'

In the organizational context, ethics can have the following implications:

Motivation A leader's staunch belief in certain values, which can improve productivity, can be transcended to his subordinates. The motivating power should be the benefits attached to adopting a particular set of values.

Interpersonal ethics In an organization, if the commitments between various departments are kept, deadlines are adopted, and work gets done, then surely we can have more efficient organizations.

Customers A word of commitment made by the organization with customers, if kept, can win loyal customers, e.g., companies proclaiming service time of 4 hours in case of breakdown must stand up to it. In the long-run, these are the factors which shape the organizational futures.

The case in point is summed up in the following lines by Vaslav Hand, in his inaugural address as President of Czechoslovakia:

'A better system will not automatically ensure a better life. In fact the opposite is now true; only by creating a better life can a better system be developed.'

The value management may, therefore, be precisely said to be the development of an individual's self-management in a community. It involves the development of personal commitment to the company as well as to a set of necessary rules and to psycho-social responsibilities.

Thus, every profession has certain professional ethics, which must be adhered to. A person deviates when his/her perception of reality varies and the ends become more important than the means themselves. The pursuit of ethics by employees can only be possible when the top management approves it and leads by example. Everyone wants to identify with a dependable person, a person who carries conviction and stands by his/her word. It is a commitment which makes all the difference.

The relevance of values is highlighted by the following *shloka* from Hindu scriptures.

> *Ye'sam no vidya na tapoh na danam*
> *Gyanam na sheelam guno na dharma*
> *Te martyja loke bhuvibhar bhuta*
> *Manusya rupena mriga's charanti*

The aforementioned *shloka* highlights that a person's life without a set of values is simply meaningless. The state of abject happiness can only be attained by certain commitments in life, the most important being commitment to self. Finally, the sense of judgement can be facilitated by the gospel according to St Matthews.

Everything you want others to do to you, you shall do unto others. (Matthew 7:12)

According to Hinduism, 'Do not do anything to others that if done to you would cause you pain.'

Bhattacharya (1995) remarks about the observations of Frank Kristol, a leading American intellectual, on the consequences of the unbundled pursuit of 'having more'—independent of ethical, moral, and even political considerations.

Economic progress has been accompanied by an unforeseen tidal wave of social disintegration and moral disorientation. Whoever expected that the successful creation of a welfare state in an affluent economy would be accompanied by an incredible increase in criminality, so that our streets would be blanketed with fear, a sharp increase in teenage pregnancies and drug addiction, the creation of a dependent, self destructive under class, or two million abortions a year?

Learned et al. (1959) have described spirituality as making a continuing conscious effort to rise above these inevitable human limitations—a maximum endeavour or to comprehend the ultimate values, the truth, and the reality of the orderliness of the universe—and to live in accordance with the reality.

This, if kept in mind, can lead to a better understanding of any situation, removing many a doubt. Exhibits 17.1 and 17.2 discuss 10 myths about business ethics and benefits of managing ethics in the workplace, respectively.

Exhibit 17.1   Ten myths about business ethics

McNamara (1999) has discussed 10 myths related to business ethics. Business ethics in the workplace is about prioritizing moral values for the workplace and ensuring behaviours are aligned with those values—this is value management. Yet, myths abound about business ethics. Some of these myths arise from general confusion about the notion of ethics. Other myths arise from narrow or simplistic views of ethical dilemmas.

Myth 1: Business ethics is more a matter of religion than management. Diane Kirrane, in 'Managing values: A systematic approach to business ethics,' (*Training and Development Journal*, November 1990), asserts that, 'altering people's values or souls isn't the aim of an organizational ethics programme—managing values and conflicts among them is.'

Myth 2: Our employees are ethical so we don't need attention to business ethics. Most of the ethical dilemmas faced by managers in the work-place are highly complex. Wallace explains that one knows when they have a significant ethical conflict, when there is presence of a) significant value conflicts among differing interests, b) real alternatives that are equality justifiable, and c) significant consequences on 'stakeholders' in the situation. Kirrane (1990) mentions that when the topic of business ethics comes up, people are quick to speak of the golden rule, honesty, and courtesy. But when presented with complex ethical dilemmas, most people realize that there is a wide 'grey area' when trying to apply ethical principles.

Myth 3: Business ethics is a discipline best led by philosophers, academics, and theologians. Lack of involvement by leaders and managers in business ethics literature and discussions has led many to believe that business ethics is a fad or movement, having little to do with the day-to-day realities of running an organization. They believe business ethics is primarily a complex philosophical debate or a

Contd

Exhibit 17.1 Contd

religion. However, business ethics is a management discipline with a programmatic approach that includes several practical tools. Ethics management programmes have practical applications in other areas of management, as well. (These applications are listed later on in this document.)

Myth 4: Business ethics is superfluous—it only asserts the obvious: 'do good'! Many people assert that codes of ethics, or lists of ethical values to which the organization aspires, are rather superfluous because they represent values to which everyone should naturally aspire. However, the value of a code of ethics to an organization is its priority and focus regarding certain ethical values in that workplace. For example, it is obvious that all people should be honest. However, if an organization is struggling around continuing occasions of deceit in the workplace, a priority on honesty is very timely, and honesty should be listed in that organization's code of ethics. Note that a code of ethics is an organic instrument that changes with the needs of society and the organization.

Myth 5: Business ethics is a matter of the good guys preaching to the bad guys. Some writers do seem to claim a moral high ground while lamenting the poor condition of business and its leaders. However, those people well versed in managing organizations realize that good people can take bad actions, particularly when stressed or confused. (Stress or confusion are not excuses for unethical actions—they are reasons.) Managing ethics in the workplace includes all of us working together to help each other remain ethical, and to work through confusing and stressful ethical dilemmas.

Myth 6: Business ethics is the new police person on the block. Many believe that business ethics is a recent phenomenon because of increased attention to the topic in popular and management literature. However, business ethics was written about even 2,000 years ago—at least since Cicero wrote about the topic in his *On Duties*. Business ethics has received more attention recently because of the social responsibility movement that started in the 1960s.

Myth 7: Ethics can't be managed. Actually, ethics is always 'managed', but, too often, indirectly. For example, the behaviour of the organization's founder

or current leader is a strong moral influence or directive, if you will, on behaviour of employees in the workplace. Strategic priorities (profit maximization, expanding market share, cutting costs, etc.) can be very strong influences on morality. Laws, regulations, and rules directly influence behaviours to be more ethical, usually in a manner that improves the general good and/or minimizes harm to the community. Some are still sceptical about business ethics, believing that you can't manage values in an organization. Donaldson and Davis (*Management Decision*, vol. 28, no. 6) note that management, after all, is a value system. Sceptics might consider the tremendous influence of several 'codes of ethics', such as the 10 Commandments in the Christian religion or the US Constitution. Codes can be very powerful in smaller 'organizations' as well.

Myth 8: Business ethics and social responsibility is the same thing. The social responsibility movement is one aspect of the overall discipline of business ethics. Madsen and Shafritz refine the definition of business ethics to be: (a) an application of ethics to the corporate community, (b) a way to determine responsibility in business dealings, (c) the identification of important business and social issues, and (d) a critique of business. Items c and d are often matters of social responsibility. (There has been a great deal of public discussion and writing about items (c) and (d). However, more needs to be written about items (a) and (b), about how business ethics can be managed.) Writings about social responsibility often do not address practical matters of managing ethics in the workplace, e.g., developing codes, updating polices and procedures, approaches to resolving ethical dilemmas, etc.

Myth 9: Our organization is not in trouble with the law, so we're ethical. One can often be unethical, yet operate within the limits of the law, e.g., withhold information from superiors, fudge on budgets, constantly complain about others, etc. However, breaking the law often starts with unethical behaviour that has gone unnoticed. The 'boil the frog' phenomenon is a useful parable here: If you put a frog in hot water, it immediately jumps out; if you put a frog in cool water and slowly heat up the water, you can eventually boil the frog. The frog doesn't seem to notice the adverse change in its environment.

Contd

Exhibit 17.1 Contd

Myth 10: Managing ethics in the workplace has little practical relevance. Managing ethics in the workplace involves identifying and prioritizing values to guide behaviours in the organization, and establishing associated policies and procedures to ensure those behaviours are conducted. One might call this 'values management'. Values management is also highly important in other management practices, e.g., managing diversity, total quality management, and strategic planning.

Source: Adapted from McNamara (1999). Reprinted with permission from Carter McNamara, Authenticity Consulting, LLC.

Exhibit 17.2 Benefits of managing ethics in the workplace

Many people are used to reading or hearing of the moral benefits of attention to business ethics. However, there are other types of benefits, as well. The following list describes various types of benefits from managing ethics in the workplace.

1. **Attention to business ethics has substantially improved society.** A matter of decades ago, children in our country worked 16-hour days. Workers' limbs were torn off and disabled workers were condemned to poverty and often to starvation. Trusts controlled some markets to the extent that prices were fixed and small businesses choked out. Price fixing crippled normal market forces. Employees were terminated based on personalities. Influence was applied through intimidation and harassment. Then, society reacted and demanded that businesses place high value on fairness and equal rights. Anti-trust laws were instituted, government agencies were established, unions were organized, and laws and regulations were established.

2. **Ethics programmes help maintain a moral course in turbulent times.** As noted earlier, Wallace and Pekel explain that attention to business ethics is critical during times of fundamental change—times much like those faced now by businesses, both non-profit or for profit. During times of change, there is often no clear moral compass to guide leaders through complex conflicts about what is right or wrong. Continuing attention to ethics in the workplace sensitizes leaders and staff to how they want to act, consistently.

3. **Ethics programmes cultivate strong teamwork and productivity.** Ethics programmes align employee behaviours with those top priority ethical values preferred by leaders of the organization. Usually, an organization finds surprising disparity between its preferred values and the values actually reflected by behaviour in the workplace. Ongoing attention and dialogue regarding values in the workplace builds openness, integrity, and community—critical ingredients of strong teams in the workplace. Employees feel strong alignment between their values and those of the organization. They react with strong motivation and performance.

4. **Ethics programmes support employee growth and meaning.** Attention to ethics in the workplace helps employees face reality, both good and bad, in the organization and themselves. Employees get full confidence that they can admit and deal with whatever comes their way. Bennett, in his article, 'Unethical behaviour, stress appear linked' (*Wall Street Journal*), explained that a consulting company tested a range of executives and managers. Their most striking finding was that the more emotionally healthy executives were, as measured on a battery of tests, the more likely they were to score high on ethics tests.

5. **Ethics programmes are an insurance policy—they help ensure that policies are legal.** There are an increasing number of lawsuits in regard to personnel matters and to the effects of an organization's services or products on stakeholders. As mentioned earlier, ethical principles are often state-of-the-art legal matters. These principles are often applied to current, major ethical issues to become legislation. Attention to ethics ensures highly ethical

Contd

Exhibit 17.2 Contd

policies and procedures in the workplace. It is far better to incur the cost of mechanisms to ensure ethical practices now than to incur costs of litigation later. A major intent of well-designed personnel policies is to ensure ethical treatment of employees, e.g., in matters of hiring, evaluating, disciplining, firing, etc. Drake and Drake (*California Management Review*) note that 'an employer can be subject to suit for breach of contract for failure to comply with any promise it made, so the gap between stated corporate culture and actual practise has significant legal, as well as ethical implications'.

6. ***Ethics programmes help avoid criminal acts 'of omission' and can lower fines.*** Ethics programmes tend to detect ethical issues and violations early on so they can be reported or addressed. In some cases, when an organization is aware of an actual or potential violation and does not report it to the appropriate authorities, this can be considered a criminal act, e.g., in business dealings with certain government agencies, such as the defence department. The recent Federal Sentencing Guidelines specify major penalties for various types of major ethics violations. However, the guidelines potentially lower fines if an organization has clearly made an effort to operate ethically.

7. ***Ethics programmes help manage values associated with quality management, strategic planning, and diversity management—this benefit needs far more attention.*** Ethics programmes identify preferred values and ensure organizational behaviours are aligned with those values. This effort includes recording the values, developing policies and procedures to align behaviours with preferred values, and then training all personnel about the policies and procedures. This overall effort is very useful for several other programmes in the workplace that require behaviours to be aligned with values, including quality management, strategic planning, and diversity management. Total quality management includes high priority on certain operating values, e.g., trust among stakeholders, performance, reliability, measurement, and feedback. Eastman and Polaroid use ethics tools

in their quality programmes to ensure integrity in their relationships with stakeholders. Ethics management techniques are highly useful for managing strategic values, e.g., expanding market share, reducing costs, etc. McDonnell Douglas integrates their ethics programmes into their strategic planning process. Ethics management programmes are also useful in managing diversity. Diversity is much more than the colour of people's skin; it is acknowledging different values and perspectives. Diversity programmes require recognizing and applying diverse values and perspectives; these activities are the basis of a sound ethics management programme.

8. ***Ethics programmes promote a strong public image.*** Attention to ethics is also strong public relations. Admittedly, managing ethics should not be done primarily for reasons of public relations, but, frankly, the fact that an organization regularly gives attention to its ethics can portray a strong positive to the public. People see organizations that value people more than profit, as striving to operate with the utmost of integrity and honour. Aligning behaviour with values is critical to effective marketing and public relations programmes. Consider how Johnson and Johnson handled the Tylenol crisis versus how Exxon handled the oil spill in Alaska. Bob Dunn, president and CEO of San Francisco-based Business for Social Responsibility, puts it best: 'Ethical values, consistently applied, are the cornerstones in building a commercially successful and socially responsible business'.

9. ***Overall benefits of ethics programmes.*** Donaldson and Davis, in 'Business ethics? Yes, but what can it do for the bottom line?' (*Management Decision*, 1990) explain that managing ethical values in the workplace legitimizes managerial actions, strengthens the coherence and balance of the organization's culture, improves trust in relationships between individuals and groups, supports greater consistency in standards and qualities of products, and cultivates greater sensitivity to the impact of the enterprise's values and messages.

10. ***Last, and most important, formal attention to ethics in the workplace is the right thing to do.***

Source: Adapted from McNamara (1999). Reprinted with the permission of Carter McNamara, Authenticity Consulting, LLC.

Unethical behaviour carries with it a stigma that can alienate markets and create massive employee-moral problems. These consequences are often unmeasured side effects of unethical behaviour that can linger long after the fine has been paid. They are consequences that require additional expenditures to correct and in some cases cannot be totally corrected.

Work is not something detached from the rest of human life, but rather 'man is born to labour as a bird to fly' (Pope Pius XI 1985).

Gini (1998) raises the question, what work and business are? Is it about earning a living? Yes. Producing a product or service? Sure. Making money or profit? Absolutely. In fact, most ethicists argue that business has a moral obligation to make a profit. But business is also about people—the people you work for and work with. Business is an interdependent, intertwined symbiotic relationship, where life, labour, and business are all of a piece. They should not be seen as separate 'games' played by different 'rules'. The enterprise of business is not distinct from the enterprise of life and living; they share the same bottom line—people. Therefore, as in the rest of life, business is required to ask, 'What ought to be done in regard to others'?

Gini (1998) says that conventional wisdom has it that two of the most glaring examples of academic oxymorons are the terms 'bu siness ethics' and 'moral leadership'. Neither of these terms carries credibility in popular culture and when conjoined, they constitute a 'null set' rather than just a simple contradiction in terms. At best, both these terms remain in the lexicon as wished for ideals rather than actual states of being.

Ciulla (1998) argues that the definition question in leadership studies is not really about the question 'What is leadership?', but about the question, 'What is good leadership?' By good, I mean morally good and effective. That is why it is fair to say that ethics lies at the heart of leadership studies. Researchers in the field need to be clear on the ethical elements of leadership in order to be clear on what the term leadership connotes. This has been pointed out by existing theories and empirical literature which have strong normative implications that have not been fully developed by their authors. Normative theories of leadership, such as transforming leadership and servant leadership, are not well developed in terms of their philosophic implications. They need more analysis as ethical theories and more empirical listing. Research into leadership ethics should not only help us with question like, 'What sort of person should lead?' or 'What are the moral responsibilities of leadership?' It should also give us a better understanding of the nature of leadership.

It is pointed out that the ultimate question in leadership studies is not 'What is the definition of leadership?' The ultimate point of studying leadership is, 'What is good leadership?' The use of the word good here has two connotations—morally good, and technically good or effective.

Transforming leadership is concerned with end values such as liberty, justice, and equality. Transforming leaders raise their followers up through various stages of morality and need. They turn their followers into leaders, and the leader becomes a moral leader.

Dunlop (1996) says that the dimension, which has been conspicuously omitted by the *Cadbury Committee* (this committee had put forward recommendations on corporate governance) is the one which is said to be the underlying principle of all corporate regulatory legislation in this country, i.e., that of accountability to the owners of the companies—the shareholders. Companies seem to have become synonymous with their board of directors, with shareholding having become a marginalized, disadvantaged group. Rather than enabling the organization to become more accountable to its real owners, not to mention the other groups who may have an interest in its financial and operating performance, the recommendations address only one side of the corporate paradigm.

The ethical issues exist at three levels (Hoffman and Moore 1990; De George 1987; Epstein 1989; and Goodpaster 1993):

1. At the macro level, there are issues about the role of business (public sector organizations) in the national and international organization of society. This will differ depending on the socio-political system, the type of enterprise, and between national and international operation.

2. At the corporate level, the issues concern corporate social responsibility, which is concerned with the ethical issues facing individual corporate entities when formulating and implementing strategies. The third section deals with philosophy and content of a corporate social responsibility (CSR) approach.

3. At the individual level, the ethical issues concern the behaviour and actions of individuals within organizations. This is clearly an issue which affects both the formulation and implementation of strategy since these are important management tasks in most organizations (Carr 1968).

ETHICS AND SERVICE FIRMS

This section offers insights to managers on issues around ethics. Different management sectors are chosen and problems are highlighted.

The pursuit and understanding of ethical issues is critical for service and product firms. The boundaries between traditional manufacturing and service firms are diminishing because the manufacturing firms also look at the service dimension of the products that are being offered. Any cost-intensive product such as automobiles, computer, electricity, and generators, when purchased, also has an after-sales service dimension to it. So, the services attached to the product have a huge revenue generation capacity.

Ethics play an important role in being the foundation for conduct of business and fostering relationships with the consumers. The perception of quality of service relies on factors such as reliability and integrity, which are based on both personal and professional ethics. Every industry has certain professional ethics, which must be adhered to in order to foster lasting relationships with consumers and the society at large. The driving force for long-term sustenance of the businesses will not come from mere marketing gimmicks and promises but from value delivered to the stakeholders, and most importantly, relationships fostered with the communities.

To gain a deeper insight into the range of issues involved in ethics, a few examples will provide issues which could be raised in the domain of service firms.

Management Education

India is a flourishing market for higher education. There are both private and public players. There are nearly about 1,000 management institutes and university departments. Foreign direct investment and liberalization measures have opened up immense opportunities for management jobs. The demand–supply gap has led to an increasing level of entrepreneurship in the service industry. There is still no foreign direct investment in the education segment and there are ambiguities in the regulatory mechanism. The accreditation of private technical institutions is under the purview of All India Council of Technical Education. There have been a lot of cases involving student anxiety over the validity of their degrees. The University Grants Commission (UGC) and All India Council for Technical Education (AICTE), which are responsible for ensuring proper planning and coordinated development of technical education system throughout the country, have identified a lot of institutions that are providing engineering and management education without their approval. Apart from these, there are universities which have closed down indefinitely and created havoc among students and parents alike. There have been cases of severe depression among students. This makes it all the more important for AICTE to keep a check on these unapproved institutions and the so-called 'deemed' universities without UGC's approval. The ethical factor to understand here is whether it is fair on these institutions to play with student's useful years for the sake of their business and profits.

The last few years have witnessed the mushrooming of numerous private institutions. Management institutes face severe dearth of faculty, lack of systematized mechanism for quality control, lack of research orientation, inadequate research infrastructure, poor delivery mechanism, and hence, poor output. These problems are a major challenge for Tier II and Tier III management schools. The Tier I schools include the IIMs, IITs, and other premium management institutions in India. The signalling effect of education is lost and firms have to make massive investments in de-learning and re-training the graduates emanating from some of these institutions.

The Private University Bill has been passed in some of the states in India. There are a few private universities which have been set up in India. However, in Chhattisgarh there were over hundred universities created in a span of less than one year. This resulted in small time institutes registering themselves as universities and admitting students in various programmes.

There was then a Supreme Court ruling which took away the status of private university from many of these institutions. This created a lot of confusion in the market and many of the students who had already taken admission in the so-called universities had to confront a lot of problems later, as the existence of that university was no long valid.

This raises further, the ethical issues of motive of existence for such service firms. There are issues of charging hefty fees without offering corresponding student experience. There have also been issues on offering placement for such students.

Admissions to Primary Schools in Delhi

Admissions of students to primary schools in Delhi have been a very contentious issue. Most of the private schools in Delhi had cumbersome admission procedures. There are long queues for filling up forms, questionnaires to be filled, with complex questions assessing ones view on the philosophy of life. Parents as well as children are interviewed. The court intervened and has now mandated certain criteria for regulating admissions to the primary schools. The question is, should a three and a half year-old child and his parents be interviewed for admission to the primary school? What ethical issues are involved here?

Healthcare

This is another sector wherein lots of ethical debates have arisen. Some of the questions which have been raised are:

1. Should tests on animals be banned?
2. What should the firms disseminate to people who are willing to go in for clinical trials for new drug development?
3. Should patients be advised of the consequent side effects of drugs administered to them?
4. What are the consequences of carelessness on the part of hospital staff when a patient is undergoing treatment in the hospital?

Also, another issue dominating the Indian healthcare scenario is the rampant illegal trade of organs. China and India are the leading nations in terms of illegal organ trade. The ethical issues arising in this case are kidneys being removed without informing the patients and refusal to pay as promised for the donation.

Exhibit 17.3 explains clinical trials done on babies.

Telecom

This is an emerging area in services and hence then are a lot of issues, which may lie in the domain of ethics, and which could be discussed. Some of these issues are:

- Should firms be offering lifetime connections for mobile phones? The tenure of licensing to operate in a region is fixed. So, is it ethical to make offers which may not hold valid when external circumstances change?

Exhibit 17.3 Clinical trials on babies

Right to Information (RTI) reported in early 2008 that the All India Institute of Medical Sciences (AIIMS) conducted about 42 sets of trials on 4,142 babies—2,728 of them, below the age of one—since January 2006. The hard fact that emerged in this case was that about 49 babies died during the trials. The question that they had no answer for was, 'How many of them were from the lower strata of society?' While the authorities deny any such bias, the fact was cleared when it was accepted that before these trials happen the 'consent form' is read out in case the parents do not know how to read and write. The ethical implication that arises is that when the parents of the newborn do not even know how to read or write, how do authorities expect them to understand the implications of these trials.

Source: Adapted from Rtindia (2008).

Exhibit 17.4   Importance of good ethics and corporate governance

Good ethics and corporate governance are considered important behaviourial traits that can help an organization to build brand equity and ensure stable growth for the company. As companies globalize, marketing, manufacturing, and distribution networks are being set up abroad. But as this happens, ethics and governance are topics that should gain more importance. It represents the responsibility of the company towards all its stakeholders, employees, and the government. But the fact is that making ethics part of the organizational culture has to be an ongoing process. Training programmes can help employees to consider their value systems when they are faced with ethical dilemmas. Global companies have customers who demand to see and expect ethical behaviour and governance; 90 per cent of Americans aim to do business that is right and profitable. This refers to documentation, systems, and processes such as ISO 9001 and CMM. This essentially helps establish credibility and governance policies and processes, to help the company be the next 'wave' globally. Thus, it becomes the company's responsibility to put in place some strong governance policies and help them lead by example. These policies go a long way in helping them to establish best practices in the industry.

The trend in India is very positive as it has been seen that the corporate sector in India is moving towards zero tolerance towards instances of misconduct or erratic behaviour of employees. For example, in companies like Coca-Cola, TCS, and KPMG, a recruit whose ethics are suspect, are refused. Companies like Motorola expect their employees to under commit and over-deliver, while Infosys puts in value systems on the wall to ensure that everybody follows them.

Source: Adapted from Raghavan (2006) and Kaushik (2008).

- Mobile phone users in India get numerous promotional SMS messages and automated calls for product promotions. Is it not an invasion of privacy for a consumer? Is it ethical for mobile phone companies to share the mobile number database for commercial purposes?
- Mobile service operators offer free phones at lower prices clubbed with service, which may already be obsolete in terms of technology. Is it ethical to offer that stock at subsidized prices to the consumers?

Exhibit 17.4 mentions the importance of ethics and corporate governance for organizations.

SUMMARY

This chapter introduces the concept of ethics and values and provides an overview of the same. The sources of ethics have been explained and its importance in an organization is discussed. While explaining the concept of ethics in an organizational context, the guiding principles around ethics are also provided. The chapter also provides an insight on issues of ethics in service firms.

There could be a range of ethical issues which could arise related with a service offering. These could be related with keeping up the promises made to the consumer, or the delivery mechanism of the same, or other aspects related to the conduct of the business. The service firms need to be extremely cautious of the perception that they are creating in the mind of the consumer.

This chapter also addresses some of the myths associated with ethics. The code of ethics in an organizational context has also been discussed. The benefits of managing ethics at the workplace have also been discussed.

KEY TERMS

Code of conduct A set of conventional principles and expectations that are considered binding on any person who is a member of a particular group.

Corporate governance The manner in which organizations, particularly limited companies, are managed, and the nature of accountability of the managers to the owners.

Ethics A science that deals with morals.

Myths A fiction or half-truth, especially one that forms part of an ideology.

Personal ethics They reflect one's value system and feelings about a number of issues.

Professional ethics They reflect ethics or commitment of word in the worklife. It relates to one's commitment to professionally laid out principles and objectives.

Values They are moral or professional standards of behaviour, principle, artistic, legal, or scientific.

CONCEPT REVIEW QUESTIONS

1. What interventions should firms initiate to create the perception of being an ethical organization?

2. What are the common elements of ethical issues raised in select service sectors as enumerated?

3. Evaluate the principles which govern ethics in an organization.

4. What is the difference between personal and professional ethics?

5. What are the key sources of ethics?

CRITICAL THINKING QUESTIONS

1. SMS (short messaging services) in India are an acceptable way of communicating. Consumers are constantly bombarded with SMS messages by various firms. Consumers can choose the 'do not disturb' facility offered by mobile service operators, but even then the customer has no respite. Please analyse the situation from an ethical perspective.

2. Is it right to overbook an aircraft an then off-load passengers at the last minute in a budget airline? Please evaluate from an ethical perspective.

3. In India, the demand for higher education is greater than the supply. Higher education institutions use various techniques for eliminating applications for various courses. Please analyse the situation from the ethics viewpoint.

INTERNET EXERCISES

1. Browse through the website of Infosys and Tata Consultancy Services. Compare and contrast the ethical principles followed by the two firms.

2. Identify issues of ethics for the hotel industry by choosing a particular country's context.

CASE STUDY

Information Technology, Corporate Business Firms, and Sustainable Development: Lessons From Cases of Success From India*

This paper critically analyses some cases of success of interventions initiated either by corporate firms or supported by the corporate firms which lead to community development. These cases highlight practices, which can be adapted in any part of the world. These interventions are a win–win situation both for the firms and the communities involved. A multiple case study approach has been adopted. The range of interventions vary from being very specific to being very wide in their approach, and help the grass-roots level communities to emerge out of the poverty trap. The analysis culminates in development of a framework, which attempts to link the nature of the intervention with the stage of development. The study concludes that the interventions have to be linked with the stage of development and resource strength in a particular geographical location. The resource may be a raw material or manpower, which can lead to the turnaround of that region. Where the stage of development is low and where people do not even have access to basic amenities, the nature of interventions have to be wide so as to simultaneously have positive impacts on food, shelter, water, education, employment, and women empowerment (as in SWRC Barefoot College initiative). In such cases, sophisticated technologies may not generate the desired effect. For areas which have some basic resources, IT and other related technologies can be channelized as in the case of HP and TARAhaat for evolving new commercial products and services. The ITC case study is an outstanding example of self-sustaining intervention which leads to identification of a new business channel, and which also empowers rural communities and brings in efficiency in the business processes. The policy implications are suggested and pointers towards aspects that need to be taken care of to

make these interventions successful have also been delved upon.

Background

The pictures presented by poverty are grim. By 1999, 1170 million people lived in extreme poverty (World Bank 2003). 'Though the poverty levels have declined in East Asia and the Pacific, in sub-Saharan Africa, the number of people steeped in extreme poverty increased by 74 million. For 1998–2000, the FAO estimates that 799 million people or 17 per cent of the population in developing countries were undernourished. Additionally, there are another 30 million undernourished people in transition economies of Eastern Europe and the former Soviet Union. One hundred and fifteen million children remain out of school. In South Asia, where only 61 per cent of girls complete primary school, the average woman has 3.4 years of schooling. In 2002, 42 million adults and five million children were living with AIDS. Lack of clean water and basic sanitation is the main reason for so many health-related problems. In 1990, diarrhoea led to three million deaths; 85 per cent of them were children. In 2000, 1.2 billion people still lacked access to an improved water source' (*Human Development Report* 2003).

In a world where there are amazing technological achievements at one end, there are also issues of people living in abject poverty. The idea is to include people at the bottom of the pyramid in the economic development process. The corporate sector has a distinct role to play in bringing out this change. The poor pose a lot of challenges for the public sector, which has neither the expertise nor the resources to provide goods and services on a scale sufficient to reach the approximately four billion people who currently

* Jauhari, V. (2005), 'Information technology, corporate business firms and sustainable development: Lessons from cases of success from India', *Journal of Services Research*, vol. 5, no. 2, October 2005–March 2006. Reprinted with the permission of *Journal of Services Research*.

earn less than $2,000 a year. The private sector has both. Prahalad and Hammond (2004) point out that there are some innovative initiatives undertaken by the private sector which aims at products and services targeted at the poor (bottom of the pyramid). In their study, they have pointed out the following:

○ The poor live in very high cost economies. For most products and services that they buy, they end up spending more money. Costs to the poor can be dramatically reduced if they can benefit from the scope, scale, and supply chain organization of large enterprises, as do their middle-class counterparts.

○ Many interventions end up exploiting the poor rather than doing them good in the long-run.

○ The poor have a purchasing power.

○ Many of the bottom of the pyramid (BOP) markets are geographically concentrated. A slum such as the one located in Dharavi in just 175 hectares, generates $450 million in manufacturing revenues.

○ The poor welcome new technologies.

Sustainable Development and Profitability

The World Commission on Environment and Development (1987, p. 8) states, 'Sustainable development meets the needs of the present without compromising the ability of future generations to meet their own needs'. Reinhardt (2003) indicates that there are issues in measuring sustainability at the firm level and there is also confusion about the term 'sustainable development' itself. When one talks about the term sustainable development at the firm level, there are issues about its measurement. Reinhardt (2003) quotes the two DuPont formulas about measuring sustainability. One is the private cost test and the other is the social cost test. Under the first test, a sustainable firm is one that augments its shareholders value when all stocks and flows are measured at the prevailing private costs, as those costs are determined by market forces and by current government regulations. Companies deliver profits to their shareholders by creating value (Holliday 2001). Under the second test, a sustainable firm is one that creates value when all of its costs and revenues are measured at their

social costs. This test is exactly analogous to the national level sustainability requirement. To be sustainable from a social cost perspective, a firm must be creating value and re-investing enough of that value to maintain its capital stock at an undiminished level. As was true for national economies, to test for a firm's sustainability, it is essential to consider conventional accounting measures as well as environmental performance. If a company has to pass this test, it also delivers profits that are measured not according to social costs but by market prices.

For a corporate firm, profitability is important for survival and existence. The challenge is about being able to identify the right kind of business product, which not only creates a lasting value for the organization but also involves people at the grass-roots who have not been included in the development process. World statistics indicate that poverty has been a curse for mankind, which deprives people of self-esteem, empowerment, and denies basic rights. The corporate world has a huge capacity to initiate meaningful initiatives for human beings. There have been a few experiments in India, which demonstrates a faith in the power of networking and the capacity of shaping their own destiny by some communities. There are diverse initiatives by NGOs, the corporate world, and the support by the government.

Research Objectives

The objective of this research is to analyse the different interventions initiated by the corporate firms and NGOs which help the development of communities living in poverty. The objective is to identify interventions which can be replicated, are sustainable, and can help the under-developed regions to move to a level of economic prosperity. The study also assesses the role of the corporate sector and MNCs. The objective is to develop frameworks which could work in areas with different levels of development.

Research Methodology

Each country has a unique historical background and a culture which needs to be preserved. Blind aping of western models for initiating development is not healthy as that replicates the same culture diluting the individualistic characteristics. This research uses the multiple case study approach, which reflects the participative approach directed to alleviate poverty and empower people at the grass-roots levels. In all these cases, the corporate sector has had a distinct role to play. These are interventions which have been initiated and targeted at various stages of development. The nature and extent of intervention varies as it moves from a lower stage of development to a higher stage. The development in a country can be sustainable if strategies are aligned to the resources available in abundance. The study proposes models for development and links the nature of intervention with the stage of development of that geographical area. The paper makes policy recommendations for different category of interventions.

Corporate Interventions

Competitiveness is important for a nation's prosperity (Porter 2003). The framework developed by Porter (2003) links competitiveness to—quality of factor conditions, context of firm strategy and rivalry, the quality of local demand conditions, and the presence of related and supporting industry. However, the low income countries can shorten their learning curve and leapfrog to the status of developed countries. This can be done by establishing linkages with local strengths. India has witnessed some of these unique experiments, which bring to light some interesting displays of innovation and strengths at the grass-root levels. These are communities which found tremendous strength by identifying their own strengths and utilizing them to create brands, which have given the multinationals a run for their money.

The ITC E-Choupal Initiative

This is an experiment which demonstrates the identification of strengths that exist at village level, identification of a methodology which results in higher incomes, use of information technology which creates empowerment, and redefines the roles of individuals. It also demonstrates a unique innovation on the part of the corporate firms to redefine the supply chain management practices, which contributes to added value.

ITC is an Indian diversified firm which operates in the area of tobacco, hotels, consumer products, and agri-based products. The corporate aim was to:

○ become India's largest agri-produce processor, servicing 1,00,000 villages covering 10 million farmers by 2007

○ create an information superhighway to the rural economy

○ establish a single point of contact between farmers and a range of suppliers of agri inputs and consumer goods—Monsanto, Eicher, and Nagarjuna Fertilizers.

The Indian Backdrop

One of the interventions suggested to alleviate poverty is to increase the productivity of small farmers. Seventy per cent of the world's poorest farmers live in rural areas and depend on agriculture (Human Development Report 2003). A typical village in India does not have basic amenities such as electricity and water. Illiteracy levels are high. However, the same group became adept at using e-commerce, which changed their lives. At the same time it is also interesting to see how the rural market in India behaves with regard to the demand for consumer goods (Table 17.2).

Table 17.2 Distribution of villages in India

Population	Number of villages	% of Total villages
Less than 200	1,14,267	17.9
200–499	1,55,123	24.3
500–999	1,59,400	25.0
1000–1999	1,25,758	19.7
2000–4999	69,135	10.8
5000–9999	11,618	1.8
10,000 and above	3,064	0.5
Total number of villages	6,38,365	

Source: Adapted from Kashyap (2003).

In agricultural products, there are *mandis*, which are agricultural markets set up by the state governments to procure agricultural produce directly from the farmers. Table 17.3 lists the number of villages and *haat*s in India. Located in high production centres of different crops, these markets can be categorized as grain mandis, cotton mandis, soya mandis, etc. There are about 6,800 mandis in India (Table 17.4). The average population catered to by each mandi is 1.36 lakh. Most agricultural areas with population more than 10,000 have mandis.

Annamalai and Rao (2003) have criticized the mandi system, stating that it does not serve the farmer well and is burdened by inefficiency. Depending on the geographic proximity, the farmer takes his goods to the nearest mandi. The system is viewed as based on exploitation. There are multiple points before the supplies are bought that contribute to wastage.

Dadar & Nagar Haveli	0 (6)
Maharashtra	43,722 (3,578)
Karnataka	29,483 (1241)
Andhra Pradesh	8,183 (NA)
Goa	359 (8)
Lakshadweep	24 (0)
Kerala	1,364 (670)
Tamil Nadu	16,317 (1169)
Puducherry	92 (0)
Andaman & Nicobar	547 (0)

Source: The Marketing Whitebook.

Table 17.4   Regulated agri produce markets (mandis) in India

State	Number of mandis
Andhra Pradesh	23
Assam	35
Bihar	828
Goa	5
Gujarat	30
Haryana	75
Himachal Pradesh	29
Karnataka	44
Kerala	5
Madhya Pradesh	84
Maharashtra	827
Orissa	123
Punjab	667
Rajasthan	384
Tamil Nadu	270
Tripura	21
Uttar Pradesh	645
West Bengal	456
Chandigarh	3
Delhi	17
Pondicherry	5

Table 17.3   Villages and haats in India

State/UT	Number of villages (number of haats)
Jammu & Kashmir	6,652 (NA)
Himachal Pradesh	19,831 (10)
Punjab	12,729 (16)
Chandigarh	24 (0)
Uttarakhand	16,805 (NA)
Haryana	6,955 (0)
Delhi (rural)	165 (28)
Rajasthan	41,353 (261)
Uttar Pradesh	1,07,440 (14,121)
Bihar	45,113 (10,681)
Sikkim	452 (19)
Arunachal Pradesh	4,065 (NA)
Nagaland	1,315 (46)
Manipur	2,391 (7)
Mizoram	817 (49)
Tripura	870 (736)
Meghalaya	6,023 (319)
Assam	26,247 (4,044)
West Bengal	40,783 (456)
Jharkhand	32,615 (NA)
Orissa	51,352 (3,887)
Chhattisgarh	20,308 (NA)
Madhya Pradesh	5,392 (NA)
Gujarat	18,544 (NA)
Daman & Diu	23 (0)

Contd

The Business Model (ITC)

The model is centred on a network of *e-choupals*, or information centres equipped with a computer connected to the Internet, located in rural villages. ITC appointed *sanchalaks* (coordinators) and *samyojaks* (collaborators) into the system as the provider of logistics support. Each e-choupal serves about 10 villages within a five-kilometre radius. There are a million farmers being served in nearly 11,000 villages through 2000 e-choupals in four states (Madhya Pradesh, Karnataka, Andhra Pradesh, and Uttar Pradesh).

Traditionally, the soya or wheat crop would be traded at mandis. Farmers were exploited by traders, who often bought the wheat at low prices claiming it to be of poor variety. Storage, transport, and handling facilities were limited. So, intermediaries like traders were needed.

Intermediary margins were high, accurate market signals were non-existent, wastage was rampant, and processing yields were low. Conventionally, a typical farmer would sell to a small trader called the *kaccha adat*. This man in turn, sold it to a larger trader called the *pakka adat*. From here the produce found its way to the local mandi where a large trader came into the picture. Going through a loop like this meant procurement costs were as high as Rs 700 per tonne of soya. In addition, there were losses in transit and a tax burden as well. This is reflected in Fig. 17.1.

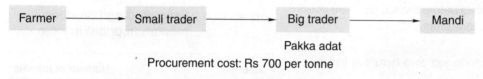

Pakka adat

Procurement cost: Rs 700 per tonne

Fig. 17.1 Conventional channel for selling soya

Brokers compare these statistics with the American mid-west market. Its farmers produce 36 bushels of wheat per acre, one of the highest yields per acre and its millers achieve flour extraction levels of 75 per cent. Average waste levels are 2 per cent, which are the lowest in the world and well ahead of the 8–11 per cent in India. Wheat farmers in the US now get 92 per cent of the delivered mill price as opposed to less than 70 per cent that Indian farmers now take home. ITC started the process of disintermediation. So, by providing the information access to the farmer rather than the intermediary, the value is added directly.

The ITC Model for Soya Procurement

So, ITC identified co-ordinators at the village level who were called sanchalaks, who used the net to provide spot quotes after examining the produce sample. If the price was right, the farmers would take the produce to the ITC collection centre. The samyojaks were the collaborators who would co-ordinate the group of villagers. They would perform the documentation work and supply farm inputs from ITC and partner companies to sanchalaks. They would also build relationships with the sanchalaks and farmers.

When ITC started the experiment it was the middle of 1990s. ITC first leased few centres and started scouting for villages around these centres. The computer was placed at the *sanchalak's* house who would head each *choupal*. He was trained to use the computer. He was carefully chosen so that farmers could trust him—neither too big, which would distance him, nor so small that he may not be respected. ITC started to pump information on mandi prices through the Internet to the sanchalak's home. Information on best farming practices and weather forecasts were also made. The sanchalaks were paid 0.5 per cent for each tonne of soya that originated from their choupal. There were commission agents in mandis whose role was redefined by ITC. They were called samyojaks or co-ordinators. They would use their ties to nominate sanchalaks but also do the relevant mandi documentation. For villages situated far off, the samyojaks would aggregate the grain and bring it to ITC. For this he was paid a commission of 1 per cent. As a result, ITC reduced the cost of procurement from Rs 700 a tonne to Rs 200 per tonne. This is reflected in Fig. 17.2.

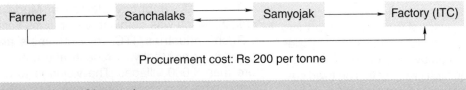

Procurement cost: Rs 200 per tonne

Fig. 17.2   e-Choupals

Financial Feasibility

On an average it cost Rs 40,000 to set up a basic choupal. In places where connectivity was poor ITC had to invest in VSATs. These investments escalated the costs to Rs 1 lakh. In Madhya Pradesh alone, when the experiment started ITC had 1,045 e-choupals spread over 6,000 villages serving over six lakh farmers. This was for soya crop which was a five million tonne crop in Madhya Pradesh. For it wheat was 14 times bigger.

ITC's Game Plan

There would be 1.5 million outlets in the country. There would be an army of mobile traders and cycle distributors. There would be a huge earning on transaction fees for every deal that took place. The market for agricultural products is valued at Rs 1,75,000 crore. The tobacco market is just Rs 15,000 crore. So, it makes a lot of business sense to diversify the risks and add new business areas, which also contribute not only to the bottom lines but to the profitability as well. The investment made by ITC would be recovered in five years for wheat procurement. The infrastructure created can be used for other purposes as well. It also sets up a relationship at the grassroots level. In years to come, this can open doors for more revenues to come in as it will also expose the community to new products.

ITC had tied up with Monsanto for seed selling. The FMCG products and consumer durables could be delivered through the same network.

The investments in the e-commerce initiatives are different as compared to the normal manufacturing operations. The cost curves for e-based businesses also behave differently. Choi et al. (1997) and Choi and Whinston (2000), discuss investments in the e-businesses. The total cost curves of many physical products and services are U-shaped. First, as the quantity increases the cost declines; but later, the cost increases due to the growth of both the fixed and the variable costs (especially administrative and marketing costs). In contrast with digital products, the variable costs per unit are low and almost fixed, regardless of the quantity. Therefore, cost per unit declines as quantity increases due to pro-ration of the fixed component of the cost over more units. This results in increasing returns with increasing sales (Turban et al. 2002).

Most FMCGs currently operate where they are viable while servicing populations above 1,00,000. There are enormous pockets of widely dispersed markets where population sizes are below 2,000. ITC with 1.5 million outlets across the country, an army of mobile traders, and cycle based distributors, claim to understand the nuances of catering to these populations. By collaborating with ITC, a potential seller does not have to invest in infrastructure. ITC simply takes a small transaction fee for every transaction, for every deal taking place on its network. The market for agricultural produce is Rs 1,75,000 crore, out of which ITC only accounts for Rs 15,000 crore.

Comparison with Traditional Models

The agribusiness initiatives taken by some of the other farmers have not been successful. Initiatives by some of the well-known companies such as Mahindra and Mahindra, Tata Chemicals, EID Parry, Rallis, and Nagarjuna Fertilizers took up agribusiness ventures by setting their own models. Most of them faced problems for growth. The 'Shubh Labh' venture started by Mahindras had set up 36 centres in 10 states by the end of 2002. Even ikisan.com (Nagarjuna Fertilizers), Indiagriline.com, and Parry's corner (EID Parry), which tried to create an e-marketplace could not scale up.

Problems

Firstly, there was a lack of trust from the farmers as these models depended on the intermediaries who were not trusted by the farmers. Secondly, these models had high fixed costs. The fixed cost of a Rallis Kendra was Rs 0.5 million to 0.6 million, whereas the variable cost came up to Rs 1 million (this included the cost of a PC, telephone, furniture, 2–3 motorcycles for field staff, rentals, and salaries). Rallis covered 20,000 acres but could not scale up. Every centre had 6–8 employees. For 10 centres, 60 people were to be employed. Taking an average salary of Rs 0.15 million would mean an outflow of Rs 100 million per month in salaries itself. Unless volumes went up, operating costs would be high.

Thirdly, there were issues of channel conflict. Also, many companies did not have enough knowledge in procurement. Corporations need the organizational knowledge of handling samples. The market does not reward you for scaling, but for taking positions.

From the organization's perspective, profits do not come easy in the agribusiness unless the organization has sufficient control over the supply chain of the agricultural produce. In Madhya Pradesh, the farmers were located in remote villages scattered throughout the state. The next issue before the organization was that of the middlemen for obtaining good quality products. The middlemen exerted influence on the farmers by concealing the prevailing market prices and other related information. They made large profits for themselves by blocking access to such information.

On the farmers' side, there were issues such as they were trapped in a vicious circle of low investment, low productivity, weak market orientation, low value addition, low margin, and low risk-taking ability. So the paradoxical condition was that despite abundant natural resources, Indian farmers remained globally uncompetitive. This was evident in Indian performance on the global scale. The immediate aim for the e-choupal initiative was to integrate ITC's association with rural suppliers as well as to develop new markets for its own and third-party goods.

The rural symphony started in Madhya Pradesh, which was dominated with firms such as Ruchi Industries. ITC soya choupals are located all over Madhya Pradesh and cater to more than 6,000 villages. The vision is to get farmers a better price for their crops.

TARAhaat—A Case Study

This case study highlights an attempt to achieve connectivity for the poor. TARAhaat comprises a commercially viable model for bringing relevant information, products, and services via the Internet to the unserved rural market of India, from which an estimated 50 per cent of the national income is derived. TARAhaat is promoted by Development Alternatives and its alliance partners include Hughes Escorts Communication, KLG Systel, jaldi.com, James Martin, Hewlett–Packard, Oracle, and the Global Development Gateway sponsored by the World Bank and the Gates Foundation. Excelsior Ventures Management and James Martin & Co., are providing initial equity capital together with management and operational resources. TARAhaat is a business enterprise of Development Alternatives (DA), an NGO focused on sustainable rural development in India, and its marketing arm, Technology and Action for Rural Advancement (TARA). TARAhaat uses a franchisee-based business model to bring computer and Internet technology to rural regions, and plans to use these technologies to create revenue streams leading to financial viability for itself and its franchisees. These business objectives are balanced with the social objective of uplifting rural India through easy access to relevant local and global information, and propelling it into the twenty-first century. TARAhaat also hopes to find the right balance of rural and peri-urban franchisees to be able to subsidize rural locations with lower potential.

The initiative includes the development of a mother portal, TARAhaat.com, supported by franchised networks of village cyber cafes and delivery systems to provide a full range of services to its clients. The portal has the following subsidiaries:

TARAdhaba: provides connectivity and access to new world

TARAbazaar: provides access to products and services needed by rural households, farmers, and industries

TARAvan: delivers goods

TARAdak: connects the rural families to the daughter married far off, and the son posted on the front

TARAguru: is a decentralized university providing mentoring and consultancy to village-based mini enterprises

TARAcard: enables the villagers to order goods and services on credit

The effort is directed at attracting and retaining all kinds of users—farmers, traders, housewives, senior citizens, and children. The initial interface is both graphic and voice-based to ensure that everyone regardless of their level of literacy can learn to take advantage of the system.

Business Model

The business combines a mother portal, TARAhaat.com, with a network of franchised village internet centres, or TARAkendras. TARAhaat will deliver education, information, services, and online market opportunities to rural consumers via the Internet and its kendra outposts. It also hopes to provide a cost-effective gateway by which larger corporations can reach rural customers. It will offer information, e-mail, and web services, and eventually e-commerce and fulfilment services, earning revenues through membership fees and commissions.

Infrastructure

Where possible, TARAhaat will use existing telephone lines to connect its franchise internet centres. But it also plans to install VSAT links where necessary to provide connectivity, utilizing satellites operated by others. Thus, TARAhaat is largely dependent on India's existing commercial infrastructure, which is less than ideal. Dependence on the satellites has already caused interruptions in service for some franchises, and is a relatively high-cost solution. Connectivity, and bandwidth capable of supporting a graphics-rich Internet experience, is likely to remain in short supply for the near future, posing a continuing challenge to the venture. In addition, electric power outages are frequent, so much so that the company provides a diesel-powered generator as part of the franchise infrastructure, adding considerably to costs and maintenance needs. However, one factor that bodes well for success is the company's flexibility in developing its products. TARAhaat has shown high sensitivity to customer needs, allowing products to evolve to meet these needs. For example, TARAgyan products, TARAhaat's education offerings, came into being only recently to address the strong demand for computer and computer-based education in the initial customer base. In addition, each franchise has latitude in developing products and services that meet local market needs. TARAhaat hopes to create a brand image in which the local TARAkendra is seen as the place for a family to find products aimed at the entertainment, information, and commercial needs of each member. The company provides content in two local languages as well as English, and expects to provide content in other local languages (India has 18 official languages) as well.

Human Capacity

TARAhaat provides extensive support for its franchisees, including assistance with financing, internet connections, business and IT training, and marketing. It plans to create a TARA university for franchisee training. Many franchises offer computer or other IT classes. Nonetheless, the lack of literacy among many of its intended customers poses continuing challenges to its business strategy.

Policy India's telecom regulatory policies are improving, but fall short of fully open competition. As a result, prices are relatively high and service is generally quite poor, especially in rural areas. Since TARAhaat is largely dependent on commercially available infrastructure, this poses a substantial challenge to the venture. However, the company faces no major regulatory hurdles.

Enterprise TARAhaat's association with Development Alternatives brings a wealth of rural expertise and a resilient attitude towards overcoming all hurdles. Some of the initial challenges described in this report have been handled with creative solutions, both at the franchise level and at the enterprise level. However, the venture has substantial financing needs and faces long-term challenges relating to product development and franchise operations that still await resolution. Unlike many start-ups, however, its management team is seasoned and strong.

Key Lessons

Interviews with users of TARAhaat's services demonstrate the venture's social benefits, including empowering the education of girls, inspiring confidence and higher aspirations among rural children, and enabling farmers to gain market information and substantially higher prices for their crops.

The staying power of TARAhaat's business model is not yet proven, but the positive customer response is an early indication of viability. The venture's franchise model seems likely to harness local entrepreneurial energies to the benefit of both. Its emphasis on locally-relevant content, in local languages, and strong orientation to product development based on customer feedback is also an important characteristic, one that takes advantage of India's large rural middle-class. Finally, the company combines both commercial and NGO characteristics, potentially giving it an advantage in pioneering the relatively risky Internet market in rural India, and is unlikely to face major competition in the near future.

Financial Feasibility

The financial feasibility is worked out as reflected in Table 17.5.

Table 17.5 Financial working for TARAhaat initiative

Year	Cost ($ million)	Revenues ($ million)
1	0.3	5.9
2	6.6	15.9
3	32.1	39.0
4	72.4	55.5
5	121.6	80.2
6	182	109.7

The revenues and costs vary from centre to centre. The larger centres achieve profitability in year 1, the medium village achieved profitability in year 3, and the smaller village never achieves sustainable profitability. The small village kendras, which TARAhaat management considers social investments and not profit generators, will rely on subsidies from TARAhaat, which will be offset by profits from larger kendras.

Tata Group's Community Initiatives

The Tata Group's commitment to contribute substantially to the community led to the formation of the Tata Council for Community Initiatives (TCCI). With the active participation and contribution of Tata Group companies, TCCI has helped communities to become strong and self-reliant. TCCI has evolved Tata Corps of Volunteers who serve as a bridge between the company's explicit intent to develop the community and its employees to provide a broad support. TCCI will strive to evolve simple but business compatible procedures to evaluate the impact of community programmes in terms of their outcome in human development. The procedure will be titled Tata social evaluation, responsibility, and accountability (Social–ERA).

The M.S. Swaminathan Research Foundation (MSSRF), with the help of the Tatas, has set up the Virtual Academy for Food Security and Rural Prosperity. As a part of this project, the foundation has set up knowledge centres at 10 villages around Puducherry using information and communication technologies. There is a hybrid wired and wireless network comprising PCs, telephones, VHF, duplex radio devices, spread spectrum, e-mail connectivity, VSAT, and a public address system. Not only are electronic media like the Internet, cable television, ham radio, and loudspeakers used, but traditional methods like yellow pages and community pamphlets, and the good old notice board, also ensure that the information reaches the intended audience. It is not the hardware that changes the lives of the have-nots. What brings them to the knowledge centre in droves is the data relevant to their lives. MSSRF focuses on helping them convert this know-how into do-how.

At Veerampattinam, the fisher folk earlier used meteorological reports provided by the state's fisheries department. But these sometimes came in too late. The foundation now downloads the wave height and wind direction from the US Navy website, and sends an online message in the local language from the main hub to the village centre, which then makes announcements throughout the day on the public address system. Residents of Embalam, among other villages, receive not just weather reports and information on the government schemes, but also availability of agricultural inputs, market potential, and prices of their produce. The project is directed towards meeting the needs of the local community. It works according to the guidelines for sustainable development issued at the 2002 World Summit at Johannesburg. It concentrates on climate management, water energy, health, agriculture, and on biodiversity, and the ecosystem. The positive impact on women and child education is clearly visible. The people have been helped to develop numerous skills.

Hewlett Packard's Global Citizenship Initiative

Hewlett Packard's (HP) global citizenship is built around the core of ethics and governance. Fundamentally, the heart of global citizenship is about engaging the communities that the organization works and lives in. As a part of their citizenship agenda the priority areas are three-fold—the environment, privacy, and e-inclusion. According to HP, the three enablers of citizenship effort are the government policy, philanthropy, and communication. On the environmental front, HP has an explicit goal of designing new products so as to minimize their ecological impact, from production through disposal. The e-inclusion and education programme focuses on using technology to give people access to social and economic opportunities. Regarding privacy rights, HP was the first company in the Fortune 50 to join Safe Harbour, the international data protection agreement outlining rules for transfer of consumer data across international borders.

In their quest for technology solutions for the emerging markets, they developed a solar powered digital photographer's backpack. It takes the standard digital photography equipment—digital cameras, and a digital printer which does not require a computer but has lots of intelligence embedded—in a kit that runs on solar power. The package is being piloted to stimulate the community in Kuppam by creating jobs for women's self help groups. One of the solutions is an information system for agriculture, a major livelihood in Kuppam, where the women may be employed to take photos of crop problems. The government uploads them on the web, allowing local farmers to tap into advice on their crops from experts in other parts of the world. The government is also interested in potentially hiring the women for a broader project to create photo IDs for citizens. Clearly, everyone in Kuppam will not have a digital camera or a photo printer, but individuals can be employed in ways that enable them to earn a living using HP's products and stimulate the overall economy.

HP has designated a senior executive with the set of responsibilities associated with the global citizenship programme. When at the HP executive council, anything related with HP strategy is discussed this executive can raise issues about the citizenship agenda. In their quest towards a prototype solution, they initiated an experiment at Kuppam in India. HP has a matrix structure for such initiatives. For example, for the e-inclusion initiative, the e-inclusion market solutions team has a big role. The strategy process has been driven through the creation of horizontal teams made up of key members from each of the departments that has a role in various initiatives.

The Kuppam i-community initiative demonstrates HP's commitment to e-inclusion and community engagement, and makes a great deal of business sense. As a high priority growth market for HP, India has many potential customers for its technologies. Kuppam was also chosen because it could help HP learn about nascent or white space opportunities—the high potential opportunities that lie between markets, or outside HP's current focus areas. HP feels that their richest opportunities and best chances for innovation lie in regions that rank user and organizational needs very differently from the way established markets and customers do.

When global citizenship efforts and business efforts are being fused, it is important to choose initiatives based on the strength of the local leadership. The Kuppam i-community now encompasses five physical community information centres with more on the way, where students, teachers, parents, and others can learn skills and get access to information and services via the Internet. It features a government portal, usable from a web-enabled device, which gives access to government services through the net. The i-community also features a mobile service centre with wireless access and new technology empowered social programme.

Social Work Research Centre

The Social Work Research Centre (SWRC) has been working in rural communities in India to improve the quality of life of the rural poor. SWRC has worked to address basic needs—water, health, education, employment, social awareness, and conservation of the ecological system—while enrolling individuals in the processes that govern their lives. A voluntary agency, SWRC's main centre is in the village of Tilonia in the Silora block in Ajmer district of Rajasthan. The organization began its work in 1972 in Tilonia, by opening a barefoot college, because a rural development agency could and should not work from a village. Rural development required living among the people who would effect and be affected by that development process. SWRC programmes were initially started with urban expertise from outside the area.

The college benefits the poorest of the poor who have no alternatives. It encourages practical knowledge and skills rather than paper qualifications through learning by the 'doing' process of education. The college is spread over 60,000 square feet and consists of residences, a library, dining room, meeting halls, marketing outlets, an open theatre, a blacksmiths workshop, solar fabrication workshop, water testing laboratory, an audio visual unit, handicraft production centre, a puppet workshop, and a 4,00,000 litre rainwater harvesting tank, entirely built and supervised by the local people. It serves a population of over 1,00,000 people, both in immediate as well as distant areas.

Philosophy

The philosophy at the barefoot college is that people are encouraged to make mistakes so that that they can learn humility, curiosity, have the courage to take risks, to innovate, to improvise, and to constantly experiment. It is a place where all are treated as equals and there is no hierarchy. The barefoot college believes that development programmes do not need urban based professionals because para-professionals already exist in the villages whose wisdom, knowledge, and skills are neither identified and mobilized, nor applied just because they do not have an educational qualification:

The barefoot college is developed in the following manner:

○ First, by reposing faith in the competencies of rural poor community anywhere in the world, that the community has members who have the knowledge, the skills, the wisdom, and the faith to identify and solve their own problems.

○ Second, by creating an environment and a situation where these skills and knowledge can be applied for the community's own development.

○ Third, by informal, non-structured, on-the-job practical training until such time as the person has acquired the confidence, the competence, and the capacity to provide the service without any help from outside.

○ Fourth, by choosing an area, which is remote, inaccessible, and very difficult to reach physically, so that there is peace, mental space, and non-interference from the so-called experts who are dying to make sure you fail.

Today, people who have no formal educational or professional degree run all the programmes. An individual's will to learn and aptitude for learning is more important than any formal degree or paper qualification. The new campus at Tilonia was designed and built by one of the villagers, who can barely sign his own name. The campus itself reflects the adaptation of both traditional as well as new methods and technologies. Old traditional methods have been used to keep the buildings cool, while solar energy is used to provide electrical power to the campus. People with minimum paper qualifications work as night school teachers, health workers, computer operators, solar engineers, or hand pump mechanics. Basic literacy, health, and first-aid skills are also taught. In this way, each individual learns about the entire organization, its mission and its functioning.

Sustainability:

o It generates employment.

o It involves people in the process.

o It helps to take care of the basic minimum needs.

The centre does not provide free services. A nominal fee is charged for all services including health services, training, and installation of hand pumps, or solar electrification for lighting. Almost 98 per cent of the workers are from neighbouring rural areas.

Technology Orientation

Social Work Research Centre believes that new trends in technology and high-tech machines are not always synonymous with development. Social Work Research Centre does not believe in imposing technology on people in rural villages or using technology which deprives people of employment. Adapting and improving on pre-existing, traditional ways is often more effective than using newer technologies.

Reliability of the barefoot concept:

o It will work anywhere; in any poor rural community, anywhere in the world where there is extreme poverty.

o The rural communities are neglected, deprived, and forgotten so they have no choice but to develop and depend on each other, and not on people from outside; thus all knowledge and all skills are useful, necessary, and respected

o Where the percentage of illiteracy is high, the oral tradition is rich and knowledge skills are traditionally passed down from one generation to another.

The barefoot college encourages the following people to participate:

o Those who are dropouts, cop-outs, washouts, and who are rejected by society because they cannot pass exams and obtain a degree.

o Those who have no possibility of getting the lowest of the low government jobs. They have no choice but to stay and the investment in the training is not wasted. They will earn the respect of the communities they serve because of the service they provide.

Organization

The barefoot college concept is percolated to the communities in the 110 villages of the Silora block through the 12 SWRC field centres. The field centres have the freedom to decide their own course of action. Each serves between 9 and 35 villages. The college has over 400 staff members working full time in various activities related to basic services. They have no formal qualifications for the job they are doing. With the help of a cadre of barefoot engineers, doctors, teachers, designers, chemists, accountants, and traditional communicators, communities are using the expertise they acquired from their ancestors. The concept of communities depending on themselves has revived. Indigenous institutions and decision-making processes have been activated, and villagers have gained new confidence. They increasingly recognize their own strengths and assign value to their own skills; something that was never felt before.

The Barefoot College and Children's Parliament of Tilonia, Rajasthan has won the Children's World Award (Sharma 2001). The award, considered the 'Children's Nobel Prize' is a unique global award for organizations that champion the rights of children through their activities. Queen Silvia of Sweden presented the award at Gripsholms Castle in Marie Fred, Sweden, on 18 April 2001. The award carries a prize of $12,500. The prize money is to be spent on activities conducted by the college for the rights of the children.

Interventions in Education

The college runs a series of night schools in several villages in and around Tilonia where children are taught in the evenings, after they finish their day's work. The college students have their own parliament and the representatives to it are elected from among the boys and girls attending the different night schools.

Night Schools

More than 80 night schools have been set up for the benefit of working children. Nearly 1,200 girls and over 1,500 boys who tend cattle during the day attend these schools after dark. Solar lanterns maintained by rural solar engineers, power more than 68 per cent of these institutions. All teaching aids and learning materials used in the night schools are made from waste materials. Instruction is informal and curriculum is focused on practical knowledge and experience. Since most children tend cattle, they learn basic husbandry along with reading Maths. They attend night schools for five years. Children monitor their own schools by electing their own representatives.

Children's Parliament

The children's parliament controls and supervises the night schools. It is based on the belief that giving power to the people who have a vested interest in the school is the best way of ensuring its success as well as making the children aware of the political structure and processes. This form of education-related activism provides a heightened awareness of the system, its workings, and avenues for redressal of local grievances.

There is also a provision for teacher training, and there is a mobile library which goes from village to village and from where children from the night school can borrow books.

Concrete Outcomes

Hand pumps More than 1,500 India Mark II hand pumps were installed between 1979 and 1995. Over 3,00,000 people continue to benefit from these hand pumps. Despite claims by the government that it was technically impossible, 28 hand pumps were installed at 15,000 ft above sea level in Ladakh and operate at −40°C.

Since 1993, the college has focused on water harvesting and dipped water systems as the emphasis has moved beyond providing clean water, to providing easy access to drinking water. Twelve villages, 12,000 connections, and 15,000 people now benefit from community piped water systems that have been designed, planned, and implemented entirely by the village people. These communities pay Rs 20 per month for two hours of water per day

Other water initiatives include:

o Twelve million litres of rainwater collected in 155 schools and community centres. This water is the only safe option in areas of brackish water with high iron and fluoride content.

o 1,400 samples of drinking water covering 78 villages in eight states tested using mobile testing kits.

o Thirty-five rural youth trained as barefoot chemists in eight states.

o 753 hand pump mechanics trained to carry out all repairs for the 45,000 hand pumps in Rajasthan; 40 of these mechanics are women.

Contribution to Health

The barefoot college has remarkable achievements in the health sector too. Begun in 1973, the health centre served as a small dispensary. Villagers are now charged a nominal amount for medicines. A team of doctors pays regular visits to villages for routine health examinations. Today, more than 200 health centres serve villages throughout India. Since 1986, the barefoot college has been using biochemical medicines. Biochemical medicines are a set of 12 medicines, which can be combined and used for different ailments. The college has developed 28 medicines using the twelve root medicines. At least one field staff member in every village has been trained in this alternate system of medicine and serves as the field centre's *svasthya karyakarta*s or health workers.

Today, more than 200 health workers serve a network of Indian villages trained to tackle the health issues and minor injuries. The health workers can give artificial respiration in emergencies and take a patient to the nearest government hospital when necessary. Health workers also teach villagers about basic health issues including hygiene, the importance of vaccinations, and other preventive measures. Barefoot midwives are trained in proper delivery methods as well as pre- and post-natal care of the mother and the child. In case of birth complications that cannot be tackled in the village, the *dai* (midwife) escorts the expectant mother to the nearest hospital.

Environmental Initiatives

Barefoot solar engineers have installed solar photovoltaic units across 10 states of India in 300 adult education centres. The results include:

- ○ 500 solar lanterns manufactured at the college for 200 night schools across the country.
- ○ 104 fixed solar units at night schools have replaced kerosene lamps, which have a negative impact on children's eyesight.
- ○ 25 remote and inaccessible villages in Ladakh have 36 KW of solar panels that provide three hours of light to 930 families in the bleakest winter.
- ○ In Leh and Kargil districts, solar energy initiatives have saved a total of 59,000 litres of kerosene.
- ○ 79 rural youth operate as barefoot solar mechanics, with absolutely no aid from urban professionals.
- ○ 1,30,000 litres of kerosene have been saved by replacing generators and oil lanterns with solar power.

Funded by the European Commission, the college is working with Programme Asvin to develop and disseminate solar energy systems for villages in the Himalayan region of India. The project is bringing solar powered lighting to 30 villages in Sikkim, Uttar Pradesh, and Ladakh, as well as demonstrating how local knowledge and practical skills can make these villages completely self-sufficient, technically and financially.

Wasteland Development

Most of the land owned by the government or village and reserved as fodder ground is wasteland. Most of the wasteland in Rajasthan is barren because of overgrazing and desert-like conditions. The barefoot college helps rural communities to regenerate this land. The college provides seedlings from its nursery of drought-resistant trees, shrubs, and grasses. The villagers themselves plant the trees and shrubs, which will become a source of fuel and fodder. Every wasteland has a watchman who prevents trespassing or misuse.

The barefoot college aims to drought-proof these areas by employing various strategies:

- ○ wasteland development
- ○ popularizing traditional systems of water storage
- ○ re-charging old wells from rainwater harvesting units
- ○ preserving desert culture and mobilizing people's actions.

The rainwater harvesting initiatives have achieved:

- ○ 207 underground tanks with a total capacity of 11.5 lakh litres built for rainwater collection in Rajasthan, thereby employing 4,000 persons.
- ○ 12 million litres of water collected in 1996–7 in rural schools and centres where rainwater harvesting units have been installed.
- ○ Because of the availability of potable water the attendance of girls in these schools has increased significantly.
- ○ 2,325 landless labourers have given 93,500 days of employment to build these tanks.
- ○ Ninety lakh litres of water was collected at Re 0.25 per litre in 1996–97 with individuals contributing over Rs 5 lakh worth of their labour.

Conclusion

The interventions discussed in the paper can be summed up as indicated in Table 17.6.

There is no unique solution for development efforts. Different geographical areas are at different stages of development and therefore, one solution cannot be an answer. A mix of interventions is required. The solution may have technology

Table 17.6:   Interventions and their context

Initiative	Objective	Stage of development	Geographical area	Beneficiaries	Financial feasibility	Dependence on grants	Self-sustaining	Range of intervention	Areas where impact is created	Network with others
ITC	Supply chain management	Medium	Central and north India	Rural farmers	Yes	None	Yes	Narrow	□ Distribution network □ Information access □ Community exposed to IT networks	Yes Primarily with community fertilizer firms, government, and other business organizations
TARAhaat	Information products and services through Internet	Varies from region to region	Wide-spread	Rural markets	□ Yes, for more developed areas □ No, for less developed areas	Yes, for underdeveloped areas, primarily managed by equity investments from the corporate sector	Yes, in the long-run	Narrow	□ Village connectivity □ Access to products and services needed by the farmers	Employment Empowerment Delivery of products Decentralised university
M.S. Swaminathan Research Foundation	□ Corporate intervention along with an NGO □ Used IT for generating food security and rural prosperity	Low	South India	Rural communities	NA	Yes	Still evolving	Narrow	Climate management, water, energy, health, agriculture biotechnology	NGO and corporate networking

Contd

Table 17.6 Contd

		Medium	South India	Rural communities	Yes	No	Yes	Narrow	▫ IT usage for re-employment ▫ Women empowerment	Corporate and community networks
HP's Global Citizenship	Engaging communities at grassroots levels for product development	Medium	South India	Rural communities	Yes		Yes	Narrow	▫ IT usage for re-employment ▫ Women empowerment	Corporate and community networks
SWRC (Barefoot College)	Wide range of interventions targeted at extreme poverty conditions	Low	Initiated in north west and then shifted to different parts of India and other countries as well	Rural areas	Yes, in the long-run, if coupled with corporate initiatives	Yes	Yes	Wide	Education, agriculture, food, wasteland development, solar energy, women empowerment, shelter, water	Networking of community, government, NGO, and international agencies

which is very basic or a technology which is high-tech. Also, for implementing such solutions, there is a need for interaction between the community, corporate firm, NGO, and the government.

Intervention such as Barefoot college:

o The case in point is the barefoot college where very basic technologies have been used.

o The interventions were initiated by an NGO, which raised funds from international organizations.

o It is a remarkable case of community-led intervention, with a wide scope of activities.

o It did not involve any experts, but individuals who felt that the community would benefit if they themselves identified with the place and the people with whom they worked.

o At a later stage of development, initiatives such as those undertaken by HP or ITC can bring it to the next stage of development.

Intervention such as HP Global Citizenship Programme or TARAhaat:

o Initiatives such as those initiated by HP are directed at a community who have some resource base for survival. Here, there are people who have some means for living and have some level of literacy, and access to food and water.

o An initiative such as the one initiated by HP makes sense as it provides employment and empowerment for the communities.

o It helps the firm develop and align products, which cannot only be directed at the urban population but also at the grassroots levels.

ITC Initiative:

o The initiative such as the one taken by ITC in India is an interesting case. There is a resource base available.

o The effort is directed at system inefficiencies and then linked with improving procurement from the villages. It results in cost savings for the farmer.

o It opens new doors of opportunity for the firm for additional revenues. It gives impetus for expanding into more areas for procurement. ITC started with soya procurement and then moved over to wheat procurement.

o Here, initiatives such as those by HP and the barefoot college can bring in a holistic development and empowerment of communities.

The interventions that are initiated have to be sustainable and self-propagating. So, an important dimension is the financial feasibility to create a spiral effect that leads to that region's growth. ITC's model is an indication that being commercially savvy and also having community orientation is possible. There is a huge potential to convert the latent demand into an active demand and bring in new numbers in the list of potential consumers.

The involvement of the local community and their role makes a huge difference. There is a need to redefine the roles and also make them understand the outcome of such interventions. When there is a realization that such interventions will lead to a larger good of the community, then their motivation levels are higher. Corporates will have to look for such unique value drivers, which may not just come through artificial means such as expenditure on advertising. After all, many products that actually sell in the market do so because of the superficial differentiation. So, efforts which are directed at doing things differently, which lead to a positive impact on the resource usage and recycling the existing resources, will be desirable.

ITC management of the bureaucracy is also unique. When e-choupals were conceived, they faced a fundamental regulatory obstacle. The Agricultural Produce Marketing Act, under whose aegis mandis were established, prohibits procurements outside the mandi. ITC did not use the mandi infrastructure and invested on building the electronic infrastructure. Since ITC paid the tax on the produce sourced, it did not risk the relationship with the government and mandis.

Proposed Framework for Development

Based on the studies quoted in this paper a framework is being proposed, which links various geographical areas on the basis of their stage of development with the nature of intervention that may work.

Different geographical areas are at different stages of evolution. They differ in infrastructure, literacy levels, availability of basic amenities, employment opportunities, environmental conditions, and presence of industry. With all these factors, it is important that there is a match between the intervention and the state of development. We can take technology as one of the tools which can facilitate development. It alone may not be sufficient to determine the complete intervention. For an intervention to be complete, it will need softer components and some technology as well. Consider an area which has low levels of literacy, limited resource base, dependence on basic produce, and lack of basic amenities of life. Such an area will need interventions targeted at the basic needs to which people do not have access. Such efforts will require the efforts of an NGO, the local community, and international organizations as well. Such an intervention must be broad based in its approach. Another aspect is the use of sophisticated technologies, which can be tapered to the needs of the local community. The most important aspect is the matching of the environmental strengths and needs of the local community with products which result in a win–win situation for both. India has many strengths. It is one of the world's largest providers of fruits and vegetables, while our share in the global food industry is negligible. India has a large resource base, so interventions that create larger markets make these communities economically independent, enabling them to have a sense of self-esteem.

The broad framework which seems to emerge is depicted in Fig. 17.3.

Low Stage of Development

In this state of development, people live in poverty, there is a scarcity of resources, low literacy, scant availability of water, food, and shelter is an issue. Such areas are also characterized by high levels of child mortality, ill-health, and low women empowerment.

As indicated in Fig. 17.3, in such areas interventions like the barefoot college can be initiated and they seem to bring a ray of hope where there is none. When the basic self-esteem is built in, then technology and corporate firms need to pitch in to take the intervention to the next stage of development. Such interventions require a very close networking of the community, NGOs, government, and the business firms (Fig. 17.4).

Medium Stage of Development

This intervention is targeted at a socio-economic scenario characterized by medium stage of development. People have basic education and are aware of external opportunities. A basic intervention which offers employment opportunities can be very helpful.

When initiatives such as Kuppam are initiated, they can have a spiral effect leading to providing opportunities for people and corporate firms as well.

Higher Stage of Development

The next stage is where there is resource base; economic activity is taking place, but there are still areas where there is exploitation. Looking at areas which bring in efficiency into the system, by making supply chain interventions as done by ITC, can help the community leapfrog into the next stage of development (see Fig. 17.5). This can have an immense consequence. At this time, if support is provided by NGOs and initiatives comparable to the barefoot initiative are undertaken, they can lead to a holistic development.

Critical Factors for Success

Synchronization

All these interventions need to be in synchronization and various stakeholders have to work together. A lack of support from any one of them can hamper the overall development process.

Use of local resources

There are issues about access to information and actual initiation of efforts. There are many institutions, NGOs, trusts, and voluntary organizations which initiate numerous efforts. There needs to be documentation effort on the part of the

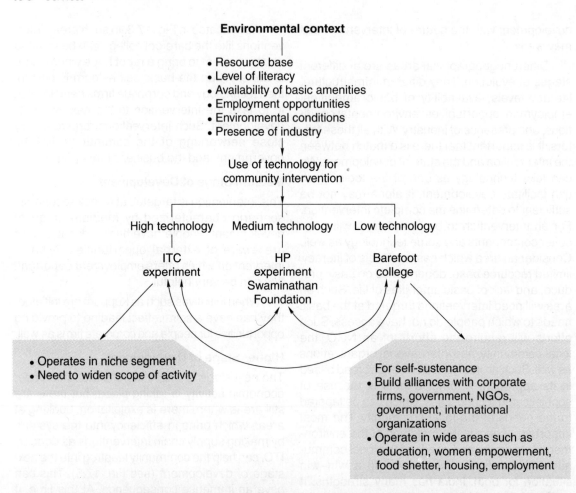

Fig. 17.3   Nature of sustainable development initiative

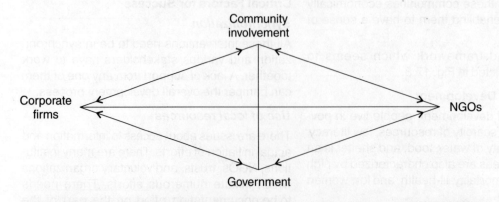

Fig. 17.4   Nature of intervention

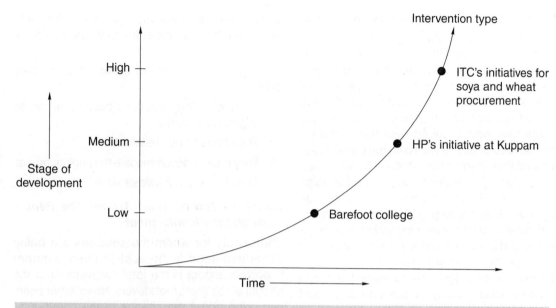

Fig. 17.5 Types of interventions

government wherein all the contact points and areas where work is carried out is clearly indicated. Consultants and experts need to be kept out of such interventions. A study reported in the *Harvard Business Review* points out some alarming facts about the intervention initiatives. There is a pointer towards the foundations.

'When a donor gives money to a foundation, most of the gifts sit on the sidelines. On an average, foundations donate only 5.5 per cent of their assets to charity each year, a number slightly above the legal minimum of 5 per cent. The rest is invested to create financial, not social returns (Only 0.01 per cent of foundation investment portfolios are invested to support philanthropic purposes). Most of the $330 billion currently held by the foundations, then represent a future benefit to society; one that could be realized only when the money is given away.'

Fewer than 9 per cent of all foundations make 75 per cent or more of their grants in a single field. Only 5 per cent focus more than 90 per cent of their grants in one field. Also, there is criticism related with foundations expressing a strong interest in innovation and advancing the state of knowledge about society's problem, but very few of them fund studies that explore the relative effectiveness of different approaches to a given issue.

Policy Implications

So, for areas where resources are limited some of the following interventions are suggested.

Simple Technologies

Infusion of capital or technology alone is not a solution to the problem of poverty. It is a multifaceted issue and requires interventions at various levels. Merely putting computers in the villages is not a solution. The reality is that there are a large number of people who are illiterate and unemployed, and need to be employed meaningfully so that they can earn their livelihoods. In the cases seen above in various sectors, it has been observed that the technologies which were used were very basic, were easy to understand, and people have known these for a long time. So, the solutions were not imposed from outside but were generated by the communities themselves. The case of the barefoot college at Tilonia indicates that even illiterate people can be trained if the technology is easy to understand. The simpler the technology is the higher will be its acceptability by the people.

Documentation of Indigenous Technologies

This points to the understanding of the importance of indigenous knowledge. Despite technology advances, the problem of drinking water and sanitation is still prevalent. In the olden days, they did not have trained doctors, architects, or biologists. They did not depend on theory but applied the wisdom they had acquired over the centuries. Many communities are tired with the current situation that they want to be left alone to solve their own problems. The indigenous knowledge helps to arrive at solutions. Greiner (1998) defines *indigenous knowledge* (IK) as 'the unique, traditional, local knowledge existing within and developed around the specific conditions of women and men indigenous to a particular geographic area'. Indigenous knowledge can provide insights into the area of food security, health, education, and natural ecological initiatives. The advantage of indigenous knowledge is that it is dynamic in character, as it has the capacity to evolve, since people have been using it in the past to survive through centuries. It needs to be documented and stored in a systematic manner as it has been passed on from generation to generation. The solution does not lie in inflicting western solutions on communities. Interventions fail to induce people to participate because of the absence of instruments and mechanisms that enable them to use their own knowledge.

The use of traditional knowledge, skills, and wisdom, promotes active community involvement because people depend more on each other. The use of traditional knowledge demystifies the local technologies that will be the basis for sustainable solutions in the future. The more people understand and try out a technology, the greater the chance of the technology getting accepted. In 1997–8, through the use of century-old technologies, a total of 12 million litres of rainwater was collected in 100 schools, attended by 3,000 children, at the barefoot schools. The cost was a mere $0.10 a litre. The schools have teachers with no qualifications. Over 150 young people from nine states of India have been trained as barefoot solar engineers. They have equipped over 2,000 houses in the Himalayas with solar electricity. The

practice can be transferred to other places and situations, but it is essential that several conditions be met.

The characteristics of these solutions have to be that:

○ The technology solutions have to be rooted in ground realities.

○ They have to be sustainable.

○ They have to accommodate the huge numbers.

○ They have to tap investments.

Solutions too be Built Around the People through their Involvement

The people for whom the solutions are being generated need to be kept in mind. Another important aspect is the total involvement of the people at the grassroots levels. No external agent can bring about the change in the community. Unless the people stand up for themselves, nothing can change. They would have to be united together to stand up for their rights and there is a need for facilitators rather than consultants. These should be the people who can identify themselves with these people and live with them so as to experience what it means to live a life they live. The solution for any community has to be a sustainable solution that leads to a process, which is self-sustaining. This can only happen if the use of the local know-how is usefully channelized so that it can be sustained in the long run. The case of Tilonia as discussed in the paper is an example of this. The people need to be sensitized to the change. Acceptance of change is far easier when there is a suitable climate created for it.

Dissemination of Information to the Poor

The biggest problem for poor people is the lack of information on what is happening around them. The government starts so many programmes for the poor but the benefits never reach down to them. The government needs to communicate information regarding the programmes to them and most important, monitor the implementation of these. For example, the much hyped Swarna Jayanti Sahari Yojana and Swarn Jayanti Swarojgar Yojana, which were launched in April 1999, have failed to benefit even 5 per cent of the target in Orissa. Bamboo craftspersons in Bhubaneshwar were to be the beneficiaries of the Swarna Jayanti Sahari Yojana, which was meant to help people rise above the poverty line. In the last two years, since the scheme began, not a single person received even a rupee as a loan.

Better Management of Resources

A recent news reported in the press is an eye opener. The drought-affected people in 10 districts of Rajasthan protested in order to highlight the fact that though the Food Corporation of India (FCI) godowns were bursting with food grains, people remain hungry. In godowns in India, the FCI has nearly 410 lakh tonnes of food grains; nearly an estimated 139 lakh tonnes in excess. It costs the government Rs 4,20,000 lakh just to store these food grains in Rajasthan (www.ndtv.com, 17 May 2001). The FCI has in recent years been grappling with the problem of how to take care of the huge surplus food grain, which is fattening an ever-growing army of rodents or simply rotting away in its badly managed warehouses (*The Times of India*, 11 May 2001). So, there is a need for better management of the resources. With little changes in the way things are operated, it can become quite easy.

Political will to Take Pragmatic Decisions

The income and consumption patterns of the poor are changing. The shift is away from coarse grains to wheat, paddy, and oilseeds. Singh (2001) has analysed the dynamics of the cropping patterns. A drop of 50 per cent in the cultivated area of *sorghum*, little millet, and finger millet has come about just in the past decade. It was in the 1980s that the Public Distribution System (PDS) became a welfare instrument to provide essential items at nearly half the market price. Neither crop loans nor crop insurance are available for these groups. Also there are no subsidies. The promised minimum support price of coarse grains is denied to farmers due to government non-intervention. The chemical composition of coarse grains is better than rice and wheat in many cases. Pearl millets have a higher concentration of protein, fat, and minerals, particularly calcium.

The 1999–2000 Union Budget projected a cut in the central deficit of 0.9 per cent of GDP. Achieving this target depends on substantial rise in tax revenue and containing revenue expenditure growth to only 9 per cent. The interest costs of the debt have increasingly crowded out infrastructure, maintenance, and social spending in central and state budgets. Implicit and explicit subsidies at the centre and especially at the state levels are a major factor in the deficit (World Bank Report, 2000). The ministry of finance estimated these subsidies at over 14 per cent of GDP in 1994–5. In addition to increasing the deficit, they are distortionary, non-transparent, and at best have uncertain equity consequences. At worst, they are anti equity.

Transparency

Transparency in operations is required. A review of literature suggests that poverty has a relationship with political corruption. Oyen, in Human Development Report (1997) mentions that poverty often serves the vested interests of the economically powerful, who may depend on the poverty stricken to ensure that their societies run smoothly. A mobile pool of low-paid and unorganized workers is useful for doing the 'dirty, dangerous, and difficult' work that others refuse to do. Corruption in government increases poverty in many ways. Most directly, it diverts resources to the rich people who can afford to pay bribes, and away from the poor people who cannot (Transparency International 1996). Corruption also skews decisions in favour of capital-intensive enterprise and away from labour-intensive activities more likely to benefit the poor. Corruption also weakens the government and lessens their ability to fight poverty. It reduces tax revenues and thus the sources for public services. Most generally, corruption eats away at the fabric of public life, leading to increased lawlessness and undermining social and political stability.

Where corruption is rampant and evidence is in place that development funds have never reached the target segment, it is all the more required. The barefoot college is evidence where, through the *Jansunwai* (public hearing) it shared all the financial details with the people for whom the development work is being done. It must involve participation by the poor if it is to yield meaningful inputs. It is necessary to vitalize the community media with the involvement of people (Sharma 2000). It is important to bring information to the doorsteps of the poor people. There is an urgent need to ensure access to modern information technology in rural areas or disadvantaged communities to disseminate simple, practical knowledge, which will save their lives, increase awareness, and stimulate development. Properly used, media can help reduce the conflict and strengthen local organization. It can help reduce poverty through providing information on how people of their type somewhere else are handling their situation. The poor have inadequate access to information, technology, expertise, and resources.

Linkages between Different Sectors

Interventions taken in one sector have an impact on the other sector and there are strong inter-linkages between the same. Improving health outcomes not only improves well-being but also increases income-earning potential. Increasing education not only improves well-being but also leads to better health outcomes and to higher incomes. Providing protection for poor people not only makes them feel less vulnerable, it also allows them to take advantage of higher risk and higher returns opportunities. Increasing poor people's voice and participation not only addresses their sense of exclusion, it also leads to better targeting of health and education services to their needs.

Survival within poverty includes many strategies, which are combined in a process aimed not just at income in the broadest sense but also at assurance against the stresses and shocks to which poor people are particularly vulnerable. One such strategy is a mixture of jobs, some temporary, some full-time, some self-employed, and some working for others. Technology can play a vital role in the elimination of illiteracy. For example, information technology can be utilized to make education reach the most distant location. It can create a difference by dissemination of information using various means in the rural areas. It can address concerns like the problems faced by craftsmen, farmers, or a person who runs a leather tannery, among others. Another important aspect that can be addressed by IT can be converting the entire literature into a language which the masses understand. But IT alone cannot be a solution. The solution has to be rooted into the reality of the situation.

Areas Where Resource Base is Stronger

In such areas it is important, that technology is incorporated which improves productivity. Some interesting conclusions can be drawn from ITC's experiment. These are as follows:

Have a Clear Focus

Business firms need to have a clear sense of direction. Risk analysis is important. From ITC's perspective, the risk was high if it were to continue with the tobacco business. By diversifying into areas where India is resource rich and by imbibing requisite technology, ITC ventured into an area which can fetch good returns for the firm and also bring in tremendous goodwill. Profits are important to add value to the investments made in firms. They have their own role. They generate employment and bring in development as well. But such initiatives have inclusion effects and also expand the potential market of the firm.

Identification of the Customer Needs

Need identification is important. Here, customers need branded products, which assure them of quality and value for money. However, the organization at any point of time is always trapped in tradeoffs between profits through market research and investments in innovation and societal benefits. It is not just advertising expenses but also other value drivers that can contribute towards organizational excellence. In ITC's case the entire product line may shift. In its attempt to streamline the supply chain, it has not only made the procurement process more effective, but has made a tremendous contribution to the society as well. It has improved the wages that the farmer carries home for his hard work. This assures a better quality of life for him. Also, it meant replicating the experiment for not only soya crop but also extending it to wheat. So, this experiment takes the entire concept of branding and development to a new paradigm, which is not just caring for profits but developing products that ensure sustainability.

Redefine Roles

The idea is not to take away from people but modify the roles and responsibilities so that they have a sense of self-esteem and feel involved. Such efforts can be successful if the community has a feeling of trust and feels that it will benefit from the process. So, community involvement and re-defining the roles are important.

Networking of Different Stakeholders

At some point different stakeholders have to work in synchronization with each other. Each intervention will have a range of activities and will be constrained by the state of development. The initiatives for the overall development must include simultaneous interventions by many firms, government, and NGOs. More than institutions, individuals will have to come forward and take a lead in such initiatives. The bigger organizations have a lot of administrative costs. The benefits need to trickle down to the lowest level for a real change to happen, which is self-sustaining in character.

Notes

1. The World Bank (2003) report indicates that in the year 2001, 72 per cent of the people residing in India were the rural population (p. 121). The population density was 454 (people per sq km of arable land) in the year 2000. In India, in 2000, the land area was 2973 sq. km. Out of this, arable land was 54.4 per cent. Permanent cropland was 2.7 per cent of the land area. The use of agricultural machinery is low in India as compared to the developed countries. In India, the number of tractors per 1000 agricultural workers was 6 in 1998–2000 as against 2 in 1979–81. The number of tractors per 100 sq. km of arable land in 1998–2000 was 93 against 24 in 1979–81. Compare this with the figure in Israel where it stood at 734 per sq. km or 4,691 in Japan, 1,549 in Norway, and 2,512 in Austria. Poor farming practices can cause soil erosion and loss of soil fertility. Productivity improvements through excessive use of chemical fertilizers can lead to pesticide poisoning and alter the chemistry of the soil.

2. There have been sporadic corporate experiments which have resulted in success for some firms. These have been tailored to suit rural requirements Arvind Mills in India found that even the cheapest jeans were out of reach for most Indians. It introduced the ready to stitch Ruf & Tuf jeans kit, priced at Rs 195 against the organized sector price of Rs 300. The product was available in local retail outlets serving the hamlets with populations ranging up to 5,000. Village tailors were trained and provided with additional machine accessories needed for stitching heavy denim. The result was that five million kits were sold within 18 months. Products need to reach the villages with over 2,000 people (there are about 65,000 of these) accounting for 40 per cent of the rural population and 60 per cent of the rural consumption.

3. Terms used in the text

Choupal	A Hindi word which connotes a village gathering place
1 crore	Indian term for the number 10,000,000
Lakh	Indian term for the number 100,000
Kendras	Centres
Madhya Pradesh	An Indian state in central India
Mandi	A government-mandated marketplace where farmers sell their crops, or other things are bought and sold
Rajasthan	An Indian state in north west India

Quintal	One hundred kilograms
Rupee	Indian currency
Samyojak	Commission agent in his role as a collaborator

Sanchalak	Village farmer who runs the e-choupal and acts as ITC's representative in the state
VSAT	Satellite based technology, which helps in wireless connectivity

Questions

1. What are the lessons on ethics that you have learnt from the discussion of numerous corporate firms listed in the case study?

2. Compare and contrast the efforts of SWRC and corporate firms. What lessons on ethics can be derived from SWRC's work?

SELECT REFERENCES

Al Gini (1998), 'Moral leadership and business ethics', in *Ethics the Heart of Leadership*, Joanne B. Ciulla (ed.), Praeger, London.

Annamalai, K. and Sachin Rao (2003), *What Works: ITC's E–Choupal and Profitable Rural Transformation*, World Resources Institute.

Assisi, C. and I. Gupta (2003), 'ITC's rural symphony', *Business World*, 10 January.

Bhattacharya, P. (1995), 'In look as a counterpoint to outlook: Reflections on value systems workshops', in S.K. Chakraborty (ed.), *Management by Values towards Cultural Congruence*, Oxford University Press, New Delhi.

Buchholz, R.A. (1989), *Fundamental Concepts and Problems in Business Ethics*, Prentice Hall, Englewood Cliffs, New Jersey.

Carr, A.Z. (1968), 'Is business bluffing ethical', *Harvard Business Review*, vol. 46, no. 1, pp. 143–153.

Chakraborty, S.K. (1991), *Management by Values towards Cultural Congruence*, Oxford University Press, New Delhi.

Choi, S.Y. and A.B. Whinston (2000), *The Internet Economy: Technology and Practice*, Smartcon.com, Austin, Texas.

Choi, S.Y. et al. (1997), *The Electronics of Electronic Commerce*, Macmillan, Indianapolis, Indiana.

Cooke, R.A. (1986), 'Business ethics at the crossroads', *Journal of Business Ethics*, vol. 5, pp. 259–263.

Datta, S.K. (1995), 'Efficacy of workshops on value based management: The Reserve Bank of India experience', in S.K. Chakraborty (ed.), *Human Values for Manager*, Wheeler Publishing, New Delhi.

Davis, M. (1982), 'Conflict of interest 2', *Business and Professional Ethics Journal*, vol. 1, no. 4, pp. 17–29.

De George, R.T. (1986), 'Replies and reflections on theology and business ethics', *Journal of Business Ethics*, vol. 5, pp. 521–524.

De George, R.T. (1987), 'The status of business ethics past and future', *Journal of Business Ethics*, vol. 8, pp. 201–211.

Doft, Richard L. (1985), *Management*, Dryden Press, Chicago.

Donaldson, T. (1989b), *The Ethics of International Business*, Oxford University Press, New York.

Dunlop, Alex (1996), 'Corporate accountability: More form than substance', in K. Smith and P. Johnson (eds), *Business Ethics and Business Behaviour*, International Thomson Business, London.

Dunn, D. and K. Yamashita (2003), 'Micro capitalism and the mega corporation', *Harvard Business Review*, August.

Epstein, E.M. (1989), 'Business ethics—Corporate good citizenship and the corporate social policy process: A view from the United States', *Journal of Business Ethics*, vol. 8, pp. 583–595.

Goodpaster, K. (1993), 'Business ethics and stakeholder analysis', in E.R. Winkler and J.R. Commbs (eds), *Applied Ethic—A Reader*, Blackwell, Oxford.

Goodpaster, K.E. and Matthews (1982), 'Can a corporation have a conscience?', *Harvard Business Review*, vol. 60, no. 1, pp. 132–140.

Grenier, Louise (1998), 'Working with indigenous knowledge', *A Guide for Researchers*, IRDC.

Hoffman, M. and J.M. Moore (1990), *Business Ethics: Reading and Cases in Corporate Morality*, 2nd edn, McGraw-Hill, New York.

Hofstede, G. (1991), *Culture and Organization: Software of the Mind*, McGraw-Hill, London.

Holliday, C. (2001) 'Sustainable growth, the DuPont way', *Harvard Business Review*, pp. 129–134.

Hornsby, A.S. (1993), *Oxford Advanced Learners Dictionary,* Oxford University Press, Calcutta.

Human Development Report (2003), Oxford University Press, New Delhi.

Joanne B. Ciulla (1998), 'Leadership ethics: Mapping the territory', in B. Ciulla (ed.), *Ethics: The Heart of Leadership*, Joanne Praeger, London.

Learned, E., P. Dooley, R. Arch, and R.L. Katz (1959), 'Personal values and business decisions', *Harvard Business Review*, March–April.

MacIntyre, A. (1989), *A Short History of Ethics*, Macmillan Press, London.

Mahoney, J. (1990), 'An international look at business ethics', *Journal of Business Ethics,* vol. 9, pp. 545–550.

McHugh, F.P. (1988), *Keyguide to Information Source in Business Ethics*, Nichols, New York.

Miller, Samuel H. (1960), 'The tangle of ethics', *Harvard Business Review*, Jan–Feb.

Ozar, D.T. (1979), *The Moral Responsibility of Corporations in Ethical Issues in Business*, in T. Donaldson and P. Werhane (eds), Prentice Hall, Englewood Cliffs, New Jersey.

Payne, S.L. and R.A. Giacalone (1990), 'Social psychological approaches to the perception of ethical dilemmas', *Human Relations*, vol. 43, no. 7, pp. 649–665.

Peterson, C., V. Sandell, and A. Lawlor (2001), *What Works: Tarahaat's Portal for Rural India,* World Resources Institute, July.

Pope Pius XI (1985), 'Quadragesimo Anno (On reconstructing the social order)', in David M. Byers (ed.), *Justice in the Marketplace: A Collection of the Vatican and U.S. Catholic Bishops on Economic Policy, 1891–1984*, United States Catholic Conference 61, Washington DC.

Porter, M. (2003), 'Building the microeconomic foundations of prosperity: Findings from the Microeconomic Competitiveness Index', *The Global Competitiveness Report 2002–03*, Oxford University Press, New York.

Primeaux, P. (1942), 'Experiential ethics: A blueprint for personal and corporate ethics', *Journal of Business Ethics,* vol. 11, pp. 779–788.

Raphael, D.D. (1981), *Moral Philosophy*, Oxford University Press, Oxford.

Reinhardt, F. (2003), 'Tests for sustainability', *The Global Competitiveness Report 2002–03*, Oxford University Press, New York.

Shah, N.B. (1995), 'Value/ethics in management: Relevance and application', in S.K. Chakraborty (ed.), *Human Values for Manager,* Wheeler Publishing, New Delhi.

Small, M.W. (1993), 'Ethics in business and administration: An International and historical perspective', *Journal of Business Ethics*, pp. 293–300.

Smith, Ken and Phil Johnson (1996), *Business Ethics and Business Behaviour*, Thomson, London.

Srinivas, M.N. (1996), *Indian Society through Personal Writings*, Oxford University Press, New Delhi.

Stace, W.T. (1988), *Ethical Relativity and Ethical Absolution in Ethical Issues in Business: A Philosophical Approach*, 3rd edn, in T. Donaldson and P.H. Werhane (eds), Prentice Hall, Englewood Cliffs, New Jersey.

Steiner, G.A. (1975), *Business and Society*, Random House, New York.

Sumner, W.G. (1988), 'A defence of cultural relativism', in T. Donaldson and P.H. Werhane (eds), *Ethical Issues in Business: A Philosophical Approach*, 3rd edn, Prentice Hall, Englewood Cliff, New Jersey.

Transparency International (1996), 'Sharpening the response against global corruption', *Transparency International Global Report 1996*, Berlin.

Turban, E., D. King, J. Lee Warkentin, and M.H. Chung (2002), *Electronic Commerce*, Prentice Hall, New Jersey.

Velasquez, M.G. (1988), *Business Ethics: Concepts and Cases*, 2nd edn, Prentice Hall, Englewood Cliffs, New Jersey.

World Bank (2003), 'World development indicators', The World Bank, Washington.

HP.com (2004), 'Global citizenship', http://www.hp.com/cgi-bin/hpinfo, accessed on 12 July 2004.

http://www.barefootcollege.org/html/water.htm.

Levine, J. (2004), 'The citizenship agenda at Hewlett Packard: An interview with Debra Dunn, Knowledge Centre', http://www.be.edu/centers/ccc/pages/resources/kn_resart_dunn.html, accessed on 25 June 2006.

Meghani, S. (2004), 'A village comes of age', http://www.tata.com, accessed on 27 August 2004.

Roy, Bunker (2001), 'Management of water resources at local level—The repair and maintenance of hand pumps', http://www.unv.org/projects/sl/collect/swrc1.htm.

Sarvani, V. (2003), 'ITC's e-choupal: Taking e-business to farmers', *Case Folio*, July. Also available on www.icfaipress.org.

Sharma, M. (2000), 'Information technology for poverty reduction', www.ouhk.edu.hk/cridal/wrapup/discuss/messages/22.html.

Tarahaat (2004), 'What works: Tarahaat's portal for rural India', http://www.digitaldividend.org/case/case_tarahaat.htm, accessed on 1 September 2004.

www.ndtv.com (2001), 'Pro poor policies let down by the lack of reform', accessed on 1 March 2001.

www.unesco.org/most/bpik16.htm, 'The barefoot college—Promoting productive employment for youth'.

18 Strategies for Business Growth

OBJECTIVES

After reading this chapter you will be able to understand the:

- strategic management framework for service industry
- options available for growth of a service firm
- concepts related to green field ventures
- meaning of joint ventures
- concepts related to mergers and acquisitions (M&A), strategic alliances, franchising, and licensing
- relevance of management contracts
- emerging forms of entrepreneurship

INTRODUCTION

This chapter elaborates on the strategic management framework for the service industry. It traces the evolution of the strategic management framework. This chapter discusses the various strategic options for growth of a service firm. These options could be green field ventures, joint ventures, mergers and acquisitions (M&A), strategic alliances, franchising, licensing, and management contracts. The factors affecting the choice of entrepreneurship have also been elaborated upon.

STRATEGIC MANAGEMENT FRAMEWORK

Strategy, as has been treated in the conventional management literature, is associated with the growth of the business—keeping in mind the vision and matching external environmental dynamics with the internal resource base in the organization. Andrews (1971) defined the strategy as a match between what a company *can do* (organizational strengths and weaknesses) within a framework of what it *might do* (environmental opportunities and threats). Strategic management literature has postulated several frameworks to further the understanding of the concept of strategy. External business environment influences the strategic behaviour of a firm. For example, a mature industry has a relative stable business environment, which then elicits behaviour that focuses more on cost-saving and process-related improvements in business. A high-tech industry, however, is characterized by a lot of changes. In such an industry, the product life cycles are short, customer aspirations change very fast, the competition is aggressive, and customers have to be educated about new products—their features and advantages. Examples of these product categories are electronics products, telecommunications, wireless-based products, aeronautics, chemicals, pharmaceuticals, etc.

Since the beginning of strategic management discipline, the four major corporate strategy frameworks that have emerged are strengths, weaknesses, opportunities, and threats (SWOT) in the 1960s, strategic planning matrix in the 1970s, competitiveness in the 1980s, and core competencies in the 1990s (Karki 2004). There is also abundant literature available on style of leadership, which has an impact on the behaviour and orientation of a firm. The leadership may vary from being bureaucratic to entrepreneurial. The organization structure and the business environmental behaviour have also been explored in strategic management literature.

Resource-based View of the Firm

It combines the internal analysis of the phenomenon within companies with external analysis of the industry. The resources may be tangible, intangible, and in a form such as supply chain management or managerial capacity. Based on the resource-based framework, the firm can assess its portfolio of products or services on the BCG framework or Ansoff grid parameters. Also, all these resources can be assessed on the following dimensions (Collis and Montgomery 1995):

- Test of inimitability
- Test of durability
- Test of appropriability
- Test of substitutability
- Test of competitive superiority.

In all these tests the focus is on this resource base, keeping in mind the market conditions and competitive factors.

Porter's (1980) view on competitive advantage discussed the competitive dynamics of the firm. He has postulated various frameworks which facilitate a better understanding of the firms in light of the competitive dynamics. For instance, the five-force framework or the value chain analysis helps firms to understand the sources of competitive advantage for the firm.

Collis and Montgomery (1998) have even discussed the context in which the resource-based view of the firm could be further analysed. They have pointed out that the resource continuum can be extended across numerous factors such as:

- nature of resources which can vary from general to specialized
- scope of resources which can vary from wide to narrow
- coordination mechanisms which vary from transferring to sharing
- control systems which can range from financial to operating systems
- corporate office size which can vary from small to large.

McKinsey's 7-S framework also prescribes a model for managing organizations, which considers the following factors:

- strategy
- skills
- staff
- shared values
- styles
- systems
- structure.

The strategic view of the firm suggests that there should be a source of competitive advantage. This source should be sustainable in the long run.

Sustainable Competitive Advantage

The main reason for analysing competitors is to enable the organization to develop competitive advantages against them, especially advantages that can be sustained over time. The real advantages come from advantages that competitors cannot easily imitate, not those that give only temporary relief from the competitive battle. To be sustainable, competitive advantage needs to be more deeply embedded in the organization—its resources, skills, culture, and investment over time. Sources of sustainable competitive advantage can take many forms, for example:

- differentiation
- low costs
- niche marketing
- high performance or technology
- superior quality
- superior service
- vertical integration.

Lynch (1997) offers the following examples of competitive advantages in different types of businesses (Fig. 18.1).

OPTIONS FOR GROWTH OF THE SERVICE FIRM

Strategic management takes a long-term perspective of the firm. It helps to chart out long-term plans for growth of the firm. Some of the different options for growth for national and international expansion of the firm are as follows:

- green field ventures
- joint ventures
- mergers and acquisitions
- strategic alliances
- franchising
- licensing
- management contract.

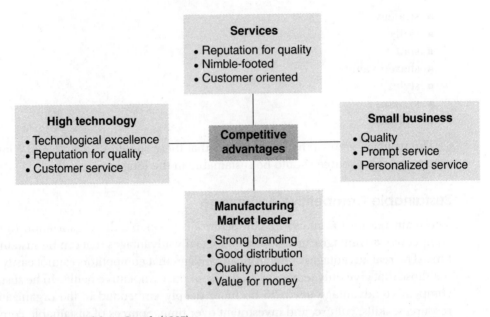

Source: Adapted from Lynch (1997).

Fig. 18.1 Types of competitive advantages in different types of businesses

GREEN FIELD VENTURES

A *green field venture* is a firm, which has been started from scratch. It is a new venture created by bringing in capital, land, and labour, and is often a painstaking exercise. The risk in creating a new venture is substantially high. It also varies from industry to industry.

Many firms have grown only by internal or organic development. This means starting the firm's operations from scratch. The advantages of organic growth may be summarized as follows:

- The cost of development is spread over time.
- The firm experiences minimal disruption.
- The firm can build up its own internal team (it does not need to inherit resources, as in an acquisition or merger).

However, there are also obvious disadvantages:

- It can be a slow process and the final cost may be high.
- The means of development is perceived by some to be conservative and cautious.
- There may be operational and bureaucratic delays.
- It may take many years to build up a brand.
- It may be entirely dependent on the promoter's initial vision and his experience may be a limiting factor.

External growth on the other hand is perhaps more visible and can be more risky. Mergers and acquisitions also offer speed in development. They also provide immediate access to necessary resources, knowledge, and competitive position, which are the other benefits.

JOINT VENTURES

A *joint venture* is an entity that is formed by a legal agreement between two or more parties. The various parties have a financial stake and the profit-sharing arrangement is agreed in advance.

It is also a manifestation of an organization's entrepreneurial orientation. India took the initiative to start joint ventures in the late 1950s. The first Indian joint venture was sanctioned as early as 1959. This paved the way, and opened new vistas, for closer economic and trade ties between India and other developing countries.

Joint ventures benefit the investing firm, the investing country, and the host country. Some Indian firms had earlier invested abroad due to severe cuts imposed on the expansion of large houses under the Industries Development and Regulation Act and the MRTP Act prior to liberalization, but most of them are lured by the attractive incentives offered by many developing countries in the form of tax holidays, export incentives, freedom to remit profits and repatriate capital, and in many cases, protective tariffs. The Indian entrepreneur gets first-hand market information, widens his contacts, and thus gets an opportunity to increase his exports. For example, Indian joint ventures can be established in Mauritius, to take advantage of the benefits offered by the government.

Joint ventures may have the following advantages:

- Lead to increased export of capital goods, spare parts, and components from India.
- Exports of technical know-how and consultancy services also increase.
- It helps in projecting India's image as a supplier of capital goods and technology.
- They can help in the utilization of idle capacity in the capital goods sector and thus in reducing costs in general.
- They may lead to greater employment.
- The country also gains by greater inflow of foreign exchange in the form of dividends, royalties, and technical know-how fees.
- These also help to achieve India's aim of achieving collective self-reliance and annual cooperation among the developing countries.

Developing countries generally welcome India's joint venture because intermediate labour-intensive technology developed by India is more suited to their requirements, and they can adopt it directly without any or slight modifications. Moreover, most developing countries, because of their limited home market, may not be able to afford large-scale capital intensive technology provided by developed countries and thus prefer the medium-scale technology developed by India. Finally, host countries perceive little threat to their political or economic independence from Indian joint ventures.

Joint Ventures in India

Indian companies convince their partners of their clout and influence. The business is secondary; the priority is having a tie-up. However, after the initial enthusiasm, the ardour begins to wane. The transnational—almost invariably, a company with superior financial, managerial and technological muscle—begins to ask the basic question, 'What can my Indian partner contribute that will endure?' In most cases, the answer is straightforward: nothing. The foreign investor then wants control, whereas the Indian company, with its access to the media and politicians cries foul. This is the first set of problems that are visible. Not enough time is spent by either party to identify their complementary core competencies. The Indian companies keep looking for alternative collaborations. A clash of managerial cultures and styles is inevitable. The problem can be overcome over time if there is investment in training and the development of skills. But this is not something Indian companies are comfortable with. A third set of problems arises when foreign companies want management control since they are bringing in the technology. So, in technology-driven businesses Indian companies might have to play second fiddle initially. However, there is nothing wrong in this. If Indian managements believe in sustaining their presence in a particular industry, they will see the value of investing in research, technology, and networking, and earn the right to be equal partners.

Joint ventures obviously bring together contrasting management styles. Generalizations are tricky, but it would not be an exaggeration to say that the managerial ethos in Indian companies reflects that of our society—inegalitarian, stratified, secretive, and top-down. In the final analysis, it is this that creates strain and tension. Transparency is unwelcome not only to Indian politicians but also to Indian industrialists, used as they are to a feudal system of management. Nationalist slogans are used to garner public support, but the root of the problem lies in the fear of exposure and the loss of control. A joint venture is not a black box; it is exactly like a marriage. The alliance will have its ups and downs, but given a measure of trust, communication, and sensitivity of both sides, things can be managed smoothly.

MERGERS AND ACQUISITIONS

This section discusses mergers and acquisitions (M&A) in detail

Takeover and Merger—Some Definitions

Takeover of a company means assumption of management control of that company by getting substantial powers of management (Thakur 1995). This is normally done through an acquisition of a sufficient number of shares carrying voting rights and then taking charge of the management of the company by getting appointed to the Board. The purpose of takeover is generally unilateral and the offer company decides the maximum price (Verma 1995).

The draft regulation of SEBI on takeovers does mention takeover and an informal definition of a takeover bid is also given. A *takeover bid* is generally understood to mean: an offer made to the holders of securities carrying voting rights in a company or convertible into securities carrying such rights, to acquire their securities for a consideration, the purpose of the offer usually being to acquire control of the company, or consolidate control by the existing management.

The omission of a formal definition seems to be conscious. It seems that the legislature does not want to enter into disputes on whether the acquisition of shares is for a takeover or is a genuine investment. The provisions of law are triggered as soon as shares exceeding the specified limits are acquired. However, the flip side of this is that when a person purchases shares for a genuine investment, he has to adopt the same procedure as required for a takeover.

Merger or *amalgamation* on the other hand, refers to the physical joining of two companies. This takes place either by dissolving both the companies or forming a new one to take over their businesses, or by one company dissolving and transferring its existence to the other. In a sense, takeover may precede a merger, though a takeover is not necessary for a merger to take place.

Verma (1995) defines merger as the combination of two or more companies into a single company, where one survives and another loses its corporate existence. The survivor acquires the assets as well as liabilities of the merged companies or company. The company which survives is the buyer and retains its identity, while the seller company is extinguished. Merger is also defined as amalgamation. It is the fusion of two or more existing companies. All assets, liabilities, and stock of one company stand transferred to the transferee company in consideration of payment in the form of equity shares of the transferee company, or debentures, or cash, or a mix of two or three modes.

Amalgamation is used interchangeably with merger. The common literal linkage between these two terms is through the word combination. The Oxford dictionary defines both these words as combinations, carrying a sense of mixing or uniting two or more things together, or in the corporate sense, uniting or combining two undertakings together. The essence of amalgamation is blending of two or more existing undertakings into one undertaking, which may take one of the following forms:

- Absorption: This occurs when one or more undertaking blends with another.
- Merger: Two or more undertakings blend to form a new one. This is precisely known as merger, since the blending companies merge their respective separate identities to form a new undertaking.

MERGERS AND ACQUISITIONS IN INDIA

The Indian economy has seen a rise in the mergers and acquisitions (M&A) activity since the liberalization process gathered momentum from 1991 onwards. The number of M&As has increased and each industry is witnessing change. The privatization of industries such as power, steel, and telecom has opened new opportunities. The Monopolistic and Restrictive Trade Practices (MRTP) Act, 1969 that was implemented to check concentration of economic power and control the growth of monopolistic and restrictive trade practises has been weakened. The industrial policy, announced on 24 June 1991 by the government, assured the dismantling of the shackles of the regulatory system. Amendments were made in the MRTP Act, omitting all restrictive sections discouraging the growth of the industrial sector. To attract foreign investment in industry, relaxations were made for foreign direct investment (FDI) up to 51 per cent foreign equity in high priority industries that has further been enhanced in many sectors. The spate of M&A activity in the industry has increased, led by changes in economic policy.

The study initiated by Jauhari and Misra (2001) elaborates on the trends in M&A activity from 1993 to 1999. There are two time segments in which this study has been conducted. The first is from January 1993 to 1996. The second phase is from 1997 to 1999. The information on the acquisitions has been painstakingly collected from the various publications such as CMIE, leading Indian newspapers, and business publications. This methodology was adopted, as there is no single source in India, which records all these M&As. For the period 1993–96, information on 80 M&As was collated. For the period 1997–99, information on 323 M&As has been collated. For international M&As, data was collated for the year 1994–95. The data for international M&As has been updated till the year 2000. The comparison of trends for these years gives an insight into the dynamics of M&A activity.

Significance

The study assumes significance, as the very nature of Indian industry coupled with the liberalization of economy will lead to more M&A activity. This is because of the excess capacities in Indian industry, over-fragmentation, lack of requisite size of the firm, the firm's viability, lack of financial resources, and commercial orientation. All these factors characterize Indian industry, as the environment was such that a long period of licensing regime ensured that industry could not expand beyond a particular size and political influence helped getting licenses for setting up industry. In many industry sectors in India, this led to monopolies as a result of which there was little competition. The industry did not really invest on R&D and innovation as it was able to sell whatever was being produced. So, there was no incentive for making any improvements, which led to stagnation in Indian industry. Suddenly, in 1991 the liberalization process initiated by the government changed the rules of the game. Profitability coupled with productivity and customer orientation became important terms, which Indian industry had been evading for long years. Since the shakeout in Indian industry is inevitable on account of increased competition, M&A activity is bound to take place. So, it becomes necessary to understand what needs to be kept in mind to manage these better.

As per the current statistics of M&A activities in India and abroad, the first six months of M&A deals in 2008 stands at 265 with a value of $18.54 billion as against 335 deals amounting to $43.97 billion in the corresponding period in 2007.

The acquisitions in the services sector have been largely driven by IT and ITES. The figures are as high as 84 per cent for overseas acquisitions in number terms, and 85 per cent in value, during the period 2001–07. See Table 18.1 for figures in service sector acquisitions.

Table 18.2 gives the number of overseas acquisitions by Indian multinationals upto 2007.

Table 18.3 gives the top 10 acquisitions made by Indian firms worldwide.

Table 18.1 Service sector acquisitions

Year	Banking & financial services	Business advisory	Hospitality and tourism	Telecommunication services	Media and entertainment	IT and ITES	Services
(Acquisitions in number)							
2000					4 (15.4)	22 (84.6)	26 (100)
2001					1 (5.3)	18 (94.7)	19 (100)
2002	1 (10.0)					9 (90.0)	10 (100)
2003		1 (5.0)		1 (5.0)		18 (90.0)	20 (100)
2004		1 (5.0)		1 (5.0)		18 (90.0)	20 (100)
2005	4 (7.7)	1 (1.9)	3 (5.8)	2 (3.8)		42 (80.8)	52 (100)
2006	2 (2.8)		4 (5.6)	2 (2.8)	9 (12.5)	55 (76.4)	72 (100)
2007		2 (4.2)	1 (2.1)	3 (6.3)		(42) (87.5)	48 (100)
All years	7 (2.6)	5 (1.9)	8 (3.0)	9 (3.4)	14 (5.2)	224 (83.9)	267 (100)
(Acquisitions in value, $ million)							
2000					25 (5.56)	425 (94.44)	450 (100)
2001						140 (100.00)	140 (100)
2002	4 (6.34)					58 (93.66)	62 (100)
2003		3 (0.79)		207 (62.62)		121 (36.60)	331 (100)
2004				130 (26.14)		367 (73.80)	497 (100)
2005	17 (2.32)	5 (0.68)	85 (11.62)	239 (32.67)		386 (52.71)	732 (100)
2006			174 (11.66)	60 (4.01)	76 (5.06)	1186 (79.27)	1496 (100)
2007	21 (0.34)	9 (0.35)	60 (2.48)	303 (12.48)		2053 (84.69)	2424 (100)
All years		16 (0.27)	319 (5.21)	939 (15.31)	101 (1.64)	4734 (77.23)	6130 (100)

Source: Adapted from Pradhan (2007).

Table 18.2   Number of overseas acquisitions by Indian firms

Year	Overseas acquisitions	Value ($ million)
2000	33	896
2001	23	188
2002	21	2536
2003	38	649
2004	44	2787
2005	135	3564
2006	177	7658
2007 (up to August)	123	32,858
All above years	594	51,136

Source: Adapted from Pradhan (2007).

Findings

The following are the findings of the study.

M&A Activity in India (1993–99)

Table 18.4 gives the segmentation in terms of the number of acquisitions and mergers in different timeframes in India and abroad. It also gives details about the M&A activity abroad.

Table 18.3   Top 10 acquisitions made by Indian firms worldwide

Acquirer	Target company	Country targeted	Deal value ($ml)	Industry
Tata Steel	Corus Group plc	UK	12,000	Steel
Hindalco	Novelis	Canada	5,982	Steel
Videocon	Daewoo Electronics Corp.	Korea	729	Electronics
Dr Reddy's Labs	Betapharm	Germany	597	Pharmaceutical
Suzlon Energy	Hansen Group	Belgium	565	Energy
HPCL	Kenya Petroleum Refinery Ltd	Kenya	500	Oil and Gas
Ranbaxy Labs	Terapia SA	Romania	324	Pharmaceutical
Tata Steel	Natsteel	Singapore	293	Steel
Videocon	Thomson SA	France	290	Electronics
VSNL	Teleglobe	Canada	239	Telecom

Source: Adapted from http://trak.in/tags/business/2007/08/16/indian-mergers-acquisitions-changing-indian-business/.

Table 18.4 Profile of mergers and acquisitions in India and abroad

Category	India (1993–96)	India (1997–99)	International (1995–96)
Number of M&As	80	323	270
Number of acquisitions	65 (81%)	251 (71%)	200 (74%)
Number of mergers	15 (19%)	72 (29%)	70 (26%)
Related M&As	64 (80%)	318 (99%)	193 (71%)
Unrelated M&As	16 (20%)	5 (1%)	77 (29%)

The total number of M&As has been increasing every year, though there is a change in the composition of the same. An analysis of M&A activity reveals that the number of acquisitions as a percentage of total M&A activity declined vis-à-vis the number of mergers. This is probably because many more Indian firms are restructuring themselves and are merging different group entities, which explains the increased number of mergers in the second phase. Basant (2000) also echoes a similar viewpoint when he suggests through his research that over 50 per cent of mergers in the 1990s were horizontal in nature. He also suggests that firms were consolidating operations. This is suggested as about 74 per cent of the merging companies belonged to the same business group. Over-diversification, resulting from earlier business strategies, is being corrected. In the pre-reform period, companies within the group often competed with each other for market share. The dominant pattern is, therefore, consolidation at the business of group levels to derive economies of scale, increase market share, reduce costs, achieve focus, and eliminate intra-group competition (Venkiteswaran 1997).

During 1995–96, the analysis of the M&A activity internationally reveals that 76 per cent of the activity was confined to US and Europe in the given sample. Asia and Australia comprised 19 per cent of the M&A activity and the balance was attributed to other countries. In line with the trends in India, acquisitions (74 per cent) were far higher than mergers (26 per cent). The related M&As (71 per cent) were far higher than unrelated M&As (29 per cent), which indicates a drive towards focusing on core competence.

Figure 18.2 reveals the value of the M&A activity worldwide.

The value of cross-border M&As completed in 2000 rose to $1.1 trillion, nearly 50 per cent higher than in 1999. Cross-border M&A has been a driving force behind the recent growth in FDI. According to the Securities Data Company, the year 1998 witnessed M&A deals worth $2.4 trillion worldwide, a 50 per cent increase on 1997, in itself a record (*The Economist* 1999). Figure 18.3 illustrates the trends in the growth of cross-border M&A.

1993–96 During this phase, some of the largest M&A were reported. Some of these are Brooke Bond with Hindustan Lever in April 1996, leading to the formation of the biggest food conglomerate in India. The merger of Whirlpool with Kelvinator in March 1996, SRF's acquisition of Ceat's nylon tyre cord division, Union Carbide's acquisition by BM Khaitan, and the Heinz takeover by Glaxo, are all examples in this category.

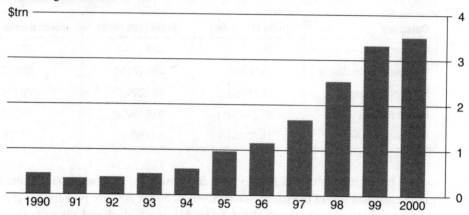

Source: Adapted from *The Economist* (2001).

Fig. 18.2　M&A activity worldwide

In this period 20 per cent of the M&A activity was in the consumer non-durable sector, in areas such as food, soaps, and cosmetics. The multinationals played a predominant role in acquiring the brand names, distribution strengths, and enhancing market shares. The next category was pharmaceuticals and chemicals, and the electrical and power segment.

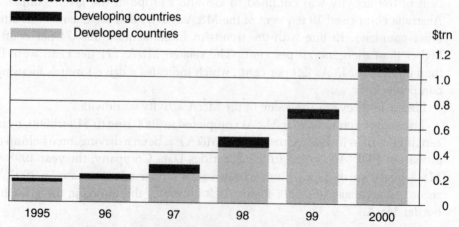

Source: Adapted from *The Economist* (2001).

Fig. 18.3　Cross-border acquisitions

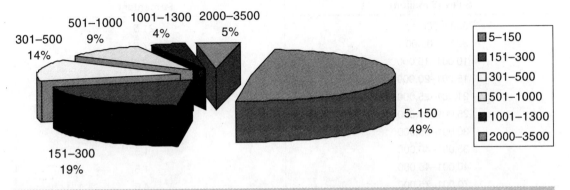

Pie chart representing distribution of companies involved in merger and acquisitions activity according to their sales turnover (Rs crore)

Fig. 18.4 Size of the companies involved in M&A activity

The distribution of the firms according to the size, which were involved in the M&A activity, is shown in Fig. 18.4.

Figure 18.4 indicates that about 49 per cent of the companies being taken over or merged with the acquiring company in the sample involved, have a sales turnover of less than Rs 150 crore (one crore equals 10,000,000). Only 19 per cent of the sample companies that have been taken over have their turnover between Rs 151 crore and Rs 300 crore. Ninety-five per cent of the M&A activity involves companies that have been merged or acquired with sales turnovers up to Rs 1,300 crore. Only 5 per cent of the companies have turnovers between 2,000 and 3,500 crore.

1994–95 International M&As

The world's largest firms involved in the M&A activity analysed here is Mitsubishi (1995 sales were $175.83 billion). The distribution of US firms involved in M&A activity during this period based on sales turnover is given in Table 18.5.

In 1995, an analysis carried out by the Securities Data Company revealed that 55 per cent of the M&As announced was attributed to just 41 deals or less than 1 per cent of the total number of deals. Since 1991, the deals valued at over $1 billion represent 45 per cent of domestic M&A activity in US.

Table 18.6 indicates the distribution of the M&A activity in different industrial segments.

Exhibit 18.1 presents an insight into the new M&A activities in India.

Reasons for M&A Activity

This section illustrates the reasons for M&A activity since the liberalization of the Indian economy.

Table 18.5 US companies involved in M&A activity (1994–95)

Sales ($ million)	Percentage
900–5000	21.5
5001–10,000	27.6
10,001–15,000	9.2
15,001–20,000	7.6
21,001–25,000	3
25,001–30,000	1.5
30,001–35,000	4.6
35,001–40,000	1.5
40,001–45,000	1.5
70,001–75,000	4.6
75,001–80,000	1.5

Table 18.6 Industry-wise distribution of M&A activity in India and worldwide

Sl. no.	Industry	Number of M&As in India				Number of M&As worldwide	
		1993–96	%	1997–99	%	1995–96	%
1	Consumer non-durables	16	20	29	9	15	7.1
2	Chemicals	8	10	100 (includes pharma)	31		
3	Pharmaceuticals	7	9			15	7.1
4	Textiles	5	6	15	5		
5	Consumer durables	4	5				
6	Engineering	4	5	29	9		
7	Electronics	4	5	24	7	34	16.1
8	Steel	4	5				
9	Automobiles	4	5	15	5	6	2.8
10	Group companies	4	5				
11	Power/Electricity	3	4	5	2	10	4.7
12	Packaging	3	4				
13	Energy	2	3				
14	Others	12	14	20	6	15	7
15	Finance			30	9	36	16.5
16	Entertainment/Media					15	9.5

Contd

Table 18.6 Contd

17	Telecom				10	3	7	3.3
18	Retail						9	4.2
19	Cement				14	5		
20	Marketing research				11	3		
21	Agribusiness				9	3		
22	Metals				12	4		

1993–96

In this phase, most of the M&A activity was restricted to the consumer non-durable and chemical sectors. After liberalization of the Indian economy, many MNCs started increasing their stakes in Indian companies.

During this phase, the major reasons were as follows:

Quest for market leadership   For example, Hindustan Lever Ltd (HLL) merged with Brooke Bond India Ltd. HLL bought brands such as Dollops from Cadbury's, Kissan products, tea estates, Doom Dooma Ltd, and Kwality and Milkfood's distribution assets were also taken over by HLL. Other examples are the takeover of Wiltech by ISPL and a stake in Damania Airlines by NEPC.

Expansion of portfolio   For example, the takeover of TOMCO by HLL which gave it a penetration into the lower end of the market in the soaps and cosmetics category; the acquisition of Tata's Lakme by HLL and the latter's merger with Ponds are also examples in this category.

Acquisition of brand names   The acquisition of oral hygiene unit Cibaca, owned by Hindustan Ciba Geigy by Colgate Palmolive in 1994–95, the acquisition of Eveready

---

Exhibit 18.1   M&A activities in India

'A rallying rupee and slowdown in the US may result in a number of overseas acquisitions by Indian companies such as Mahindra & Mahindra and Ranbaxy Laboratories.

Analysts believe that as the rupee appreciates it does become cheaper to acquire companies overseas.

Mahindra & Mahindra	Ranbaxy Laboratories	Tata Steel
Aims to expand its tractor making and auto parts business by buying overseas competitors or building plants. It plans to compete with Tata Motors to acquire British auto brands Jaguar and Land Rover.	It plans to acquire rivals in emerging markets. Takeovers aim to propel 20 per cent revenue growth next year.	Its acquisition of Corus accounted for almost a third of the record $39 billion of cross-border takeovers this year.

Source: Adapted from *Hindustan Times Business* (2007).

owned by Union Carbide by Williamson Magor group, and the acquisition of Lauffenmuehle by Arvind Mills are also examples in this category.

Access to new markets The takeover of Merind by Tata Pharma helped it to gain access to markets in North-east India and Russia. Titan bought a plant in Switzerland to have higher acceptability in European markets. Many Indian companies bought firms in US, which have helped them gain access to NAFTA partners, Canada and Mexico.

Encash upon new opportunities SRF, for instance, took over an ophthalmic lens plant, which does not bear synergy with its current tyre cord business.

Operational synergy Many firms took over other firms as it led to either backward or forward integration, e.g., the takeover of Sesa Goa by the Ruias, which led to operational synergy. The takeover of Lakme by HLL also led to access to Lakme's excellent distribution channel, which HLL could capitalize for its other consumer products as well.

The other acquisitions were takeovers of sick companies and group consolidations.

1997–99

Most of the mergers in this phase took place in the pharmaceutical segment. The number of M&As in this sector increased because there is a massive fragmentation in the industry with about 24,000 drug manufacturers, with the eight top players holding less than 30 per cent of the market share (Jauhari 2000). Of these, only 250 units were in the organized sector. The reason for this situation is the lack of product patents and price controls. The reason for higher M&A activity is the achievement of higher market share, acquisition of brand names, and wide portfolio of products.

During this phase, the reasons for M&As primarily remain the same as narrated earlier; only, the M&As became more expensive. Also, in 1996–98, FDI in India through the M&A route was $1.3 million. The global flow of FDI rose from $60 billion in 1985 to $350 billion in 1996. Out of that $275 billion was spent in M&As in 1996.

Worldwide, the highest number of M&As were taking place in the computer industry. The computer industry along with the electronics segment contributed to 16 per cent of the M&A activity. The other groups, which saw a considerable amount of M&A activity were the banking sector, food, and the pharmaceutical segment. This phase saw the merging of Pharmacia and UpJohn, Glaxo and Welcome, and Ciba Geigy and Sandoz leading to the formation of Novartis. As far as the numbers are concerned, there were more acquisitions and also related M&A was higher than unrelated. The top three bank mergers total nearly 6 per cent of the domestic volume in the commercial industry in the year 1995. The top bank mergers were:

- NBD Bancorp/First Chicago
- First Union Corp/First Fidelity Bancorp ($5.4 billion)
- Fleet Financial Group/Shahmut National Corporation
- Chase Manhattan/Chemical Banking ($10 billion)
- PNC BankCorp/MisAtlantic Corp ($3 billion)
- UJB FinancialCorp/Summit Bancorp ($1.2 billion)

- Fifth Third Bancorp/Kentucky enterprise ($64.3 million)
- National City Corp/Integra Financial Corp ($2.1 billion).

The figures in brackets indicate the cost of the acquisition of the second bank by the first. Davidson (1985) argues that there are ways other than mergers for a comprehensive financial institution to develop, but such ways are too difficult, unreasonably costly, or simply unnecessarily slow. The cost advantage of new institutions simultaneously requires nationwide credit profiles, full investment services, and large collection of funds to lend, and then mergers may be the only way for economic viability. Banks worldwide are realizing the greater need for a range of services, and also the newer business opportunities arising in the Asian region. They need to be of a large size in order to expand their operation, and hence the quest to become bigger in terms of their asset base. *The Economist* (1996) reveals that during the past two decades the global network of computers, telephones, and televisions has increased its information carrying capacity a million times over. Computing power doubles every 18 months or so in line with Moore's law. The technologies are converging. So electronics, telecommunication, and biotechnologies are converging, which is leading to a number of firms in these segments taking over to reap the benefits of synergy.

It can be deduced from the above examples, therefore, that the underlying reasons for the M&A activity in this segment can be consolidated as follows:

- To go in for complementary products, which help to expand the product portfolio.
- Helps satisfy the customer demand by providing a complete range of solutions.
- By virtue of making available a wide expanse of solution at a single point, it gives the customers also a competitive edge and enhances customer satisfaction.
- Access to better technology.
- Tapping new markets.
- To be known as the market leader in its area of operations.
- Maximization of investment.
- Consolidation of market situation.

However, in the post-liberalization phase some of the important reasons for M&A activity, as in 2008, are as follows:

- Globalization strategy adopted by many international firms and various economies inviting FDI.
- For similar developed economies market growth rate is stagnant, hence firms look for growth opportunities in emerging markets.
- Expanding product portfolios offering complete solutions.
- Access to new technologies as the time between various technologies is diminishing. The convergence of technologies is opening new doors of opportunities.
- Divestment in light of changed market scenarios, such as recession in US markets, has led to firms like Merrill-Lynch being acquired by Bank of America, and Morgan-Stanley being up for sale in 2008.

Conclusion

A KPMG report concluded that half of the mergers destroyed shareholder value and a further third made no difference (*The Economist* 2000). Study after study of past merger waves has shown that two out of every three deals have not worked; the only winners are the shareholders of the acquired firm, who sell their company for more than it is really worth (*The Economist* 1999). There are a number of considerations that need to be kept in mind while managing the M&A process.

The merger/acquisition is just the beginning of the real challenge. The signing or physical transfer of assets is just the tip of the iceberg. Integration of operations is extremely important. It is a simple fact, which is overlooked in most cases. For instance, the merger between Union Pacific and Southern Pacific in 1996 was supposed to deliver a seamless rail service and $800 million in annual savings by using Union Pacific's top-notch computer system. Aetna and US Healthcare had problems with combining the back office computer systems.

Managing Cultures

The managing of cultures between different merging entities is also extremely important. There are a number of issues which need to be addressed.

Sharing of power at the top   When two companies merge, decisions need to be taken regarding who will be at the helm of affairs at the top. This transition has to be smooth and in the interest of the organization. Also, several sensitive decisions need to be taken regarding which employees will stay and who will leave. An acquisition/merger is accompanied by a sense of fear in the employees about their survival in the organization. This leads to the management of another important aspect—the communication process.

Communication channels   These need to be set up right in the beginning. Asea Brown Boveri had handled the acquisition of ABL in India very well. Letters from the CEO had been sent to employees at ABL giving them information about the proposed change. Such communications instil a lot of confidence in employees. In contrast, the merger of Compaq with Digital was fraught with uncertainty and suspicion, and many employees from Digital left. Such a scenario can be devastating, as losing good employees is a far bigger loss.

Setting up a code of conduct   There can be differences in work cultures. These are more striking if a cross-border merger is involved. For instance, in the merger between Daimler and Chrysler, there was clearly a difference between the work styles. Chrysler liked to pride itself on a buccaneering approach, where speed and ingenuity is prized. The engineers, designers, and marketing people all worked together on each model. While Daimler has a more traditional chimney structure in which designers and marketing people mix less, and engineers are in charge.

Mergers should not be a strategy in their own right. Many mergers are undertaken in the name of cost cutting. A study by Anthony Santomero of the Wharton School examined the cost-cutting performance of banks in America and found that the merged banks had generally cut performance more slowly than their non-deal making peers.

Many companies went in for a merger as it was difficult to survive. McDonnell merged with Boeing as its biggest customer was cutting its spending to half. Chrysler merged with Benz as it was finding it hard to survive.

There are industry sectors where size matters. According to some estimates, an automobile maker has to produce a minimum of four million cars to survive (JETRO 2000). There has been substantial restructuring in recent years as a result of weak demand, over-capacity, and environmental pressures. In 1999, five automobile manufacturers in the world produced 30,637 units constituting 54 per cent of the world's production and the 10 largest manufacturers constituted 80 per cent of the world's total production (UNCTAD 2000).

In the banking sector, the largest 25 banks measured by assets, accounted for 33 per cent of the assets of the 1000 largest banks in 1999, compared with 28 per cent in 1996. The abolition of the Glass Stegall Act in US in 1999 dismantled the wall between banking and securities. Deregulation and the introduction of the single currency in the European Union, financial liberalization in Japan, and restructuring of banking in countries affected by financial crisis, all contributed to large scale M&As (*Banker* 2000).

In the pharmaceutical industry, costs for expensive R&D and to derive synergies have been the driving force for acquisitions. All large pharmaceutical firms have grown bigger in size through the M&A activity rather than through organic growth. In 1999, the top five and ten largest TNCs accounted for 28 and 46 per cent of the world sales of pharmaceutical products, respectively, compared to 19 and 33 per cent, respectively, in 1995 (*The Financial Times* 1997).

However, despite the talk of a lot of activity taking place in the domain of M&A, one needs to look at its total contribution in the world economy. In developing countries, the advantage of M&As is rarely access to proprietary technology or skills. The advantage lies more in rapid market entry, local market knowledge, established distribution systems, and contacts with the government, suppliers, or customers (*World Investment Report* 2000). In cross-border mergers/acquisitions, the acquisition offers saving of time as compared to setting up a green field venture along with other reasons advocated earlier. However, from a developing country's perspective, foreign acquisitions do not add to productive capacity but simply transfer ownership and control from domestic to foreign hands accompanied by laying-off employees, or closing production or functional activities. However, any country where M&As are being looked at, should also take into account the development priorities of the country. Not only the financial implications, but other social and cultural implications must also be weighed when evaluating a merger/acquisition (Exhibit 18.2).

STRATEGIC ALLIANCES

Global networking, partnership alliances, and information sharing are utilized by world-class organizations. Alliances enable companies to focus on their core skills and competencies (Thompson 1995). Globalization and technology are changing the nature of business like never before. Both technology and globalization are intimately linked. By reducing the costs of communication, IT has helped to globalize production and

---

Exhibit 18.2 Air India–Indian Airlines merger

As the costs pertaining to airlines increase, the merger between Air India and Indian Airlines, two major national carriers, will help both to rationalize costs by synergizing their operations. Apart from savings in terms of separate offices and manpower, the inventories, engineering, and IT areas can also be combined and can lead to large savings.

As crude oil prices are at an all-time high, airlines in India are facing turbulent times. Apart from this, airport and hotel charges and manpower costs, especially for pilots and engineers, are also part of the problem. To add to the problem, air travel became more and more affordable with the entry of several low-cost carriers such as Spice Jet and Indigo, among others. Through the latter, the government aimed to increase capacity into India but tried to solve the problem of over-capacity by selling below cost. New National Aviation Company of India Ltd (NACIL) continued to use older aircraft, which is not the right way to attract customers in a highly competitive environment. If the earlier governments had allowed the airlines to renew their fleets, the hardware problem could have been resolved. The software issue is basically associated with the operation of separate networks of domestic and international passengers. The two domestic carriers, Air India and Indian Airlines competed with each other rather than collaborate. There is now an opportunity for both entities to cooperate and work together to provide better services for the passengers. Though the process will not be easy and there will be disagreements and issues, one should consider this as a part and parcel of the merger process, and find innovative solutions to overcome the same. The success of the merger depends on a shared vision of overcoming individual issues and looking at the larger picture. When that happens, not only will Indian aviation gain, but so will all the employees of the national carrier.

Source: Adapted from http://www.blonnet.com/2008/07/02/stories/2008070251050900.htm (2008).

---

financial markets. In turn, globalization spurs technology by intensifying competition and by speeding up the diffusion of technology through FDI. Together, globalization and IT crush time and space. During the past two decades the global network of computers, telephones, and televisions has increased its information carrying capacity a million times over. Today, a $2000 laptop is more powerful compared to a $10 million mainframe computer in the mid-1970s. A fibre optic cable can carry 1.5 million conversations, whereas a transatlantic telephone cable could carry only 138 conversations simultaneously. No communication medium has grown as fast as the Internet. Anybody with a computer, a modem, and a telephone can teleshop, telebank, and telelearn, 24 hours a day.

Traditionally, the concept of the firm came in because different functions had to be co-ordinated. Ronald Coase, a Nobel prize-winning economist in 1937, asked why workers were organized in firms instead of acting as independent buyers and sellers of goods and services at each stage of production. He concluded that firms were needed because of the lack of information and the need to minimize transaction costs. A world without firms, in which production was organized entirely through markets, would require full information and no transaction costs; but in the real world it takes time and money to find out about the product being bought and sold. A firm resolves these problems. The size of firms is determined by the relative costs of buying in services from outside and the overhead cost of providing them in-house. For instance, a car firm can either make the tyres itself or buy them from a supplier. The tyres will probably cost less if bought in the competitive marketplace, but some of this saving may be offset by higher transaction and coordination costs. The higher these costs are, the greater the likelihood that firms will find it more profitable to provide services internally, which will increase their size. However, IT—in the form of e-mail, Internet, fax machine, and computerized billing—reduces these costs, and so increases the attraction of buying goods and services from outside. As these costs fall, the traditional logic of the firm becomes less persuasive. All kinds of goods and services can be outsourced and many employees replaced by outsiders, linked by electronic networks. In this way, IT encourages vertically integrated corporate giants like AT&T to break themselves up into smaller more efficient firms loosely connected by networks. Two opposing forces are therefore at work. In industries such as software and entertainment, where network externalities are powerful, IT will favour a greater concentration of business to exploit larger economies of scale, so the firm will tend to increase in size. Elsewhere, falling communications costs will favour de-centralization and one would see the emergence of a lot of strategic alliances.

Another factor driving the concept of strategic alliances is customer focus. Organizations are now focusing on providing complete solutions rather than offering isolated products. For instance, Kodak, Intel, and Canon have little in common except digital technology, but they can all come together to provide a complete solution to the customer. Kodak can click pictures, Intel can process them using the microprocessor, and Canon can make multiple copies using its photocopiers. There are also some other reasons which lead to strategic alliances. For instance, Bowersox (1991) points out the forces for impetus for strategic alliances.

- The political legal terrain of the 1980s stimulated the development of integrated-services practices. Deregulation of transportation and communications, coupled with relaxed anti-trust enforcement—intended to give productivity a change—generated an atmosphere conducive to innovation.
- The explosion in IT has made computerization cheap and computers hold logistic alliances together.
- Today's emphasis on lean organizations (cost conscious and focussing on areas of expertise) makes managers more likely to turn to external specialists to solve problems or perform tasks outside the organization's sphere of expertise. The objective of competing more effectively—through greater asset utilization, higher leverage, and faster responsiveness—is a prime stimulant towards logistic collaboration.
- An escalating competitive environment forces the players to do all they can to become lowest cost competitors. Efficiency in logistics is particularly important for companies that are doing business abroad.

Strategic Alliances—The Concept

Different researchers have delved upon various aspects of strategic alliances. Some of them have propounded a specific definition while others have deliberated upon the form of manifestation of strategic alliances. The different perceptions are outlined in Table 18.7.

Table 18.7 Perceptions on strategic alliances

Author	Year	Definition/Manifestation
Forest and Martin	1988	Strategic alliances could take a form of operational joint venture, equity investment, client sponsored research contract, marketing distribution agreement, research institute agreement, collaborative R&D, R&D Limited partnership, and technology licensing.
Thomson	1990	Strengthening of competitiveness in terms of technology, cost, or marketing with an aim to increasing competitive advantage without either merger or acquisition, primarily because of inherent problems. Thompson has cited six categories of strategic alliances—mergers, new business, development of business jointly, special agreement between marketers and their suppliers, making strategic investment in another firm, and international trading partnerships.
Bowersox	1991	Has delved upon logistic alliances: ▫ extended organization ▫ concentration of relationship continuum instead of series of single transactions ▫ combine resources of service providers ▫ vertical alignment between two or more proprietary markets ▫ horizontal alignment of product marketers.
Mohr and Spekman	1994	Firms comprising the alliance share costs, risks, and benefits of exploring and undertaking new business opportunities.
Orsino	1994	Alliances with supplier, horizontal integration, new product or market access, and mutual marketing relationship.
Raphael et al.	1995	Classifies the types of alliances as machine, entrepreneurial, complementary, and customer partnerships.
Luffman	1996	Type of business partnerships in which the firms concerned, each of which retains its own corporate identity, provides its partners with particular skills, competencies, and resources for their mutual benefit. It can also involve equity investments.
Wright et al.	1996	Define strategic alliances as partnerships in which two or more firms carry out a specific project or cooperate in selected areas of business. According to them, the strategic alliances can take one of the following forms—joint ventures, franchising, licensing, joint operations, joint long-term supplier agreement, joint marketing agreement, and consortium.
Rangan and Yoshino	1996	An arrangement that links specific facets of the business of two or more firms. The basis of the link is a trading partnership that enhances the effectiveness of the participating firms' competitive strategies by providing for mutually beneficial exchange of technologies, products, skills, or other types of resources. They suggest that strategic alliances simultaneously possess the three following characteristics: (1) Two or more firms that unite to pursue a set of agreed upon goals, yet remain independent subsequent to the formation of the alliance. (2) The partners share control over the performance of assigned tasks associated with the alliance and in the benefits derived from it. (3) The partners contribute on a continuing basis to the alliance.
Dacin and Levitas	1997	Strategies for firms from multiple countries to share risks and resources, to gain knowledge, and to obtain access to new markets.
Das and Teng	1997	Inter-firm cooperative arrangements aimed at pursuing mutual strategic goals, e.g., joint ventures, joint R&D, product swap, equity investment, sharing, licensing, and others. They do not consider internalization, including M&As, as a strategic alliance.

Contd

Table 18.7 Contd

| Harrigan | 1998 | Diversification by strategic alliance refers to arrangements in which corporations join forces to form a cooperative partnership. Typically, neither company owns the other, though often they create a third commercial entity usually referred to as a joint venture, that they co-own. |
| www.Business Dictionary.com, Web Finance, Inc. | 2008 | Agreement for cooperation among two or more independent firms to work together towards common objectives. Unlike in a joint venture, firms in a strategic alliance do not form a new entity to further their aims, but collaborate while remaining apart and distinct. |

Table 18.7 provides an insight into the concept and views of the various researchers on strategic alliances. It is observed that strategic alliances are seen as distinctly separately from the M&A activity. It could be seen as a step towards strengthening of competitiveness, sharing of risks and resources, gaining knowledge, obtaining an access to new markets and technology, and carrying out a new project. It has also been seen as a partnership in which each partner retains his own individual identity. Joint ventures are seen to be a manifestation of strategic alliances. Thompson, however, in contrast to the others does considers mergers to be a manifestation of strategic alliance.

Rangan and Yoshino (1996) base their premise for analysis of alliances on the argument that an alliance-seeking firm acts in two dimensions—cooperation and competition—that generally play out as cooperation and conflict. They examine the strategic alliances on four dimensions:

1. Flexibility
2. Protection of core competencies
3. Learning
4. Value addition

Burton (1995) delves into two paradigms of business strategy—competition and collaboration. In the competitive paradigm, he credits Porter (1980) who in the conduct of business strategy equated it with execution of competitive strategy and achievement of sustainable advantage for the business. The alternative paradigm emphasizes the positive role of cooperative arrangements between industry and participants, and the consequent importance of what Kanter (1994) termed collaborative advantage, as a foundation of superior business performance. Burton has propounded that an all or nothing choice between a single-minded striving for either competitive or collaborative advantage would be a false one. The real strategic choice problem that all businesses face is where (and how much) to collaborate and where (and how intensely) to act competitively. He has provided a framework of analysis to explore issues concerning the coherence of the firm's composite strategy. It seeks to overcome the one-sided application of the competitive strategy model, which can lead the firm down strategic routes that do not optimize its overall advantage.

A study carried out by McKinsey examined the partnerships of 150 top companies—50 each from the US, Europe, and Japan. Of these, 49 cross-border strategic alliances were studied in detail. This study was published in HBR in 1991, and was reprinted in the 1993 book, *Collaborating to Compete,* edited by McKinsey consultant Joel Bleeke. The major findings are as follows:

- Alliances between strong and weak companies usually do not work because they do not provide the skills needed for growth. This leads to mediocre performance.
- The hallmark of lasting alliances is their ability to grow beyond the initial goals. For this, ventures need autonomy and flexibility.
- Alliances with equal financial partnerships are more likely to succeed than those in which one partner has a majority interest.
- Clear management control is what matters more than financial ownership.
- More than 75 per cent of the alliances that terminated ended with an acquisition by one of the partners.
- The hallmark of successful alliances is their ability to evolve beyond initial expectations and objectives.
- Corporate partnerships with an even or nearly even financial stake are more likely to succeed than those in which one partner holds a majority interest. Nearly 65 per cent of the joint ventures that had partners with different geographic strengths, succeeded. The story is different in cross-border acquisitions where the success rate was just 9 per cent, when the acquiree and the target company did not have significant overlapping in the same geographic markets.

Forms of Alliances in India

Alliances in India take one of the following forms:

- marketing tie-ups
- operations handling
- joint ventures
- technology licensing
- manufacturing
- MoUs
- services
- supply
- setting up a new business.

There is, however, no data to support that a particular form of alliance will be more successful than others. The alliance may or may not involve an equity stake. In joint ventures there is certainly an equity stake, which makes each of the partners more responsible and hence there is a greater sense of commitment. However, in India there is a lot of problem with joint ventures. One of the reasons is the level of liberalization, which has removed restrictions from a lot of industrial segments as a result of which many foreign companies that earlier were going in for joint ventures prefer to set up a 100 per cent subsidiary.

Breaking a Strategic Alliance

The number of newly forged alliances has been growing at more than 25 per cent annually in recent years (Bleeke and Ernst 1995). The failure rate of these alliances has been consistently very high (Parkhe 1991). Inter-firm trust, managerial coordination, and opportunistic behaviour of the partners, are just a few issues that complicate the management of these alliances (Alexander 1995).

A lot of reasons emerge as being a case for breaking these alliances. Some of these are:

- consolidation of business
- increase in stake by the foreign partner
- cash crunch
- difference in business priorities
- change of business focus
- lack of trust
- lack of ability to stick to the deadlines
- government policy
- mismatch of corporate cultures.

Dacin et al. (1997) remark that approximately 50–60 per cent of alliances formed are unsuccessful in accomplishing the partners' objectives. Besides the inherent risk, one of the most often cited reasons for alliance failure is the incompatibility of partners. The choice of the right partner can yield important competitive benefits, whereas the failure to establish compatible objectives can lead to insurmountable problems. Corning Glass Works, which has developed numerous successful strategic alliances, has undertaken a long courtship with potential partners to assess their motives and the quality of their management as one of its guiding principles in selecting partners (Slocum and Lei 1993).

Dacin et al. (1997) identify the following reasons for incomplete agreement on alliance objectives:

- cultural heritage
- level of economic development.

On one hand, partners from developed countries look to partners from developing countries to provide access to local knowledge, including customs and business practices, political connections, as well as the ability to satisfy the host government's foreign investment requirements. On the other hand, partners from lesser developed or developing countries seek access to technology, export opportunities, and an opportunity to gain international alliance experience. Thus, partners differ by level of economic development, motives for setting up alliances, and expected benefits (Beamish 1988, 1994). Differences in government support and foreign policies can influence the alliance process.

The difference in value systems too has an impact on the nature of an alliance. For instance, the US has a cultural heritage based on rugged individualism and belief in free market, whereas Korean culture is strongly influenced by Confucian ideology. It has been suggested that Koreans are less egocentric than the Americans; Korean's standards of success and failure are more closely associated with the approval or disapproval of others than with inner personal standards or goals, more common among Americans (Brandt 1987). Korean managers have a stronger long-term orientation than

US managers (Kim et al. 1990). Korean culture is more concerned with the interests of the community. In Korea, state run capitalism operates with a vast network of institutionally defined relationships between business and government. Korean managers have had to develop the requisite partnering skills needed to be effective in collaborative ventures. In sharp contrast, there is a clear separation between private business and public government in the US. There have been few attempts by the US government to foster industry. Relations between government, business, and labour are often adversarial (Lodge and Crum 1985).

Way to Go Ahead with Alliances

The following are the recommendations which seem to emerge:

- There is a greater need to have an objective before going in for an alliance.
- There is also a need for assessing the strengths and contributions by both the partners.
- There is a need for ensuring a cultural match between the different partners involved in the alliance.
- There needs to be a commitment from all the partners involved in the alliance, and the roles of the partners must be clearly identified.
- A level of trust needs to be built up between the partners. This can only be done if the business processes are documented, the procedures for decision-making are fair, and financial transactions are transparent. Financial irregularities can be disastrous for the partnership.
- Indian companies also need to put their value systems in place. Unless that happens, no amount of technical excellence can really lead to an improvement in the working of any enterprise. As Ghosal (1999) points out arrogance, lack of respect for individual dignity—one's own and that of others—an opportunistic relationship with employees within the organization and with customers and suppliers can be detrimental in the long run. These companies must commit to a process of shaping and embedding a new set of values within their organizations.
- If equity stakes are involved then the level of commitment becomes higher and there is a greater degree of seriousness in the venture.
- Both the partners must ensure a greater degree of value addition.
- There should also be a clear identification of critical success factors in the alliance.
- When forming alliances between international partners the differences in culture, infrastructure, and economic development and government policies should be incorporated (Dacin et al. 1997).
- Certain variables should be avoided when choosing a partner for strategic alliance. Alliances should not be formed to correct a weakness because the weaker party ends up at the mercy of the stronger, e.g., GM's alliance with Toyota. GM entered the alliance with an inability to manufacture high quality cars. Ten years later, GM was still not able to strengthen the weakness.
- Proprietary technology should not be licensed. Sony acquired transistor technology from Bell Labs for a small price of $25,000 and there are literally no radio manufacturers in US.

Some of the aforementioned aspects will help to sustain the alliance for a longer time. Alliances will be formed as there is a trend towards subcontracting activities in which the organization does not have core competencies. The duration of the alliance, however, depends on the degree of trust and adjustments, which both the partners are willing to make.

FRANCHISING

Franchising is one of the many ways in which a business can grow. It is being adopted by a number of businesses and has led to an emergence of international brand names such as Wimpy, Kentucky Fried Chicken, Coca Cola, Pepsi, and retail chains such as Pierre Cardin, Benetton, Van Heusen, and Bata.

The following sections attempt to explain the concept of franchising, the advantages it offers to the franchiser (one who owns the brand), and the franchisee (one who buys the business concept and the brand name from the franchiser). It also elaborates upon the relationship of franchising with entrepreneurship and the franchising trends in India.

Organizations have to find new mechanisms for growth from time to time. Different organizations have gone in for different strategies for growth. Franchising has emerged as one such strategy for growth among other prevalent activities. It is a way of expansion of one's business after establishment of a brand name, by lending it for a royalty on sales. On a macro-level, franchising can serve to widen the entrepreneurial base of the country. It is a concept, by virtue of which one invests one's own money for buying an established brand name for selling a particular product or service, to become a part of a retail chain or an established business but retain the ownership of the business. It, therefore, gives an entrepreneur access to an established business format, thereby reducing the chances for failure.

Bidlake (1990) remarks that franchising is gaining an increasingly respectable image as more large professional companies use it as a route to rapid expansion with low capital outlay. Franchising has been adopted as the predominant route for expansion by firms such as Kentucky Fried Chicken, McDonald's, Bennetton, Holiday Inn, and Wimpy, to name a few international giants, in their area of operation. Jarillo (1993), for instance, traces the emergence of the Kentucky Fried Chicken chain, which was started in 1956, when an old native of Kentucky, Colonel Saunders started selling to some of his friends the right to open restaurants to cook and sell a chicken dish after a Southern recipe, which he had perfected in the previous 20 years. Just eight years later, he presided over the entrance of 700 Kentucky Fried Chicken restaurants throughout the world, selling the same menu to the same standards. This is what is called franchising. Orsino (1994) writes that franchises are built on the premise of superseding regional differences—no matter where you travel across the country, when you go to a franchise operation you know exactly what to expect in terms of quality, pricing, and service. Uniformity and predictability are paramount.

Franchising is one of the most creative of the various marketing techniques. The key to a successful franchise operation is a strong system. It is a system that provides the appearance that all outlets belong to a chain, the know-how to franchisees to keep one step ahead of the competition, and abundant opportunities to all who want to fulfil the dream of owning ones own business.

Definition

Franchising is a system or method of marketing a product or service, wherein the franchiser who has developed a special product service or system that has gained national recognition grants a right or license to small independent businessmen throughout the country to merchandise this service or product under the national trademark and in accordance with a proven successful format. This increases the franchiser's exposure to more national business and gives the franchise a greater chance for success in a given field with a smaller amount of capital investment.

The franchise system of distribution is a significant part of the US economy and is viewed as a dynamic, growing, business activity, increasingly accepted and respected by the public, all levels of the government, and by the business community. It has become a powerful force because of the following reasons (Ayling 1988):

- overcomes shortage of capital
- overcomes high interest rates
- attracts highly motivated operators
- fast growth of operating units
- greater market penetration.

Franchising also offers advantages to the person who buys an existing franchise, i.e., the franchisee. Pecenko (1993) elaborates it as follows:

Data from the US illustrate that after one year in business, 97 per cent of franchisees are successful business operators, as compared to a 62 per cent rate in the case of fully independent entrepreneurs. After five years of franchise operation, 92 per cent of the participants observed are still successful, compared to only 23 per cent of the independents. Entrepreneurs, when going in for a franchise operation as a franchisee, find it less risky to enter the market due to the following circumstances:

- The enterprise concerned starts an already established business.
- Consumers are accustomed to franchiser-sold products.
- The entrepreneur concerned is assisted by his franchiser throughout the creation of the new company and later on in its operation.
- The entrepreneur gets access to fields of activity too expensive to venture into on his own (due to R&D and/or promotional costs).
- The entrepreneur may also get access to foreign funds when needed, since he has become part of an already established business organization.

The word franchising is derived from a French verb '*franchir*', which means 'to free' (used in the context to express freedom from servitude or restraint) (Hall and Dixon 1989). The definition of franchising as given by the International Franchising Association is: 'A franchise operation is a contractual relationship between the franchiser and the franchisee in such areas as know-how and training, wherein the franchisee operates under a common trade name, format, and procedures, owned or controlled by the franchiser, and in which the franchisee has or will make a substantial capital investment in his business from his own resources.' Ayling (1988) mentions that the definitions for franchising given by International Franchise Association and British Franchise Association have a number of things in common:

- There must be a legal contract outlining the terms and obligations agreed between franchiser and franchisee.
- The franchiser must initiate and train the franchisee in all aspects of his business prior to its opening.
- After the franchisee's business has opened, the franchiser will continue to provide him with support in all aspects of the operation.
- The franchisee is permitted, under the control of the franchiser, to operate under a particular brand name, business format, and procedure, and with the benefit of the goodwill generated by the franchiser.
- The franchisee will be required to make a substantial capital investment from his own resources.
- The franchisee will own his business.
- The franchisee will pay the franchiser for the rights he acquires, through the front-end 'license fee' and ongoing management services fees for continuing support.
- The franchiser will generally grant the franchisee a geographical territory and/or a vertical market sector in which to operate.

Hall and Dixon (1989) have delved upon some of the prerequisites to expand through franchising:

- The business must be capable of standardization.
- It must have a unique selling point.
- There should be a relatively high profit margin.
- It should be simple for the franchisees to operate.

For franchising effectively, the following are some of the essential points to observe. To set up the franchise, the franchiser will have to:

- market the franchise
- set up at least one pilot operation
- have sufficient capital and skills to support the network
- draw up a comprehensive operating manual
- draw up a detailed contract
- select suitable franchisees
- train them and give continuing assistance.

The franchise operation accompanied by complete business management assistance is called *business format franchising*.

Scope of Franchising

Looking at the present trends in the US, it seems that franchising can be attempted with nearly any type of business. Perhaps, more than any other method of marketing, franchising has reflected the demographic changes in society as well as the prosperous economic climate of recent years.

However, the Indian scenario is very different. In India, it all started in the soft drink industry with Coca Cola, in 1954. The soft drink industry is one area where franchising has really worked well; the other being bakery, as illustrated earlier. For example, Parle had 60 franchisees in India and 14 abroad. It was the leading soft drink industry in India.

In the soft drink industry Pure Drinks, UB group, and the Pepsi Company have all taken up franchising. Of these, UB and Pure Drinks have not been able to create a strong foothold. In the bakery industry, MFIL has a very strong foothold. It has a good system of franchising which has proven to be a success. Britannia, Spencer's, and Bakeman's had also undertaken franchising, though Bakeman's moved out of the bread industry and restricted itself to biscuits and other confectionery items.

Franchising has been adopted as a route to growth by many firms operating in India such as Archies, McDonald's, Dominos Pizza, NEXT Stores, Ferns and Petals, NIIT, schools such as Delhi Public School, hotel brands such as Radisson, Country Inns and Suites, and Park Plazas.

LICENSING

Licensing is also one of the corporate entrepreneurial activities undertaken by organizations for growth. There are organizations, which do not have the resources to develop their own technology. Ramu (1995) remarks that many MNCs use licensing for entry into foreign markets. There may be factors such as:

- prohibition of FDI
- absence of a large market
- scale not being attainable
- general lack of interest in international operations
- limited availability of resources.

He has talked about four forms of licensing:

- basic licensing
- management contract
- franchising
- contract manufacturing.

Basic Licensing

Here, an organization allows another firm to use its technology, patents, or trade-marks for a fee.

Management Contract

This entails the responsibility for the operation of one enterprise by another. The latter takes over the responsibility of management and training of personnel. This is primarily a non-market relationship.

Kotabe et al. (1996) identify technology licensing as a step toward or an alternative to wholly-owned subsidiaries. They remark that the recent trends in technology licensing indicate that it is used increasingly as a conscious, proactive, component of a technology-based firm's global product strategy. Barney (1991) mentions that the resource-based view of the firm implies that technology is a combination of physical, capital, and organizational capital resources. The firm uses such resources to gain sustained competitive advantage. Recent anecdotal evidence such as Philips, Matsushita's Digital Compact (Kotabe 1992), and Motorola's licensing of proprietary microprocessor technology to Toshiba (Hamel et al. 1989), implies that technology licensing is being used as an explicit, proactive element of the firms' global market strategy. This includes the use of technology licensing as a tactic to achieve rapid market penetration (Lei and Slocum 1991), a means of established standards (Hagedoorn 1993), and a method of amortizing R&D costs (Ohmae 1989).

In India, there are a lot of licensing agreements under various kinds of technology transfer agreements. Dubey (1996) examines the use of Sierra Industrial Enterprises, which have snapped up a license in 1996 for representing the $5.6 billion Beaverton (US)-based Nike in India. Nike has adopted the licensing route, which only involves lending its brand name designs and marketing experience in return for a fee amounting to 5 per cent of sales, net of tax.

Sierra has further entered into a sourcing arrangement with Moja Shoes, a company floated by US-based non-resident Indians Dilip Mathur, Mahesh Nathani, and Ravi Akhori. Sierra has also forged alliances with 20 small units in and around Delhi, Bangalore, and Ludhiana for sourcing apparel and sports accessories.

Management Contracts in the Hotel Industry

The management contract is a business format which separates ownership from operation. In the hotel industry, it has provided the opportunity for much-needed capital to fund the demand for new construction in world markets, while creating the vehicle for hotel management companies to expand their networks and market shares with reduced exposure to investment and political risks. The growth in contacts has also been driven by hotel owners; the need for experienced and established operators for their own peace of mind and to satisfy investors' demands.

There is no standard definition of a hotel management contract; however, it is usually defined as a formal arrangement under which the owner of a hotel employs the services of an operator to act as his or her agent to provide professional management of the hotel, in return for a fee. The operator assumes full responsibility for the management of the business, while the ultimate legal and financial responsibilities, and rights of ownership of the property, its furniture, and equipment, its working capital, and the benefits of its profits (or burden of its losses) remain those of the owner. The owner may be a private individual, a financial institution, a real estate company, or a government. The operator is most likely to be an established hotel chain offering marketing strength, brand names, bargaining power, systems and procedures, project design and management, technical services, training, and management development. However, the rate of growth in the number of independent hotel management companies is increasing; these include groups that do not have their own international brand and reservations system, and who operate hotels for a variety of owners.

The owner usually seeks an effective return; the contractor an effective earnings stream. Typically, the fee structure is in two parts: a base fee of around 3 per cent of hotel turnover and an achievement fee of around 10 per cent of gross operating profit or earnings before debt, interest, and tax (EBDIT).

Economic changes impacting upon the hotel industry, accelerated competition among operators worldwide, and greater performance demands by owners and lenders, are leading to adjustments in contract provisions and increased owner bargaining strength.

Management Contracts in the Food Service Industry

A management contracting arrangement, relevant to this industry sector, is defined by Sharma (1984) as 'An arrangement under which operational control of an enterprise, which would otherwise be exercised by the directors and managers appointed or elected by its owners, is vested by contract in a separate enterprise that performs the necessary management functions for a fee'. This fee may be made up in several ways. These include a straight fee; one linked to the turnover of the business; one in which purchasing discounts are returned to the client organization to offset against the fee; or a combination of the above. It is not uncommon for contractors to gain as much income from purchase discounts obtained, but not passed on to the clients, as it earns from the fees charged. This will result in local management following a strict policy of using authorized suppliers in order to maximize such discount earnings to the contracting organization. Contracts are usually of the following types, or may be a combination, dependent upon the nature of the client's business:

- management fee (sometimes called 'cost plus')
- fixed costs
- full cost recovery (nil cost)
- commercial return
- guaranteed performance
- an increasing trend is for contractors to offer a range of services in addition to catering, such as office cleaning, and accommodation and grounds maintenance, which will save the client having to deal with several different organizations for different services. Therefore, the term 'food service' may be too narrow.

Most of these business formats have implications for the organizational and operational tie between the hospitality firm and the unit or subsidiary, particularly related to the degree of control. The formats chosen depend upon whether the business is based on assets or cash flow.

All these forms of growth put a strain on the head office organization in terms of the extent and range of support services offered. All methods stretch the managerial and operational capabilities of the firm. However, they do make contractors and franchisers quite different types of competitors.

CHOICE OF EMERGING FORMS OF ENTREPRENEURSHIP

As discussed in the previous section, a firm can choose between a range of options. The choice of these strategies may depend on numerous factors. These may depend, for instance, on the resources of the firm. A resource-intensive firm will like to expand through green field ventures. It may also license its brand name. Franchising offers opportunities to the firm wherein the resource constraints are taken care of by franchisees making their own incentives. Mergers and acquisitions help to give access to established businesses, which help to enhance market share or quick access to complementary services. However, the culture match offers a huge challenge to the success of the merger. Outsourcing helps to manage costs better. Information technology enabled services are being increasingly outsourced. India is emerging as a very strong destination for outsourcing of ITES. Outsourcing helps firms to focus on core competencies and to outsource certain functions. The outsourced businesses range from very simple tasks such as call centre management, data entry, and customer processes, to high-end research-based functions.

Technology helps to go in for outsourcing solutions, especially in the case of managed services through the use of IT. Firms that offer outsourcing services also adopt specific strategies wherein they work for one major firm as an in-house outsourced services or another firm which deals with multiple vendors.

There is no unique recommended strategy. The strategy depends on the context, market, resource access, and long-term situational advantage. The success of a strategy lies in implementation and control. Great strategies will not turn into a success in reality, if the implementation is flawed.

SUMMARY

This chapter analyses the strategic options available to a firm for expansion of their operations. There are numerous strategies which a firm can adopt—green field ventures, joint ventures, franchising, strategic alliances, and M&As, among others. There are advantages and disadvantages in each case. A green field venture option is time consuming and tedious but has advantages of a fresh start and does not come along with cultural baggage. However, the time taken to start the operation varies from state to state and also across various countries. Merger and acquisitions may be a faster route for growth. However, in this case there may be challenges with regard to the culture of the two firms, and also the actual financial situation and competencies of firms in question. The time for an acquisition/merger may depend on the legal environment in a country. However, in this decade, Indian firms have been very aggressive about identifying firms abroad, and steel plants, automobile manufacturing, IT firms, research-based firms, pharmaceutical operations, etc., have been acquired by Indian entrepreneurs. This has been facilitated by a changing legal environment, which governs the M&A activity. The airlines sector has also seen M&A activity on account of a better coverage of geography and economies of scale.

Franchising in India has also seen tremendous growth across various segments such as hotels, restaurants, schools, and retailing. It is a quick way of getting access to a brand and

Contd

Summary Contd

standardizing one's operations. However, a pilot operation is essential before embarking upon franchising as a strategy for growth.

Strategic alliances also have been witnessing lot of growth and there are several manifestations of these alliances—manufacturing, marketing, R&D, supply chain, etc. There are challenges like agreement on terms by the partners and also, levels of trust play an important role.

To conclude, there is no best strategy that can be suggested. The choice of a strategy depends on the context, types of firms involved, investment, and timeframe in consideration.

KEY TERMS

Acquisitions   The act of contracting, assuming, or acquiring possession of something.

Entrepreneurship   The assumption of risk and responsibility in designing and implementing a business strategy or starting a business.

Franchising   A system, in which a license is given to a manufacturer, distributor, trader, etc. to enable them to manufacture or sell a named product or service, in a particular area, for a stated period.

Green field ventures   A green field venture is a firm, which has been started from scratch. It is a new venture creation by bringing in capital, land, and labour.

Management contracts   The practice in which a domestic firm supplies the management know-how to a foreign company that provides the capital in order to create a joint venture.

Mergers   A combination of two or more businesses on a relatively equal footing that results in the creation of a new reporting entity.

Strategic alliances   Agreements between two or more firms to engage in an activity on a shared basis. The outside activities of each partner are not affected by the alliance, which is designed to build on the expertise of each.

Strategic management   The process of managing, in a way that is consistent with the corporate strategy or in such a way as to capitalize on the opportunities that present themselves.

Strategy   Growth of the business considering the vision, and matching the external environmental dynamics with the internal resource base of the organization.

CONCEPT REVIEW QUESTIONS

1. What are the alternate strategies for growth, which service firms can adopt?

2. In a financially constrained situation, which is a better strategy to adopt—franchising or acquisition?

3. Critically analyse strategic alliances as a strategy for growth of a service firm.

4. Evaluate the advantages and disadvantages of setting up green field ventures.

CRITICAL THINKING QUESTIONS

1. A small entrepreneur is making an investment of Rs 50 crore in setting up a restaurant. What alternatives should he evaluate before venturing from a strategic perspective?

2. Franchising a brand has its advantages and disadvantages. Take the case of a successful and an unsuccessful enterprise, which opted for franchising. Identify reasons for the

success and failure of franchising as a strategy for each enterprise.

3. A small restaurant owner offering Indian cuisine is running his business in an upbeat mall in South Delhi. He wants to expand his brand nationally. Suggest a strategy for expansion given the context that he has financial constraints.

4. A fast food chain with a similar brand offers different experiences to consumers at its outlets in Delhi and Mumbai. These are franchised outlets. Identify the underlying issues.

INTERNET EXERCISES

1. Access the website of McDonald's and Domino's. Compare and contrast the franchising information available on these chains.

2. Carlson Hospitality owns a number of brands such as Radisson Country Inns and Suites. Evaluate the strategies adopted by the Radisson chain for growth, globally.

CASE STUDY

Biocon: A Strategic Insight

Biocon

Biocon is India's leading biotechnology enterprise. Over the past 28 years, it has evolved from an enzyme manufacturing company to a fully integrated biopharmaceutical enterprise, focused on healthcare. Biocon applies proprietary fermentation technologies to develop innovative and effective biomolecules in diabetology, oncology, cardiology, and other therapeutic segments. Biocon's success lies in its ability to develop innovative technologies and products and to rapidly leverage them to adjacent domains. This unique 'integrated innovation' approach has yielded a host of patented products and technologies that have enabled multi-level relationships with their global clientele.

Biocon Limited has three subsidiary companies:

1. Syngene International Private Limited provides chemistry and molecular-based custom research services in early stage drug discovery and development. Kiran Mazumdar Shaw formed Syngene in 1994 when she learnt that there were opportunities in the field of contract research. She floated Syngene as a separate business and did not expect Biocon to put in funds frequently. Kiran usually pauses before entering another space, testing the waters first, and expanding only when she is sure of its potential. Hence, for four years Syngene progressed at a slow pace and took off only in 1998.

2. Clinigene International Private Limited conducts longitudinal research in diabetes and offers a wide range of comprehensive services in drug development and clinical trials. In the late 1990s Gordon Ringold, a former business associate who had formed Surromed in the US, told Kiran about the exciting possibilities of clinical research, and Clinigene was formed in the year 2000 (Biocon Annual Report 2006; Hari 2002).

3. Biocon Biopharmaceuticals Private Limited (BBPL) was set up on 17 April 2006 in collaboration with CIMAB, representing the Centre of Molecular Immunology, Cuba. The state-of-the-art cGMP compliant facility is designed to manufacture a broad range of novel and bio-similar therapeutic products through large-scale cell culture fermentation for the treatment of cancer, autoimmune, and metabolic diseases. It was decided that commercial operations would commence in the second quarter of financial year 2007 (Capitaline database).

In 1978, Biocon started with extracting two enzymes—papain and singlass, from papaya and catfish. It produced low-cost enzymes for the food and beverage industry to increase the translucence of fruit juices, for example, or to lighten the structure of bread. It then moved into pharmaceuticals, supplying generic ingredients used in the manufacture of cholesterol-lowering statins to companies such as Myland in the US and Sandoz in Germany (Elliott 2005). In the 1980s, Biocon started R&D to manufacture enzymes through fermentation. Biocon also decided to focus on solid-state fermentation at a time when only the Japanese could handle it with ease. The R&D team knew nothing about designing a manufacturing plant, let alone about solid-state fermentation. The first blueprint for a fermenter was ready in 1989 and Biocon commissioned its first commercial plant in 1991 (Hari 2002). Initially, Kiran had promoted the company as a joint venture with Ireland based MNC, Biocon Biochemicals. However, in 1989 Unilever Plc acquired Biocon Biochemicals Ltd in Ireland and merged it with its subsidiary Quest International (Biocon Annual Report 2006). In 1998, Unilever inked a deal with ICI to sell its speciality chemicals division of which Quest International was a part. This year was crucial for Kiran as it was the year she married John Shaw (then the Managing Director of Madura Coats). Shaw with his wide experience and large savings helped Kiran to buy Unilever's share in the company. Unilever had let Kiran float other companies but did not allow her to veer it away from its original business of making and selling enzymes. Thus, Biocon became an independent entity.

By the late 1990s, Biocon had become well entrenched in the fermentation space. It designed a new reactor called the PlaFractor for solid-state fermentation, which could contain micro-organisms well, and its contents could be mixed while fermentation was going on. Things could be added and removed without disturbing the fermentation process. To top it all, it consumed less energy than the Japanese model. In 2001, Biocon became the first Indian company to be approved by US FDA for the manufacture of lovastatin, a cholesterol-lowering molecule. In the same year, it also received the US2001 worldwide patent for its PlaFractorTM.

In 2004, Biocon announced a strategic partnership with Vaccinex Inc to discover and co-develop at least four therapeutic antibody products. In the same year, Biocon created a buzz in the stock market with its hugely successful IPO. Biocon closed day one of the listing with a market value of $1.11 billion. It became the second Indian company to cross the $1 billion mark on the day of listing. After this success, Biocon announced research collaboration with North Carolina's Nobex Corporation to jointly develop oral insulin for the treatment of diabetes on a global scale. It then launched Insugen TM, the new generation bio-insulin, manufactured in Asia's largest human insulin plant. Currently, 75 per cent of insulin sales come from overseas markets such as Latin America, the Middle East, and Southeast Asia. Biocon is also planning to finalize marketing tie-ups to sell insulin in US and Europe by the fiscal year ending March 2007. In April 2006, Biocon invested Rs 1 billion in a new facility at Bangalore to make monoclonal antibodies for cancer and autoimmune diseases (*The Financial Express* 2006). Table 18.8 shows Biocon's drug discovery pipeline. In June 2006, Kiran set up the Biocon Park, which is India's largest biotech hub comprising an integrated cluster of research labs and manufacturing facilities on a 90-acre expanse in Karnataka Area Industrial Board in Bommasandra Industrial Estate Phase IV, on the outskirts of Bangalore. The park was built with an investment of Rs 600 crore and is the single largest capital investment made by Biocon in 27 years of its history. The multi-product facilities cater to cardiovascular cholesterol reduction, immunosuppressant in organ transplants, diabetes, and cancer (*Pharmabiz* 2006).

The People

Biocon has a flat management structure. Kiran realized that for such a structure to work she had to adopt a 'networking management' style wherein there is high level of networking and communication, thus helping people to make their

Table 18.8 Biocon's drug discovery pipeline

Biocon's drug discovery pipeline				■ Novel ■ Generic	
Drug	Preclinical	Phase I	Phase II	Phase III	Launch
IN 105	————————→ Diabeties				
BVX 10	——→ Inflammation				
BVX 20	——→ Oncology				
BIOMAb EGFR™	————————————————————→ Oncology				
TlhT	——————→ Oncology inflammation				
Oral BNP	——→ Cardiovascular				
Streptokinase	——————————————————→ Cardiovascular				
GCSF	——————————————→ Oncology				
Insulin	————————————————————→ Diabetes				

Source: Adapted from Biocon Financial Report (2006).

own decisions. This has inspired her employees, as is evident from their long tenures at Biocon and the less than 1 per cent attrition rate (Elliott 2005, Biocon Annual Report 2006). Most of the top executives at Biocon have been there since the beginning. Kiran started the R&D division with Shrikumar Suryanarayan from IIT-Madras whom she had met in the early 1980s when he was a student and wanted enzymes for his project. When Suryanaranyan completed M. Tech., he had a number of offers for Ph.D. programmes and wanted Kiran to help him choose. Instead, she offered him an opportunity to start an R&D division for her and today he heads this division. Murali Krishnan is another example. He was helping Biocon in 1981 while studying to become a chartered accountant. He joined the company soon after, without completing his CA, and is the president of Biocon Group Finance. Biocon, Syngene, and Clinigene together employ approximately 2000 qualified personnel—from biologists, chemists, IT specialists, medical practitioners, pharmacologists, engineers, and finance/legal/marketing analysts, to general administrators. Ten per cent of the employees hold a Ph.D. degree, 30 per cent have a Masters degree in science, and the remaining are graduates with a Bachelors degree in science, commerce, or arts. Thirty per cent of Biocon employees are women. The em-

ployee attrition rate is less than 1 per cent and the average age of employees in the company is 28. The employees say they enjoy working at Biocon because of the leadership style Kiran has adopted. Her husband, who has worked in several countries as a senior manager with Coats Viyella, marvels at the open culture at Biocon. According to ICICI Ventures who have closely studied Biocon, all the senior managers of the company have a say in the business.

Competition

The Associate Chamber of Commerce and Industry of India estimates that over $4 billion is likely to be invested in the Indian biotech industry by 2010, primarily in the areas of healthcare, agriculture, environment, and food processing. It further stated that India would become a global player through export of bio-products, particularly to neighbouring countries, West Asia, Southeast Asia, and certain developed countries. In June 2003, a study on biotechnology by Frost and Sullivan pegged the value of the domestic biotechnology market at $2.5 billion in 2002, which would zoom to $6.75 billion by 2010. In 2005, there were 265 domestic biotech firms of which 131 were in Karnataka; of these 127 were in Bangalore alone, giving it the sobriquet of biotech cluster of India. In 2005,

46 new companies came up in India. The distribution of companies also seems to be evenly spread—18 per cent were agri-biotech firms and 17 per cent were biotech firms. Supply companies (those who supply raw materials to the biotech firms) accounted for 30 of the biotech companies, while outsourced R&D including clinical development firms, accounted for 14 per cent. The takeover of Lotus Labs by Iceland-based Aciavis for 25 million Euro is another noteworthy development (*The Economic Times* 2005). According to the latest industry figures, the Indian biotechnology industry crossed the $2 billion mark in revenues with bio-services contributing $250 million, bio-agriculture $250 million, bio-industrial $100 million, bio-informatics $32 million, and bio-pharma forming a major part of the biotechnology pie at $1400 million (ABLE 2007). The revenue of the top 10 biotech companies in India is given in Table 18.9.

Table 18.9 Top ten biotech companies in India (2006–07)

Rank	Company	Revenue (Rs crore)
1.	Serum Institute of India	950.95
2.	Biocon	823
3.	Panacea Biotec	607.87
4.	Rasi Seeds	340
5.	Nuziveedu	226.42
6.	Novo Nordisk	222
7.	Venkateshwara Hatcheries	190.50
8.	Indian Immunologicals	157.90
9.	Mahyco Morsants Biotech	150.30
10.	Glaxo Smithkline Pharmaceuticals	120

Source: Adapted from http://www.biospectrum india.com.

A brief description of the top 10 biotech companies that compete with Biocon is important in order to understand the competitive horizon for the company.

At number 1 position is Serum Institute of India. Amidst stiff competition, Serum Institute of India Ltd continued its leadership position in the vaccines business with a record sales of Rs 950.95 crore in 2006–07, registering a growth of 35 per cent over the previous year's sales revenue of Rs 703 crore. Over 80 per cent of its sales are from the overseas market. Serum Institute supplies vaccines to more than 130 countries across the world and it leads in MMR and Hep B vaccines in India. Its subsidiary company, Serum International, generated Rs 42 crore in 2006–07 against the previous year's sales of Rs 36 crore, registering a growth of over 16 per cent. With this, the group turnover of Serum Institute has touched Rs 992.95 crore for 2006–07.

Biocon is placed second in the competitive landscape, reporting total sales of Rs 823 crore for the year ending March 2007 from the sale of biopharmaceuticals and enzymes. As a group, the company ended the year at Rs 990 crore. Revenues from the biopharmaceuticals and enzymes business grew 20 per cent to Rs 823 crore from Rs 688 crore, contributing 83 per cent to operating revenues in FY 2007. Revenues from research services and licensing grew 63 per cent to Rs 163 crore from Rs 100 crore, contributing 17 per cent to operating revenues in FY 2007.

The number 3 competitor Panacea Biotec has added new drugs to its product basket such as Siropan, Lower A, Myelogen Forte, Inrica, TOFF Expectorant, Toff DC, Upright SP, and Trepro. Rasi Seeds is the number 4 competitor and a leading seed company located at Attur near Salem in Tamil Nadu. The company is committed to serving the needs of farmers across India by supplying quality seeds of various crops. Number 5, Secunderabad based Nuziveedu Seeds Ltd (NSL), had the commercial release of two Bt hybrid cotton varieties following the approval from the Genetic Engineering Approval Committee (GEAC). The two Bt hybrid cotton varieties, Bt Bunny and Bt Mallika, are being sold in Maharashtra, Gujarat, Madhya Pradesh, Andhra Pradesh, Karnataka, and Tamil Nadu. Number 6, Novo Nordisk India is the Indian subsidiary of Novo Nordisk, a focused healthcare company and a world leader in diabetes care. The number 7 competitor Venkateshwara Hatcheries Pvt Ltd (VHL), a group company of the VH Group, continued to dominate the Indian poultry vaccine market with a market share of over 60 per cent. Coming in at number 8 is Indian Immunologicals Ltd (IIL), a wholly-owned subsidiary of National Dairy Development Board (NDDB). It was established in 1983 with the objective of making foot and mouth disease (FMD) vaccine available to farmers at an affordable price. The number 9 competitor, Mahyco Monsanto Biotech (India) Ltd is a 50:50 joint venture with Mahyco and Monsanto Holdings Pvt Ltd (MHPL). Mahyco Monsanto Biotech (India) Ltd (MMB) is not a listed company and was created to bring the benefits of Bollgard cotton technology to farmers in India. In 2002, Bollgard cotton was the first biotech crop to be approved for commercialization in India by the GEAC. MMB registered a fall in its sales revenue to Rs 150.30 crore in 2006–07 over the previous year's sale of Rs 391.25 crore. The sudden fall in the revenue was mainly because of government intervention in fixing the price for Bt cottonseeds during the 2006 kharif season. In 2005, it had generated revenue of Rs 391.25 crore by transferring the technology to the Indian seed companies. Last, but not the least is the number 10 competitor, GlaxoSmithKline Pharmaceuticals (GSK), which continues to lead the Indian representative vaccines market by registering a growth of over 27 per cent, with its biotech sales reaching Rs 120 crore for the year 2006–07 against the previous sales revenue of Rs 94 crore.

After examining the top 10 biotech companies, we see that Biocon is today a biopharmaceutical company with strong capabilities in statins, immunosuppressants, recombinant insulin, and a wide product range across key therapeutic segments including diabetology, cardiology, and oncology. Biocon extended its R&D to new domains of knowledge, spanning bioprocess development, gene expression technologies, secondary metabolites, bioconversions, and proteomics. Today, it leverages its multiple expertise to leading-edge recombinant biopharmaceuticals and human therapeutics. The invention of the PlaFractor and through it, the ability to pioneer novel production processes for therapeutic molecules, is testimony to Biocon's path-breaking R&D capabilities and exceptional engineering skills.

Biocon's subsidiary Syngene has entered into a research partnership with Bristol Myers Squibb. This is expected to significantly increase the scope of Bristol Myers Squibb's existing relationship with Syngene to further develop integrated capabilities in medicinal chemistry, biology, drug metabolism, and pharmaceutical development. Through this symbiotic global partnership, Biocon's Syngene will provide R&D services for discovery and early drug development. Biocon is developing Nasulin, an intra-nasal insulin spray with Bentley Pharmaceuticals. Nasulin is the second non-injectable insulin that Biocon is working on, besides the oral tablet-form insulin IN 105, which is almost on a parallel track at phase 1C. Both the drugs may be 3–4 years from the commercial stage.

Biocon and Abu Dhabi's NMC Group signed a MoU to establish a JV to manufacture and market a range of biopharmaceuticals for the GCC region (Gulf Co-operation Council). This landmark agreement between the two companies heralds the region's first foray to develop and market life-saving biopharmaceutical products and will expand Neopharma's (NMC Group) existing portfolio with a range of Biocon's therapeutic products. These products will be in the cardiovascular, diabetes, and oncology segments, which represent the fastest growing class of drugs in the $5 billion GCC pharmaceutical market. This JV is a key milestone for Biocon's marketing foray in the Gulf.

Biocon launched BIOMAb-EGFR, a therapeutic monoclonal antibody-based drug for treating solid tumours of epithelial origin, such as head and neck cancers. The drug is the first of its kind to be clinically developed in India and is the first anti-EGFR humanized monoclonal antibody for cancer to be made available commercially anywhere in the world. The product has shown consistent positive outcome in clinical trials initiated both in India and globally, and is being studied in global clinical trials for colorectal, lung cancer, glioma, and pancreatic cancers. BIOMAb-EGFR is produced at Biocon's state-of-the-art manufacturing facility, Biocon Park. Biocon has also granted an exclusive license to Ferozsons Laboratories for marketing BIOMAb-EGFR in Pakistan. Ferozsons Laboratories is a leading oncology company.

Biocon has a pipeline of 12 molecules that could be out-licensed over a period of 12–24 months. The company is in an advanced stage of discussion on three molecules. It is keen to out-license an oral insulin molecule called IN105 for type II diabetes and potential drug for congestive heart failure. The others range from a monoclonal antibody for rheumatoid arthritis to a squamous cell antibody for non-Hodgkin's lymphoma.

Biocon launched a comprehensive portfolio of renal therapy products, which are priced 35 per cent lower than those available in the market. Biocon's nephrology division is committed to finding solutions to kidney disorders using the highest standards of biotherapeutics and will simultaneously strive towards reducing the risks of the disease in the future through progressive research and innovative therapies. The new immunosuppressant drugs for renal therapy include Ranodapt, Tacrograf, Cyclophil ME, Rapacan, and Erypro. *Immonusuppressants* are medicines that inhibit or prevent the activity of the body's immune system. The company's newly carved nephrology division expects to release more drugs in the market. To achieve this, Biocon will continue to increase investments in the R&D division and expects to double its R&D spend in 2007–08.

'Biocon truly believes that non-injectable insulins will drive the future of diabetes therapy the world over. The company wants to play a big role in the insulin market, currently valued at nearly Rs 300 crore in the country,' said Rakesh Bamzai, president, marketing, Biocon.

Biocon's new product pipeline includes therapeutic biomolecules ranging from small molecules (for example, statins, and immunosuppressants) to recombinant proteins (human insulin and monoclonal antibodies) derived from microbial and mammalian cell culture based fermentation technologies (*Biospectrum* 2007). Thus we see that in comparison to other competing firms Biocon's portfolio is wider.

Many firms

Biocon is the first Indian company to manufacture and export enzymes to USA and Europe, which it started in 1979. In 1989, it became the first Indian biotech company to receive US funding for proprietary technologies. It is the first company to have solid substrate fermentation technology from pilot to plant level. The commercial success of Biocon's proprietary fermentation plant has led to a threefold expansion. In 1993, its R&D and manufacturing facilities received ISO 9001 certificate from RWTUV, Germany. In 2002, Clinigene's laboratory became the first in India to receive CAP accreditation. In 2003, Biocon became the first company worldwide to develop human insulin on a Pichia expression system.

Biocon's Business Model

Biocon is India's largest biotech company with a presence in biopharmaceuticals, enzymes, customs research, and clinical research. It is difficult to say whether it is an enzyme company, a biotech company, or a pharmaceutical company. Biocon has a multi-business revenue share model with pharmaceutical products forming 75 per cent of its revenue, research services constituting 13 per cent, and enzymes 12 per cent (Fig. 18.5). Thus, we can say that Biocon is a biotech-turned-pharmaceutical company (Hari 2002). However, Chairman Kiran Mazumdar Shaw says that Biocon is rapidly transforming into an innovation-led organization where they have developed a balance between all-round revenue growth and risk mitigation in order to build a strong and sustainable business for the long term.

The integrated business approach has enabled Biocon to establish a significant presence in the global biopharmaceutical market. From early stage drug discovery to clinical development and commercialization, Biocon leverages its collective expertise and resources to provide an innovative range of products and services. This integrated business model allows it to offer its strategic global partners customized, high-value solutions at any stage in the life cycle of a

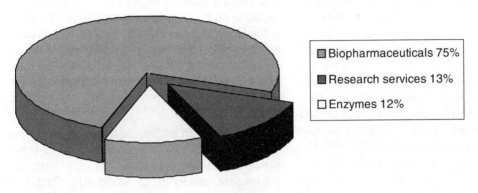

Biocon's multi-business revenue share

- ▨ Biopharmaceuticals 75%
- ▨ Research services 13%
- ☐ Enzymes 12%

Source: Adapted from Biocon Annual Report (2006).

Fig. 18.5   Biocon's multi-business revenue share

drug—right from discovery to market. The three stages are as follows (Fig. 18.6).

Step 1: Early stage drug discovery At Syngene, a Biocon subsidiary, Biocon offers outsourced, high-value R&D—from target identification and validation to small molecule and library synthesis. With its reputation for meticulous intellectual property right protection, it provides pharmaceutical and biotechnology majors customized solutions in the areas of synthetic chemistry and molecular biology.

Step 2: Clinical development At Clinigene, another Biocon subsidiary, Biocon specializes in Phase I–IV clinical trials and studies, using well-characterized clinical databases in diabetes, oncology, lipidemia, and cardiovascular diseases. It offers its services at its CAP (College of American Pathologists) accredited (CAP is widely recognized as the 'gold standard') and NABL (National Accreditation Board for Testing and Calibration Laboratories) accredited central reference laboratory and the state-of-the-art bioavailability and bioequivalence centre (BA/BE centre).

Step 3: Commercialization Biocon's track record of commercialization has been outstanding.

Syngene
- Molecular sociology
- Synthetic chemistry

Clinigene
- Clinical research
- Clinical development
- Clinical trials

Biocon
- Biologicals
- Small molecules
- Dosage forms

Biocon
- Microbial fermentation
- Biodiversity
- Bioprocessing

- Microbial fermentation
- Chemical synthesis
- Protein purification
- Mammalian cell culture

Source: Adapted from http://www.biocon.com.

Fig. 18.6   Biocon's business model

It has commercialized in excess of 25 enzymes over two decades. In the past five years, its chemical synthesis skills have enabled it to leverage its proprietary fermentation expertise to the manufacture of biopharmaceuticals. Biocon's biopharmaceutical foray began with statins and immunosuppressants. Their commercial success is evident in the rapid market share they have gained in the US and Europe. In fact, Biocon continues to be the only Indian company to have US FDA qualification for Lovastatin. FDA has inspected and accepted Biocon's facilities for Simvastatin, Pravastatin, Pioglitazone HCl, and Lovastatin (submerged fermentation). Biocon has also commercialized human insulin (rDNA) based on the Pichia expression system and submitted a drug master file for the same to the US FDA (http://www.biocon.com).

Biopharmaceuticals have been and will continue to be the mainstay of the company, promising exciting growth opportunities. This segment is involved primarily in manufacture and marketing of active pharmaceutical ingredients (APIs) that require advanced fermentation and other skills and that offer significant market potential in the regulated markets once the product goes off patent. Within this segment, statins constitute major products. Biocon has received US FDA acceptance for its Pravastatin, Simvastatin,

Lovastatin, and Pioglitazone manufacturing facilities. This acceptance allows Biocon to access the lucrative $6 billion market slated to go off patent in the United States in 2006. Biocon has already established itself as a leading exporter of Lovastatin to the US and Simvastatin to Europe. Apart from statins, other major biopharma's APIs are for immunosuppressants and anti-diabetic drugs.

The focus on statins augurs well, as statins are cholesterol-lowering agents used to treat/prevent coronary diseases, and are amongst the largest selling drugs worldwide. Patent at expiration of Pravastatin in Europe will augment statin growth in the year ahead followed by a quantum jump in the US markets in 2006 when both Pravastatin and Simvastatin go off patent. Biocon perceives the recent announcement of Simvastatin going OTC as an additional opportunity. It intends to further differentiate its statin strategy through initiating supply arrangements with innovator companies (Fig. 18.7).

Biocon has also successfully developed recombinant human insulin at a commercial scale, and the success of this technology has been endorsed by its long-term supply agreement with Bristol-Myers Squibb as well as its ability to file a drug master file with US FDA. The company is

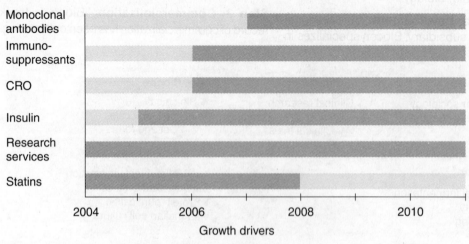

Source: Adapted from Biocon Annual Report (2006).

Fig. 18.7 The growth drivers

confident that finished formulation 'Insugen' due to be launched soon will compete very effectively in the market, and it is also addressing global opportunities for generic insulin in the semi- and non-regulated markets in the near term, and to the regulated markets in the medium term.

Financial Analysis for Biocon

All these efforts are reflected in Biocon's income statement, which in the first quarter of 2007 showed an increase of 22 per cent, with total sales standing at Rs 212 crore (Table 18.10).

Table 18.10 Profit and loss statement for Biocon, 2006

Biocon Limited (consolidated) Profit and loss statement				
Particulars	Q1 FY 2007	Q1 FY 2006	Variance Q1 FY 07 VX Q1 FY 06	Full year ended 31 March 2006
Income				
Sales biopharmaceuticals	161	135	19%	603
Sales-enzymes	22	20	10%	85
Contract research	29	19	52%	100
Total sales	**212**	**174**	**22%**	**788**
Other income	1	2		5
Total income/revenues	**213**	**176**	**21%**	**793**

Source: Adapted from Biocon Annual Report (2006).

The financial figures for Biocon are indicated in Table 18.11. The data is from March 2003 to March 2007. The capital employed has increased at an exponential rate and sales have also increased almost four times during the last five years. The profits have also increased exponentially.

Table 18.11 Financial figures for Biocon, March 2003–March 2007

Year end	Mar 2007	Mar 2006	Mar 2005	Mar 2004	Mar 2003
Equity	50	50	50	50	1.84
Net worth	940.53	801.77	694.51	540.04	124.8
Enterprise value	4,953.64	4,564.04	4,154.92	0	0
Capital employed	1,047.30	906.81	770.85	604.73	193.36
Gross block	860.08	314.83	268.77	189.64	153.4
Sales	887.15	725.75	684.35	531.55	275.16
Other income	23.63	11.72	23.41	13.93	3.69
PBIDT	236.83	186.19	209.29	163.79	64.79
PBDT	228.66	183.71	206.6	161.33	59.74
PBIT	179.22	163.34	191.2	149.94	52.77
PBT	171.05	160.86	188.51	147.48	47.72

Contd

Table 18.11 Contd

RPAT	158.35	133.48	174.39	124.67	35.87
APAT	158.32	133.31	174.21	124.62	35.75
CP	215.96	156.33	192.48	138.52	47.89
Rev. earnings in FE	480.03	358.95	378.04	300.57	108.53
Rev. expenses in FE	264.14	259.93	237.82	204.62	77.66
Book value (Rs)	94.05	80.18	69.45	54	678.26
EPS (Rs.)	15.33	13	17.16	12.34	194.95
Dividend (%)	60	50	40	20	0
Payout (%)	19.58	19.24	11.66	8.1	0
Debt–equity	0.12	0.12	0.11	0.2	0.64
Current ratio	1.29	0.97	1.64	2.25	1.18
Inventory turnover	6.93	8.22	8.82	8.14	7.85
Debtors turnover	3.69	3.83	4.74	5.6	4.04
Interest cover	21.94	65.86	71.08	60.95	10.45
PBIDTM (%)	26.7	25.65	30.58	30.81	23.55
PBDTM (%)	25.77	25.31	30.19	30.35	21.71
APATM (%)	17.85	18.39	25.48	23.45	13.04
ROCE (%)	18.34	19.47	27.8	37.57	30.56
RONW (%)	18.18	17.84	28.25	37.5	34.11
EV/EBIDTA	20.92	24.51	19.85	0	0
Net worth	17.31	15.44	28.6	332.72	45.93
Sales	22.24	6.05	28.75	93.18	70.27
PAT	18.63	−23.46	39.88	247.56	76.61
M cap	8.82	9.28	0	0	0

Table 18.12 indicates the R&D expenditures of the biotechnology industry, which has increased over the last five years. A key value driver for the biotechnology industry is the investment on R&D.

Reason for Success

Ever since Biocon became the buzzword in the market for the emerging field of biotechnology, Kiran has been a much-quoted personality. According to her, her belief in the field, a magnificent team of people who shared her passion for the subject, determination, and urge to succeed have all contributed to Biocon's reputation as the leader in the field. Another reason is that Biocon extends its friendliness to its customers. It not only gives customers a product but also provides information on the market, a strategy, and a future. According to the managing director of Delhi-based Harvest Gold Foods, 'only Biocon works with the customer to reduce costs' (Hari 2002).

The primary reasons for the success of the firm are explored as follows:

o The firm had a distinct strategy and focus area. It focused on a gap in the market and was able to expand its market around the area. It focused on enzymes and steadily extended its operations in the field. Initially, it

Table 18.12 Biotechnology industry R&D expenditures

					(Rs in crores)
	March 2007	**March 2006**	**March 2005**	**March 2004**	**March 2003**
Capital expenditure	9.8	21.6	10.34	8.99	3.4
Recurring expenditure	38.1	18.5	13.75	14.34	8
Total expenditure	47.9	40.1	24.09	23.33	11.4
Total R&D expenditure as percentage of net turnover (%)	5.5	5.8	3.7	4.6	4.48

sourced technology and even acquired the stake from Levers in order to retain its competitive edge.

o The business model of the firm is very sound. It offers and maps the entire value chain in the drug development and delivery process. It covers the entire spectrum from discovery and development to commercialization. The focus on diseases such as diabetes and cancer is appropriate as there is a lot of room for development. Over the years, it has evolved from a firm focused on enzyme manufacturing to a fully integrated biopharmaceutical enterprise. It followed an integrated innovation approach to yield patented products and technologies, which enabled multi-level partnerships. It also tapped the global market and was not restricted to the Indian market. The export orientation of the firm enabled it to prepare itself for a global strategy rather than have a micro perspective. The firm prepared itself for discovery, clinical development, and commercialization.

o The creation of a high performing team. The team dynamics and the complementary roles played by team members are critical to the success of any venture. The firm clearly demonstrates that it has used the networks of the founding entrepreneur as well as its employees to have a committed team at the top, who have stayed with the firm for an extended period thereby lending stability, and building and nurturing the R&D culture and a penchant for innovation.

o Capitalizing on the university linkages.

The firm has strong linkages with the academic community and thereby works closely with the educational system as well.

Questions

1. What are the key strengths and challenges for Biocon?

2. Critically evaluate the growth strategy adopted by Biocon.

SELECT REFERENCES

'After the deal', *The Economist*, 9 January 1999.

'B.K. Modi sells entire telecom equipment JV stake to Alcatel', *The Economic Times*, 23 March 1999.

Banker (2000), 'Top 1000', July.

Basant, R. (2000), 'Corporate response to economic reforms', in Nagesh Kumar (ed.), *Indian Economy Under Reforms*, Bookwell, New Delhi.

'Barista brewing aggressive expansion plans', *Express Hotelier and Caterer*, 6 December 2004.

'Barista Coffee sets up new company in Sri Lanka', *Express Hotelier and Caterer*, 22 December 2004.

Beamish, P.W. (1988), *Multinational Joint Ventures in Developing Countries*, Routledge, London.

Beamish, P.W. (1994), 'Joint ventures in LDC's: Partner selection and performance', *Management International Review*, vol. 34, pp. 60–74.

Bhandari, A. (1996), 'Survival of the fittest', International Times, *The Economic Times*, 13 August.

Bhargava, V. (1997), 'TCS, Microsoft, and NIIT to jointly launch EX-NGN', *The Economic Times*, 19 December.

Bleeke, J. and D. Ernst (1995), 'Is your strategic alliance really a sale?', *Harvard Business Review*, vol. 73, no. 1, pp. 97–105.

Brandt, V.S.R. (1987), 'Korea', in G.C. Lodge and E.F. Vogel (eds), *Ideology and National Competitiveness: An Analysis of Nine Countries*, Harvard Business School Press, Boston, Massachusetts, pp. 207–239.

Brown, M. (1997), 'Outsourcery', *Management Today*, January.

Burton, J. (1995), 'Composite strategy: The combination of collaboration and competition', *Journal of General Management*, vol. 21, no. 1, Autumn.

Capitaline (2005), '300 More Café Coffee Day outlets by 2007', *Capitaline*.

Chandrashekharan, A. (1998), 'A Twist in the noodle battle', The Strategist, *Business Standard*, 15 September.

Das, T. (1996), 'MNCs: India's strategy needs rethink', *Economic Growth and Social Change*, March.

Financial Times, 6 April 1997.

Forrest, J.E. (1990), 'Strategic alliances and the small technology based firm', *Journal of Small Business Management*, July, pp. 37–45.

Ghosal, S. (1999), 'The value of values', Corporate Dossier, *The Economic Times*, 5–11 March.

'Global IT giants in pact supply equipment to ISP's', *Business Standard*, 30 November 1998.

Goyal, M. (1999), 'Public bond, private life', *The Economic Times*, 26 February–4 March.

Gupta, N.S. (1995), 'Alliances emerge as the 90s weapon', *The Economic Times*, 10 September.

Haldipur, R. (1998), 'Management and strategy lessons from Microsoft and Bill Gates', *Indian Management*, October.

Hari, P. (2002), 'The World of Biocon', *Business World*, 2 December.

Hodgetts, R.M., F. Luthans, and S.M. Lee (1994), 'New paradigm organizations: From total quality to learning to world-class', *Organizational Dynamics*, Winter.

'How mergers go wrong', *The Economist*, 22 July 1999.

Jauhari, V. and K. Misra (2001), *Business Strategy*, Excel, New Delhi.

Kanter, R.M. (1994), 'Collaborative advantage: The art of alliances', *Harvard Business Review*, July–August, pp. 96–108.

Kim, K.J., H.J. Park, and N. Suzuki (1990), 'Reward allocations in the United States, Japan, Korea: A comparison of individualistic and collective cultures', *Academy of Management Journal*, vol. 33, pp. 188–198.

Levitas, E. (1997), 'Selecting partners for successful international alliances: Examination of US and Korean firms', *Journal of World Business*, vol. 32, no. 1.

Lodge, G.C. and W.C. Crum (1985), 'The pursuit of remedies', in B.R. Scott and G.C. Lodge (eds), *US Competitiveness in the World Economy*, Harvard Business School Press, Boston, Massachusetts, pp. 479–502.

Mathai, P.G. and T. Surendar (1999), 'Pharma drama', *Business World*, 7–21 April.

Mitra, A. (1999), 'Zee may tie with French firm for DTH network', *Business Standard*, 26 March.

Mohr, J. and R. Spekman (1994), 'Characteristics of partnership success: Partnership attributes communication behaviour and conflict resolution techniques', *Strategic Management Journal*, vol. 15, pp. 143–152.

Mukherjee, S. (1999), 'Posing a challenge to BHEL', *Business Standard*, 24 March.

Ohmae, K. (1989), 'The global logic of strategic alliances', *Harvard Business Review*, March–April.

Parkhe, A. (1991), 'Inter firm diversity, organizational learning, and longevity in global strategic alliances', *Journal of International Business Studies*, vol. 22, pp. 579–601.

Peters, T. (1993), *Liberation Management*, Pan, London.

'Pharmaceuticals: On tonic of mergers', Data India, *Business Standard*, March 1998.

Porter, M.E. (1980), *Competitive Strategy: Techniques for Analyzing Industries and Competitors*, Free Press, New York.

Rajadhyaksha, N. (1994), 'Are Indian brands worth so much', *Business World*, 5–18 October.

Retail Yatra (2004).

Roy, R. (1999), 'Philip Morris set to acquire Godfrey Phillips', *Business Standard*, 2 April.

Thakur, J.M. (1995), *Takeover of Companies: Law, Practice, and Procedure*, Snow-white, Bombay.

Hakusho, Toshi (2000), *Japan External Trade Organization*, JETRO, Tokyo.

Venkiteswaran, N. (1997), 'Restructuring of corporate India: The emerging scenario', *Vikalpa*, vol. 22, no. 3, July–September.

Verma (1995), *Corporate Mergers, Amalgamations and Takeovers*, Bharat, New Delhi.

Verma, Vinnie (1999), 'Indian pharmaceutical industry: Some perspectives and issues in the coming decade', *Chemical Industry Digest*, January.

World Investment Report (2000), 'Cross Border Mergers & Acquisitions and Development', United Nations, Geneva.

Wright, P., M.J. Kroll, and J. Parnell (1996), *Strategic Management Concepts*, Prentice Hall, Englewood Cliffs, New Jersey.

Asia Times (2004), 'Fresh entries stir up Indian coffee market', http://www.atimes.com/ind-pak/DD30Df03.html., accessed on 8 December 2008.

'Award for Biocon CMD', *Business Line*, 11 October 2005, http://www.thehindubusinessline.com.

Biocon Annual Report (2006), Capitaline Database. http://www.biospectrumindia.com, accessed on 2 July 2007.

'Biocon chief tops poll of biotech personalities outside US, Europe', *Business Line*, 10 March 2006. http://www.thehindubusinessline.com/2006/03/10/stories/2006031003290800.htm.

Business Standard (2004), http: indiacoffee.org/newsletter/2004/jn/news_eyes.html, accessed on 25 June 2006.

Elliot, John (2005), 'Biotech Queen', *Fortune*, 14 November 2005, press releases on www.biocon.com.

http://www.virtualbangalore.com/Ppl/PplKiranM.php> http://nrcw.nic.in/shared/sublinkimages/166.htm, accessed on 25 September 2006.

Indiacoffee.org (2004), 'Coffee consumption in India: Perspectives and prospects', http://indiacoffee.org/newsletter/2004/april/cover_story.html.

'Kiran Mazumdar is Eminent Businessperson', *The New Indian Express*, 25 February 2006, press releases on www.biocon.com.

Pharmabiz (2006), 'President Kalam dedicates BioMAb EGFR to the nation', 7 June, www.pharmabiz.com.

Shaw, Kiran Mazumdar (2006), 'We aim to make healthcare affordable to masses', *The Financial Express*, 29 January, press releases in www.biocon.com.

'Tata Coffee sells stake in Barista', http://in.news.yahoo.com, accessed on 5 March 2005.

http://trak.in/tags/business/2008/07/15/indian-mergers-acquisitions-full-private-equity-funding-growth/, accessed on 22 September 2008.

http://www.biocon.com, accessed on 28 September 2006.

The Economic Times (2005), 'Biotech turnover could touch $5bn by '10: Shaw', *The Economic Times*, 23 April 2005, press releases on www.biocon.com.

'Biocon to sell insulin in US, Europe; up R&D', *The Financial Express*, 14 September 2006, press releases on www.biocon.com.

19 Emerging Service Sectors in India

OBJECTIVES

After reading this chapter you will be able to understand the:
- various issues in healthcare industry
- factors responsible for the growth of the biotech industry
- dynamics of retailing industry
- emerging trends in the banking sector

INTRODUCTION

According to Organisation for Economic Co-operation and Development (OECD) forecasts for the year 2050, India will be the world's third largest economy after China and USA. The Indian economy is set to grow at the rate of 10–11 per cent. In 2007–08, the size of the Indian economy is set to cross $1 trillion (India Economic Survey 2007–08). The contribution of services to GDP is expected to be 9.9 per cent, while agriculture and industry contribute 4.1 per cent and 10.5 per cent, respectively. In contrast to the sharp fluctuations in agriculture, industry and services have continued to expand steadily. Since 2002–03 with annual growth of 7 per cent or more, industry and services have acted as twin engines propelling the overall growth of the economy. The services sector accounts for 54 per cent of GDP and has been growing at the rate of 9 per cent since the mid 1990s (Eleventh Five Year Plan 2007–12). The services sector in India continues to be broad-based. The growth of financial services comprising banking, insurance, and business services in the year 2006–07 was 13.9 per cent (India Economic Survey 2007–08). Services exports have shown an average growth rate of 28 per cent since the last decade. India has about 65 per cent share of the global offshore market and a 46 per cent share of the global business offshoring industry (BPOs). According to the NASSCOM study, software and services exports grew by 29 per cent (in dollar terms) and crossed the $40 billion and the domestic market grew by 26 per cent (in rupee terms) after posting revenues of $11.6 billion in FY08. With only 10 per cent of the global potential tapped so far, the future is very promising. The industry targets to achieve $60 billion in software and services exports, and $73 billion in overall software and services revenues by FY2010.

The following topics cover four major sectors in India, such as biotechnology, healthcare, retailing, and banking.

Healthcare is an important emerging sector with many large corporate hospitals being created. India's big pharmaceutical firms such as Ranbaxy have also forayed into speciality hospitals. India has earned a name for itself in heart care and other specialized streams such as ophthalmology. Medical tourism is also booming. The case study on healthcare management in India gives an insight into the dynamics of this segment.

The section on retailing gives an insight into the dynamics of the retail segment. In India, the segment has been dominated by the unorganized sector for centuries. With the emergence of specialty malls it displays a huge potential for growth. The case study brings out the nuances of managing this sector.

The section on banking gives a perspective on the nature of services offered by this segment. It compares the role of the public and the private sectors. It also delineates the role of technology in this segment. An insight into the service mix elements—product, price, place, promotion, people, physical evidence, and process has also been delved upon.

HEALTHCARE SECTOR IN INDIA

The healthcare segment has an immense bearing on the growth of an economy. It is an extremely competitive global industry. Patients are prepared to travel to remote parts of the world in order to receive the service quality they hope for, and prefer to go to private hospitals for better service. There is little research comparing service opportunities in the private and public sector segments. Health service quality is a multidimensional variable and one can use SERVQUAL to measure the service quality. SERVQUAL represents six dimensions of service quality: tangibles, reliability, assurance, responsiveness, empathy, and accessibility.

Different research studies indicate that the analysis of healthcare can be broken into various segments such as (Jabnoun and Chaker 2003):

- patient confidence
- business competence
- treatment quality
- supportive services
- physical appearance
- waiting time
- empathy.

The experience of patients in the public and private healthcare segment may be very different. The most significant and widespread global trend in healthcare over the past decade has been the increasing share of for-profit healthcare and its commercialization across societies. This has paralleled the process of economic globalization and is intrinsically linked to it. The process of the private sector entering into the healthcare segment began in the late 1970s, and early 1980s and 1990s. The factors which influence private participation in the healthcare segment are as follows (Baru 1998):

- Global actors including bilateral and multilateral agencies, pharmaceutical, medical equipment industries, insurance companies, and research institutions have played a critical role in shaping health policies across the world.
- The role of the state in each country, especially in terms of investments in public health services, pharmaceuticals, medical equipment, and insurance sectors in each of these countries.
- The growth of the middle-class and their influence on both the demand and supply of private health services.

The trends in public investments have been similar to those in Pakistan and Bangladesh. While the Bhore Committee had recommended that 12 per cent of total outlay must be earmarked for health, the figure never crossed 3 per cent. Over the years it has witnessed a decline and is clearly inadequate for expansion of facilities. This gets reflected in the stagnation of public services from the 1980s through the 1990s. There is a shortage of paramedical staff in rural areas and this has negative consequences for the quality of services in the public sector.

As per the government's national health policy, the size of the healthcare sector in India stands at $17 billion (Rs 78,200 crore) and accounts for 5 per cent of the GDP. According to a CII–McKinsey study on healthcare, the expenditure on healthcare will more than double by 2012 and is expected to increase from Rs 86,000 crore (Rs 860 billion) at present, to Rs 1,94,000–2,70,000 crore (Rs 1,940–2,700 billion) over the next 10 years.

Healthcare in India

The late 1980s saw the mushrooming of a number of corporate hospitals. However, the boom remained short-lived and out of the 22 listed hospital scrips, most are trading below par today. Most of the corporate hospitals failed because they emerged in isolation and were not part of a larger picture. However, with liberalized health insurance and increasing awareness, and the spread of corporate hospitals, things are looking up.

Industry Structure

States such as Maharashtra, Gujarat, Kerala, Tamil Nadu, Karnataka, and Orissa in India have surplus hospital beds, whereas Punjab, Haryana, Rajasthan, Uttar Pradesh, Madhya Pradesh, and Bihar face acute shortages in this respect (Capitaline Plus Report 2006). In states such as Maharashtra, Gujarat, Kerala, and Andhra Pradesh, 85–95 per cent of the total hospitals in the state are private hospitals. On the other hand, in states such as Rajasthan, Madhya Pradesh, and Haryana, private hospitals either do not exist or form a very small proportion of the total number of hospitals. This leaves a lot of scope for private players to enter these states.

Major Players

Major players in the hospital sector are the Apollo Group of Hospitals, Fortis Healthcare, Max India, Escorts (now Fortis Escorts), Wockhardt, and Duncans.

Table 19.1   Ranking of various hospitals in India

Ranking	Hospital	Location
1	All India Institute of Medical Sciences	Delhi
2	Apollo Hospitals	Chennai
3	Post-Graduate Institute of Medical Education and Research	Chandigarh
4	Christian Medical College	Vellore
5	Sankara Nethralaya	Chennai
6	Bombay Hospital	Mumbai
7	National Institute of Mental Health and Neurosciences	Bangalore
8	Jaslok Hospital	Mumbai
9	Sanjay Gandhi Post-Graduate Institute of Medical Sciences	Lucknow
10	Tata Memorial Hospital	Mumbai

Source: Adapted from *Business World* (2005).

A survey by *Business World,* a leading business publication in India, categorized the following hospitals as the leading hospitals offering healthcare in India. The findings are indicated in Table 19.1.

The survey interviewed 663 general practitioners and 1013 specialists in 20 cities for the ranking.

Table 19.2 gives the results of an online survey conducted jointly by All India Management Association (AIMA) and Yellowjobs.com India Limited. This survey reflects the choice of today's Internet-savvy customer. The criteria were accessibility, brand awareness, customer service, performance, and price.

Table 19.2   Online survey of favourite healthcare companies

Favourite healthcare company	Votes (%)
Apollo Hospitals	28
All India Institute of Medical Sciences	24
Max Hospitals	11
Fortis Healthcare	7
Dr Batras	3
Fortis Escorts Heart Institute and Research Centre	2
VLCC	1
Lilavati Hospital	1
Sankara Nethralaya	1
Christian Medical College	1
Others	20

Source: Adapted from AIMA (2008).

Government Policy

In the mid-1980s, the healthcare sector was recognized as an industry. Hence, it was possible for the players to get long-term funding from financial institutions. The government also reduced the import duty on medical equipment and technology, paving way for technological upgradation in the industry.

Since the national health policy, with its main objective of 'health for all' by the year 2000, was approved in 1983, little has been done to update or amend the policy even as the epidemiological profile of the country changed and new health problems arose from ecological degradation. The focus so far has been on medical care and not on comprehensive healthcare.

The hospitals are also handicapped with government regulations, which do not allow them to advertise. As hospitals spend millions of rupees in technology and infrastructure, it becomes necessary for them to attract patients and generate funds.

In India, approximately 60 per cent of the total health expenditure comes from the self-paid category as against government's contribution of 25–30 per cent; the contribution from insurance companies is negligible.

The majority of private hospitals are expensive for a normal middle-class family. The opening up of the insurance sector to private players has helped improve the access to healthcare establishments. Health insurance will make healthcare affordable to a large number of people.

Health insurance premium collections in India increased by 55 per cent during 2007–08 and touched Rs 5,133 crore ($1.2 billion). The fact is that health insurance in 2008 was the single largest business segment (after motor insurance) in the non-life insurance sector. With a share of 24.3 per cent, New India Insurance is the largest player in the health insurance segment, followed by ICICI Lombard with 17.7 per cent market share. The other leading players are Bajaj Allianz, Royal Sundaram, IFFCO Tokio, and Reliance General Insurance.

Despite this, if the world figures are considered, only 2 million people (0.2 per cent of a total population of 1 billion) are covered under Mediclaim, whereas in developed nations like the US, about 75 per cent of the total population are covered under such insurance schemes. One reason could be that the agencies that offer the scheme have never marketed health insurance aggressively. Moreover, agencies like GIC take up to six months to process claims and to reimburse customers after they have paid for treatment out of their own pockets.

Issues Related to Private Health Insurance in India

Mahal (2002) in his outstanding work on private health insurance in India suggests that the introduction of private health insurance can contribute to increasing the aggregate costs of healthcare in several different ways. In their interactions between the healthcare providers and customers' such as doctors and patients, it is given that the former have much better information about their patient's health status and future course of treatment than the latter. The patient is fairly dependent on the course of treatment recommended by a physician. One consequence is that in a regime of pure indemnity insurance, providers have an incentive to provide more care than may be medically appropriate. The problem will arise when the patient can choose his/her doctor and treatment freely and then present the bill to the insurer for reimbursement. There is another dimension to the whole process. Once insured, an individual faces a reduced incentive to take health precautions. Also, a sick person may feel less compelled to control her consumption of healthcare and expensive diagnostic examinations if medical care costs are covered by insurance.

Key Success Factors

Location of the hospital is a key success factor. The major factors in deciding the location of a hospital are:

- a central place having easy accessibility
- space around the hospital for future expansion
- space to make provision for residential quarters for the staff
- hostel facility, if there is to be a college on campus.

It is also beneficial if the hospital is located in a place where there is no other hospital in the vicinity. For example, when Apollo opened in Delhi, there was no other hospital for 200 km, which proved to be a boon for them.

Also, diseases which are characteristic of a certain region, can affect the location. For example, studies conducted by Fortis show that north Indians are more prone to cardiac diseases and so it has set up a 200-bed cardiac hospital and 12 smaller cardiac centres in and around Mohali (Chandigarh).

In case of Mumbai, where space is a problem and there are already a lot of hospitals, super-speciality hospitals make more business sense. Technology plays an immense role in delivering better quality healthcare through application of telecommunications technology or rather tele-medicine. This will help transfer of electronic medical data, including high-resolution images, sounds, live video, and patient records from one location to another through telephone lines, ISDN, modem, Internet, satellites, video-conferencing, etc.

Mathur (2003) has evaluated the impact of IT on healthcare management in India. The role of IT in healthcare and its impact through services trade depends on three related aspects:

1. Power and reach of telematic connectivity, which determines who will be included.
2. Legitimacy of service providers seeking return on investments.
3. Structure of responsibilities for healthcare, which are a part of the government frame in local and national jurisdictions.

The stakeholders' goals by performance criteria as postulated by Mathur (2003) are indicated in Table 19.3.

Hospitals need to have long-term understanding with Preferred Provider Organizations (PPOs), which further have an understanding with corporates. In case an employee in

| Table 19.3 | Stakeholder goals by performance criteria | | |

Healthcare stakeholders	Criteria: Choice	Criteria: Efficiency	Criteria: Cost
Consumers	Does choice of healthcare commodities, services, and facilities expand?	Countervailing institutions? Quality standards? Competition?	Pricing? Safety? Data privacy?
Service providers	Which cross border networks?	Synergy effects in innovation of production and distribution?	Reduced costs on development and delivery?
Insurers (Firms, employers)	Data-based calculus for financing? Consolidation?	Scale effects? Cross border delivery?	Reduced costs? Health maintenance organizations? Moral hazards? Leakages?
Governments	Designing health systems with national/global scope?	Side effects/spillovers? Equitable norms?	Burden on public finances? Trade balance? Investment flows? Human capital?

Source: Adapted from Mathur (2003).

any of these corporates has an illness, it is referred to the PPOs, which sends them to the hospital for check-up and treatment.

The success rate of crucial operations and surgeries reflect the technological and knowledge-based edge of a hospital over its competitors. Such successes are discussed in health magazines and newspapers, which becomes a natural advantage for the hospital.

Some hospitals by means of their past track record have created a niche market for themselves. For example, the Hinduja Hospital in India is known for its high-quality healthcare at reasonable rates, whereas Lilavati Hospital is known for its five-star services. Hospitals can also promote medical colleges. This helps them to generate extra resources in the form of fees, using the same infrastructure.

Sources of Revenue

The general perception that large hospitals with high bed-occupancy rate are profitable is misleading. Experience from around the world shows that hospitals with more than 250 beds do not do well. Many Indian hospitals are following the US healthcare industry practice by decreasing the average length of stay of patients and increasing patient turnover. Research conducted in the US shows that 80 per cent of the revenues from a patient comes within the first 72 hours of admission. Hospitals generate a lot of revenue from general inspection if the patient turnover is very high.

A large percentage of revenue comes from specialized services like operations and surgeries. For these reasons, many corporates are planning for small, 100-bed specialized hospitals, which cater to specific diseases such as cardiac, cosmetic surgery, and neurology.

Research has also shown that there is a lot of scope for super-speciality hospitals with 100–50 beds, which generate revenues equivalent to a large 500-bed general hospital. Typically, large hospitals with approximately 500-bed capacity take about 9–10 years to break even, whereas super-specialty hospitals with about 100 beds only take about 6–7 years to break even.

General room charges do not contribute significantly to the hospital revenues, unlike intensive care units (ICU). The general room to ICU/ICCU room ratio depends upon the type of the hospital. In case of general hospitals, the ratio is about 8:2, whereas in case of a specialized hospital, it is about 6:4. Hospitals have in-house doctors and visiting consultants. The visiting doctors contribute a certain percentage (approximately 15 per cent) of their billings to the hospital revenues. Hospitals can also generate revenue from medicines if they are supplying them in-house. Some hospitals make it mandatory for their patients to buy medicines from the hospital's chemist shop. A margin of 15–20 per cent can be charged for such medicinal supplies.

Though many hospitals run by trusts do not earn this way, new entrants or corporates, for whom the private healthcare sector is a direct extension of their line of business (for example, pharma companies), can generate good returns from the supply of medicines. Hospitals promoting medical studies generate extra resources in the form of fees, using the same infrastructure. For example, Manipal Hospital charges a fee of $20,000 annually from foreign students.

More and more overseas Indians fly home to visit their doctors here because they have complete confidence in them. They get world-class treatment at a fraction of the cost they would have to pay abroad, as liberalization has speeded up the entry of the latest state-of-the-art equipment.

Medical charges in India are between one-tenth and one-thirtieth of that in the US. For example, a bypass surgery, which costs $3000 in the US, costs only Rs 35,000–40,000 in India, with the same technologies and facilities.

This is also because Indian doctors are amongst the best in the world. They prefer to consult these doctors for their chronic diseases such as high blood pressure, diabetes, neurological problems, and even dentistry.

Modern Healthcare Management

Third-party administrator (TPA) can play a major role by managing the healthcare needs of groups of individuals. A TPA will negotiate better deals for their customers and sort out the medical claims for a fee. On the other hand, a PPO can manage almost all the healthcare needs of their customers. However, PPOs cannot provide insurance cover, as they do not assume the risk of their clients. But now, with private insurance operators coming into the picture, most PPOs and TPAs will turn into health maintenance organizations (HMO), by linking their products with insurance companies, or even hospitals. (As of today, HMOs are not allowed in India).

A key aspect of HMOs is that they carry the risk of their customers, and hence they will want to know the bio-informatics and the epidemiological data of clients. Understanding the disease trends of their clients helps them to know which risk to carry, how much, and at what price.

Experience, mostly in the US, has shown that HMOs have lowered the cost of treatment (it is in their interest to make sure payouts to hospitals are reduced), ensured preventive care, and made the healthcare industry, by and large, more professional.

For the healthcare boom to succeed, it is imperative that hospitals do not fail. Overseas, where the HMOs have a say in the way hospitals are run, they keep a tight control of costs and revenues. HMOs have still not made their entry in to the country, but PPOs, thanks to the sheer quantum of business they bring, are already influencing the way hospitals are managed, in the same way that mutual funds keep the companies they invested in on their toes.

Hospitals can become integrated healthcare systems, i.e., when medicines, food services, laundry, and linen, will become 'purchased' services. These third-party operations will increase the profit margins.

A World Bank report of November 1999 points out the emergence of large-scale, investor-owned hospitals in the country as a 'dramatic' development. The corporate hospitals will play a positive role in the healthcare sector by taking the load off government hospitals, whose performance has not been up to the mark.

In the last five years, approximately 750 mergers and acquisitions have occurred in hospitals in the US. A major advantage of these mergers is the move towards more integrated healthcare systems, which can achieve economies of scale by rationalizing capacity and amalgamating functions such as information technology, consultants, emergency transport, database, and research and development.

But healthcare is primarily a local market business and it is very important to consider the following factors before going in for mergers:

- relative sizes of the hospitals
- their geographical proximity
- the relationship between individual hospitals and physicians
- degree of unity in leadership structures of separate institutions.

Again, research in the US has shown that merged hospitals in narrowly defined geographic areas, with few or no competitors, have succeeded in exerting a favourable influence on the services.

The key to success appears to be a strong orientation to performance, as well as standardizing and integrating work processes, functions, suppliers, and investments, but not necessarily on a centralized basis. For example, Apollo in Chennai, Hyderabad, and Delhi will be separate hospitals postmerger, but functions will be centralized.

Some type of mergers can be for synergy of skills. For example, to help the merged organizations benefit from one another's individual strengths by applying them across the board. It also helps them to make joint investments in branding or information technology and also to react effectively to the changed market forces.

Alternatively, hospitals can go in for group purchases, as in America. The buying power of large PPOs in USA such as Premier, VHA/UHC and AmeriNet gives them the clout to exert price pressure on suppliers, particularly for products in lower demand. As PPOs have become consolidated, manufacturers have to offer bigger discounts in order to hold on to their contracts. So, there exists a lot of supply management opportunity, which will affect spending productivity.

Outlook

Demographic data available from the National Centre for Applied Economic Research (NCAER) states that the national average of the proportion of households in the low income group (annual income < Rs 25,000) has declined from 58.84 per cent in 1990 to 49 per cent in 1996. On the other hand, the middle and higher middle income group (annual income > Rs 50,000) has increased from 14 per cent to 20 per cent.

With the opening up of the insurance sector, a lot of private players will come out with innovative insurance products, which will further drive the healthcare revenues.

Considering the middle and higher middle income groups, we get a conservative estimate of 35–38 million households or 200 million insurable lives. They provide a ready market for corporate hospitals. The Indian healthcare industry can replicate the success of the IT industry if the resources are utilized well and the demand–supply gap is reduced. The fact that patients from about 55 countries are treated in Indian hospitals and more than 5000 international patients visit Apollo Hospitals and Fortis healthcare annually, indicate that the potential of this industry is huge. It is important that the healthcare facilities are made accessible to more and more people. The future step towards this should be expansion, that is, to set up private hospitals and healthcare facilities in Tier II and Tier III cities and towns of India. For this to become a reality, creation of better infrastructure for increased access to these locations is extremely important.

BIOTECHNOLOGY INDUSTRY IN INDIA

Biotechnology holds a lot of promise for India. As a stream of science, it has the ability to deliver the next wave of technological change. The growth of the sector can usher in employment generation, intellectual wealth creation, enhance industrial growth, and generate entrepreneurial opportunities. According to the national biotechnology development strategy draft put together by the Department of Biotechnology, Ministry of Science and Technology:

'Biotechnology as a business segment for India has the potential of generating revenues to the tune of $5 billion and creating one million jobs by 2010 through products and services.'

Comparisons can be drawn between the growth of the IT sector and the biotechnology sectors in India:

- In the biotech area, the assets are more capital intensive.
- The return on investment takes a longer time to materialize.
- Intellectual property assets are important.
- A high level of skill and education are required.
- There are strong roots in the education system. In a lot of incubation projects, academics have taken a lead in setting up new ventures.

- There are gaps in the competencies available and the skill set required by the industry.

There are three main segments in the biotechnology segment:

1. Biopharmaceuticals
   - vaccines, therapeutics, diagnostics, and animal healthcare products
2. Bioindustry
   - enzymes, organo-amino acids, and yeast-based products
3. Bioservices
   - Clinical research, contract research, contract manufacturing, and bioinformatics

Insight into the Biotech Industry in India

In the year 2005–06, the biotech industry in India crossed $1 billion (Rs 4,745 crore) in revenues. The exports accounted for 51.48 per cent of the total industry.

Biopharmaceutical exports accounted for 74.33 per cent of the total exports. Bioagri's share was 1.07 per cent. Bioindustrial and bioinformatics sector accounted for 1.23 per cent and 3 per cent of the total exports, respectively.

The biotech industry revenues are given in Table 19.4. The top 10 biotech companies as ranked by biotech turnover are provided in Table 19.5.

Government Interventions

The government of India has over the years been spending higher amounts of money on the department of biotechnology (Fig. 19.1). The government has decided to initiate the following strategic actions for the promotion of the biotechnology sector in India in order to:

- create a national task force on education and training
- formulate a human resource development strategy
- deploy initiatives towards curriculum development

Table 19.4 Biotech industry revenues

Segment	2005–06
Biopharma	4708
Bioservices	720
Bioagri	598
Bioindustrial	375
Bioinformatics	120
Total	6521

Source: Adapted from www.biospectrumindia.com (2006).

Table 19.5 Top 10 biotech companies by turnover

Rank (2006)	Company	Biotech turnover (Rs) (crore)
1	Serum Institute of India	703
2	Biocon	688
3	Panacea Biotec	437.82
4	Mahyco Monsanto Biotech	391.25
5	Rasi Seeds	309.49
6	Venkateshwara Hatcheries	280
7	Novo Nordisk	175
8	Mahyco	117.76
9	Aventis Pharma	114.5
10	Indian Immunologicals	102.67

Source: Adapted from www.biospectrumindia.com (2006).

- take measures to strengthen the teaching and R&D in life sciences and biotechnology in universities
- create science and technology leaders for the industry.

India's Strengths in the Sector

India's strengths in the biotech segment are as follows:

- Availability of skilled and educated manpower.
- Indian companies are committed to global standards.

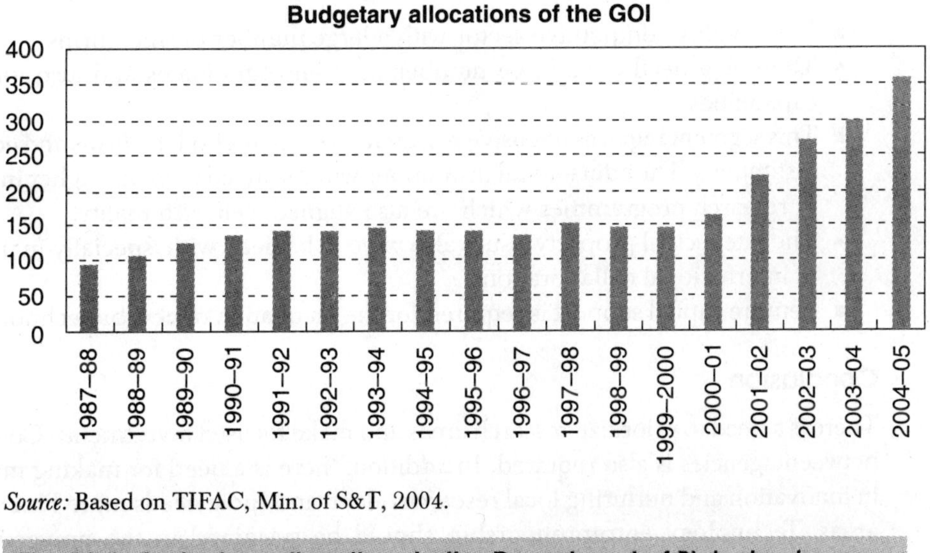

Budgetary allocations of the GOI

Source: Based on TIFAC, Min. of S&T, 2004.

Fig. 19.1 Budgetary allocations to the Department of Biotechnology (millions of $ PPP)

- Availability of venture capital and a growing economy.
- There are a large number of companies operating in various areas.
- There is a strong MNC presence, which helps firms to compete.
- Have competencies in specific areas such as vaccines.
- There are enormous strengths in areas of bioinformatics.
- Have capabilities to manage clinical trials. There is a high incidence of infectious/ lifestyle diseases and an excellent pool of doctors and physicians.
- There is a huge network of research laboratories.
- Rich biodiversity is available in India.

The government is committed to supporting biotechnology parks and at least 10 parks will be promoted and supported by 2010. The Department of Biotechnology will support the creation of incubators in biotech parks promoted by private industry or through public–private partnerships. Concessions will be provided to firms located in biotech parks.

According to the Technology Information Forecasting and Assessment Council of India (TIFAC) there were 2378 biotechnology patent applications which were filed between 1995 and 2003 (TIFAC 2004).

There is evidence of a large number of alliances being fostered between academia and industry.

The outsourcing of clinical trials is on the rise. Also, there are a large number of alliances being forged with foreign firms in different areas such as agriculture, healthcare, environment, and industrial biotechnology. There are clusters of biotech firms in Hyderabad, Bangalore, Mumbai, Delhi, and Chennai.

Challenges

The biotechnology sector faces the following challenges:

- It is a highly competitive sector with a large number of small firms.
- There is a need for a large number of science graduates and also for research capabilities.
- This segment requires intensive research investments both by firms and educational institutions. The educational institutions will also need to make higher investments in research programmes which are also aligned well with reality.
- The intellectual property issues also have to be dealt with, specially in the context of international collaborations.
- Venture capital support is required for the incubation of new biotechnology firms.

Conclusion

There is a need to prioritize research areas and make focused investments. Coordination between agencies is also required. In addition, there is a need for making investments in innovation and nurturing local research talent, and India needs more Ph.D.s in these areas. Technology entrepreneurship should be sustained in the universities. The regulatory framework needs to be strengthened. Entrepreneurship in this sector should be encouraged and firms should be more open to collaborations and networks.

THE RETAILING SECTOR IN INDIA

Modern retail globalization is accelerating. Since 2001, more than 89 new markets have been entered by more than 49 new retailers. According to AT Kearney's 2006 report, Asia has overtaken eastern Europe to become the dominant region in global retail expansion. This shift is not surprising seeing the fact that Asia represents 26 per cent of global GDP and 32 per cent of global retail sales. Its annual retail sales grew at a rate of 7 per cent in 2005. Apart from the economic considerations, modern retailers have just tapped 28 per cent of the Asian region in comparison to 42 per cent of eastern European markets. The latest edition of India Retail Report, brought out by private research firm Images F and R along with the Confederation of Indian Industry (CII) and other organizations says that the domestic retail market will touch Rs 18.1 trillion (Rs 18,10,000 crore or $402 billion) by 2010. About 328 new shopping malls are expected to come up in Indian metros and Tier 1 and Tier II cities. Real estate consultancy firm Jones Lang LaSalle Meghraj also predicts that northern India will lead the retail boom. If we see the country-wise retail overview, we see that China's retail market grew by more than 12 per cent in 2005 but still slipped to number five, as market saturation is on the rise with more than 40 foreign retailers entering the market. 'Success stories are on the rise in China. Do-it-yourself retailer B&Q entered China in 1999 and has enjoyed double-digit growth every year since then. Last year, sales grew by about 50 per cent to nearly $550 million, and it purchased the China operations of Germany-based home decor company OBI. Looking ahead, B&Q plans to open 100 stores in China in the next five years. Another example is Tesco. Although the UK-based retailer didn't move into China until 2004—long after Wal-Mart and Carrefour entered in the mid-1990s—its performance has been strong. Tesco is planning to open 16 new stores in China, and also operates 41 hypermarkets in the country through a joint venture with Ting Hsin' (AT Kearney 2006).

AT Kearney (2006) studied that successful retailers:

- enter a high potential market early
- take their time to develop
- are willing to experiment with a variety of store formats
- assemble a team comprised mainly of local nationals who know the market and the culture, and then
- give these local managers substantial authority to find the formula that works.

But speed to market alone doesn't equal success and 19 markets were exited in 2006, and many retailers still struggle to achieve profitability in emerging markets in less than five years.

INDIAN RETAIL INDUSTRY

The Indian retail industry, traditionally dominated by the family-run *kirana* stores, has faced a tremendous metamorphosis both in format and structure. Indian retailing has the highest retail density in the world (Vishvas and Murugaiah 2006) and the past few years have witnessed the evolution of organized retailing with numerous players, both national and international, joining the fray. The total retailing market in India in 2005 stood at Rs 10,000 billion, i.e., 9–10 per cent of the country's GDP. The organized sector accounted for Rs 350 billion, i.e., 3.5 per cent of the total (www.icmr.icfai.org). This organized retailing is expected to cross Rs 1,000 billion mark by 2010. Today, the organized retail sector has 300 malls, 1500 supermarkets, and 325 departmental stores (Vishvas and Murugaiah 2006).

Retailing is India's largest industry and accounts for 14 per cent of GDP. It is the second largest source of employment, next only to agriculture, but is still the least evolved of all the industries (Kanwar 2005). According to AT Kearney's 2006 Global Retail Development Index, India occupied the first ranking which has now been taken over by Vietnam. The rise of the double income family (resulting in increased purchasing power), higher mobility, availability of credit cards, changed lifestyle, and scarcity of time, necessitate the need for convenience shopping. Organized retailing in India is predominantly an urban phenomenon and is likely to remain so. Many players are trying to recreate the ambience and experience of foreign shopping malls and are providing wide product range, quality, and value for money to create a memorable shopping experience (Kaushesh 2002). Please see Exhibit 19.1.

Exhibit 19.1   Vietnam replaces India as the most attractive emerging retail destination (AT Kearney)

The country has ended India's three-year reign as the most attractive emerging market destination for retail investment according to the seventh annual Global Retail Development Index (TM) (GRDI), a study of retail investment attractiveness among 30 emerging markets conducted by management consulting firm AT Kearney. This leap from rank fourth in the 2007 GRDI to first place in 2008 was driven by strong GDP growth, changes to the country's regulatory structure favouring foreign investors, and increasing consumer demand for modern retail concepts. India, Russia, and China, which were the top three countries in last year's GRDI, fell to second, third, and fourth respectively, in the 2008 GRDI. While these countries will remain important retail investment destinations, the high real estate costs in large cities and growing competition have decreased their attractiveness relative to prior years and has forced retailers to look for opportunities in Tier II and Tier III cities.

The GRDI helps retailers prioritize their global development strategies by ranking the retail expansion attractiveness of emerging countries based on a set of 25 variables including economic and political risk, retail market attractiveness, retail saturation levels, and the difference between gross domestic product growth and retail growth. It also focuses on opportunities for mass merchant and food retailers, which are typically the bellwether for modern retailing concepts in a country.

Though Vietnam's $20 billion retail market pales in comparison to India or China, the absence of competition and 8 per cent GDP growth make it an attractive expansion opportunity for global retailers. Another advantage for Vietnam is that its people are among the youngest in Asia, with 79 million below the age of 65, and have increased their consumer spending by more than 75 per cent between 2000 and 2007. The country is becoming increasingly urbanized and concentrated with more than one million people a year migrating into the two large cities of Ho Chi Minh and Ha Noi. The Vietnamese government is expected to remove controls on 100 per cent foreign ownership of retailers in the country and has established a new programme to develop wholesale and retail real estate by 2010. The region has already seen the recent emergence of modern retail in neighbouring countries such as Thailand, Philippines, and Malaysia.

Source: Adapted from Reuters (2008).

Retail Defined

Gilbert (1999), defines *retail* as, 'Any business that directs its marketing efforts towards satisfying the final consumer based upon the organization of selling goods and services as a means of distribution', and *international retail* as, 'the process of a retailer transferring its retail operations, concept, management expertise, technology, and/or buying function across national borders'.

'Any retail outlet chain (and not a one-stop outlet) which is professionally managed (even if it is family run), has accounting transparency (with proper usage of MIS and accounting standards), and organized supply chain management with centralized quality control and sourcing (certain part of sourcing can be locally made), can be termed as organized retailing in India' (Vishvas and Murugaiah 2006).

Indian Retail Structure

The Indian retail industry is divided into organized and unorganized sectors. *Organized retailing* refers to 'trading activities undertaken by licensed retailers, i.e., those registered for sales tax, income tax, etc.' This includes retail chains, hypermarkets, large retail business, etc. The *unorganized retailing* sector refers to local *kirana* stores, mom-pop stores, *paan/beedi* shops, convenience stores, hand-cart and pavement vendors, etc. There are more than 12 million mom-pop stores in India (*Retail Merchandiser* 2006). According to KSA Technopak, organized retail constituted just 2 per cent of retail sales in India in 2002, which is bound to grow to 12–3 per cent by 2010 (Table 19.6).

The initial growth in organized retailing was slow and concentrated in the metros. Due to the high investment required for real estate, the real estate developers have been the major players in organized retailing in India such as DLF, Rajan Raheja, K. Raheja, and DS group (Fitch Report 2003).

The study of development of retailing in India brings forth some interesting facts.

Region-specific retail   Retailing is region-specific with players making their presence felt in a particular region, for example, Apna Bazar has 75 stores in Mumbai only, and Subhiksha has 112 stores, Foodworld has 75 outlets in South India, and Wills Sport has 29 stores in Delhi (*The Economic Times* 2003).

Emergence of discount formats   As Indians are more price conscious and look for value-for-money, large discount format stores, i.e., hypermarkets have emerged as major competition to both organized and unorganized retail.

Table 19.6   Retail industry in India

	2002	2010
Estimated size of retail in India	10,700	14,000
Share of organized retail in India (%)	2	12–13
Size of organized retail in India	225	1700–1800

Source: Adapted from KSA Technopak (2005).

In 2006, there was a major breakthrough for the retail industry in India. The government finally allowed international brands to set up their retail chains with majority stake instead of having to depend on local franchisees. This move will also help the already existing international brands that have a major influence, such as Nokia and Adidas. The fate of companies such as Adidas, which acquired Reebok, is unknown as the retailing of multiple brands has not got the government's go ahead. This is believed to be the first significant step towards the entry of foreign retail majors such as Wal-Mart, Target, and Carrefour in the domestic market. The advantages of retailing in terms of creating jobs are known, but the guidelines should be made very clear.

Source: The Times of India (2006).

Large number of international players   With the government announcing that international brands can now set up their retail chain with majority stake, a large number of international players are eyeing India. Some of the international players already in the market are Landmark Group, Dubai; Metro, Germany, Nanz, Germany, Mango, Spain; McDonald's, USA; Dominos, USA, etc. (Fitch 2003).

Mall development   Malls started developing in India in the late 1990s with Crossroads in Mumbai and Ansal Plaza in Delhi taking the lead. According to an ASSOCHAM report (2009), there is close to 40 million sq ft of mall space in India today.

Exhibit 19.2 cites the entry of foreign retail majors in the domestic market.

Business Models for Retailing

Every product/process has a life cycle. If we analyse the global retail trends we see that in the past 11 years (i.e., 1995–2006) the market attractiveness follows the same consistent pattern, i.e., opening, peaking, declining, and closing. This usually happens over a period of 5–10 years.

Marketers can plan the business models when they are entering a country based on which life cycle stage the country is in at that point of time. The business model or retail format is the type of mix the retailers adopt regarding the nature of merchandise and services offered, pricing policy, advertising and promotion, store design, store size, and location (Lamba 2003). However, AT Kearney (2006) says that the business model chosen should match with the market stage of the country you are entering. Some of the different business models for retailing are as follows:

Convenience stores   These are the modern version of the friendly neighbourhood stores, easily accessible and having the essential items; for example, 7-Eleven chain of convenience stores.

Department stores   These are usually multi-tiered large stores that stock a vast range of products in a variety of departments. Their number in India has grown by '24 per cent per annum over the past five years and their sales have grown even more rapidly by about 34 per cent annually over the period 1999–2003. The upper-middle and high income classes predominantly frequent these stores. Most department stores stock a range of branded goods to cater to the customer's demands. Examples are Shoppers Stop and Lifestyle' (Jhamb and Bhardwaj 2006).

Specialty stores   As the name suggests these stores offer a particular line of merchandise and cater to a niche market. They offer lower prices than other types of retailers selling similar items.

Supermarkets   These are departmentalized self-service stores offering a wide variety of food and household goods. They offer products at lower prices by reducing the margins. In India, there are no major national supermarket chains and most of the organized retailers prefer to operate in particular regions, for example, Foodworld. In 2007, Reliance Fresh was also launched by Reliance Industries in the supermarket format (INR News 2007).

Superstores   These are also called combination stores and are larger versions of supermarkets. They are usually situated on the outskirts of the city and occupy a large area. Popular examples are Wal-Mart, K-Mart, and Target.

Discount stores   As the name suggests, in this format the consumer gets the items at a discounted price. Indian customers have already experienced these discount stores like Giant by the RPG group and Big Bazaar from Pantaloon. Big Bazaar's promoters did not have the product expertise in all the products offered at their stores. So they came up with 'consolidator' concept where different national players were given a space in the stores with the understanding that they would provide the best deal in town (Shah 2002).

Hypermarkets   These are larger retail stores which combine superstores and discount stores. Hypermarkets result in a colossal retail facility carrying an enormous range of products. They have the potential to satisfy all the routine weekly shopping needs of the customers in a single trip. Big Bazaar and Giant are the main players in India. Reliance announced its entry in the retailing sector with an investment of Rs 25,000 crore (*The Economic Times* 2006). This retail rollout expected to be functional by the year end and in a hypermarket-led format (Kurian and Rao 2006), was launched on August 14, 2007 as India's largest hypermarket under the name 'Reliance Mart' in Ahmedabad. It carries a range of over 95,000 products catering to the entire family (INR News 2007).

Warehouse stores   Just like the low-cost airlines, warehouse stores project a low price image by offering their merchandise in a no-frills environment. They carry limited merchandise, displayed in simple cut boxes and price them low by cutting on the profits.

Shopping malls   These are a common mall where a variety of retailers are located and are not retail stores in the true sense. Recent times have seen the emergence of many malls in India. One of the reasons for this can be the convergence of retail and entertainment sectors (*The Economic Times* 2003). The first malls to develop in India were Spencer Plaza in Chennai (1998), Crossroads in Mumbai (1999), and Ansal Plaza in Delhi (2000). 'A mall without walls is the latest innovation in mall formats to hit India in the form of Bangalore Central launched by Pantaloon Retail (India) Ltd in May 2004 in Bangalore. Unlike the regular malls which are consortiums of clearly demarcated shops, the seamless mall is akin to an enormous trail outlet housing hundreds of well-known brands, sharing space with each other. The brands are showcased category-wise and once the customer focuses his attention on a desired category, competing brands vie with each other for a share of his mind space and pocket. Common facilities such as centralized billing, marketing, and loyalty programmes benefit both, the customers and participating brands. Besides this, it also houses a coffee shop, a food court, a supermarket, a pub, a fine-dining restaurant, a discotheque, and even India's first in-house radio station Radio Central' (Bharwani and Bhushan 2005).

Cash and carry   This is generally targeted towards small wholesale customers who buy in bulk and pay in cash. Whereas the other models concentrate on business to customer, this model targets business to business customers. Hotels, restaurants, caterers, and exporters generally prefer this model as they get products at a price lower than the market price. The basic concept is a retailer selling to another retailer and not competing with it. German giant Metro AG has entered India as a cash and carry store (Marketing Whitebook 2005).

Direct catalogue retailing   This is a successful business proposition as entrepreneurs can set up the business without going into the heavy investment of owning/renting an elaborate showroom. They can successfully run the venture of mail order retailing even from their warehouse. However, this is not a good idea in India where customers like to feel the product and satisfy themselves before going for the final purchase, and where there is scepticism about getting the product after having made the payment in advance to an unseen company.

Web stores   With the widening and ever-increasing use of the Internet non-store retailing is also spreading at a fast rate. In India, Internet shopping has become a 'Rs 3,500–4,000 crore market with almost 28 per cent or 5.9 million people buying online in the last one year' (Dobhal 2006). According to Assocham, 2008, 'e-shopping in October–November 2007 had impacted shopkeepers' sales in major hubs of economic activities to the extent of Rs 5,500 crore. It is expected to surge 175–180 per cent during Dussehra and Diwali this year and traders will lose Rs 15,000 crore to online shopping (*The Economic Times* 2008).

Future of Retailing

According to AT Kearney (2006), the decision to allow FDI of up to 51 per cent in single-brand retailers has fuelled retail investors' interest in India. 'This has triggered market-entry announcements from retailers such as Gap, Zara, UCB, and Timex, among others. Wal-Mart has announced it will open an Indian office for market research, and Tesco has entered the market through a partnership with Home Care Retail Mart Pvt. Ltd, launching a hypermarket format called Magnet. Not to be outdone, local retail conglomerates are rising to the challenge and racing to capture the best locations. Reliance Industries has announced a $3.4 billion investment to develop about 1,575 stores between December 2006 and March 2007' (AT Kearney 2006).

'India is at the peak of attractiveness for retailers right now, with a $350 billion retail market expected to grow 13 per cent this year,' said Mike Moriarty, a vice president in AT Kearney's consumer industries and retail practice, and leader of the Global Retail Development Index study (AT Kearney 2006). Thus, we can say that the Indian retail industry is standing at the threshold of a successful innings.

THE BANKING SECTOR IN INDIA

The banking sector is the backbone of any financial system and economy. Commercial banks play an important role in the development of underdeveloped/developing economies by mobilization of resources and their better allocation. The Indian banking system has changed a lot over the last five decades, especially in the last 15 years, with India taking to the path of free market economy and globalization. From private ownership and control of commercial banks to public ownership and government control by way of nationalization, the system changed further in the wake of liberalization and introduction of new players in the shape of private sector banks and foreign banks. This brought the element of stiff competition in the environment with the introduction of new technologies and ideas, new perceptions of quality, along with a high degree of professional management and marketing concepts, in to the Indian banking system.

The public sector banks, which still account for the major part of the Indian banking industry in terms of size and reach (Table 19.7), are facing stiff competition from private and foreign banks as also from the non-banking financial institutions.

The foreign banks which form only 0.26 per cent of the total number of branches in India still manage to gather 5 per cent of the total deposits. (See Table 19.8 for more details on the financial figures of public, private, and foreign banks).

Banking Trends in India

The banking system in India has undergone major changes in the last century. The Indian banking system is regulated by the central bank of the country, i.e., Reserve Bank of India (RBI), which was nationalized in 1949. RBI is the primary regulator for the banking sector and the government exercises direct and indirect control over banks

Table 19.7 Banking sector in India

	Public sector banks	Private sector banks	Foreign banks
Number of banks	28	29	31
Number of branches (as % of total)	88.4	11.33	0.26
Total deposits (%)	78	17	5

All figures for the period 2004–05.

Source: Adapted from Indian Bankers' Association (2006).

Table 19.8 Financial figures of banks in India

(Rs in Crores)

	Public sector banks		Private sector banks		Foreign banks	
	31.03.05	31.03.06	31.03.05	31.03.06	31.03.05	31.03.06
Deposits	14,36,537	16,22,479	3,13,967	4,23,337	86,389	1,13,845
Investments	6,86,211	6,33,962	1,40,272	1,78,312	42,858	5,35,662
Advances	8,56,062	11,06,347	2,20,542	3,09,578	75,318	97,556
Total assets	17,73,634	20,14,880	4,26,614	5,65,094	1,53,529	2,01,587
Gross NPA	48,405	42,105	8,546	7,720	2,183	1,919
Net NPA	16,903	14,384	4,094	3,141	648	806
Interest income	1,20,358	1,37,615	26,265	34,529	9,168	12,236
Other income	24,204	23,332	6,367	9,097	3,864	5,194
Total income	1,44,561	1,60,946	32,633	43,627	13,032	17,430
Interest expenses	68,754	80,272	16,273	21,416	4,042	5,149
Operating expenses	37,040	41,531	8,675	11,514	4,417	5,620
Total expenses	1,05,794	1,21,803	24,948	32,930	8,458	10,769
Operating profit	38,767	39,143	7,684	10,697	4,574	6,660
Provisions & contingencies	23,072	22,357	4,151	5,682	2,587	3,592
Net profit	15,137	15,979	3,533	5,014	1,987	3,068

Source: Indian Bankers' Association (2006).

through RBI to protect the depositors and to stabilize the banking system. Extensive powers have been conferred on RBI under the RBI Act and Banking Regulations Act.

RBI, as banker to the government, transacts government business and manages public debt besides giving temporary (ways and means) advances. It is the sole agency in India to issue currency notes. As the controller of banks, RBI grants licenses to conduct banking business and issues directions to carry on banking business. It carries out inspection of banks for financial supervision and exercises management control. Being a bankers' bank, RBI keeps deposits of the commercial banks and provides financial assistance to them as lender of last resort and also by refinancing their outstanding export credit. As controller of credit, RBI fixes bank rates and interest rates, and also exercises selective credit control and other methods for monetary control through tools of maintenance of statutory reserves, as banks have to maintain credit reserve ratio (CRR) and statutory liquidity ratio (SLR), i.e., a certain percentage of their assets with RBI in the form of cash/eligible securities.

In 1947 there were 558 commercial banks in India, which were reduced to 91 in 1967 due to liquidations and mergers. State Bank of India, the biggest Indian commercial bank was formed in July 1955 to break the ownership and control of few leaders of commerce and industry over the economic power and banking system. These consisted of mainly private banks under the ownership of big industrial houses, catering primarily to the needs of a few big leaders in commerce and industry. Also, in order to have balanced geographical growth of banks, especially in rural areas and small towns that accounted for the majority of the population, 14 major banks were nationalized by the government in 1969.

The government as the owner of the banks decided the agenda for the banks and directed the flow of credit. The focus changed from class banking to social banking. The thrust of the banking system was on extensive branch network in unbanked areas, promotion of savings and tapping more deposits, providing credit to priority sector of the economy, which while contributing a lot to the economy was not getting adequate credit, and for rural development.

This social transformation process resulted in unprecedented expansion of the banking and financial system. However, the regulated business environment, poor quality of credit portfolio due to social lending without adequate safeguards against defaults, thin margins on social lending, disruptive tactics of trade unions, increasing number of loss-making branches due to unmindful branch expansion in rural areas, and other factors, resulted in sacrifice of service quality, operational productivity, and profitability of these organizations, which still survived due to the regulated business environment. The regulated environment killed the scope for competition among banks.

However, the acute financial crisis at the beginning of the 1990s, which brought India on the verge of default in its foreign exchange repayment commitments for the first time since independence, necessitated liberalization. The Narasimham Committee set up to suggest ways and means to reform the financial sector to avoid recurrence of the above situation, recommended the adoption of transparent accounting procedures (prudential norms) by banks in line with international norms and entry of private players into the market. The later recommendations dealing with restructuring of the financial sector to make it more robust included interest deregulation as one of the important measures. In the wake of liberalization, the decision to take the path of free market economy and globalization, necessitated reforms in the financial sector to become internally viable and internationally competitive.

To strengthen the banking system, a lot of measures have been taken to restructure banking in India with the introduction of prudential norms on capital adequacy, asset liability management, asset classification, income recognition and provisioning, accounting standards and transparency in disclosures, corporate governance, risk management, etc. The entry of foreign/private banks, deregulation of interest rates, disintermediation, and other policy measures initiated competition in the banking industry. The government support in the shape of recapitalization has been provided to a very few weak banks only. To meet the capital adequacy requirements the public sector banks are resorting to raising capital from the public, leading to reduction in the government shareholding. Public sector banks were forced to focus on improved quality, greater efficiency, and higher productivity. Profitability has taken the centre stage. Globalization has rendered it necessary to be cost-effective, customer-oriented, and technology-based.

The reforms after 1991 have resulted in widening and deepening of the financial system. The growing competition and highly stressed profits have not only introduced new marketing concepts in the Indian banking sector but has also brought customer satisfaction to the centre of the focus. It has become very important for banks to retain their existing customer base as well as to enlarge it.

Marketing Mix for the Banking Sector

The key marketing mix elements for the banking sector are as follows:

Product   Banks offer different types of products. In addition to the traditional products like plain vanilla deposit accounts and loans banks have now added a wide portfolio of products, a large number of which are technology enabled. Some of these are as follows:

- car loans
- housing loans
- education loans
- services of saving/current accounts
- discounting/underwriting of bills
- corporate banking products specifically designed for each key account.
- credit and debit card instruments
- fund transfer mechanisms
- issuance of drafts and banker cheques
- investment advisory services
- cash management services
- investment products
- consumer loans.

This form of retail banking is a fairly new concept in India. It is at a level which is still far below the other Asian markets and thus, the scope for growth continues to be immense (Goyal et al. 2004). Within the retail portfolio there is not much difference in the products being offered by most of the players in the Indian banking sector.

Pricing   Pricing management is significant in India because other non-banking financial institutions charge least possible fees for services rendered. However, RBI and Indian Banker's Association (IBA) regulate pricing policies of banks in India. Thus, the rate of interest and rate of other services are fixed by RBI and IBA. Hence, there is not much scope for differentiation based on pricing and product.

Promotion   Despite interest deregulation to some extent, banks still do not have much leverage in price discrimination and as the products also are very similar, the banks have to actively promote/market themselves in order to gain business. Also, the introduction of different international players in the market and the increasing variations of products being introduced, promotion now occupies an important place. Online banking is also an effective medium of promotion for the various bank schemes and acts as a marketing tool (IIBF 2005). They are promoted actively through the print media, radio, television, outdoor hoardings, and banners. Banks also organize customer meets, which is a forum to mobilize business and provide promotional materials such as pens, calendars, and diaries.

Place Banks are easily accessible from the different branches present in an area. Changing technology has also brought about changes in the channels of distribution of banking services. Services are being increasingly distributed via the following means:

- ATMs: The automated teller machines (ATMs) have come up as an alternative to new branches and reduce the operating costs. They are located at convenient locations in cities, provide easy access to consumers, and have helped banks in market penetration. Banks have also been gaining synergies through ATM sharing arrangements.
- Tele-banking: Telephone banking or tele-banking is another delivery medium for banking services, which is accessible 24 hours. A customer can call the bank any time and inquire about balances or transaction history, or can even transfer funds between accounts. Telephone banking has led to growth of call centres, and many banks such as ICICI, HDFC, Standard Chartered, and American Express have deployed call centres for better customer support and care. Public sector banks are also following suit with SBI and PNB taking the lead.
- Cards: These are also called plastic money. A number of options are now available like:
    - Credit card—These are a source of revolving credit. They allow the user to make payment on purchases by using this card (at a fixed rate of interest) without having to go through the hassles of managing hard cash.
    - Debit card—This also allows the user to make purchases or obtain cash by debiting the payments to the cardholder's bank account where credit balance exists.
    - Gold card—This is a credit card aimed at more affluent customers.
    - Smart card—These cards have integrated chips (IC) installed and have a memory and a processor. They have to be paid for in advance and can be reloaded with funds and used for a range of purposes.
- Online banking or e-banking: This is also referred to as anywhere banking. The customer can transact business from any corner of the world via the Internet. Thus, any computer having an internet connection can provide banking facility to the customer. This allows:
    - faster
    - more efficient
    - more personalized

service to the customer. At the retail end, banks offer internet banking through a large number of branches, e.g., account enquiry, money transfer requests, etc. Corporate customers are also being offered internet banking services, e.g., online funds transfer facility, trade finance management, funds management, upload features, MIS/reconciliation, multi-level authorization, etc.

Process With the basic product offered by different banks being the same, the differentiation comes in the form of mode of delivery. The foreign/private banks score in this area by having a better organized delivery. However, banks as a whole are making an effort to be more consumer responsive by providing a time-bound delivery

(Goyal et al. 2004). Installation of a number of electronic mediums such as ATMs and tele-banking, has caused less crowding in the counters at the banks, helping the bank employees to deliver a more personalized and quicker service to the customers. They are hence able to deliver customer value.

People   When banks upgraded their technology they realized that they did not need the number of staff they had. By announcing attractive schemes to the employees so that they could take voluntary retirement, different banks were able to retain the quality staff that was open to adapting to the new technologies being introduced. Still, the public sector banks are saddled with a de-motivated, ageing workforce, lacking in attitude towards productivity, and service to customers. These act as a major deterrent for the customers who increasingly prefer to deal with the private sector banks that have young, high-performing, tech-savvy, and motivated personnel who are open to mould with the changing scenario effectively. Since people are an important component in the service delivery, public sector banking needs to have an effective human resource management.

Physical evidence   In keeping up with the change in technology the ambience of the banks were also paid attention to. The growing competition from foreign banks, which had a well appointed and standardized office (Goyal et al. 2004) forced the public sector banks to sit up and take note of their ambience. Keeping in mind that the surroundings in which customers make transactions has a lasting impression on them, banks concentrated on proper maintenance of premises, cleanliness, basic amenities, decor, sitting arrangements, placement of vouchers at convenient locations, and all counters had signboards prominently displaying the nature of transactions being handled at those counters for the convenience of the customers (PNB Monthly Review 2005).

Critical Factors for Success

Consumers find banks to be preferred places for monetary transactions. Safety, better interest rates, and ease of management attract customers for money deposits and on the other hand, attractive interest rates and flexibility of payment along with pleasing and friendly services make them a good borrowing option also. Customers seeking other services, say, like locker services are interested in friendly service and operational facility for longer hours. Some of the critical factors for overall banking success are:

- Ability of the services product: The needs of the customers are varied and banks providing a whole portfolio of services are required to satisfy these needs.
- Availability or services distribution: The availability of the services at an arms length is what the customers are looking for. These include the branch networks, ATMs, computerized and IT enabled services, etc.
- Incidence of affable services.
- Use of the Internet: Using the Internet as a service channel rather than a pure sales tool is required (KPMG 2006).
- Recognition of and relationship with the customer.
- Mature, enthusiastic, knowledgeable, friendly, and cooperative staff providing prompt and reliable service.

- Reward for the customers in the form of interest rates.
- Management of customer perceptions about the bank.
- Trust and confidence in the bank.
- Ambience.
- Complaint redressal mechanism and availability of help desks for customer convenience.

CONCLUSION

Public sector banks have the advantage of having reach and a long history, which brings credibility, but at the same time the quality of services provided is questionable in the mind of the customers. They are further disadvantaged by being bureaucratic, having social obligations, lending to priority sectors at low rate of interest, having an ageing workforce with a low level of motivation, and low per employee business. They further lack expertise and are faced with delayed decision-making. Attitudinal differences affect the productivity and performance of employees and thus affect the overall profitability of the banks.

The private/foreign banks on the other hand, are at an advantage as they have started afresh, are thin and lean, have a tech savvy, young, and highly motivated workforce. However, the disadvantage is that they have fewer traditional channels of distribution, thus causing lower reach and are unable to tap the big rural market/agriculture sector. They are also facing a quicker turnover of their employees.

Product and pricing are still very much regulated and there is not much difference in the products; it is only the quality of services mainly, which makes considerable difference in the Indian banking sector at a time when the expectations of the customers are on the rise. The public sector banks are changing but there is still a gap between the level of services expected by the customers and the services being provided to them.

SUMMARY

This chapter gives an insight into the four sunrise services sectors—healthcare, biotechnology, retailing, and banking. For each section, the overview of the industry and the government policies affecting these sectors along with the major players have been highlighted.

There are certain similarities across all the sectors. All these sectors other than banking have large number of small players. In healthcare and biotechnology there is a need for investment in research and development (R&D) as that would lead to competitive advantage. There is also a need for a very strong university–industry relationship. There is a need for trained manpower and more research oriented output from academic institutions in these segments. The large players in these two segments have focused on issues such as international expansion, fostering strategic alliances, investing in R&D, and undertaking global operations. Technology entrepreneurship should be sustained in the universities; regulatory framework needs to be strengthened; entrepreneurship in these sectors should be encouraged; and firms should be

Contd

working towards opening collaborations and networks. All these have been dealt in detail in this chapter.

The retailing sector also promises huge opportunity for growth in India. Characterized largely by unorganized sector, the country finally sees emergence of malls and organized retailing is slowly gaining firm ground. There are different models which retailers deploy for operations. India has seen a large number of domestic brands that have created a foothold in the domestic market. The entry of foreign players will make the Indian market even more competitive. However, addressing people's issues is a key challenge in this segment. As the business grows, finding the right talent and utilizing technology to enhance productivity would be important factors that need to be addressed.

The banking section shows that the product and pricing are still very much regulated. It is mainly the quality of services and not the services themselves, which makes a lot of difference in the Indian banking sector at a time when the expectations of the customers are on the rise. The public sector banks are changing but still there is a gap between the level of services expected by the customers and the services being provided to them. There is a lot that needs to be attended to in providing better experiences to customers in banks. All other aspects, such as technology deployment, can be replicated but the element of a distinct service culture and customer focus creates a unique advantage for the banks along with their portfolio of offerings.

KEY TERMS

Critical success factors The strengths and weaknesses that most affect an organization's success. These are measured relative to those of its competitors.

Intellectual property (IP) An intangible asset such as copyright, patent, trademark, or design right. Intellectual property is an asset, and as such it can be bought, sold, licensed, or exchanged.

Marketing mix The factors controlled by a company that can influence consumers' buying of its products.

Reserve Bank of India (RBI) This is the central bank of India and the preamble to the RBI describes the basic functions of the bank with regard to regulating the issue of bank notes and keeping of reserves with a view to securing monetary stability in India, and generally operating the currency and credit system of the country to its advantage. It is also the sole agency in India for issue of currency notes.

Retail Any business that directs its marketing efforts towards satisfying the final consumer based upon the organization of selling goods and services as a means of distribution.

SERVQUAL A service quality measurement model that is used to compare customers' expectations before a service encounter and their perceptions of the actual service delivered. It represents six dimensions of service quality, namely, tangibles, reliability, assurance, responsiveness, empathy, accessibility, and affordability.

CONCEPT REVIEW QUESTIONS

1. Discuss the major challenges in the healthcare sector in India.

2. Critically discuss the success factors in a healthcare sector using conceptual and practical aspects.

3. Analyse the role of paying capacity of a consumer and issues of the insurance sector in enabling the wider consumption of healthcare services.

4. Profile the major challenges across the service mix elements in the healthcare segment in India.

5. What are the key factors that have contributed to the growth of the biotech industry in India?

6. Critically assess the strengths and challenges for the biotech industry in India?

7. Compare and contrast the similarities and dissimilarities between the IT and biotech industry and state the factors that biotech firms should consider when setting up operations in India.

8. What is retailing? Critically evaluate the concept of retailing, globally.

9. What are the different models of retailing and how do they vary over the product life cycle?

10. If a consumer durable firm is entering the Indian market which model of retailing should it adopt and why?

11. 'Retailing is here to stay'. Critically discuss in context to the Indian scenario.

12. Critically discuss the best segment to enter for retailing, the part of the country, and the format it should adopt.

13. What are the reasons for the nationalization of banks?

14. Discuss the impact of the nationalization of the banks on the Indian economy.

15. What further changes can you suggest to improve the functioning of the banking sector?

16. Critically evaluate the impact of information technology on the functioning of banks.

17. How has the paradigm shift occurred in 'place' of the marketing mix for the banking sector?

SELECT REFERENCES

Baru, Rama V. (1998), *Private Healthcare in India: Social Characteristics and Trends*, Sage Publications, New Delhi.

Bharwani, Sonia and Sudhanshu Bhushan (2005), 'The emergence of malls as a retail format in India—Some perspectives, trends, and paradigms', Paper presented at the International Conference on Services Management, 11–12 March 2005, New Delhi.

Capitaline Plus Report (2006) on 'Healthcare in India'.

'Changing gears: Retailing in India', *The Economic Times*, 2003.

Dobhal, Shailesh (2006), 'Net's cast wider than you thought', *The Economic Times*, 5 July, p. 1.

'E-shopping to get festive boost in metros: Assocham', *The Economic Times*, 6 October 2008, p. 4.

Gilbert, David (1999), *Retail Marketing Management*, Pearson Education, pp. 6–7, Harlow, England.

Goyal, Parul, Kirti Sharma, and Vinnie Jauhari (2004), 'The State Bank of India: A progressive study of transformation of a socialistic welfare organization into a market entity', *Journal of Services Research*, vol. 4, no. 2.

Indian Institute of Banking and Finance (2005), *Principles of Banking*, Indian Institute of Banking and Finance, Mumbai.

Jabnoun, N. and M. Chaker (2003), 'Comparing the quality of private and public hospitals', *Managing Service Quality*, vol. 13, no. 4, pp. 290–299.

Jha, S.M. (2000), *Bank Marketing*, Himalaya Publishing House, Mumbai.

Jhamb, Sujata and Astha Bhardwaj (2006), 'The case for FDI in the retail sector—India', presented at Fourth International Conference on Globalization and Sectoral Development, 17–19 February 2006, IILM, New Delhi.

Lamba, A.J. (2003), *The Art of Retailing*, Tata McGraw-Hill, New Delhi.

Mahal, Ajay (2002), 'Assessing private health insurance in India: Potential impacts and regulatory issues', *Economic and Political Weekly*, 9 February.

Mathur, A. (2003), 'The role of information technology in designs of healthcare trade', Indian Council for Research on International Economic Relations, New Delhi.

Padhy, Kishore C. and Manoranjan Padhy (2002), *Banking Future: The Coming Shape of Money and Finance*, Dominant Publishers and Distributors, New Delhi.

Punjab National Bank, *Monthly Review*, June 2005, New Delhi.

'Reliance now sells retail tale to India', *The Economic Times*, 28 June 2006.

Shah, Kinjal (2002), 'Discount stores: Is it the answer?', *Marketing Series, Retailing the Sunrise Sector*, Institute for Chartered Financial Analysts of India.

Sobti, Renu (2003), *Banking and Financial Services in India*, New Century Publications, Delhi.

The Marketing Whitebook 2005, *Business World*, New Delhi.

Toor, N.S. (2006), *Handbook of Banking Information*, Skylark Publications, New Delhi.

Vishvas, Radhika and V. Murugaiah (2006), 'FDI in retailing—Challenges and opportunities,' *Marketing Mastermind*, July.

Bhushan, Ratna (2003), 'Food for retail thought', *The Hindu Businessline*, http://www.thehindubusinessline.com, accessed on 1 July 2006.

http://economictimes.indiatimes.com/News/News_By_Industry/Services/Retailing/Organised_unorganised_retailers_can_co-exist_in_India/articleshow/3564943.cms.

http://en.wikipedia.org/wiki/Store, accessed on 10 October 2008.

http://icmr.icfai.org/casestudies/catalogue/Marketing/MKTG114.htm, accessed on 14 July 2006.

http://www.aima-ind.org/AIMA_Yellojobs_Online_survey_16 May 2008.pdf, accessed on 10 October 2008.

http://www.assocham.org/prels/shownews.php?id=1865, accessed on 22 January 2009.

http://www.atkearney.com, accessed on 17 July 2006.

http://www.biospectrum.com, accessed on 14 June 2006.

http://www.domain-b.com/organisation/Nasscom/20080211_indian_it.html, accessed on 10 October 2008.

http://www.domain-b.com/organisation/Nasscom/20080709_NASSCOM.html accessed on 21 January 2009.

http://www.expresshealthcare.in/200809/market28.shtml, accessed on 12 October 2008.

http://www.fitchindia.com, accessed on 14 December 2006.

http://www.icmr.ucfau.org, accessed on 14 July 2006.

http://www.imagesretail.com/india_retail_report.htm, accessed on 10 July 2006.

http://www.iba.org.in, accessed on 13 July 2006.

http://www.inrnews.com/realestateproperty/india/ahmedabad/reliance retail_launches_hyper.html, accessed on 12 November 2008.

http://www.kpmg.no/?aid=9166399, accessed on 21 December 2006.

http://www.livemint.com/2008/03/24002940/328-new-malls-by-2010-retail.html, accessed on 12 October 2008.

http://www.rbi.org.in, accessed on 15 July 2006.

http://www.rediff.com/money/2002/oct/26heal.htm, accessed on 12 October 2008.

http://www.rediff.com/money/2002/oct/26heal.htm.

http://www.retail-merchandiser.com, accessed on 11 July 2006.

http://www.reuters.com/article/pressRelease/idUS123461+02-Jun-2008+PRN20080602, accessed on 15 October 2008.

Kanwar, Onkar S. (2005), 'Retailing in India: FDI and policy options for growth', http://www.ficci.com/media-room/speeches-presentations/2005/feb/feb23-retailing-onkar-htm.htm, accessed on 8 August 2006.

Technology Information Forec- ting and Assessment Council (2004), *Intellec... Property Rights*, vol. 10, nos 6–7, June–July, http://www.pfc.org.in/fac/june04.pdf, accessed o- ~8 July 2006.

Index